# The Collected Papers of James Meade

***The Collected Papers of James Meade***

Volume I
*Employment and Inflation*

Volume II
*Value, Distribution and Growth*

Volume III
*International Economics*

Volume IV
*The Cabinet Office Diary 1944–46*

# The Collected Papers of James Meade

## Volume IV

*The Cabinet Office Diary 1944–46*
Edited by Susan Howson

Routledge
Taylor & Francis Group
LONDON AND NEW YORK

First published by Unwin Hyman Ltd in 1990

This edition published by Routledge in 2005
2 Park Square, Milton Park, Abingdon, Oxfordshire OX14 4RN

Simultaneously published in the USA and Canada
by Routledge
711 Third Avenue, New York, NY 10017

*Routledge is an imprint of the Taylor and Francis Group, an informa business*

First issued in paperback 2015



Typeset in Times by Keystroke, Jacaranda Lodge, Wolverhampton



*British Library Cataloguing in Publication Data*
A catalogue record for this book is available from the British Library

ISBN 978-0-415-35049-5 (set)
ISBN 978-0-415-35053-2 (hbk) (volume IV)
ISBN 978-1-138-99150-7 (pbk) (volume IV)

**Publisher's Note**

The publisher has gone to great lengths to ensure the quality of this reprint, but points out that some imperfections in the original may be apparent.

# The Collected Papers of James Meade

## *Volume IV:* The Cabinet Office Diary 1944–46

*Edited by*

SUSAN HOWSON and DONALD MOGGRIDGE

*University of Toronto*

London
UNWIN HYMAN
Boston Sydney Wellington

# Contents


| | | |
|---|---|---|
| | Introduction | *page* ix |
| | Abbreviations | xiii |
| | *The Cabinet Office Diary* | |
| 1 | November 1944 | 1 |
| 2 | December 1944 | 11 |
| 3 | January 1945 | 25 |
| 4 | February 1945 | 39 |
| 5 | March 1945 | 48 |
| 6 | April 1945 | 58 |
| 7 | May 1945 | 73 |
| 8 | June 1945 | 87 |
| 9 | July 1945 | 101 |
| 10 | August 1945 | 114 |
| 11 | September 1945 | 122 |
| 12 | October 1945 | 139 |
| 13 | November 1945 | 157 |
| 14 | December 1945 | 174 |
| 15 | January 1946 | 193 |
| 16 | February 1946 | 210 |
| 17 | March 1946 | 229 |
| 18 | April 1946 | 247 |
| 19 | May 1946 | 261 |
| 20 | June 1946 | 270 |
| 21 | July 1946 | 292 |
| 22 | August 1946 | 308 |
| 23 | September 1946 | 318 |
| *Dramatis Personae* | | 332 |
| Index | | 357 |

# Introduction

This fourth volume of *The Collected Papers of James Meade* is rather different in form and content from the previous three volumes (*Volume I: Employment and Inflation, Volume II: Value, Distribution and Growth, Volume III: International Economics*). It consists of a single previously unpublished work, the diary of Meade's life in the Economic Section of the Cabinet Office which he kept for nearly two years, from the time, November 1944, when he was appointed to succeed Lionel Robbins as Director of the Section at the end of the Second World War until September 1946. This period encompasses the last few months of the war in Europe, the unexpectedly brief 'Stage II' (between the end of the European war and the defeat of Japan) and the first year of peace and of a majority Labour government under Prime Minister Clement Attlee. The work of the Section under Meade was thus centred on the implementation of the war-time coalition government's White Paper on post-war *Employment Policy* (Cmd 6527, May 1944) and the post-war international economic and financial settlement, which involved in 1944–6 discussions with the US Administration on commercial policy, the negotiation of the 1945 Anglo-American Financial Agreement, and the setting up of the International Monetary Fund and the World Bank. The commercial policy discussions led to the UN Conference on Trade and Employment in Havana, Cuba, in 1948, following two sessions of a Preparatory Commission in London and Geneva in October 1946 and April 1947 respectively. The diary ends three weeks before the London meetings of the Preparatory Commission, on which Meade was a British representative.

Meade had joined the Central Economic Information Service, the forerunner of the Economic Section and the Central Statistical Office, in the summer of 1940, after he and his wife Margaret and their three children had escaped from France ahead of the invading German Army on their way back from Geneva where Meade had been working for the League of Nations since 1937. His first achievement in the Section was to prepare with Richard Stone, who joined him in September 1940, the official national income and expenditure accounts for the UK which were first published in the White Paper, *An Analysis of the Sources of War Finance and an Estimate of the National Income and Expenditure in 1938 and 1940* (Cmd 6261), in April 1941. He then turned to the problem of post-war employment policy, to which he was to give much thought and attention in the following six years, writing the first draft of what eventually became the White Paper on *Employment Policy* in April 1943. (For Meade's war-time work on national income accounting and post-war employment policy see *Collected Papers*, Vol. I, Chapters 7–10 and 11–15 respectively.)

Over the same period he was equally concerned with the international aspects of post-war planning. In 1942 he drafted a proposal for an international 'commercial union' (reprinted in *Collected Papers*, Vol. III, Chapter 3) to complement Keynes' 'clearing union' plan, a proposal which, eagerly taken up by the President of the Board of Trade, Hugh Dalton, was adopted by the UK Government as the basis for Anglo-American talks on post-war commercial policy. Meade was himself a member of the Mission headed by Minister of State Richard Law, which went to Washington in September-October 1943 to begin those conversations and which agreed on the need for an international trade organisation on the lines proposed by Meade. (Meade also kept a diary of the Law Mission, which at his suggestion is to be published with Lionel Robbins' diaries of his wartime official visits to North America.) Discussions resumed in London in December 1944 shortly after Meade's Cabinet Office Diary opens, continued in Washington in September-December 1945, and culminated in a set of *Proposals for Consideration by an International Conference on Trade and Employment* (Cmd 6709, December 1945). The Preparatory Commission for the conference then drew up a draft Charter for an International Trade Organisation, which was adopted at the Havana Conference in March 1948; although the Charter was never ratified, the principles were incorporated into the General Agreement on Tariffs and Trade negotiated in Geneva during 1947. Meanwhile Meade had decided to leave the Section and return to academic life, as Professor of Commerce with special reference to International Trade at the London School of Economics. He was succeeded as Director of the Economic Section by Robert Hall, who arrived part-time from the Board of Trade on 1 June 1947, full-time from 1 September. Meade's work for the Section ended with his 'triumphant return' (Mrs Meade's words) to Geneva which he had left to join the Section seven years before. (For further biographical details see Meade's own account of his life published in Vol. I, Chapter 1.)

On the domestic front, the Economic Section was responsible to the Lord President of the Council (Sir John Anderson 1941–3, Clement Attlee 1943–5, Lord Woolton in the brief caretaker government of 1945, Herbert Morrison in the first post-war Labour government), whose Lord President's Committee was the main ministerial committee concerned with economic policy. Many of the Section's day-to-day tasks consisted of briefing the Lord President on whatever topics were coming up at his committee. In accepting the Directorship of the Section Meade ensured that he should also be a member of the Treasury's Budget Committee (otherwise composed of senior Treasury, Inland Revenue and Customs and Excise officials). He and Robbins were also members of the 'National Debt Enquiry' set up on the initiative of Meade and Sir Richard Hopkins (Permanent Secretary to the Treasury, 1942–5) to report to the Chancellor of the Exchequer (then Sir John Anderson) in early 1945 on post-war monetary policy and management of the national debt (including the future of 'cheap money' in the light of the *Employment Policy* White Paper, and the possibility of a capital levy after the war).

At the same time the Section began to prepare the surveys and analyses of current and prospective economic conditions called for by the *Employment Policy* White Paper (paras 81, 83–4). The preparation and contributions to economic policy-making of the first two such surveys, which were not published, are fully described in Meade's diary. In this activity, known as 'economic planning' under the Labour government, the Section worked closely with Sir Edward Bridges, Secretary to the Cabinet 1938–45 and Permanent Secretary to the Treasury in succession to Sir Richard Hopkins from 28 February 1945 (to 1956), Norman Brook, Permanent Secretary to the Ministry of Reconstruction 1943–5, and Treasury officials such as Sir Wilfrid Eady, Sir Bernard Gilbert, Sir Herbert Brittain, R. W. B. (Otto) Clarke and Dennis Proctor. Lord Keynes was also an adviser to the Chancellor of the Exchequer (Sir John Anderson 1943–5, Hugh Dalton from July 1945) until his death in April 1946. Under the Labour government another set of tasks in which the Section worked closely with other parts of Whitehall was in connection with the nationalisation programme which was co-ordinated by Morrison as Lord President. Last but not least Meade had to concern himself with staffing the post-war Section, since academics in war-time government service were returning to the universities, as well as to foster good working relations with the Treasury and the rest of the Whitehall machine. The diary is thus a rich source of information on the evolution, administration and outcome of economic policy-making – domestic and external – in an especially critical period of Britain's economic history, as well as on Meade's contribution to that process.

Meade at first wrote up his diary weekly, later – under the pressure of work in 'Stage III', the transition from war to peace – normally fortnightly, usually on a Sunday, Saturday being a working half-day in war-time and early post-war Whitehall. The 'chapters' into which we have divided the diary are, therefore, each a month's entries. An important feature of the diary is that Meade usually explained the nature of the issues and problems that came up as he saw them. As editors we have therefore generally – but not invariably – confined our footnotes to identifying the committees, documents, decisions and events referred to in the diary, adding when possible sources – in government records, the Meade Papers in the British Library of Political and Economic Science or elsewhere – where interested readers can obtain further information on the incidents and episodes recorded. Our major source of references has been the Cabinet Office and Treasury records in the Public Record Office at Kew. The Section's own files are among the Treasury records since the Economic Section was taken over by the Treasury in 1953, but the Lord President's and Lord President's Committee papers came under the Cabinet Office's filing system. We have also searched files of the Board of Trade, Colonial Office, Foreign Office, Ministry of Agriculture and Fisheries, Ministry of Food and Prime Minister's Office, for various memoranda – not always with success, however. It has to be admitted that not all the documents mentioned by Meade have been found: some of the informal committees – and the 'top secret' Budget Committee – did not keep minutes, some of the briefs the Section prepared for the Lord President seem to have vanished, and other memoranda known or suspected to exist are in files not yet open under the thirty-year rule for British official records. With respect to persons mentioned in the text, we have provided a *dramatis personae* (pp. 332–356 below) in order to reduce the number of footnotes. Apart from the correction of minor inconsistencies of spelling and obvious slips of the pen and on eleven occasions breaking up very long paragraphs,[1] the printed text follows the copy of the manuscript in the British Library of Political and Economic Science, except that some of the deletions Meade made when depositing the copy in the library have with his permission been added back from the original. Editorial additions to the text (mainly dates) are indicated by square brackets.

We should like to thank Dr Angela Raspin of the British Library of Political and Economic Science for assistance in using the Meade and Dalton Papers, the Controller of Her Majesty's Stationery Office for permission to cite government documents in the Public Record Office, Sir Alec Cairncross for letting one of us read drafts of his and Nita Watts' forthcoming history of the Economic Section, Professor Leslie Pressnell for much encouragement and advice, our excellent research assistant Catherine Schenk for preparing the *dramatis personae*, Noreen Anderson for typing the manuscript with skill and accuracy, and the Social Sciences and Humanities Research Council of Canada and the Humanities and Social Sciences Committee of the Research Board of the University of Toronto for financial assistance in support of the project. Most of all we should like to thank James Meade for agreeing to the publication and editing of his diary, and him and Margaret for all their help of various kinds in enabling us to carry out our editorial tasks.

Susan Howson
Donald Moggridge
*November 1988*

[1] On pages 81, 115, 178, 201, 251, 289, 290, 309 and 310.

# Abbreviations

| | |
|---|---|
| **BoT** | Board of Trade |
| **cif** | cost insurance and freight |
| **CSO** | Central Statistical Office |
| **EIPS** | Economic and Industrial Planning Staff |
| **EJ** | *Economic Journal* |
| **EPT** | Excess Profits Tax |
| **FAO** | Food and Agriculture Organisation |
| **FBI** | Federation of British Industries |
| **FO** | Foreign Office |
| **fob** | free on board |
| **FSSU** | Federated Superannuation Scheme for Universities |
| **HMG** | His Majesty's Government |
| **HMSO** | His/Her Majesty's Stationery Office |
| **ILO** | International Labour Office |
| **IMF** | International Monetary Fund |
| **ITO** | International Trade Organisation |
| **LP** | Lord President (of the Council) |
| **LPC** | Lord President's Committee |
| **LSE** | London School of Economics |
| **MAF** | Ministry of Agriculture and Fisheries |
| **MAP** | Ministry of Aircraft Production |
| **MEW** | Ministry of Economic Warfare |
| **MFN** | most favoured nation |
| **MP** | Member of Parliament |
| **NDC** | National Defence Contribution |
| **NDE** | National Debt Enquiry |
| **PAYE** | Pay-as-you-earn |
| **PEP** | Political and Economic Planning |
| **PM** | Prime Minister |
| **PPS** | Parliamentary Private Secretary |
| **RAF** | Royal Air Force |
| **TUC** | Trades Union Congress |
| **UNESCO** | United Nations Economic Social and Cultural Organisation |

| | |
|---|---|
| **UNO** | United Nations Organisation |
| **UNRRA** | United Nations Relief and Rehabilitation Administration |

In the footnotes documents in the Public Record Office are identified by their call numbers, BT, CAB, T, etc.

# 1

# November 1944

## *5 November 1944*

Last Friday [3 November] after very many weeks of indecision I at last cast the die, deciding to stay on in Govt service after the war instead of going back to academic life. It was a difficult decision. The attraction of academic liberty was very great and I felt that I should very much like to devote my time to the academic task of writing a 3rd edition of *Economic Analysis and Policy*[1] to become a new *Economics of Welfare*[2] and to expound the possibilities of a 'Liberal-Socialist' economy. On the other hand, there was the prospect that nearly all economists would desert Whitehall for the Universities and the experiment of the Economic Section (which has undoubtedly been useful during the war) might come to grief not because Whitehall, but because the economists, were unwilling to continue it. This argument was forcibly stated to me by Sir Richard Hopkins, and I do not believe it would be answered by anything short of staying in Whitehall. That the possibility of a group of economists at the centre, giving expert advice during the first critical years of reconstruction, should go by default was more than I could calmly contemplate.

Moreover, it does not seem that the preparation of a 3rd edition of *Economic Analysis and Policy* need be wholly incompatible with the direction of the Economic Section. I have taken Bridges' advice, who considers that it would not be impossible to publish such an edition while I was in Govt service. I have obtained from him agreement to the idea that I might spend, for example, Saturday mornings at home working on it. My intention is, therefore, to see if the following arrangement might work. I should work from 7 to 8 a.m. daily on it and on Saturday mornings, and I should devote four out of the eight weeks of annual leave to it. By this means I might be able to get a solid amount of fundamental economic work done while enjoying at the same time the interest and experience of economic co-ordination and the formulation of economic policy at the centre of Whitehall.

But can the Economic Section continue to be a success in peace-time? When we return to party politics (each party having its own economic

[1] *An Introduction to Economic Analysis and Policy*, 1st edn. Oxford: Clarendon Press, 1936; 2nd edn, London: Oxford University Press, 1937. A draft of an appendix and a chapter on national income and expenditure for a third edition is in Meade Papers 3/15.

[2] A. C. Pigou, *The Economics of Welfare*. London: Macmillan, 1920.

programme and economic advisers) and to the more familiar economic issues of peace-time, will Ministers listen to an Economic Section? Moreover, what will be the attitude of the Treasury to the Economic Section? In war-time the Treasury has in many ways played second fiddle, the fundamental economic instruments of control being the direct 'real' controls (consumer rationing, labour controls, raw material controls, etc.); and the Treasury has tagged along behind trying to mop up the purchasing power made redundant by the 'real' controls. In peace-time the 'real' controls will presumably go, and financial inducements will come into their own again. To take an outstanding example, employment policy will inevitably again become mainly a financial problem of maintaining total monetary demand at an adequate level; control through a manpower budget and labour direction will recede into the background. The Treasury, willy-nilly, will become the central economic Dept.

Accordingly, before accepting the Directorship of the Economic Section, I made certain by means of a formal minute to Bridges[3] that it was not the intention of the Treasury to maintain its own group of economic advisers, but to rely upon the Economic Section, and that it was the intention of the Treasury that the Director of the Economic Section should be consulted on budgetary policy and on external finance.

The central task round which the work of the Economic Section must, I think, be built is the duties of the central economic staff mentioned in the White Paper on *Employment Policy*.[4] It must be our central routine job to forecast and to advise on the control of employment trends (largely through the forward planning of the national expenditure and so the national income). This will involve financial policy, both internal and external. It will involve manpower statistics and wages policy.

If we are successful in this, we should naturally (if somewhat illogically) find our way into industrial efficiency, restrictive practices and the location of industry.

The other great block of subjects are the external economic and financial problems, including the Article VII range of topics (long-term financial, commercial and commodity policies);[5] the short-run transitional problems (such as the future of Lend-Lease and the temporary arrangements

[3] Meade to Bridges, 1 October 1944, quoted in Butt, 'Notes on the History of the Economic Section', 11 August 1953, T230/283.

[4] *Employment Policy*, Cmd 6527, 1944.

[5] Article VII of the Mutual Aid Agreement signed on 23 February 1942 committed Britain as follows: 'To that end, they shall include provision for agreed action by the United States of America and the United Kingdom, open to participation by all other countries of like mind, directed to the expansion, by appropriate international and domestic measures, of production, employment, and the exchange and consumption of goods . . .; to the elimination of all forms of discriminatory treatment in international commerce, and to the reduction of tariffs and other trade barriers; and, in general, to the attainment of all the economic objectives set forth in the Joint Declaration made on the 14th August 1941 . . . [the Atlantic Charter]'. Under Article VII, Anglo-American negotiations had by November 1944 resulted in the United Nations Monetary and Financial Conference at Bretton Woods, New Hampshire, which drafted the Articles of Agreement for the International Monetary Fund and the International Bank for Reconstruction and Development. Discussions had also taken place in Washington in September-October 1943 on trade, commodity and employment policies, but no agreed schemes had emerged.

necessary to keep our balance of payments in control); and the immediate problems of European reconstruction (including the future of Germany from the point of view of economic security and reparations and the rebuilding of the economies of the liberated territories).

I am frankly appalled by the magnitude which the task which I have undertaken will assume if it is successfully undertaken and by the responsibility which is involved in giving serious advice on these problems, when one knows that the advice may really influence decisions and action. The first thing to do is to try to make sure that there is a really competent team of economists in the post-war Economic Section.

## 12 November 1944

I have spent the week on the tiresome matter of establishments. The prospects of getting together a decent team for the post-war economic section seem better than I had imagined. A. J. Brown, Jack Stafford and [Donald] MacDougall, with whom I have talked this week, all seem much attracted by the idea. Marcus Fleming may stay. Even Stanley Dennison, who always maintained that he was going, has been sufficiently shaken by my decision to stay on to consider (rather by way of duty than of pleasure) staying on himself for a bit. The above would certainly make a first-rate team. My real headache starts with Tress and Chantler, both of whom are thinking seriously of staying on and both of whom I should like to keep. But the Treasury will not let me overdo the top grade and both T. and C. (with considerable justification in my view) do not want to stay on if it involves their staying in an inferior grade (i.e. as plain Economic Assistants when all the rest will be Chief Economic Assistants). Lionel [Robbins] is being very helpful and has devised the idea of having only one grade of Economic Assistants with a salary scale covering both the existing grades, and giving T. and C. an appreciable rise in salary but not right up to the others. We have tried to sell this idea to Bridges for him to sell to the Treasury. I shall be wild with anger if, having persuaded me to stay on, the Treasury now make it impossible to keep the team together.

The main work I have been concerned with is the preparation of the paper on how quantitative import controls can be made to work in a non-discriminatory manner. The Economic Section have been trying to sell the idea that the import licences should be sold to the highest bidder in an auction on the lines of the Treasury Bill tender. This would not only ensure non-discrimination but would enable one to measure the protective incidence of the quota (by relating the import licence fee to the value of the goods imported). The only person in the official committee concerned (Eady, Hubert Henderson, Liesching, Shackle, Clutterbuck, Broadley, Blagburn, Fergusson, Enfield, Robbins and myself, with Gorell Barnes as secretary) who is willing to contemplate the auctioning of licences experimentally for some commodities is – *mirabile dictu* – Fergusson.[6]

[6] The committee of officials, consisting of representatives from the Treasury, Dominions Office, Board of Trade, Ministry of Agriculture and Fisheries, Ministry of Food and the

On the motion of Hubert Henderson who has 'stability' on the brain, the committee were going to suggest that this country should commit itself to a formula for non-discrimination which would prevent it shifting its purchases quickly from one source of supply to another.[7] Lionel and I protested vigorously against such an arrangement which – in the name of non-discrimination – would prevent us from buying in the cheapest market. This we argued (and, I believe, to some effect) was not really a very sensible proposal for a country which expected to experience serious difficulties in its balance of payments. The result is to be a very general paper for Ministers merely arguing that a set of rules for non-discrimination can be worked out, and that we should urge that it should be permissible (but not obligatory) for a country to move only gradually from a more expensive to a less expensive source of supply, but that it would have to shift at least gradually.[8] The hope is that, on the basis of this paper and of the ones which we have already submitted to Ministers on the position of Agriculture under the proposed commercial policy convention, we shall at last (some 14 months after the Washington conversations on commercial policy in September 1943) be permitted to talk again to the Americans on the subject. This Ministers are under an obligation to do; and Hawkins of the State Department who has recently been transferred to the American Embassy in London is patiently waiting to take up the problem with us.

## *19 November 1944*

The week has again been spent largely in making arrangements to get a team of economists together for the Economic Section after the war. There is clearly going to be difficulty – in fact great difficulty – in persuading the Treasury to offer sufficiently attractive terms to tempt economists to stay. They do not, I think, realise the great scarcity of economists; the attractiveness to economists of academic life; the additional income that economists can earn outside by examination, by extra teaching and by writing. There would be a very good chance of getting a really good team together if the Treasury would compete with the Universities (which are offering more and more additional jobs for economists) by offering really attractive terms. All this I have to try to make clear (with the very greatest help from Lionel Robbins) to Bridges, in order that he may himself be persuaded to take on the task of

Economic Section, had been set up on 27 September 1944 to 'examine as a matter of urgency the needs of the agricultural industry for stable prices after the war, in relation to the Anglo-American scheme for commercial policy. In particular . . . to examine levy subsidies, bulk purchase and other forms of state trading and quantitative regulation of imports and to report to what extent arrangements to ensure the stability of price levels deemed necessary by the Agricultural Departments would involve modification of the Washington proposals [of September-October 1943].' (T230/127)

7 Draft Report on Non-Discrimination in Relation to Programming of Imports, 9 November 1944, T230/9.

8 Meade to Eady, 9 November 1944, T230/7; Commercial Policy and the Needs of Agriculture: Report by a Group of Officials, November, 1944 T230/127.

persuading the Treasury. Meanwhile, Stafford, Chantler and Miss Watts have said that they will definitely come if a sufficiently attractive offer is made to them. A. J. Brown and Marcus Fleming are likely to come if they don't get the new chair at Liverpool. Others are still hesitating.

The suggested method of reconciling the requirements of Agricultural Policy with the Washington Commercial Proposals has been presented by our official committee to the Chancellor's Ministerial Committee which approved it with no difficulty.[9] It now goes to the Cabinet next week. We shall then at last be able to talk to the Americans again (in the person of Hawkins) after an interval of no less than 14 months. (Incidentally Eady from the chair at the last meeting of the official group [16 November] with everyone else present said that he had been lunching with Hawkins who had expressed the opinion that James Meade was a man of 'incorruptible honesty'. This from a man of Hawkins' incorruptible honesty and undoubted intelligence is an honour indeed!) For the first time we now have proposals which have the definite support of Fergusson and the Agricultural Departments. If we can pull this off with the Americans, the outlook is at least reasonably bright again.

There was one last-minute threat of a hitch (there will be many more last minutes before the goal is reached) when at the last official meeting we were discussing the draft of a telegram for the Dominions explaining the proposal we were about to make to Hawkins.[10] I had suggested a redraft making it clear that, while we desired to give agriculture rather more latitude than industry in respect of a moderate and limited quantum of production both by allowing a rather higher level of protection and by allowing the use of quantitative restrictions as a normal method of protection, we intended to restore the balance by ensuring that all forms of protection and support to agriculture (including subsidies) would be continuously and progressively reduced so long as agricultural production exceeded the limited quantum. At this last moment Enfield argued that the MAF did not mean this, but merely that the degree of protection should be somewhat reduced by a sliding scale as agricultural production exceeded the limited quantum. After some argument Fergusson, I am glad to say, accepted my emendment which, if it goes to the Dominions, will definitely commit the Agricultural Departments. I spent 2½ hours the next morning at the Ministry of Agriculture trying to persuade Enfield to let it go and not to insist on his point. I think I made some impression on him.

In the course of the week I wrote a draft paper on the statistics which will be required on capital investment after the war for the purpose of Employment Policy. This was in answer to a paper by Coase of the Central Statistical Office in which it was argued that we should collect statistics of national expenditure by products – e.g. how much is spent on engineering

[9] Committee on Commercial Policy, CCP(44) 4th Meeting, 15 November 1944, CAB87/97, T230/127.

[10] 16 November 1944, T230/127.

products, how much on building, etc.[11] These output figures will in any case be collected by the annual census of production after the war. What is wanted in expenditure forecasts, in order to stabilise *total* national expenditure and not merely on one type of product or service, is to get figures of future expenditure by categories (e.g. consumers' expenditure, government current expenditure, private investment, public investment, the foreign balance) according to the types of control and of policy by which they are affected. This is an important principle of post-war employment policy.

Beveridge's long awaited report on 'Full Employment in a Free Society' is out. I am reading it and am under a promise to write a paper on it (particularly comparing it with the Government's White Paper on the same subject) for the Reconstruction people. It would, I think, be useful to employ this opportunity for a little further instruction of Ministers and of officials on this subject.[12]

In the course of the week I received copies of the pamphlet which Stone and I have written on the National Income and Expenditure.[13] I hope that it may be yet one more drop in the bucket, which – when full – will enable us so to understand the working of the system as to be able to prevent fluctuations in total national expenditure and, in consequence, in employment. I sent copies to Bridges and Eady, from the latter of whom I got a most disarming letter saying that he had had no training in economics but was trying to master the subject. When one looks at it objectively, what a state of affairs it is when the man chiefly responsible for internal and external financial policy has had no technical training. I am sure that in our grandchildren's days this will be considered very odd.

## *25 November 1944*

Some part of the week (but not enough, I fear) has again been spent on considering a future team for the Economic Section. I have spoken with Tom Wilson and G. L. Shackle of Lord Cherwell's staff.[14] Both are possibilities but uncertainties. I don't think that either Bridges or the Treasury fully realise how desperately difficult it is likely to be to get a first-class team together for this really difficult but vital job. I must take the matter up really vigorously with them next week.

I have finished and despatched my note on Coase's memorandum on

[11] Meade, 'Notes on Mr Coase's "Statistics of Capital Expenditure and Employment Policy" ', 16 November 1944, R. H. Coase, 'Statistics of Capital Expenditure and Employment Policy', 28 October 1944, T230/69. A revised version of Meade's paper was circulated on 27 November as EC(S) (44)17 (T230/16).

[12] Sir W. Beveridge, *Full Employment in a Free Society*. London: Allen and Unwin, 1944. See below p. 7.

[13] J. E. Meade and Richard Stone, *National Income and Expenditure*. London: Oxford University Press, 1944 (reprinted in *The Collected Papers of James Meade*, Vol. I, chapter 10).

[14] The Prime Minister's Statistical Branch, set up by Churchill when he was First Lord of the Admiralty in September 1939.

the investment statistics required for post-war Employment Policy.[15] One more drop in the bucket, persuading people to tackle the problem through national expenditure forecasting and planning. But I have been rather depressed by a discussion with Stone later in the week on this subject. He is, alas, taking a rather perfectionist line, and seems unwilling to start in boldly and do a forecast and improve the information and technique later *ambulando*. I argued that this was what we in fact did in September 1940-March 1941 with the estimates of the national income and expenditure themselves and that if we had not allowed the Budget speech of 1941 to be based on our hurried and slipshod estimates we should never have got the idea started at all.[16] He may, nevertheless, be right. But if so, we must give up any idea of controlling depressions by foreseeing them and planning ahead. We must devise methods of jumping in to squash a depression after it has started and as soon as we are sure from first evidence (e.g. movements in unemployment indices) that it has actually started. We must, of course, be ready to do this in any case, since we certainly cannot rely upon perfect forecasting and completely effective planning ahead of expenditure.

I have been continuing my paper on Beveridge's book.[17] So far I have done a first draft of a section showing (what is really a most remarkable fact if one casts one's memory back to the doctrinal bedlam of the 1930s that the basic principles of Beveridge's book and the Government White Paper on *Employment Policy* are exactly the same: maintenance of aggregate demand with freedom of consumer's and worker's choice as the main instrument, supplemented by measures to stimulate the mobility of labour and to guide the location of industry. I have also done the first draft of a section arguing that Beveridge's target of an average unemployment percentage of 3 per cent is really too much of a good thing. Surely it is merely playing to the gallery. It assumes that seasonal unemployment is halved without saying by what means; it assumes literally no structural or depression unemployment except such as may result from inevitable instabilities in our exports; and it is only half as much as pre-1914. I should have thought that we should be doing extremely well if we can get back to the 6 per cent of pre-1914.

Early in the week Lionel Robbins and I went to visit Sir Bernard Gilbert in the Treasury in order to discuss certain points in our forthcoming Economic Survey on the problems of reconversion in 1945.[18] The highlight of the visit was a strange little exordium from Gilbert before we got down to business. – Do not be in too great a hurry. Remember the striking address given by Jeans as [the] presidential address to the British

[15] See p. 6, note 11.

[16] For the story of the 1941 estimates see J. R. N. Stone, 'The Development and Use of National Income and Expenditure Estimates' in D. N. Chester (ed.), *Lessons of the British War Economy*. Cambridge: Cambridge University Press, 1951.

[17] 'Sir William Beveridge's "Full Employment in a Free Society" and the White Paper on Employment Policy (Command 6527)', 1 December 1944, EC(S) (44)20, T230/20, Meade Papers 3/2, and *The Collected Papers of James Meade*, Vol. I, chapter 15.

[18] The first draft had been produced in October: 'Economic Survey October 1944', EC(S) (44)15, T230/16.

Ass[ociation] or the Royal Society (G. could not remember which) in which Jeans had likened the probable life-time of man on this planet to the four score years and ten of an individual life and had pointed out that we were now only 21 months old and had been civilised only for 4 months.[19] Was it not being in too much of a hurry to try to put right in the next second all the conditions which would affect the rest of our life merely because we had spent the last five seconds quarrelling with our equally baby brother? One must not try to go too quickly in our social institutions. We proceeded by going a little forward here, a progress which set up a tension over there, which tension we relieved by yet another small advance in some other part of the system. But might not Beveridge speed cause a break instead of a tension? What was to be the position of the striker under a universal social security system in which no one was to be in want? Did this tension involve giving up the right to strike or would there be a break? – After this we turned in a wise and patient manner to a few verbal changes in our draft! There *is* something admirable in this philosophy of slow-but-sure; and if there were never any wars, I believe it would have it every time. But I suspect that major wars both set up abnormal tensions and also present unique opportunities, which justify or indeed necessitate putting on rather more than usual speed after them.

On the international front one serious set-back and one partial offset to this set-back. Under the influence of Beaverbrook the PM has taken a line on our proposed compromise between Agricultural Policy and Commercial Policy which resulted in a Cabinet decision which will make it impossible for us to discuss in detail the compromise with Hawkins, when the time comes to talk with him again.[20] But it seems that we shall be able to talk, very unofficially and non-committally of course, and even to see how he reacts to the idea that agricultural protection should be rather more than industrial for a limited quantity of production, but less than industrial for anything over this quantity. Before the Cabinet Lionel and I had been to see how to explain the proposed compromise to him; Lionel had briefed Attlee; I had briefed Woolton and had explained the situation to Weeks who was briefing Lyttleton.

As against this, the idea that we should sponsor an international conference (à la Hot Springs[21]) on employment policies has prospered with Ministers. This may prove important, since international conversations and progress on the subject might help to break the jam in which the other schemes seem temporarily at least to have got themselves. I have drafted an agenda for such a conference, which Lionel is sending round for discussion among officials.[22]

This morning Penrose of the US Embassy rang up and asked whether he

[19] Gilbert's reference was probably not to Jeans' Presidential Address to the British Association for the Advancement of Science on 5 September 1934 ('The New World-Picture of Modern Physics', supplement to *Nature*, no. 3384, 8 September 1934, pp. 355–65), but to his Royal Institution Lectures at Christmas 1932, which were expanded and published as *Through Space and Time*. Cambridge: Cambridge University Press, 1934.

[20] WM153(44)4, 22 November 1944, CAB65/44.

[21] The UN Conference on Food and Agriculture at Hot Springs, Virginia in 1943.

[22] Not located.

and Hawkins could come round to see me. Naturally I could not say no, and was in fact delighted to see Hawkins.[23] But I felt very inhospitable that my attempts not to speak to him until our lips were a bit unsealed in commercial policy should have meant that he had to take the first steps to renew contact in this country. Hawkins expressed a strong desire that we should get talking again in order to avoid reaching a position in which formal delegates should confront each other without previous informal preparation and then reach a deadlock. He asked whether any substantial part of our difficulties would disappear if it became clear that under the proposed multilateral arrangement (and we convinced the Americans at the Washington talks of the need for a multilateral treatment of tariffs) the Americans were prepared to make a really very large cut in their tariff. I pointed out – what must be obvious to him – that our three main political and psychological obstacles were Agricultural Policy, the Imperial problem and the fear that by tying our hands internationally we might be unable to carry out our domestic policy of employment. I kept the conversation very much on employment policy, and argued that one important strand in our difficulties would be broken if it became clear that other countries (and in particular the USA, of course) were determined, on the lines of our White Paper on *Employment Policy*, not to allow a domestic slump in their buying power. Hawkins said that they were working on this employment policy problem in Washington; and he said that he agreed with what I said except that the general principles of the international set-up should be agreed first, so that the domestic full employment policies should be made to fit into this structure. I replied that I thought that there was a difference between a country (like the USA) which would never be prevented on balance of payments grounds from prosecuting a domestic full employment policy but which might like to use protection to export unemployment and a country (like the UK) which, if it tied its hands internationally too strictly, might in conditions of a world depression be positively compelled to give up its domestic policy of stabilisation. To which Hawkins replied (very pertinently) that he did not see what more was needed than the various let-outs on balance of payments grounds which they considered to be perfectly justifiable. Penrose and Hawkins agreed that they thought full employment of first-rate importance; but was it not really being somewhat overdone? There were other things also of importance. I could not have agreed more with them, particularly when Hawkins went on to add that he thought that one thing – namely Peace – was even more important, and that he could not see how Peace could be assured in the world of trade wars which would result from discriminatory bilateral practices adopted to maintain stability in foreign trade.

The conversation was made more piquant by the fact that in the middle Richard Law rang me up to say that he had been to Bath yesterday for his aunt's funeral and had met mother, Margaret and Diana. He then proceeded to ask me what I thought of the Cabinet decision on Commercial

[23] The substance of the conversation is reported in Meade to Robbins, 27 November 1944, T230/173.

Policy.[24] As I was speaking in front of Hawkins, I had to mumble some incomprehensible remark, ring off and ring up later when Hawkins had gone, in order to explain my embarrassment.

[24] See above p. 8.

# 2

# December 1944

*3 December 1944*

In the course of the week I have made a little further progress with the problem of building up a post-war Economic Section. Bridges has been to see Wilson Smith (the head of establishments at the Treasury) and has left with him a very satisfactory aide-memoire[1] (very much on the lines of a minute sent by Lionel to Bridges) emphasising the need to offer good salaries at an early date to economists if they are to be tempted from University life, and suggesting (what I am sure is right for the Economic Section) that one should have a single grade of Economic Assistant with a very wide salary range (covering the grades corresponding to Principals and Assistant Secretaries). The Economic Section should be very much like the Fellows of an Oxford College, equal status but variations in stipend according to seniority. In the course of the week I had lunch with E. Devons, at present in charge of the Statistics and Programmes Division of the Ministry of Aircraft Production. I feel sure that he would be an ideal person for the Planning and Timing of Public Investment. He seemed at least willing to consider joining the Section in this capacity. I have heard that Gilbert Walker (at present posted to Washington by the M[inistry] of Supply) wants to join the Section after the war. He might do this job if Devons is not available.

We have had some considerable discussion about the organisation of Overseas Economic Intelligence after the war. Nigel Ronald of the FO has written raising the subject,[2] which involves (i) the absorption of some of the MEW intelligence work by the FO and (ii) the setting up of some central machinery in the Cabinet Offices to co-ordinate all overseas economic intelligence (which covers India, Dominions and Colonies as well as foreign countries). The danger from our point of view seemed to me that there might be set up in the Cabinet Offices a new organisation dealing in the end with external economic policy, which would usurp many of the functions of the Economic Section. But after conversation with Lionel Robbins, Bridges and Laithwaite I think this danger will be avoided.[3]

[1] Not located.

[2] Ronald to Robbins, 28 November 1944, CAB 21/2562.

[3] On 1 December 1944: Robbins to Bridges, Laithwaite and Meade, 1 December 1944, CAB 21/2562.

I have spent most of the week writing a vast Memorandum on Beveridge's recent book on Full Employment.[4] The thesis of my Memorandum being that the general principles of policy in B's book are the same as those in the Government's White Paper, so that one can assume (in direct contrast to the inter-war period) that the general principles of Employment Policy are now agreed. But B's book, by setting the impossible target of 3 per cent average unemployment, is doing a grave disservice to the conscientious and responsible treatment of this difficult problem. It is merely playing to the gallery and embarrassing HMG. Further, B's section on international policy and employment is most unsatisfactory. It does not recognise any of the real advantages which the type of external world which we are building up through Bretton Woods and Article VII has for the prosecution of internal economic employment policies. For example, astonishing as it may sound, the whole chapter on the international implications of full employment does not have a single reference to exchange rates! Contrast the Bretton Woods rules which, if applied 1929–39, would have allowed us to depreciate in 1931 (regardless of our domestic policy) and would have ruled out the subsequent unnecessary competitive exchange depreciation of the Americans.

In the middle of the week Bruce, the High Commissioner for Australia, asked me to call on him. He said that Copland, Professor of Economics at Melbourne who is also Prices Commissioner and Economic Adviser to the Prime Minister at Canberra, was coming to London and would I introduce him to the economists in Whitehall? Later in conversation with Bruce I realised that for some reason or another he had not seen the telegram to the Australian and New Zealand Govts, in which we accepted their idea of an international conference on employment policies and offered to broach the idea with the Americans.[5] I verified from Clutterbuck of the Dominions Office afterwards that Bruce should have seen this telegram and that I might speak freely about it to Copland.

The next evening Copland came to dine with me at the Reform Club and I went on to see him after dinner in his room in the Grosvenor House Hotel. Copland was very appreciative of the White Paper on *Employment Policy*. He thought it was a marvellous document for economists to have got accepted as a White Paper. He was interested to learn our views on the technique of the forward planning of national expenditure and national income and to hear of the future prospects of the Economic Section. The conversation then turned to the international aspect of this problem, and I was able to surprise him (very agreeably and again to the credit of this country in being the champion of employment policy) with the news that we had agreed to their views on an international conference to promote suitable domestic employment policies. I then turned the conversation to the other aspects of international economic policy (monetary, investment, commercial policies, etc.). Copland clearly showed that he did not sympathise fully with the Australian extremists (like Coombs) who will not

[4] See page 7, note 17.

[5] The telegrams, nos. 338 and 276, from the Dominions Office to Australia and New Zealand, 24 November 1944, are on FO371/40949.

touch obligations to fix exchange rates or to lower trade barriers; but he went on to the defensive and explained how he was confronted in Washington and Ottawa with the accusation that Australia was playing a selfish nationalist game in not being willing to go ahead with these international obligations. To such critics, he said, he replied that, whereas the Australians and New Zealanders could not for political reasons sell these international schemes to their electorates without getting the first and main emphasis on full employment, so the North Americans, again for political reasons (e.g. to avoid accusations of New-Dealism), would not go ahead with discussions on the important subject of full employment; they were, therefore, just as much to blame as the Australians for any deadlock.

At this I let loose a general offensive. I said that I fully agreed with the need to get all the main countries to accept domestic employment policies. But how, I asked, could the Australians be so blind as to fail to see that these other international obligations, far from being of a character which might endanger their and our domestic employment policies, had in fact been carefully devised to safeguard such policies if there were, in spite of all our efforts à la Australienne, in fact some general world depression. Assuming an American depression to cause the Americans to have a seriously favourable and us a seriously unfavourable balance of payments (and this was its only real danger), then under the International Monetary Fund (i) we could depreciate and the Americans could not, a position vastly superior to that of the 1930s, (ii) we could prevent the export of hot money or other forms of capital, which did so much damage in the 1930s, and (iii) the scarce currency arrangements were a miracle which would enable us to refuse American goods without their being free to refuse ours and this regardless of any existing MFN clauses. Under the Commercial Policy arrangements we in balance of payments difficulties could regulate imports and the Americans could not. From his reaction I do not believe that Copland had ever before heard the argument that the Article VII arrangements would prove a positive help (instead of a positive hindrance) to domestic employment policies. I am sure that this is the way to tackle the Australians.

We have received the directive from the Chancellor [of the Exchequer] (agreed by the PM) for the talks with Hawkins.[6] We are to be very tentative and non-committal; but we can outline very provisionally the main lines of the proposal suggested for agriculture provided that no figures at all are mentioned except by way of example. It might be worse after all. Dean Acheson I see has meanwhile made a public statement to Congress in Washington emphasising the fact that the Roosevelt Administration is really sold on getting a general commercial policy convention in line with our Washington proposals.[7] Sooner or later I expect the Americans will turn the heat on.

[6] For its contents see WM153(44)4, CAB65/44, and CCP(44)8 Committee on Commercial Policy, FO371/40949.

[7] On 30 November 1944 to the Sub-committee on Foreign Trade and Shipping of the Special Committee of the House of Representatives on Post-War Economic Policy and Planning: Department of State, *Bulletin*, 3 December 1944, p. 656.

## 10 December 1944

This week the conversations with Hawkins on Commercial Policy started.[8] Personally I was very sorry indeed not to be present at this very memorable (and what turned out to be almost dramatic) occasion, particularly when I think back to the summer of 1942 when I drafted the first version of the Commercial Union and began to sell it to the Board of Trade.[9] But my absence from the party was inevitable: Liesching had, of course, to lead; it was essential that the Treasury and the Ministry of Agriculture should be present (in the persons of Eady and Fergusson) so that those departments should be involved in the negotiations; and Lionel as director of the Economic Section had to be there. As we were to meet only Hawkins and Penrose on the other side, our party could not be enlarged. At the meeting, I am told, Liesching made a few introductory remarks on our political difficulties and asked Hawkins if he had anything to say. We were expecting him to probe our position, and Fergusson had been primed to go on to expound our agricultural difficulties and the particular let-outs which we had devised for them. Instead of this Hawkins replied that he would like to make a statement. He had with him a draft convention which [had] gone very far up in Washington (although not yet naturally through the President's Office).[10] He did not want actually to hand it over. But would we like to be informed of its contents? The rest of the meeting was taken up with an explanation by Hawkins of some of its main contents: a declaration about domestic employment policies; a cut in all tariffs by 50 per cent with a floor of 10 per cent; preference margins to be squeezed by applying these tariff cuts to the non-preferential rates and not to the preferential rates, with a maximum percentage limit to preference margins; quantitative restrictions to be permitted for five years from the signing of the Convention (provided the quotas were not less than actual imports in a pre-war base period) and then to be continued only with the agreement of the proposed International Commercial Policy Organisation on a 'tailing-off' basis; and such quantitative restrictions could be imposed again later with the permission of the ICPO (which would be bound to allow them if they were necessary to ease a re-adjustment of industry due to some structural change) again on the basis that they would be 'tailed-off' over a period of years. The other clauses (including a joker to cover the balance of payments difficulties) are to be explained next week. This, of course, puts commercial policy on the map again. It is difficult to see how we can lightly refuse an offer to halve the American tariff, when the Americans have gone out of their way to meet us (i) on employment policies, (ii) on not demanding the total elimination of imperial preference and (iii) on the quantitative regulation of trade. Eady and Fergusson are

[8] On 7 December 1944. There were twelve subsequent meetings between then and 30 January 1945. Records of the meetings are on BT11/2504.

[9] Meade's first draft, 'A Proposal for an International Commercial Union', 25 July 1942, EC(S)(42)19, is on T230/14 and 125 and in Meade Papers 3/2, printed in *The Collected Papers of James Meade*, Vol. III, chapter 3. Later drafts, including the Board of Trade version, 'Project of a Commercial Union', 5 November 1942, are on T230/125.

[10] See the 'Synopsis of the American Draft Convention', on FO371/40949.

said to have been most impressed with Hawkins' attempt to meet us. This, together with the recent pamphlet by the Federation of British Industries urging the acceptance of Bretton Woods,[11] puts an entirely new light on post-war international arrangements in the economic and financial fields.

I have had two more sessions with Copland this week. First, he came to the office to meet Chester who explained to him (really brilliantly) our problems of fiscal control. Secondly, I went up with Marcus Fleming to call on him at the Grosvenor House Hotel, where we explained the problems of our White Paper on *Employment Policy* and managed again to expound to him the view that the proposed Article VII international settlement (through the rules covering exchange rate adjustments, scarce currency, import restrictions on balance-of-payments grounds, etc.) would be positively helpful to domestic policies for full employment. It will not be for want of trying on my part if he does not take this message back to Australia!

Noel-Baker asked me to lunch and explained how he had to speak to a motion at the Labour Party Conference on Full Employment, which was to be moved by Shinwell. I explained to him how he could argue that the Bretton Woods Agreements and a commercial policy which generally cleared the channels of trade without preventing countries in special balance of payments difficulties from regulating their imports would positively help the domestic policy of full employment. I referred to the rules about exchange depreciation, the scarce currency arrangements, the right to control capital movements, and the provision of untied loans. It will be good to hear of an internationalist like Noel-Baker, as a member of the Party Executive, following a speech by Shinwell on this subject. I told Noel-Baker that it was a speech which no one yet had ever made and encouraged him to do it.[12]

There have been some more developments in the post-war organisation of the Section. I had lunch with Gilbert Walker who is most keen on the work of the Section on post-war employment policy. In spite of his rather crude manner, I believe that he might make a very useful member of the Section. There has also been a reply from the Treasury to Bridges' suggestion that there should only be one grade of economic assistant for the first years after the war. They accept the general idea but wish to maintain that the numbers of those put on a salary scale equivalent to that of Assistant Secretary should be limited in number and above a certain age. This must be carefully considered.

There has also been a very satisfactory meeting with the Secretary, Laithwaite, Campion, Robbins and myself to discuss the functions at the centre of overseas economic intelligence. The Central Statistical Office is to produce a statistical digest of overseas figures and the Economic Section a periodical survey of the overseas situation and its implications for UK policy. There is to be an interdepartmental official committee, with

[11] Interim Report of the Federation of British Industries on the Final Act of the United Nations Monetary and Financial Conference, November 1944.

[12] Shinwell's and Noel-Baker's speeches (on 14 December) are in the Report of the 43rd Annual Conference of the Labour Party, pp. 160–3 and 167–8.

secretariat from the CSO and the ES and with representation also from the CSO and ES to co-ordinate the overseas economic intelligence work done in the various departments.[13]

Some preliminary moves on the organisation of the post-war use of National Income and Expenditure figures have not been so successful. Indeed, from my purely personal point of view they threaten to approach disaster. During the week Stone came to tell me that Campion (during Stone's absence in Washington) had started to split up the National Income and Expenditure work, and had given the Balance of Payments to Fowler, Home Investment to Coase, etc. Stone is most anxious, of course, to see a proper National Income and Expenditure Unit set up in Whitehall which will give him the assurance that the whole work can be carried on, under his control, as a coherent unit. I, considering him to be by far the best man for this job and knowing that a coherent and logical use of this instrument is essential for the post-war work of the ES, did all I could to help. I discussed it for hours with Lionel, who discussed it with Bridges, who had an hour's interview with Stone, who came away very pleased as Bridges had said to him that the initiation of the post-war employment policy might form an appropriate occasion on which the work on the National Income and Expenditure could be re-orientated a bit towards the Economic Section, who would want to use it much more than before.

The implication and intention of all this was that, by emphasising the genuine need of the Economic Section to take a close part in the logical make-up of the estimates and in the process of forecasting, Stone's hand would be strengthened in his desire to preserve and develop a unified National Income and Expenditure enquiry somewhat independent of the rest of the CSO. Accordingly, I prepared a note for Lionel emphasising the special interest and responsibility which the Economic Section would have in using these estimates for the purpose of forecasting and in seeing that the classifications were suitable for employment policy.[14] My conclusion was that, in view of the Statistical and Economic interests in these estimates, some very special form of co-operation between the CSO and ES would be necessary in this field. This was intended to make way for a solution by means of a special National Income and Expenditure Unit with the CSO with Stone as its head. Bridges and Lionel were both ready to hint this idea to Campion. . . .

## *16 December 1944*

. . . On Monday an Egyptian called Ami appeared with a letter of introduction from E. M. H. Lloyd in Cairo. He is from the Egyptian Ministry of Finance and has come to study our methods of measuring the national income and expenditure. I have him a copy of Stone's and my recent pamphlet,[15] talked to him generally on the subject and sent him off

[13] The meeting took place on 1 December (CAB21/2562). The minutes of the inter-departmental committee are on CAB134/204.

[14] Meade, 'Estimates of National Income and Expenditure', 7 December 1944, T230/69.

[15] *National Income and Expenditure*, op. cit.

to Stone, who in turn rang me up after his visit to say that he thought that we were going to find him a willing but backward pupil. On Tuesday I went to a lunch at the National Institute of Economic and Social Research where there were a number of American economists for us to meet. On Friday Stone rang me up to say that, on his suggestion, Brittain of the Treasury asked me to go round with Stone to his room to discuss the forecast of the national income for 1945/46 which Stone was doing in preparation for the next Budget.[16]

I was rather amused at this meeting with Brittain, because at the end of it Brittain said that he thought that he realised now how to put the general financial outlook to the meeting of high-ups who were to consider it in the next few days. Lionel and I had just been invited by Sir Richard Hopkins to attend that meeting.[17] This is the first entrée of the Economic Section to Budgetary Policy. Lionel had been speaking to Bridges who had, I believe, spoken to Brittain about the relations between the Economic Section and the Treasury on Budgetary Policy. As a result here is the first move on the part of the Treasury to honour its undertaking (see my entry for 5 November 1944 [p. 2] that we should be consulted on Budgetary Policy. I hope that this works out well. It is essential if the Economic Section in the post-war world is really going to play an effective part in general economic policy.

Early in the week I went out of my way to invite Coase over from the CSO to discuss his views on the statistics of capital investment required for post-war employment policy. (See entries of 19 and 25 November 1944.)[18] We agreed that one wanted figures both by products and by the general categories (e.g. consumer's expenditure, public current expenditure, private investment, public investment, foreign balance). I am determined to keep on friendly and co-operative terms not only with Stone but with all the members of the CSO whom Campion sets to work on different sections of the statistics required for employment policy.

My main tasks this week have been to revise my long paper on Beveridge's recent book on Full Employment,[19] and to consider the revision of our Economic Survey. As a result of changing the assumed date of the end of the German war from end-December 1944 to end-June 1945, the whole thing needs revision.[20] We are determined if possible to get it out in the course of next week, but it will be rather a rush.

In the course of the week the Section (in the persons of Chester and Chantler) have prepared a long brief for Woolton on the report of a committee of officials on how public utility corporations in general and

[16] The forecast appeared in B(45)1, 'Budget 1945: Note by Sir Herbert Brittain', 14 December 1944 (T171/369).

[17] This was the first meeting of the Budget Committee for the April 1945 Budget. Robbins and Meade did not in fact attend that meeting (on 21 or 22 December 1944), but see below, p. 21.

[18] Above pp. 5–6. Coase, who had regretted the wide circulation of Meade's memorandum, had written a reply to Meade's paper: 'A Reply to Mr Meade's Comments on Statistics of Capital Expenditure and Employment Policy', 5 December 1944 (T230/69).

[19] See page 7, note 17.

[20] See below, p. 20.

the electricity industry in particular should be constituted.[21] One aspect of this matter interests me very much. If prices of the output of such monopolies are equated to marginal costs (as they should be) and not to average costs (as everyone assumes they will be), they may properly make considerable losses. This means that such public monopolies should be financed by the state taking over the ownership of their assets and compensating the previous owners with fixed interest national debt, thus leaving the public utility free to make such profit or loss as is in the public interest. This outcome would be gravely hampered if public utilities were so financed that they had to meet out of their own profits the fixed interest on their debt. After considerable argument a paragraph in our brief was inserted to keep the door open on this point; but there is a *very* long way to go indeed before this sensible principle of pricing policy becomes at all generally accepted. Incidentally, the symposium which Fleming and I have written on this subject appeared in the *Economic Journal* last week.[22] It had been Keynes' idea to have it published and it may set a useful precedent for the view that members of the Economic Section should be allowed to publish papers of general interest even on subjects of economic policy.

The talks with Hawkins have been continued. He has finished outlining the American proposals, which do not mention anything more very startling, but are bold and sensible. There was then a meeting of UK officials to decide how to proceed. Lionel tells me that this meeting was terrible. At it Liesching produced a paper by Shackle which was certainly lamentable – all full of the difficulties of a general multilateral agreement and emphasising every difficulty and disadvantage in the American proposals and overlooking all the many advantages of them.[23] I really believe that the professional economists are the only people among officials (apart from Clutterbuck of the Dominions Office) who really wish to get an agreement. And yet an agreement is so patently in our interests and failure to agree with the Americans on this so patently dangerous. At another meeting with Hawkins our proposal for a separate treatment of agriculture was unfolded, and apparently after a sticky start it went down well. The Americans realised that it was not just a bad joke but was a truly serious and perhaps rather promising way out of the worst agricultural difficulties in exporting as well as in importing countries.

I have now submitted a list of persons and proposed salary scales to the establishments officer here, and he is to discuss it with Bridges and attempt to get Treasury agreement. One thing has become urgent. MacDougall (of Lord Cherwell's office) has been offered a fellowship and lectureship

21 'Public Utility Corporations (R(44)199)', 16 December 1944, EC(S)(44)22, T230/96. The Report of the Official Committee on Public Utility Corporations, 30 November 1944, R(44)199, was considered by the Reconstruction Committee of the Cabinet on 20 December 1944 (R(44) 80th Meeting, CAB 124/427).

22 'Price and Output Policy of State Enterprise, A Symposium', *Economic Journal*, Vol. 54 (December 1944), pp.321–39, reprinted in *The Collected Papers of James Meade*, Vol. II, chapter 3. Meade's and Fleming's original papers on the subject had been circulated in the Section as EC(S)(44)2, 'Pricing of State Products', 4 January 1944, and EC(S)(44)3, 'Criteria of Operation of State Enterprises', 8 January 1944 (T230/16).

23 R. J. Shackle, 'Points for Discussion on American Draft Convention' (with annotations by Meade), 14 December 1944, T230/31.

at Cambridge. I have painted a picture of the counter attractions of the Economic Section. He is at present on a razor's edge and may go either way. He is to make up his mind in the next day or two, and I have impressed upon the establishments officer here that we must be able to make him a definite and attractive offer very early next week.

## *22 December 1944*

I spent Monday finishing off final revisions to my document on Beveridge's book on *Full Employment in a Free Society*. The idea is that Woolton should circulate it to Ministers as a paper for his Reconstruction Committee.[24] This seems all to the good provided that Beveridge does not himself become Lord President in a future government and himself see the paper – an event which might somewhat cramp the style of the future Director of the Economic Section in advising the future Lord President on Employment Policy but which is, I am given to understand, safeguarded by the constitutional principle that Ministers in one administration may not read the Cabinet papers of a previous administration.

Waley of the Treasury called a meeting in his room on Tuesday afternoon to consider the UK reply to the latest telegram from Australia on the proposal for an International Conference on Employment Policy.[25] On the whole all went well in discussing details of future procedure. But I was alarmed to discover (in response to some observations which I made to probe the situation) that Leggett of the Ministry of Labour was still seriously convinced that the ILO [International Labour Office] was the body which should be charged with arranging for international conferences to consider what national and international measures should be taken if a general depression threatens to develop. I vigorously opposed this idea, the absurdity of which is obvious when one considers the sort of questions which will be at issue: budget deficits, fiscal policy, taxation and state expenditure, adjustment of exchange rates, commercial policy, banking policy, etc. What is wanted (I argued) is some organisation (e.g. of the Social and Economic Council of the Dumbarton Oaks proposed organisation)[26] on which governments and international bodies (such as the International Monetary Fund, Development Bank, Trade Organisation and, of course, Labour Organisation) would come together to consider appropriate action. Waley was in one of his pleasant, but essentially cynical and flippant, moods, and on the grounds that the only purpose was in any case to let popular opinion let off hot air on a subject on which governments would in any case go their own ways supported

[24] It was circulated at Norman Brook's suggestion to 21 Ministers plus Sir Richard Hopkins, Sir Wilfrid Eady, Sir Alan Barlow, Keynes and Sir Edward Bridges: Brook to Robbins, 11 December 1944 (T230/69) and 21 December 1944 (CAB 124/831).

[25] For the telegram, no. 335, from Australia to Dominions Office, 15 December 1944, and the meeting, see FO371/40949.

[26] The conference of representatives from the UK, USA, USSR and China at Dumbarton Oaks in Washington, DC in August-September 1944 had laid the groundwork for what became the United Nations Organisation.

Leggett's proposition. I find this a truly irresponsible line for a high Treasury official to take.

On Monday evening I had dinner with Lionel Robbins, Fergusson and Hawkins to discuss Agriculture and Commercial Policy. In their different ways, what charming men Fergusson and Hawkins are. Fergusson explained how he used to be a liberal free-trader, was secretary at the Treasury to successive Chancellors (Snowden, Churchill, Chamberlain), used to be an idealist out to reform the world. But he has obviously been completely disillusioned by the events of the 1930s. What has made Waley flippant, cynical and irresponsible, had made Fergusson throw himself heart and soul into the anti-intellectual, hard-headed, tough organisation of the Ministry of Agriculture, on non-liberal, non-free-trade, non-economic lines. But he remains a charming man of irrepressible vitality and good humour. Hawkins, on the other hand, is the quintessence of the quiet, fresh, new-world outlook of the best balanced and most cultured Americans, with a large strain both of their generous idealism and of their hard-headed business sense. Nothing very memorable occurred at the dinner except that one watched these two men getting to know one another, each expressing his free-trade or his anti-free-trade point of view openly and frankly. But it might be of momentous importance if these two men could really get to know one another, and if this resulted in Fergusson being weaned again to what is really the more adult fare of international liberalism in economic policy. Hawkins in the course of the evening made a very sad remark which wrung my withers. He argued how, if the USA and the UK really agreed together on the desirability of a liberal commercial policy, it would be irresistible throughout the world; and he said with a sigh that just as now the USA was turning rapidly towards the old English tradition of liberalising trade, just at that very moment the UK seemed to be moving as rapidly towards the evil old American tradition of high protectionism.

The Cabinet has recently decided that plans should be made on the basis of the assumption that the German war will go on until the middle of 1945. This involves the complete revision of our Economic Survey which has now been in proof and just about to be issued to Ministers for over two months! As a result of this I called a meeting to discuss revisions necessary in the 1945 forecast of the Balance of Payments:- Thompson-McCausland of the Bank of England, Leak of the Board of Trade, Stone of the CSO, Austin Robinson of the Ministry of Production, and Edgar Jones of the Treasury.[27] The Balance of Payments estimates, which the Bank now do, need great development and improvement; and I was able to suggest (with Stone's full approval!) that this should be done through a working party of officials for which the Bank of England and the CSO should be responsible.

The most important event of the week from the point of view of the

[27] Notes of a meeting on 20 December 1944 on Annex C of the Economic Survey 'Overseas Liabilities and the Balance of Payments', T230/6. The Cabinet decision was taken following a special meeting of the War Cabinet with the Chiefs of Staff on 13 December 1944: WM(44) 167th Conclusions, CAB65/44.

Economic Section was the fact that Sir Richard Hopkins had sent Lionel and myself copies of the first paper of the Treasury Budget Committee for this year, and had asked us to go and see him about it.[28] This, the first occasion on which we had been called into consultation on the Budget, was due to backstage work by Bridges. In the course of our interview Hoppy made it clear that it was the definite intention of the Treasury to invite the Director of the Economic Section to become a member of the Budget Committee next year (when the Treasury economists would presumably no longer be there). We were able to read Hoppy two lectures: the first on the importance of regular, periodic reviews by the Treasury, CSO and Economic Section in forecasting the National Income and Expenditure; and the second on the desirability this year of starting to move from real controls (e.g. labour direction, raw material controls, etc.) to financial inducements (e.g. by some lowering of EPT [Excess Profits Tax] together with even more severe taxation on inessential domestic consumption) in order to increase the incentive for producing those things which were really wanted (e.g. exports and essential domestic supplies) at the cost of those which were not. It is quite essential for the health of the future Economic Section (particularly, but not only, for its work on Employment Policy) that we should enter fully into budgetary and fiscal policy; and for this reason the importance of this meeting can, I think, scarcely be overestimated. We are now in a very strong position vis-à-vis the Central Statistical Office.

## *31 December 1944*

I have only been back from the Christmas holiday for the last day or two of this week. The immediate task is to get our Economic Survey completely rewritten on the new assumption that the German war will end in the middle of 1945. I have set Miss Watts on the task of revising our 1945 Balance of Payments estimates and Tress on that of revising our guesses about inflationary pressure in 1945.[29] I have myself worked mainly on the question of the post-war National Debt and how to deal with it (Sinking Fund, Capital Levy, Annual Capital Tax, etc.). At our meeting last week Hopkins had said that the committee (of Treasury, Inland Revenue and Economic Section) which has been projected on this subject since the summer will now definitely meet early in the New Year.[30] We must be prepared on this important subject.

Had lunch with Noel-Baker and A. A. Evans (of the ILO and now of the

[28] B(45)1, 'Budget 1945: Note by Sir Herbert Brittain', 14 December 1944, T171/269.

[29] Their memoranda are on T230/162 and T230/17.

[30] Meade had proposed an enquiry into a post-war capital levy and related matters to Hopkins in July 1944. In August the Chancellor of the Exchequer had agreed to a joint Treasury-Economic Section-Inland Revenue Committee on post-war management of the national debt and interest rates, whose meetings were then delayed by the absence overseas of many of the participants first at Bretton Woods and subsequently in Washington negotiating the arrangements for Stage II of Lend-Lease (the period between the end of the war with Germany and the defeat of Japan) (T230/94 and T273/389). The National Debt Enquiry first met on 19 February 1945 (see below p. 45).

Ministry of War Transport) on Thursday. They were most anxious about the restoration of European transport, arguing with great persuasiveness that the restoration of their transport was the essential preliminary, since until this was done the Europeans could do nothing to help themselves. They had, however, come up against Treasury opposition to any schemes whereby we should provide transport equipment to these countries on tick or on credit. I explained that I very fully sympathised with the Treasury attitude here because of our extreme balance of payments difficulties. It was, I said, an outstanding case for an untied reconstruction loan from the USA, the proceeds of which could be spent on our equipment (which Noel-Baker gave me to understand the Europeans would prefer on grounds of cheapness and for other reasons). Such an arrangement would restore European transport and at the same time serve to adjust the American and British balances of payments. It was an obvious case for a loan through the proposed International Reconstruction and Development Bank or – if that could not be set up in time – for a special transport reconstruction loan on similar principles. I promised to speak to Keynes on the subject.

Had dinner on Friday [29 December] with Hawkins and Marcus Fleming. We had a very interesting discussion after dinner.[31] Marcus and I gave Hawkins a little lecture about the need for flexible exchange rates to adjust balances of payments, if all the necessary adjustments were not to be pushed by the Treasuries of the various countries (who wished to stabilise exchange rates) onto the Boards of Trade or State Departments (who would be forced to envisage rigid trade controls as the only alternative methods of adjusting balances of payments in a world in which internal wage levels were not easily reduced). Hawkins took this point very well – a point of which he was, of course, well aware in Washington. The most interesting part of the conversation was, however, Hawkins' assertion that the US Administration, Congress and public opinion were all moving very strongly in favour of removing trade barriers; his statement that an international trade conference was quite inevitable, since the pressure of public opinion for it was irresistible (Hull was always being asked in his Press Conferences when the trade conference was to be held); his illustration of this fact by explaining that New York bankers such as Aldrich considered that the International Monetary Fund (which *they* regarded not as a mechanism for returning to gold and fixing exchange rates, but as a mechanism for adjusting balances of payments by means of flexible exchange rates) might conceivably be acceptable if it was preceded by an international agreement to lower trade barriers, since in that case smaller exchange rate movements would be required to achieve any required change in balances of payments; his explanation that he had coached the other American states to the point at which they would, he believed, reach the conclusion at the forthcoming Pan-American conference[32] on this subject that their commercial policy problems could not be settled on a regional basis but required an all-round multilateral

[31] Recorded in Meade to Robbins, 1 January 1945, T230/173.

[32] The Conference was to be held in Mexico City in February 1945.

treatment (but he made it quite clear at the same time that if we went regional, there would be the world's greatest trade war which, in his opinion, might make political co-operation between the USA and the UK impossible); his regret that we had not yet reached agreement in time, when the Trade Agreements Act came up in Congress in February for renewal, for new legislation to be submitted which would give them the power to adhere to a multilateral convention; and finally his breathtaking admission that he was advising his government to introduce legislation in February in Congress for powers to reduce duties on such a wide scale and in such general terms that under it the Administration could in fact implement any multilateral convention. He thought this legislation would pass, and said (as he well might) that it would make it clear to the world that the USA meant business.[33]

Piquancy was added to this conversation by the fact that just beside us were sitting Oliver Franks and R. L. Hall (of the Ministry of Supply) and Fennelly (of the Ministry of Production) to discuss a perfectly dreadful paper on the line which we should take in conversation with the USA on international cartels.[34] 'Stonewalling made up half of negation and half of indecision' was Franks' description of it to me later. This is to be discussed at a meeting of UK officials next week [on 1 January], and Franks, I am glad to hear, is going to submit an alternative and less negative draft.

Had a long talk with John Maud first on the subject of an article which he wanted me to write for *The Round Table* on export policy (I was able soon to convince him completely that it would not do for the Director-designate of the Economic Section to write an article on so politically controversial and issue) and secondly on what line Christians should take on Employment Policy.[35] I argued that the technical scientific problem was largely solved. The ethical problem consisted in:- (i) suitable people taking the trouble to understand the technical problem; (ii) persuading people that they must have the will to see that something was done about it this time, and not just let unemployment continue as they did last time: one must not just get used to an evil; and (iii) in those cases where there was a conflict between private interest and the social interest persuading people to restrain the former in preference to the latter. I argued that Employment Policy probably raised this third essentially moral problem less acutely than most other economic issues, since, in general, greater employment by leading to a larger national income could make everyone simultaneously better-off, whereas problems involving the distribution of the national income or the control of monopoly raised immediately the question of the conflict of class interests. Nevertheless there were instances of this type of conflict in Employment Policy. For example, workers in work must exercise self-control in industrial discipline, in wage policy, in restricting entrance to new workers, etc., if the high demand for their

[33] In seeking renewal of the Reciprocal Trade Agreements Act the Administration requested and obtained authority to reduce tariffs to 50 per cent of their existing levels.

[34] International Cartels: Draft Brief for Possible Discussion by American Officials, circulated by Sir Percivale Liesching, 18 December 1944, CAB 124/496; see below, p. 25.

[35] Maud wrote a paper, 'Full Employment and the Responsibility of Christians', 9 January 1945, which he sent to Meade on 18 January (T230/69).

labour which would be associated with Full Employment was not to lead to the evils of reduced productivity, inflation, exclusion of the underpaid or unemployed from the best-paid employment. Similar restraints would be needed on the part of producers who might, through certain restrictive practices, gain at the expense of others the high demand associated with full employment. It was to explain the reasons for this kind of self-restraint and 'unselfishness', if the employment policy was to succeed, that required a special moral appeal.

# 3

# January 1945

*7 January 1945*

Early this week there was a meeting in Eady's room in the Treasury to discuss papers by the Board of Trade on the lines to be taken in future discussions with Hawkins on International Cartels and Commercial Policy. On the former we had before us a Board of Trade paper which was, I think, almost the most lamentable paper I have yet seen in Whitehall, being (in the words of Oliver Franks) a pure stonewalling effort compounded of negation and indecision.[1] Franks . . . made it clear that he thought the purely negative line of the BoT unhelpful. Lionel Robbins (on my previous prompting) developed the three points: that if we did not do anything to meet the American and Dominions desires to curb the misuse of cartels in manufactured products, we could not hope to be successful in our campaign against restrictionism in the case of primary products; that for a country which had to expand its manufactured exports by 50 per cent over pre-war it could not be reasonable to start off with rigid quotas of manufactured exports; and that we stood to endanger our diplomatic relations seriously by taking a line unacceptable both to the USA and the Dominions. Jewkes, who has been largely in charge of the work on international policy on this subject, backed us up. I suggested that we might at least see whether Ministers would not be willing to go as far internationally for international cartels, as they were domestically for domestic cartels, and agree to some form of international arrangement whereby countries would agree to investigate either jointly or severally any international cartels to which their nationals were parties, if a *prima facie* case could be made out to the International Trade Organisation for their investigation. In the end the BoT were asked to redraft their paper on rather more positive lines; but I realised with horror that, almost without exception, everyone who had taken at all a decent line on this subject was a temporary civil servant, and imagined the desolate isolation in which I might find myself when they had all disappeared. Afterwards the meeting discussed the line to be taken with Hawkins in the next conversations with him on Commercial Policy. Again the BoT took a terribly negative line, emphasising every difficulty in the way of Hawkins'

[1] For a record of the meeting of 1 January 1945 and the Board of Trade paper see CAB 124/496 or BT64/317.

draft convention. I fear that they have really lost (if they ever had) any faith in the general multilateral convention. It is very depressing when the Americans are in such forthcoming mood.

Had a long conversation with Keynes. He was very amusing, calling me 'the only rat that was not deserting the ship' and inveighing against the Treasury officials who (with the exception of Hoppy [Sir Richard Hopkins]) he said were utterly incapable and incompetent to deal with technical economic matters. How have they the face to write long documents on economic matters! He (Keynes) would not take it upon himself to write a treatise on electricity. Economics was not yet taken as a serious subject. Hoppy, who understood the issues, was now too old and tired to do more than give his love and good wishes. All this was *à propos* of the report of the official committee on the future of the public utilities and of the electricity industry, in which – he said – they did not even show themselves aware of the economic problems of pricing which Marcus Fleming and I discussed in our symposium in the current *EJ*. He said that he had just written such a stinker on this subject that Sir Alan Barlow had spent the whole morning trying to get hold of a copy of the *Economic Journal*.[2] At length I turned the conversation to the problem of Commercial Policy and the official conversations to prepare for Hawkins. As often on this subject, Keynes was not at his best. He seemed to think that the thing to do was to go for a general 'gentlemen's agreement' or statement of principles as to what countries would or would not generally do. He also said that he had got the impression from Pasvolsky in Washington that the Administration was intending to put the problem of commercial policy late on their list of priorities. None of this squares at all with what Hawkins says, as I pointed out. Moreover, I maintained that many senior officials here were not simply trying to show Hawkins our very real difficulties; but they wished to put off the whole question, and this, I maintained, was riding for certain catastrophe as the USA certainly intended sooner or later to have some real liberalisation of commercial policy. To this he assented. I went on to try to sell to Keynes the idea of untied reconstruction loans to Europe from the USA which would be used to spend on our goods particularly for the vital purpose of the restoration of the European transport system. Keynes said, as I thought and hoped he would, that this was essentially a job for the proposed Reconstruction Bank. He welcomed the proposal to lunch with Noel-Baker, Hurcomb and myself next week to discuss this possibility.[3]

Have spent considerable time in the course of the week on the problem of the post-war national debt, capital levy, etc. I intend soon to draft a paper on this subject,[4] but meanwhile I have got Miss Watts to work out

[2] Report of the Official Committee on Public Utility Corporations, 30 November 1944, R(44)199, CAB 124/427; Meade and Fleming, 'Price and Output Policy of State Enterprise, A Symposium', op. cit.; Keynes, 'Electricity, Treasury Guarantees', 6 January 1945, reprinted in *The Collected Writings of John Maynard Keynes*, Vol. 22, London: Macmillan 1978, pp. 472–7. For Keynes' views on the official committee's views see also ibid., pp. 455–68.

[3] See below pp. 28–9.

[4] See below p. 36.

rough estimates of the net saving to be expected from various forms of levy after the war.

Lunched with Radice early in the week. He seems uncertain whether he wants to stay in Government Service after the war. He is at present engaged in turning the MEW [Ministry of Economic Warfare] enemy intelligence service into the new FO economic intelligence department. He would think of staying if only the FO would drop their absurd idea of staffing the department not with permanent experts but with a rotation of ordinary diplomats serving two-year periods and then passing on. What an absurd idea! Lunched with David Owen at the Athenaeum. We discussed the organisation of the Economic and Social Council of the Dumbarton Oaks Organisation. We agreed that what was wanted was a series of permanent technical commissions (e.g. on health, economic problems, social problems, etc.) to report to the council. The problem of Employment Policy would be tackled in this way but would need a commission on which were represented not only technicians from national govts (to discuss the way in which the USA, UK, etc. meant to meet a depression) but also from the relevant international bodies (International Bank, Fund, Trade Organisation etc.). It was at this level that the ILO (like all other technical international bodies) should come into the picture. But Owen said that that was certainly out of the question. The ILO went so far that it wanted to be at least on an equality with the Economic and Social Council itself.

Attended a meeting of the official committee on industrial problems of reconstruction to discuss the disposal of surplus machine tools.[5] An interesting debate took place in which the Ministry of Supply alone was resisting a proposal pressed by nearly all other departments (Treasury, BoT, MAP [Ministry of Aircraft Production], etc.) that the Government should have the power not only to subsidise the production of new machine tools to save the vital tool-making industry during the hard period when the surplus stocks of tools were being fed into the system but also to buy up and take off the market second-hand tools. This is a very difficult problem when the tool-producing industry is admittedly vital and when there is such a surplus stock of their products; but my sympathies always go out to those who (whatever their motive may be) are against causing scarcities by taking resources off the market and immobilising them.

The symposium between Marcus Fleming and myself in the *EJ* on the pricing of socialised production seems to have given rise to more controversy than I had suspected, partly because economists have further to go in realising the implications of the economic calculus than I had imagined. Plant is really shocked at the idea that a concern should not cover total costs. Coase has been writing a short reply to our symposium on the same theme, and argues vehemently that our principles would redistribute income unfairly in favour of people who spent a large proportion of their income on goods produced under Increasing Returns.[6] Roy Harrod

[5] Reconstruction Committee, Official Sub-Committee on Industrial Problems, R(IO)45 1st Meeting, CAB 124/357.

[6] Coase's note, which he sent to Meade on 1 January 1945 (T230/115), was published in the *Economic Journal* in April 1945: R. H. Coase, 'Price and Output Policy of State Enterprise: A Comment', *Economic Journal*, Vol. 55, pp. 112–13.

has sent me a series of letters and paid me a visit – not, however, on the main issue but on my footnote saying that if the population were at the optimum the result of the marginal principle of pricing would mean that the whole national income would go to labour. There was some considerable misunderstanding because Roy did not realise that I was assuming factors other than labour (i.e. capital and risk-bearing) constant. Of course, if capital and risk-bearing varied with capital [labour], the supply of labour which maximised output per head would not be that at which the marginal product of labour was equal to the average product of labour.

Had a talk with Bridges. We agreed that MacDougall might well say that he would provisionally join the Economic Section and yet remain free to take a job at, say, Oxford later if one appeared. This would enable him to refuse the Fellowship now offered to him at Cambridge with the certainty that he could come to the Economic Section, and yet he could put in later for an Oxford Fellowship. I took the opportunity (rather boldly) of hinting to Bridges that he ought to consider the possibility of getting Hoppy and the Chancellor to put pressure on Lionel Robbins to stay on in Government service, not in the Economic Section but in a central position in the Treasury. Bridges took the point at once. Indeed, it seemed to me that it was already in his mind. What a difference if this would be brought off! Imagine the difference between Eady and Lionel Robbins, for example, from the point of view of the Economic Section's contact with the Treasury. How bleak the prospect for the post-Keynes Treasury is, unless something of this kind can be pulled off.

## *14 January 1945*

The chief event of the week has been that Treasury sanction has come through to make definite offers to the various potential future members of the Economic Section on the terms and conditions which Lionel and I had worked out together. I have spent a good part of the week on this. On the whole the offers have gone down remarkably well. Miss Watts has definitely decided to stay on, so the Director-designate has one member for his Section. The others are still considering it. The idea of having only one main grade from the point of view of status, but with a very wide salary range with members of different seniority starting at different rungs of the salary ladder has, in particular, gone down well. MacDougall has turned down the Cambridge Fellowship, but rather I fancy to leave himself free for a job which he hopes to get at Nuffield College [Oxford] than in order to join the Economic Section.

I learn that Woolton has circulated to Ministers my long paper on Beveridge's *Full Employment in a Free Society*.[7] The paper is unsigned and said merely to have been written in the Economic Section. I have not yet heard whether any Minister has read it!

Went to lunch at the Mayfair Hotel with Noel-Baker. Keynes, Hurcomb

[7] See above, p. 19.

(Permanent Secretary of the Ministry of War Transport) and Archie Evans were there. Subject for discussion: the possibility of reconstruction finance for the rehabilitation of European transport. Keynes seemed hopeful that the International Reconstruction and Development Bank might be in operation in the second half of this year, which should be soon enough from the point of view of financing the reconstruction of European transport. At present it is scarcity of supplies, not finance, that is holding things up. The idea is that a Bank loan should be used to provide an international pool of rolling stock to be operated by the proposed International Transport Organisation (which it is hoped will soon materialise in spite of the usual Russian inscrutable procrastination), so that the rolling stock can move freely across frontiers for use in all countries. But as the Bank can only lend on the guarantee of borrowing governments this will require some consortium of European Governments to guarantee quotas of the ITO's loan. Permanent way etc. would remain the concern of the national governments who would finance it out of their own funds or through national loans from the International Bank. There remain other points to be worked out. How much finance would ITO want for rolling stock? Who would guarantee Germany's quota of the loan? Apparently it must be the Allied Control Commission, which means that Russian agreement will be necessary. But clearly Germany must be treated as an integral part of Europe for the reconstruction of European transport.

Keynes gave me a lift back to the Treasury in his car, which gave me an opportunity of discussing with him his views on the International Monetary Fund. Last week Keynes circulated a terrible document, being his report of proceedings with Harry White in Washington on Articles IV and VIII of the Fund Articles.[8] Article IV 4(b) gave no difficulty. White agreed that it put no more obligation on us than to make black markets illegal. Article VIII 2(a) raised a storm. Keynes maintains that it does not mean that we are obliged, if we monopolise foreign exchange dealings, to find foreign exchange for those who wish to make current payments. The Americans maintain that it clearly does, and they are obviously right. Keynes argues that he cannot recommend the Chancellor to accept the Bretton Woods Agreement in this case unless it is qualified (on the lines of VIII 4(b)(v)) so that the obligation ceases when we can draw no more foreign exchange from the Fund. White says that they must put the Agreement through Congress without any amendments, since if they start proposing amendments there is no knowing what Congress will do with it. Anyhow, he argues, we can safeguard our balance of payments by import restrictions instead of by foreign exchange restrictions. As a matter of fact this has all along been precisely our line, and for this reason we have insisted (and the Americans have agreed) on the balance of payments let-out in the commercial policy agreement. Keynes has been in one of his silly moods. I worked on this early in the week and produced minutes arguing that we should accept the agreement as it stands and rely on import restrictions for our balance of payments, but that if we started amendments we ought to

[8] 'The International Monetary Fund', 29 December 1944, T247/39 and *The Collected Writings of John Maynard Keynes*, Vol. 26, pp. 146–55.

write Articles IV 4(b), VIII 2(a) and VIII 4 into one consistent and lucid Article of which I produced a draft.[9] At present they are obscure and inconsistent. Keynes had looked at these minutes and the well-known process has started. Within a week, I don't mind betting, he will be as violently in favour of accepting without amendment as he is at present against doing so. At present he is, I believe, advising the Chancellor to write to Morgenthau to put our doubt on record, but in the end to accept with the warning that a satisfactory interpretation of VIII 2(a) will be one of the things that will make it possible for us the sooner to accept the full obligations of convertibility.[10]

I had lunch with Jenks of the ILO. He is over here in connection with meetings to start next week of the ILO Employment Committee and the Governing Body. I received from the Ministry of Labour papers prepared by the ILO office on the ILO and Employment Policy.[11] They really make ridiculous claims. The ILO and its Employment Committee seriously think of themselves as being *the* international body for co-ordinating international monetary, economic, commercial policy, investment policy, etc. from the point of view of employment. I had a friendly dispute with Jenks on this subject in the course of which I said that in fact the ILO was claiming to usurp the whole of the functions of the Dumbarton Oaks Social and Economic Council; and from the reserved way in which he replied to this I suddenly realised that what I had spoken in jest was seriously contemplated by some at least of the ILO officials (though not I think by Jenks). But it really would be ridiculous for the ILO to be the international body to co-ordinate monetary policies, for example. I have stirred Lionel up on this and he has prodded the Treasury on it. I expect there will be a meeting on it, though whether there will be time to get proper instructions given to our representatives at the Governing Body meeting, I don't know. As Leggett himself favours the inflated view of the ILO and is strongly backed by Bevin, I doubt it. But I don't see how any Chancellor of the Exchequer (much less Anderson) would stand for it if he really knew what was at stake.

In the course of the week I attended with Philip Chantler a meeting of the Exchange Requirements Committee at which Keynes gave one of his superb conversational lectures on our post-war external financial position, the purpose of which was to familiarise departments with the idea that after the war we should be in an infinitely more difficult foreign exchange position than before the war or than we were now, when with both Lend-Lease and the piling up of sterling balances it was real scarcities and not external finance that determined the war economy.[12] I also attended with Miss Watts a meeting called by Campion to discuss the statistical

[9] Meade, 'International Monetary Fund Articles VIII 2(a) and 4', 10 January 1944, T247/39.

[10] See below pp. 32–3 and 37.

[11] ILO Governing Body, 94th Session, Questions arising out of the Resolutions concerning Economic Policy adopted by the Conference at its 26th session, 1 December 1944, FO371/50621. The ILO Governing Body's 94th session was to take place in London 25–31 January 1945.

[12] Meeting of 9 January 1945, T231/156: see also L. S. Pressnell, *External Economic Policy since the War, Volume I: The Post-war Financial Settlement*. London: HMSO, 1986, p. 236.

problems involved in improving our knowledge about the UK balance of payments.[13] I hope at last we are going to put an end to the scandal whereby the Bank of England's figures of our adverse balance of payments on current account show an excess each year of anything from £100 to £150 million over their capital figures of foreign disinvestment. I am pretty sure that Leak's pre-war Board of Trade figures also overestimated our adverse balance on current account. This which is going to be one of our most important problems ought to be measured more accurately. The Bank are at last taking it seriously.

## *20 January 1945*

During the week-end and the first part of the week I prepared a document, on the basis of statistics which the Board of Trade have prepared, on the balance of advantage and disadvantage to our trade of the proposals for tariff and preference reductions and other changes in the draft Commercial Policy Convention.[14] If one takes into account (i) the freedom which we should have under our agricultural counter-proposals to give moderate increased protection to our agriculture, (ii) the direct effect upon our invisible exports (e.g. shipping, financial commissions, etc.) of a stimulus to our international trade, (iii) the fact that our tariff structure on imports is not so high as that of foreign countries on our exports and (iv) the fact that greater latitude is to be given to countries with unfavourable, than to countries with favourable, balances of payments in the use of import quotas, it is clear that on balance (even on the most narrow mercantilist view that anything which increases our demand for imports or decreases the foreign demand for our exports is necessarily bad) we stand to gain much. But even if the mercantilist balance were exactly equal, we should stand to gain (perhaps more than any other individual country) (i) from the increased division of labour brought about by the general clearance of trade barriers and (ii) from the greater efficacy of exchange rate adjustment and similar measures in restoring equilibrium to balances of payments in a world in which rigid obstacles to trade are removed. The paper has been circulated to Liesching, Eady and Clutterbuck. I am hoping that it may have some effect in persuading officials to report more favourably than would otherwise be the case on the outcome of their talks with Hawkins.

The Board of Trade have circulated a revision of their draft paper for Ministers suggesting the lines which officials should take in their talks with Hawkins on the subject of International Cartels. It is a truly lamentable document, – a catalogue of musty and unimpressive arguments against doing anything, without any of the arguments on the other side. Lionel Robbins is going to prepare a draft minority report for the Economic

[13] Minutes of the Meeting of the Interdepartmental Committee on Estimates of the Balance of Payments, 10 January 1945, T236/306.

[14] 'The Balance of Gain and Loss to United Kingdom Trade from the Proposed International Multilateral Commercial Policy Convention', 17 January 1945, EC(S)(45)1, T230/17.

Section to submit to Ministers, in which we shall emphasise (i) that the problem is pressing because we must know what to do with German cartels, (ii) that we cannot hope to achieve a successful commodity policy which will limit the use of restriction schemes in the case of the foodstuffs and raw materials which we import if we take a completely *non-possumus* line about restriction of manufactured exports, (iii) that we have to get an overall expansion of 50 per cent of our exports and it is not likely to be to our interest that our exporters should all tie their hands to quantitative quotas based presumably in large measure on pre-war trade, and (iv) we have the Dominions and the United States against us on this. We shall argue that our right line is to resist the American proposals on the ground that they are too elaborate and far-reaching for countries (like us) which have not had their experience of trust-busting to be able to adopt, but that we should be willing to agree to some organised international machinery for investigation and publicity when complaints are made about the abuses of international cartels. There is to be a meeting in Eady's room next week to discuss this before it goes to Ministers.[15] I have tried to interest the Ministry of Production in all this through Richard Kahn.

Early in the week Lionel Robbins, Chester and I discussed a confidential report submitted by the Iron and Steel Federation to the Ministry of Supply on what the Iron and Steel Industry wants out of the Government after the war.[16] This document certainly shows the need for a strong policy on cartels. As one might expect, the Industry wants cartelised international trade with plenty of protection (quite apart from its horrifying suggestions for completing its system of monopolistic organisation and price control at home). The Report does, however, contain one reference to the fact that many, if not all, of the protective devices which it desires might be unnecessary if all countries would stick to principles of Fair Trade. Lionel and I explained the main provisions (such as rules against export subsidies etc.) which an international commercial policy convention would probably contain, so that Chester (who is working for Oliver Franks at the Ministry of Supply in preparing an official report for Ministers on the future of the Iron and Steel Industry)[17] might be able to guide the conversations with the industrialists on the right lines. Chester looked into my room later in the week to say that he had successfully persuaded them of the rightness of the approach. But it would be naive, I feel, to have much confidence in this! Still every little bit helps; and where reason is strong, even the most brazen may be shamed into a more moderate attitude!

I received from Keynes in the course of the week a minute in answer to my letter on the International Monetary Fund together with a copy of a draft letter from the Chancellor to Mr Morgenthau on this subject.

[15] Board of Trade, 'Draft Brief for Discussion with American Officials on Cartels', 16 January 1945, Robbins, 'International Cartels: Comment on the Draft Brief for Possible Discussion with American Officials', 20 January 1945, BT64/317. On the meeting, on 23 January, see below, pp. 34–5.

[16] British Iron and Steel Federation, Report by the British Iron and Steel Industry to the Ministry of Supply, December 1944 (Appendix A to R(45)36, CAB87/10).

[17] R(45)36, 'Iron and Steel, Joint Memorandum by the Minister of Supply and the President of the Board of Trade', 6 April 1945, CAB 87/10.

Progress is in the right direction. The suggestion now is to accept the draft of the Fund as it now stands, but on the understanding that some satisfactory clearing up of the meaning of the obligations under Article VIII 2 and 4 is reached during the transitional period, on the grounds that we should not be in a position to accept multilateral convertibility for our currency under Article XIV until we were sure that the let-out to convertibility under VIII 4(b)(v) would also refer to any obligations to convertibility which may be implied in Article VIII 2. I still believe that we should be sufficiently safeguarded to rely upon import restrictions as opposed to exchange controls when we were in balance of payments difficulties, and that the Chancellor would assert this in the House of Commons if the question is raised. Both I and Lionel have written to Keynes to this effect.[18]

I went to dinner with Lionel to Mr and Mrs Spearman. He is a wealthy City man; Conservative Member for Scarborough; the maker of the very sensible speech on the International Monetary Fund in the last debate on the subject in the House of Commons.[19] A very modest, intelligent and charming man, a Conservative of the Richard Law type, though not, I should imagine, with quite the same ability as the latter in speaking and writing. His wife, who was a pupil of Lionel at the LSE, is to stand at the next election as a Conservative at Hull. After dinner we discussed the International Monetary Fund at some length. Apparently there is to be a debate in the House at an early date. This will presumably be just before, or simultaneous with, the discussion of the Fund in Congress. I hope that the wires don't get crossed. The prospect of a simultaneous attack on the Fund by MPs as being a capitulation to the Americans and the Gold Standard and by Congressmen on the grounds that it is a clever plot of Lord Keynes to get money out of the Americans is not a very happy one.

The great excitement of the week to me was receipt of a minute from Sir Richard Hopkins setting up, under his chairmanship, a committee of the Treasury (Eady, Brittain and Keynes), the Board of Inland Revenue (Gregg, Chambers) and the Economic Section (Lionel Robbins and myself) to consider the future of the National Debt – Capital Levy, Sinking Fund Policy, Conversions etc.[20] Not only is the subject of quite central importance for post-war economic policy, but this is really the first occasion on which the Economic Section has been invited into the hidden recesses of the Treasury to discuss essential fiscal problems. I am determined that we should prepare a really good study on this subject. Lionel, with great generosity, has offered to take over the re-writing of our Economic Survey (which as a result of the continuation of the German War will have to be completely rewritten) so that I can concentrate on this.

Having come to Bath for the week-end, on Saturday morning I received

[18] 'Bretton Woods (Interpretation of Article VIII): Draft prepared by Lord Keynes', January 1945, T247/39 and *The Collected Writings of John Maynard Keynes*, Vol. 26, pp. 156–9; Meade to Keynes, 17 January 1945, T247/39; Robbins to Keynes, 17 January 1945, T247/39 and *The Collected Writings of John Maynard Keynes*, Vol. 26, pp. 171–3.

[19] *House of Commons Debates*, Vol. 399, 10 May 1944, cols. 2012–15.

[20] Hopkins to members of the National Debt Enquiry, 17 January 1945, T230/94 and T273/389; see above, p. 21, note 30.

from an Admiralty messenger a packet containing a draft report on the future use of the Purchase Tax by the Board of Customs and Excise and asking me to attend a meeting there on Monday morning next to discuss it. I believe that the very existence of a committee and draft report on this subject was due to my insistence at various Reconstruction meetings that if we are during the transitional period (i) to restrain inflation, (ii) to give an incentive to export, and (iii) give an incentive to produce essentials rather than inessentials for domestic consumption, we shall have to turn progressively from real controls (such as labour direction, allocation of raw materials, etc.), which will not on political grounds or for reasons of administrative personnel be easily maintained, to financial inducements. This means some reduction in EPT (since a 100 per cent marginal tax on profits removes *all* financial inducement) and an increase in taxation on unnecessary consumption, which will not only mop up purchasing power but increase the attraction to producers of less heavily taxed exports and essential consumption. From some oversight I was not invited to the earlier meetings on the subject, but have now been invited at the eleventh hour to discuss the draft report.[21]

One more person (Philip Chantler) has definitely decided to join the post-war Economic Section. So now I have two members for my staff. Slow, but I hope sure, progress.

## *28 January 1945*

A busy, but profitable week. The most important development was on International Cartels. At a meeting in the Treasury under Eady's chairmanship [on 23 January] we had before us a lamentable Board of Trade paper which still merely stone-walled on the subject and a paper by Lionel Robbins saying that we should do something about it (i) because the problem of German cartels would soon become acute, (ii) because we would not hope to maintain an anti-restrictionist front on primary products if we were not willing to do something on the cartelisation of manufactured exports, (iii) because a country like us which had to expand its exports by, say, 50 per cent should not start off by tying its hands by quantitative quotas based on previous experience, and (iv) because diplomatically we had both the USA and the Dominions against us on this point. The paper went on to argue that we should resist the extreme American proposal for an international Sherman Act on the grounds that they were utterly impracticable, but that we should go as far internationally as we were proposing to go nationally, – i.e. set up an international machinery for complaint, discussion, investigation and publicity about the ill effects of international cartels. After some wrangling the Board of Trade capitulated, and Liesching actually asked Lionel Robbins to draft a paper on the above lines to go to Ministers as the directive for our officials to follow when they talked with Hawkins on the subject. This draft is completed and

[21] See below p. 36.

is now with Ministers.[22] Before the Treasury meeting I had carefully briefed Richard Kahn and Austin Robinson of the Ministry of Supply; and the whole atmosphere was radically changed by the fact that they were able to persuade Lyttleton to approve action on these lines.[23] As Lyttleton has been up to now the most difficult Minister on the internal problem of Restrictive Practices, this marks a revolutionary change for the better. Gossip has it that Lyttleton is scared at the prospect that he personally and through him the Conservative party will be branded as the monopolists' friends. Within the Board of Trade there has been a severe struggle going on. Liesching has for long really wanted to do something. But Miss Kilroy, Watkinson and Overton have been very sticky. At last Liesching has broken through on this front. But there is a sad story of Dalton. Apparently it took a two-hour meeting to make him accept the draft directive before it was sent from the Board of Trade to Woolton for the latter to submit to his Reconstruction Committee. That night, without consulting his officials, Dalton wrote a personal letter to Woolton saying that the paper went further than he thought most of his ministerial colleagues would want to go – and this after Lyttleton's acquiescence had been made known to him![24] Our socialist President does not seem to dare risk offending any monopoly-capitalists! This has enraged even Overton and Dalton was persuaded to withdraw his letter.

I attended a meeting in Caine's room at the Colonial Office to discuss the vexed question of Jamaican Bauxite. The Reynolds Metal Box Co. are using their lobbying power in the States to get the State Department to turn the heat on us (on the grounds of the Atlantic Charter right to equal access to raw materials) to guarantee a concession to them to work bauxite deposits in Jamaica. We want the Jamaica legislative body to pass legislation nationalising the working of these deposits and then to let out their working to one or two companies. Does the right of free access to raw materials mean equality of right to purchase them when produced or does it grant an equal right to exploit their production? If the latter, what does equality of right to produce them mean in a case where, on technical grounds, there is only room for one (or at the most a few) producing concerns? We are drafting a reply to Winant saying that we cannot immediately guarantee that the Reynolds Co. will obtain a concession, but I got inserted a paragraph saying that in the choice of companies for this purpose no regard would be had to the nationality of the producing company.[25] This is clearly the correct principle; but what does it mean in practice? A very difficult question.

[22] Board of Trade, 'Draft Brief for Discussion with American Officials on Cartels,' 16 January 1945, Robbins, 'International Cartels: Comment on the Draft Brief for Possible Discussion with American Officials', 20 January 1945, and minutes of meeting on 23 January 1945, BT64/317 and CAB124/496; Robbins, 'International Cartels', 24 January 1945, R(45)18, CAB124/496.

[23] Meade to Robbins, 19 January 1945, T230/174; Robbins to Liesching, 24 January 1945, BT64/317.

[24] Dalton to Woolton, 24 January 1945, CAB124/496.

[25] The meeting was held on 22 January 1945 to consider Winant to Eden, 8 January 1945; the draft reply after further redrafting was sent as Law to Winant, 31 January 1945 (CO852/619/2).

I attended a meeting early in the week at the Board of Customs and Excise with Sir Archibald Carter in the chair to discuss their report on the future of the Purchase Tax. There had been a muddle which prevented us from being invited to earlier meetings, which was unfortunate as the two main points of the report were to dismiss (i) the suggestion which I had made at earlier reconstruction meetings that as the real controls (e.g. on labour and raw materials) became less strict during the transitional period we should have to turn progressively from real controls to financial inducements, and that a high rate of purchase tax on inessentials in domestic consumption would give an inducement to producers to concentrate on production for export or for essential domestic consumption and this in a way which would mop up redundant purchasing power in so far as any inessentials were bought on the domestic market; and (ii) a suggestion of the Board of Trade that rates of purchase tax should be reduced (or removed) on a wide range of utility goods and of price-controlled goods during the transitional period in order to re-enforce the Board's efforts to control qualities and prices. As a result of the meeting the report was revised so as to give a much better statement of our proposals. It has now gone to Sir Richard Hopkins and the Budget Committee and we wait to see if our opinions will be canvassed by the Treasury.[26]

I have spent a great deal of time and trouble this week, together with Miss Watts, getting on with our paper on the post-war National Debt. I have now drafted the sections on the effect of changes in the rate of interest, population, employment, prices and productivity on the burden of the debt. I have now to do the fundamental sections on Sinking Fund, Capital Levy, Annual Capital Taxes, etc., i.e. on methods of repaying the debt. I hope that we shall be able to produce a paper which will encourage the Treasury to believe that we might be of real assistance to them on financial policy.[27]

I have had conversations in the course of the week with Carter Goodrich (chairman of the Governing Body of the ILO), Lubin (President Roosevelt's brains truster who represents the USA on the G[overning] B[ody] of the ILO when Goodrich is in the chair) and Dupriez of the Institute at Louvain. I have found all three conversations encouraging. Goodrich and Lubin have both reassured me that the claims which are apparent in some ILO quarters that the ILO should take on the main tasks of international co-ordination of economic and financial policies are not to be taken too seriously or tragically. It is partly a question of bargaining tactics and partly a question of a few extremists who do not properly represent the sound opinion in the ILO. Both Goodrich and Lubin agreed with my proposition that the right way to deal, for example, with employment policy internationally was to have a commission of experts (probably

[26] The revised report, dated 23 January 1945, was circulated by Sir Richard Hopkins as B(45)8, 'Purchase Tax Policy, Memorandum by the Board of Customs and Excise', on 24 January 1945, for the Budget Committee meeting on 29 January (T171/369); see also below, pp. 41–2.

[27] Drafts of the papers, which became NDE Papers 4, 5 and 6 (see below p. 46), are on T230/94. The final version is printed in *The Collected Papers of James Meade*, Vol. II, chapter 15.

under the Economic and Social Council of the Dumbarton Oaks organisation) made up both of representatives of the main international institutions concerned (e.g. the Fund, the Bank, the ILO, the International Trade Organisation, etc.) and of representatives of the main countries (e.g. Treasury representatives from the UK, USA etc.) to discuss both the international and the domestic aspects of employment policy. Goodrich, however, added two points: (i) the ILO would probably want to send a tri-partite delegation to any such commission and (ii) the ILO would want the right to appeal beyond the Economic and Social Council to the Assembly of the Dumbarton Oaks organisation. With Goodrich, Lubin and Dupriez I discussed employment policies. The two former have both convinced me that the USA won't in fact again allow a depression to develop unchecked of the kind that occurred after 1929. Both (particularly Lubin) were talking of employment policy in terms of the forward planning of national income and expenditure; and though they are New Dealers and therefore going through some partial eclipse of their ideas, I feel pretty confident that if we can continue on these lines these ideas have already a sufficient bridgehead on the North American continent for one more serious threat of depression to bring them to the fore. Dupriez was enthusiastic for these ideas. He spoke incidentally about their goings on during the occupation: how they ignored all German ideas about economic policy and reconstruction; how they heard of our ideas on Social Security and Employment Policy through the wireless and through Switzerland; how they had study groups to work out the application of these ideas to Belgium; how they had not properly heard of our work on National Income and Expenditure but were now going all out to fill this gap in their knowledge. Already in Belgium they are taking steps to get important business to plan their investment ahead at a stable rate. If all this is at all typical of Western Europe, what an opportunity we have of establishing an efficient liberal economy if only we can set an efficient liberal example!

On the Bretton Woods front the Cabinet has, most sensibly, decided not to have a debate now but to wait and see how things develop in Congress.[28] Meanwhile, the Chancellor's letter to Morgenthau on Article VIII and all that has, I hear, been revised in a most desirable sense, – i.e. simply putting on record our difficulties in that respect as an obstacle to the early assumption of the full obligations of convertibility but not asking at this stage for a definite commitment on the part of the Americans to accept our interpretation.[29]

I have been spending all my spare time in the evenings over the last weeks reading Lerner's *Economics of Control* and writing a review-article of it for the *Economic Journal*.[30] Here is a real Liberal-Socialist-Welfare-

[28] WM9(45)4, 25 January 1945, CAB65/49.

[29] Anderson to Morgenthau, 1 February 1945, T247/39, and *The Collected Writings of John Maynard Keynes*, Vol. 26, pp. 175–7.

[30] Abba P. Lerner, *The Economics of Control: Principles of Welfare Economics*. New York: Macmillan, 1944; Meade, 'Mr Lerner on "The Economics of Control" ', *Economic Journal*, Vol. 55 (April 1945), pp. 47–69, reprinted in *The Collected Papers of James Meade*, Vol. II, chapter 4.

Marginalist economist. The real thing. He has a definite tendency to dress even the simplest things up in novel and paradoxical disguises, which makes the book a queer book. Also, as I point out in my review (which I have at last managed to finish), there are a number of technical imperfections. But when all is said and done, what a breath of fresh air it is, after the dreadful arbitrary and authoritarian quantitative planning of a Balogh on the one hand and the extreme *laissez-faire* attitude of a Hayek on the other, to read an economist who starts out from the simple and fundamental economic proposition that the purpose of economic policy should be to make the economic calculus work and that the particular uses of planning or of *laissez-faire* should then be judged as means towards this end.

No progress this week on the make-up of the post-war Section. On the contrary, much to my disappointment (and, I confess, my surprise) Tress has told me that he definitely wants to go for an academic job. I desisted from pressing him as I have no desire to have people in the Section who will sub-consciously bear a grudge if they feel, when things go wrong, that they were pressed to stay against their better judgement. But I should not put it beyond the bounds of possibility that Tress may himself change his mind.

# 4

# February 1945

### *4 February 1945*

Some small progress this week with the make-up of the Economic Section. Edgar Jones, who was lecturer before the war at [University College] Swansea and during the war has been dealing with foreign-exchange and balance of payments matters in the Treasury, has let it be known that he might like to join the Section. The same has happened with a young man called Jefferies, at present in the RAF who got a good First at the London School of Economics in 1940. It appears to me that one will probably be able to get together a quite decent staff of good competent workers, but the great question is whether one will be able to get one or two real mature high-flyers like Fleming and Devons. Really to pull off the potentially decisive influence that the Section might have one must have one or two people of this calibre.

Ministers have passed the official proposals on International Cartels and Hawkins has been informed that, while we couldn't accept the US proposals for what amounts to full-blooded international trust-busting, we will contemplate some international machinery for investigation, review, publicity, consultation, etc.[1] A feather in the Economic Section's cap, I venture to think; without Lionel Robbins' intervention we should have adopted a completely *non-possumus* attitude. At the Ministerial meeting Lyttleton took the line that the only quarrel which he had with the officials' proposals was that they didn't go far enough, whereas Dalton advised caution. What a transposition of the roles of monopoly-capitalist and radical trust-buster!

I attended a meeting at the Foreign Office to discuss the relations of the Directors and Staffs of the new international economic organisations with unofficial institutions (such as universities) and individual experts.[2] The problem arose over the rules of procedure of the Food and Agriculture Organisation with a duel between Sir Donald Fergusson of the Ministry of Agriculture and Sir Henry French of the Ministry of Food. The former (backed by Colonial Office, Ministry of Health) was taking the strictest

[1] The meeting of Ministers was on 29 January 1945 (R(45) 6th Meeting, Minute 2 Confidential Annex, CAB124/496); the meeting with Hawkins on 30 January 1945 (AS(US)(44) 13th Meeting, BT64/317).

[2] 'Record of a meeting held at the Foreign Office on 30 January 1945', FO371/50833.

line that these organisations should have no formal contacts whatsoever with any body except the governments of the member countries, while the latter (backed by the FO, Treasury, Research Depts and Councils and Economic Section) took the more liberal view that it was impossible to lay it down that these international bodies should not be permitted to consult scientific bodies and experts. Much of Fergusson's attitude was due, no doubt, to the natural but reprehensible desire of a very efficient bureaucrat not to be embarrassed by outside ideas too much. But there was this element of force in his argument: after this war international institutions were not going to be the same as after the last war; all these subjects were going to be matters of great ideological and political difference of opinion; the Food and Agriculture Organisation might have an ideologue in the form of Mr Wallace or of a Russian communist as its enthusiastic head; they might use their influence to stir up ideological propaganda with bodies and individuals which were not really scientific; the right solution was to look upon these international bodies as strictly bodies for contacts between different governments which might be of widely different ideological complexion. The compromise solution reached was that the international bodies should be bound to consult with the member government before they sought the advice of any private individual institution or individual in the member's country. In a decent liberal world there would, of course, be no question that an international body should be able to consult private bodies or individuals in countries in any part of the world. But (dreadful thought) in a world of conflicting ideologies (many of which are highly illiberal), is there an element of truth in Fergusson's contention: It would, however, be a counsel of despair to build the foundations of the new world on definitely predetermined illiberal lines.

In the course of the week I had an SOS from Lord Woolton's secretary: the Minister was concerned, as a result of the recent Cabinet discussion on the Bretton Woods International Monetary Fund,[3] lest if there were an inflation in other countries this country would be bound to follow suit; could I not write him a Minute on this subject? It is heart-breaking work. If I have written one, I have written a dozen notes, papers, minutes and memoranda, copies of which have been sent to his Lordship on the very question of the way in which the exchange rate rules and other provisions of the Fund should help us rather than hinder us in preserving domestic stability in an unstable world. But – never say die – I wrote another and sent it off. Half of this confusion is due to the fact that, whereas the Cabinet would never discuss difficult military or diplomatic problems without a military or FO expert there, they discuss economic or financial matters with no expert help or guidance.

Attended a meeting in Keynes' room to discuss yet once more with the Bank, CSO, etc. the improvement of our Balance of Payments statistics so as to get rid of the at present large gap of £150-£250 million between the estimated balances on current and capital account.[4] Went over all the same old ground. Nevertheless it all helps to make the Bank take the problem

[3] On 25 January 1945: WM9(45)4, CAB65/49.
[4] 'UK Balance of Payments, Note of a Meeting of 30 January 1945', T230/306.

very seriously. Humphrey Mynors was there representing the Bank. It was nice to meet him again. I do not believe that I had seen him since the year I spent at Cambridge (1930–31) when he was a Fellow of Corpus [Christi College].

In the course of the week Lionel Robbins has sent a letter to Sir Richard Hopkins about the Customs and Excise report on the future of the Purchase Tax.[5] We are taking very seriously the point that in the transitional period, as it becomes increasingly difficult to operate the real controls (over labour, raw materials, etc.), we must shift increasingly to financial inducements, among which the heavy taxation of inessential domestic consumption with lower taxation or exemption of essentials and exports must play a big part. Lionel and I are to attend the Budget Committee in the Treasury next week to put our point of view.[6]

Most of my time this week has been spent on the paper I am preparing on the post-war treatment of the National Debt. This week I have drafted the section dealing with the repayment of debt and employment policy: the maintenance of employment may demand fiscal policies which lead to an excess of budget deficits over budget surpluses; debt considerations may require a reduction of debt in order to get a reduction in taxation and improvement in economic incentives; dilemma; what to do? I am suggesting the following principles of policy:- (1) As far as short-run budgetary policy is concerned, one should plan total expenditure and the level of taxation so as to preserve the general level of aggregate demand and so full employment. (2) If this lead to an excess of deficits over surpluses or to too slow a rate of debt repayment, one must take special long-run measures (a) by reducing interest rates, (b) by a policy of gently rising, or at any rate not falling, prices and wage-rates, (c) by foreign investment and (d) by a change in tax structure which has announcement effects such as encourage expenditure. (a) and (b) will not only stimulate private investment, but will simultaneously reduce the burden of the existing debt. (d) may take the form of discouraging savings by distributing income more equally, but this if carried too far may have restrictive effects on work, risk-bearing and investment; but there are surely changes in the tax structure (e.g. heavy taxation of undistributed profits with special tax exemptions in respect of expenditure on capital development) which will discourage savings and encourage investment. (a) (b) (c) and (d) are all ways of stimulating private expenditure without a budget deficit.[7]

Received some interesting literature from Lubin (in particular a full version of President Roosevelt's recent budget message to Congress with tables of national income and expenditure at the end)[8] which illustrate the growing interest in the USA in the use of the technique of national income-national expenditure planning for the maintenance of domestic stability. This is encouraging.

Had lunch with Jenks, Legal Adviser of the ILO. In the course of our

[5] Robbins to Hopkins, 1 February 1945, T171/369.

[6] See below p. 42.

[7] See page 35, note 27.

[8] *Budget of United States Government, fiscal year 1945: Budget message of the President and summary budget statements.* Washington DC: US Government Printing Office, 1944.

conversation we got on to demographic problems, which I maintained were likely to take the place after the war which problems of employment had taken in the inter-war period. That is to say, employment policy had been the important problem requiring intellectual solution and agreement last time; this stage was now passed and the stage of application was now approaching. But demographic issues (i.e. the terrifying prospect of a fade-out of population in the West combined with most serious over-population in the East) was an underlying problem of the first importance (demanding both control in the East, stimulation of fertility in the West and increased migration) on which the preliminary work of general education still had to be done. I suggested to Jenks that the ILO should now go all out to play the part of preliminary education on this subject which they had last time played on employment policy. He said he would try to get the Indian and Chinese workers to suggest a general ILO investigation into Population and Welfare in the East. I have later had a hurried note from him saying that he thought something might come of this idea.[9]

## *10 February 1945*

The week has been almost entirely spent on internal finance. On Monday [5 February] Lionel Robbins and I attended the Budget Committee in the Treasury to argue our case for the heavy taxation of inessentials under the Purchase Tax in order to give a financial inducement in the transitional period to export and to the production of essentials. Keynes argued that while this was on the right lines the best we could hope to do would be to hold the Purchase Tax as it is and to resist demands for reductions and exemptions for new lines of utility goods which were not really essential. We were inclined to agree with this, with the proviso that if it became impossible to resist the pressure for the introduction of new differentials into the Purchase Tax for the encouragement of new lines of utility goods, this should be done as much by raising rates on non-utility as by lowering rates on utility lines.[10]

Most of my time this week has been taken completing the first draft of the third main section of my paper on the Post-War Treatment of the National Debt, namely on the Capital Levy and Annual Capital Taxation.[11] It is clear that with the high and progressive rates of income tax, sur-tax and death duties and with the low rates of interest on the debt which are probable after the war the net yield from a very progressive

[9] Meade's interest in population problems persisted: see, for instance, his Presidential Address to the Royal Economic Society on 'Population Explosion, the Standard of Living and Social Conflict', *Economic Journal*, Vol. 77 (June 1967), pp. 233–55 (*The Collected Papers of James Meade*, Vol. II, chapter 26).

[10] The views of the Budget Committee (Hopkins, Eady, Keynes, Brittain, Gregg, Sir Archibald Carter, and Padmore) and of the Section are recorded in B(45)11 Revise, 'Budget Committee, Purchase Tax', 10 February 1945, and Robbins to Hopkins, 8 February 1945, T171/369.

[11] See page 35, note 27.

capital levy would be small (though it must not be forgotten that even if there were no net yield to make possible a reduction in the schedules of taxation after the levy, the very levy itself would reduce marginal rates of surtax and death duty – which are what matter from the point of view of economic incentives – by shifting people to lower tax brackets). But a proportionate levy with a moderate exemption limit (e.g. a levy of 33⅓ per cent on all holdings, the first £1000 being exempt) would have a substantial net yield. I also have an idea for collecting such a levy by instalments (e.g. 4 per cent in each of eight successive years). On grounds of equity (since capital even if it yields little or no income confers advantages) and on grounds of economic incentive (since taxation assessed on capital does not fall on the reward for risk-bearing) there is much to be said for substituting a permanent annual tax on capital for part of the income tax. If on these grounds a permanent tax of, say, ½ per cent per annum were levied on all individual holdings of property with exemption of the first £1000, a capital levy could be collected by instalments by an additional charge of 4 per cent for the first eight years. This instalment system would, as compared with a single huge levy, cause less disturbance in the capital and money markets and therefore be both more practicable and more equitable. [Incidentally a study of this problem has suggested some new ideas about the theory of liquidity preferences. One must consider three types of asset: Money, Bonds (i.e. assets with safe fixed interest) and Machines (i.e. assets with uncertain yield). The choice between Money and Bonds depends upon the pure rate of interest, and between Bonds and Machines on the risk premium. But the risk premium, just as the rate of interest, will depend upon the quantities in which the various types of asset are forthcoming in the market. If I have time sometime, I must write a note on this for publication.][12]

Had a visit from Gilbert Ponsonby of the Ministry of War Transport[13] (alias lecturer in the economics of transport at the London School of Economics). Most encouraging. Without any prodding that Ministry is taking the problems of the White Paper on *Employment Policy* seriously; and they are considering in detail the problems of the planning and timing of public investment on Roads, Railways etc. If all departments behaved like that, there would be a real chance of success for the policy.

There has been another series of indications this week of the interest which other countries are showing in these same problems. It all makes one think that the problem of employment policy is now merely a matter of working out in practice. The main issue of policy (state action to preserve the general level of aggregate demand) commands very wide if not universal acceptance. A New Zealander called Middleton, who is second in command of their reconstruction outfit, came to call. He seemed to be mainly interested in the shape of the administrative machinery here which would be necessary to carry out the White Paper policy. Tait of the

[12] Brackets in original. A development of these ideas appears in Meade's later article, 'Is the National Debt a Burden?', *Oxford Economic Papers*, Vol. 10 (June 1958), pp. 163–83 (*The Collected Papers of James Meade*, Vol. II, chapter 17).

[13] On 7 February: Ponsonby to Robbins, 5 February 1945, T230/69.

ILO, whom we used to know in Geneva[14] and who is now head of the Employment Section of the ILO, came to call and to exchange views on these general issues. I have received a letter from Copland (the Australian Prime Minister's Economic Adviser) sending estimates and forecasts of the Australian national income and expenditure done on the lines of our Budget White Paper for the purpose of Australian employment policy.[15] Much the most interesting exchange of ideas, however, came from a discussion with Americans – Lubin and Leon Henderson – who asked myself, E. A. G. Robinson and Lionel Robbins to an evening party. Both Lubin and Henderson are convinced of the enormity of the problem which the USA has to face almost immediately after the war (an excess of savings with full employment of, perhaps, $20,000 millions!!) and of the essential importance from the point of view of world economics that they should solve this problem. They themselves had all the right ideas; and we discussed such matters as prohibitive taxation on undistributed profits, consumers' credits, reductions in hours of work and longer holidays (which would not only decrease the income from which to save but also increase the opportunities for expenditure). But they were themselves depressed because of the intellectual and political background in the USA which made it difficult to get any of these ideas accepted. Still, I personally cannot help suspecting that when the depression does seriously start in the USA, after the experience of 1929–31 and with the much greater familiarity with Keynesian ideas which does after all now exist, they are likely to take measures (perhaps of a very unorthodox kind) which will certainly prevent the depression going anything like as far or lasting anything like as long as it did last time. Nevertheless the impression is inevitable that the US will certainly have a serious depression and will not be 100 per cent successful in meeting it. God help the rest of the world if it really gets out of hand!

Have given my review-article of Lerner's *Economics of Control* to E. A. G. Robinson for the *Economic Journal*.[16] A very queer book, but good hunting to all such economists who really see the point in a 'Liberal-Socialist' economy. It is perhaps a pity that Lerner should make such a sane policy look so strikingly paradoxical and queer; but as his book is only addressed to technical economists, perhaps this does not matter.

Had lunch with Marcus Fleming and Dennis Robertson to meet the American economist Marget, who is now dressed up as a soldier ready to move to Vienna as a member of the Austrian Control Commission when the time comes. What a voluble gas-bag! He never stopped talking. A very pleasant man, but the flow of words was stunning, and I haven't the slightest idea now what it was all about. I noticed that it had much the same effect upon Dennis.

The great news of the week is, of course, the appointment of Bridges to succeed Sir Richard Hopkins at the Treasury, and of Norman Brook to succeed Bridges at the Cabinet Offices. With the two most consistent

[14] When Meade was working in the Economic Intelligence Service of the League of Nations 1937–40.

[15] Copland to Meade, 30 January 1945, Meade Papers 1/9. The tables sent by Copland are on T230/99 (see Meade to Stone, 14 February 1945).

[16] See page 37, note 30.

friends of the Economic Section in the two most central positions the prospects may be said to be good.

## 19 February 1945

Very little to record this week. I have spent quite a lot of time catching up with the reading of papers, minutes etc. which I had allowed to accumulate for some time unread. The main job has again been the preparation of the paper on the post-war treatment of the national debt,[17] and we had a long and interesting meeting on the subject after dinner one evening (Lionel Robbins, Marcus Fleming, Tress, Miss Watts and myself). The net saving from a levy seems to be very exiguous with present low rates of interest and high rates of taxation; and I suspect that the right policy is (1) to reduce interest rates as far as is compatible with the avoidance of inflation, since as the debt approximates towards interest-free debt the burden of internal debt tends totally to disappear, and (2) to introduce an annual capital tax (which will avoid disadvantageous effects upon risk-bearing) and possibly to use this as a basis for a 'capital levy by instalments', i.e. a series of specially heavy payments under the annual capital tax, the proceeds being used for the repayment of debt.

Lunched with Gilbert Ponsonby of the Ministry of War Transport. The fashion in the transport world is, apparently, more and more in favour (so he tells me) of 'co-ordination', 'orderly organisation' etc. – i.e. preventing the competitive processes of the market from working. Surely the correct policy is (1) to nationalise the railways or other systems of transport which for technical reasons must be monopolies and consciously to run them on the correct price-cost principles (e.g. prices = marginal cost) and (2) to encourage competition on the roads where competition is possible. The present licensing restrictions on road hauliers and passenger bus services are, of course, quite opposed to these principles; and Ponsonby tells me that the tendency is likely to be to make them even more restrictive in future.

## 26 February 1945

On Monday afternoon Sir Richard Hopkins held the first meeting of his committee on the post-war treatment of the National Debt. Sir Wilfrid Eady, Sir Herbert Brittain, Lord Keynes from the Treasury; Sir Cornelius Gregg and Chambers from the Board of Inland Revenue; and Lionel Robbins and myself from the Economic Section. Plus two secretaries, Shillito (who was at Oriel [College, Oxford] with me) from the Treasury and another from the Board of Inland Revenue.[18] A most successful meeting. The problem is apparently to be taken really seriously and we are

[17] See page 35, note 27.
[18] The minutes of the meetings of the National Debt Enquiry are on T230/94 and 95, and T233/158. The first meeting was on 19 February 1945.

to meet twice a week as soon as we really get down to it. Not only are we to deal with the Capital Levy, Sinking Fund, Annual Capital Taxes, etc., but Keynes is also going to give us a series of lectures on what determines the market rate of interest and what rate of interest should be set for the debt. This is most important. The more I examine the problem, the more certain it seems to me that the proper radical solution is to get interest rates down to or towards zero, thereby killing two birds with one stone: avoiding economic stagnation and removing the burden of debt interest on the budget. The only argument against this would be if it led to inflation; but within reason such a development could be counteracted by running a budgetary surplus. Only if the 'natural' rate of interest were really pretty high might it be necessary to set a market rate of any considerable height, and in this case a Capital Levy might provide a worthwhile yield. Conclusion: either a high rate of interest + capital levy, or else a very low rate of interest and no attempt to repay debt. Lionel Robbins and I went round to Keynes' room after the meeting to hear his views on the problem. He has ideas on a reform of taxation, raising 2*s* 6*d* [12½p] in the £ as a corporate tax, 2*s* 6*d* in the £ as a tax on personal incomes and the equivalent of an income tax of 2*s* 6*d* in the £ as a tax on capital values. I am not at all clear what this really comes to. My first reaction is to consider any movement retrogressive which goes away from taxation on persons, either on *personal* incomes or on *personal* capital. Keynes on the rate of interest showed himself in a typical mood: revolutionary in thought and very cautious in policy. He seemed to justify a 3 per cent rate of interest as being socially desirable in order to maintain pensions etc., whereas in my mind the real social revolution is to be brought about by the most radical reduction of interest rates which is necessary to prevent general deflation. This would have the great secondary advantage of removing the debt interest from the budget and removing the rentier without disturbing either the entrepreneur or the man who wished to hoard money.

Incidentally I hear that Bridges when he takes over his new duties will take the chair at the committee on the post-war debt, and Hoppy who is to stay on as one of the Chancellor's advisers will also remain a member of the Committee. It is going to be fun! Bridges very able and competent but without much technical knowledge of these subjects; Hoppy very wise and learned as the elder statesman making way for new blood; Maynard perverse, brilliant and wayward; Eady muddled and uncertain; and the Economic Section – can one hope – sane and scientific!! At any rate the Economic Section has quite definitely gate-crashed into the arcana of internal finance.

I have spent the rest of the week working away at our paper on this subject. I have turned them into three separate papers: one on 'The Fiscal Problem set by the Debt' giving the statistical position of the debt interest as a proportion of the taxable income and discussing how various developments (fall of interest rates, rise of prices, decreased population, increased output per head) might affect it; one on 'The Capital Levy' discussing the Equity, Financial Effects and Yield of various kinds of Capital Levy and tending to the conclusion that with present low interest rates and high and progressive income taxes and death duties, the levy is not worthwhile; and one on 'Debt Repayment and Employment Policy' discussing by what means (Price Policy, Interest Policy, Foreign Investment, Change in Tax Structure) a policy of debt repayment might be reconciled with one for the maintenance of a high and stable level of employment.[19]

[19] See page 51, note 7.

# 5

# March 1945

### *11 March 1945*

Have settled down to work again after a week's leave. We have had another meeting of the committee on the Post-War National Debt, this time with Bridges in the chair in his new capacity as Permanent Secretary to the Treasury. The meeting [on 8 March] was devoted to a long academic lecture by Keynes on the whole of the *General Theory* – the equality between savings and investment; the inducement to invest; the propensity to consume; and liquidity preference.[1] It must have been very difficult for the layman and a terribly hard introduction for Bridges. Keynes still goes out of his way to give the maximum stress to the difference between his theory and old-fashioned orthodoxy. I felt definitely uncomfortable at his conclusions. He now almost holds the view that variations in the rate of interest (at any rate when it is as low as 3 per cent) have no effect upon investment. His conclusion is that the correct policy is to hold the rate at 3 per cent and not to let it rise in the short inflationary transitional period because any moderate rise in it will do little or nothing to restrain investment, and not to let it fall in the long run because a reduction will do little to promote investment and it is socially desirable that rentiers (i.e. universities, widows and orphans, etc.) should get some return on their capital. I am inclined to dispute this both for the transitional period and for the long run. In the transitional period it will be difficult to maintain the real controls and some rise in interest rates may be inevitable if we are to avoid inflation. In the long run I doubt whether it is true that a lot of investment (e.g. housing, public utilities and the non-profit-making developments of local authorities) is not greatly affected by the rate of interest. Also a long-run reduction in interest rates is (apart from a capital levy) the best way of reducing the budgetary burden of the national debt and the best way of getting fundamental improvement in the distribution of income. Indeed in the papers on the post-war debt (on which I have again spent a considerable time this week)[2] I am coming to the fundamental conclusion that (i) the capital levy is the way to proceed when

[1] J. M. Keynes, *The General Theory of Employment, Interest and Money*. London: Macmillan, 1936. Keynes' notes for his 'lecture' are in *The Collected Writings of John Maynard Keynes*, Vol. 27, London: Macmillan 1980, pp. 388–96; see also 'National Debt Enquiry Note of Second Meeting . . . on 8th March 1945', T230/94.

[2] See above, p. 46.

interest rates must be high to prevent inflation and (ii) that where interest rates are low and can be safely reduced towards vanishing point without leading to inflation the burden of the debt will automatically disappear and the fundamental redistribution of income will take place without the necessity for the capital levy earthquake. I suspect case (ii) applies to the present position but it must not be upset by assuring 3 per cent for ever as a 'just price' for savings.

Some time has been spent on the post-war central organisation for employment policy, involving future relationships between the Treasury, the Economic Section and the Central Statistical Office. Very encouraging progress has been made. Lionel Robbins, Campion and I met one evening after dinner to discuss the whole problem and a very happy concordat was reached. Campion has no desire to inflate the functions of the CSO as far as policy formation is concerned, nor to see the work on the National Income and Expenditure absorbed in the Treasury in a way which would short-circuit the CSO and the Economic Section. We agreed that the structure to aim at was: (i) an administrative division in the Treasury charged with the control of the timing and planning of public investment; (ii) a high-level official committee (of the status of the Budget Committee) which might be called the Employment Committee to advise the Chancellor through the Permanent Secretary of the Treasury on general policy; and (iii) the CSO and the Economic Section working for the Employment Committee in preparing surveys, proposing policies and 'brains-trusting' on the subject. It is at this point that the joint charge to the CSO and the Economic Section to forecast by means of the National Income and Expenditure would come in. By one of those coincidences which appear to be providential, just as we had concluded our discussion a message came through from Bridges saying that he wanted to fix a time to discuss just this problem. We went down straightaway to Bridges' room and Norman Brook joined us. Bridges agreed to the whole of our proposals and another meeting is to be held next week with the Treasury people present to finalise the arrangements.[3] It is indeed most gratifying to find Bridges within a week of his appointment taking the initiative to arrange these matters and in a manner so favourable to the Economic Section. . . .

I have also spent a considerable time this week on the future establishment of the Section including a 1½ hour talk with Norman Brook on the problems involved. He is clearly very keen on the Section and is going to give it every support. I have had interviews with two men, Brian Tew and Campbell Secord, both of whom have let it be known that they might be interested in jobs in the Section. Campbell Secord is a very exceptional man who has done a great deal in the RAF and in the Ministry of Aircraft Production to win the Battle of the Atlantic. He is a great mountaineer also, among other things. A very charming man who immediately strikes you as being an exceptional person, but I am not altogether clear that he would be suited for the patient and quiet existence of a member of the Economic Section. Tew is a very different type – quiet, industrious and capable. I think that we ought probably to offer him a junior post in the Section.

[3] See below, pp. 52–3.

Lunched with Blaise Gillie of the Ministry of Town and Country Planning. We had an interesting discussion. He is convinced that there is need for the application of economic analysis to the problems of planning, and that his department is suffering from the lack of this. So I let go on the need for a solution of the problem of compensation and betterment which did not completely destroy economic incentives and the pricing system in determining land-use – such as may be the result of prohibitive taxation on development value. I suggested that you could get this result either (a) by outright land nationalisation, the state then taking steps to see that the land (within the framework of the plan) was let out to the highest bidder or (b) by leaving land in private ownership and paying full compensation at market prices for all planning restrictions, the necessary funds being obtained (à la War Damage Contribution) by means of a small levy on the Schedule A value of all real property. I don't know whether he will take this message back to his Ministry, but the present proposals will, I am sure, not really work.[4]

It seems that Article VII and Commercial Policy may soon get a move on. The President approached the PM at the Crimea conference to get a move on with it.[5] Hawkins had scarcely returned to London from Washington when he was summoned immediately back to Washington to go over the Commercial Policy ground with Harry Hopkins whom the President has charged with the subject. And now the Canadians have sent some most important telegrams on the subject of Canadian financial aid to this country and commercial policy. They are naturally afraid that, being outside the sterling area, there will be serious discriminations against their trade. They suggest easy terms for Canadian credits (which would only be repaid as and when our balance of payments was favourable) which would make it possible not to discriminate in favour of sterling as opposed to Canadian goods. I have written a minute on this. It gives chapter and verse for two propositions which we have always held in the Article VII disputes, namely – (i) that a bilateralist restrictionist policy on our part would split the Empire and (ii) that the amount of financial help which we can expect to get from North America (and we shall badly need such help) will depend upon our attitude on commercial policy. It is sometimes forgotten that Article VII is after all in fact the 'consideration' for Lend-Lease. Sterling is only 'soft' and dollars are only 'hard' so long as in face of our very adverse balance of payments the sterling area countries will lend to us (by accumulating sterling balances) on terms which are more acceptable to us than those on which other parts of the world will lend. But we must remember that the sterling area countries will not forever continue to lend to us on such easy terms and we must make sure that the dollar countries do lend to us on very easy terms. As soon as the terms of lending approximate, the distinction between 'hard' and 'soft' currencies logically disappears. The Canadian attitude is so satisfactory because it so clearly relates the Canadian demand for an Article VII Commercial Policy with

[4] The 'present proposals' were contained in the coalition government's White Paper on *The Control of Land Use*, Cmd 6537, June 1944. On this subject see further below, pp. 123–4.
[5] Churchill, Roosevelt and Stalin met at Yalta in the Crimea between 7 and 12 February 1945.

the recognition that the terms of Canadian lending to us must be made to approximate towards those of war-time sterling area lending.[6]

## *17 March 1945*

This has been a very full and exciting week from the point of view of the future work of the Economic Section on internal financial policy and employment policy.

First, after yet another discussion of them in the Section I have finished what I hope are the final drafts of our three papers on the post-war treatment of the National Debt.[7] The third of these, on the problem of debt repayment and employment policy, is really little more than an enumeration of the main ways in which it might be possible to resolve the problem of secular unemployment without incurring budget deficits, namely:- Low Interest Rates, Rising Prices, Foreign Investment and Changes in the Tax Structure. Each of these four subjects require separate additional papers which the Economic Section will, I hope, undertake at some time. The *first* would discuss what sets the technical minimum to Interest Rates, by what means Interest Rates might be raised or lowered, and the extent to which different lines of investment would be likely to be affected by changes in interest rates. The *second* would be a very fundamental paper. It would point out that, from the point of view of stimulating investment, the expectation of a rise of money prices of 2 per cent per annum should have the same effect as a reduction in the rate of interest by 2 per cent per annum, and that if rates of interest have reached their technical minimum it may be best to operate on prices. But this paper would have a more fundamental purpose. The main danger and difficulty in carrying out successfully a policy for full employment is that the continued pressure of demand in the labour market will cause a wage inflation. The responsibility of the government should be to maintain, not full employment, but such a steady and expanding level of demand that full employment can be maintained provided that there is a sensible wage policy. In other words, I would have the Govt say: 'We are going to take general financial measures to ensure that the level of demand expands in such a way that the money price level rises continuously by, say, 1 per cent per annum. This will ensure full employment provided that there is a moderate wages policy.' To ensure this the Govt would incur any budget deficits which were necessary; but the 1 per cent rise in prices would stimulate private investment, and if continued budget deficits proved necessary to achieve this price objective and it was not possible still further to reduce interest rates, the Govt would set the objective of money prices rising at, say, 2 per cent per annum. This would all have the advantage of restoring the mechanism of rises or falls in money wage-rates in restricting

[6] Mackenzie King to Churchill, Telegrams 45, 46 and 47, 23 February 1945; Meade to Robbins and Fleming, 7 March 1945, T230/174.

[7] NDE Paper 4, "The Fiscal Problem set by the Debt", NDE Paper 5, 'The Capital Levy', NDE Paper 6, "Debt Repayment and Employment Policy", T230/95 and T233/159, Meade Papers 3/10, and *The Collected Papers of James Meade*, Vol. II, chapter 15.

or expanding the demand for labour – a matter which is especially important when one thinks of unemployment in particular industries, occupations or localities. The *third* paper would discuss the mechanisms (a) for controlling the balance of current payments (e.g. exchange rates) and (b) for influencing capital movements (e.g. interest rates), and would try to lay down an international code of principles for distinguishing between a favourable balance of payments which merely resulted in exporting unemployment and one which was to everyone's advantage. The *fourth* would consider such matters as taxes on undistributed profits to stimulate consumption expenditure or taxes assessed on capital instead of on income to stimulate investment.

We spent some time (Lionel Robbins, Tress and myself) at the beginning of the week preparing some comments on the draft of a new form for the White Paper on National Income and Expenditure to be published with this year's budget. The draft by Dick Stone is a brilliant piece of work, the main feature of which is a long first section showing how the different balancing tables of income and expenditure for the different sections of the economy (personal, public authorities, overseas accounts, etc.) can be put together in order to construct the different national incomes and other aggregations. . . . We prepared a note on the draft saying how good and useful we thought it to be and making a number of detailed suggestions.[8]

The next development on this matter was a meeting in Bridges' room with Barlow, Eady and Proctor from the Treasury, and Norman Brook, Lionel Robbins and myself and Campion from the Cabinet Offices to represent the Economic Section and the Central Statistical Office. A most satisfactory meeting. There is to be a special division within the Treasury, of which Proctor is to be in charge, to deal with the planning and timing of public investment. Meanwhile the Economic Section and the Central Statistical Office are jointly charged with the preparation of a paper showing the technique and statistics required to make forecasts of the 'target' national income (i.e. of the non-inflationary full employment income) and of the various categories of national expenditure (i.e. personal consumption, current public expenditure, private investment, public investment and the foreign balance).[9] Eady showed concern, as a result of a series of articles in *The Economist*,[10] that the Govt might have committed itself to too large an amount of total capital expenditure and wanted us to undertake a re-examination of these commitments. I tried to take the opportunity of showing that one could not usefully do this (i.e.

8 Stone to Meade and Robbins, 3 March 1945, T230/69 and 99; 'Draft National Income White Paper, Comments by the Economic Section', T230/99, Robbins to Campion, 13 March 1945, T230/70. According to Stone, the re-arrangement had been undertaken 'So as to provide a more connected and explicit account of the subjects with which it deals and so as to tidy up the logical form of presentation in such a way that its uses for peace-time purposes are made more apparent'.

9 The meeting was held on 15 March: 'Employment Policy, Note for Record', 17 March 1945, T230/70. On the Section-CSO paper see p. 58.

10 'Capital for Reconstruction', *The Economist*, 20 January 1945, pp. 83–4; 'Post-War Arithmetic', *The Economist*, 24 February 1945, pp. 235–6; 'Capital for Industry', *The Economist*, 10 March 1945, pp. 303–4. On the second of these articles Tress wrote a note circulated in the Section on 24 March as EC(S)(45)4 (T230/17).

measure this particular slice) unless simultaneously attempts were made to forecast the 'target' national income (i.e. the size of the cake itself) and the other categories of expenditure (i.e. the size of the other slices). It is from all points of view a good thing that this technique is now starting at a time when we are faced with an inflationary rather than a deflationary pressure for a series of years. For we shall be able to build up our reservoir of postponed projects; and the Treasury will be broken in gradually, since they will exercise the technique at first in conditions where they will be required to undertake the congenial duty of causing expenditure to be restricted rather than stimulated.

Campion with members of the CSO and Lionel Robbins with members of the ES are to meet in Proctor's room to make a start with our joint task. Campion has now circulated to us a draft paper by the CSO on the statistics required for post-war employment policy.[11] It is, on the whole, a good and ambitious paper which would have the effect of vastly improving UK statistics. But there are certain *lacunae* particularly from the point of view of forecasting and of controlling investment. We must now prepare ourselves to suggest the necessary changes and also to draft our Economic Section paper on the technique of using the national income and national expenditure for the purpose of forecasting and control [of] the total demand for goods and services.[12] (It is to be remarked that Campion's paper, which has apparently already been agreed with Norman Brook, Proctor and the statistical divisions of the main departments, had not been previously seen by us. . . .)[13]

The day after the meeting in Bridges' room Lionel and I had lunch with Dennis Proctor. We had a general talk about the whole problem of controlling national expenditure and, in particular, public investment. He is clearly going to be very keen on his job, but he and the Treasury are starting right from scratch in all this.

The day before I had lunched with Ponsonby of the Ministry of War Transport and with his chief, Wilson. Here is one of the main spending departments from the point of view of public investment which is dead keen itself on planning and control and timing. They are the only department which has itself taken a constructive initiative on the basis of the *Employment Policy* White Paper. In the course of our conversation five main points arose:- (1) Wilson maintained that a main thing was to get it laid down that the acquisition of land for public works (which might take up to two years) must be considered part of the blueprint stage and not part of the works themselves, and that departments must be authorised (and indeed made) to acquire the land well in advance; (2) he argued that the principle of varying the rate of central grant as a means of getting capital expenditure undertaken at the right time was important; (3) he argued that the form of contracts between public authorities and contractors needed examination in order to see how expenditure could be

[11] 'Statistics for Full Employment', CS(S)(45)15 (Revise), 8 March 1945, CAB139/124.
[12] See below p. 56.
[13] The first draft and the correspondence with the departments is on CAB139/124.

made most flexible; (4) he wholeheartedly agreed with me when I suggested that departments should be asked to prepare their programmes ahead, not in the form of a single figure of their capital expenditure, but in the form of 3 or 4 tiers, showing the maximum they could usefully spend, the amount they would normally spend if they were not being encouraged to turn the tap on or off in the interest of employment policy, and the minimum level of expenditure without which they could not get on; and (5) he noted for further thought my suggestion that the various public authorities should be asked to show at what rates of interest their various projects would become profitable. Altogether a most heartening lunch, but I doubt whether many of the main spending departments will prove to be so enlightened.

Laughlin Currie of the US Foreign Economic Administration and one of the 'New Deal' brains trusters has been in London this week on his way back to Washington from Berne, where the Americans together with the British and French have been reaching a new economic agreement with the Swiss.[14] He invited me to dinner *à deux* in the Savoy on Monday, when we discussed in rather general terms the familiar topics of commercial policy, the UK balance of payments and employment policy. He, like Lubin and Henderson a few weeks ago, showed that he realised the immensity of the problem facing the United States. He invited me to lunch the following Wednesday, and when I got there I found that the other guests were Ambassador Winant with Penrose from the US Embassy and Minister of State Law with Nigel Ronald from the Foreign Office. Winant was very interesting (and sensible) on the international labour situation, pointing out that the AF of L [American Federation of Labor] had as its officials Irish anti-British ex-isolationists. It was, therefore, very important that they, who had been brought into international co-operation through their membership of the ILO, should not be antagonised through the side-tracking of the ILO in favour of any new organisation that might proceed out of the recent international trade union conference which the Russians and the CIO [Congress of Industrial Organizations] attended.[15] The main conversation was, however, entirely on international political questions. Winant and Currie argued strongly the case for believing that Russia truly intended to co-operate with the West – Winant illustrating his points with some very interesting backstairs Geneva gossip relating to the time when Russia attacked Finland and was herself kicked out of the League [of Nations][16] and the ILO and Currie putting forward a very weak argument that we should not form a Western bloc with Norway, Holland, Belgium, France, etc. As he had strongly argued the Russian case for the annexation of the Baltic States and for taking bases in Finland on the ground of strategic needs against the great German menace, I could not refrain from asking him (a) whether we were not justified in arranging by *friendly*

[14] For Currie's report of his London conversations between 10 and 16 March, including his meeting with Meade, see *Foreign Relations of the United States*, 1945, Vol. VI, Washington: Department of State, pp. 36–40.

[15] Held in London 6-17 February 1945.

[16] Russia invaded Finland on 30 November 1939 and was expelled from the League of Nations the following month.

*agreement* with a country only 21 miles from us for common military defence and (b) whether we were wrong in not having seized the Irish ports in 1940, '41 or '42? Winant openly rebuked Currie by asking him whether he realised that the State Department had invited Southern Ireland (which was a military menace to us) and had failed to invite the Argentine (which was in South America) to the Chicago Civil Aviation conference[17] without previously consulting us, and whether he thought that this was the way to discourage us from making our regional security arrangements in Europe? And when Currie argued that if we formed a Western bloc it would be against Russia and not against Germany, which would never again be in a position to threaten the world, Law sagaciously asked whether this argument did not also refer to the World Security Organisation, on which Currie had spoken with such enthusiasm. Security against whom, if not against Germany? At any rate we all agreed that a Western bloc would not offend if (i) it were done with Russian participation or agreement, and (ii) it were done as part of the regional mechanism of the World Organisation and (iii) it did not mean economic discriminations and exclusiveness. Law maintained throughout that, although it was not HMG's policy to form a Western bloc, he thought it would in fact be a good thing to do and need not be anti-Russian. We had common traditions of liberty and democracy; and recent history had shown that these small states of Western Europe could not stand alone against Germany and that we needed them for our own defence.

## 25 March 1945

At last the three papers on the post-war National Debt are completed. They will be duplicated during the week-end and circulated to the committee at the beginning of next week. We have had another meeting in Bridges' room of the National Debt Enquiry committee, at which Keynes continued his lectures on the rate of interest.[18] It was all really rather embarrasing, as he continues to put his ideas on this subject in the most extreme form and to call on me and Lionel Robbins for support. He seems completely to have abandoned the idea of using the rate of interest to influence investment (an idea which I want to do my utmost to revive) and also leaves out all qualifications of the Liquidity Preference idea so as to assert unequivocally that neither thrift nor the productivity of capital have any influence over the rate of interest. (For example, he does not state that if the rate were fixed at a level much below the productivity of capital, there might be an inflation of investment which, by raising the level of the money income, would increase the demand for money for transactions purpose and so reduce the amount of cash available for other purposes with the result that the rate of interest would rise.) I fear that

[17] The International Civil Aviation Conference met in Chicago 1 November to 7 December 1944.

[18] See page 51, note 7 and T230/94 or T233/158 for the minutes of the meeting on 22 March 1945.

financial advice given to the Treasury on this basis may be misleading, and I continue to try to suggest (without any open disagreement) (a) that a post-war inflationary movement, if the controls over investment expenditure are not strong enough, may in fact give rise to a higher rate of interest and (b) that (especially in the long run if there is a general stagnation) the gradual reduction of interest rates to vanishing point may be the best way both of stimulating investment and [of] reducing the interest burden on the outstanding national debt.

I have spent a large part of the week writing a paper on 'Economic Forecasting and Employment Policy', as the Economic Section's contribution to the discussions which we are to have with Proctor of the Treasury and with all the Central Statistical Office on the next steps in Employment Policy. The paper is a straightforward statement of the need (a) to forecast in advance the 'target' national expenditure which will serve to maintain employment without leading to inflation and (b) to forecast the five main constituent elements of actual national expenditure – personal consumption, government current expenditure, private investment, public investment, and the foreign balance – in order to see what measures may be exercised on these items in order to make the total of these five items sum up to the 'target'. The paper discusses very briefly the main problems to be met and the main procedures to be adopted in forecasting the 'target' total and each of these five elements in turn.[19]

Richard Law took me out to dinner with him to his flat in Dolphin Square. I was very pleased to meet Mrs Law who seemed to me to be a very nice person but a little shy and reserved in manner. Having discussed our respective children at some length, we got on to the subject of post-war internal economic policy. Law was in a thoroughly depressed mood, but I think I managed to persuade him that it was at least probable that after this war we should be more successful than last time in preventing mass unemployment. I suggested that we should try to lead the world morally in a more or less liberal internal economic New Deal and argued that our Education, National Health, Social Security and Employment Policies (all accepted by the coalition government) were really a very good start. He has obviously been persuaded by the Tory progressives to consider these matters. He asked how were we to pay for such policies, and this led to a discussion on the best use of scarce resources (as the general consideration) and the level of taxation (as the more special consideration). Law went on to speak about the need for increasing the efficiency of British Industry by a wholesale rebuilding of industrial equipment on the most up-to-date lines. This argument is now very popular both with the Beveridgites such as Nicky Kaldor, with *The Economist* and with the young ginger group in the Conservative Party. I explained how the highest technical efficiency did not necessarily mean the greatest economy, and how it only paid the community to replace old plant with new when the total costs on the new were lower than the prime costs on the old. (This always seems paradoxical to non-economists, but I think that Law took the point.) Moreover, it is out of place to go all out

[19] Drafts of the paper are on T230/70. See also below, page 58.

for a rapid rebuilding of British Industry just after the endurances of six years of war privations and when all the houses need rebuilding. Surely it is in these circumstances economic to rebuild industry when consumption is somewhat restored and the population is somewhat rehoused. Also in the interests of Employment Policy it is desirable to keep these industrial projects up one's sleeve until the pressure of total demand slackens off somewhat. I fear that there is an element of the hysterical in the present shout for immediate rebuilding of all British Industries.

Lionel Robbins and I spent an hour on Monday evening with Attlee briefing him on the Canadian Government's telegrams suggesting that we should accept loans on any terms from Canada as a means of adopting more quickly and easily an Article VII non-discriminatory commercial policy.[20] We stressed the three points: first, that the difference between scarce (dollar) currencies and the sterling area was merely that the sterling area countries were willing to lend to us on more easy terms than the North Americans, and that if the North Americans would lend on easier terms and if (as very probable) when shipping and supply difficulties no longer made it impossible for the sterling area countries to spend in the dollar area the sterling area no longer was willing to lend so easily to us, the margin of the distinction between scarce dollars and the sterling area would disappear; secondly, that it was one thing for the Canadians on these grounds and conditions to ask us to give up discrimination against their goods, but it was going much further (and probably too far) for them to suggest that, as long as our balance of payments as a whole was difficult, we should not be free to restrict our total imports as much as possible; and thirdly, that the whole incident showed most clearly (i) that Empire Unity would really be promoted by an Article VII policy and not by a policy of regional blocs and (ii) that North America as a whole would only give us the support which we should need after the end of the Lend-Lease and Mutual-Aid period if we played ball on Article VII. At subsequent meetings of Ministers it was decided to send a non-committal but friendly reply to the Canadians, and I hear that in these discussions Attlee took very much the right line.[21] This is very gratifying, since when one talks to him Attlee says all the time 'Yes, Yes' in a mechanical sort of way which leaves one quite in the dark as to whether one is making any impression or not. I think that the stage is rapidly being set for the beginning of real decisions on Article VII and all that. But one never can tell.

[20] The meeting was on 20 March 1945. The basis for the briefing was 'Commercial Policy and Related Questions', 19 March 1945 (T230/174).

[21] The meetings were on 20 and 21 March 1945 (PREM4/18/4).

# 6

# April 1945

### *1 April 1945*

In the course of the week I finished the paper which the Section is preparing on 'Economic Forecasting and Employment Policy'.[1] It is the statement of first principles on so planning and forecasting total national expenditure as to make it add up to the 'target' level necessary to maintain employment without inflation (the only logical snag being that if the Trade Unions do not adopt a moderate wages policy it might be impossible to maintain high employment and avoid inflation. In this case presumably one chooses a compromise 'target' which will involve not-too-much inflation with not-too-much unemployment). This paper has now been sent to the CSO and to Proctor in the Treasury and we all meet on it next week. Meanwhile it has invoked a strange response from that 'silly boy' (to use a phrase which Maynard Keynes uses of me when I get on his nerves!) Ronnie Coase of the CSO, who is convinced that one should analyse national expenditure for employment purposes industry by industry and product by product rather than by the 'White Paper' categories of total personal consumption, total public current expenditure, total private investment, total public investment, and the foreign balance. These latter categories are essential because they correspond to the broad classes of motives and incentives determining national expenditure. Thus personal consumption depends on personal tax-free income; public investment is consciously planned and timed; the foreign balance depends on incomes and prices at home and abroad, commercial policy, etc. Coase's classification is useful for structural unemployment (for which incidentally an analysis of expenditure by localities would be as important as an analysis by products), but if it were made the primary method it would lead inevitably to most undesirable policies stabilising employment by rigidly maintaining every individual separate line of production. Having had some written controversy with Coase on this subject in the past,[2] I am being urged by Coase to prepare an agreed statement 'for the record' (silly boy!). I was quite prepared to do this and had in fact written something for this purpose; but Lionel Robbins is most insistent that, as the method of dealing with this

[1] The first draft and related correspondence is on T230/70. A later version was circulated in the Section as EC(S)(45)5 (Second Revise), 21 April 1945, T230/17; the final version, of 4 June 1945, is on T273/317 and in Meade Papers 3/2.

[2] See above pp. 5, 6–7, 17.

problem is a matter for the Economic Section and not for the CSO, I should not do more than write a letter to Coase stating my views as amended by the points which Coase has made. But as Tress tells me that nothing short of a complete recantation of my views will in fact have any effect, I fear that this stupid dispute with the 'silly boy' will continue. I fear that I am perhaps tarred in Coase's eyes (perhaps with a soupçon of justification) with the arrogance of Maynard Keynes. . . . This impression I wish to do everything in my power to remove. My letter will be a very reasonable and conciliatory one.[3]

We have had another meeting of Bridges' committee on the National Debt Enquiry at which Keynes continued to talk about the rate of interest.[4] This time he was talking on implications of his theory for post-war interest policy. He was very good and very persuasive and I thoroughly agreed with his prescriptions. His desire is to see new long-term issues take the form of bonds which the state has the option to repay in a moderate period (say 10 to 15 years) without being obliged to repay at any specified date (cf. 2½% Consols.). This would give the state the opportunity of obtaining any possible budgetary relief which becomes possible if and when interest rates have properly to be reduced as a part of long-term employment policy. He contrasted this policy with that lying behind the present 3 per cent issues which the state has not the right to repay for a considerable period of years. At the other end of the scale he would like to see the short-term rate reduced, say, from 1 per cent to ½ per cent. The floating debt is held in 3 parts of about £2000 million each: (i) by the Bank of England and Government Departments, (ii) by the joint-stock banks and discount market, and (iii) by the overseas holders of sterling balances. As far as (i) is concerned, it is merely a question of the right hand paying the left. As for (ii) there is no longer any reason to go on paying the banks so high a commission for the manufacture of the vast new deposits, particularly as their profitable source of income (namely advances) will begin to expand again soon. (iii) presents a great opportunity, since it would represent not only a considerable budgetary saving but also an appreciable saving in the balance of payments. But the danger here might be that a reduction of short-term interest rates might drive the overseas holders into still more profitable long-term assets. The question therefore arises whether the treatment of the short-term debt should not wait until comprehensive arrangements have been made with our creditors about the war-time sterling balances.

Have spent a good deal of time on establishments again. I have spoken to Hugh Weeks of the Ministry of Production and to Sir George Turner of the Ministry of Supply about Gilbert Walker, of whom both these persons spoke most highly. I am now writing to Gilbert Walker to make him a definite offer to join the Section. Campion has now made dispositions about the offers he is going to make to his CSO men. He is making a very high bid for Jack Stafford, and I must make up my mind whether I should raise the offer to him to the same level. I have an idea that it would be a

[3] Meade sent the letter on 9 April: see Coase to Meade, 12 April 1945, T230/70.
[4] On 28 March (T230/94, T233/158).

very good thing to try first of all to get Robert Hall to come to the Economic Section at the highest level in place of Stafford and to compete for Stafford if Hall will not come. Campion has also set me one or two other problems. He is offering a ceiling of £1250 to his second layer (as opposed to our £1200). This must be adjusted. He is also giving his men the choice of establishment or of temporary posts (with FSSU pensions). If so, I am not sure that our men should not be given the same choice. These points need further thought.

## *7 April 1945*

In the course of the week we have made some progress on the plans for forecasting national expenditure for purposes of Employment Policy. Stafford sent Robbins and myself a minute on the Economic Section paper on 'Economic Forecasting and Employment Policy', rather on the lines of Coase's ideas that one should consider employment industry by industry and locality by locality rather than by the global aggregates of national expenditure (making personal consumption plus government current expenditure plus private and public investment plus the foreign balance add up to a 'target' national income).[5] Against this there are the conclusive arguments – first, that you cannot hope to forecast the individual items but you may hope for more success in anticipating movements in the big aggregates; and secondly, that if you try to stabilise employment industry by industry and locality by locality you will be adopting the most extreme and rigid form of planning which will destroy initiative, remove freedom of choice, and eliminate movement of factors from less to more desirable uses. Lionel Robbins, Marcus Fleming and I had a discussion with Stafford on these lines.

In the course of the week we have had two meetings in the Treasury in Proctor's room of the Treasury-Economic Section-CSO group which is to prepare a document on the subject of the statistics and use of statistics required for Employment Policy. Those present were Proctor, Lionel Robbins, myself, Marcus Fleming, Campion, Stafford and Stone. The first meeting was devoted to discussing the CSO paper on Statistics required for Employment Policy and the second to a discussion of our paper on Economic Forecasting and Employment Policy. . . . We all wanted to liven up the CSO paper a bit by high-lighting one or two of the salient needs – e.g. for uniformity of statistical classification, synchronisation of statistical returns, speed in making results available, etc. – but Campion was much too terrified of upsetting the equilibrium of the department statisticians. . . . We proceeded to decide that we should revise our paper, the CSO should revise theirs and Proctor would then submit them with a covering note to Bridges.[6]. . .

[5] Stafford to Robbins, 29 March 1945, T230/70.

[6] Proctor's note was sent at the beginning of May 1945 (Proctor to Bridges, 'Employment Policy', 2 May 1945, T273/319). The minutes of the Working Party on Statistics for Employment Policy are on a file closed until 1990 (CAB108/124).

We have had another meeting of the National Debt Enquiry,[7] at the opening of which there was a very shy-making scene. Somehow Keynes raised the question of the Capital Issues Control, arguing that it should be greatly relaxed in order that firms might raise the necessary funds in anticipation of the time when they would be able to obtain the necessary permits for labour, raw materials, building, etc. for reconstruction. Sir Herbert Brittain tentatively defended the policy of only permitting new issues on those cases in which firms had the necessary building permits, raw material allocations, etc. Keynes said that Brittain was 'intellectually contemptible', that he was 'talking rot' and that he (Brittain) wouldn't allow him (Keynes) to see any of the papers on this question because 'you realise what nonsense I consider your ideas to be'. Brittain defended himself with dignity and effect, but it was all most awkward and really quite indefensible behaviour on K's part. It was not a very propitious opening to a meeting at which Robbins and I were billed to produce our 'confession of faith' on the rate of interest and at which we intended to counter some of Keynes' more extreme remarks in the previous meeting such that 'productivity of capital and thrift have got nothing to do with the rate of interest' and his view that the rate of interest should no longer be used to control inflation or deflation. I tried to point out that the demand for money was increased both by an increase in the volume of transactions and by a fall in the rate of interest on other assets; that for this reason a rise in the volume of transactions with the amount of money constant would cause a rise in interest rates; that if there were an increase in the incentive to invest or the propensity to consume, at any given rate of interest there would be an increase in the demand for capital goods or consumption goods which both immediately and also because of the effects of the multiplier would increase the volume of transactions; and that in consequence the indirect effects of an increase in the incentive to invest or in the propensity to consume would be a rise in the rate of interest unless the monetary authorities increased the supply of money. I argued that, apart from control by variations in interest rates, inflation and deflation could be controlled by tax policy or by direct controls or interventions (e.g. rationing in times of inflation or public investment in times of deflation). All methods had their disadvantages, but were we really wise to foreswear entirely the use of the rate of interest as a means of control? After his outburst with Brittain, Keynes was quite calm and reasonable with Lionel and myself, thank goodness![8]

Again much time has been spent this week on establishments. The short and the long of it is that I have sent off a letter to Washington to Gilbert Walker definitely offering him a job in the Section, and I have had a long talk with Robert Hall offering him a job (in charge of the General Problems but to be ready to consult with Devons and Fleming on Employment Policy and External Economic Problems and to take the place of the Director when

[7] On 5 April 1945 (T230/94, T233/158).

[8] Brittain subsequently prepared a memorandum for the committee on 'Capital Issues Control After V-E Day' (NDE Paper 10, 20 April 1945, T233/158). For Meade's views see his handwritten notes and 'Note of Fifth Meeting . . . on 5th April, 1945' on T230/95.

the Director is away). Hall was obviously very moved to accept, but he said that Margaret Hall was so attached to the society of dons' wives at Oxford and to her own teaching of economics at Oxford that he thought he would have to refuse. I suggest that Margaret Hall should build up her circle in Hampstead and teach at Bedford College. He is going to let me know in some weeks' time.

## *15 April 1945*

I have had another talk with Robert Hall about his joining the Economic Section, after having sounded out Lionel Robbins on the prospects of getting a job teaching economics for Margaret Hall at the London School of Economics, University College, Bedford College or somewhere else in London. Apparently the prospects are not at all bad, and I have got Lionel Robbins to talk to Robert Hall on the subject. So there is just a chance we may persuade him to come. I have received a letter from Gilbert Walker from Washington, crossing mine to him and hinting broadly that he might like to come to the Economic Section. So he appears quite a probability. Meanwhile I have heard what seems to be a fairly well substantiated rumour that Dick Stone has definitely decided to leave the Central Statistical Office for Cambridge. This will be a very serious blow, as he is certainly a genius at the National Income and Expenditure and will be very difficult to replace. It is true that his replacement may ease some personal tensions both within the CSO and between the CSO and outside bodies; but it will be a major disaster if this part of the work of the CSO falls into incompetent or unsympathetic hands, – and I am pretty sure that Campion is fundamentally unsympathetic towards it. Tress has dropped one or two broad hints that this is a job which might interest him, and I think it would be a very good thing if he took it on. He has not the same imaginative genius as Stone. But he understands its purpose, is very hard-working and gets on well both with myself and Campion.

I attended a meeting under the chairmanship of John Maud of the official reconstruction committee on industrial problems, at which we were discussing papers by the Board of Trade and the Ministry of Aircraft Production on the setting up in this country of industries to produce goods previously imported.[9] Most of the proposals were pretty innocuous and at this stage were completely non-committal. But Lionel and I put in a vigorous plea that the Departments in discussing with the industries should at this stage confine themselves as far as possible to discovering how much support or protection each scheme would require rather than going into details on the methods of support (tariffs, quota restrictions, etc.) which the industries wanted. It is, we argued, most important not to get tied up at all on this subject until the general commercial policy arrangements which may (or may not!) come out of Article VII have been decided. We should almost certainly be able to do all the reasonable things under these

[9] The minutes of the meeting (R(IO)(45) 7th meeting, 10 April 1945) and the two memoranda discussed (R(IO)(45) 12 and 14) are on CAB87/18.

arrangements, but we might have to choose one method (e.g. subsidies) rather than another (e.g. import restrictions). This was a hard doctrine for the officials who (like Sir George Turner of the Ministry of Supply) are responsible for carrying on the negotiations with particular industries; but I am sure that it was right. But alas! Since then Roosevelt has died,[10] and I wonder how long that will postpone decisions on Article VII. One knew that Roosevelt had an international trade conference high on his list of priorities. What about President Truman?

We have had another meeting of Sir Edward Bridges' 'National Debt Enquiry', the main feature of which was a statement by Sir Richard Hopkins of his personal views.[11] He spoke mainly about the interactions of external economic events on our domestic policies. Suppose we decided on an internal policy of cheap money in the interests of domestic employment policy. What was to happen if there was a serious external slump? Our exports would fall off; our balance of payments would deteriorate; should we really be able to maintain our domestic policy of full employment and cheap money? Keynes immediately leapt into the breach: (i) he did not think that we could or should completely offset our loss of external markets by internal expansion, and for this reason he thought that Beveridge went too far in setting an inviolable objective of 3 per cent for unemployment;[12] (ii) we should have to take steps in such circumstances to restrict imports and thus divert demand from overseas to domestic markets; (iii) exchange depreciation was no good either as a cyclical or as a secular measure for putting us right, as if it failed to expand appreciably the volume of our exports the fall in their price might well make matters worse; and (iv) in the last resort we must turn to the Russian system of foreign trading (by which I think he meant bilateral balancing of imports and exports). I could not stand this reference to exchange depreciation, and argued that as we produced manufactured goods in competition with many other exporting countries and in competition with the home industries of many of our customers it seemed to me highly improbable that a decline in our export prices relatively to others would not cause a very substantial expansion of our exports. This, I said, could be particularly the case if we could achieve (i) a Bretton Woods monetary agreement which would allow for exchange depreciation in the case of a country whose balance of payments was in fundamental disequilibrium without permitting offsetting competitive exchange depreciation in the case of a country with a favourable balance of payments, and (ii) a commercial policy agreement which allowed a country with an unfavourable balance of payments to restrict imports but did not allow the exports of such a country to be rigidly held from expansion by high tariffs, quotas, etc. in countries with favourable balances of payments. Eady then took up the tale and argued that the American proposal (in their latest draft convention)[13] by which countries would be able to impose quantitative restrictions in cases in which excessive imports hurt any of their home

[10] On 12 April 1945.

[11] See Minutes of 6th meeting, 10 April 1945, T230/95 and T233/158.

[12] In his *Full Employment and a Free Society*, op. cit.

[13] See above, p. 14.

industries offended against the conditions which I mentioned. I did not think it proper to continue the discussion in detail at Bridges' meeting; but subsequently I wrote a long letter to Eady[14] (which was really meant for the eyes of Bridges, Hoppy and Keynes to whom I sent copies) taking these points up. The American proposals I pointed out (i) made this use of import restrictions subject to the approval of the International Trade Organisation except in the transitional period; (ii) made it necessary for the ITO to give its sanction only if increased imports were harming a domestic industry, whereas in the case under discussion (in which our exports to the USA were falling off because of an American slump) our problem would be *not* to expand our exports to the USA above the pre-slump level but merely to maintain our exports at the pre-slump level; (iii) emphasised the importance of this last point by stating that the limitations on imports could not be to a level less than that of a previous representative period and must in any case allow for progressive relaxation of the restrictions. Therefore, I wrote to Eady, I stuck to my main contention that we should expect exchange depreciation in a regime of Bretton Woods-cum-Article VII commercial policy convention to be a very powerful weapon. I added that I should not be persuaded by those who said that exchange depreciation would diminish the volume of our exports until I heard the self-same people taking the logical step of arguing that the way to correct our balance of payments was to make our export industries *less* efficient and *more* costly and to impose special taxation on them!

After the meeting I went to call on Sir Herbert Brittain and persuaded him to send us information about the composition of the national debt – stock prices, amounts subscribed etc. This made a useful contact and enabled me to exchange a few words which made it clear that the Economic Section was not agreeing with all of Keynes' extravaganzas.

A sub-committee of the National Debt Enquiry has been set up consisting of Sir Richard Hopkins, Sir Cornelius Gregg, Lionel Robbins and myself to take our paper on the Capital Levy as the basis of a paper for the Chancellor to send to other Ministers on this subject.[15]

I have spent the week-end rewriting our paper on 'Economic Forecasting and Employment Policy' to take more account of (i) structural unemployment and (ii) the fact that employment policy will have in fact to rely a good deal on the close watching of current trends of employment and their prompt correction (as opposed to forecasting and planning ahead so that nothing ever begins to go wrong). I hope that these adjustments of the paper will help to meet the misgivings of the Central Statistical Office.[16]

[14] Not found.

[15] See below pp. 65, 69–70.

[16] This version of the paper was circulated as EC(S)(45)5 (Second Revise) on 21 April 1945 (T230/17). For the CSO's misgivings see Campion to Meade, 10 April, and Stafford to Meade, 21 April 1945, T230/70.

## *22 April 1945*

Having made a few further alterations in the paper on 'Economic Forecasting and Employment Policy', I have now sent it on to be retyped for the CSO and Proctor of the Treasury. I hope we shall soon be able to submit it to Bridges with the CSO paper on Statistics for Employment Policy, so that he can get the Departments ready to start up on this subject.

We had a sub-committee meeting of the National Debt Enquiry (Lionel Robbins, myself, Sir Richard Hopkins and Cockfield deputising for Sir Cornelius Gregg of the Board of Inland Revenue). We (that is to say the Economic Section in close consultation with the Board of Inland Revenue) are now to redraft the paper for submission to Ministers.[17] It is clear that Hoppy would simply love to be in charge of a Capital Levy. He believes that the thing is practicable if (i) no attempt is made to collect in money but the state becomes a gigantic investment trust taking over a proportion of all forms of capital and (ii) all private valuers etc. are taken on as temporary civil servants for the duration. As an artist in financial administration he is as disappointed as I am that the arithmetic of the yield of a levy shows it not really to be worthwhile. Meanwhile we have had further confirmation of what a millstone the debt is going to be round our neck in the post-war world. At another meeting of the National Debt Enquiry [on 19 April] we discussed a draft paper by Keynes on what should be the future policy of interest rates.[18] The fear of the effect of a rise in interest rates on the burden to the budget in a higher annual debt service is clearly going to inhibit everybody from using the rate of interest as a regulator of the general economic situation. For example, Keynes is all for an immediate reduction in short-term rates, although the immediate post-war period will be one of inflationary pressures in which the real controls over prices, uses of materials, labour, etc. may for political reasons be becoming less and less effective. If we are quite unready to use the two great price mechanisms (the rate of interest and the rate of exchange) for maintaining internal and external equilibrium we shall be driven more and more to quantitative real controls and authoritarian interventions unrelated to prices. As a Liberal-Socialist economist I regard it as my function to fight the battle of the use of these two central price mechanisns. As a result of the meeting Hoppy was asked by Bridges to do a draft on the basis of Keynes' draft for submission to the Chancellor on the subject of the future of cheap money. We shall have a chance of restating our views to Hoppy.

The future of the Iron and Steel Industry has come up in an acute form as the result of a report prepared in the Ministry of Supply by a group of officials under Oliver Franks, D. N. Chester of the Economic Section having assisted in its preparation.[19] The theme of the report is that costs

[17] Drafts of the report on the capital levy are on T230/95 and T233/158.

[18] NDE Paper 7, 'Summary by Lord Keynes of his Proposals', 18 April 1945, T233/159 and *The Collected Writings of John Maynard Keynes*, Vol. 27, pp. 396–404.

[19] R(45)36, 'Iron and Steel, Joint Memorandum by the Minister of Supply and the President of the Board of Trade', 6 April 1945, covering the Report on the Iron and Steel Industry (CAB124/789). The Section discussed the report on 17 April (EC(S)(45)8, Minutes of a

must be reduced to make the industry competitive; that this can be done partly by new investment to increase productivity though a considerable part of the reduction must be brought about by reduced prices for coal; that the industry should draw up a programme of large-scale capital investment (£100 million); that this should receive high priority over the next five years; and that during this period as a temporary measure the industry should be given substantial protection as a *quid pro quo* for this extensive modernisation. All this has been discussed and, I believe, informally accepted by the leaders of the Industry. There is much that is good in the Report. In particular, the idea of a programme for capital investment, provided it is drawn up in a way which leaves the timing of the expenditure as flexible as possible, might be most useful for so timing expenditure as to fit in with the requirements of Employment Policy. But in many respects the Report is a good illustration of the dangers of tackling the economic problem industry by industry. First, how can one say whether a particular industry will be competitive or not unless one knows what the rate of foreign exchange is to be; but this is a problem which can properly be discussed only in the context of the total of imports and exports. Secondly, the emphasis in the Report is naturally on the need to re-equip the industry instanter in order to increase its productivity; but there are a large number of considerations which suggest that expenditure on such re-equipment should be spread out and should be light at first and heavier later. Such timing would be in the interests of employment policy, would allow some reconstitution of civilian standards to take place before more savings are made to benefit future generations, and could allow some immediate relief from the endurances of the war. Thirdly, the question of the protection of the Iron and Steel Industry must be considered in relation to the whole of Commercial Policy; and shall we be able to achieve the removal of foreign obstacles in the way of our other exports if we insist on absolute protection for the Iron and Steel Industry? Moreover, what is the logic of giving the Industry protection for five years in respect of capital developments which will be made during that period but which will produce output only after that period? Of course, one must suspect that the Industry hopes that having once got protection it will keep it for good and it hankers after a reconstitution of the international cartel. The right policy surely is (i) to encourage the formulation of an investment programme but of a very flexible timing and on the presumption that little can be done at once, (ii) to ensure that the rate of exchange is such that our most productive industries and the most productive plants in each industry (the iron and steel industry having clearly some very productive and some very inefficient plants) have a sufficiently competitive position to keep our balance of payments in equilibrium, (iii) to rely on international competition to put a check on monopolistic practices, (iv) *not* to guarantee any protection, beyond a very moderate tariff (which the Article VII proposals will permit) and the possible use of import controls for a time so long as the balance of payments is acutely out of equilibrium, (v) to point

Staff Meeting held on 17th April to discuss the Report on the Iron and Steel Industry (R(45)36)', T230/17).

out that the world demand for steel will be high during the period of reconstruction and that the German industry will be out of the market, and (vi) on the basis of these facts to get the industry to undertake the most obvious and productive projects of capital re-equipment. Tress is to write a note rather on these lines.[20]

Marcus Fleming has gone off with Attlee to the San Francisco Conference to advise him on the Social and Economic Council.[21] Meanwhile, I am to take on Marcus' work for EIPS (the Economic and Industrial Planning Staff which is a group of officials trying to advise on what should be done economically with Germany). I shall not be able to cover this huge and revolting subject at all adequately. This week produced one of the most absurd proposals. An EIPS paper proposes that we should disallow the German scheme for family allowances because it encourages births and we don't want Germans![22] Really, what nonsense. On both humanitarian grounds (since the Germans are going to have a very low standard in any case for some time, in which case the children will need family allowances) and on the most brutal grounds for the collection of the maximum of reparations (since you will not be able to get the most out of the Germans if you have to allow the bachelor German worker to have a wage high enough to 'prevent disease and unrest' among married workers with families), you should insist on the Germans having family allowances. Moreover, what a wonderful handle for German propaganda if, just as we are introducing the social reform of family allowances in this country, we deny them to the Germans. As far as the encouragement of births is concerned, the removal of the laws against contraceptives would be a quite reasonable and much more efficacious measure; but there is one feature of the German family allowance scheme (namely, the great bonus given to large families by not paying the allowances for the first three children until the fourth is born) which might be disallowed. But I hope as a general rule we shall not interfere with German life and arrangements except where it is essential, and this is not an essential. Otherwise we shall find ourselves held responsible for every detail of the horrible time which is undoubtedly coming to the Germans in the chaos of their disintegration with all their productive equipment smashed. I got Lionel Robbins to make these points over the telephone to Mark Turner (chairman of EIPS) as I could not attend the meeting.

I have spent part of the week-end writing a long letter to Lucius Thompson-McCausland of the Bank of England who had sent me a copy of a paper which he has written on 'Cheap Money'. It is a criticism of Keynes' Liquidity Theory; and then it goes on to argue for the dangers of what he calls 'flabby' money by which he means excessive money. But he does not give any definition of excessive money. I have tried to argue (i) that in a mature economy as capital development takes place there must be a progressive reduction of interest rates (towards zero in the extreme);

[20] See below p. 71.

[21] The Conference prepared the United Nations Charter at meetings that began on 25 April and lasted until 26 June.

[22] The story of this proposal is on FO942/154. For the results of Meade's intervention see also below, pp. 78, 92.

(ii) that with very low rates of interest people will hold a larger amount of money to finance any given volume of monetary transactions, so that one must expect a larger and larger proportion of money to business transactions, and that in this sense there is no excessive supply of money; and (iii) that the only criterion of excessive (or deficient) supplies of money is whether there is a general upward (or downward) movement in such general economic indices as prices, national income, etc., and that if one could once stabilise general economic conditions there would be a great improvement in business confidence on which Lucius puts so much stress. I am lunching shortly with Lucius to discuss these matters with him.[23]

Roy Harrod has sent me a manuscript of an article by him suggesting that we should combine automatic 'commodity money' (i.e. the purchase and sale in unlimited quantities of a basket of commodities for money by the central monetary authority) with the use of new interest-free money to balance a budget deficit created by reduced rates of taxation, so long as purchases of commodities for new money is continuing (and the use of a budget surplus created by higher tax rates for the redemption of such interest-free credits so long as the monetary reserve of commodities is declining). It is an ingenious and attractive idea.[24] It so happens that this very week I have read Benjamin Graham's *World Commodities and World Currency*[25] suggesting an international scheme for a commodity currency to form, as it were, the international monetary reserve for the International Monetary Fund. These are very good ideas. The one thing against this (apart from costs of storage of which I am ignorant) is that full employment may require rising prices if the trade unions raise wages more rapidly than productivity. But it is dangerous to allow any rise to take place; and there might be much to be said for saying in effect to the trade unions: 'We are going to take absolutely certain and effective action so to control total demand that there will always be an unlimited demand for goods and services at a constant price level. Now it is up to you to decide how much or how little unemployment you are going to cause by immoderate wage demands industry by industry or locality by locality'. The wage mechanism would then come into its own again.

I hear confidentially from Norman Brook that Stone is definitely going to leave the CSO and go to Cambridge. In many ways this is a real disaster for Whitehall; for it will not be possible to replace him by anyone of comparable ability both in statistics and in the logic of the national income and expenditure; and, moreover, since the CSO have no faith in, and little understanding of, the technique of the use of the national income and national expenditure for Employment Policy. Thus we may be in for a disastrous development . . . Campion wished at once to offer Stone's job to Fowler; but I strongly cautioned Brook not to let him do this. I am personally most anxious that Tress should take over the National Income and Expenditure. He knows and understands the work; he is an intelligent

23 Thompson-McCausland sent Meade his 'Cheap Money: A Critique of Lord Keynes' Theory and an Alternative View' on 28 March 1945. The paper and Meade's reply of 23 April are on T230/70 and Meade Papers 1/9. For their lunch see below, p. 74.

24 See Meade to Harrod, 25 April 1945, T230/70 and Meade Papers 1/9.

25 New York: McGraw-Hill, 1944.

and hard worker; he understands the sort of use which we want to make of it in the Economic Section; and he gets on very well both with Campion and myself. Lionel Robbins is of the same opinion on this matter.

## *27 April 1945*

The main event this week has, I think, been the preparation of a definitely final version of our paper on 'Economic Forecasting and Employment Policy'. There was a meeting of Lionel Robbins and myself from the Economic Section and of Stafford and Taplin from the Central Statistical Office in the Treasury with Proctor in the chair. After this meeting Stafford and I agreed upon a final version of our paper and of the CSO paper on the statistics required for Employment Policy. At the meeting we decided on the next steps to be taken. Proctor will send our papers to Bridges, who is going to hold a meeting of the heads of departments to tell them about the organisation of Whitehall for employment policy and to direct them now to get on with the job. Our two papers will be given out at the meeting as a general note on what is required. (I am to have no less than 100 copies of our paper typed!)[26] This will give the CSO and us full authority, together with the Treasury, actually to prepare – and to demand the assistance of all departments in preparing – estimates of a future 'target' level of national expenditure over the next five years and of the future course of the main categories of actual national expenditure. The great steamroller of the Whitehall machine will thus actually have been put in motion to undertake national expenditure forecasting for the purposes of Employment Policy. Thus is five years' labour finally rewarded. But one realises with a shock one's responsibility. As a pure academic one can have an idea, publish it – and next year have a new idea which supersedes the first and publish it in turn without a blush. But once the Whitehall machine has been well and truly put into motion on these lines, it is no good one's having a totally fresh idea next year.

I have had a visit from Jussiant of the Belgian Economic Mission who brought me two young Belgians, one from the Belgian National Bank and the other from some part of the Belgian Civil Service, who have come over here specially to study our methods of measuring the national income and expenditure for purposes of their own employment policy. The idea is spreading.

I have redrafted our paper on the Capital Levy, incorporating statistical information from the Board of Inland Revenue and laying emphasis on Sir Richard Hopkins' point that the levy should not be paid in cash but by the surrender of an appropriate part of all forms of asset to the state which would hold them as a gigantic investment trust and would only very gradually realise them for the redemption of Government debt. The ideas

26 The final version of Meade's paper was in fact printed and circulated in June. On 2 May Proctor sent copies of the two papers to Bridges, who sent the CSO paper to Departments on 11 May (see letters and memoranda in T230/70 and T273/319). Bridges' meeting with the Departments was held on 1 June: see below pp. 87–9.

in the paper are otherwise unchanged but the form has been simplified to make it more readily understandable to busy and uninstructed Ministers.[27]

Lionel Robbins and I went round to see Sir Richard Hopkins who is drafting a document to go to the Chancellor to express the views of Bridges' National Debt Enquiry on the subject of Cheap Money.[28] This distinguished man, having just retired at the age of 65 from his position as head of the Civil Service and Permanent Secretary to the Treasury, having just received the most signal honour for a Civil Servant of being made a Privy Councillor, having been head of the Board of Inland Revenue and chief financial adviser in the Treasury, with an unexampled modesty and flexibility of mind, which I pray that I may still retain when I am his age, is now sitting down seriously to study economics, having read Keynes' *General Theory* twice and Dennis Robertson's *Essays on Money* once in the last month![29] But he retains the skill (and the delight in the skill) for which he was famed in the Civil Service of drafting a document in the form of words with which everyone can agree. But working with so fine a man is a real pleasure, and he clearly has some sympathy for the point of view intelligently on the most difficult financial problems and has so acute an understanding of the practical and now also of the theoretical issues involved; and yet, where an academic would attempt to state precisely and pungently the points at issue where agreement could not be reached, he instinctively and, indeed, avowedly attempts to find a meaningless form of words with which evryone can agree. But working with so fine a man is a real pleasure, and he clearly has some sympathy for the point of view which we have been putting – namely that although Keynes may be right in saying that one can fix the rate of interest where one likes it is not necessarily therefore wise to give up its conscious use as a means of controlling booms and slumps. But this would mean taking action to increase the authorities' powers of varying the long-term rate (for example, I said that the long-term rate could be fully controlled if the Bank of England announced – like the Bank Rate – the price at which it would freely buy and sell 2½% Consols until further notice) rather than merely coaxing the market into thinking that a rate of, say, 3 per cent on long-term bonds was going to rule in the market unchanged. We said that we did not wish to have a policy of dear money in the transitional period; but how were we to get through this most inflationary period? We deny ourselves the weapon of dear money; the Chancellor in his Budget speech this very week has hinted at considerable tax reductions as soon as the European War ends;[30] can we really rely on no crumbling of the real controls over quantities and prices of goods and services and factors of production? This elicited the admission from Hoppy that he was not altogether comfortable about what the Chancellor had said on the subject of tax remissions.

27 After further revision (see below p. 74), this became NDE Paper 13, 'The Capital Levy' (T230/95 and T233/159).

28 Hopkins' draft report was circulated as NDE Paper 9, 'Draft prepared by Sir R. Hopkins of an interim report for the Chancellor's eye only' (T230/95 and T233/159).

29 Keynes, *The General Theory of Employment, Interest and Money*, op. cit.; D. H. Robertson, *Essays in Monetary Theory*. London: P. S. King, 1940.

30 *House of Commons Debates*, Vol. 410, 24 April 1945, cols. 721–3.

We have had another meeting of the Section on the subject of our note on the Iron and Steel Report, which Tress has now finished.[31] The note is now, I think, a really good document. We suggest: (i) that the Industry should be encouraged to prepare a programme of capital expenditure on re-equipment etc., since this is just what the Govt has stated that it wants in its White Paper on Employment Policy. But we point out that in the interests of employment policy such programmes must be drawn up in such a way that the timing of the expenditure is as flexible as possible and that on general economic grounds the years immediately after the German War are years in which it will be necessary to damp down all forms of expenditure; and (ii) that no special or particular guarantee should be given to the Industry in the matter of protection. The history of the effect of the very vague promise of a 'healthy and well-balanced agriculture' should be enough to warn one of the dangers of any such action.[32] What can properly be done is to give the Industry a general idea of the conditions which the Government foresees, namely:- (a) a high world demand for Iron and Steel products for some years; (b) a destroyed German industry; (c) the probable need for us for some time to control imports on balance of payments grounds; (d) the fact that the Government does not intend to go Free Trade, although the actual height of duties must of course depend on international negotiations; and (e) the fact that the Government intends to get rid of export subsidies by international agreement and, in the absence of such agreement, intends to remain free to impose anti-dumping duties to protect the home market at least from such action.

Tress has dropped a very broad hint that he might like to stay on in the Economic Section if either he were offered a rather higher salary or were given a rather more definite guarantee about continuing employment in Whitehall after the end of his five-year appointment. He also suggested that he would rather work on the National Income than on Manpower (which was the subject which I had proposed to him). I am going to go all out to keep him. He is very good. I think that it would be a really good thing if he would work on the National Income and also would be responsible as editor for the production of a regular Quarterly Economic Survey on internal economic conditions.[33] Meanwhile I shall try to persuade Brook to give him some more positive assurance about his position at the end of his five-year period; and I think that Tress, Chantler and Brown might properly all be offered £50 a year more than their present offers. But this last will be a difficult matter to put across the Treasury.

I have lunched with Dennis Robertson between two sessions of his Royal

[31] EC(S)(45)9, 'Minutes of a staff meeting held on 23rd April to consider a draft memorandum by Mr. Tress'; EC(S)(45)7, Tress, 'Report on the Iron and Steel Industry (R(45)36), Observations by the Economic Section', 26 April 1945, T230/17. For the earlier meeting see page 65, not 19.

[32] The promise was given by the Minister of Agriculture in the House of Commons on 26 November 1940 (*House of Commons Debates*, vol. 367, cols. 91–2). The history of the promise up to March 1945 is contained in T230/1.

[33] On which see pp. 74–5.

Commission on Equal Pay for Equal Work.[34] We discussed many matters, among which I tried to interest him in the idea of 'commodity money'.

On Tuesday [24 April] I went to hear Dick Stone read his paper to the Royal Statistical Society on Consumer Demand – a most impressive performance. It is a really first-rate, path-breaking paper.[35]

*The Economic Journal* has come out this week with my review of Lerner's *Economics of Control* in 23 pages, which Keynes tells me is the longest review that there has ever been in the Journal![36] I have also been flattered to be invited to become a member of the Council of the Royal Economic Society, an invitation which I have not hesitated to accept.

[34] The Royal Commission on Equal Pay was set up in 1944 and reported in October 1946 (Cmd 6937). Its chairman was Sir Cyril Asquith; its terms of reference 'to examine the existing relations between the remuneration of men and women in the public services, in industry and in other fields of employment, to consider the social, economic and financial implications of the claim for equal pay for equal work'.

[35] 'The analysis of market demand', *Journal of the Royal Statistical Society*, Series A, Vol. 108 (1945), pp. 286–382.

[36] 'Mr. Lerner on "The Economics of Control" ', *Economic Journal*, vol. 55 (April 1945), pp. 47–69, reprinted in *The Collected Papers of James Meade*, Vol. II, chapter 4.

# 7

## May 1945

### *6 May 1945*

We have been working again largely on internal finance. There have been two meetings of the National Debt Enquiry. At the first [on 1 May] we discussed a draft by Sir Richard Hopkins of a paper for the Chancellor on cheap money. We continued to make our point that the danger of inflation was very real and that it was wrong to rely wholly on the direct control over prices and quantities of commodities and factors of production. One should certainly rely on heavy taxation as well, even if on grounds of budgetary difficulties and of the need for preserving social priorities (e.g. not making housing impossible) a rise in the rate of interest was to be avoided. I have prepared a note on these lines, which Lionel Robbins and I have circulated to the committee. In particular our note tries to refute by statistical illustration an argument which Keynes brought up, namely that any reasonable relaxations of taxation released sums which were negligible in comparison with the idle sums of purchasing power which consumers would in any case have at their disposal from accumulated small savings, demobilisation gratuities and the like.[1] At the second meeting of the NDE [on 3 May] we discussed a paper by Sir Herbert Brittain on the future of the control over New Issues. The control is to go on; but there is to be a long list of objects (e.g. promotion of exports, production for housing needs, etc. etc.) for which permission to make new issues of capital will normally be given. But, in addition to this, the Bank of England will exercise some control over the timing of those new issues which are permitted, in order to prevent the capital market from becoming clogged up. All this is a quite sensible form of control which will be of some use in preventing unnecessary expenditure on investment and so in preventing inflation. But it is a very limited form of control because it only catches those firms which have no resources of their own and must, therefore, go to the new issue market; and there are many firms which are not in this position. Nevertheless these same principles are to guide the granting of overdrafts by the banks also; and when we may need all the weapons in the

[1] NDE Paper 9, 'Draft prepared by Sir R. Hopkins of an interim report for the Chancellor's eye only', NDE Paper 10, 'The Control of Inflation: The Three Alternatives, Note by the Economic Section', 3 May 1945, T230/95 and T233/159.

armoury to meet the threat of inflation, it is not for us to despise this little one.[2]

I have revised yet once more our paper on the Capital Levy! I hope and believe that we are nearing the end now. It will now go for comments to the Board of Inland Revenue, then to Hoppy, then to the full National Debt Enquiry and then to the Chancellor to send to Attlee and to any other of his colleagues whom he may think should revise it.[3]

I lunched with Lucius Thompson-McCausland of the Bank of England,[4] and tried hard to persuade him that the correct criterion for an expansionist or restrictionist monetary policy was whether the total national expenditure was showing signs of declining or rising too rapidly. Beneath a general stability of the total national expenditure one could let private enterprise go ahead on its own, and general confidence would grow even though particular firms and particular industries would from time to time burn their fingers. But Lucius persists in thinking in terms of pools of what he calls 'flabby' money which rushes from commodity to commodity causing speculative booms and slumps, undermining confidence and thus leading to a general slump. He wishes to drain away such stagnant pools, keeping money what he calls 'taut'. But the danger is, of course, that the general process of keeping money 'taut' will maintain the rate of interest at an unduly high level so that there is a more or less permanent deficiency of total national expenditure. I would, however, admit this much justification in Lucius' ideas:- in a mature economy the rate of interest must be very low to maintain equilibrium; but a very low rate of interest means (a) a large demand for liquidity (i.e. an abnormally large ratio of money stock to money transactions) and (b) a large investment in working capital (i.e. an abnormally large ratio of commodity stocks to commodity turnover). (a) may mean that people have a lot of spare money to speculate in price changes if a speculative situation develops, and (b) means that there is a large buffer of stocks between demand and production, so that over- or under-production in particular lines may be more possible; but it would indeed be throwing the baby out with the bath-water to tighten up the supply of money and interest rates (and thus cause a certain and permanent depression) in order to avoid the possibility that (a) and (b) above may cause speculative troubles which might possibly lead to a temporary depression.

We have decided to try to write an Economic Survey again and we have held a staff meeting to discuss it. Tress is to be its Editor, and certainly the end of the European War [on 8 May] and the beginning of Stage II deserves and needs a general survey of economic affairs. Our last Survey could never be issued because we made the mistake of writing it in one definite assumption (namely that the European War would end on December 31st

[2] NDE Paper 8, 'Capital Issues Control After V-E Day (Note by Sir Herbert Brittain)', 20 April 1945, T230/95 and T233/159. The policy was implemented by means of the issue of *Capital Issues Control, Memorandum of Guidance to the Capital Issues Committee*, Cmd. 6645, May 1945, and a letter from the Chancellor of the Exchequer (Sir John Anderson) to the Governor of the Bank of England (Lord Catto) on 24 May 1945.

[3] See below p. 84.

[4] On 3 May 1945 at the Reform Club.

1944); and as soon as it was clear that this was probably very wide of the mark, the whole Survey was useless.[5] This time we cannot make such an error about the time of the end of the German War! But I urged at the meeting that we should take warning from this experience. Whitehall when it plans makes a single assumption and then plans to that. This is in principle wrong. If the assumption is false, everything may be widely and *rigidly* out of line. What Whitehall must learn to do is to prepare very *flexible* plans to meet various ranges of possible alternative assumptions. This will, for example, be very important in Employment Policy. Our Economic Surveys should start the fashion. We should state not merely what we think is most likely to happen, but also how wide of the mark we may turn out to be and how prepared we are likely to be to cope with the unexpected.

I have spent a large part of the week on Establishments again. A. J. Brown is, I am glad to say, almost certainly joining the Section. After speaking to MacDougall, who is almost certainly going to Nuffield College [Oxford], I have told Tress that if he stays he will work on the National Income and Expenditure statistics (in so far as the Economic Section will have a hand in these) and will be the regular editor of our Economic Survey on internal economic matters. I have suggested that he should talk to Norman Brook about security of tenure and to Lionel Robbins about the general question of the choice between the Economic Section and academic life. I think that he was moved and may join the Section. We shall see. I have had another very long discussion with Brook and Robbins and am to write Brook three minutes: one on the general establishment of the Section (jobs to be done and number of persons needed to do them), one on the application of the Federated Superannuation System for Universities to men in the Section, and one on the appropriate pay for our 'apprentices'.[6]

On Thursday evening I met a man called (I believe) Zenkl who was Lord Mayor of Prague and has just been released from Buchenwald after 6 years in German concentration camps.[7] The stories he told me were so terrible that, although they are somewhat out of place in this diary, I cannot refrain from recording them. He spoke of the day on which he arrived at the camp in 1939. They were all kept waiting out in the open in bitterly cold weather for 27 hours. Then the camp commandant made a speech to them saying that they had not come there for pleasure; they were political criminals not fit to live with their fellow men and they had come to be politically re-educated; 'and we shall succeed' said the commandant; they were to understand that there were no longer any titles or distinctions of degree among them; all were equal; and they would start off by setting the most distinguished among them to clean the latrines. Upon hearing that they would all be equal a young communist next to Zenkl murmured blissfully 'at last' – thereby showing, said Zenkl, how easily idealists and inter-nationalists could be pleased! In December 1939 in the bitter frost and

[5] Above, p. 20. On the preparation of the new Survey see T230/162 and below pp. 77–8.

[6] For some of the results of this activity see L. N. Helsby, 'War Cabinet Economic Section', 4 May 1945, T217/205.

[7] He had arrived in London from Paris on 29 April 1945: *The Times*, 3 May, 1945, page 3.

snow 40,000 Poles were brought to the camp. There was no room for them indoors so a piece of ground was wired off for them. At the end of a fortnight 400 of them alone survived. The most terrible stories he told were of the medical officer in charge of Buchenwald.[8] This man was not really a doctor at all. He had done some medical study and at the camp he wished to finish his studies and qualify for his degree. So he decided to write a medical thesis. It was to be a first-rate thesis with real original work in it. He got hold of one of the prisoners, a Privat-Dozent in medicine from the German University of Prague, and made him do the actual writing of the thesis which was to be on tuberculosis. The medical officer first procured a batch of perfectly sound prisoners, killed them, removed their lungs; he then procured a batch of prisoners with a certain degree of tuberculosis, killed them, removed their lungs; and so on. By these experimental means his Czech Privat-Dozent was able to write a very illuminating thesis which was sent up *with the specimens* to the University of Freibourg which in turn conferred the degree on him *summa cum laude*. Some time later a medical school at Graz which was confined to the training of SS men made use of the Buchenwald medical officer. For demonstration purposes for the students they formed the idea that it would be useful to have a collection of perfectly sound normal specimen organs (hearts, livers etc.) to compare with specimens of diseased organs. But the difficulty in forming this collection in the ordinary course of things was that corpses for dissection died as a result of disease or accident, or in any case had been dead some little time during which physiological changes might have taken place. What was wanted was a set of really freshly preserved human organs. So they wrote to the medical officer at Buchenwald who picked out some completely healthy prisoners and provided them. Another officer in the camp had a passion for tattoos. He used to have the prisoners examined for their tattoos; and when he saw an interesting one, he had the man killed and flayed and the tattooing added to his collection. Zenkl learned on 6 April that he was to be hanged. He and about forty others were asked to parade at a certain hour to do some task. All the others were communists who according to Zenkl (who remained doggedly a bourgeois liberal) as a party managed to run the camp very largely through their hidden cells. (Zenkl seemed as opposed to communism as an orthodox liberal-bourgeois can be.) The communists had discovered that they were all to be hanged if they turned up to the parade. They sent a messenger to Zenkl to warn him of this, saying that they (the communists) had their plans laid to go into hiding in the camp and that Zenkl must act on his own initiative. Zenkl admitted that it was very decent of the communists to have warned him and to have trusted him sufficiently, since he might have tried to save his own life by going to the camp officials and telling them that the communists were forewarned of their danger; but they then left him to shift for himself. He managed to hide in a small hole in the ground at the end of a small tunnel, where he was off and on for five days, unable to stand or even to sit up, until the Americans liberated the camp on 11 April. They

[8] Dr Erwin Ding (UN War Crimes Commission, *Staffs of the German Concentration Camps, No. II Buchenwald*, November 1945).

heard the battle approaching; the SS guards were ordered to retire; they crept out of their hiding places and he watched the last stages of the battle from under a table; and then the Americans arrived. It was very strange sitting in the Reform Club in an armchair next to this little tough man who throughout those six years had preserved his political opinions, his sense of humour and his intelligence if not his physical health (he had a bad cough but did not look terribly starved); but I expect it was a great deal stranger for him.

## *13 May 1945*

The most interesting job this week has been the drafting of a very short statement on Wages Policy and Employment at the request of Sir Alan Barlow of the Treasury.[9] The Ministry of Labour wish to send out a statement to all their local branches to guide them on problems of fixing wage-rates in the light of the White Paper on *Employment Policy*. My draft goes on very familiar lines:- the Govt's policy is to expand aggregate demand to absorb unemployment; but if wage-rates start an upward spiral before the unemployed are absorbed the Govt will be put in the cruel dilemma of either giving up its employment policy or allowing a general inflation to develop; this makes a moderate wages policy essential. If in each particular industry, occupation and locality wage-rates do not rise, or even fall, so long as there is substantial unemployment in that particular labour market, and if at the same time moderate wage increases take place where there is an excess of demand over supply for labour, the following three advantages will accrue: first, there will be no general rise in wage-rates so long as there is general unemployment to be absorbed by an expansionist policy; secondly, wages will rise as productivity rises because the Government policy of maintaining aggregate demand will provide a market for increased output and competition among employers will then serve to increase the demand for labour above its supply; and thirdly, there will be wage differentials between different labour markets which will help the transfer of labour to those jobs where the demand is greatest and of capital and enterprise to those labour markets where the supply of labour is most abundant. It is going to be one of the most important, and most difficult, parts of employment policy to get wage principles of this kind applied. It will be interesting to see what the Treasury does with my draft.

We have had a meeting to discuss the general line to be taken by Tress in writing our new Economic Survey.[10] The main formal point at issue is how far and how quickly we should shift from an analysis in terms of a Manpower Budget (typifying the allocation of scarce real resources by means of direct controls) to an analysis in terms of the main elements of National Income and Expenditure (typifying the freer economy in which financial inducements rather than direct controls must be the order of the day). The transitional period into which we are entering will be a bridge

[9] 'Wages Policy and Employment', sent by Meade to Barlow, 14 May 1945, T230/111.
[10] See T230/162.

period, in the course of which direct controls will diminish in importance and general financial policy will become increasingly important. Our Survey must itself reflect this bridge.

I attended a meeting of the Economic and Industrial Planning Staff (better known as EIPS, the group of officials who discuss what to do with Germany economically) to consider the suggestion that the German system of Family Allowances should be disallowed on the grounds that it was a racial measure for stimulating births.[11] I urged the points that it would be psychologically a very great mistake to disallow this German piece of social legislation just as we were to introduce family allowances ourselves; that both in the interests of humanity in a country like Germany where standards would certainly be reduced to a very low level and in the interests of toughness so as to be able to reduce German consumption in order to collect reparations, a distribution of income according to family needs was essential; and that if it were desired to check German fertility it might be desirable to remove from the German scheme the element of abnormal stimulus to large families (at present allowances are paid in respect of the first three children only when a fourth is born) and it would certainly be desirable to remove the laws against contraception. I was horrified at the meeting to realise that Phillips, the representative of the Ministry of Labour, contemplated that there should be no public relief paid to German wage-earners with large families except when they were unemployed. If German standards are low, as they are bound to be, this will lead to the disastrous position that a wage-earner with a family will be little better off, and may be even worse off, in work than out of work. The result will be a rigidity and lack of movement in the labour market just at the time when such movement will be most necessary.

I have also attended a meeting in the rooms of Hugh Weeks (of the Ministry of Production) to discuss the problem of supplying the Americans regularly with information about the reconversion of our economy.[12] It is clearly going to be of great importance that we should reveal the whole truth to them frankly and regularly. From the point of view of domestic politics here the tendency will all the time be to show how quickly we are restoring peace-time conditions; while from the point of view of Lend-Lease etc. the need in the United States will be to show how tight our belt still is. I think that Weeks, who is a good friend of the Economic Section, has in mind that if and when the Ministry of Production disappears, the Section might inherit some of its duties in these centralising respects.

Lionel Robbins and I went out to dinner with Alec Spearman (a Conservative MP with very enlightened views) to meet Captain Peter Thorneycroft, the chairman of the Tory Reform Committee. Thorneycroft seems a very intelligent man, though by no means familiar with economic modes of thought. We gave him a vast tutorial, first on Bretton Woods and all that and secondly on domestic economic policy. On the latter subject I was astonished to realise that both Spearman and Thorneycroft had been

[11] Note of an informal meeting of EIPS, 7 May 1945, to discuss Report of the Working Party on Problems of German Employment and Unemployment, FO942/154.

[12] No record found.

reading the first part of my *Economic Journal* review of Lerner's *Economics of Control*.[13] They were searching for a conservative 'middle way' between complete socialist planning and complete liberal *laissez-faire*. So I let them have it! If these intelligent, enlightened and young Conservatives can be persuaded to include the right measures, and to exclude the wrong measures, of state intervention in their 'middle way', it would be grand. I explained that being a Civil Servant I really could not discuss details of economic policy, but that I was not precluded in an informal after-dinner conversation with friends from explaining my own personal general philosophy of economic policy. My argument ran on these lines:- there are three main ways in which the state should intervene, first, it should take general financial measures (e.g. timing of public expenditure, monetary policy, tax policy) to see that the general level of money demand for goods and services was high enough to give good employment but not high enough to lead to inflation; secondly, that where on technical grounds competition was possible, production should be left (behind the general level of demand maintained by state influences) to the free competition of private enterprise and risk-bearing; but that there were many cases where for technical reasons (e.g. the railways, public utilities, etc.) there was not room for a large number of independent competing plants and in these cases at least state control, and probably even state ownership and management, was necessary; and thirdly, that by social security measures, taxation, etc. the state should intervene to improve the distribution of income. We had a very considerable discussion on competition, monopoly, socialisation, etc. We made it clear to them that there was need for a large range of legislation (i) removing all sorts of statutory restrictive schemes (agricultural boards, herring boards, Part I of the Coal Mines Act [1930] etc.), (ii) reform of the law of libel which would allow real consumers' research, (iii) some form of check on advertisement expenditure, and (iv) reform of the patent law, in order to set the stage for really constructive free enterprise once more. None of this was incompatible with the out and out state control or ownership of those industries which could not compete. I think we made a definite impression.

I have lunched with a Professor Rousseaux, professor of economics in the Belgian University of Louvain. He is over here to re-establish contacts after five years of German occupation with the academic world here. I explained how nearly all UK academic economists had been in Government service during these years; told him something about the Economic Section and the Central Statistical Office and of the White Papers on National Income and Expenditure and on Employment Policy. In return he told me that Belgian students during these years had been avidly consuming my *Economic Analysis and Policy*, which was very gratifying.[14] Have we really a chance of developing an efficient Liberal-Socialist economy in Western Europe and the English-speaking world?

[13] 'Mr. Lerner on "The Economics of Control" ', op. cit. The Tory Reform Committee had been set up by 36 Conservative MPs, including Thorneycroft, in March 1943.

[14] *An Introduction to Economic Analysis and Policy*, op. cit. Rousseaux's letter of thanks to Meade is in Meade papers 1/9.

I am glad to say that Tress has after all decided to remain a member of the Section after the war. He is to work on the statistics of National Income and Expenditure and to try his hand at being the regular editor of our Economic Surveys. He is attracted by this work and should be a great acquisition, I think. Meanwhile I have written Brook three notes on our establishment problems: one on the application to members of the Section of the Federated Superannuation System for Universities; one on the rates of pay which we should offer to 'Apprentices' in the Economic Section; and one on the general size of establishment which we shall want.[15]

---

This week has marked Victory in Europe. I went to Bath to celebrate the two VE holidays [8 and 9 May 1945] with the family. But since coming back I have seen something of the crowds in London. I spent an hour on the top of the tower of the Ministry of Health building at the corner of Whitehall and Great George Street watching and listening to a huge crowd which was yelling for Churchill. Dusk was falling after a brilliant sunny day. At first the crowd was a patchwork of bright colours; but by the time I went in it was dark and the floodlighting of St. Paul's, Nelson's Column, the London County Council building, Buckingham Palace, etc. had started. Still the crowd sang and shouted. At each false alarm that Churchill had come out onto the balcony an ear-splitting roar went up. The mood was so good-humoured, patient and happy; the floodlighting was so striking after the blackout; the sense of relief from danger and tension so marked; and the evening itself so balmy that I climbed down from the tower with tears in my eyes. Alas! I did so five minutes too soon, because Churchill appeared on the balcony and made a speech just after I had gone in. Next day, again from the roof of the office, I watched the King [George VI] and Queen [Elizabeth] and the two princesses [Elizabeth and Margaret] drive down Birdcage Walk and Great George Street on their way to visit SE London. On Saturday evening I wandered round Whitehall, Trafalgar Square and St. James's Park to see the floodlighting. As I came down by Duck Island in the Park, between the lake and the Horseguards' Parade, the floodlights were suddenly switched on in the Horseguards' Parade on Dover House. It made one catch one's breath. There were soft coloured lights already shining in the trees in Duck Island which made it look too 'Hansel and Gretel' for words; and suddenly out of the gloom of Horseguards' Parade there stood out a huge white castle as if by magic. It is strange that in the celebration of Victory over Germany one's mind should turn with infinite pleasure to such things which, I must admit, remind one more definitely of a sentimental Germanic fairy story than of anything else.

## *21 May 1945*

There have been two more meetings of the National Debt Enquiry this week [on 14 and 18 May]. At the first we discussed the final version of Sir

[15] Not found.

Richard Hopkins' draft document for the Chancellor on the future of Cheap Money.[16] There is a great tendency to overestimate the budgetary burden which would be caused by a rise in the rate of interest. In Hoppy's draft it was argued that a rise of ½ per cent in the rate of interest would impose a burden of £100 million a year on the budget. But this calculation omitted three facts: (i) that debt would only have to be converted to the higher interest level as it matured for repayment; (ii) that a large part of the increased interest would come back to the Exchequer in income tax and sur-tax; and (iii) that an appreciable part of the debt was in any case held by public departments. It is most necessary to correct such misapprehensions, because if we are not going to pay off the debt in a capital levy our hands must not be too rigidly tied against using the rate of interest as a means of controlling inflations and deflations. We also made one other intervention on this paper. It was argued in Hoppy's draft that if people shifted their preferences from long-term to short-term securities, the authorities should take the opportunity of saving interest by reducing the rate of interest on short-term debt. I pointed out that to reduce short-term rates might cause people to go on buying long-term instead of short-term securities, and the loss of interest involved in frightening people off short-term securities might be greater than the saving of interest on the outstanding short-term debt. I said that this desire to frighten people off short-term debt was a new form of funding complex – a malicious remark as I knew that this passage was in fact drafted by the arch-anti-funding Keynes!

At the second meeting of the National Debt Enquiry we discussed two Economic Section papers: one on the general factors (such as reduction of interest rates, growth of population and employment, growth of productivity per head or a rise in prices) which might help to reduce the burden of debt; and the second on the general problem [of] how to reconcile Debt Policy (i.e. the repayment of debt) with Employment Policy (under which the state must be willing to run a Budget Deficit if necessary to maintain demand).[17] In this second subject we had suggested that in the short run (i.e. in budgetary policy from year to year) the Government must think primarily of Employment Policy and run the Deficit or Surplus which is necessary to maintain employment; but that if these short-term policies appear to be leading to chronic deficits then long-term measures must be taken to enable demand to be maintained with a smaller average budget deficit. We suggested that such measures might be on the four following lines: (i) a reduction of interest rates, (ii) rising prices to stimulate investment, (iii) stimulation of foreign investment, and (iv) an overhaul of the tax structure so as to encourage people to invest and to spend money but not to save. Keynes attacked our last paper, saying that it should have

[16] NDE Paper 11, 'Revised draft prepared by Sir R. Hopkins of an interim report for the Chancellor's eye only', T230/95 and T233/159. The version that went to the Chancellor is also to be found in the same files.

[17] NDE Paper 4, 'The Fiscal Problem Set by the Debt', and NDE Paper 6, 'Debt Repayment and Employment Policy'. On their drafting see above, pp. 36, 41-3, 46-7, and 51–2.

dealt with Lerner's 'functional finance';[18] but as this consists in trying not to have a budget deficit, our paper would in that case have been worthless! Sir Richard Hopkins then let us have his views on employment policy and sound finance. His desire was to appear at least to be adopting a policy of sound finance, even though one was borrowing for employment policy. His policy was only to borrow (outside the Budget) for productive capital expenditure and to attach to all such loans a sinking fund which, together with the interest on the debt, would have to be met from the ordinary Budget. But this would, in fact, be open to at least two most serious objections. In the first place, as time goes on there would be a larger and larger sinking fund to be met out of current taxation; and this enforced state saving might make the maintenance of employment more and more difficult. Secondly, for the reason given immediately above, there would be, under this system, an ever-increasing need for more and more public investment to mop up the ever increasing state savings, while – on the other hand – at the same time the outlets for profitable investment might be becoming fewer and fewer; and for these reasons this type of employment policy is likely to lead to 'digging holes and filling them up again', when from the point of view of the community the most sensible thing might be to induce ordinary consumers to buy more goods and services (e.g. by reducing rates of taxation). Hoppy also maintained that there might in the Budget be a sinking fund equal to the annual revenue from Death Duties because the latter were paid out of capital. This argument begged two questions: first, whether the Death Duties are paid out of savings or consumption; and secondly, whether the state wishes in its Budget to be neutral and not to influence the net saving of the community. I found it very difficult to sit silently through Hoppy's remarks.[19] I really think that the Economic Section must reply on this Sinking Fund question.

We have had two more Section meetings to discuss the main lines to be taken in our forthcoming Economic Survey which Tress is preparing.[20] The outlook is really rather grim for the immediate future. The *labour* situation is likely actually to get worse for some time, as women are expected to be leaving industry more rapidly than men are demobilised from the forces or from munitions industries; *foodstuffs* are likely to get shorter as Europe is opened up for large-scale relief and as we have lived on our stocks in the last year; and *coal* is likely to be worse in the coming winter than in any other year of the war. I wonder whether the populace are really prepared for these fruits of victory.

I attended a meeting of the R(IO) (the interdepartmental committee of

[18] Abba P. Lerner, 'Functional Finance and the Federal Debt', *Social Research*, February 1943 (reprinted in A. Smithies and T. Keith Butters (eds.), *AEA Readings in Fiscal Policy*. Homewood, Ill.: Richard Irwin Inc., 1955, pp. 468–78; *The Economics of Control*, op. cit., chapter 24.

[19] See also the minutes of the 11th meeting of the National Debt Enquiry on T230/95 and T233/158.

[20] There were in fact three meetings, on 15, 16 and 17 May 1945, whose minutes were circulated as EC(S)(45)17 and 19 (T230/17 and 162).

officials set up to serve the R(I), which is the Ministerial committee dealing with Industrial Problems of Reconstruction).[21] We were discussing our future programme of work now that the German war is over. There ensued a very interesting discussion about industrial reconversion. It seems clear that the Ministry of Labour is very frightened of imposing labour controls, with the result that people will stay in relatively well paid jobs (e.g. light engineering for the export or home markets) and will not move to the less well paid jobs (e.g. textiles) though their products may be much more essential in the restoration of civilian standards. Nor did there appear to be any controls other than labour controls which would do the trick. We shall be driven, willy-nilly, to restore the price system and profit incentives; but this will involve a really substantial rise in prices.

Had lunch with Dupriez of the University of Louvain who was in London on his way to Canada for an ILO meeting. He is chairman of the ILO Employment Committee. I think that he realises that the proper ILO function in this sphere is very limited.

Had lunch with Noel-Baker and Gilbert Ponsonby, in order – so I thought – to discuss Employment Policy. But we discussed politics and the prospects of an early election at lunch and after lunch Noel-Baker (as always) had to rush away in a hurry, so that no word was exchanged on Employment Policy! Noel-Baker is extremely nice, but he is the typical politician, so busy that one cannot apply one's mind consecutively to any one subject for more than five minutes.

I have been spending some time this week thinking of arrangements for a personal secretary for myself for the future. The establishments want me to take an ordinary typist-secretary, and the particular person whom they suggest for a start will probably only be staying a few months. But I think that I must have someone who has some technical knowledge of economics and who is likely to stay some time. We have an immense amount of papers etc. on every conceivable economic subject coming into the Section, and the Director's secretary must be someone who is really competent to deal with all of this.[22]

## *27 May 1945*

The National Debt Enquiry this week discussed the paper which Lionel Robbins and I had put in on the control of inflation during the transitional period.[23] Our point of view was that there were three methods of control – (1) Higher Interest Rates, (2) High Taxation, (3) Direct Controls over Prices and Quantities to be bought. Admitting reluctantly that one must abandon (1) because of the cost to the Budget and the effect on social priorities (e.g. housing), we argued that you should *not* abandon (2) and rely only on (3), as Keynes seems to want. We argued that it was going to be

[21] R(IO)(45) 9th meeting, 15 May 1945, CAB87/18.

[22] See below p. 113.

[23] NDE Paper 10, 'The Control of Inflation: The Three Alternatives', 3 May 1945 (T230/95 and T233/159), was discussed at the 12th meeting of the Enquiry on 24 May.

difficult to maintain the direct controls, particularly in the case of inessentials; and that both as a weapon against inflation and also in order to prevent resources from being drained away into the production of inessentials, it was desirable to restrain buying power as much as possible through fiscal measures. Keynes opposed us vigorously. He wants to see a considerable reduction in taxation in an autumn Budget and to rely almost solely on the direct controls to prevent inflation. He argues that a reduction in taxation is necessary to restore incentives (this is no doubt true in the case of 100 per cent EPT [Excess Profits Tax]) and that the accumulated capital sums in the hands of consumers are so great that any additional sums made available by reduced taxation would be neither here nor there. But I do not believe that people will be anything like as ready as he supposes to live on their past savings; and increased tax-free incomes are undoubtedly likely to cause a serious intensification of our difficulties. The net effect of our intervention was undoubtedly to introduce a note of caution into the minds of the permanent Treasury officials (Bridges, Hopkins, Eady, Brittain) in the matter of the autumn Budget.

Next week in the National Debt Enquiry we are to discuss the redraft of our paper on the Capital Levy, which I have spent some time with Cockfield of the Board of Inland Revenue in titivating this week.[24] The Inland Revenue have now agreed on the points of detail; but I suspect that at next week's meeting Gregg will demand a major change in the form of the paper. He just wants a short note saying that the levy will not lead to a sufficient net budgetary saving to make it worthwhile, whereas our paper argues all the points for and against the levy at some length. But we are all agreed that the yield of a levy would be so disappointingly low (even in the case of a non-progressive levy with a low exemption limit) as to make it for practical political purposes practically a non-starter.

We have had some further discussion in the Economic Section about our forthcoming Economic Survey.[25] In this connection Tress and I went to call on Sir Herbert Brittain in the Treasury to discuss with him the possibility of revising the estimates given by the Chancellor in his Budget Speech of the probable Vote of Credit expenditure on the war in the course of 1945/46.[26] It appears that there is not as yet any great reason for any very significant revision of the estimate (or – should one say? – guess). We were able to take the opportunity of suggesting to Brittain that in a short time we should hope, in accordance with the letter which Bridges had circulated to Heads of Departments on the subject,[27] to be coming to him to get more help and information on forecasting government expenditure, as part of our work in forecasting the National Income and Expenditure for the purpose of Employment Policy. Brittain was very friendly and

[24] NDE Paper 13, 'The Capital Levy', which was discussed at the 13th meeting of the National Debt Enquiry on 31 May (T230/95 and T233/159). On the 'titivating' see Robbins to Hopkins, 23 May 1945, T233/159.

[25] Minutes of the discussion on 22 May were circulated as EC(S)(45)20 (T230/18 and T230/162).

[26] *House of Commons Debates*, Vol. 410, 24 April 1945, cols. 717–18.

[27] Bridges, 'Employment Policy: Administrative Arrangements', 11 May 1945, T230/70 and T273/319.

helpful on all this. But what a funny place the Treasury is! It turned out that Brittain had never seen Bridges' letter until we showed it to him; and yet Brittain is the Under-Secretary dealing with Home Finance which is the division in the Treasury most intimately concerned with National Income and all that. Incidentally in this connection, I have this week had a very revealing conversation with Proctor (who has been put generally in charge of the co-ordination of Employment Policy in the Treasury). For the purely accidental reason that the Treasury started to organise itself for Employment Policy purely in terms of the control of Public Investment, Dennis Proctor (although he is now to concern himself with *all* Treasury aspects of Employment Policy, including presumably budgetary aspects of such policy) is to report through Sir Bernard Gilbert, who deals with Supplies, Local Authorities, etc., and not through Brittain and Eady, who deal with High Finance.[28] Proctor was concerned because, in his words, Sir Bernard Gilbert just does not believe in Employment Policy and Hale, who deals with local authorities under Gilbert, does so even less. Thus the outlook is not promising until some reshuffling of duties takes place in the Treasury. But I told Proctor that time was on our side, because Bridges believes in it, Parliament will certainly demand it, and there are a number of other elements – such as the Economic Section, Proctor himself and, I believe, Brittain – who are on the side of the angels.

I attended a meeting of EIPS (the Economic and Industrial Planning Staff) to discuss the future of German patents. In the paper under discussion the very sensible line was taken that German patent rights in this country should simply be abolished, so that everyone and anyone could use the inventions without charge, provided that other important industrial countries would agree to the same course. If, however, other countries would not adopt this course, it was argued that we should put our manufacturers at a disadvantage if we adopted it in this country while our competitors did not do the same. In this case the paper recommended that we should go to the other extreme; namely, that HM Government should take over the German patents and hire them out to 'a few selected manufacturers'.[29] I argued strongly against this course and obtained a little support from Miss Jennings of the Treasury and someone (name unknown to me) who represented the Control Commission in Germany. I was stoutly opposed by Saunders, the Comptroller of the Patent Office and by sundry other men (many with spanners sticking out of their pockets and oil dripping from their fingers – or so it seemed to me) from the Supply Departments. I wanted a system of Licences of Right (possibly with the exception of producers or importers of the commodity if produced in another country which did not give us as favourable treatment in the matter of German patents in their country), so that everyone could make use of the German inventions and no unnecessary monopolistic positions need be built up. Saunders and the others argued that the patents would in fact

[28] For the Treasury discussions on internal organisation, see the 'Note of a Meeting of 21 March to discuss arrangements for dealing with employment policy with special reference to the internal organisation of the Treasury' on T273/319.

[29] The paper, 'Patent Rights in Germany and German Owned Patents Abroad', appears in two later drafts dated 31 May and 29 September 1945 on BT11/2654.

never be exploited unless they were given only to a 'few selected manufacturers' who knew that they would be protected from outside competition if they did exploit the idea. I admitted that this might be the case in particular cases, but could not believe that it was the general rule. They seemed to me to be incapable of seeing the contradiction in their own case; they were advocating the (very sensible) first choice of abolishing altogether existing German patent rights, if they could get all countries to agree to this; but did they really do this believing that this was a certain way of ensuring that no one would ever benefit from these German inventions; and, if not, how could they hold that they must be confined to a 'few selected manufacturers' if they were to be exploited? It was a good fight; but all I achieved was the insertion in one paragraph of a tiny sentence saying that if the course of abolishing German patents did not obtain general agreement, there might be a case for reconsidering the matter. But the rest of the document was all written on the basis that the only feasible alternative was the 'few selected manufacturers'.

# 8

## June 1945

*3 June 1945*

This week has marked important developments in the organisation of Employment Policy. Bridges had already sent out to the departments concerned a copy of the Central Statistical Office paper on the statistics required for Employment Policy with a covering letter asking for their comments.[1] Apart from details the replies raised two main points: first, whether the statistics which we were asking for from industry would not be too great a burden on industry and how industry might best be approached to make them willing to provide the necessary information; and, secondly, (a matter of really fundamental importance) how far Employment Policy should be conceived in terms of deciding how many people ought to be employed in each particular industry or occupation. This latter point was raised in a letter from Ince of the Ministry of Labour who stated baldly that the Ministry of Labour's view was that after the war, as during the war, there should be a Manpower Budget allocating definite amounts of labour to the various departments in charge of different industries and occupations. During the war period of labour shortage, it had been the duty of each department to see that the industries for which it was responsible did not employ more labour than its allocation. In the view of the Ministry of Labour each department in a peace-time surplus of labour should be given the obligation of seeing that the industries for which it was responsible employed as much labour as was allocated to it. By this means, so it was argued, two advantages would be achieved: first, each department would be given a definite responsibility for making its contribution towards the maintenance of employment; and, secondly, due recognition would be given to the fact that unemployment would always show itself in the form of particular unemployment in particular occupations and industries.[2]

Bridges called a preliminary meeting of the Treasury (Gilbert, Barlow, Proctor), the CSO (Campion, Stafford) and the Economic Section (Robbins and myself) to consider the points raised in the departmental

[1] Bridges, 'Employment Policy: Administrative Arrangements', 11 May 1945 enclosing the CSO paper 'Statistics for Employment Policy', 1 May 1945 (T273/319).

[2] The replies to Bridges' letter are on T273/319. Ince's letter, of 23 May 1945, is also on T230/70.

replies to his circular letter.[3] On the problem of the quantity of statistics to be collected from industry we agreed that we could not aim at anything much less than was proposed in the Central Statistical Office paper, but that it was important to make a single joint approach to such bodies as the FBI [Federation of British Industries], which were representative of industry, in order to explain the general nature of the corpus of statistics which the Government needed for Employment Policy and to avoid a piecemeal and unco-ordinated search for statistics department by department, industry by industry and subject by subject. On the fundamental point raised by the Ministry of Labour it was agreed that the system of labour allocations could not be effectively used in conditions of labour surplus in the more or less free economy for which one must prepare. The following were agreed to be the decisive points against the Ministry of Labour's proposals: first, that in the absence of a system of extensive socialisation or particular intervention in all industries there would be no means whereby the department in charge of each industry could make an industry take on more labour than it was willing to absorb; secondly, that under the general type of policy envisaged in the White Paper on *Employment Policy* the action to be taken in a period of unemployment and which might result in the expansion of employment in, say, the textile industries would not take the form of a Board of Trade directive to the textile industry to employ more workers, but the form of a general policy (e.g. by the remission of taxation, or more expenditure on public investment) to expand consumers' purchasing power which would result in the purchase of more textiles; and thirdly, that a policy of allocating labour industry by industry or department by department would provide the maximum incentive to ossify and rigidify the industrial structure, since vested interests would be encouraged to insist that particular measures should be taken to ensure that profits and employment were not allowed to decline in their particular sector of the economy, however much some such adjustment might be fundamentally in the social interest.

The following day [30 May] Bridges held a meeting at which this matter was discussed with Ince (accompanied by Hitchman and Reeder of the Ministry of Labour), the others present being Sir Bernard Gilbert of the Treasury and myself. Bridges asked Ince to express his views and then called on me to put the other case which I did on the lines indicated above. The meeting was extremely friendly and it was agreed that much of this *solvitur ambulando*. We agreed on our side that a Manpower Survey was most desirable both to examine past movements and to forecast as far as possible the available supply of future manpower and the probable supply and demand developments (the latter resulting largely from the types of general policy adopted to stabilise total money demand for goods and services) which were likely to take place in each of the main particular labour markets. On being pressed we went so far as to admit that actual targets for future employment might usefully be set in some special occupations, particularly in those cases (such as the armed forces or road-making) where the Government was the employer. Bridges later sent a

[3] See 'Note of a Meeting in Bridges' room on 29 May 1945', T230/70 and T273/319.

letter to Ince on these lines after discussing the draft with Gilbert and myself.[4] The point at the moment is not, of course, really finally settled. It is clear that the Treasury and the Economic Section are going to think of Employment Policy primarily in terms of general measures to sustain general demand and the Ministry of Labour primarily in terms of particular measures to deal with particular pockets of unemployment. There is, of course, an infinite gradation of compromise possible.

Later in the week Bridges held a general meeting of heads of departments to discuss the Central Statistical Office paper on the statistics needed for Employment Policy.[5] At this meeting none of the Ministry of Labour-Treasury difference of opinion came to the surface. The most significant point was undoubtedly the demonstration to all departments that the Treasury intended to take a really serious lead on Employment Policy and to regard itself in the future as a real central economic department. Bridges suggested at the meeting (in addition to an interdepartmental working party to go over in detail the problem of the statistics required) a standing interdepartmental committee of officials to deal with problems of Employment Policy and reporting to a Ministerial Committee of which the Chancellor of the Exchequer would probably be the chairman and which would eventually absorb the present Manpower Committee. The other main question discussed at this meeting was the problem of the joint single preliminary approach to industry on the question of the statistics required from them. Some departments (such as the Ministry of Works) had already begun separately to approach their industries. But the main difficulty came from the Board of Trade which are on the point of setting up public committees of officials and businessmen to examine (i) the question of additional information required in the post-war census of production and (ii) the question whether there should be a census of distribution. (Incidentally they have invited me to serve on this latter committee, an invitation which I have now accepted.) Preliminary soundings had already been taken by them of retailers and wholesalers on this second question, if not also on the first. They were most anxious that their enquiries should not be held up while a working party of officials first worked out a complete programme of the information required and subsequently a general approach was then made to the FBI and similar bodies. It was finally decided, if my understanding is correct, that there should be a general approach to industry at as early a date as possible on the general subject, and that meanwhile the Board of Trade might continue with their two projected committees.[6]

We (i.e. Lionel Robbins, Tress and myself from the Economic Section with Stafford from the Central Statistical Office) spent a morning with Dr W. A. Mackintosh of the Canadian ministry of reconstruction (or whatever is the corresponding organisation in Ottawa) who was the author

[4] Bridges to Ince, 31 May 1945, T273/298.

[5] Minutes of the meeting of 1 June 1945 are on T273/319 and T230/70.

[6] Meade was invited to serve on the committee on the proposed Census of Distribution at Dalton's instigation (Overton to Bridges, 10 May, and Note by Dalton, 11 May 1945, BT70/99). On the establishment of that committee and the question of its postponement see BT70/99.

of the Canadian White Paper on Income and Employment.[7] We exchanged views and information on our ideas about post-war Employment Policy and I gave Mackintosh informally a copy of our Economic Section paper on Economic Forecasting and Employment Policy.[8] These meetings are very useful as one may hope gradually to build up a common basis of action. Nothing very exciting turned up except the information that the Canadians in their annual census of production have already introduced a question asking businesses to state not only their capital expenditure in the past year but their plans for capital expenditure in the coming year. This is an interesting attempt to start forecasting private investment. We should consider it for this country.

The Canadians (i.e. Mackintosh; Towers, the Governor of the Bank of Canada; and McKinnon, formerly head of their tariff board) have been in London talking to the Treasury about the financial problems of the period after the Japanese War, when they are most anxious to see a solution to our Balance of Payments problem which does not make it necessary to discriminate against imports from hard-currency countries.[9] They invited me to dine with them at the Savoy hotel where they were staying. We spoke about employment policy and also to some extent about post-war commercial and financial policy. They have been informed of recent developments in our conversations with the Americans. Later in the week when Mackintosh lunched with me I tried to convince him that our proposals for special treatment for foodstuffs in international trade, whereby quantitative restriction would be permitted, but there would be an overall ceiling on protective devices of a price-raising character and, in addition, all forms of support (including subsidies) would have to be tailed off so long as production exceeded a certain datum level, was a serious and reasonable compromise. It gave agriculture greater latitude than industry to protect and quantitatively to regulate up to a certain level of production; but beyond that point it treated agriculture much more severely than industry. (Incidentally, in the conversations which have been proceeding with Hawkins,[10] the Americans have now made it clear that they have a definite programme: first, they wish to agree with us behind the scenes a statement of principles on commercial policy; secondly, they intend then to publish it on their own initiative as their own document, after some discussion with Congress behind the scenes and possibly after some discussion with other countries; and finally, they intend to call a trade

[7] The 'organisation' was the Department of Reconstruction and Supply. On the preparation of the Canadian White Paper, 'Employment and Income, with Special Reference to the Initial Period of Reconstruction', presented to Parliament on 12 April 1945, see W. A. Mackintosh, 'The White Paper on Employment and Income in its 1945 Setting', in S. F. Kaliski (ed.), *Canadian Economic Policy Since the War*. Ottawa: Canadian Trade Committee, 1966, pp. 9–21.

[8] EC(S)(45)5, T230/17; see above, p. 69.

[9] For the Canadians' discussions with the Treasury see T236/31–2, and, for a memoir of the meetings, Douglas LePan, *Bright Glass of Memory*. Toronto: McGraw-Hill Ryerson, 1979, pp. 55–101. The Canadians also discussed commercial policy with Sir Wilfrid Eady and officials from the Board of Trade ('Article VII: Commercial Policy. Summary of Discussion with Canadian Officials on 25, 29 and 31 May 1945', T230/174).

[10] On 18 May 1945: *Foreign Relations of the United States*, 1945, VI, pp. 47–50.

conference on the subject, this latter stage to be reached early in 1946. Now that Bretton Woods is sailing through Congress; that the House of Representatives has passed their new trade agreements act giving power for a further 50 per cent [cut] in the USA tariff; and that we are coming to realise that both on political grounds and because we need American financial support after the end of Lend-Lease, the prospects for an international economic solution à la Article VII must be considered not too bad, although an adverse political movement in this country as a result of the forthcoming election might still, of course, do untold harm.)[11]

There has been a meeting of the National Debt Enquiry this week at which my redraft of the paper for the Chancellor of the Exchequer was up for discussion. The outcome of the meeting was quite satisfactory in that with certain changes, none of a very essential character but all tending to play down the arguments for a Capital Levy rather more than I had been willing to do, the paper was approved.[12] Nor do I dissent myself from the general conclusion that the yield from a levy would be so small that a progressive levy is no use at all, while a fairly heavy proportionate levy which reached down to all properties above £1000 (if it were politically feasible, which it almost certainly isn't) would only just be worth considering. But the atmosphere of the meeting was most disconcerting. It consisted of a series of facetious remarks (or of what Keynes called Capital Levity) from the assembled heavyweights – Bridges, Eady, Keynes, Gregg, etc. Thus all my pet arguments were swept aside in a tide of laughter. I find nothing so disconcerting as being laughed at! Bridges made a pretty little speech at the end saying how nice the draft was as a whole, and in fact with minor changes it is thought worthy of being sent to the Chancellor as expressing the views of the Treasury, the Board of Inland Revenue and the Economic Section on the subject. Nevertheless I would have preferred them not to have laughed so uproariously!

I had a visit during the week from F. G. Lee of the Treasury delegation in Washington, who is home on a visit. He came to impress on us the great importance of our having new estimates and forecasts of the Balance of Payments ready before the autumn when it was possible that talks might start on the problems of the post-Lend-Lease world. Miss Watts is going to get down to this next week.[13]

## *10 June 1945*

I have had a meeting with Proctor and Vinter in the Treasury on the next stage in Employment Policy. I suggested that we should now do two

[11] The US Bretton Woods Agreements Act was approved by the Senate on 18 July 1945 and signed by the President on 31 July. On its passage through Congress, and that of the 1945 Reciprocal Trade Agreements Act, see Richard N. Gardner, *Sterling-Dollar Diplomacy*. London: Oxford University Press, 1956, pp. 129–43 and 158–60 respectively.
In the UK the coalition government had been ended on 23 May, Churchill forming a caretaker Conservative government; a general election was to be held on 5 July (see below, p. 114).

[12] See 'Note of 13th meeting . . . on 31st May 1945', T230/95 and T233/158.

[13] See below, p. 111.

things:- *first*, that the Economic Section, Treasury and Central Statistical Office should meet together to clear their own minds on the actual form in which we should like to get the programmes of Public and Private Investment prepared in order that a meeting might then be called by the Treasury to induce the departments mainly concerned to approach the public authorities and industries concerned in the right way after we had discussed with them their views on the way in which these programmes might best be formulated; and *secondly* that the Economic Section and Central Statistical Office should now sit down in co-operation and start to forecast the 'target' total national expenditure, required to give full employment, over the next five years. I think that we shall now probably proceed on these lines.[14]

I have now revised our paper on the Capital Levy and it has been circulated in printed proof to the members of the National Debt Enquiry. I hope that this is more or less the end of it as far as I am concerned.[15]

There has been a meeting in Sir Richard Hopkins' room of the officials (namely, myself; Dick Stone; Leak, Reddaway and Hicklin of the Board of Trade) who are to be members of the public committee to enquire into the desirability and feasibility of having a Census of Distribution. The meeting was entirely one to decide upon tactics. The great concern of Sir Richard Hopkins, who is to be chairman of the Committee, being to ensure that the whole thing looks as attractive as possible, or as little distasteful as possible, to the small shopkeeper.[16]

I attended a meeting of EIPS (the Economic and Industrial Planning Staff) to discuss the final redraft of the section of their document on social insurance in Germany which dealt with Family Allowances. I managed to persuade them to keep the draft as it stands at present which is in a form which does properly set out the advantages of permitting the Germans a scheme of children's allowances.[17] We then went on to discuss whether or not there was likely to be a long period of mass unemployment in Germany or not. I expressed the view that there would be a limited period of heavy dislocation-unemployment; but that that period should be fairly short and, in view of the great need for reconstruction in Germany and of demands for reparations, there should in fact therefore be very good employment prospects for a long time. I received considerable support in this view from E. A. Radice as opposed to those who seemed to expect a very prolonged period of mass unemployment.

I had dinner with Oliver Franks and Robert Hall to meet an Australian called Murphy, who is head of their department of Commerce. He has been concerned over here with talks on the future of wool and how to dispose of the vast surpluses of wool. But he wished to exchange views on Commercial Policy before he went back to Australia. He revealed some illuminating, if indiscreet, incidents about Australian policy on this subject. He explained how, at the time of the signing of Article VII [23

[14] See Proctor to Bridges and Gilbert, 'Employment Policy', 9 June 1945, T273/319 and T230/70.

[15] See below, p. 95.

[16] On the choice of the official members of the Committee see BT70/99.

[17] The draft is on FO942/154.

February 1942] in spite of the fact that it was realised that it meant a radical modification of Imperial Preference, Evatt had torn up the draft cable which he (Murphy) had prepared to be sent to the UK to back up the UK in signing Article VII and had drafted the one which was actually despatched urging the UK to sign; and not only this, but Evatt had actually allowed the Americans to see the draft of this telegram so that they might know that the Australians were pressing the UK to sign.[18] All this, because the Japs were at Australia's doorstep and American aid was needed. Later, however, Evatt did all he could to prevent any modification of Imperial Preference. Melville, when he represented Australia at the last official Dominions talks on the subject in London, was so strictly bound by his instructions not to give anything away that when he sent back a cable to Australia saying that he had stated that Australia could not consider any modification of Imperial Preference except in return for very far-reaching counter-concessions, Evatt had insisted on a reply being sent to Melville severely reprimanding him for going so far![19] The conversation with Murphy was rather depressing, as it is clear that it is going to be very difficult to get much progress from Australia on this subject. Murphy was very anxious that there should be imperial talks at the Ministerial level in order that we might get a common Commonwealth policy before going into any world conference on commercial policy, since if we did so unprepared there would only be a first-rate Commonwealth dispute in front of everybody else. I gave reasons for the view that the Americans were likely to press ahead quickly now for discussions, if not a world conference, on this subject; that there would be no use in having a Commonwealth conference unless there was some general agreement as to the hypotheses on which the conference should work (e.g. was it the object of the conference to increase Imperial Preference or to reduce it?); that the only basis for an Imperial conference would be to consider the ways in which Imperial Preference might be reduced and the counter-concessions by other countries which would be necessary (i.e. to discuss the implementation of Article VII); and that on these conditions a conference might be most useful and most desirable.

In the course of the week Norman Brook sent for me and said that the Chancellor of the Exchequer had expressed the desire that Lionel Robbins should stay on in the Cabinet Offices for some months yet to be available to advise on Article VII and other matters of Anglo-American economic and financial relations. He had already talked with Lionel and they were suggesting that I might take over the Economic Section very soon and that Lionel should stay on in the office in an independent position for the other purpose. I objected strongly to this arrangement on the grounds that it would imply that Robbins had been dealing with Article VII etc. *qua* Lionel Robbins and not *qua* Director of the Economic Section, and that it would therefore be very undesirable from the point of view of the future of the Section. On the other hand, I said that I would be very pleased if

[18] The telegram sent is No. 130, Australia to Dominions Office, 12 February 1942, T175/123.

[19] For a summary of the talks, February-April 1944, see WP(44)192, 6 April 1944, CAB66/48; cf. Pressnell, *External Economic Policy since the War*, op. cit., pp. 134–5.

Lionel stayed on as Director of the Section. I have persuaded Lionel that there is force in this argument and I hope therefore that the proposed arrangement can be avoided.

I have, alas, heard from Robert Hall that he does not want to join the Section; from Devons that he will probably wish to go to Manchester; and of Tom Wilson that he is putting in for a position at the London School of Economics. I expect that Stafford will stay in the Central Statistical Office and that MacDougall will go to Oxford. So the prospects of staffing the Section really adequately look, at the moment, pretty grim.

## *16 June 1945*

The week has been dominated by problems of establishments and of staffing the Section. Gilbert Walker has now told me that he does not want to join the Section, and I hear that the Cassel Chair at the London School of Economics is being offered to Fleming who is bound to be very attracted by it. The position begins to look rather desperate. I am going to make a tentative approach to R. S. Sayers. The great difficulty is clearly going to be to get one or two of the more senior people, and I really require three – one to deal with Employment Policy, one with External Economic affairs and one with the day-to-day work of briefing the Lord President of the Council. Meanwhile the Treasury Establishments are now denying that they have authorised the offers that have been made and, in particular, are asserting that they cannot pay Miss Watts the salary which has been promised to her. They also maintain that all our junior grade (Economic Assistants as opposed to Economic Advisers) must be recruited on the ordinary basis of an entrant to the Civil Service with the ordinary pay of an Assistant Principal. The week has been taken up with a series of meetings and discussions with Norman Brook, Lionel Robbins, Colonel Walker (our establishments officer) and the Treasury establishment officials.[20] But the tangle is still unresolved.

Otherwise there is not much to record this week. We have had a series of staff meetings to discuss Tress' first draft of our new Economic Survey.[21] This draft is constructed on the basis of first considering the total demands on the country's resources under the heads appropriate for forward planning in terms of the National Income and Expenditure, that is to say in terms of (i) public demand for goods and services (for the war against Japan), (ii) export demands to get our balance of payments into equilibrium as soon as possible, (iii) public and private investment (e.g. house-building) and (iv) the demand of persons for consumption goods and services. The Survey then considers the total resources available to meet these demands. It is not yet possible to quantify these estimates in *£ s d* so that the demands on resources and the supply of available resources can be properly compared (such quantification is, of course, one of the highest priority jobs of the Section); but there is no difficulty in

[20] See Helsby, 'Cabinet Economic Section', 16 June 1945, T217/205.

[21] A draft appears on T230/162.

making plain that there will be a strain on our total resources. A third part of the Survey discusses three main problems which arise from this situation:- the problem of obtaining a smooth and rapid reconversion from war to peace economy, so that there is no unnecessary waste of resources; the problem of deciding on the priorities to be observed in the use of the available resources; and the problem of avoiding inflation. Tress is now redrafting.

The week has seen the final approval and printing of two papers on which I have expended a great deal of effort in the last months – (i) the paper on the Capital Levy, which was finally approved at a meeting of the National Debt Enquiry [on 14 June] and which is now to be given to the Chancellor and by him, probably, to Attlee as well as to a number of Ministers; and (ii) the paper on Economic Forecasting and Employment Policy.[22] This latter paper caused a little more trouble. At the last moment Sir Bernard Gilbert in the Treasury took exception to the passages in which we suggested that local authorities and other relevant public authorities should be asked to plan their capital expenditure ahead in a three-tier programme – i.e. a maximum which they could reach if they had to stimulate expenditure in order to avoid depression; a minimum below which they would not go without gravely impairing the service concerned even if work should be restricted in the interests of employment policy; and a normal level which they would adopt in the absence of stimulation or restriction of expenditure on grounds of Employment Policy. He also took exception to our discussion of the fact that the rate of interest and the rate of grant paid would affect the amount of capital expenditure undertaken by the public authorities. He was only willing to say that the local authorities would be asked for a single figure programme and that the central authority would then try to turn it into a three-tier programme. I argued that in order to do this one must at least ask the authorities concerned to give one some indication of the variability of their programmes – e.g. to specify what part of their programme (a) had the plans ready, (b) had the necessary land already acquired, (c) was sanctioned by their finance committees etc. Otherwise one would have no idea of the amount by which their programmes could be speeded up. At a meeting between Gilbert, Lionel Robbins, myself, and Bridges, we agreed a draft which really left all these matters unresolved. In this form our paper will go forward with the full backing and approval of the Treasury; and as it contains in the large the whole argument for the forward planning of the national income and expenditure, this is a tremendous advance. The next stage will be a meeting of heads of departments to discuss our paper; and at this stage the Economic Section will be free to bring forward its own ideas on the subject.[23]

[22] A proof of the report on the capital levy is on T230/95. The final version of 'Employment Policy and Economic Forecasting, Note by the Economic Section of the War Cabinet', 16 June 1945, is in Meade Papers 3/2.

[23] The dispute is recorded in Bridges to Robbins, 11 June, Meade to Robbins, 13 June, Robbins to Bridges, 13 June, Gilbert to Bridges, 14 June, Eady to Bridges, 14 June 1945, T274/319. See also below, pp. 96 and 102.

## 25 June 1945

Some little further preparatory work has been done for Employment Policy. I went to a meeting with Proctor of the Treasury and Campion of the Central Statistical Office to discuss the future procedure of the interdepartmental 'working party' which is to consider the CSO paper on the statistics required for Employment Policy. Meanwhile inside the Economic Section we have been discussing, on the basis of a paper submitted by Chester, the questions which ought to be asked of Local Authorities for the purpose of forming a programme of Public Investment.[24] The issues here really turn on the amount and the form of the information which one would ask them to give in order to be able to judge how readily their expenditure could be expanded or contracted if and when the need arose. We consider that it is no use asking them merely for a single figure of proposed expenditure for each of the years in question. One must at least ask them to give indications of their state of preparedness in respect of this expenditure – e.g. in respect of how much of the planned expenditure has the local council (a) itself approved the expenditure, (b) obtained loan sanction and (c) actually started the undertaking? In respect of how much has it already acquired the land? We propose to prepare a paper on this subject, which is now very urgent because a first questionnaire must shortly go out to local authorities. A second paper, which is rather less urgent but even more fundamental, we intend to prepare on the subject of the means by which the Central Government can actually influence the timing of local authorities' expenditure:- e.g. by rates of grant which are higher when it is desired to stimulate expenditure than when it is desired to restrict [it]; by higher or lower rates of interest; or merely by persuasion. It is on this subject which we are most likely to clash seriously with Sir Bernard Gilbert and other Treasury pundits, I suspect. The Treasury itself is, in fact, divided on all this. Lionel Robbins and I lunched this week with Proctor of the Treasury who works under Gilbert.[25] Proctor is entirely of our way of thinking that one must get serious indications from Local Authorities about the variability of their expenditure and also that one must consider means (such as variable grants-in-aid) of controlling the timing of their expenditure. It is clear, however, from what Proctor says that Gilbert is very cautious and unwilling to go ahead on these ideas and that Proctor is being prevented from getting on in his own way on this subject. It is clear also that Gilbert wishes as a next stage to call a meeting of officials at the highest level to discuss the approach to Local Authorities, whereas Proctor and we think that it is most desirable that we (i.e. the Treasury, Economic Section and CSO) should thrash out these issues among ourselves first.[26] Otherwise at a full interdepartmental meeting the Economic Section will be seen to be at variance with the Treasury and we shall not get anything very sensible done.

[24] Both draft and final version of Chester's paper, 'Capital Expenditure by Public Authorities', are on T230/18 (EC(S)(45)22 and 25, 6 and 27 June 1945).

[25] On 20 June 1945 (T230/70).

[26] See Robbins to Bridges, 21 June 1945, T230/70 and T273/319.

Cockfield (who is acting as director of statistics in the Board of Inland Revenue while Chambers is away as Financial Adviser to the Control Commission in Germany) was sent to call on me by Sir Cornelius Gregg to leave with me copies of correspondence between the Board of Inland Revenue and the Federation of British Industries on the subject of the publication by the Inland Revenue of statistics of industrial profits and costs arising out of the income tax. In 1930 in the then fashionable obscurantism the FBI had successfully prevented any such publication. Apparently now in the fashionable 'Joy through Statistics' era they have consented to publication.[27] The only contention now is exactly how much should be published, whether – for example – industrial costs should be split down showing labour costs and raw material costs separately. There were two causes for rejoicing: first, that these statistics, which will be of great use from the point of view of economic policy, were at last to be made available; and, secondly, (a very parochial consideration) that Gregg should see fit to consult the Economic Section at once on the question of what detailed figures were and what were not required.

We have continued during the week a series of staff meetings on the Economic Survey which Tress is preparing. The Survey is becoming shorter, less repetitive and more to the point; and Tress is behaving very well under a constant barrage of criticism. The draft was clumsy at first; but it is now much improved.[28] I still hope that Tress (who learns by experience) will prove a good regular editor for what I hope will be a regular periodic production of the future Economic Section.

I with Lionel Robbins attended a meeting of officials about the setting up of a 'Joint Intelligence Board' after the war.[29] This is to be a small permanent staff of officials in the Cabinet Offices to work for the Joint Intelligence Sub-Committee of the Chiefs of Staff Committee in preparing appreciations of military intelligence. This will all, of course, have an important economic side (e.g. on the war potential of various countries) and the idea is that the Economic Section should be prepared to aid the JIB where general economic issues are involved.

The other day at lunch at the Reform Club, Sir Arthur Salter who is now Chancellor of the Duchy of Lancaster with special responsibility for the problems of European Reconstruction, came to sit next to me. His object was to see whether the Economic Section was the sort of body which might help him. He had two problems in mind. In the first place, he wanted to start off his Ministerial work on this subject with a general paper reviewing the whole problem of European Economic Reconstruction. Were we the sort of body which might help him on this? I said I thought that we were.

[27] This correspondence has not been found. On the FBI's attitude to the publication of official statistics in 1930 see the information from Colin Clark reported by Don Patinkin in his *Anticipations of the General Theory?*. Chicago: University of Chicago Press and Oxford: Basil Blackwell, 1982, p. 260. The phrase 'Joy through Statistics' comes from Keynes ('Post-war Employment: Note by Lord Keynes on the Report of the Steering Committee', 14 February 1944, in *The Collected Writings of John Maynard Keynes*, Vol. 27, pp. 364–72, which also refers to the FBI problem).

[28] Drafts are on T230/162.

[29] No minutes of this meeting have been located.

Secondly, he wanted to read over the central documents on the subject of Article VII both as background to his work on European Reconstruction and also because he hoped to play a part in any Cabinet discussions on this subject. In this connection he told me that when the PM sent for him to offer him a position in the Government, the PM had said that he wanted someone in the Cabinet who understood economic issues and asked him whether he was interested in Bretton Woods and Article VII in general. Salter replied that he was, but himself suggested that he would rather at first concentrate on the problem of European economic reconstruction. I felt that I must consult Norman Brook before giving Salter the back papers on Article VII, since this involves the principle of the availability of the papers of one Cabinet to a Minister in a succeeding administration. I have spoken to Brook on this and it appears probable that he will authorise me to give the papers to Salter. In any case we must keep Salter briefed on Article VII in the future. He should be a useful, if not a heavyweight, ally in the Cabinet.

Talking of Article VII I must record two things. First, the US Senate has this week passed the Bill renewing their Trade Agreements Act in a form which gives the President the power to negotiate a further 50 per cent cut in the US tariff. This is indeed a great stimulus to a successful final outcome to the Article VII negotiations. Secondly, Roy Harrod – the courageous, noble fellow – is standing as a Liberal candidate in Huddersfield on the sole plank of Article VII. The sitting member is Mabane, the Liberal National Minister of State in the Foreign Office. For long Mabane met Harrod's accusation that the Tories intended to throw over Article VII in silence. But at last to Harrod's great joy he replied with a statement in which he said that HMG stood by Article VII. To which Harrod replied that this could not be so in view of the statements of the Lord Privy Seal (Beaverbrook) and the Secretary of State for India (Amery). I happened to be in Norman Brook's room when I heard one repercussion of this. Mabane apparently wished to issue a statement saying that his previous statement was issued 'with the full authority of the Prime Minister'. Brook, however, was taking the line that the PM should not be bothered with this, but that Mabane should get out of his own electioneering difficulties. Roy Harrod has come nearer to driving a wedge into the Conservative Party than he himself realises!

The outstanding event of the week has been a dinner given by the Royal Economic Society to Keynes who, after 30 years continuous service, is this year retiring from the positions of Secretary of the Society and editor of *The Economic Journal*.[30] First of all there was, at tea time, the annual meeting of the Society at which Dennis Robertson read a paper on the problem of exports, with Keynes in the chair as the newly elected President. In this paper[31] Dennis dealt with three main topics: first, he debunked the view that you must first develop a large home market in order to spread your overhead costs before turning to the export market

[30] Keynes had been editor since 1911, secretary since 1913.

[31] D. H. Robertson, 'The Problem of Exports', *The Economic Journal*, Vol. 35 (December 1945), pp. 321–5.

(this is very important. The motor-car manufacturers are, for example, trying to get the purchase tax on motor-cars removed in order to foster home sales in order to get a good basis from which to export. But this is quite absurd. In present conditions in which they could sell abroad every single car which they could produce, a restriction of home sales cannot fail to encourage exports); secondly, he dealt with the question of justice versus efficiency in the problem of whether all manufacturers should be required to make their contribution to exports or whether some should be allowed to produce for the home market while the most suitable were made to concentrate solely on exports; and, thirdly, he dealt very beautifully with the modern fashion of suggesting that it does not pay to reduce the price of British exports in order to expand the value of British exports, since the fall in price might more than outweigh the consequent increase in volume. He pointed out that to be consistent one must use this argument not only to deny the utility of exchange depreciation but also to deny the utility of wage reductions or of increases in industrial efficiency as means of increasing the value of our exports. In the course of this section he made a very shrewd dig at Keynes. Keynes during the speech kept on catching my eye at the points on which we had had recent discussions in Whitehall; and during the discussion after a number of businessmen had spoken he called on me to speak for the professional economists. But this invitation I felt bound to decline, as one could not speak at all freely on this controversial issue at what was virtually a public meeting.

That evening at dinner Keynes was quite superb. Attending the dinner in addition to Keynes were Hawtrey (in the chair), Sir Arthur Salter, Sir Walter Layton, Lionel Robbins, Carr-Saunders, Hubert Henderson, Joan Robinson, Piero Sraffa, Geoffrey Crowther, Arnold Plant, Claude Guillebaud, A. G. B. Fisher, C. R. Fay, Dick Stone, John Hicks, Richard Kahn, Noel Hall, Henry Clay, John Jewkes, Sargant Florence, Hayek, Roy Harrod, Dennis Robertson and J. H. Jones. Keynes gave the most superb speech starting with reminiscences of the Council of the Society in 1912 when he first became editor. Then going back to even earlier days when, as the son of J. N. Keynes in Cambridge, he claimed to have been kissed by 25 per cent of the first council of the society. After a series of the most delightful sketches of all the well-known economists he came to the serious side of his speech. He emphasised, through these reminiscences, the great value of continuity of tradition in English economics as in all things English; stressed the fact that recent events must have convinced us all that what our forebears had achieved was harder to achieve and easier to lose than we had perhaps realised previously; and underlined the great responsibility that now lay upon the economists to carry on and develop this tradition because they were – and were coming to be recognised to be – not the guardians of civilisation but the guardians of the possibility of civilisation. Harrod, as the new editor, was called on to speak and made a delightful speech in which he said that the wonder of Keynes was his combination of the scientist and the artist. In the course of his remarks he referred to 'the arithmetic of pleasure' according to which Keynes the artist had given delight to so many throughout the world. Henderson added a third ingredient to Keynes' character, his humanity. Then many joined in, making reference to Keynes' many excellencies or reminiscing with him about past times. I kept silence; but as the party broke up, I felt compelled to go up to Keynes privately to tell him that my silence did not mean that I in any way failed to realise that I owed more to him than perhaps to any single man. Keynes was really moved by the evening's proceedings.

# 9

## July 1945

### *1 July 1945*

The week has been quite a profitable one from the point of view of post-war Employment Policy. In the first place, there has been a meeting of the National Debt Enquiry to discuss papers by Brittain and Keynes on the question whether there should be a post-war Capital Budget as well as a Revenue Budget.[1] Keynes divided the problem into four parts:- (i) an Exchequer Capital Budget (i.e. a Capital Budget for the Central Government), (ii) a Public Capital Budget (i.e. a Capital Budget for all Public Authorities), (iii) an Investment Budget (i.e. a Budget for all Private and Public Capital Expenditure) and (iv) a Remanet Budget (i.e. a special Budget for special receipts and expenditures – such as War Damage Payments – remaining over from the war). We were able to reach a very satisfactory agreement on all this. Everyone was agreed that some form of Investment Survey must be prepared of all forms of public and private capital expenditure; that the past figures must be published each year at the time of the Budget White Paper; that for internal purposes forecasts of capital expenditure must be prepared, but that it was questionable whether they should be published, since such forecasts might help to cause a boom or slump. It was also agreed that for internal purposes it was desirable to prepare figures of what Keynes called Exchequer and Public Capital Budgets; but it was pointed out that most of this information was already available in the Budget White Paper on National Income and Expenditure.[2] There was, however, great opposition to the idea that the Exchequer accounts should formally be recast into a current budget and a capital budget. This opposition came, on the one hand, from people such as Sir Richard Hopkins who argued that in fact the ordinary budget contained very little capital expenditure which was already financed almost entirely by borrowing 'below the line', and that it was wrong to disturb age-long traditions when there was so little point in doing so. On the other hand, I opposed the idea strongly on the grounds that it would encourage a very dangerous new financial orthodoxy. It would come to be

[1] The fifteenth meeting of the National Debt Enquiry was held on 28 June 1945; the papers discussed were NDE Paper 12, 'Proposals for a Capital Budget', by Brittain and NDE Paper 14, 'The Concept of a Capital Budget', by Keynes (T230/95 and T233/159). Keynes' paper also appears in *The Collected Writings of John Maynard Keynes*, Vol. 27, pp. 405–13.

[2] First published in April 1941.

considered essential that in all circumstances the revenue budget should be balanced each year, and that employment policy could operate only by the variation of expenditure in the capital budget. It was, moreover, proposed that all the 'productive loans' issued to finance public investment through the capital budget would have sinking funds attached to them which would have to be met out of the revenue budget. In consequence as time went on, it would become necessary for the state to raise taxation for an ever growing sinking fund while at the same time the opportunities for profitable public investment would probably become more and more restricted. This new financial orthodoxy might thus lead to the need to dig holes and fill them up as a legitimate means of encouraging purchasing power through the capital budget, whereas the most sensible thing might well be to run (temporarily at least) a deficit in the revenue budget to encourage ordinary consumers' purchases. For these reasons I think that it was fortunate that it was decided not to have a formal Exchequer Capital Budget.

We have also had a meeting in Sir Bernard Gilbert's room in the Treasury with Campion and Stafford from the CSO; Lionel Robbins, Chester and myself from the Economic Section; Proctor from the Treasury; and George and Cross from the Ministry of Health; on the subject of the questionnaire and form to be sent out to Local Authorities in connection with the programming of their future capital expenditure. The results were really very satisfactory. The decisions taken were practically exactly what the Economic Section wanted: an attempt is to be made to get the forms out and filled up in time for analysis before the April 1946 Budget; the programmes are to cover maintenance expenditure as well as new capital investment; the figures are to be given for the three years 1946/47, 1947/48 and 1948/49; the authorities are to be asked to give their suggested expenditure on the assumption of current prices and costs, current rate of grants, current rate of interest etc.; expenditure on land or other existing property was to be shown separately. The only point which gave any difficulty was our proposal that the expenditures should be subdivided into the amounts which had been approved by the local council; which had received loan sanction; which referred to works for which tenders had already been accepted or on which work had already started; and in respect of which the necessary land had already been acquired. It seemed to us essential to have this analysis according to the degree of preparedness of the works in order to know how variable the works in fact were. Proctor was asked to draft a circular and form to be sent to Local Authorities; and it was agreed that our proposals about the degree of preparedness should be included in this draft to see what it looked like.[3]

Lionel Robbins told me of a meeting which he had attended in Bridges' room with Eady and Keynes, at which Keynes proposed that Stone – who is going to academic life in Cambridge – should nevertheless remain in charge of the work on the National Income and Expenditure, which should be transferred from the Central Statistical Office to the Treasury and there managed by a committee consisting of Stone, Brittain and myself. This

[3] No record of the meeting has been found. On the circular to local authorities, see p. 135.

would really be a quite impossible arrangement, as Lionel fully recognised; and he managed successfully to resist. Nevertheless there are very real dangers on the other side if the National Income work remains in the Central Statistical Office under Campion, who certainly is overcautious and perhaps rather unimaginative about it. Campion must be coaxed into putting someone good in charge of it. Robbins' idea which he mentioned to Bridges is that Tress might be in charge of it, jointly responsible to Campion and myself. This has its points, but joint responsibility is a difficult thing.

Lionel Robbins and I were asked to go across to the Board of Trade to a meeting with Overton, Liesching and Helmore to discuss a paper by Keynes on the external finance of Stage III (i.e. of the period after the Japanese War is over and Lend-Lease comes to an end).[4] Keynes' paper is really brilliant. He distinguishes between three main lines of solution: Austerity, Temptation and Justice. Austerity consists in our making ourselves independent of United States financial aid by a heroic policy of belt-tightening, bilateral trade bargains, etc. etc. Temptation consists in our accepting loans from the United States which will enable us to tide over our balance of payments difficulty without, however, any ultimate scaling down of our total external liability. Justice consists in all countries (i.e. the USA and the sterling area countries) making some contribution to our external liabilities (which will be somewhat greater than the largest figure yet mentioned for German Reparations) since we alone of all the Allies will have incurred some liabilities in the common war effort, the remaining liability being treated on very reasonable terms as to interest, repayment etc. Austerity would be incompatible with, while Temptation and Justice would be compatible with, an Article VII world. Part of Keynes' proposals about Justice were that the sterling balances should be divided into three parts: one part would be made fully and completely convertible, one part would be completely cancelled, and a third part would be funded and released gradually over a period of years for expenditure on additional UK exports. Overton was disturbed from the point of view of the UK export trade at the size of the sums which Keynes said should be immediately made fully convertible; he was afraid that these sums, which were certainly more than the values which we could hope to export to the sterling area countries over and above our need to purchase from them, would encourage them to purchase American goods instead. This would enable the Americans to build up goodwill and export connections in these markets in advance of our exporters; whereas, if these sterling balances could be released only after a period of years, their owners might be encouraged to economise in overseas purchases for some time so that our exporters would have a more equal start with the American exporters. Lionel Robbins and I had a different sort of worry over Keynes' proposals. Keynes suggested that the funded part of the sterling balances should be released over a period for expenditure on UK goods. But, so we argued, it was only possible to ensure that they were spent exclusively on

[4] 'Overseas Financial Policy in Stage III', May 1945, PREM 4/17/15 and *The Collected Writings of John Maynard Keynes*, Vol. 24, pp. 256–95.

UK goods by taking action (which would occur in a period long after any transitional let-outs were operating) incompatible either with the Bretton Woods agreement against multiple-currency practices or with the proposed commercial policy rules against discrimination. If the sterling balances were owned by a Govt (e.g. the Govt of India) which itself wished to indulge in overseas expenditure, purchases by this government of UK goods regardless of the prices or costs of alternative goods would be discriminatory. If (the more usual case) the sterling balances were owned by a Govt or by individuals which did not themselves wish to make overseas purchases, they must be sold to those who did wish to do so. But these purchasers could only be induced to buy UK as opposed to US goods regardless of UK and US prices if *either* the blocked sterling balances were, if necessary, at a discount (a multiple-currency practice) *or* by import restrictions directed against US goods the purchasers were forced to buy from the UK or some similar commercial policy discrimination. I proposed, as a method which might meet Overton's point as well as ours, that (i) part of the sterling balances should be cancelled, (ii) only a small part should be made immediately freely convertible, and (iii) the rest should be completely blocked for all payments but should be released and made completely convertible by small amounts each year. I have been asked to draft a joint Board of Trade-Economic Section note on these lines.[5]

The whole of Tuesday [26 June], morning and afternoon, was taken up with the first meeting of the Census of Distribution Committee. Sir Richard Hopkins has started on his campaign of trying to coax the representatives of the small shopkeepers into acquiescing with the taking of a Census of Distribution. The meetings were taken up with much preliminary matter including the reading of a letter from Lyttleton, the President of the Board of Trade, giving a wide interpretation to our terms of reference. We are to concern ourselves not only with retail and wholesale business but with service trades such as entertainments, hairdressers, etc. etc. A Board of Trade document stating the general case for a Census was read out. Everyone in turn was asked to make a statement giving their general views on the matter; and to my delight it appeared that everyone was in favour of a Census except the representatives of the small shopkeepers, and even they seemed ready to acquiesce provided they weren't asked for too much detail. It seems most probable that there will be a Census. What we must really fight for is that the Census should be frequent enough; that the first one should be taken at a reasonable early date (Leak, the Board of Trade statistician, in his ultra-cautious manner was talking of not being able to hold the first Census until 1949); and that the necessary questions are all asked (of these the most necessary to watch out for is the question showing the gross profit margins of the business concerned). We ended up by spending a long time discussing the trade organisations and other bodies which should be asked to give evidence.[6]

Marcus Fleming, having been invited to take the Cassel Chair at the

[5] See below p. 105.
[6] The agenda for the meeting and the Board of Trade document are on BT70/99.

London School of Economics, is now in almost exactly the same state of dither which I was in last year. Bridges is going to speak to him to reassure him about his prospects of continuing employment in Whitehall if he does elect to stay on in the Economic Section. I sincerely hope he does; but I doubt if he will. Meanwhile, the Treasury have prepared the first draft of a document on the recruitment of economists and statisticians for the Government Service. (i) It does not seem to allow for any recruitment of more senior economists outside the ordinary civil service entrance examinations, and (ii) it proposes to appoint the more junior members by means, and on conditions, very analogous to those applying to the ordinary entrant to the Civil Service. The former point must be changed. The latter is one possible conception; but it raises the question whether the Treasury is wise in tying its hands against making any truly temporary appointments. Bridges has suggested to me that Campion and I should write a short note on this subject.[7]

## *8 July 1945*

There is not very much to record this week, which I have spent largely in reading papers and on questions of establishments.

I have drafted the note on Keynes' proposals for the overseas financial settlement for Stage III which the Board of Trade and the Economic Section are going to put in as a joint note to the Treasury. I went round to the Board of Trade to discuss the draft with Liesching and Helmore who have accepted it with very few amendments. They have proposed that we should also collaborate with Leak in preparing statistical estimates of the way in which Keynes' proposals and our modifications of them could affect our Stage III balance of payments. Miss Watts is getting down to this.[8]

Lionel Robbins, Marcus Fleming and I have had a meeting with Redvers Opie who is over on a visit from the Embassy in Washington, in order to expound to him the UK commercial policy proposals for the special treatment of agriculture in the proposed multilateral convention[9] and to attempt to get him to say something in their favour in Washington. Apparently the prospects of their acceptance in Washington are none too good. But very much turns on this because the prospects of the acceptance of the commercial policy proposals in this country are very dependent on an acceptable arrangement for agriculture.

Hawkins has now been given a UK draft Statement of Principles on Commercial Policy to illustrate (in comparison with the draft which Hawkins had shown us) what shape we thought the document should take.[10] The idea is that the US Government should put out such a statement

[7] The Treasury's draft, 'Statisticians and Economists in the Civil Service', circulated in late June 1945 is on T217/205.

[8] Joint Memorandum by the Board of Trade and Economic Section, 'Overseas Financial Policy in Stage III', 9 July 1945, T236/436. On Watts' work see below, p. 111.

[9] See above, p. 5.

[10] The draft appears as the annex to 'Article VII, Continuation of Informal Talks with American officials, 8th meeting, 21 June 1945', FO371/45680.

on its own responsibility (but in fact after agreement had been reached with us on the text). This statement would then be the subject of a preliminary conference which would then instruct a group of experts to draw up a detailed convention on the basis of the principles agreed at the preliminary conference, the convention itself being the subject of a full final conference. Our statement of principles is, of course, put forward without commitment, merely as an illustration of the form which such a statement might take, etc. etc. Nevertheless it was only put forward after consultation with the Chancellor of the Exchequer and the President of the Board of Trade and in fact it marks a very definite step forward in the negotiations. The statement covers commercial policy, commodity policy and cartel policy in a quite unexceptional manner. It does, however, also have a section on Employment Policy. It suggests that the proposed International Trade Organisation should cover the Trade Aspects of Employment Policy as well as Commercial Policy, Commodity Policy and Cartel Policy, and that the multilateral convention should include the pledge on the part of the member countries to maintain employment at home. This seems to me to be all wrong, and Marcus Fleming and I have done our best to persuade Lionel Robbins that it is wrong. Of course, we all want to get an international recognition of the fact that it is the international duty of countries to maintain their demand for others' goods. But it is quite wrong to connect this specially with the International Trade Organisation, for two reasons:-*First*, Employment Policy concerns monetary policy just as much as, if not more than, trade policy. It should, therefore, form the main task of the Economic and Social Council of the new world organisation to co-ordinate action on employment policy. This task has already been recognised as belonging to the Economic and Social Council, and we should not therefore set up the International Trade Organisation as a rival in this field. *Secondly*, there is a very dangerous trend of thought in the USA, of which Will Clayton in the State Department may be taken as the symbol, that the way to cure unemployment is to have stable exchange rates and free trade rather than (what is much nearer the truth) that the only way to achieve the conditions in which one can establish freer trade and more stable exchange rates is for countries to adopt suitable domestic policies for maintaining employment. There is already some sign of this in the preamble to Bretton Woods where it is implied that one of the main objects of stable exchanges is to achieve a higher level of employment and there is no hint of the fact that it is only if countries like the USA successfully maintain employment at home that we shall be able to stabilise exchange rates. My fear is that if employment policy is made a central feature of the trade convention we should get the cart before the horse once more and shall find the emphasis on the fact that we want free trade to give employment rather than that countries like the USA must take domestic measures to maintain employment if they want other countries to reduce trade barriers. My own view of the correct course is (i) that the trade convention should only have a passing reference to employment policy in its preamble and (ii) that the Trade Conference should pass a resolution saying that the successful operation of the trade convention depends upon domestic policies for full employment and asking the Economic and Social Council to get on with this subject.

The week has been a very busy one in the matter of establishments. First, A. J. Brown has joined the Section this week. He has started to read all the Article VII, Stage III, Reparations, etc., etc. papers. His main work will be on our projected periodical Survey of Overseas Economic conditions.[11] Secondly, Marcus Fleming is definitely inclining towards the Economic Section in preference to the Cassel chair at the London School of Economics. It will be marvellous if he stays. He will, however, be giving up an academic offer which in his case is very unlikely to recur. He feels therefore that he is making a final choice between the academic way of life and public service, and I have spent some time in consultation with Brook and Bridges in arranging for him a definite assurance of continuing employment in Whitehall at the sort of work in which he is interested, if he decides to stay. Bridges has been absolutely first-rate in helping on all this. What a friend the Economic Section has in him! Thirdly, I have written to MacDougall who is at present in Moscow with the UK delegation to the Reparations Commission offering him the job of being in charge of Employment Policy in the Section. I do hope he will accept. If I could get Fleming, MacDougall and Sayers as the three seniors to deal with External Economic Problems, Employment Policy and General Questions respectively, I should have a real team. Fourthly, I have drafted some notes for Bridges on the Treasury Memorandum on Economists and Statisticians in the Civil Service and have sent them across to Campion in the Central Statistical Office to see how he reacts to them.[12]

This week I have made a start with my plan for doing an hour's work before breakfast on real economics. I have this week read offprints of three articles by Hicks on Consumers' Surplus and a Ms. note which he has sent me on the consumers' surplus questions about Gas and Electricity which I asked in my recent review of Lerner's *Economics of Control.* I am sure that Hicks is right in asserting that one must rehabilitate the use of Consumers' Surplus to deal with welfare economics, and his notes on the subject are a real treat to read.[13]

## *16 July 1945*

This week Bridges held a meeting of the Budget Committee to discuss a paper by Gregg on the restoration of the Income Tax allowances and the

[11] See below, p. 121.

[12] Not found.

[13] The three articles were: 'The Rehabilitation of Consumers' surplus', *Review of Economic Studies*, Vol. 8 (February 1941), pp. 108–16; 'Consumers' Surplus and Index-numbers', *Review of Economic Studies*, Vol. 9 (1942), pp. 126–37, and 'The Four Consumers' Surpluses', *Review of Economic Studies*, Vol. 11 (1943), pp. 31–41. For Meade's questions see *The Collected Papers of James Meade*, Vol. II, p. 43. Meade himself later provided an answer to these questions in his 'The Optimal Balance between Economies of Scale and Variety of Products: an Illustrative Model', *Economica*, Vol. 41 (November 1974), pp. 359–67 (*The Collected Papers of James Meade*, Vol. II, chapter 11).

winding up of the post-war credits.[14] Broadly speaking the idea is to restore the personal allowances but not to restore (at any rate completely) the earned income allowances. This is to be combined with a reduction in the standard rate of income tax, such that broadly speaking the taxpayer would enjoy tax reductions equivalent to the post-war credit proportion of his tax payment. The post-war credits would then be stopped. Another idea is that, in order to avoid high marginal rates of income tax on the lowest taxpayers, there should be a two-tier graduation of reduced rates on the first slices of taxable income instead of, as at present, a single reduced rate before the standard rate of tax is imposed. There are a number of points in all this which disquiet me. First, I cannot believe that in the near future when the inflationary pressures are so great it is wise to reduce taxation as extensively as is contemplated. Secondly, it seems particularly inappropriate to wind up the post-war credits at such a time, since their existence is presumably worth something to the taxpayer; and it should therefore be possible to get away now with rather less tax reduction if the income tax credits were maintained. Thirdly, I would like to see the income tax credit maintained as a more or less permanent feature. The revenue representing the credits could be paid to a special fund and the credits released at times when it was necessary to stimulate personal expenditure in the interests of employment policy. Fourthly, we still have to discuss all this in terms of taking a decision this autumn as to what shall start to happen in April 1946. The difficulties of prompt adjustment because of PAYE are considered insuperable. This is alarming. It means that changes in the income tax can never be used as a prompt means of control of the general inflation-deflation situation.

The whole of Tuesday, morning and afternoon, was taken up with the second meeting of the Census of Distribution Committee. We continued to discuss the institutions from which we should seek evidence and the sort of evidence which we should ask them to give. It becomes more and more apparent that the whole thing is merely a very tedious drill to be gone through in the attempt to persuade the small shopkeepers to submit themselves to a Census. There seems to be no other interest which does not positively welcome the idea.[15]

The work on forecasting the national income has now at last started in earnest. Brittain of the Treasury wants to revise the Treasury estimates of post-war budgetary commitments and taxable capacity and for this purpose wants to have estimates of post-war taxable income. He has asked the Central Statistical Office to prepare these estimates. Tress is representing the Economic Section in this work and we are taking the opportunity to get the estimates done in a way which simultaneously will provide the estimates of 'target national income' for employment policy purposes.[16]

The great news of the week from the point of view of the future

[14] On 11 July: Bridges, 'Budget Committee', 10 July 1945, T171/372. Gregg's paper is in the same volume.

[15] The incomplete set of minutes of the Census of Distribution Committee in BT70/99 does not include this meeting on 10 July 1945.

[16] See below, p. 110.

Economic Section is that Marcus Fleming has turned down the offer of the Cassel Chair at the London School of Economics and has decided to stay on in the Economic Section. This is very great news. He is extremely able and very nice to work with. He has a most acute analytical brain and his strongest point is just that faculty of constructive criticism which is needed when we are examining proposals for economic policy. This week also I have heard from Sayers that he will probably join the Section, but he has raised a number of points which I am now trying to fix up with the Treasury establishments division.

Friday, Saturday and Sunday were spent in Oxford where Margaret, Bridget and I stayed with the Principal in Hertford College. The purpose of my visit was a Conference at Jesus College at which a number of men from the Foreign Service, the Colonial Service and the Indian Civil Service were taking a week-end 'refresher' course to inform them about economic developments here. Lionel Robbins was in the chair and gave a first introductory talk on the general domestic and external economic position. John Maud gave a talk, which was a general survey of what had been done in domestic reconstruction since Woolton became Minister of Reconstruction. I gave a talk on Employment Policy. Eady gave a sombre account of our very strained external financial position. Pepler gave a talk on the problems of Town and Country planning, and Helmore described the difficulties of achieving the required expansion in our export trade. I think that the week-end was a real success, and it is certainly a very good idea that the Foreign Service people should be informed of our economic problems; and they showed a very keen interest in the problems.

On Sunday evening I was asked round by Ogilvie (the Principal of Jesus College) to call. Mrs Ogilvie is a member of the Population Commission; and they have apparently been looking at the chapter which I wrote on Population in the League of Nations' *World Economic Survey*.[17] She is dead keen on doing something to raise the fertility rate; but as far as I can make out neither she nor any other member of the Royal Commission have yet had any very bright ideas as to what exactly might be done. Sir Reginald Leeper, our Ambassador at Athens, was visiting the Ogilvies; and he entertained us with some amusing accounts of Churchill's visit to Athens last Christmas when the fighting in Athens was still in progress. Ogilvie himself seems to have lost all interest in Economics. He was, however, very interested in the problem of providing 'refresher courses' for Civil Servants in the Universities and discussed this at some length with Sinker, who has just been appointed at the Treasury as Director of Education for the Home Civil Service and who was attending our week-end conference with the Foreign Office people.

## *22 July 1945*

I have prepared a note on the future of income tax deferred credits, the main points in which are to argue: (1) that as a long-run measure we may

[17] The Royal Commission on Population, which had been set up in March 1944, and reported in June 1949 (Cmd. 7695); League of Nations, *World Economic Survey 1938/39*. Geneva, 1939, Chapter VI.

well want a permanent system of deferred tax credits in order, by the rate of their release, to help to control the total national expenditure in the interests of employment policy; (2) that they may be essential if, for technical reasons, it is impossible to vary frequently and rapidly the rates and allowances of the income tax so that control of expenditure by direct variation of taxation is out of the question; (3) that in the short run it is most inappropriate to wind them up since the immediate future will be a period when, for political reasons, tax concessions will be necessary while for the control of inflation high taxation should be maintained, so that to remove from taxpayers an advantage (namely a promise of repayment of part of their taxes) which in no way helps the inflationary situation is out of place; and (4) that it might be possible, for example, to restore half the allowances under the income tax and to maintain the system of deferred tax credits on a different basis, namely by allowing as a deferred credit the first X per cent of each taxpayer's tax liability with an upper limit of £Y or merely by allowing as a deferred credit the first £Z of each taxpayer's tax liability. My note will be circulated to Sir Richard Hopkins, Keynes and Bridges;[18] but I fear that I shall be away on leave when the matter next comes up for discussion.

I find myself gradually playing the role of a Director. That is to say, I spend less time writing and thinking myself and more time directing the thoughts and writings of the other members of the Section. In particular this week, Tress's work on the forecasting of the National Income and Miss Watts's work on the Balance of Payments. Tress is going ahead with the Central Statistical Office estimating the probable taxable income in 1950 for the purpose of estimating the probable burden of post-war taxation in view of the various post-war commitments for budgetary expenditure.[19] The idea is to combine this work with estimates of the 'target' national income for employment policy purposes. This week there has been considerable coming and going over the assumptions to be made about the future course of prices – these comings and goings being partly diplomatic and partly scientific. The diplomatic problem has been due to the tendency of the Central Statistical Office and of Campion in particular to go cap in hand to the Treasury to ask what assumptions should be made for their statistical computations, a tendency which is strongly resisted by Tress as representative of the Economic Section, which holds that it is at least as responsible as the Treasury for deciding what are likely to be the future trends. The scientific point is that future prices will themselves depend upon other factors:- (a) the wage-rate level combined with (b) the distribution of income between wages and other factor incomes and (c) the output per head of labour will determine what may be called 'the factor cost of UK output'; (d) the level of indirect taxes and subsidies and (e) the terms of trade between the prices of our exports and our imports will then determine 'the market price of UK expenditure'. The point is that all these factors must be assumed to move in a self-consistent way. The idea

[18] Meade, 'Income Tax Credits', 20 July 1945, sent by Robbins on 23 July, T171/372 and Meade Papers 3/10.

[19] For the outcome of this work see below, pp. 134–5.

is to consult with the Ministry of Labour about the probable future of wage-rates, so that it would be folly then to ask the Treasury independently what to assume about prices unless indirect taxes and subsidies are assumed to be put at any level to make these various assumptions self-consistent.

Miss Watts is now going to go ahead with forecasting our balance of payments over the next five years or so. This is an essential ingredient in our forecasts for employment policy of the national income and expenditure. It is also certain that we shall want figures of this kind for the purpose of our discussions with the Americans shortly on Stage III (i.e. what happens after the Japanese War when Lend-Lease comes to an end).[20]

I have also had some talk with John Maud about the future work of the Section on Building and Housing. This is clearly going to be one of the most important issues of economic policy and is most intimately connected with, for example, employment policy. Maud is just setting up an official committee on Housing, and I believe that we ought to be on it. He explains that there is a very delicate position on the Housing Committee and is most anxious that its membership should not be enlarged. Partly, I think, his hesitation is due to the temperamental angularities of Chester, who would naturally be our representative on this subject. Chester will be going soon. So I have accepted the position for the time being; but I shall return to the charge sometime.[21]

I had lunch with Forge of *The Economist*. Some remarks which he has been making in *The Economist* on the question of the valuation of stock in trade in company accounts have been causing a good deal of correspondence.[22] Clearly it is not necessary that one should want to put down in a company's balance sheet the same figure for the valuation of stocks as is used to compute the company's profit. And from the point of view of statistics of the national income and expenditure it is essential that sooner or later we should be able to measure net investment in stocks (i.e. the value of the increment of stocks) and to *compute profits on the same consistent basis* on the other side of the national income and expenditure account. The ideal procedure would be for all companies at all times to show their stock in trade in the balance sheet at the current price (i.e. at $\Sigma p_0q_0$ where $p_0$ and $q_0$ are the current prices and amounts of each item of stock). They should also show as a footnote to the account $\Sigma p_{-1}q_0$ or $\Sigma p_0q_{-1}$ or preferably both. Investment in stocks could be measured then not as $\Sigma p_0q_0 - \Sigma p_{-1}q_{-1}$ (i.e. the change in the stock valuation from one balance sheet to another) but as either $\Sigma p_{-1}q_0 - \Sigma p_{-1}q_{-1} = \Sigma(q_0{-}q_{-1})p_{-1}$ (i.e. the increment of stock at values at the beginning of the period) or as $\Sigma p_0q_0 - \Sigma p_0q_{-1} = \Sigma(q_0{-}q_{-1})p_0$ (i.e. the increment of stock valued at the end of the period) or best of all as the average of these two. One could also adjust the actual profits as shown to any desired re-adjustment of the company's stock valuations. Forge, I think, is going to suggest in *The Economist* that

[20] Watts attended meetings (chaired by Keynes) on 'Stage III Balance of Payments (Statistical Requirements)' on 31 July and 1 August before the Japanese war, and Lend-Lease, ended abruptly in August (see below, p. 114).

[21] Maud's Committee was not in fact set up.

[22] 'Valuation of stock-in-trade', *The Economist*, 16 June 1945, pp. 821–2; 'The Cohen Report', *The Economist*, 21 July 1945, pp. 88–9.

all companies should show their stock values in their balance sheets at the actual market prices; that they should not, however, add to profit any increase in stock values due to price rises but should add this to a 'stock replacement account'; and that in each balance sheet they should show their stocks not only at end-year prices but also at end-previous-year prices.[23] This would avoid all need to squabble about 'first-in first-out' or 'last-in last-out' principles and would give enormously greater information to the economist and statistician.

Tinbergen has turned up from Holland with a delegation of three or four other Dutch economists or bureaucrats (whose names I could not catch) on an official delegation to study our methods of price control. Marcus Fleming and I spent an afternoon talking to them. Tinbergen is delightfully naive at times. He cannot believe that two civil servants from two different governments should talk to each other with any greater reserve than two scientists outside government service. Thus he kept on asking me whether Ministers in this country were going to have a Capital Levy or not!! Later Tinbergen will turn in Holland to planning the national income and expenditure in advance. He came to supper with us during the week and we asked Mr and Mrs Tress to meet him. I wanted Tress to meet him as they will both be concerned with forecasting national incomes. Luckily, however, the economists (as so rarely happens) behaved themselves and we talked practically no economics. Tinbergen described war-time conditions in Holland; and Tress (elementary school-secondary school-external London degree) and I (preparatory school-public school-ancient university) tried to tell Tinbergen something of our education problems. A very pleasant evening.

I went to call on the Robbins' family one evening after supper. John Jewkes was staying there, and Arnold Plant and his wife came in. On this occasion the economists misbehaved badly and talked about the Distribution of Industry. Jewkes and, still more, Plant were poking fun at the sort of attempt which Douglas Jay and others in the Board of Trade are trying to make to get industry to go to the Development Areas.[24] Certainly some of the instances are very ridiculous and, indeed, it is depressing to hear of businesses refusing to undertake development at all rather than go into areas where they believe that the addition to their costs would be excessive. But I wish these *laissez-faire* economists would go to the root of the matter. If the pricing system were allowed to function unhampered, depressed areas would in the end look after themselves by the following mechanism. The wage-rates would decline in the depressed areas (in the absence of unemployment benefit and of trade unions); and this would give a great incentive both to labour to get out of the areas and to enterprise to come in to take advantage of the cheap labour. In the absence of such a mechanism it is not sufficient just to sit back and do nothing. The *laissez-faire* economists should make a head-on attack on the trade unions for

[23] See 'Reform of Company Accounts' and 'And Consolidated Accounts', *The Economist*, 28 July 1945, pp. 126–8, 130.

[24] On Jay's efforts, see his *Change and Fortune, A Political Record*. London: Hutchinson, 1980, Chapter 6, and Hugh Dalton, *The Fateful Years: Memoirs 1931–1945*. London: Frederick Muller, 1957, chapter 29.

maintaining wage-rates in the depressed areas and on unemployment benefit etc. What one must do is: (i) make wages as flexible as possible and in particular avoid nationally fixed wage-rates; (ii) make unemployment benefit conditional upon being prepared to move geographically as well as occupationally; (iii) give general financial inducements for industry as a whole to set up in the depressed areas; but (iv) avoid all particular interventions which involve treating each case on its merits (i.e. arbitrarily).

Campion, Colonel Walker (our establishments officer) and I had a long talk with Helsby and Miss Sharp of the Treasury Establishments on the general question of the recruitment of economists and statisticians to government service. Miss Sharp seemed very reasonable; but Helsby wanted to raise all the old points and seemed quite inflexible. We are now putting in a list of the offers which we have made with the intention of getting the Civil Service Commissioners to OK them. This is a matter which the Treasury in its great inefficiency seems to have overlooked! But in spite of having to argue every point at least ten times with the Treasury establishments there is no doubt that progress is in fact being made.

This week Miss Howell, who has just taken her degree at Liverpool University, arrived in the Economic Section to be my personal assistant. It will be a tremendous relief to have someone to look after my papers, engagements, telephone etc.; and it certainly marks a very definite stage in one's career to have a personal assistant at one's beck and call!

# 10

## August 1945

### *26 August 1945*

We went away for three weeks' holiday in Cornwall on 26 July, – the very day on which the election results were announced! We came back to a totally different world: the UK had a Labour Government with a huge majority;[1] the future of the world had been totally altered by the dropping of two atomic bombs; and the war in the Far East was over.[2] The situation when I got back was quite transformed. In the first place, the coincidence of the end of the war with the beginning of the new Labour Government has put a strain of work on the central Whitehall machine such as I cannot remember since I came to Whitehall in 1940. The whole of the machinery and policy for the transition from war to peace must be put into operation months before it was expected to be necessary; all the Cabinet committees have had to be reconstituted and ministerial responsibilities re-allocated (a matter which has given rise to some remarkable jockeyings for position); many major issues of policy which are of urgent importance have needed to be reconsidered or reconfirmed; Lend-Lease has come to an abrupt end and urgent attention has had to be given to the problem of external finance;[3] the council of UNRRA and the interim commission charged at San Francisco to set up the new World Organisation are in session in London;[4] the Potsdam conference between the Big Three was in session when the change of government took place and all its results have now to be worked out and to be applied in detail.[5]

The result of the elections was certainly a complete surprise to me. It is clearly much too early to be able to say what the main results of the Labour Government may be; but as an incurable optimist, I will note what (if things go well) might be its main advantages in internal and in external policy. In internal policy there is already a conflict between the different main

[1] The results of the general election on 5 July, announced on 26 July to allow for the collection of servicemen's ballots etc., were: Labour, 393; Conservative, 212; Liberal, 12; Others, 11.

[2] After the bombing of the cities of Hiroshima and Nagasaki on 6 and 9 August, Japan surrendered on 14 August.

[3] On 17 August 1945 President Truman decided on the basis of a strict reading of the legislation to end Lend-Lease immediately, a decision communicated to Britain on 20 August.

[4] Their meetings took place on 7–25 August and 16 August–27 October respectively.

[5] The Potsdam Conference ran from 17 July to 2 August.

meanings that may be given to the idea of Socialist economic planning. Broadly speaking, there are on the one hand those (led by Cripps at the Board of Trade) who believe in the quantitative planning of the economy commodity by commodity. Such a Gosplan could not, in my opinion, be carried out without socialising all or most industries (which is expressly not the policy of the Labour Party)[6] and, possibly, without losing freedom of choice of consumers and workers as to what they will consume and what they will work at. On the other hand is what I think of as the Liberal-Socialist solution under which certain industries which must in any case be large-scale monopolies (e.g. electricity, railways, etc.) are completely socialised and run on 'market' principles of pricing and costing, while the rest of industry is made to compete by anti-restrictive practice legislation. Steps are taken to maintain total aggregate demand – partly (i.e. in the case of the socialised sector of the economy) by quantitative planning and programming and partly by planning certain categories of demand by such means as tax and subsidy policy, the rate of interest, the rate of exchange, etc. to see that private investment, consumers' expenditure or exports are of the desired magnitude. I am pretty sure that Morrison, who most fortunately as Lord President is the Economic Section's Minister, is going to be the leader of this second school of thought.

In the general jockeying for position among the top Ministers this conflict is already apparent. Cripps made an effort to absorb the Economic Section and the Central Statistical Office, lock, stock and barrel into the Board of Trade and to become responsible for Employment Policy – a clear indication to me that he thinks of all this in terms of planning the real resources of the community in the sense of deciding how many pairs of boots, how many shirts, how many bicycles, etc., etc. shall be produced, imported and exported in each of the next five years. Morrison has very strongly resisted the idea that we should be absorbed into the Board of Trade (which would indeed be absolutely fatal since it would cut us off completely from the Treasury and from questions of finance). This may, of course, be due solely to the fact that he obviously intends that the Lord President's Committee should revert to the central position which it enjoyed under Anderson and which it lost under Attlee. He regards himself as the central economic co-ordinator and is not going to give up the Economic Section.[7]

Incidentally he had a curious conversation with me about the Economic Section. He first hinted that he wanted to find employment in the Govt Service for Schumacher. I made it clear that on grounds of S's temperament and background and, above all, on the grounds that I had already largely made up the team and allocated the topics I did not think that it would do. Morrison went on to ask whether the members of the

[6] See the Party's manifesto, *Let Us Face the Future*, April 1945.

[7] For Cripps' initiative see Armstrong to Blaker, Padmore and Pimlott, 19 August 1945 concerning a meeting of the Prime Minister, Chancellor of the Exchequer, Lord President and President of the Board of Trade on 20 August to discuss the future of the Economic Section and the CSO, T273/298; on the Lord President's Committee and its wartime role see S. S. Wilson, *The Cabinet Office to 1945*. London: HMSO, 1975, Chapter 9, para. 950.

Section all agreed on the need for the state to undertake the sort of interventions of which I had been speaking to him earlier in our conversation. He was clearly worried with the idea – which is certainly widespread and due to the pre-war reputations of Robbins, Jewkes, Dennison etc. and which has moreover some element of truth in it – that the Economic Section would be *laissez-faire* and anti-economic planning. I replied (a) that we were all agreed on the main lines of policy to maintain aggregate demand and would probably all in fact welcome as economists any extra drive which the new government might give to this type of policy (e.g. by greater willingness to vary the rate of income tax as a means of influencing consumers' expenditure – a device which Morrison himself on his own initiative mentioned to me without any prompting much to my delight, confirming me in my opinion that he is a Liberal-Socialist); (b) that we were all agreed in the main on external economic issues; but (c) that there would be more difference of opinion on the question of industrial organisation, all economists agreeing that at the one extreme there were certain activities which should be publicly run and that at the other there were industries which should compete, but each drawing the dividing line at a different spot. I added, however, that he could take it for granted that if it were decided to socialise an industry which some of the economists would themselves have placed in the private enterprise sector, he could nevertheless rely on the fact that the decision would be loyally accepted and that the economists would then turn their attention to the scientific question of the most economic way to take the industry over and to run it. We should give him economic advice, but no political advice. The outcome of all this at the moment is that there was a meeting of Ministers with the PM at which, after much talk by Cripps about complete planning and considerable opposition by Morrison, Bridges was asked to put forward a scheme of organisation for preparing and carrying out a five-year economic plan. Bridges has accordingly sent a letter to Norman Brook, John Maud, Campion, myself, Gilbert (of the Treasury), Woods (who has taken Overton's place as Permanent Secretary at the Board of Trade) and Ince (of the Ministry of Labour).[8] This really suggests a development of the machinery which was already being set up in embryo form under the previous government to deal with Employment Policy. There is to be a high level steering committee of officials to prepare and present to Ministers an overall five-year plan of the main uses of our economic resources. I have drafted, after consultation with Dennison, Fleming, Tress and Chantler, an answer to Bridges trying to fill in the details a little bit so as to make it a machinery for a Liberal-Socialist Plan rather than an authoritarian Gosplan in terms of quantities of commodities etc.[9]

In internal economic policy we have given Morrison advice on the day-to-day issues as they have come up. In particular, Tress had under the previous Government just finished the Economic Section's General Survey on the Economic Situation at the end of the German War. Morrison

[8] Bridges to Meade, 22 August 1945, T273/298 and T230/18. The Ministerial meeting had taken place the previous day (21 August).

[9] See below, page 122.

has not only circulated this (with a short supplementary note on the effect of the end of the Japanese War) to departments for their comments. He has put it down for discussion at the Lord President's Committee and is obviously intending to make it the occasion of a grand 'second reading' discussion among Ministers on the urgent economic problems of the day. Tress and I spent an hour with the Lord President briefing him on these.[10] Earlier in the week John Maud and I had spent an hour with Morrison discussing with him the line which he should take in his closing speech in the debate on the address. I suggested that he should divide this into two main sections – the first dealing with the grim and immediate economic difficulties which had got to be surmounted in the immediate future and the second with the long-run economic reforms which the Labour Party was planning now to bring to fruition as soon as present circumstances permitted. In the first group, I placed (i) the overall shortage of manpower; (ii) the misuse and temporary unemployment of certain pockets of labour which was bound to occur because of the dislocation due to the enormously rapid shifts which the practically simultaneous end of the war in Europe and the Pacific would bring about; (iii) the very grave problem of our foreign balance of payments and the continued austerity which the necessary restriction of imports and expansion of exports would entail; (iv) the problem of controlling inflation during the transitional period in which there would be great shortages of goods and abundance of monetary purchasing power; (v) the world food shortage; and (vi) the coal shortage. In the second category I placed (i) the intention to carry out an effect[ive] Employment Policy; (ii) Social Security; (iii) Industrial Organisation, – covering on the one hand the intention to socialise certain major industries which would have to be large-scale monopolies in any case and, on the other hand, the intention to prevent restrictive practices and to enforce competition in the unsocialised sector; and (iv) the intention to control the use of land in the interests of the community. I was extremely gratified to learn that Morrison had used this outline fruitfully for his speech.[11] It was on just the same lines as these six immediate grim difficulties that we have briefed Morrison for the discussion of our Survey at the Lord President's Committee. Incidentally I was called down to the Lord President's Committee on Friday to hear the discussion of our Survey, but this item of the Agenda was never reached. Instead I heard Ben Smith (the Minister of Food) give a good summary of our food position; and I must say that the discussion seemed to me to be on a very sensible and intelligent level. It was by no means the disorderly and unintelligent bear-garden which I have been told is the character of many Ministerial meetings.[12]

The Section has also just written briefs to the Lord President on many particular issues which have come up to his Committee – a Hydro-Electric

[10] EC(S)(45)23 Final Revise, 'Survey of the General Economic Situation', 25 July 1945, and EC(S)(45)26, 'Survey of the General Economic Situation: A Supplementary Note', 20 August 1945 (T230/18) circulated to the Lord President's Committee as LP(45)138 and LP(45)139 (CAB71/21). For the Lord President's briefing see Tress to Lord President, 'Survey of the Economic Situation (LP(45)138 and LP(45)139)', T230/162.

[11] *House of Commons Debates*, Vol. 413, 21 August 1945, cols. 573–81.

[12] LP(45) 29th meeting, 24 August 1945, CAB71/19; see also below, p. 128.

Power Scheme for Scotland; the Wool Agreement recently reached with the Dominions; the future of the Regional Boards;[13] and (for discussion at the Cabinet) the effect of the early introduction of the higher school-leaving age on the manpower and building shortages (teachers and schools).[14]

I have also asked Philip Chantler to prepare a few notes on the issues of economic principle involved in the question of nationalising coal. My idea is to stimulate a general discussion throughout the Section on these issues, so that our ideas may be crystallising gradually in time to advise the Lord President when the issues come to his committee.[15]

In external policy it is difficult to say yet what is likely to be the effect of the new government. One real danger is that so much attention will be given to internal reform that the external economic problems will not receive due attention. (I already feel myself – who am, I believe, essentially an internationalist – prone to this temptation.) And yet not only, with the passing of Lend-Lease, is our external economic position our gravest immediate headache, but also from the long-run point of view our welfare depends probably more essentially upon a sound and lasting economic and political settlement internationally than upon our internal policy. Apart from this, the effect of the Labour Government upon the external economic settlement will depend very largely upon whether the Liberal-Socialists or the Gosplanites win the internal struggle. If the Liberal-Socialists win out, an economic settlement with the USA *à la* Article VII would not be impossible. Prices and costs would exist and would be used to measure discrimination and protection in those trades which were conducted by the state; the rate of exchange would be a meaningful price and the Bretton Woods rules about exchange rates would be applicable; and much trade would in fact be left to private initiative. If the Gosplanites won, it would seem difficult to attach much meaning to the Article VII discussions, since there would be no internal system of prices and costs on which degrees of protection or discrimination could be measured. If the Liberal-Socialists win internally, the result of the election might exercise a very wholesome effect on the international political scene. There will then be an alternative progressive socialist but liberal government to set

13 The Lord President's Committee discussed these topics on 21 and 24 August 1945 (LP(45) 28th and 29th meetings, CAB71/19), when they considered a memorandum by the Secretary of State for Scotland; a joint memorandum by the Chancellor, the Minister of Supply, and the Parliamentary Undersecretary for the Dominions of the previous government (on the Wool Agreement); and a memorandum by the President of the Board of Trade (on the regional boards) (LP(45)140, CAB71/21; CP(45)31, CAB66/66; LP(45)145, CAB71/21). For the Section's briefs see Chantler to Lord President, 'North of Scotland Hydro-Electricity Board Constructional Scheme No. 2: Memorandum by the Secretary of State for Scotland (LP(45)140)', 28 August 1945, CAB124/428, and Dennison to Lord President, 'The Future of the Regional Boards and of the National Production Advisory Council (LP(45)145)', 23 August 1945, CAB124/349.

14 The Cabinet discussed the raising of the school leaving age (to 15 years as from 1 April 1947) on 23 August, deciding that the Lord President should appoint an *ad hoc* committee to examine the practical implications; the Cabinet subsequently (on 4 September) endorsed the Lord President's recommendation that the school leaving age should be raised (CM(45) 25th and 28th meetings, CAB128/1).

15 See below, pp. 122–3.

against authoritarian Russia. The forces of the left in Europe will have a free as well as a totalitarian point of attraction. We might perhaps even set a bridge between the United States, with which we should share all the fundamental English-speaking ideas about individual liberty, and the Russians, since we should not be a purely *laissez-faire* capitalist regime.

Meanwhile the abrupt ending of Lend-Lease has caused real trouble this week. I fear that the recriminations due to the feeling on this side of being left in an intolerably difficult position and on the other side of feeling that it is unreasonable for us to expect to live on charity after the end of the war may cause a bad atmosphere for the Article VII talks. Dalton, as Chancellor of the Exchequer, has circulated to a small group of Ministers a paper (which is in reality Keynes') on a solution of our external financial position in Stage III. It is very like the solution proposed in the paper by Keynes of which I have written in my entries of 1 July and 8 July this year, except – as a result of our intervention as recorded in those entries – that he accepts the view that as we gradually unblock the sterling balances they should be unblocked for all purposes of payment in all currencies.[16] Marcus Fleming wrote a brief for Morrison on this financial settlement, and he and I went to discuss it with Morrison for an hour. I have spent a great deal of time preparing a brief for Norman Brook which he sent on to the Prime Minister on the whole of this financial settlement in relation to Article VII. My thesis being: We can't do without American assistance in Stage III. We shan't get such assistance except in return for implementing Article VII. In any case we have certain great advantages to gain from Article VII such as: (i) possibility that a country in a balance of payments difficulty can depreciate currency or impose import restrictions while other countries cannot do so; (ii) Scarce Currency Article [VII] of Bretton Woods Agreement; (iii) untied loans by USA through the reconstruction bank; (iv) clearance of barriers against our exports which we must expand by at least 50 per cent. The main question to look at is whether the latest American proposals for commercial policy can be made to bring us these advantages.[17] Unfortunately the answer to this last question is now not as obvious as it was. During the three weeks of my leave events had moved fast and had much deteriorated. The Americans, headed by Clayton of the State Department, had produced very nearly final proposals on commercial policy.[18] These were incidentally very satisfactory in so far as Employment Policy is concerned in that they suggest a form of commitment to which nations would subscribe for taking domestic measures to maintain employment which goes miles beyond anything which the Americans have previously been willing to contemplate. But on commercial policy they show a terrible backsliding in that the Americans propose that the

[16] Keynes' paper, 'The Present Overseas Financial Position of the UK', 13 August 1945 (T247/50 and *The Collected Writings of John Maynard Keynes*, Vol. 24, pp. 377–98) was circulated by Dalton on 16 August 1945 as CP(45)112 (CAB129/1). For Meade's intervention, see above, pp. 103–4 and 105.

[17] 'Article VII and the Overseas Financial Position of the United Kingdom', 22 August 1945, forwarded to Attlee by Brook on 23 August 1945 (T230/276).

[18] The American 'Proposal to Establish an International Trade Organisation' was handed over by Clayton on 4 August 1945 (BT64/414).

multilateral commercial policy convention should cover everything (including the abolition of imperial preferences) except tariffs, which would be covered only to the extent that the signatory countries would commit themselves to negotiate bilateral treaties covering tariffs on MFN principles. They admit, of course, that the obligations under the multilateral part of the convention would be conditional upon the effective negotiation of such treaties. Nevertheless the difficulties are immense; the time needed for negotiations would be very long; and the whole psychology is wrong, since the great creditor nation the USA would be asking all other countries to undertake a single dramatic renunciation of their favourite protective devices, whereas the US tariff would be the subject of a series of nibbles. Moreover, the whole multilateral convention would, in my opinion, be threatened. We should find it very difficult not to insist that tariff-preferences should be treated bilaterally with tariffs; and in their turn countries which had relied mainly on, say, quota restrictions might well insist that quotas should be treated on a par with tariffs and preferences; and so on, until no part of the multilateral convention remained. Meanwhile Keynes and the financial pundits are to go to Washington to try to negotiate a financial arrangement for Stage III;[19] and the commercial policy pundits are only to follow later if the Americans refuse (as I am willing to bet that they will) to talk about other financial assistance without simultaneously talking about the implementation of Article VII.

The Interim Commission set up by the San Francisco Conference to prepare the way for setting up the new United Nations World Organisation is now meeting in London.[20] Marcus Fleming and I went out to dinner with Gladwyn Jebb (who is head of the Interim Commission's Secretariat), David Owen (also of the Secretariat), F. L. McDougall of Australia House and three of the Americans (Stinebower, Fowler and Tomlinson) who are interested. The subject of our talk was the Economic and Social Council. Whether it is really effective will depend upon whether it has real powers to co-ordinate on such matters as the international aspects of employment policy; and this will depend upon such things as whether its commissions are academic study groups or effective bodies representing the national treasuries and the other specialised international organisations (such as the proposed International Monetary Fund and the Bank), whether its constitutional relations with these bodies are close enough, whether its geographical position is the same as that of these other bodies, etc. We had an interesting conversation on all these matters. The Executive Committee of the Interim Commission is now about to set up a series of sub-committees to deal with the various aspects of the world organisation, one is to be on the Economic and Social Council and one on relations with other specialised international organisations. Spurred on by Marcus Fleming I called on Ronald, Hall-Patch and Ward in the FO, only to find out literally nothing had been done in the way of preparing ideas as to who should represent the UK or what policy the representative should take on these

[19] See below, p. 132.

[20] See note 4 above.

two sub-committees. Whether or not in part or in whole as a result of this intervention, on Saturday at 12 noon a meeting was called in the FO of all departments concerned, with Philip Noel-Baker (now Minister of State) in the chair to arrange for representation and policy on all these sub-committees.[21] Clearly the Economic Section is going to be asked to play an important if unobtrusive role as far as ideas on the Economic and Social Council are concerned. Noel-Baker in the chair was a treat! His idealism and enthusiasm ran away with him. Whenever there was a choice between a cautious and an incautious line, he chose the incautious, and he seemed to want the sub-committees of the Executive Committee of the Interim Commission, set up to advise Governments on how to institute the new World Organisation, themselves to do the first ten years' work of the organisation itself!

Meanwhile in the Section we are preparing for our first Overseas Economic Survey. This might prove of great importance if we can do it well. I am sure that the present set of Ministers, with their eyes naturally on the domestic scene, might be much influenced by a readable Survey of the Overseas Economic Position which brought the external factors before them. I have had a meeting of the people concerned in the Section to see that A. J. Brown is properly briefed in preparing the Survey.[22]

I went out to lunch with Alec Spearman, the Conservative MP who is to my knowledge unique not only in being enthusiastically pro-Article VII but also in having increased his majority in the last election. He wanted to discuss points to make in the speech which he contemplates making in favour of Bretton Woods when it comes up for discussion in the House, as it is bound to do soon since we have to give notice whether we will join by December of this year.[23] (Incidentally Bevin, I am told, is resolutely opposed to Bretton Woods. There [are] going to be difficulties here, which will become involved in the Stage III Finance-Article VII complex of questions).[24]

The stream of overseas visitors to learn about our economy continues. This week I have had to lecture an Australian banker about our immediate transitional period difficulties and a Swiss bureaucrat about our Employment Policy. The Germanic heaviness and the Swiss stodginess of the latter so overcame me that I could scarcely think of anything to say.

I have had a long session with Norman Brook and Colonel Walker on Establishments questions. I want very much to get MacDougall and Sayers, and am going to sound out Tew of the Ministry of Aircraft Production again to try to strengthen our staff on the side of industrial problems. We shall have to be ready now to deal with radical measures of industrial reorganisation.

[21] Minister of State's Advisory Committee on the United Nations Organisation, Minutes of Meeting of 25 August 1945, T236/428.

[22] See below, p. 192.

[23] The debate took place on 12–13 December 1945 (*House of Commons Debates*, Vol. 417, cols. 421–558 and 641–74).

[24] Bevin had publicly expressed doubts about Bretton Woods in Parliament in June 1945: *House of Commons Debates*, Vol. 411, 4 June 1945, col. 581 (quoted in Alan Bullock, *The Life and Times of Ernest Bevin, Vol. 2, Minister of Labour 1940–1945*. London: Heinemann, 1967, p. 386). But he was to defend the agreement in the Commons debate on its ratification in December 1945 (Alan Bullock, *Ernest Bevin, Foreign Secretary*. London: Heinemann, 1983, p. 205.)

# 11

## September 1945

### *1 September 1945*

Another very full week. I have completed and sent off to Bridges the Economic Section's views on the machinery required for carrying out a five-year Economic Plan. Our general line is an official working party which will survey probable future economic developments in terms of total national income and expenditure, will assess any overall inflationary or deflationary gap, will comment on the major implications from the point of view of the impact of future events on particular regions or industries, and will present to Ministers the alternative lines of policy which they might adopt to overcome the problems. Such an Economic Survey would go, through a top-level official Steering Committee, to Ministers for broad decisions of policy and then it would become the duty either of individual departments to carry out the policy (e.g. the Treasury might be asked to adopt a tax policy to restrict or stimulate consumers' expenditure by a certain amount) or of interdepartmental working parties under the official Steering Committee to carry out the policy (e.g. a working party on Public and Private Investment might consider how to stimulate or restrict Investment to a given degree or a working party on Exchange Requirements might vary the Import Programme to a given degree).[1] Morrison sent for me to have a long talk again on the problem of Economic Planning, and I took it on me again to try to show him the difference between sensible global planning which allows a large measure of freedom and flexibility and senseless quantitative planning of output and employment in every single line. I have sent him copies of Bridges' letter and of my reply to it as a means of showing him how we are thinking of this problem. It is my intention to write to him a considerable paper on this topic, and I have actually made a series of notes for it.[2] (This by dint of working for an hour before breakfast, but not – I fear – as I had hoped on rewriting *Economic Analysis and Policy* but on the ordinary work of the Economic Section.)

Another major internal topic which will, of course, come up is the question of Nationalisation. I summoned a meeting of Dennison, Fleming, Tress, Chantler, Chester and Tom Wilson to discuss the general issues and

[1] Meade to Bridges, 29 August 1945, T230/18 and T273/298.

[2] This became 'Economic Planning', 10 October 1945, EC(S)(45)28 Second revise (T230/18, Meade Papers 3/2 and *The Collected Papers of James Meade*, Vol. I, chapter 16). On its preparation see below, p. 127.

how we should prepare our minds on the subject. The danger is, of course, that a nationalisation scheme will come forward from the Department concerned (e.g. for coal from the Ministry of Fuel and Power) when it is already in the form of a detailed bill and when the legislative time-table is such that there is no time to consider any radical changes. What we must do is to get the Lord President to persuade what he calls 'my socialising Ministers' to put forward at an early stage their ideas on the general principles which they intend to adopt for their particular schemes, so that there can be discussion of the main issues centrally and interdepartmentally. We considered these points at our meeting; then considered some of the main principles involved in such matters as Compensation, Capital Structure, Administrative Structure, Price Policy, Import and Export Policy, Capital Development Policy, etc.; then decided that Philip Chantler should finish his notes on these principles with special reference to coal[3] and that Chester should prepare some notes on these principles with special reference to Iron and Steel. By a strange coincidence we had scarcely finished our meeting before Turpin (one of Morrison's secretaries) came up to me with some papers from the Lord President on this very subject suggesting that he should call a meeting of 'my socialising Ministers'. I am to see him early next week on the subject.[4]

When I came into the office on Monday morning this week I found that a paper from the Minister of Town and Country Planning had come in to the Lord President on Compensation and Betterment to be discussed at a meeting on Tuesday [28 August] of Ministers. It was an attempt to rush through what is in essence the policy outlined in the Coalition Government's White Paper on the Control of Land Use. I briefed Morrison myself very strongly against it.[5] In the first place, on the grounds of this extraordinary theory of 'floating value' it proposes to compensate owners for only ½ of the market value of any development rights which are lost – although full market value is taken for the purpose of Death Duties. I cannot believe that it is sensible to start off with principles of compensation of that kind, when the Govt will want businessmen to undertake capital development and re-equipment in a whole series of industries which they will not socialise but which may fear that socialisation is round the corner. In the second place, the paper maintained the proposal that whenever a change in land use took place 80 per cent of the increased value of the land should be taken away in a Betterment Tax. But this is not in fact a charge on Betterment. All increments of value to land in its present use due to an act of a public authority (e.g. an improvement in the value of existing houses in an existing residential area due to the removal of factories from

[3] See below, p. 141.

[4] See below p. 130. The 'socialising Ministers' were the President of the Board of Trade, the Chancellor of the Exchequer, and the Ministers of Supply, Fuel and Power, and Transport (Cripps, Dalton, Wilmot, Shinwell, and Barnes). On the whole nationalisation programme of the Labour Government see Sir Norman Chester, *The Nationalisation of British Industry 1945–51*. London: HMSO, 1975.

[5] LP(45)134, Minister of Town and Country Planning, 'The Control of Land Use', 14 August 1945, CAB71/21; Cmd. 6537, *The Control of Land Use*, June 1944; Meade to Lord President, 'Compensation and Betterment', 27 August 1945, CAB124/382.

the residential area) go untaxed. The charge is a tax on development and when development takes place it is taxed whether the increase in value is due to social factors or to the enterprise of the landlord. In a mixed economy a large amount of development will be undertaken privately and it is most dangerous to remove 80 per cent of the incentive to develop. Good planning can only be brought about in the private enterprise sector of the economy by leaving the maximum incentive to develop but taking every necessary power to prohibit undesirable development. I suggested that a totally new scheme should be considered under which full compensation was paid and the necessary funds were raised by a general charge on all real property (e.g. on the lines of the War Damage Contribution assessed on Schedule A values). I heard before the meeting that Morrison was convinced of the need to reconsider the whole scheme; but at the meeting itself the whole thing seems to have gone through practically unchanged.[6]

Cripps this week has put in a paper to the Lord President's Committee on how to encourage Industrial Efficiency. He wants to set up a series of commissions industry by industry to review the position, these commissions being formed of the employers and employed in each industry under examination.[7] Dennison (with some changes which I suggested to his draft) briefed the Lord President to the effect that such 'self-government-in-industry' bodies were much more likely to want to consider how to make the industry profitable to them than how to make it technically efficient; that certain general overall measures (such as the restraint of restrictive practices, state encouragement for research, taxation as it affects new capital development, etc.) were most likely to encourage efficiency; and that if special enquiries were desired industry by industry they should be technical rather than economic and should be carried out by those who were not directly concerned with the industry in question.

I have attended another meeting of the Budget Committee.[8] The political pressure will clearly be for very substantial alleviations on the small incomes. The question to my mind is how much we can stand without the danger of serious inflation. Presumably the controls will be better maintained under this government than under a Conservative Government, so that the taxation defence against inflation may be less essential. Keynes being away in the USA, no one seemed at all ready to consider the probable movement in aggregate national income and in the various forms of national expenditure in order to see what was the probable degree of inflationary pressure with which we have to deal. I argued that we ought to do this, and it has rather been left to me to organise this with the CSO. There is certainly no time to do more than make a rough guess – which in any case was all that Keynes usually did! There is a real taxation problem

[6] CB(45) 1st Meeting, Ministerial Committee on Compensation and Betterment, Meeting of 28 August 1945, CAB124/382. See also below, pp. 135–6, 287.

[7] 'The Government Plan for Encouraging Industrial organisation and efficiency', 27 August 1945, LP(45)152 (CAB71/21), which was discussed at LP(45) 30th meeting, 30 August 1945 (CAB71/19).

[8] On 31 August (Bridges, 'Budget Committee', 29 August 1945, T171/372).

in the next years of this government. 100 per cent EPT [Excess Profits Tax] removes all incentive from industry to reduce costs etc., etc. 19s 6d [97½p] in the £ on the higher incomes removes incentives from businessmen and professional men. Yet if on grounds of distribution of income major relief from taxation must be given to the smaller incomes, on grounds of revenue and of inflation no great reduction in these 'disincentive' forms of taxation would appear possible. The only solution is to find a 'soak-the-rich' form of taxation with less adverse incentive effects than 100 per cent taxation of profits or high incomes. The answer, I believe, is an annual tax on capital to replace part of these excessive rates on highest incomes. Incidentally, such a tax might enable one (since it differentiates against unearned income) to avoid raising the earned income allowance above its present level and this might save much revenue. The problem of motor-car taxation has also been re-opened. I had taken the opportunity to send a letter (drafted and prompted by Chantler) to Gilbert in the Treasury strongly urging the case for reconsidering this question in the interests of encouraging the mass-production of a rather higher horse-power car in the interests of the export trade.[9] This matter was discussed and may be re-opened.

Chester (with some suggestions from me) has prepared a brief for the Lord President for a speech which he intends to deliver to some Labour meeting at Leeds.[10] The theme is the need to raise the standard of living over the next years; the fact that something but not all can be done by a redistribution of income, which if it goes too far will remove economic incentives; two sets of factors working adversely to an increased production of goods and services – the first set being the increase in leisure (shorter hours, higher school [leaving] age, lower retiring age, holidays with pay) which is desirable in itself, and the second set being real adverse factors such as aging of population, need to use factors to restore our pre-war capital (e.g. housing) and loss of foreign investments and possible adverse change in the terms of trade; output can be increased by employment policy and by increasing technical efficiency of industry.

I have spent a considerable time this week on the problem of an international cotton agreement. A study group has been meeting in Washington at which the Americans have produced a draft agreement based on restriction by export quotas which the importing countries are to police.[11] It is much against our interest since it may raise the price of raw cotton to us, and also because export controls are likely to be much more effectively worked than internal production or price controls in the producing countries, with the result that the producers of raw cotton may enjoy cheaper cotton for their new textile industries than will Lancashire. The agreement is one which will tend to make international balances of payments worse rather than better by putting a further strain on our unfavourable balance and by improving still more the US favourable

[9] Meade to Gilbert, 29 August 1945 (enclosing EC(S)(45)2 Revise, Chantler, 'British Motor-Car Taxation and the Export Problem', 29 January 1945), T161/1291/S51207/5.

[10] Not found.

[11] The American Draft International Cotton Agreement of 20 July 1945 and the discussions of the Cotton Study Group in Washington are on T230/36.

balance. Moreover, the agreement is not in the spirit of Article VII in which discussions it has always been recognised that no such agreements should be reached unless there are *pari passu* measures to remove the underlying disequilibrium and to shift production from the high-cost to the low-cost producers (i.e. in this case from the US producers). The great diplomatic danger that we run is that by a series of agreements such as this the USA will contract out of all their difficulties under Article VII, while we contract out of none of ours. Then the Americans will demand that we implement Article VII if we want any financial assistance. Such things as a cotton agreement must remain part of the total Article VII bargain. This week Leslie Wheeler of the US Department of Agriculture has been in London and we have had a couple of informal meetings with him. I argued strongly that we should make it perfectly clear that we couldn't go on on the present basis and that the next meeting of the international Study Group should be postponed until there has been a satisfactory Anglo-American discussion and agreement on the subject. But it appears that the Americans have with difficulty managed to persuade the Brazilians to come to the next Study Group meeting (24 September) and therefore cannot put it off. It was agreed that the Study Group meeting should be held, but that it should really be held to hear the views of the Brazilians (who could not attend the first meeting) and that it should be understood between us that no agreement should be sought at it.[12]

Marcus Fleming has prepared a paper on the set-up of the Economic and Social Commission [*sic*] under the UN World Organisation and on the relations between it and the specialised organisations, our main idea being to make the Council a reality from the point of view of international co-ordination of national and international policies on such questions as the maintenance of employment and the restoration of equilibrium to balances of payments. A meeting of the Depts concerned was held in the FO with Nigel Ronald in the chair and it is clear that Fleming's paper will be taken as the basic draft for the preparation of papers to be put in by the UK to the relevant sub-committees of the executive committee of the Preparatory Commission now at work setting up the World Organisation. Marcus Fleming will, I think, attend the meetings of the sub-committee.[13] The outlook seems good, since Noel-Baker (now Minister of State) who is the UK chief delegate to the Preparatory Commission is all in favour of central co-ordination by the World Organisation. But it remains perhaps a trifle undecided whether this is his policy or the policy of HMG! And there are certainly very difficult rocks ahead. Will it be possible for the Economic and Social Council really to do anything effective to influence the Bretton

[12] A summary of the informal meetings on 29 and 30 August is on T230/36; for further developments, including informal bilateral talks between the UK and the US in January 1946, see the same file.

[13] The meeting was on 1 September. Fleming's paper 'Some Points Affecting the Economic and Social Council and the Relations with Specialised Agencies, Note by the Economic Section', 31 August 1945, became 'Commissions of the Economic and Social Council, Draft Memorandum for Submission by HMG to Sub-Committee 3', 4 September 1945 (T236/428). For the meetings of the sub-committee, which Fleming did attend, see T236/427.

Woods organisations? And will it be possible to see that all the specialised organisations in the economic field (including the Bretton Woods organisations) are all housed in the same place?

A strange occurrence this week, when Bridges sent for me urgently. He showed me a copy of a minute by Bevin, Dalton and Cripps to the PM saying in effect that no work had been done on the possible effects of the end of Lend-Lease on our economy and suggesting that the Cabinet Offices (i.e. the Economic Section) should be asked to do something. He showed me at the same time a draft paper prepared by Eady, R. W. B. Clarke and other Treasury officials on the subject of its effect on our Balance of Payments.[14] He was clearly very annoyed that the Chancellor should have so minuted the PM without first finding out what Treasury officials were doing. He then asked me to read the paper and to tell him what I thought of it. I did so and said that I could not comment just at a moment's notice on the figures and that there was an anti-Article VII tone about the concluding paragraphs which I did not consider entirely justified. I was in a difficult position since I did not want to be unco-operative, but I also wanted to make it clear that we were in fact being kept carefully out of all the discussions on Stage III finance. Overnight it occurred to me that Bridges might be thinking that the suggestion of the three Ministers might be due to intrigue on the part of the Economic Section, so I went back to assure him that this was not the case.

A good deal more work this week on establishments seeing Sayers, Tress and MacDougall. Sayers, I think, is coming. MacDougall will, I fear, probably go to Oxford if, as is most probable, a Fellowship is offered to him. Tress is attracted but has other irons in the fire.

## *16 September 1945*

The last fortnight has again been an exceedingly busy one. The idea of a five-year plan for our internal economy has progressed somewhat. I have discussed with the Lord President our ideas on the subject and promised to prepare him an Economic Section paper on the subject. I have written a first draft of this and circulated it as a Staff paper.[15] The main idea is that proper planning falls into three parts:- *first*, a general forecast of what our resources are likely to be over the next years and of the demands that are likely to be made on them in the light of existing policies and programmes, thus showing an overall inflationary-deflationary gap; *second*, the setting of economic targets, i.e. a set of general policy decisions as to the extent to which the various main categories of demand (e.g. public or private investment, personal consumption, foreign balance, etc.) should be adjusted in an upwards or downwards direction; and *thirdly* the remoulding of policies (e.g. the speeding up or postponement of public investment, changes in the taxation on personal incomes) to fill the gap. Bridges has

[14] Bevin, Dalton, and Cripps to Attlee, 22 August 1945, 'End of Lend-Lease, Balance of Payments, Memorandum Prepared in the Treasury', 31 August 1945, T230/142.

[15] See page 121, note 2.

prepared a note which he has circulated to all the economic departments and on which he has held a meeting, on the subject of the administrative machinery necessary to carry out the Plan.[16] The meeting went well from our point of view. There is to be a top-level Steering Committee with Bridges in the chair and of which the Treasury, the Board of Trade, the Ministry of Labour, the Office of the Lord President and the Economic Section are to be members. There was a great cry from Sir Donald Fergusson (ex-Agriculture and now at Fuel and Power) that the industries producing basic commodities were overlooked (e.g. coal and agriculture) and that we must plan these in order to become as autarchic as possible and save imports, and that one of the departments representing this point of view should be on the Steering Committee. It was agreed that one of them should be so represented. A series of working parties are to be set up under this steering committee, the first of which (of which I am to be chairman) is to forecast future economic developments and in fact to survey the position on the basis of current programmes and policies and to suggest alternative methods of filling an inflationary or deflationary gap.[17]

The Lord President's committee has at last taken our general Economic Survey.[18] I attended the meeting, and demurely took my seat at the bottom of the table; but the LP made me come up and sit between him and the Chancellor so as to be able to brief him in the course of the discussion. There was a long and general discussion about our immediate economic problems. As practical results of the meeting it was decided (1) to set up a working party under the Treasury to examine all import programmes from the point of view of saving foreign exchange, (2) to set up a working party under the Board of Trade to review the problems of forecasting our exports, and (3) to ask the Treasury with the Board of Trade and the Ministry of Labour to prepare an examination of the future of the stabilisation policy and of the subsidisation of the Cost of Living Index. The Economic Section was to be associated with each of these. (1) and (2) above will presumably cover exactly the same ground as two of the working parties which will ultimately be set up under the Steering Committee on the Economic Plan. The setting up was a result of a note which I passed to the LP during the meeting, and my idea had been to set up bodies which would simply foreshadow and automatically turn into two of the Steering Committee working parties. But I hear that, at least as far as (1) is concerned, Rowe-Dutton of the Treasury who is to be in charge of the party, is procrastinating by saying that nothing should happen until the Steering Committee machinery is set up. I fear that this is all part of the Treasury desire to keep overseas finance and all that is concerned there-with a dark Treasury secret with which no other department should be concerned. I have discussed this with John Maud and Murrie and we have

[16] Bridges, 'Planning of Economic Development', 6 September 1945, T273/298 and CAB21/2215; the meeting was held on 12 September.

[17] For Fergusson's views see Fergusson to Bridges, 11 September 1945, T273/298; on the Economic Development Working Party see below p. 133.

[18] LP(45) 31st Meeting, 7 September 1945, CAB71/19. On the interdepartmental examination of the future of the stabilization policy see below, pp. 194–5.

agreed that we should maintain the line that the Treasury must fulfill the decision of the LP's Committee and undertake the survey of import programmes together with the other departments concerned.

The Industrial Sub-Committee of the Lord President's Committee has discussed a long-winded document by an interdepartmental group of officials on the future of the Economic Controls. All are agreed that certain controls (e.g. food and clothing rationing, building licensing, etc.) must be continued in order to ensure a fair share of certain very scarce commodities; also that certain controls over and above this (e.g. price controls) must be maintained against inflation. But with the labour controls crumbling and about to disappear, doubt arises whether one will be able effectively to use the controls in order to direct economic resources into those areas in which they are most required. There was a meeting of officials before the document was sent in to Ministers, which I attended and at which there was an interesting discussion on such points as (1) whether it was possible to supply and effectively to administer production controls (e.g. controls requiring producers to export a given percentage of their output) without the sanction of a raw material or labour control so that offenders could be brought to heel by the simple process of turning off the supply of their raw materials or labour, and (2) whether it was possible or desirable to maintain a raw material control after the material had become plentiful merely as a means of backing up a production control.[19] Chester who had been a member of the interdepartmental committee on the subject and I both briefed the LP.[20] I drew his attention to two salient points: *first*, that taxation was to a large extent an alternative to direct economic controls as a means of preventing inflation and that a high level of taxation would make it much easier to maintain price controls, and *secondly* that the extent to which it was desirable to maintain controls as a means of allocating resources to the uses with the highest social priority depended upon the following two factors at least:- (1) the speed with which labour and other resources were to be transferred from war-time to peace-time uses. If, for example, it were decided to increase substantially the speed of demobilisation, there would be so much the less need to maintain controls which restricted the employment of labour and other resources in inessential uses, both because the overall shortage of labour would be the less so that it was less necessary to take special measures to see that essential uses were met and also because the more rapid transfer would give rise to the greater danger of pools of dislocation unemployment, which might be prevented from finding work by restrictions maintained on inessential production; and (2) the extent to which it is possible to maintain effective restrictions on the most inessential employments. Thus, controls which prevented the production of the rather less essential commodities in the hope that this would make more labour available for

[19] The Ministerial sub-committee discussed the report (LP(45)162, 'The Immediate Future of Controls, Report by Official Committee', 6 September 1945, CAB71/21) on 11 September 1945 (T230/35); the officials met on 6 September (GEN 87/ 1st meeting, CAB78/37).

[20] Chester to Lord President, 'Future of the Economic Controls (LP(45)162)', and Meade to Lord President, 10 September 1945, CAB124/687.

the most essential lines might merely do more harm than good if they drove labour in effect into the most inessential employments of all which it was not in effect possible to control (e.g. retail service or domestic service).

Chester and I went to see the LP on this subject. It was a very hurried meeting in which there was hardly time to discuss the subject at all. In the course of the conversation Morrison objected to the use of the term 'negative' or 'restrictive' controls and said that he wished we could make it clear that the controls should properly be operated in an expansionist and constructive manner. I held my fire; but on returning to my room I wrote Morrison a minute on the general theory of the subject.[21] In this I argued (i) that it was not a question of phraseology since most of the war-time controls were in fact restrictive in that they limited the amount which a man might produce, buy, sell or employ, and that they could not be used to induce him to produce, buy, sell or employ more than he wished to; (ii) that they were useful for a period of shortage but that they were worse than useless and merely an impediment when demand fell short of supply; (iii) that economic expansion in those latter circumstances could be brought about by three types of state intervention, (a) the direct planning of extensive programmes of development in the socialised sector of the economy (e.g. roads, municipal housing, investment in socialised industries), (b) the adoption of financial policies (rate of interest, rate of foreign exchange, rates of tax, subsidies) to stimulate total demand, and (c) the prevention of restrictive practices in the private sector of the economy.

I went to see the LP on the question of the future of policies for the nationalisation of various industries. I persuaded him to send round to the 'socialising' Ministers a letter in which he stated that the principles to be observed in each scheme of nationalisation were a matter of common interest to a number of departments and in which he sent a list of the sort of general questions (drafted by us) which they would have to have in mind in tackling each nationalisation scheme (e.g. principles of compensation, financial structure, price policy, etc.).[22] He has held one meeting of his 'socialising' Ministers [on 10 September], but I am not sure what the outcome was.

The LP has sent to us for our comments a PEP pamphlet on Economic Controls from the point of view of the promotion of our exports.[23] I have asked Tom Wilson to do a brief on this subject. Wilson and I accordingly called on George Owen and Richard Pares at the Board of Trade to discuss what views they had on this subject. The obviously effective controls are those (such as clothes rationing, purchase tax, need to obtain a Ministry of War Transport licence before purchasing a new motor-car, Limitation of Sales Orders, etc.) which limit sales or purchases on the domestic market but leave the foreign market free. Also price control which makes sales in

[21] Meade to Lord President, 13 September 1945, CAB124/687.

[22] Johnston, 'Note of a Meeting in the Lord President's Room, 3 September 1945', CAB124/915; Morrison to Cripps, Dalton, Wilmot, Barnes and Shinwell, 3 September 1945, CAB124/915. The eight questions enclosed with each letter had been drafted by Chantler (Chantler to Meade, 3 September 1945, T230/106).

[23] Political and Economic Planning, *Planning* no. 236, 22 June 1945.

the home market less profitable. The question is how large a field can be covered in this way, and whether it is possible to use direct production controls or what will remain of raw material and labour controls to force producers to export. We had an interesting discussion.

I have spent some time putting A. J. Brown, who is in charge of our Overseas Economic Survey, into touch with the various officials in the departments concerned with overseas economic intelligence. A tedious, time-absorbing activity which may bear fruit months hence!

During the week-end I went to Oxford and stayed in Jesus College for another FO conference at which members of the Foreign Service (diplomatic, consular, colonial, Indian, etc.) were present to listen to speeches from Whitehall officials on problems of economic reconstruction. I spoke again on Employment Policy with much the same results as last time. Again I think that the conference served a very useful purpose. It is certainly an admirable idea that these men should really learn something about the economic issues which face us. This time we enjoyed a typical speech from the new Minister of State (Noel-Baker) – an extraordinary mixture of idealism and realism and of economic good sense and fallacy. Many of the stock economic fallacies of the internationalist utopians were trotted out – the economic harmony of interests (i.e. that it was to our interest as well as Germany's that she should have export industries to compete with us), the economic clap-trap of the ILO (i.e. that we should benefit and raise standards in the backward countries by not allowing them to undercut us by low wages). But he has a superb faith and a really firm-based conviction in the real need for effective international organisation. It was a real breath of fresh air to hear him talk about the Great Power Veto in the new [United Nations] organisation. He poured scorn on the view that you couldn't in fact do anything effective to preserve the peace if one of the Great Powers decided to run amok, so that the veto question did not really matter. Did anyone really believe that if we ran amok the USA and the USSR in combination could not stop us! He was very interesting and realistic on Russia. He admitted that owing to the brutal conduct of the Russians in Europe our troops had passed from admiring the Russians through a process of embitterment to out-and-out hatred. He explained how in his view we should go ahead with organising world institutions, should invite the Russians in but should not hold up matters merely because they were not coming in at once. He asserted that there were two fundamentally different schools of thought in Russia – the imperialistic generals who wished to dominate Eastern Europe and to prepare for what they thought was the inevitable clash with the West and the descendants of the old Litvinov tradition of co-operation with the League [of Nations]. The latter school was most likely to be strengthened if we went ahead and made it clear beyond any shadow of a doubt that we really intended to make the new international institutions a reality.

The question of the future of shipping has been up to the Cabinet.[24] Marcus Fleming provided a brief for Morrison on the subject. I also sent him a short note on the subject which raises very important issues in the

[24] CM(45) 29th Conclusions, 6 September 1945, CAB128/1.

matter of Article VII. We obviously have an enormous amount to gain by applying Article VII principles to shipping, so that the Americans cannot subsidise their uneconomic war-time merchant fleet. Similarly, we have much to gain from the application of Article VII principles to cotton, where we are an importer of a raw material of which the USA is a high-cost producer. The danger is that the Americans will treat separately from the general Article VII talks the things in which the application of Article VII principles is most difficult to them (Wheat Agreement, Cotton Agreement, Shipping) and will then call on us to fulfill Article VII in the rest of the field in which we find difficulties (Imperial Preference, Home Agriculture). It is, therefore, most important that in season and out of season we should insist that such matters as Cotton and Shipping be dealt with under Article VII. This magnificent brief was duly sent to the LP, who arrived at the Cabinet *after* this item had been taken! He had, however, the decency to send up a note to Marcus Fleming and myself to inform us that his ill-behaviour was due to the fact that an aeroplane which was bringing him from Leeds where he had been delivering an oration had been delayed!

Meanwhile there are some fine goings on in the matter of Article VII. Keynes has really excelled himself. He got himself sent to Washington without the commercial policy boys (Liesching, Lionel Robbins and Enfield) on the grounds that the mission was solely a financial one. He has now got set up in Washington an Anglo-American committee to discuss commercial policy, which he proposes to conduct himself, having at the last moment in England (while Liesching and Lionel Robbins were on leave) more or less sold to Ministers the crazy, lunatic, self-contradictory idea that we should join in with America in a general convention to reduce obstacles to trade all round but should maintain completely unfettered rights to programme (i.e. to restrict) our imports *ad infinitum* to any extent we desire![25] This week there has been a most resounding counter-attack on the part of Liesching and Lionel Robbins. Cripps at the Board of Trade has been magnificent, insisting on the need for a convention which prevents other countries from restricting their imports of our goods. (Query: How does this anti-import restriction view square with his apparent desire to 'plan' everything quantitatively?) Dalton to whom I sold the idea of the Commercial Union in the first place, who himself first launched the idea in Whitehall, who used to rant against us for not being willing to brush aside import restrictions quickly enough, and who used to pour scorn on Keynes' excursions into this field – now that he has moved from the Board of Trade to the Treasury seems to have swallowed this Keynes nonsense at least temporarily. But he was completely routed at the Ministerial meeting. Definite instructions have been cabled to Keynes instructing him not to touch commercial policy and to wait for a properly constituted team on this subject.[26]

[25] Keynes' instructions for the Washington discussions were agreed at a meeting of Ministers on 23 August 1945 (T236/436, and *The Collected Writings of John Maynard Keynes*, Vol. 24, pp. 420–5).

[26] 'Commercial Policy and the Lend-Lease Negotiations in Washington, Memorandum by the President of the Board of Trade', 13 September 1945, and GEN89/1st Meeting, 14

I have spent a fortnight of lunches with economists. Polak, the Dutchman now with UNRRA and with whom I used to work at the League of Nations in Geneva; Roy Harrod of Christ Church [College, Oxford]; Abba P. Lerner, with whom I discussed my *Economic Journal* review of his book;[27] Beckhart, economic adviser of the Chase National Bank of New York and Professor at Columbia University; Richard Stone and Derksen, of Tinbergen's section in the Hague, who measures the national income of Holland; Alec Cairncross, whom I tried in vain to persuade to come to the Economic Section; Martin Hill with whom I used to work at the League in Geneva and who is now working for the Preparatory Commission for the new United Nations Organisation; and Sir Theodore Gregory, economic adviser of the Government of India who wants to discuss the possibility of some world conference to encourage countries to measure their national incomes and expenditures on uniform lines.

## *23 September 1945*

There have been a number of developments this week in connection with the proposed five-year economic plan. We have held a staff meeting to discuss the draft paper which I had prepared for the Lord President on the principles of economic planning, in which I try to emphasise the desirability of 'liberal-socialist' planning (i.e. overall planning to preserve the balance between total national demand and the available resources within a framework of the economic calculus of prices and costs as determinants of what particular things shall be produced) rather than a rigid quantitative authoritarian 'Gosplan'.[28] I have now to rewrite the draft in the coming week. Meanwhile, Bridges has submitted his report to the PM on the administrative machinery required for carrying out the plan, as a result of the meeting which he held last week [on 12 September].[29] In the first draft of this report words were chosen which apparently laid on the Economic Section an inappropriately grandiose position. The 'economic development working party' of which I am to be chairman seemed to be given the duty of 'planning the use to be made of the country's economic resources'. This might have suggested that the Economic Section should have acted as arbiter when there was a difference of opinion as to whether, for example, consumption standards should be improved at the expense of investment or *vice versa*. Clearly this would have been an impossible position. So I went to Bridges and explained that the Section's task should be merely to survey the available resources and, on

September 1945, CAB78/37. Present at the meeting were the Prime Minister, Foreign Secretary, Chancellor of the Exchequer, President of the Board of Trade, Secretary of State for India, the Ministers of Agriculture and Fisheries and of Fuel and Power, the Parliamentary Undersecretary to the Dominions Office, plus Bridges, Liesching, Vandepeer, Robbins, Shackle, Stirling and Grant. On the Commercial Union see T230/125.

27 See above, p. 37.

28 See page 122, note 2.

29 See above, p. 128. Revised versions of Bridges' paper were circulated after the meeting, on 14, 15 and 19 September 1945 (T273/298).

the basis of present policies and programmes, to survey the probable demands upon them and to analyse the implications of various alternative ways of filling the deflationary or inflationary gap. I explained that in my opinion our working party should be a very humble and small affair consisting practically solely of the Economic Section and the Central Statistical Office, and that our duty would be to bring reports on this subject for the Steering Committee, who in turn would hold the great 'auction sale' to decide to which uses the resources would be put. This was slightly complicated by a letter which I received from Broadley of the Ministry of Food as a result of Bridges' meeting last week, in which Broadley stated that if the Ministry of Food was not to be on the Steering Committee he understood (from Bridges' meeting) that they should be on my 'Economic Development Working Party' which would be the appropriate place for them to assert the claims of food consumption and of consumption standards in general on the resources of the community. This letter illustrated the danger (a) of inflating the position of the Section into a high executive organ and (b) of having all the departments on my working party. I have drafted a reply to Broadley, which Bridges has approved, arguing that the two operative places at which Broadley must state the Ministry of Food's case are (i) at the import programming working party at which food import programmes must be drawn up which take into account both national considerations and the home agricultural output and (ii) at the Steering Committee itself when any questions of allocating resources as between consumption standards and other uses may arise. I also explained the more limited role which the Economic Development working party would have to play.[30]

Meanwhile the actual preparation of the plan itself, as it were, has made some progress. Tress and Stafford have now completed estimates of the future national income for 1946, 1947 and 1948 on certain assumptions about movements in wage-rates, profit margins, unemployment, total manpower, etc. These have been sent in a preliminary form to Brittain who (after their conversion from figures of 'net national income at factor cost' to 'total taxable income') will presumably be using them for the budgetary purpose of seeing what a normal post-war taxable income (say in 1948) is likely to look like. On this basis he can start to say what rates of taxation some four or five years hence may have to be to meet the total level of national expenditure which will then be probable. Meanwhile, I have written on this basis a minute to Brittain on the balance between spendable personal incomes in 1946 (after deduction of tax at current rates and at possible lower rates) and the probable available supplies of consumption goods. The result, I must confess, shows a position which is likely to be somewhat less inflationary than I had feared. Nevertheless the general moral still is that reductions of taxation should be kept within the narrowest bounds which politics will permit. These estimates of future national income, which are now being written up into a paper by Tress in consultation with Stafford, will form the basis of my Economic Development

[30] Broadley to Meade, 15 September, and Meade to Broadley, 24 September 1945, T273/298; Meade to Bridges, 18 September 1945, CAB21/2215.

Working Party's estimates of future 'target' national incomes.[31] We must now turn from the estimate of the available resources to estimates of future demands on these resources.

In this connection there has been a meeting this week to discuss the circular and form which is to be sent out to Local Authorities asking them for their programmes of capital development over the next three years. These forms are now, I hope, at last reaching the stage at which they will be sent out.[32]

Bridges sent for me this week to explain that the Treasury were preparing a Bill to make the control of new issues and foreign exchange control a permanent feature of the economy. In this connection they have persuaded the Chancellor that only the Whitehall machine can really be responsible for planning investment (since it is only one part of the total problem of planning the whole of the national demand for resources and since in any case the state must be responsible for the decisions to be taken); but the Chancellor is bound for political reasons to go a little way towards a National Investment Board. The proposal is therefore to set up a National Investment Consultative Council consisting of the Chancellor, the permanent secretaries of the main departments concerned with investment, and outside representatives of industry, finance, etc. Bridges asked me to draft the first paragraphs of a White Paper which they intend to issue with the Bill briefly explaining the position of investment planning and thus of the Consultative Council in relation to the total economic plan. I have tried a draft and have advised Bridges strongly that the Chancellor should make no attempt to pretend that the Consultative Council would perform the functions which others wish to put on an Investment Board but should defend his position by saying that these executive functions should be and will be carried out by HMG itself.[33]

I have prepared a paper on the present proposals for a Betterment Tax (of 80 per cent on all development value when land is developed).[34] I have attacked it (a) because it does not collect betterment on land whose use is not changed and (b) because it will act as a most undesirable restraint on development during a period when great development is needed. I have proposed as an alternative a periodic tax on increments of land value. If this is ruled out because (a) of the difficulty which landowners may have of raising the funds to pay such a levy on land which is ripening for development but has not yet been developed and (b) of the difficulties of a periodic valuation of all land, I have suggested as a modification that the

[31] Meade to Brittain, 23 September, and Brittain, 'National Income and Budget Forecast for 1948', 27 September 1945, T171/371; CS(S)(45)77 and EC(S)(45)32, 'The net national income in 1946, 1947 and 1948', 25 September 1945, T230/18.

[32] See below, p. 148.

[33] Dalton's Investment (Control and Guarantees) Bill passed into law as the Borrowing (Control and Guarantees) Act in July 1946; on its preparation and passage through Parliament, see files T233/25–29. (The exchange control provisions were saved for a later Bill, which became the Exchange Control Act 1947.) For the National Investment Council's membership and proceedings see files T233/161–166. Meade's contribution, 'Draft White Paper (to be presented with the Investment and Exchange (Controls) Bill)', is on T233/25.

[34] This became 'The Proposed Betterment Tax', 26 September 1945 (T273/340).

tax on the increment of value should be levied only when the land was sold, was inherited or was developed. If this is impossible, I suggest that there should be instead merely a small annual contribution of the Schedule A value of all real property (à la War Damage Contribution) to feed a fund for the compensation of landowners who suffer damage as a result of town and country planning. This issue is quite important for 'liberal-socialist' planning. We must maintain the private incentive to develop, and guide development in the social interest largely by saying 'No' to undesirable development.

On Monday [17 September] the Chancellor of the Exchequer took me out to lunch *à deux* in a Soho restaurant. I took the opportunity of giving him a violent lecture on the line which he was allowing the Treasury to take on Import Quotas under the commercial policy proposals. He seemed to be backing up Eady and Keynes' idea that we should stick out for the right to programme (i.e. to restrict) imports in all circumstances. He said that he wanted to be able to say 'No luxury motors to be imported. Only necessities such as wheat.' I told him that either this restriction was needed on balance of payments grounds because we could not afford the foreign exchange or it was required on manufacturing grounds. In the first case, we must rely on the balance of payments let-out for import quotas in the commercial policy convention, which was devised by himself when he was President of the Board of Trade to give us the best of both worlds – namely to allow us to control our imports so long as this was essential to us without giving foreigners the power of restricting our exports. In the second case, it was not import of luxury cars but the domestic consumption of luxury cars (whether imported or home-produced) which he should restrain e.g. by sumptuary taxation. How on earth could we hope to get agreement to a general commercial policy convention whose purpose was to remove or reduce obstacles to international trade, which contained a general clause allowing all countries to restrict imports *ad lib*?

He also spoke to me about the coming Budget.[35] His proposals seem quite reasonable to me – particularly so after the forecast of 1946 national income and supplies of consumption goods which I did not then have. He, however, is thinking of the timing of possible tax reductions from the point of view of its political repercussions. I argued strongly for their consideration from the point of view of the need to control the inflationary or deflationary gap, and I strongly emphasised the need to get a reform in PAYE so that it will not be necessary to decide each year in September what the rate of tax is going to be for a twelve-month period starting the following April. Supposing, I said, a major slump started when he was Chancellor in October a year or so before a general election! Could he stimulate an increse in consumers' demands in time to avert catastrophe?

He asked me whether my present job was a full-time one or whether I might have time to sit half-time on a Public Corporation. I said that my job was a full-time one; but afterwards I went to see Bridges about this. What the Chancellor has in mind, I think, is that one might serve as an

[35] To be presented on 23 October 1945 (*House of Commons Debates*, Vol. 415, cols. 1875–1902).

economic adviser to the nationalised Bank of England.[36] I left Bridges in no doubt that I should like this if it were possible. The Chancellor told me to go and see him whenever I wanted to bring anything to his attention. This also I mentioned to Bridges, who was most considerate about it. My God, would that it could really be so! What could I not do with access to the Chancellor as free as my present access to the Lord President!

In external matters, Lionel Robbins, Liesching and Enfield have now gone off to Washington to join Halifax and Keynes and to be responsible for commercial policy.[37] More power to them! In the fight for 'liberal-socialism' perhaps nothing is more important than this external commercial policy settlement, since a more or less liberal settlement there would necessitate and be made possible by 'liberal-socialism' at home. On the other hand, I do not see how a Gosplan socialism which pays no regard to prices and costs can possibly be made compatible with rules against excessive protection or discrimination in international commerce. We must do absolutely everything we can to aid these negotiations at home while the delegation is away. Our first basis is to stuff Morrison hard with the subject.

Meanwhile A. J. Brown has been making contacts with officials in other departments on the subject of overseas economic intelligence. Marcus Fleming has written a note on this subject which has now been sent to the Foreign Office,[38] and has held a Section meeting on the topic. A. J. Brown has also prepared a brief on the Treasury paper (of which Bridges showed me an advance copy some weeks ago) about the effect of the termination of Lend-Lease on our balance of payments. This requires a little more polishing to bring out some of the points about the legitimacy of distinguishing as rigidly as the Treasury do between dollars and other currencies. I must get A. J. Brown to revise this next week and then I will send it to Bridges.[39]

Murrie, John Maud and I paid a depressing visit to Eady, who it appears is to be chairman of the working party on the balance of payments which is to form part of the set-up for the Economic Plan. The purpose of the visit was to coax the Treasury to prepare a report for the Lord President's Committee on our import programmes in the coming months or years as had been promised at the meeting of the LP's Committee when they discussed our Economic Survey.[40] Eady twisted and shifted as usual. There was no sign of a desire to have an above-board and scientific enquiry into our import programmes. It was all to be kept in the murky subterranean shadows of the Treasury (i.e. of Eady and R. W. B. Clarke). But this is quite wrong. The Treasury must have the main responsibility in saying

[36] The Bank of England Bill was published on 10 October 1945 and the Bank came into public ownership on 1 March 1946. On the Bank nationalisation see Chester, *The Nationalisation of British Industry 1945–51*, pp. 27–8, 237–40.

[37] See above, p. 132; the party sailed from Southampton on the *Queen Mary* on 22 September 1945.

[38] Not found. For some related correspondence see CAB21/2206.

[39] 'The Treasury Memorandum on the End of Lend-Lease, Balance of Payments (Gen. 83/1), Note by the Economic Section of the Cabinet Secretariat', T230/142.

[40] See above pp. 128–9.

how much we can afford in total to spend on imports (just as the Ministry of War Transport used to have the main responsibility in saying how much we could ship in total into the country), but within this total whether we should import food, raw materials or manufactured goods remains an issue of overall interdepartmental policy. We must remain patient. Our opportunity will come at our own Economic Development Working Party, where we can bring out these implications. Nevertheless Eady remains the real menace to the effectiveness of the Economic Section.

# 12

## October 1945

*6 October 1945*

This has again been an exceedingly full fortnight. One of the main preoccupations has been the proposed Economic Plan. I have sent Bridges a copy of the revised draft of the paper which I am preparing for the Lord President on Economic Planning. We have held another staff meeting on this draft. And I am now going to prepare a final version of it. I hope that this may be ready in time to be circulated to the Lord President's Committee together with the report which Bridges has now submitted to the Prime Minister and which has been accepted by the Ministers concerned (the Lord President, the Chancellor, the President of the Board of Trade and the Minister of Labour) for the administrative machinery to look after the Plan. Our paper on the purpose and methods of planning would go well with Bridges' report on administrative machinery.[1]

Meanwhile Bridges has held what was in fact a first meeting of the Steering Committee to deal with the Plan (Gilbert of the Treasury, Ince of the Ministry of Labour, John Maud of the Lord President's Office, Murrie of the Cabinet Office, and myself). It was decided that a plan for the calendar year 1946 should be prepared by the middle of November and that departments should be asked to provide the necessary information by the end of October. The idea is to do the plan both in terms of the availability of manpower and the departmental demands for manpower and also in terms of the 'target' national income and the national expenditure which will be involved by current programmes and policies of all kinds. The difficulty at the moment is to decide in what sense the departmental 'demands' should be drawn up. For example, should the departmental demands in the case of building show all the building which those whose interests they represent would like to undertake if there were no acute shortage of building resources; or should they represent the amount of building which they already have (or expect to have) allocated to them? If the first, the gap between overall supply and demand will be so great as to be meaningless. If the latter, there should be from the beginning no gap between demand and supply. The decision was to seek

[1] Meade to Bridges, 26 September 1945 (enclosing EC(S)(45)28 Revise, 'Economic Planning'), T273/298; 'Planning of Economic Development, Memorandum by Sir Edward Bridges', 19 September 1945, CAB21/2215 and CAB124/890.

something between the two, i.e. something which included only what departments considered really essential or of very high priority but which was not necessarily confined to what they expected to be able to get. This would leave the Steering Committee and Ministers the function of deciding what should proceed and what should not.[2]

I was asked as a result of the meeting to draft a letter to be sent to all departments to get this information. I have held two meetings with Tress and with Campion and Stafford of the Central Statistical Office to start deciding what we shall actually need from departments for the Plan; and meanwhile I have prepared a draft of the letter for Eady to send to departments.[3]

There has also been a meeting in Proctor's room in the Treasury to discuss with the Board of Trade how to get figures from industry of private investment. It was a long and rambling meeting; but the final outcome was not unsatisfactory.[4] In the immediate future it is intended that all that one can do is to get some indications of what investment private industry is likely to undertake by examining the supply side; i.e. by considering how much building they will be allowed to undertake and by considering how much of the output of the engineering industries will be made available for these purposes. Any attempt to start from the demand side, i.e. to consider how much private industry would like to invest, would (so the Board of Trade argues) lead to quite ridiculously high figures and the information would in any case be impossible to obtain. We in the Economic Section and the Central Statistical Office maintained that sooner or later the Board of Trade must go to the demand side; i.e. enquire by sample of all firms in all industries about their future programmes of expenditure on capital development in the form of building or machinery. In the end Leak agreed that this would have to be done, but there was no conclusion as to when it should start. Leak seemed to imply not before 1948. I suspect that during 1946 we should enquire about intentions for 1947. Otherwise we may be threatened with deficient demands for investment by private industry before the machinery for collecting investment programmes from private enterprise is at all well exercised.

I have sent to Brittain and discussed with him my minute on the probable outcome between personal spendable incomes in 1946 and the supply of goods and services then likely to be available for personal consumption, with indications of the amount of tax reduction which this suggests might be possible without too great a danger of inflationary pressure upon the available supplies. I confess that the figures when worked out suggest that there is rather more scope for tax reduction without undue inflationary pressure than I had previously expected. In discussing this minute with Brittain I took the opportunity of asking him whether the time had not come to prepare estimates of future public expenditure not only for 1946/47 but for future years as part of the preparation for the Economic Plan. He promised to send me what figures they had got together (and I believe

[2] The minutes of the meeting, on 29 September 1945, are on T273/298 and CAB124/890.

[3] See below p. 147.

[4] No minutes have been located.

that they already have some for 1946/47 and some figures for a 'normal' post-war year such as 1950); but I have not yet received anything from him. The preparation of the Plan for 1946 will, however, give me an opportunity of returning to the charge. Tress has completed a paper on our estimates of the net national income at factor cost for 1946, 1947 and 1948 which is really a first draft of the 'target' national income for the Economic Plan. We have sent a copy of this to Brittain for his information.[5]

Meanwhile the Section has had its ordinary routine of preparing briefs for the Lord President on the economic questions which come up to his committee and to the Cabinet. I cannot remember all which have occurred in the last fortnight; but among the subjects have been Future Building Programmes, the Future of the Labour Controls, the Future of the Royal Ordnance Factories, and the Foreign Financial Control of British Companies.[6]

By far the most important was the problem of the nationalisation of the coal mines. The Minister of Fuel and Power had put in to the Lord President's Committee a paper outlining the broad principles on which he intended to nationalise the coal mines. We (Chester, Chantler and I) prepared a long brief on this subject. The proposals are on the whole much better than might have been expected. There is to be a National Coal Board, whose members are *not* to represent particular interests. This Board will operate the industry on instructions as to broad principles which are laid down by the Minister. Compensation is to take the form of Govt stock (i.e. not of Coal Stock secured on the profits of the coal mines). In our brief we emphasised the need for a board which did not represent particular interests, and the need for paying compensation in the form of Govt stock, because to tie the reward of the past owners to the earnings of the industry over which they no longer had any control might be (i) more expensive, (ii) unfair to previous owners, and (iii), above all, stultifying to the state in deciding what policy was the best to adopt in the national interest. In the case of an increasing returns industry which was socialised, the state might wish to charge a price equal to marginal cost and so make no profit. If there was stock outstanding on the profits of the concern, either previous owners would obtain no compensation or else the state would be precluded from doing this. But the main point in our brief was that the real economic problems arose when you came to discuss not the taking over of the industry but the principles on which it should then be run. We laid great stress on the present position in which the low-cost coal fields were in fact being taxed in order to subsidise the high-cost coal fields, and we inveighed against such 'pooling' systems on the grounds that you

5 Meade to Brittain, 23 September 1945, T171/371; Meade to Brittain, 28 September 1945, enclosing 'The Net National Income in 1946, 1947 and 1948', CAB21/2215.

6 The first three of these topics were discussed at the Lord President's Committee on 5 October (LP(45) 30th meeting, CAB71/19), which considered memoranda by the Minister of Labour (on labour control), the Minister of Works (building programmes), and the Minister of Supply (Royal Ordnance Factories) (LP(45)187 and 180, CAB71/21, and LP(45)193, CAB71/22). Dennison's minute on LP(45)187, 4 October 1945, is on CAB124/692. A joint Treasury-Ministry of Supply-Board of Trade memorandum on 'Foreign Control of British Companies', LP(45)168, 13 September 1945 (CAB71/21), was not discussed in the LPC.

could not expect to get efficient production and high standards of living unless you produced in the lowest-cost manner. As a result, the Lord President's Committee has asked for an account from the Minister of Fuel and Power of the principles upon which he intends to run the industry.[7]

The Lord President has it in mind to deliver this autumn and winter a series of six speeches on economic matters. We have prepared an outline for this series – Immediate Problems of the Transition, Economic Planning, Industrial Efficiency, Social Services and Distribution of Income, External Economic Problems, and General Summary. This is a great opportunity to get the LP to look at these problems as a whole, to commit himself publicly to the proper policies, and to educate the public. I have sent a minute round the Section to get members to prepare notes. We must take this seriously.[8]

There have been two meetings (John Maud in the chair, Vandepeer of the Ministry of Agriculture, Broadley of Food, Palmer of the Board of Trade, and myself) to discuss the future of the Food Controls and, by implication, of the Ministry of Food. This was one of those unsatisfactory occasions in which there was so little precision of analytical thought on an economic subject that one just did not know where one was going. The Ministry of Food are preparing a paper to say that under the previous government the presumption was that Food Controls would all go and the Ministry of Food would be wound up at the earliest opportunity, but that with a Labour Government that is no longer so. That was about all there was to it. When it came to why one wanted to control food or by what means in normal peace-time when acute war shortages were over, there was so little precision that one did not get any idea where one was going. One object of Food Policy is, for example, to preserve high prices, production and profits for home farmers without restricting imported supplies or raising prices to consumers – without any mention of subsidies!!![9]

Another day has been taken up with yet another meeting of the Census of Distribution Committee. We have received evidence from bodies representative of small shopkeepers which is definitely opposed to the idea of a Census. I believe that we have probably made an error in the first communication which we sent round to trade associations etc. in asking

[7] Minister of Fuel and Power, 'Nationalisation of the Coal Mining Industry', LP(45)179, CAB71/21; 'Nationalisation of the Coal Mining Industry, Memorandum by the Minister of Fuel and Power (LP(45)179), Note by the Economic Section of the Cabinet Secretariat', 1 October 1945, EC(S)(45)33, T230/106; LP(45) 35th meeting, 2 October 1945, CAB71/19 and CAB21/2207. See also Chester, *The Nationalisation of British Industry 1945–51*, pp. 47–8.

[8] According to his biographers, Morrison 'devoted a number of speeches up and down the country, and abroad, to educating the public on the facts of Britain's economic plight and needs . . . explaining Britain's economic and industrial problems and urging greater savings, exports and production' (Bernard Donoughue and G. W. Jones, *Herbert Morrison, Portrait of a Politician*. London: Weidenfeld and Nicolson, 1973, p. 377).

[9] No minutes of the two meetings have been found. The Ministry of Food's paper (LP(45)196, 'Government Controls and Food Policy', 10 October 1945, CAB71/22) recommended the continuation of food controls until the end of the post-war food shortage; the Lord President's Committee approved the proposals on 12 October 1945 (LP(45) 37th meeting, CAB71/19).

their evidence solely on what use the Census would be to them and on what questions they would like asked, etc. The point is that the real use of the Census is going to be for national policy (e.g. the improvement of national income and expenditure estimates for employment policy or for analysing the efficiency of distribution). Someone has got to sell the idea to the small shopkeeper on these grounds. At present he looks upon it as an inquisition which has little or no purpose whatsoever. We had before us a paper by Stone on the use of the Census information from the point of view of the National Income and Expenditure, and on this Reddaway and I (in the absence of Stone who has gone off to the USA) were cross-examined. (Reddaway also said something about the Bank of England retail trade statistics.)[10] Our idea now is to get the people who are opposing the Census to come and give evidence, and informally at the end to ask them whether they would care to see Stone's paper, as representing evidence which we were receiving to the effect that there was a real national interest in obtaining a Census.

In external matters the fortnight has been dominated by the repercussions of the financial talks now going on in Washington. I have got A. J. Brown to revise his note on the paper which the Treasury had prepared on the subject of the effect of the end of Lend-Lease on our balance of payments, in which they came to the conclusion that we must indulge in the maximum possible shift away from dollar purchases of all kinds. We have questioned this conclusion on various grounds. (i) First, as the Treasury admits, we cannot save much of our 1946 deficit by austerity and restriction of imports. We must, therefore, borrow from others if we don't borrow from the USA. But as far as terms of borrowing are concerned, this would probably cost us more. Our sterling creditors are not now thinking in terms of lending us more but of getting their existing debts repaid. If we borrow, say, £500 million more from them in 1946 instead of from the USA this will mean that we must compare the terms on which we could borrow £500 million from the USA *not* only with the terms on which we could borrow £500 million more from the Sterling Area but also with the worsening of the terms on which we can settle for the whole of the outstanding £3,000 million or more which we already owe them. (ii) If we shift from dollar purchases to other purchases regardless of costs, we shall have to buy at higher prices and, therefore, shall have to borrow more to obtain the same real supplies. (iii) The real question is the question of repayment later. As far as our total balance of payments with the rest of the world is concerned (which is the fundamental thing for us to restore) it makes no difference whether our debts are to the USA or not. We shall only find difficulty in obtaining dollars for the other currencies which we obtain from our exports if there is a *world* shortage of dollars. But for this we must rely on the Scarce Currency Clause of the Bretton Woods agreement, which in this case would allow us to discriminate against

[10] Stone, 'Usefulness of a Census of Distribution to National Income Statistics', 22 September 1945, CDC10, BT70/99. The retail trade statistics were published in the *Bank of England Statistical Summary* each month from January 1932 to December 1945. The *BESS* ceased publication when the CSO began to publish its *Monthly Digest of Statistics* in January 1946.

American goods. I have sent a copy of this note, which is now I think really effective, to Bridges.[11]

Whether as a result of this or not, I do not know, but this week Eady (much to my surprise) has called me into consultation on the question of the Washington talks and the terms of aid from the United States. Keynes has cabled back to ask whether it would be acceptable if he could get $5,000 million of assistance from the US provided that the annual service of this did not exceed £100 million a year.[12] Eady called me round to ask my opinion on this (whether because Bridges or the Chancellor had told him to do so or – what I find difficult to believe – because he thought it would be of value from his own point of view I do not venture to guess). R. W. B. Clarke was there. He and Eady were taking an impossible line. We must refuse to countenance such an arrangement. When one considers (i) the extreme, indeed impossible, degree of austerity which would be involved if we tried to do without borrowing; (ii) the fact (see above) that borrowing from other sources would probably be more expensive (added to the fact that we must in any case borrow something – ?$1,000 million – from the USA for our essential minimum dollar needs and that $1,000 million alone on purely commercial terms might involve an annual service of practically $100 million); and (iii) the fact that we can ill afford either the economic or the diplomatic conflict with the Americans which a failure to reach a general financial and commercial settlement would involve, it becomes clear that the case for accepting such a proposal if it were forthcoming is overwhelming, provided that the conditions attached to the loans were not intolerable. One condition will almost certainly be some liberalisation of the present Sterling Area arrangements. But in this connection we have ourselves suggestions for proposing a general settlement involving scaling down part of the balances, releasing a part forthwith for expenditure in any currency (including dollars) and releasing the rest gradually over a series of years for expenditure in any currency. All this should be acceptable to the Americans. Another set of conditions will probably be some general commercial policy statement. The difficulties here are still to come. It is already clear from the first meeting of the commercial policy committee in Washington that the Americans are going to go all out for a complete elimination of imperial preferences as part of a general commercial settlement.[13] But the immediate point at issue was whether we could face the obligation to find $100 million a year in the future to service an American loan.

Eady and Clarke said No. I said Yes on certain conditions. One must draw a clear distinction between (i) getting our balance of payments with the rest of the world into equilibrium and (ii) finding dollars. As for (i) £25 million a year was not really much in comparison with the £1,500 million of exports which we shall in any case need to put our overall balance right.

[11] 'The Treasury Memorandum on the End of Lend-Lease, Balance of Payments (GEN83/1), Note by the Economic Section of the Cabinet Secretariat', T230/142; see also above, p. 137.

[12] Cable 6490, 27 September 1945, T236/439 and CAB78/57.

[13] This meeting was held on 2 October: see *Foreign Relations of the United States 1945*, VI, p. 137.

Our problem may be very difficult and we must be free to restrict imports on a non-discriminatory basis so long as our overall balance was not in equilibrium. But a £25 million addition was not really very formidable. As for (ii), if our balance with the rest of the world as a whole was right, we should have difficulty finding dollars only if there was a *world* shortage of dollars. In this case we should have to insist on our right under Article VII of Bretton Woods (the Scarce Currency Article) to restrict imports from the USA on a discriminatory basis; and it may be that we should be wise to insist on the right to suspend payments on the American loan if and when the dollar were scarce. But with such safeguards it would be madness to refuse $5,000 million because of an annual payment of £25 million.

Next day I received the papers which were to be submitted to Ministers on this issue. It included a draft cable to Keynes (written by Eady) which was totally wrong. It suggested that we could not accept assistance on these terms. It confused in an inextricable tangle the issue of our balance of payments with the rest of the world and the issue of a world shortage of dollars. It insisted that we should have completely unfettered rights to restrict imports on a discriminatory basis whenever we ourselves thought this necessary. Then Eady sent for me alone and discussed this telegram. He had already decided to withdraw it twelve hours after submitting it to Ministers! He made himself as pleasant and as flattering as possible to me. He listened with care (and with intelligence) to my exposition of the necessary safeguards which should enable us to accept such terms. The next day he called me in (with Grant and Clarke present) to go through a revised version of the answer to Keynes, which while by no means perfect (it still insisted that we must be completely free to judge when we needed to restrict imports from the US on a discriminatory basis) was an enormous improvement. But it did not tell Keynes anything. It merely asked him for further information about these safeguards and whether they would be forthcoming.[14]

Meanwhile I had abandoned the domestic Economic Plan and (Marcus Fleming being on leave) sweated my guts out writing a fairly long minute to the Lord President on the issue and a shorter note for Brook to send to the Prime Minister. I spent an hour with the Lord President (Marcus Fleming who had returned accompanying me) explaining it to him. I sent a copy of the brief to Stirling at the Board of Trade. I spent some time with Douglas Jay who is now economic adviser to the Prime Minister explaining the issue and gave him a copy of my longer brief to the Lord President. In the result the Ministerial meeting came to very sensible conclusions. We should accept such terms if they were forthcoming (though Keynes should not take the initiative in proposing them), but we must have the right to suspend payments if there was a deflationary collapse in the USA and must be permitted to restrict imports so long as necessary.[15] But I have not yet

[14] GEN89/4, 'End of Lend Lease: The Washington Talks, Note by the Chancellor of the Exchequer', 2 October 1945, T230/142; Eady to Trend, 5 October 1945 (enclosing revised telegram), T236/432.

[15] Meade to Lord President, 'End of Lend-Lease: The Washington Talks (GEN89/4), Note by the Chancellor of the Exchequer', 4 October 1945, and Meade to Prime Minister, 'End of Lease-Lend-Washington Talks (GEN89/4), Note by the Chancellor of the Exchequer', 4 October 1945, T230/142; GEN89/2nd Meeting, 5 October, 1945, CAB78/37.

seen the telegram which the Treasury will feel entitled to send as a result of this.[16] It may be all right. We shall see.

We have had communications from Washington (in which I sense the influence of Lionel Robbins) suggesting that, if we are to reap the great advantages of getting the Americans to treat shipping à la Article VII and to refrain from uneconomic shipping subsidies, we had better see whether we cannot apply the same principles to Civil Aviation and Telecommunications, on which we have so far taken the exactly opposite line. A meeting of officials has been held in the Foreign Office to discuss this.[17] Marcus Fleming attended for us. He tells me that there is perhaps a chance of pulling something off if we can get some transitional period let-out for Civil Aviation while we restore our post-war position, but that the worst obstacle may be the sense on the part of the Civil Aviation boys that we shall look such fools if we go back on our previous line.

I attended a meeting earlier on at the Ministry of Labour (in Marcus Fleming's absence) [on] the line to be taken by the UK Government delegation at the ILO conference in Paris later this month. There is a long and detailed resolution on employment policy which is really quite good but which raises in rather an acute form the issue whether the ILO (rather than the Economic and Social Council as should certainly be the case) will be the body to deal with employment policy. Also the question is to be discussed at the conference of the relation of the ILO to other international bodies such as the Economic and Social Council. I made a statement on both these subjects, suggesting that we should accept the resolution only if we could put on record in one way or another our belief that the Economic and Social Council was the real operative body on this subject, and suggesting that we should attempt not to let the ILO go ahead at this stage too quickly in fixing its policy on relations with other bodies since this was much better discussed at a later stage when the constitution of the Economic and Social Council had progressed a little more.[18]

Had a long talk this week with Noel-Baker after lunch at the Reform Club. The same infectious enthusiasm as ever for making the international institutions a reality. Would that all statesmen (including the Russians) were like this. Then we might get somewhere.

Gunnar Myrdal, the Swedish economist who is now Minister of Commerce in their Labour Government, spent Saturday afternoon with us at 76 Corringham Road. He brought a young and intelligent Swedish economist called Svennilson with him. We had a very interesting conversation comparing notes on the UK and Swedish Labour Governments and their problems ranging over industrial efficiency and organisation, economic planning and full employment, and international economic

[16] 10094 PRISEC, Chancellor of the Exchequer to Keynes, 8 October 1945, T236/439.

[17] Telegrams NABOB 80, Keynes to Chancellor of the Exchequer, President of the Board of Trade and Minister of War Transport, 24 September, and Halifax No. 6439, Hall-Patch to Foreign Office, 26 September 1945, T236/52. The meeting at the Foreign Office was on 5 October; for a report of it see J. F. Cahan to Clarke, 5 October 1945, on same file.

[18] The ILO conference met 15 October-5 November 1945. The instructions for the UK delegation to the conference were approved by the Cabinet on 11 October (CM(45) 40th conclusions, CAB128/1).

and financial problems including the whole corpus on Article VII-Stage III finance-Sterling Area problems. I had to be discreet, but it is surprising how easily one can talk without being indiscreet with a fellow economist. These exchanges of general ideas are part and parcel of the way of life of the liberal Western civilisation. Why can't one meet Russians on the same basis?

## *20 October 1945*

This fortnight has been mainly taken up, as far as I personally have been concerned, with external economic affairs. On the internal side there have been some developments in the preparations for the Economic Plan. I have revised and have sent to the Lord President the paper which we have been preparing on Economic Planning.[19] Bridges has now sent out his letter to Departments concerned asking for the best information available in the limited time available to prepare a Plan for 1946 by the second half of November. This letter contains an appendix illustrating the sort of statistical information which it will be necessary to obtain from the different departments, and the drafting of this Appendix has caused us some trouble. Tress prepared a first draft; but Bridges considered it would terrify departments as it seemed to demand too much within so limited a space of time. I spent the next morning at another draft. Now the letter has gone out, and the whole Whitehall machine is at work planning its future demands on the community's resources both in terms of manpower and in terms of money expenditure.[20] Tress and Stafford have now taken over *pro tem*, going the rounds of the various departments to get out of them the sort of thing which we shall want. We have also had some discussion to ensure that there is not an awful lot of overlap in collecting information from the various departments on the same topic for different uses.[21] The most important point was the collection of figures about manpower (a) for the Manpower Committee (a Cabinet committee which is quite separate from the Lord President's Committee which is to be responsible for the Economic Plan) for the purpose of demobilisation and manpower allocation and (b) for the purpose of the Steering Committee of officials who are preparing the Economic Plan. The problem is to be solved by ensuring that the official manpower working party works both for the Steering Committee and the Manpower Committee and collects the manpower figures for both. But the whole problem is, of course, a nonsense problem, because rationally it is stupid to treat manpower allocation separate from the economic plan. The real trouble is that Bevin is Chairman of the Manpower Committee and Morrison of the Lord President's Committee and they cannot work together.

[19] Meade to Morrison, 10 October 1945, CAB124/890. Meade's paper is reprinted in his *Collected Papers*, Vol. I, chapter 16.

[20] Bridges to Heads of Departments, 'Central planning of economic development', 9 October 1945, CAB124/890 and T273/298. Some drafts are on T230/54.

[21] See Stafford to Meade, 13 October, Meade to Murrie, Proctor and Campion, 15 October, and Meade to Murrie, Proctor and Campion, 18 October 1945, T230/54.

Eady has written to me with a draft of the White Paper which it is intended to issue with the Bill setting up the National Investment Advisory Council. I have made one or two small comments; but the draft (although it is much toned down from the draft which I did for this purpose) seems to me to be on much the right lines. It stresses the point that the planning and timing of investment must be a function of HMG and must be considered as part of the larger problem of planning and timing total national expenditure. Incidentally it is proposed that the Director of the Economic Section should be a member of the Council.[22]

Gilbert has held another meeting of his official working party on public investment. The form to be sent to Local Authorities asking for their investment plans has been approved. A similar form is now to be prepared to be sent to the Public Utilities.[23]

Sir Alan Barlow of the Treasury sent for me to ask whether we could advise him on the probable future course of industrial wage-rates, as they were negotiating for a revision of the wage-rates of the lower grades of civil servants. I explained that this was necessarily one of the most uncertain prognostications; but we have sent him a short note, prepared by Tress, explaining the assumptions which we made on this score in our recent forecast of future movements in the national income and giving briefly our reasons for making those assumptions.[24]

Meanwhile we have performed our regular duty of briefing the Lord President on the hundred and one different economic topics which come up to the Lord President's Committee or to the Cabinet for decision. Among the other subjects we have sent him briefs (prepared by Tom Wilson) on the food situation, on wheat supplies and on the future of food policy, and briefs (prepared by Chester) on the nationalisation of Gas and Electricity and of Shipping.[25] In connection with this last subject I have arranged that Chester and Wilson shall prepare together a long Section paper on the problems of nationalisation.[26] In addition to the subjects

22 The LPC decided on 16 November 1945 against issuing a White Paper with the Bill (LP(45) 43rd meeting, CAB71/19). The Director of the Economic Section was added to the proposed council at a meeting of Treasury officials with the Chancellor on 3 October (T233/25).

23 Copies of the circular to local authorities dated 8 November 1945, and of the returns, are on T161/1370/S53555/03.

24 The forecast was the Section-CSO memorandum, EC(3)(45)32, 'The Net National Income in 1946, 1947 and 1948', 29 September 1945 (T230/18).

25 The LPC considered Ministry of Food memoranda on the world food outlook and on world wheat supplies as well as the Ministry's memorandum on the future of food controls (above p. 142) at their meeting on 12 October (LP(45)182 and 181, CAB71/21; LP(45) 37th meeting, CAB71/19). At their next weekly meeting the LPC gave further consideration to the Ministry of Fuel and Power's proposals for nationalisation of the electricity and gas industries previously considered by the Cabinet on 16 October, and, on the basis of a paper of the Minister of Transport, agreed to announce that it was not intended to nationalise shipping during the present Parliament (LP(45) 38th meeting, CAB71/19; CP(45)217, 'Future of Electricity and Gas Industries, Memorandum by the Minister of Fuel and Power', 11 October 1945, CAB129/3; LP(45)197, Minister of War Transport, 'Shipping Policy', 10 October 1945, CAB71/22). Chester's brief to Morrison, 'Future of Electricity and Gas Industries (CP(45)217), Shipping Policy (LP(45)197)', 13 October 1945, is on CAB124/428.

26 See below, p. 157.

which we covered in our long brief on the nationalisation of the Coal Mines[27] I want to cover the following topics: (i) the economic criterion as to which industries should and which should not be nationalised (i.e. those where for technical reasons the size of the plant must be large in relation to the market for the product), (ii) the problem (which is much to the fore now) of ensuring (both by telling each industry whether it is to be nationalised or not and by finding a basis of compensation that favours efficiency and makes allowance for new capital investment that has been installed between now and the future date of nationalisation) that industries which think they are lingering in the condemned cell may still have an incentive to invest and to raise their productivity.

The greater part of my time has been spent this fortnight on external matters. I hear that both the Lord President and the Prime Minister (duly briefed by myself) spoke up well at the meeting of Ministers recorded in the last entry in my diary; and the telegram which was sent to Washington was much more satisfactory than the Treasury draft.[28] It was made clear that Ministers would in fact probably accept $5,000 millions of aid on conditions which did not involve more than $100 millions payment annually. Certain safeguards were sought, in particular against inability to pay because of a shortage of dollars or a general world depression. Certain very unsatisfactory features remained. In particular the Treasury insisted on including the demand that in imposing discriminatory restrictions against imports from the USA on the grounds that the dollar was scarce we should be free to look ahead and on our own judgement impose such discriminatory restrictions because in our opinion there was the prospect of the dollar becoming scarce. This is, of course, totally at variance with Article VII of the Bretton Woods International Monetary Fund. Luckily it seems rather to have been overlooked by our delegation in Washington; and Eady (from subsequent conversation) seems to be in a fine old muddle about it and fails to distinguish between a right on our part to suspend payment on an American loan when the dollar is duly declared scarce and the above right to impose discriminatory restrictions against American goods because we think that the dollar will at some future date become scarce. R. W. B. Clarke is behind this latter claim on the grounds that you cannot suddenly switch from USA to other sources for your imports when there are no more dollars to be had. You must gradually switch as you see the shortage of dollars arising. There is, of course, a grain of truth in this; but the answer is, of course, that the Bretton Woods Scarcity Article refers only to the scarcity of the currency in the International Monetary Fund. In other words, when the dollar was formally declared scarce it would mean that we could not get any more dollars from the Fund; it would not mean that we had no reserves of gold and dollars ourselves, which we could rely on to tide over the period while we were switching from USA to other goods.

Since the despatch of this telegram we have received another from Keynes explaining that Clayton had in fact made an informal offer of

[27] Above, pp. 141-2.
[28] Above, p. 145.

$5000 million on terms which involved the annual payment of $150 million in fifty years beginning after a period of five years. To meet the argument that we could pay $100 million but not $150 million (an argument which it is incidentally very difficult for us to sustain) Clayton told Keynes to draft an escape clause which would in effect mean that $50 millions of the above $150 millions was completely waived (not merely deferred) when we were not in a position to pay. Keynes proposed an escape clause which made the payment depend upon the real value of our exports (i.e. at 1938 prices) being above a certain level.[29]

This approach is, of course, the best common sense. It is quite uncertain what our balance of payments position will be five years hence (to say nothing of the position 55 years hence). If the American optimists are right, we should have no difficulty in paying more than $150 millions. If the British pessimists are right, we might have considerable difficulty in paying $100 millions. Therefore, let the event decide. Let the payment depend upon what in fact happens to our export trade. (Incidentally I think that it would be an improvement on Keynes' form of escape clause to make the payment depend upon the current value of our exports converted into dollars at the current official rate of exchange. To make a dollar payment the important thing is the total dollars which we can collect from our exports. This formula would, unlike Keynes' formula, help to ensure against a deflationary collapse in dollar prices.)

I argued this as best I could at a meeting under Eady's chairmanship with Rowe-Dutton, Grant, R. W. B. Clarke of the Treasury and Cobbold of the Bank of England. Later we adjourned to Bridges' room and argued it there. I believe I should have gained the point had it not been for Cobbold. Indeed, Rowe-Dutton at first liked my suggestion, Eady seemed to accept it and Grant actually drafted a passage to incorporate it which was then handed round the meeting. Then Cobbold weighed in. We must stand absolutely pat. Escape clauses of this kind were the devil. They would lead to every kind of annual recrimination between Congress and Parliament, etc., etc. No doubt there is an element of truth in this; but (a) the criterion is a fairly straightforward one which it is difficult to dispute and (b) there would be much more recrimination if we were either to reject the present settlement because we thought we might perhaps not be able to pay $150 millions in some years in the future or were to accept the settlement and then be forced to default without an escape clause. As to the argument that the Americans would argue that we were deliberately refraining from exporting in order to get out of the payment, it is most unlikely that the value of our exports would year after year be just below the critical level. It would probably be a long way above or a long way below. In the former case the problem would not arise, and in the latter case it would not arise in an acute form and we should have to resist what criticism there was. It is only if the value of our exports were very near the critical level that the criticism could arise in a very acute form; and in that case we could, if we wished, not take advantage of the escape clause.

[29] Cables 6733 and 6772, Keynes to Chancellor, 9 and 11 October 1945, T230/142 and FO371/45103.

Meanwhile the question of Imperial Preferences has come to the fore in an acute form. Our delegation in Washington has reported the great pressure which they are under for the complete elimination of preferences. There is complete political deadlock on this issue, since the Americans say that Congress will not grant the financial aid or significantly reduce the US tariff without the elimination of preferences, and we say that we will only bargain away preferences for adequate reductions in tariffs and other trade barriers and that the reductions which the Americans can undertake within the terms of the Trade Agreements Act are not sufficient to justify the elimination of preferences. Our delegation has cabled back a proposed treatment of preferences which is aimed at breaking the deadlock.[30] We undertake as a first step towards the substantial reduction of tariffs and the elimination of preferences in the spirit of Article VII that (i) no new preferences will be introduced or old preferential margins raised, (ii) all reductions of tariffs will apply to the general rate so that the preferential margins will be wholly or partially closed by the reduction of tariffs, (iii) no existing commitments (i.e. the Ottawa Agreements [of 1932]) will be held ultimately to stand in the way of reductions in preferential margins, and (iv) at a later conference, called by the International Trade Organisation, we would be prepared to consider whether a further deal could be done moving us further towards the elimination of preferences in return for further reductions in tariffs. Bridges held a meeting of officials at which all departments agreed that we should advise Ministers to let our delegation in Washington try out something on these lines.

Marcus Fleming prepared for the Lord President a brief on Imperial Preference. I prepared one for him on Imperial Preference and on the financial issue discussed above. At the meeting of Ministers at which both these issues were discussed, our delegates were authorised to try out this solution of the Imperial Preference issue, but – as was to be feared – on the financial issue Ministers jibbed at the objective test of our capacity to pay $150 millions a year for the financial aid.[31] Tactically it may have been correct to stand fast and see if one could not get a better offer out of the Americans; but I fear that serious damage may have been done to the idea of an objective test of this kind, which in my opinion in fact holds out the greatest hope of ultimate agreement.

The outcome of all this has been that on Imperial Preferences our delegation in Washington at the official level has drafted a treatment of preferences which seems to me to be very highly satisfactory, being on the general lines suggested above but without any reference at all to a second round of preference reductions. But this has not been agreed by Clayton and may very well be rejected at the US Ministerial level as quite inadequate for Congress. On this we cannot but wait and see.

On the financial issue Keynes has replied with a superb telegram in

[30] Cables NABOB 132, Halifax, Keynes and Liesching to Dalton and Cripps, and NABOB 133, Keynes and Liesching to Dalton and Cripps, 9 October 1945, T230/142.

[31] Fleming to Lord President, 10 October 1945, T230/175; Meade to Lord President, 13 October 1945, T230/140; GEN89/3rd Meeting, 12 October 1945, CAB78/37; cables ASKEW X 226, Helmore to Liesching, and PRISEC 10274, Chancellor to Keynes, 13 October 1945, T230/142.

which he returns to the charge in favour of a solution with, say, $150 millions annual payment but with adequate safeguards or escape clauses.[32] One set of escape clauses refers to the American capacity to receive payment. Here he suggests a threefold let-out:- (i) if the dollar is scarce under Article VII of the International Monetary Fund; (ii) if less than 75 per cent of the currencies which we receive for our exports are convertible into dollars; and (iii) if there is a prolonged and serious general world depression disturbing international balances of payments and recognised as such by the International Monetary Fund. It seems probable that we shall be able to reach agreement here easily enough on these. I have argued them at length with R. W. B. Clarke of the Treasury and no one seems to object. (Personally I would be prepared to drop the third, if we had a criterion for our capacity to pay based upon the dollar value of our exports. I cannot imagine a world depression which made it difficult for us to pay or for the Americans to receive payment but which did not make the dollar scarce *or* make more than 25 per cent of the currencies received from our exports inconvertible *or* reduce the dollar value of our exports below a suitably defined critical value.)

But Keynes then turns to a measure of our capacity to pay, dependent upon the volume of our exports. Here clearly the battle will have to be joined again – with what issue, I do not dare to prophesy.

Behind all this there is another issue. There is a strong current of opinion here in London that we should borrow from the USA only enough to meet our future current deficit with the USA and, possibly, a part of our current deficit with other countries; that we should try to obtain as much as possible in additional loans from others; and in any case we should not borrow to repay existing loans from others (i.e. to unfreeze existing sterling balances). This is a very dangerous line. We could not obtain a cheap settlement of our existing indebtedness if we had to go to our creditors cap in hand asking for further loans and without the inducement that, if they make a generous settlement with us, we will treat generously the problem of the conversion of their remaining balances into dollars. We can only maintain the Sterling Area in the long run on the basis that working balances of sterling are in part freely convertible, which they can be (and most important) will be thought to be, only if we have an adequate reserve of dollars. We shall not be able to join in with the Americans in a general economic and financial arrangement on Article VII lines, unless we have a large reserve of dollars which enables us to liberalise the sterling area, and if we cannot do this we cannot hope to have lasting and firm political co-operation with the USA and in the English-speaking world as a whole. Moreover, there is little prospect that we could borrow a smaller amount without having either to pay so much more for it in interest and repayment that it would be as expensive as the larger sum on more generous terms *or* to commit ourselves to a degree of action on commercial policy and liberalisation of the sterling area which it might be dangerous for us to do without the backing of the larger dollar reserve. And in any case the whole thing is absurd because we cannot expect to borrow as cheaply elsewhere

[32] NABOB 177, Keynes to Chancellor, 18 October 1945, T230/142.

as the terms offered by the Americans and the problem of repayment in dollars (as opposed to repayment in the currencies of other lenders) can be fully looked after by safeguards on the lines of the Scarce Currency Article of the International Monetary Fund.

I am arguing all this as well as the question of the objective test in a brief which I am preparing for the Lord President.[33]

All these questions I have been arguing at length in a series of meetings which I have been holding with Douglas Jay (who is now the Prime Minister's economic adviser) and R. W. B. Clarke of the Treasury. Clarke is a case of a man who temperamentally revolts against an idealist solution or a solution based on general principle. He feels embarrassed unless he can smell out some special vested national interest at work in each particular phase of each negotiation. Accordingly he hates Article VII and all to do with it. But he is a very nice and pleasant man to argue with. Douglas Jay who is learning all this up to brief the PM thus hears both sides of the case and so far takes a somewhat middle course.[34]

The most exacting task this fortnight has been the preparation of a reply to a telegram from Robbins to myself from Washington asking me in consultation with the Treasury to consider the details of the objective test to be used by countries which desired to impose quantitative restrictions on imports on the grounds that their balance of payments was out of equilibrium. The request came in the form of asking what precise numerical figures should be inserted into a formula (which made the use of import restrictions on balance of payments grounds depend upon the height of, and the rate of change in, a country's monetary reserves expressed as a percentage of their quotas with the International Monetary Fund) which we had devised with the Treasury for the purpose of talks with the Dominions officials on this subject earlier this year.[35] This was a consciously ingenuous request, since Lionel Robbins realises well that this matter is a bone of contention between the Treasury (who now hold that each country must be more or less free to use its own judgement about restricting its imports) and the Board of Trade (who hold that the all-important thing is to curb the power of other countries to put quantitative restrictions on their imports of our exports). So I was put on the spot in this innocent way to find a solution agreeable to these two great departments of state. I started by ringing up Eady who told me to get into touch with Clarke – I spent a whole Saturday morning arguing with Clarke. We started on Keynes' tests as to America's ability to receive payment from us of the service of a dollar loan (for which see above) and soon reached agreement on this. Clarke then stated that the Treasury view was that there should be no test at all for a country's right to impose import restrictions. We argued and argued and broke up for lunch at 2:20, argued through lunch and in the Underground to Camden Town where we parted.

33 Below, p. 164.

34 On these meetings, which took place on 16 and 18 October, see Clarke to Meade, 11 October 1945 (enclosing 'The Amount and Terms of Aid from USA' which he had sent to Jay on 10 October), T230/142, Jay to Meade, 13 October, and Meade, Draft for Meeting, 13 October 1945, T230/175.

35 NABOB 158, Robbins to Meade, 13 October 1945, T230/176.

I drafted over the week-end, rang Helmore up at the Board of Trade on Monday. He rang Eady up, who said he was going to keep out of this and that Clarke was taking it up. I then had another meeting with Clarke at which we both produced drafts – his simply saying that a country could impose restrictions when either it was losing reserves or had an adverse balance of payments on current account; and mine saying (i) that a country could not impose restrictions at all if its monetary reserves were above a certain proportion of the value of its imports and exports, (ii) that below this it could impose restrictions only if its reserves were falling seriously and it would remove restrictions sufficiently to prevent its reserves rising, (iii) that the proposed International Trade Organisation could ask it to explain its action, could hear complaints against it and could in the last resort judge that its action was inadmissible and relieve other countries of their commercial policy obligations towards the offending member, and (iv) that if restrictions imposed on these grounds continued for two years or more the country would be willing to consult with other countries and international institutions to see if some better alternative means could be found of getting rid of the disequilibrium in the balance of payments. I objected strongly to Clarke's version on two grounds: first that it left countries much too free to decide for themselves so that there would be no guarantee that restrictions would not be misused to the detriment of our export trade, and secondly that the criterion of the balance of payments on current account was completely wrong since it would mean that a capital importing country could always impose restrictions on imports without limit while a capital exporting country could never do so.

Next day we had a meeting with Helmore, Clarke, Lucius Thompson-McCausland of the Bank of England, Fleming and myself at which we managed to reach an agreed text. I gave up the idea of an automatic test; but the guiding principles on which a country would act were fairly precisely laid down. Restrictions were only to be used in so far as they were necessary to avoid a large or prolonged deficit in the balance of payments, defined as the current balance adjusted for normal capital imports or exports and thus in large measure to be observed through movements in a country's monetary reserves. While each country maintained its right to judge for itself, the International Trade Organisation had the right of hearing complaints and, in the last resort, of depriving an offending member of the benefits of the convention. The principle was also maintained of the search for alternative means of putting the disequilibrium right if the import restrictions persisted.[36]

The real issue is, of course, between (a) unlimited national sovereignty, (b) making the International Trade Organisation a 'super-state' in the sense of giving it the power of deciding whether a country can or can not impose restrictions, and (c) a more or less automatic rule agreed upon in advance to determine whether a country could use restrictions or not. Our compromise is something between all three of these. It is not very good, but it is better than nothing.

[36] See Meade to Clarke, Thompson-McCausland, Helmore and Fleming, 15 October, and cables BABOON 126 and 127, Meade to Robbins, 16 October 1945, T230/175.

Another issue arose in the course of these discussions. As our draft now stands the import restrictions can be on a discriminatory basis on three occasions:- (i) during a transitional period, (ii) when a currency is scarce *à la* Bretton Woods, and (iii) in the sense that the whole of a group of territories making up a single unit of the International Monetary Fund can impose restrictions as a unit against the rest of the world (i.e. our colonies can stop the imports of American [cars] without stopping the import of UK cars). (ii) is obviously all right. I should expect the Americans to react violently against (iii) which offends against the 'open-door' trusteeship principle in colonial administration and I personally would sympathise with them if they did. I should also expect them to ask why (i) should be necessary if we obtain all the dollar financial aid for which we are asking. Should we not then be prepared to buy in the cheapest market? Again I shall be prepared to argue that in this respect we should meet the American demand if it comes.

Tom Wilson has been discussing with Pares at the Board of Trade a paper which they are preparing on export policy, and he has himself prepared a draft paper for the Lord President on the Export Drive which we have discussed at a Staff Meeting.[37]

Miss Watts has written the Lord President two admirable briefs. The first was on Migration pointing out that the talk of migration from the mother country to the Dominions, which is seriously proceeding from the Dominions Office, is nonsense in the present demographic position of this country. The second was on Civil Aviation, pointing out that it would be worth our while adopting an Article VII principle allowing free foreign competition against our Civil Aviation (with a suitable transitional period let-out for the building up in the months immediately ahead of our civil air fleet) provided we could get in return from the Americans a similar policy about shipping. Our balance of payments had much more to gain from shipping than from Civil Aviation.[38] Unfortunately on this latter problem we do not seem to have had any success so far.

I attended a meeting in Norman Brook's room at which Eady from the Treasury, Ronald from the Foreign Office and Woods from the Board of Trade were present.[39] The purpose of the meeting was to set up the interdepartmental committee to deal with the central collection and appraisal of Overseas Economic Intelligence. We move surely but slowly on this point. Helmore of the Board of Trade is to be chairman of the committee. Fleming is to be our representative, and A. J. Brown will be one of the secretaries.

I was invited to dinner at the Savoy by the Chancellor of the Exchequer to meet Gunnar Myrdal and Svennilson (who spent the afternoon with us

[37] LP(I)(45)4, 'Development of the Export Trade, Report by the President of the Board of Trade', 24 October 1945, CAB124/749; Wilson, 'The Export Drive', EC(S)(45)34, 9 October 1945, T230/18 and CAB124/749.

[38] Watts to Lord President, 'Migration, Memorandum by the Secretary of State for Dominion Affairs CP(45)198', 8 October 1945, CAB21/2260, and 'Civil Aviation Policy, Memorandum by the Secretary of State for Dominion Affairs (CP(45)221) and the Minister of Civil Aviation (CP(45)222)', 17 October 1945, T230/3.

[39] On 10 October; minutes are on CAB21/2206.

in our home the Saturday before). Douglas Jay, Evan Durbin, Hugh Gaitskell, and the Financial Secretary (Hall) were the other guests. I was a bit embarrassed in being produced as one of the young Labour Party economists. I am nothing of the sort. I am a Civil Servant.[40] The talk was mainly political and I listened with interest but kept Mum.

The next day I was asked to lunch at the Swedish Legation again to meet Myrdal and Svennilson. Professor Laski was there plus (in addition to the Swedish Minister and his wife) two Swedes whose names and occupations I do not know. Laski was in his usual lying, boastful and exhibitionist mood. I realised with a start that I had become one of the semi-great (if not actually great) when I perceived Laski taking notice of me and actually inviting me to call at his home on Tuesday evening after 8 p.m.!

Lunched with Jussiant of the Belgian Economic Mission to meet two other Belgians (names unknown), one of whom was, I believe, the senior permanent official of the Belgian ministry of economics.

Lunched with Penrose of the US Embassy at the Churchill Club. I like old Penrose. Maybe he is a trifle dull at times, but he is a really sincere and hard worker in the cause of international sanity. He is always very friendly and good humoured and, on the whole, full of good shrewd common sense and with very few prejudices.

[40] Meade had been an adviser to the Labour Party while he was a Fellow of Hertford College, Oxford (1931–7) (see Meade Papers 2/7). When he returned to England from the League of Nations to join the Central Economic Information Service in 1940 he 'decided to behave exactly as a Civil Servant without engaging in political activity of any kind' (Meade to Howson, 12 May 1986).

# 13

# November 1945

### *3 November 1945*

This fortnight has again been one of frightful pressure of work with two first-class issues (nationalisation at home and the Washington discussions abroad) piled on top of the ordinary day-to-day work of the Section.

On nationalisation we are engaged in preparing a more or less comprehensive Section paper for the Lord President. He sent out in September a list of eight questions, which we had drafted, to the Ministers likely to be responsible for socialisation schemes, covering such problems as:- the basis on which compensation should be assessed; the method by which compensation should be paid (i.e. cash, equity shares, fixed debt on the socialised industry with or without Treasury guarantee, Government stock); the form of organisation for running the socialised industry; whether or not there should be separate organisations for different regions or sections of the industry; the price policy of a socialised industry; wage policy; investment policy; and import and export policy.[1] We have had a series of staff meetings and innumerable discussions in the preparation of a series of replies by ourselves to these questions together with some introductory observations which I have tried to draft myself. Chester has worked on the problems of compensation and organisation; Tom Wilson

[1] The questions, which were sent to Cripps, Dalton, Morrison, Shinwell, Wilmot and Barnes on 3 September (T230/106), read as follows:-

(1) On what basis and on what scale of generosity should the owners of industries which are being socialised be compensated?
(2) Should compensation be paid in cash, Government stock, fixed interest stock secured on the industry, or partly equity stock?
(3) What form of organisation should be set up to run the industry?
(4) Should we in certain circumstances contemplate separate organisations for different sections or regions of the industry?
(5) How should prices be fixed? Should they pay regard to the regional or sectional differences within the industry? Should the aim be to make some profits, sell at average cost or, in certain circumstances, to sell below average cost?
(6) Should there be a single, nation-wide basis, for wage-rates or should there be regional or sectional variations? Should the rate of wages be related to productivity?
(7) What arrangements should be made for the planning and timing of new investment in the industry?
(8) On what principles should the import and export trade of the commodities concerned be conducted?

See also Chester, *The Nationalisation of British Industry 1945–51*, pp. 234–5.

on the problems of price policy; Dennison on that of wage policy; Tress on investment policy; and Marcus Fleming (who has just returned from the ILO conference in Paris) has taken on the question on import and export policy.[2]

Our line is the first shot in the fight which I intend to wage for the liberal-socialist policy in socialised industries, i.e. for the proper use of the economic calculus in determining their output, prices, wages, imports, exports etc. In my introductory remarks I have attempted three themes: first, that one of the main principles in determining whether an industry should be socialised or not is whether it is inevitably, for technical reasons, monopolistic or not and that where true competition is possible the advantages of the economic calculus can be brought about without state intervention; secondly, that socialised industries should obey the economic calculus (i.e. produce by the cheapest methods and expand production so long as cost is lower than price); and, thirdly, that they should not be afraid of competition from alternative sources of supply (e.g. let private enterprise coastal shipping compete with the nationalised railways) or from imported supplies. In our answers to questions we have expanded these themes. We have had a great debate about price policy, where Tom Wilson has wished to lay down the golden rule that prices should cover average cost (i.e. that the socialised plant should make neither profit nor loss). He does this in order to supply incentives to managers for efficiency (i.e. so that they cannot get away with losses due to inefficiency by pleading that their prices do in fact cover marginal costs) and to prevent a spate of special pleadings for the subsidisation of everything. On the other hand, so many exceptions must be admitted to this golden rule that it seems quite wrong to start off with it. In the first place, in the short run if the demand for the product of the socialised industry is much too great or much too small for the existing scale of capital equipment it would appear very wasteful not to equate price to marginal prime cost and to allow a considerable profit or loss to develop for a time. Secondly, in the case of increasing cost industries like coal-mining where the different seams are of differing productivity it would be very wasteful to make the price cover only the average cost and not to allow for any Ricardian rent. Thirdly, in decreasing cost industries like electricity it would be very wasteful not to promote consumption by appropriate devices for charging consumers only the marginal cost of their consumption. I have tried my hand at a revision of Tom Wilson's draft on these heads.[3]

We have taken the opportunity of preaching many individual lessons on the application of the economic calculus in a liberal-socialist manner. Costs of efficient and of inefficient plants must not be pooled, but low-cost

[2] Some of the drafts were circulated as Section discussion papers: Chester, 'Problems and principles of socialisation', 25 October, Wilson [Answers to questions (3), (4) and (6)], 31 October, and Meade, 'Problems and principles of socialisation', 30 October 1945, EC(S)(45)36, 37 and 38, T230/18 and 106. The final version is in *The Collected Papers of James Meade*, Vol. II, Chapter 5.

[3] Wilson, 'Price and output policy of state enterprise', 19 October, Annex I to EC(S)(45)37, 31 October 1945, T230/106 and 18.

plants in socialised industries must be permitted to drive out the high-cost plants; uniform national delivered prices must be avoided, and regional differences must be allowed in order to avoid wasteful transport; uniform wage-rates must be avoided and wages must be related to productivity in order to encourage workers to move from positions in which they are less to those in which they are more productive or else we must be prepared either to direct labour from the unproductive to productive employments or to lose the possible improvement in standards of living; we must import from abroad if we can get the goods thus at a cheaper rate than through production in the socialised industry; etc., etc.

The problem of Compensation and Betterment and the Control of Land Use has been up to Ministers again. The official committee which has been working on this has now reported to the Lord President and Chester has briefed him on it after discussing it with me.[4] We still take objection to the proposals on Betterment which suggest that when any piece of land is developed the developer will have to pay a licence fee equal to 80 per cent of the development value, which – we contend – will remove the willingness of the landowner to develop (without in fact collecting any Betterment due to increased value of land whose use is not changed). It is true that there will be a right of public acquisition of the land for the purpose of letting it out to developers if the landowner is recalcitrant; but in our view a system should be devised which does not remove so much of the private incentive to develop. The alternatives are a periodic tax on the increment of value of all land (whether its use has been changed or not) or an annual levy on all real property (like the War Damage Contribution) to form a fund for payment of compensation to those who are on planning grounds refused permission to develop or to put the burden of compensation direct on the Exchequer. Chester and I have discussed with John Maud; he and Chester have discussed with the Lord President; and I have sent to Bridges a copy of a note which I wrote on this subject some weeks ago. We managed to scare Maud and the Lord President into the view that there was real danger to the prospects of adequate development and so to employment policy in all this; but when it came to the Ministerial meeting I understand that Morrison did not press the point hard. The matter now goes to the Cabinet.[5]

On the home front there have been many other important issues under discussion; but extreme pressure of work has made it very difficult to give them the attention which they deserve. The question of future agricultural policy has been before the Lord President's Committee and there have been a series of drafts of a Ministry of Agriculture paper and a draft public announcement on it. These have been sent to us for our observations and

[4] Official Sub-Committee on Compensation and Betterment First Report, CB(0)(45)15 and CB(45)6, 23 October 1945, Chester to Lord President, 'Compensation and Betterment (CB(45)6)', 27 October, and 'Notes on Betterment', 30 October 1945, CAB124/383; Chester to Lord President, 'Notes for Meeting on Compensation and Betterment Report CB(45)6', 31 October 1945, CAB124/384.

[5] Meade to Bridges, 30 October 1945 (enclosing 'The Proposed Betterment Tax', 26 September), T273/341; CB(45) 3rd Meeting, 31 October 1945, CAB124/384; CM(45) 53rd conclusions, 15 November 1945, CAB128/2.

comments by Sir Donald Vandepeer, who has succeeded Sir Donald Fergusson as Permanent Secretary of the Ministry of Agriculture. He is certainly going all out to woo us who, under Lionel's directorship, have been regarded as the Ministry of Agriculture's *bête noir*! Tress has discussed these problems with John Maud and has briefed the Lord President.[6] The policy is not too bad. It is desired to carry out a policy of giving guaranteed prices for farm products and the paper is mainly on the mechanics of doing this. The real rub, of course, arises when it is decided what level the guaranteed prices should be fixed at, because it is this, of course, which determines the degree of protection given. There are, however, certain favourable factors at work. This present Government (as witness the perhaps rather unwise guarantee given by the Chancellor in his recent Budget speech that the cost-of-living index will not be allowed to rise during the coming year)[7] will not favour increased prices to consumers, so that the cost of protection will fall on the Exchequer. This both provides some safeguard to the amount of protection likely to be given, and makes the policy less likely to conflict with any general commercial policy agreement reached under Article VII, where the principle seems recognised that direct subsidies to production are permissible. Moreover, the mechanism adopted seems to plan agriculture less in quantities to be produced (though there are references in the Ministry of Agriculture's paper to which we have taken objection on the power to direct what crops shall be grown and on the power forcibly to eject unsatisfactory farmers or landowners) than in terms of the prices to be offered; and I am sure that planning in terms of prices, allowing producers freely to produce within that price structure, makes the achievement of a liberal-socialist economy more possible. So far, therefore, we have not quarrelled with the Ministry of Agriculture; but such are the traditions of the Economic Section that this automatically makes me ask myself whether this does not automatically prove that we have taken the wrong line!

Another issue which has been to the Lord President's Committe (the Industrial Sub-Committee) and thence to the Cabinet is the future of the Labour Controls. Here there have been two rather distinct views among Ministers. On the one hand, the Minister of Labour wishes greatly to relax the existing controls, largely on the ground that the existing controls cannot in fact be enforced because of their political implications. He wishes to reduce the whole thing to something which can be vigorously enforced (roughly speaking covering persons of military age up to 30). On the other hand are those (Cripps and Morrison) who are struck with the difficulty of manning certain industries (notably textiles) whose products are most essential but which are unattractive to labour.[8] Here is a first-rate issue

[6] LP(45) 40th Meeting, 1 November 1945, CAB71/19; LP(45)216, 'Agricultural Policy', 29 October 1945, CAB71/22; Vandepeer to Meade, 2 November 1945, Tress to Maud, 'Agricultural Policy', 29 October, and Tress to Lord President, 'Agricultural Policy: Memorandum by the Agricultural Ministers (LP(45)216)', 31 October 1945, CAB124/568.

[7] *House of Commons Debates*, Vol. 415, 23 October 1945, cols 1877–8.

[8] The Industrial Sub-committee of the LPC and the Cabinet discussed an official report on Labour Controls, with a covering note by the Minister of Labour, on 29 October and

for the liberal-socialist! Labour is not in fact going to be directed in peacetime. The only way to induce labour to go into the desired occupations is by variations in relative wage-rates. But is this to be brought about solely by a rise in the unattractive wage-rates or can some reduction in the too attractive wage-rates be brought about? If only by the former, is there to be a continual inflation of costs? If so, what about the stabilisation of the cost of living? This is a tender spot indeed. Can a liberal-socialist economy be run (a) permitting private monopolies (Trade Unions) to fix wage-rates and (b) without state intervention in the wage bargain, while (c) the cost of living is stabilised and (d) a general policy of expansion of demand is guaranteed to prevent general unemployment? At present the one outcome of the discussion is that there is to be an interdepartmental examination of relative wage-rates in which the Economic Section will, I hope, be represented.[9]

Yet another first-rate issue has been the treatment of certain localised pockets of unemployment. In the course of industrial reconversion some, still small, black spots of unemployment are appearing. Ministers remembering the 1930s are getting panicky about it. They fail to realise (a) how small these totals are, (b) how unusual and unprecedented the present labour transfer and reconversion is, and (c) how much easier these limited black spots will be to deal with if we preserve a generally high and stable level of demand and do not permit the development of general depression as in the 1930s. The Minister of Labour has put in a paper to the Lord President's Committee on the localised spots of unemployment which are now developing. Dennison briefed the Lord President on the subject, explaining how small the present amount of unemployment really was; how inevitable some local spots of unemployment were bound to be during the transition and reconversion; how impossible it was to deal with this promptly by building new factories, since one would have to wait until one had got the building labour together and until the building labour had actually built the factories. He also pointed out how the present attempts of the Board of Trade to coax industrialists to set up new firms in the development areas were really not very successful, the vast majority of applicants for permission to set up new factories preferring to wait (even in present conditions when their only hope of being able to carry out their projects is to go to a development area) rather than to go to these localities. All this led up to the moral that we must stress the mobility of labour as much as the bringing of the work to the men. The tone of Dennison's minute, however, appeared to me to be very inappropriate: "Sno use; Can't be done.' The Prime Minister (at the instigation of Jay who is an enthusiast on the other side) sent the Lord President a minute asking whether more could not be done by giving preferential treatment to these areas by giving them priority in the allocation of raw materials, and I took the opportunity

1 November 1945 respectively (LP(I)(45) 2nd meeting, CAB124/692, and CM(45) 48th conclusions, CAB128/2; 'Labour Controls, Report by Official Committee', 22 October 1945, GEN87/5 and LP(45)209, CAB124/692 and CAB71/22). Cripps' views are in 'The Future of Economic Controls', LP(45)210, 24 October 1945, CAB71/22.

[9] See below, p. 205.

of briefing the Lord President on this subject myself in a rather less doctrinaire tone.[10]

G. L. Shackle has produced an enormous work on the theoretical aspects of the problem of the extent to which changes in interest rates are likely to affect the decision to invest. I have discussed this with him and have urged him to proceed to a more realistic study of our probable actual future investment programme in this country and to consider, in the light of his theoretical analysis, how far the different parts of this programme are likely to be sensitive to changes in the rate of interest or to other devices (e.g. taxes or subsidies on investment, or the provision of equity capital by the state).[11] So far the Economic Plan has all been a matter of forecasting programmes etc. Soon we shall have to join battle on a royal scale with the Treasury as to the mechanisms (which must be largely financial and fiscal if we are to obtain a liberal-socialist solution) of influencing the rate of national expenditure as and when the real quantitative controls crumble or become irrelevant because the problem is to stimulate rather than to restrict expenditure.

This fortnight has seen the most crucial developments in the Washington talks on Finance, Commercial Policy etc. As was to be feared, the American reaction to our absurd insistence to have nothing to do with a waiver clause which would make our liability to pay on the loan dependent upon our balance of payments ability to pay has been to reduce the sum which they offer to lend us to $3½ billion at 2 per cent interest repayable over 50 years, in an attempt to bring the annual service near the mystic figure of $100 million which Ministers in their wisdom (on the advice of the Treasury) have selected as the figure below which we could pay without a waiver and above which we could not pay.[12] This figure is totally inadequate to enable us to liberalise at all the Sterling Area arrangements. Indeed we assess the deficit over the next three years in our current balance of payments at $5 billion, so that with $3½ billion only from the USA we should have to get other countries to lend us $1½ billion, which is a very different story from releasing some part of the existing sterling balances for payment in dollars or any other currency. I had been trying to push a waiver clause based on the current dollar value of our exports on the grounds that this would take account not only of the volume of our exports but also of a possible deflation of dollar prices. But Keynes has produced a much better waiver:- the interest element of the payment is to be waived whenever our visible and net invisible exports are not sufficient to finance our pre-war volume of imports. The philosophy behind this is that we cannot be considered to have restored our balance of payments position until we can finance our pre-war level of imports, and that it cannot be

[10] LP(I)(45)5, 'The Employment Situation' also circulated as CP(45)228, 13 October 1945, CAB129/3; Dennison to Lord President, 'The Employment Situation (CP(45)228)', 23 October, Minute M119/45, Attlee to Lord President, 19 October, and Meade to Lord President, 'The Employment Situation and Raw Materials (LP(I)(45)5) and Prime Minister's Personal Minute (M119/45)', 26 October 1945, CAB124/218.

[11] See below, p. 184.

[12] Cable NABOB 191, Keynes to Chancellor of the Exchequer, 20 October 1945, T236/440 and *The Collected Writings of John Maynard Keynes*, Vol. 24, pp. 557–63.

made out to be a debt settlement which, in the words of Article VII, does not burden international settlement, unless it permits us to import at least as much as before the war. I immediately abandoned my idea of a waiver and backed this wholeheartedly. This I did first of all in a minute to Bridges who had received a personal cable from Lionel Robbins in Washington urging acceptance of a waiver. But Bridges unfortunately had been persuaded of the lack of wisdom in any settlement in which our great nation was, in his words, permanently taking the temperature of another great nation. I argued that the dangers of the waiver had been much exaggerated. First, the criterion would be a more or less objective matter of fact. Secondly, as Keynes suggested, the International Monetary Fund could be given the statistical job of determining whether or not the critical point were reached. Thirdly, the probability was, of course, that our visible and invisible exports would either be much above or much below the critical point; in the former case the issue whether or not to use the waiver would never arise; in the latter case the verdict should be unquestionable; and in the improbable case of our exports hovering around the critical point we need not make use of the waiver.[13]

The Treasury then proceeded to draft a telegram giving our counter-proposal to the American offer. This was, I think, the lowest point of Eady's and Cobbold's efforts. We were to offer the Americans two alternative plans. Under Plan A we should borrow $2½ billion, at 1 per cent interest repayable over 50 years starting in five years' time and should have an option on another $2 billion free of interest, which would be used only to liberalise the Sterling Area. (This was, of course, a specious but quite bogus point. It was not as if we could use this $2 billion to release existing Sterling Balances in dollars. It would be barely sufficient to enable us to scrape through the next three years without borrowing additional sums from the Sterling Area to meet our current balance of payments deficit with them.) Under Plan B we would refuse to continue for the time being with Bretton Woods or Commercial Policy and we would borrow only $2 billion from the United States for our inevitable purchases from them on commercial terms which we were pleased to define as 2 per cent interest repayable over 50 years.[14] This was, of course, lunacy. The terms offered for cleaning up Lend-Lease are 2⅜ per cent repayable over 30 years, and the Import-Export Bank terms are still worse. Under neither arrangement would the American administration have at their disposal $2½ billion to lend to us, and there was, of course, no presumption that they would in fact lend us a bean on any terms if we would not touch Commercial Policy or Bretton Woods. I attended a meeting in the Treasury with Eady and Clarke from the Treasury, Cobbold from the Bank of England, and Helmore from the Board of Trade. They all (including Helmore) seemed to take delight in this proposed solution because the time had come to show the Americans that we could be tough. But it was not until I heard Cobbold on this occasion that I realised that he really

[13] Cable NABOB 200, Keynes to Treasury, 21 October 1945, T230/142. Neither Meade's minute nor Robbins' cable has been found.

[14] Treasury draft telegrams replying to NABOBs 177, 191 and 200, 24 October 1945, T236/440.

delighted in a wrecking proposal of this kind. Clearly he does not want any general settlement on the lines contemplated with the Americans. He would like us to snap our fingers at the Americans and to develop the Sterling Area, – though God alone knows how we could get on in this way. He is a clever ass.

I spent a long time writing a very full minute to the Lord President on the two points: first, that we were in desperate need of finance of the order of $5 billion to pay our way with the United States, to avoid having by hook or by crook to borrow more from the Sterling Area (on much worse terms than those offered by the USA and to the detriment of any settlement in respect of our existing sterling indebtedness), to avoid crushing austerity if we had to restrict imports or push exports much more vigorously, and to avoid the gradual break-up of the Sterling Area which would tend to disintegrate if the holders of sterling could not convert their sterling; and secondly, that the logical way out was a waiver clause which would mean that we should pay if we could but not if we couldn't, and that the arguments against such an arrangement had been grossly exaggerated. I had an hour's talk with the Lord President on all this before seeing the Treasury's telegram on Plan A and Plan B, but I supplemented my general minute and conversation with a short minute showing the folly of Plan B.[15]

Meanwhile a further cause of misunderstanding had arisen on the financial side. Keynes sent a telegram from Washington of what he intended to give to the Americans on the liberalisation of the sterling area.[16] On this Cobbold and Eady threw a fit saying that we could in effect give the Americans no assurances about getting our sterling creditors to scale down their balances or about the amount to which we could release sterling balances for conversion into dollars. Keynes considers that he has definitely been led up the garden path on this, that in accord with his instructions he has made some verbal assurances on this to the Americans, and that Eady is now going back on him.

At this stage not only finance but also commercial policy seemed on the point of breaking down on the question of imperial preferences. Our delegation had tried on the Americans the rules for dealing with preferences referred to in my entry under 20 October, namely (i) that no new preferences should be introduced and no old preferences raised, (ii) that all preferential margins should be open to negotiation, and (iii) that all reductions in general rates of duty should be allowed to reduce or eliminate the preferential margin (i.e. that preferential rates should not be reduced until the general rate were reduced to the level of the preferential rate).[17] After sweating blood and tears with the Americans our delegates in Washington had obtained from the Americans a 'Draft 7' on preferences, which in fact conceded this method of dealing with preferences, but the introductory and concluding words of this Draft 7 were drafted with the most skilful ambiguity so that the Americans, in

[15] Meade to Lord President, 'Washington Discussions NABOB 177, 191 and 200', 24 October, and 'Washington Discussions, Financial Settlement (GEN89/7)', 26 October 1945, T230/142. The Treasury proposals of GEN89/7 are on T230/142 and CAB78/37.

[16] NABOB 215, J. S. M. Washington to Cabinet Office, 24 October 1945, T236/455.

[17] Above p. 151.

explaining to their public, would be able to express greater hopes that in the negotiations on tariffs and preferences to be undertaken next March preferences would be completely eliminated than we should be willing to admit. The Americans have in any case abandoned completely the idea that preferences should be eliminated in return for financial assistance; they admit that they must be dealt with under Article VII and only eliminated in return for a mutually advantageous *quid pro quo* in the form of adequate reductions in tariffs and other trade barriers by other countries; but what they will not admit openly at any rate is that there is precious little prospect of us and the Dominions being offered a sufficient *quid pro quo* (particularly in view of the limitations under the US Trade Agreements Act of the extent to which they can reduce their duties) next March for us to feel able completely to eliminate preferences then. I briefed the Lord President in the sense that Draft 7 was perfectly adequate (in view of the possible ambiguities the Board of Trade wished to scrap it), that we could not conceivably expect more from the Americans, that we might in fact get a very good bargain by giving up preferences entirely if we got a 50 per cent cut in the American and a lot of other tariffs, and that in any case it would be bad faith on our part (in view of the words of Article VII) to suggest that there was no reduction of tariffs and other trade barriers, however great, which would make it possible for us to eliminate preferences, although we could, of course, make it quite clear that elimination would require the most far-reaching tariff reductions which we did not expect to get offered us in March.[18]

Ministers met on these financial and imperial preference issues and reached all the wrong decisions. The waiver (although Morrison, Addison, Pethick-Lawrence and the Prime Minister were not adverse to it) was violently opposed by Cripps and Dalton, who were supported by Bridges, and was declared out; we were to offer the lunatic Plan B as an alternative to Plan A; and Draft 7 was to be reconsidered. The Labour Ministers discovered the Empire, in which they were helped by a well-timed telegram from the Australians who argued that we should be prepared to contemplate the absence of dollar assistance and rely on the sterling area.[19] As if the contribution which Australia could make to our balance of payments was of any appreciable significance, and as if other Dominions (like Canada who is not in the Sterling Area and South Africa who would certainly sell her gold for dollars if the sterling which she obtained for it from us were not convertible) would be willing to come in or stay in such a system.

Since this point, however, there has been a vast improvement in the situation. Keynes sent a reply telegram pointing out how lunatic Plan B was; he asked why we shouldn't have Plan A plus a waiver; Bridges began therefore to change his mind on the waiver; Brand (the cautious banker and fully *au fait* with the last debt settlement) cabled from Washington on his belief in the waiver; the Treasury cabled to Keynes saying that Plan

[18] Meade to Lord President, 'Washington Discussions: Imperial Preference (GEN89/6)', 26 October 1945. For the Americans' 'Draft 7' proposals see GEN89/6, CAB78/37.

[19] GEN89/4th Meeting, 26 October 1945, CAB78/37; Cable No. 352, Government of Australia to Secretary of State for Dominion Affairs, 23 October 1945, T230/142.

A could be put forward with 2 per cent instead of 1 per cent interest on the $2½ billions for our own use.[20]

On imperial preferences too the atmosphere has completely changed. Lionel Robbins and Hall-Patch of the Foreign Office have come home from our delegation in Washington.[21] Apart from confirming in the Treasury the need for a waiver, Lionel Robbins has done heroic work on imperial preferences. Clutterbuck of the Dominions Office has been persuaded that with minor amendments to Draft 7 (which has been cabled to Washington and agreed by the Americans)[22] plus a gloss on the interpretation of Draft 7 which we shall be able to publish here and in the Dominions without fear of American contradiction, the present text is one which the Dominions Office can get past the Dominions. I have spent much time with Robbins, Clutterbuck, Helmore and Stirling of the Board of Trade drafting these amendments and glosses. This is not economics. It is the psychology of symbols and is all very mystifying. How much easier affairs of state would be if rational men having agreed on a rational course of action were then permitted to give a rational account of it!

The atmosphere has thus completely changed in the course of a day or two. The last news from Washington was that the Americans intend now to obtain agreement in the course of next week, to publish the Commercial Policy agreement next Sunday, and the financial agreement about the same time. Dates have already, I understand, been fixed for the following week for American broadcasts by Clayton and Vinson on the subject. So in the course of next week this long Article VII story (which started properly for me when I prepared the first draft of the Commercial Union – as it was then called – for Dalton as President of the Board of Trade in July 1942) may draw (not to a close, for there is much to be done yet) but to its first definite stage of full official agreement and public commitment.[23]

We have done one or two other things in the Economic Section on the external side. Tom Wilson has been briefing the Lord President on the dreadful subject of food for Germany;[24] but there the avoidance of starvation does really depend essentially upon whether the food exporting countries will cut their stocks, cease feeding wheat to animals, and not expand their own consumption. There is little that we can do; but I feel that it is of the greatest psychological importance that we should demonstrate our willingness to do that little.

Nita Watts has briefed the Lord President on the White Paper which the Ministry of Labour wishes to publish expressing the UK acceptance of certain ILO recommendations, one of which is that we should prepare

20 NABOB 230, Halifax and Keynes to Chancellor, 28 October 1945, T230/142; NABOB 235, Brand to Eady, 30 October 1945, T236/440; BABOON 158, Dalton to Halifax and Keynes, 29 October 1945, T230/142.

21 They arrived in London on 31 October.

22 BABOON 182 and 183, Robbins to Liesching, 2 November 1945, T230/142.

23 Cable NABOB 258, Keynes to Chancellor, 2 November 1945, T236/456; Meade, 'A proposal for an international commercial union', 28 July 1942, EC(S)(42)19, T230/14 (reprinted in *The Collected Papers of James Meade*, Vol. III, Chapter 3).

24 Discussed in the LPC on 5 November, on the basis of memoranda by the Chancellor of the Duchy of Lancaster, the Minister of Food and the Lord President (LP(45) 41st meeting, CAB71/19; LP(45)219, 220, 223 and 226, CAB71/22).

and communicate to the ILO programmes of public capital investment.[25] This is objectionable (a) because it should be the Economic and Social Council and not the ILO which ought to deal with Employment Policy internationally and (b) because, while we certainly intend to prepare programmes of future investment, we may well not wish to publish them and then to invite speculation by private enterprise on the probability of a future inflationary or deflationary situation.

In the course of the fortnight I dined with Eric Biddle of the American Embassy to meet Howard [*sic*] Rice (who later lunched with me at the Reform Club) who is in charge of the Statistics division of the Bureau of the Budget in Washington. The other guests were Bridges, Maud and Campion. I lunched with Professor Lindahl, the Swedish economist, who is on a mission to this country examining taxation problems. I lunched also with Nicki Kaldor. Hall-Patch also took me to lunch at the Union Club to discuss the present position of the Washington discussions.

## *18 November 1945*

The main problem with which we have been concerned this fortnight is that of the socialisation of industry. We have continued a series of staff meetings in the preparation of our paper answering the eight questions which have been circulated to departments on the principles on which they intend to carry out their socialisation schemes. Our thoughts have centred round the problem of determining prices and output in a socialised industry.[26] This is not only a question of how the socialised industry should be run; it affects the much more immediate problem of the way in which an industry should be taken over by the state. Ministers at the moment (as was made clear at a Ministerial meeting of the 'socialising Ministers' with the Lord President in the chair which I attended) take it as axiomatic that a socialised industry should be run in such a way as just to cover the annual service of the compensation money; and they, therefore, consider that it is a purely political and administrative question devoid of economic interest whether the compensation stock takes the form of government debt (in which case the socialised industry would earn and pay to the Treasury each year an amount equal to the service of this part of the national debt) or whether compensation takes the form of stock secured on the earnings of the industry with a government guarantee. I briefed the Lord President strongly against this view and strongly in favour of the view that compensation should be paid in the form of ordinary government stock, so that the industry would not be obliged to earn always an amount exactly equal to the service of the compensation money. Such a requirement would have absurd results:- (i) If there was any element of monopoly in the pre-socialisation situation in respect of which compensation had to be paid, the socialised industry would have to carry on the

[25] Watts to Lord President, 'International Labour Conference, Memorandum by the Minister of Labour and National Service (CP(45)238)', 31 October 1945, CAB21/2260.

[26] See above pp. 157–9.

restrictive policies of the private enterprise. (ii) If there were an unexpected decline in the demand for the product, the socialised industry would have to restrict output and leave labour and plant unemployed in order to maintain (and indeed raise) the price of the product so as to cover its total cost – a policy much more restrictive than even private enterprise would adopt, since profits would be allowed to decline in bad times. (iii) Similarly, if there were an unexpected increase in demand for the industry's product, the price could not be raised in the way in which the economic calculus would require; but plant would have to be overworked in order to raise average cost to the level necessary to set a price which would equate supply to the new demand. (iv) If a risky enterprise were socialised, and the state guaranteed stock bore a considerably lower rate of interest than that relevant to the industry before socialisation, the socialised industry would have to reduce prices so as to remove the risk premium which would otherwise accrue as a net profit to the state; but the economic calculus properly applied might require no such lowering of price – at any rate not until new investment had taken place. (v) The principle would, of course, mean the underemployment of increasing returns industries.[27]

The first half of the Economic Section's paper was ready and circulated to Ministers before the Ministerial meeting to which reference is made above. This part covers the principles on which compensation should be based, the question whether stock should take the form of government debt or stock secured on the industry, and some problems of organisation.[28] We have continued discussion in the Section on the second half of the paper covering the problems of running a socialised industry – how to fix prices, wages and output, how to determine investment programmes, and how to conduct foreign trade. Over this section we have had much discussion and in particular over the question of how to determine prices. For the reasons given above we have finally decided to come down against the proposition that the general rule should be to cover average costs, and to start straight off with the principle that prices should cover marginal costs. (To do it the other way round would be like the passage on the budget in the White Paper on *Employment Policy*. The great rule is to balance the budget; but the whole of the rest of the Paper is an argument for neglecting this rule!) Marcus Fleming is now doing a draft of this part of the paper.[29] He is developing five main ways of applying the rule:- (1) Socialist competition in which the individual managers are told to compete with one another and each to make as large a profit as possible. (2) Where (1) is impossible because monopolistic elements are inevitable, but where the

[27] GEN98/1st meeting, 9 November 1945, T234/1; Meade to Lord President, 'Socialisation of Industries: Question 3 – Should Compensation be Paid in Government Stock or in Stock Secured on the Industry', 12 November 1945, T230/106.

[28] 'Socialisation of Industry, Memorandum by the Economic Section of the Cabinet Secretariat', 6 November 1945, T230/106. On his copy Morrison wrote: 'It is well worth reading, though – see [marginal] notes – I don't agree with all of it. Shd. like to talk to the whole Economic Section about it.' (CAB124/916).

[29] EC(S)(45)(40) Revise, 'Note by Mr Fleming', 20 November 1945, T230/19.(Meade's reference is to para. 74 of Cmd. 6527.)

product is sufficiently storable and standardised, a central marketing organisation fixes prices at which it buys all that the individual managers of the socialised firms will produce; and behind these fixed prices the individual managers are told to maximise their profits. The central marketing organisation (allowing for margin to cover its costs) sells at corresponding fixed prices, and raises (or lowers) the price structure if stocks are declining (or rising). (3) System as at (2) except that the marketing organisation sells what it receives from the producing units at a price which will clear the market and then changes the price structure not according to whether stocks are rising or falling, but according to whether its selling price for the product exceeds or falls below its buying price. (4) Where the product cannot be stored or marketed in this way (e.g. railways, electricity, etc.), a price is fixed and the producers are told to sell sufficient to meet total demand at this price, but otherwise to maximise profits (i.e. by cost reductions). The fixed prices are then from time to time adjusted from the centre to correspond to marginal costs. (5) Where a very specialised product is made, so that central price fixing and socialist competition are impossible, one must do one's best merely by telling the individual managers to set prices equal to marginal costs. (1) (2) and (3) are comparatively easy since there need be no central measurement of marginal cost and managers can be given an incentive by making their rewards depend in part upon the profits which they make. (4) retains this incentive as far as cost reduction is concerned, but needs a central evaluation of marginal costs. (5) provides no incentive to producers and can only be judged by central evaluation of marginal costs.

The other big event on the internal front has been the first meeting of the Steering Committee on Economic Development. (Bridges, Gilbert, Woods, Ince, Franks, Johnston – representing Max Nicholson – myself and Douglas Jay.) I gave a progress report on the Plan for 1946. The position is that the departments have nearly all now sent in to the Central Statistical Office the statistical data on which the three basic summary tables for the 1946 Survey can be constructed:- (1) Requirements and supplies of manpower. (2) The 'target' national expenditure and the total expenditure likely to be incurred on the basis of current programmes and policies. (3) The balance of payments. Stafford and Tress are now busy constructing these summary tables from the material. Our intention then is to accompany these tables with (a) a commentary showing the main programmes on which the manpower requirements and the level of national expenditure are estimated (e.g. size of the armed forces, export targets, extent of restoration of consumption levels, etc.), (b) a commentary on the implications of various methods of closing the gap between supplies and requirements (e.g. what would happen to consumption levels if the whole gap were closed by an adjustment of consumption) and (c) a series of more detailed appendices giving the statistical detail for such things as investment, personal consumption, balance of payments, manpower, etc. All this was accepted by the Steering Committee, before whom we promised to have a draft plan for 1946 by the end of the present month. The Steering Committee then considered the Economic Section's paper on Economic Planning and decided to send it on to Ministers as expressing broadly the principles upon which the Steering Committee intended to conduct its work. This is to be accompanied by a Progress Report to Ministers showing them the position as regards the Plan for 1946 and promising to let them have it before Christmas, and outlining the quite considerable work which the various working parties have already done. At the same meeting of the Steering Committee we also discussed the need for some publicity for what was going on in the way of planning, and a draft is to be prepared of what might be said on this subject.[30]

I went to see the Lord President to report progress on the Economic Plan and to discuss with him our paper on Economic Planning. Mayhew (the LP's PPS), Max Nicholson and Pimlott were also there. The LP approved of the idea that our paper on Economic Planning should be sent to him from the Steering Committee as representing generally their ideas on how the thing should be done. Mayhew had raised some objections to our paper and in particular that it did not show by what means the various forms of expenditure (such as private investment) were to be controlled and influenced. These objections, however, evaporated as I made it clear that we certainly did intend to get private enterprise to join in programming its capital expenditure, and that our paper was consciously only the first bite at the cherry: it covered the problem of forecasting, programming, surveying, etc., but did not cover the problems of how to influence the various items of national expenditure.

Part of the trouble is due to the foolish behaviour of the Chancellor of the Exchequer who is just about to present to Parliament a Bill on the control of investment, which in effect does nothing more than (i) continue the restrictive control on new issues (but not on expenditure out of reserves), (ii) allow the Treasury to guarantee loans for industry up to £25 millions a year, and (iii) set up an advisory council on national investment.[31] This, if you please, he wished to present as a complete and rounded scheme for the control of investment without revealing anything that was going on in Whitehall in respect of the general economic plan. This would have been a political error of the first moment. No-one would have been deceived for one moment into thinking that it did anything at all substantial or significant for the control of investment, and in the absence of any knowledge that anything else was on foot this would have caused trouble. Tress briefed the Lord President on this subject; and the Lord President's Committee had just been meeting on the subject when I called on him to discuss the Economic Plan. It was an appropriate moment, therefore, to discuss with him the need for wider publicity and to reassure Mayhew about what was really going on. The Chancellor, by the way, is not to be permitted to make such an ass of himself.[32]

Compensation and Betterment has been up to the Cabinet. We have now tried to persuade Morrison that the way to deal with Betterment is: (i) that the planning authorities should settle the broad category of use for each zone of land; (ii) that the Land Commission should undertake

[30] ED(45) 1st Meeting, 14 November 1945, T228/20 and CAB134/186; ED(45)2, Draft Progress Report, and ED(45)1, Economic Planning, T273/298 and CAB134/186.

[31] See above, pp. 135, 148.

[32] LP(45) 43rd Meeting, 16 November 1945, CAB71/19.

(perhaps by auction) to sell the land in each zone for development (within the framework of the broad plan) to the most profitable use; (iii) the Land Commission would then acquire the land from the existing owner at its value in its present use. By this means the disincentive effects of a heavy tax on development would be avoided, and within the framework of the broad plan for the use of land the economic calculus would still direct land to its most repaying use. But this has, I think, fallen on deaf ears.[33]

I have spent a large part of two days this fortnight reading the conclusions of the Cabinet Meetings since the change of Government. This is a thing which I ought to do regularly; but somehow I have been so busy as badly to neglect it. Another whole day has been taken up with meetings of the Census of Distribution Committee, at which we heard evidence in favour of taking a census from the International Chamber of Commerce.[34]

In external matters I have not spent much time this fortnight on Article VII and the Washington financial talks. There was a terrific Cabinet meeting at which (in spite of some determined opposition from Shinwell, Aneurin Bevan and Alexander) the general lines of the commercial and financial settlement were accepted.[35] Lionel Robbins has returned to Washington, where the centre of activity now lies. There are delays both on the financial settlement and on the commercial settlement. In the latter case, although the text is now completed and agreed, publication waits on the completion of the financial talks in which (in spite of our acceptance of the waiver idea) there are still final difficulties to be negotiated. Australia is making itself a frightful nuisance on the commercial policy draft by insisting on complete and absolute freedom from any shadow of a commitment on any part of it before the trade conference foreshadowed for March of next year.

My activity in this has been very small. At the beginning of the fortnight I held a meeting with Clarke and later with Thompson-McCausland to discuss the American text in response to ours on the use of quantitative restrictions on balance of payments grounds. The main point we wished to get altered was the American statement that non-discrimination should be ensured in the use of import quotas by allowing imports from the various sources of supply on the basis of trade in a previous representative period. I, of course, want to be able to auction import licences which would ensure true non-discrimination, would enable us to get our imports from the cheapest source of supply, would let the Treasury obtain the rake-off between the buying and selling price for the restricted imports, and would remove all question of favouritism and unfairness in the distribution of licences among importers in the importing countries. More generally, I do not want this country to be tied to previous trade and thus unable to buy in the cheapest market, or to be precluded from extending its share of the trade to another country which is imposing import restrictions. Clarke

33 CM(45) 53rd Conclusions, 15 November 1945, CAB128/2; Chester to Lord President, 'Compensation and Betterment (CP(45)275 and 278)', 14 November, and Chester to Lord President, 16 November 1945, CAB124/384.

34 The meeting was on 6 November; no minutes survive on BT70/99.

35 CM(45) 50th Conclusions, 6 November 1945, CAB128/2 and Confidential Annexe, CAB128/4.

agreed with this. We tried a change on Washington, but failed.[36] The text, however, has certain loop-holes through which we shall at the appropriate moment return to the charge.

Cripps has drafted a statement which he proposes to make as President of the Board of Trade in Parliament welcoming the document on commercial policy when it is published. This is a good statement except for the passage on employment policy, in which the silly American line is taken that the clearance of barriers to international trade is an important measure providing full employment. This, of course, is not true. Increased exports give employment, but increased imports take it away again. Why we need a clearance of trade barriers is because we import necessities which we cannot ourselves make and export manufactured goods with which other countries can dispense or which they can make for themselves. The importance of employment policy in the present draft is that countries undertake to adopt domestic policies of full employment, which will in fact reduce or remove the dangers of unemployment resulting in a liberal international commercial system from depressions in other countries. I have written to Helmore on these lines and he is putting my letter before Cripps.[37]

I have at last managed to get hold (from the Cabinet Minutes, not, as promised but not expected, from Eady) of a copy of the declaratory statement which the Chancellor intends to issue when he proposes to Parliament the adoption of the Bretton Woods agreement. I am glad I have. It is a dreadful document. It says that our representatives on the International Monetary Fund will seek an interpretation of the Article governing changes in exchange rates which will permit any country to depreciate its exchange rate if it is suffering from persistent and chronic unemployment. It draws no distinction between a favourable or unfavourable balance of payments. The American depreciation of 1933 would apparently be just as justified as our depreciation of 1931. The export of unemployment by a country with a hugely favourable balance of payments but unwilling to expand domestically would be as justified as depreciation by a country which, in spite of unemployment, was being forced to domestic deflation by external pressure. I have corresponded on this with Eady who tried to persuade me to give up my point on the grounds that this was purely an internal political gesture to get the agreement through Parliament (although it committed our representatives to get a binding interpretation through the International Monetary Fund). I have, however, persisted, and my correspondence has gone to the Chancellor. Our correspondence I have also sent to Helmore, who has shown it to the President of the Board of Trade, who is himself writing to the Chancellor seeking a redraft of the statement which restricts the right to depreciate to those cases in which the unemployment is due to external pressure.[38]

[36] Cables NABOB 274, Liesching to Shackle, 3 November 1945, T236/455, and BABOON 199, Robbins and Helmore to Liesching, 5 November 1945, T236/466.

[37] 'Commercial Policy, Memorandum by the President of the Board of Trade', GEN89/11, T236/440; Meade to Helmore, 12 November 1945, T230/142.

[38] CP(45)269, 'Washington Financial Talks: Note by the Chancellor of the Exchequer', 6 November 1945, CAB129/4; Meade to Eady, 12 November, Eady to Meade, 13 November, Meade to Eady, 14 November, and Helmore to Cripps, 14 November, and Cripps to Dalton, 21 November 1945, T230/83.

There is one more struggle with Eady on the external front developing. At the meeting of the Steering Committee on Economic Development this week Bridges had called in Eady, as chairman of the Balance of Payments Working Party, to report on the work of that working party. He had, of course, nothing to report, as the whole of the work of determining an import programme for 1946 has been done in a hole-and-corner way by the Treasury with each department separately. Bridges made it fairly clear that he wanted this to be done properly through Eady's interdepartmental working party.[39] The next day a letter and document arrived from Eady calling a meeting of his working party for next Tuesday. The document was on the machinery of import programming and was very unsatisfactory. Although it made a show of having a reasonable interdepartmental machine for this purpose, it was clear that in fact the Treasury intended to do it all by private talks with each importing department separately. Marcus Fleming, who was secretary of the Shipping Committee which drew up import programmes when shipping capacity rather than finance was the bottleneck, has written me a minute explaining that we want something analogous to the Shipping Committee. The Treasury with the Bank of England should put in an estimate to the Balance of Payments Working Party of the total amount which we can afford to spend on imports; the importing departments should put in their programmes of imports; officials should then attempt to suggest alternative policies for Ministerial consideration for bringing these demands into balance with the available exchange. Marcus is coming with me to Eady's meeting. I have sent copies of Marcus' minute to Franks at the Ministry of Supply and to Broadley at the Ministry of Food.[40] We are trying to enlist the support of the importing departments (which should not, I think, be difficult) for a more sensible arrangement on these lines. The Balance of Payments Working Party is also to discuss methods of import control, and this should, I hope, enable us to give another run to the idea that in many cases the best thing may be to auction the licences to import.

Had lunch at the Athenaeum with Roy Harrod, who is writing a book on the external economic settlement. He had given me to read the MS of the first chapter which is first to be published as a separate pamphlet.[41] It is a more Harrodian production than I can remember. It is very overstated; intends to be very simple, which it often is, but is at times full of extreme Harrodian ingenuities; and the style is that peculiar product which could have come from no other pen. It is at least good to think that there are from now on going to be some economists outside who will put the pro-Article VII point of view. This has been sadly lacking all these years.

[39] ED(45) 1st Meeting, 14 November 1945, T228/20 and CAB134/186.

[40] Eady to Meade, 14 November (enclosing 'Import Control', 25 September 1945), Fleming to Meade, 17 November, and Meade to Franks and Meade to Broadley, 17 November 1945, T230/10.

[41] R. F. Harrod, *A Page of British Folly*. London: Macmillan, 1946.

# 14

## December 1945

### *2 December 1945*

In the internal field we have continued to do a good deal of work both on problems of Socialisation and on the Economic Plan for 1946.

On Socialisation we have had a series of staff meetings which started with a really sharp clash between those who wished us to recommend that prices should be equated to marginal costs and that there should be no rigid rule that a socialised industry should make earnings just sufficient to cover its total costs (in the sense of the annual service on the Government debt issued in compensation of the previous owners) and those who wished to see prices made equal to average costs. The former school was led by Marcus Fleming, whose draft was under discussion, and the latter school by Tom Wilson who made a determined counter-attack. There was some real tension. But it became clear that the majority were in favour of the 'marginal' school, though they were not willing to see the question whether an industry covered its total costs or not treated as so entirely irrelevant as Marcus Fleming was inclined to treat it. I then prepared a final draft which we discussed in the Section and which we got Gorell Barnes in the Treasury to read and to give us some comments for final revisions.[1] In this draft we kept the main divisions of five different methods of organising socialised industry so that price = marginal cost (see entry under 18 November (pp. 168–9); but I altered the last part of the document simply to cover the absurdities which would be brought about if one adopted a rule such that earnings must always just equal the cost of the compensation money:- (i) If the Government issued safe fixed-interest securities for the equity capital in a risky industry, the Government might legitimately make a net profit representing the risk premium; (ii) if there were a decline in the demand for the product of the industry, the price should fall below the average long-period cost or otherwise men and machines would be thrown into uneconomic idleness in order to restrict output so as to raise price and to spread the given overheads over a smaller output; (iii) conversely if there were a rise in the demand for the industry's product, the price should rise above the long-period average cost; (iv) if there had been an element of monopoly in the industry before socialisation for which

[1] EC(S)(45)40 Revise, 'Note by Mr Fleming', 20 November 1945, T230/19; Wilson to Meade, 'Pricing Policy', n.d., and Meade to Gorell Barnes, 28 November 1945, T230/106.

compensation had (properly) to be paid, the socialisation could not be used to expand output and remove the monopolistic restriction unless some loss were contemplated; (v) in the case of increasing returns industries the average cost principle will not permit the proper expansion of output.

While we were in the middle of our internal Section struggle on this subject the Lord President asked the whole Section to call on him to discuss problems of socialisation, which we did. We decided beforehand, in order not to display differences of opinion on this issue unnecessarily, to avoid this particular issue as much as possible and to deal with others. But the very first question which the Lord President asked us was on this subject:- should the railways be protected from other forms of transport in order to enable them to cover their capital costs? It was impossible to avoid an answer. But as a *deus ex machina*, as I opened my mouth to reply, the Lord President's secretary came in to say that Shinwell and other Ministers had arrived to discuss the socialisation of the coal mines. So we were dismissed and asked to come back in an hour's time. We spent the hour discussing our answer to this question![2]

The first meeting of the official committee which has been set up to study the problems of socialisation has been held under the chairmanship of Sir Bernard Gilbert.[3] Other members were Sir Alan Barlow and Sir Herbert Brittain of the Treasury; Sir Donald Fergusson of Fuel and Power; Sir Cyril Hurcomb of War Transport; E. A. G. Robinson of the Board of Trade; Archer of the Ministry of Supply; Hildred of the Ministry of Civil Aviation; Alec Johnston of the Lord President's Office. Luckily at this meeting we discussed only some problems of compensation; but at the next meeting we are to discuss the problem of the financial organisation of socialised industries and this will directly raise the issue whether a socialised industry should invariably cover its costs or not. If anything is to be done in the cause of the principle of marginal costs, at this meeting I shall have to confront these hard-headed and distinguished public servants with what will inevitably look like a very long-haired and academic thesis.

We have also done considerable work on the Economic Plan for 1946. Stafford and Tress have been working like niggers on the Tables and the Text of our forecasts of supplies and requirements for 1946. (The draft report is on the lines outlined in the Entry for 18 November [p. 169].) The manpower and the national income and expenditure tables both show an inflationary gap, though not a very alarming one. The thing which stands out a mile is the important relief which could be obtained by quicker and more extensive demobilisation and reduction in Govt war expenditure. We have had a series of meetings on the draft with Clarke on the Balance of Payments and with E. A. G. Robinson and Reddaway of the Board of

[2] The meeting was scheduled for 4 p.m. on 21 November. It began at 4.40 and resumed from 6.30 to 8 p.m. (CAB124/916).

[3] The Committee, which first met on 29 November, had been set up to 'examine in greater detail questions of compensation, finance and organisation' which had been generally discussed at a meeting of Ministers on 9 November (Gilbert to Robbins, 17 November 1945, referring to the conclusions of GEN98/1st Meeting, T230/106). Meade had appointed himself the Section's representative for the Committee (Meade to Gilbert, 19 November 1945, T230/106). The proceedings of SI(0)(45) are on CAB124/918.

Trade, ending up with a large meeting of Clarke, Proctor, Robinson, Reeder, Saunders, Dennison, Tress, Stafford, Campion and myself in the chair.[4]

We have also had some discussion on publicity for the Plan.[5] The Chancellor has produced a Bill on the control of investment which merely continues control over new issues and provides small Government guarantees for new capital raised for industry. This, in a short-sighted political frame of mind, he wished to present to Parliament as the Govt's scheme for the control of investment, claiming that he has thus brought into being one more of the pledges in the Labour Party's programme. This is absurd. It is no more a proper control of investment than anything we had before the war. It is pure eye-wash. The real control is the exercise of all controls and policies throughout Whitehall on the basis of the Plan. I am sure (and we have briefed Morrison to this effect) that the right course is to have fairly complete publicity for the whole Economic Plan at an early date, before it has to be given in an apologetic frame of mind by a Govt under heavy criticism.[6] I have discussed this with Bridges, Flett, Proctor and (at a lunch at the Reform Club) with Mayhew, the Lord President's Parliamentary Private Secretary. Proctor has now drafted the heads under which such publicity might be given, and this draft is to go to Ministers with the progress report on the Plan. The whole thing is complicated, I suspect, by some jockeying between the Lord President and the Chancellor as to who should give the publicity, the former being responsible for the Plan as a whole and the latter for the financial Control of Investment.

Another whole day spent at the Census of Distribution Committee hearing evidence from the Fabian Society, the Drapers and the Textile Wholesale merchants.[7] I cut the second day's proceedings.

I went to a meeting at No. 10 [Downing Street] with Douglas Jay, Norman Brook and Rowan (one of the PM's secretaries) to discuss procedure for briefing the PM for the economic papers coming before the Cabinet. The idea is to have a regular weekly meeting so that we can see that between us we cover the ground without unnecessary overlap.

The fortnight has been an exciting one so far as the Washington conversations are concerned; but I have been rather dropped from the latest activities on this subject in the Treasury, as a result – I suspect – of the very uncongenial line which I have been taking. I must say that I think that the Treasury have shown up at their worst this fortnight on this subject. It all started with the Americans handing to Keynes for submission to London a draft agreement for the financial arrangement.[8] This text was a regular lawyer's contract, it is true; (described in the Treasury as a

[4] Tress sent the first draft to Meade on 25 November. The first circulated draft was sent to Proctor, Reeder, Reddaway, Robinson and Clarke on 28 November, and the large meeting took place on 30 November 1945 (T230/54).

[5] See Woods to Flett, 30 November, Ince to Flett, 30 November, and Gilbert to Flett, 3 December 1945, T230/55.

[6] See above, p. 170.

[7] On 19 November 1944 (BT70/99).

[8] Cables NABOB 345, Keynes to Eady, and NABOB 356–62, Keynes, Brand, Robbins and other members of the mission to Treasury, 18 November 1945, T236/441.

moneylender's contract). It also contained many clauses that were very difficult for us. In particular:- (i) The statement that no part of the loan was to be used to repay sterling balances, although we were in return to liberalise the sterling area. (This, however, was of no real importance, since the total we are considering borrowing is certainly not in excess of our current adverse balance.) (ii) A definite commitment that all new current earnings of members of the Sterling Area would be free for conversion into all currencies by the end of 1946. (iii) Strict undertakings that we would not discriminate at all in our exchange controls or import restrictions (even with a doubt whether we should still be free to make use of the 'Scarce Currency' let-out under the Bretton Woods agreement if the dollar became scarce). (iv) An addition to the waiver clause which made our right to refrain from paying the interest on the loan dependent not only upon the size of our current net earnings but also on the size of our reserves of gold and dollars. (v) Clauses which gave the payments on the American loan priority over payments on other loans and then tied our hands badly in making settlements with the Sterling Area. I attended a meeting in the Treasury with Eady, Grant, Clarke, Jay and Thompson-McCausland. The Treasury and the Bank had hysterics and instead of going calmly through the document and seeing what we could accept and what we couldn't they seemed to be prepared to put an end to the whole negotiations. I lunched that day with R. F. Kahn of the Board of Trade who informed me that the officials in the Board were as concerned as myself about the line taken by the Treasury, and that Woods (the permanent secretary of the Board of Trade) was going to see Bridges to express their concern. So I took my courage into my hands and went and called on Bridges as well. Meanwhile Marcus Fleming wrote a detailed brief for the Lord President on the American draft. Then a draft telegram for Washington came round with a covering note by the Chancellor of the Exchequer suggesting that we should make a very high-level intervention to get the whole conception changed and to have a sort of high-level gentlemen's agreement rather than the moneylender's contract, thereby easing our difficulties by making the whole thing vague. Fleming and I called on the Lord President and in an hour's conversation persuaded him: (i) that this arrangement would mean that we lost the advantages of a precise waiver and would have to take on the liability of $159 million a year with no safeguard other than a vague right to approach the Americans for a revision of the agreement if necessary; (ii) that we should in fact never get the Americans to agree without fairly precise obligations on our part; and (iii) we ought in fact to go through the American draft clause by clause. The Lord President at the meeting of Ministers, as a result of this (and I suspect also as a result of jockeying for position between himself and the Chancellor on other issues), took it into his head to launch a tirade against the Treasury and the way it had conducted these negotiations – with both Bridges and Eady there and both knowing that I briefed the Lord President on all this.[9] The

[9] Fleming to Lord President, 'The Financial Negotiations at Washington', 22 November 1945, T230/142; GEN89/13, 'Washington Financial Talks: Memorandum by the Chancellor of the Exchequer', 22 November 1945, T236/441; GEN89/6th Meeting, 23 November 1945, CAB78/37.

next morning Eady sent for me and told me how the Lord President had behaved!

As a result of this ministerial meeting a strong intervention was made with the Americans as a result of which it is thought that they will be willing to drop some of the most objectionable features (e.g. the making of the waiver dependent upon the size of our gold reserves).[10] Our delegation in Washington, however, came back strongly on two points:- (i) They said that they would like to be excused from all responsibility for a settlement in which we did not have the safeguard of a fairly precise waiver in case of our inability to pay; and (ii) they said that the Americans would accept no solution which did not make it necessary for us to undertake to make all current earnings in the Sterling Area convertible by the end of 1946, and that in fact we should be going back on our previous undertakings if we withheld this concession.[11]

On this issue there is a first-class row on between our delegation and the Treasury. The Treasury maintain that the Sterling Area arrangements must be treated as a whole; that is to say, in order to get the Sterling Area creditors to scale down their sterling credits and to agree to reasonable terms for repayment of the remainder, we must be free to use the bargaining weapon not only of how much and how quickly we can release the existing sterling balances but also of how we shall treat their future current earnings. The delegation in Washington maintain that we should distinguish clearly between (a) the treatment of new current earnings by the Sterling Area after the end of 1946 and (b) the treatment of the existing sterling balances. They maintain that we have in fact already promised to free current earnings by the end of 1946 (which the Treasury deny); that in any case we can't force the Sterling Area countries to grant to us their new current earnings to be blocked in sterling, so that in fact it is not a bargaining point at all; that we shan't possibly get the American assistance unless we give up this point; and that (as the military expenditure which we shall have to make – e.g. in India and the Middle East – is exempted from this provision and is not treated as current earnings but can continue to be blocked) we shall already strike an even balance of other current payments with the Sterling Area as a whole and shall not need to force them to accumulate further current earnings in sterling balances.[12]

There was a meeting in the Treasury to discuss a draft telegram on this: Eady, Grant, Clarke, and Rowe-Dutton from the Treasury; and Cobbold and Thompson-McCausland from the Bank. I discovered once again that it was the Bank which was the real nigger in the wood-pile and I am afraid that I had a stand-up fight with Cobbold. He tried the most ridiculous

[10] Cable No. 11790, Prime Minister to Halifax, 23 November 1945, FO371/45710.

[11] Cable No. 7893, Keynes to Chancellor of the Exchequer, 25 November 1945, FO371/45710.

[12] For the Treasury's view see cables BABOON 303, Chancellor to Keynes, 26 November, and No. 11897, Eady to Keynes, 27 November; Grant to Eady, 27 November, Eady to Bridges, 27 November, and DOTEL 212, Bridges to Robbins, 27 November 1945, T236/441. For the Delegation's view see cables NABOB 400, Halifax, Keynes, Brand, Liesching, Robbins and all members of the Delegation to Chancellor, 27 November, and No. 7933, Keynes to Eady, 22 November 1945, on the same file.

arguments. He said that one couldn't distinguish between past earnings and current earnings of sterling. I said that of course one could, by saying that a country could use for all purposes all its balances above the level at the point in time at which the freedom to use current earnings was granted. He said that the statistical information on this would always be months out of date and that they would not be willing to block sterling balances, which was the alternative method. I asked him how he then contemplated carrying out the total agreements which he favoured covering past balances as well as current earnings, under which the balances could be withdrawn at a given speed? Would not this involve exactly the same dilemma between out of date statistics or blocking of balances? He had no answer. The Treasury next prepared a compromise text for the financial agreement. This text was not at all bad, if we can obtain American agreement to it. There was only one thing about the first draft of it which made my hair stand on end. The Treasury had accepted (quite properly) an obligation on our part not to discriminate in our exchange controls and import controls against American goods, if we got financial assistance on a sufficient level; but they failed (most improperly) to safeguard our rights under the Bretton Woods agreement to discriminate in our import controls against imports from a country whose currency is scarce. (I sometimes wonder on what principle the Treasury selects what is and what is not important to fight for.) The draft dropped the clause making the use of the waiver dependent on the size of our gold reserves; it removed the clause giving the American loan priority over our other external obligations; and it removed the precise obligation to make current earnings of the Sterling Area convertible by the end of 1946. I went and briefed the Lord President orally on this before the Cabinet met on the draft; and I was glad to see that as the text was sent to Washington the scarce currency clause had been safeguarded.[13] On receipt of the text the Washington delegation retorted that they could fight for all of it with some chance of success, but wanted to be allowed to make concessions on (i) the date at which current earnings in the Sterling Area would be made convertible; and (ii) the priority as between payments on the American debt and on other debt settlements. They were, however, told to present and argue for the text as it stood; but the last I heard was that Bridges was flying out to Washington.[14] Let us hope it comes off at last.

Eady has held a first meeting of his Balance of Payments Working Party. There were present: Eady, Clarke and Cahan from the Treasury; Oliver Franks from the Ministry of Supply; Broadley and Gardiner from the Ministry of Food; Woods from the Board of Trade; and myself and Marcus

[13] CM(45) 57th Conclusions, 29 November 1945, Confidential Annex, CAB128/4; CP(45)312, 'Washington Talks. Memorandum by the Chancellor of the Exchequer', 20 November 1945, CAB129/5; cables BABOON 314–315, Chancellor to Ambassador, Keynes and Brand, 29 November 1945, T236/442. Meade also briefed Morrison in writing: 'Washington Financial Talks', 29 November 1945, T230/142.

[14] Cables NABOB 417, Ambassador, Keynes, Brand, Robbins and rest of the Delegation to Chancellor, 29 November, and BABOON 325, Prime Minister and Chancellor to Ambassador, 30 November 1945, T236/442. Bridges arrived in Washington on 1 December.

Fleming. All went well. The importing departments had taken our hints and pressed for making the working party a really effective body for programming imports in the light of scarcities of foreign exchange, just as the shipping committee did in the light of shortages of shipping.[15] We shall see what happens. Can the Treasury do these things in the full light of day?

I went to a meeting in Woods' room in the Board of Trade with him, Helmore and Owen of the Board of Trade to discuss the motor manufacturers and the export market. Cripps had been making a speech which greatly upset the motor manufacturers because he said that the domestic market for motors must be much restricted and the purchase tax maintained in order to drive them to export.[16] The motor manufacturers retorted that they must have a large domestic market in order to get low costs so as to be able to compete in export markets. I argued that broadly speaking Cripps was right in the short run so long as there was no difficulty in selling what could be produced, and the motor manufacturers might be right in the long run when the difficulty was not to produce but to find markets. Apparently the atmosphere is very tense politically on this subject. I said that the sensible plan was: (i) to guarantee that the purchase tax would be removed in, say, two years' time but to retain it during the period of shortage of supplies; (ii) to alter the basis of motor taxation so as to encourage the production of more powerful cars suitable for export. Some such scheme may, I understand, now be worked out.

I am glad to record that Helmore sent me a copy of a letter from Dalton to Cripps changing the text of the proposed declaration on the exchange-rate clauses of the Bretton Woods agreement to meet the point which I raised. (See entry of 18 November.)[17] That is very good news.

Noel-Baker sent for me to a meeting in the Foreign Office with himself, McNeil, and the Foreign Office lawyers. He more or less accused me of being responsible for the fact that the proposed International Trade Organisation was to be set up as a specialised agency and not as an organ of the United Nations Organisation! I pointed out with some vigour (i) that not I, but the Board of Trade, was responsible for commercial policy; (ii) that the Economic Section had consistently done everything possible to get the closest co-ordination between the Economic and Social Council and the other economic bodies; (iii) that it was now quite out of the realm of practical politics to get the decision altered, but it was still quite possible to see that the proposed trade organisation was brought into the closest relationship with the Economic and Social Council; and (iv) that since the Bretton Woods bodies were to be specialised agencies there was positive advantage in not making the trade organisation actually part of the UNO since this might tend to suggest that the Economic and Social Council could deal with Commerce but not with Finance. Rather have Commerce and Finance both in specialised agencies, but both in close relationship with the Economic and Social Council. I hear that Noel-Baker has now called the Board of Trade to the Foreign Office for a meeting on this.

[15] The minutes of the meeting, on 20 November 1945, are on T236/1088.

[16] At a dinner of the Society of Motor Manufacturers and Traders on 15 November 1945. Cripps' notes for his speech are in the Cripps Papers (389/387) at Nuffield College, Oxford.

[17] Helmore to Meade, 22 November 1945, T230/83; see above, p. 172 and note 38.

We have had an interesting staff meeting in the Section to discuss with MacDougall, who is just back from the Reparations Commission in Berlin, the economic problems of the future of Germany. I am frankly appalled at the length to which the idea has gone that Germany's standard should be reduced in the interests of economic security and reparations. Indeed the Russians go so far as to maintain as a positive principle that Germany's standard should not be allowed to rise above the average European level; and MacDougall was seriously discussing the question whether to forbid Germany to produce more than was sufficient for this might not lead to large-scale German unemployment.[18]

## *16 December 1945*

We have now got the Economic Survey for 1946 to Bridges who has had it circulated to Departments; and there is to be a meeting of the Steering Committee on it early next week. Tress, Stafford, Jackson, Campion and I met to discuss its final revision early this fortnight. We also had a staff meeting in the Economic Section to discuss it. It was also sent to Reeder of the Ministry of Labour, E. A. G. Robinson and Reddaway of the Board of Trade, and R. W. B. Clarke and Proctor of the Treasury for their last-minute comments before it was finally submitted to Bridges.[19] Now the die is cast. We have not only sold the idea in Whitehall of setting a target national income for the future and of forecasting the main categories of national expenditure for comparison with it; but we have actually got Whitehall to do it!

There has been a good deal of activity on the socialisation front this fortnight. There have been two meetings of Sir Bernard Gilbert's official committee on socialisation problems (Fergusson from Fuel and Power, Hurcomb from War Transport, Archer from Supply, E. A. G. Robinson from the Board of Trade, Barlow and Brittain from the Treasury, Ismay from the Post Office and someone [C. W. Evans] from Civil Aviation), which I have attended. This committee has discussed a very large range of topics in which we are very little interested (such as the method of appointing to the Boards of these industries, what to do with the foreign assets of these industries, etc.). But the Committee has also discussed the problems of financial structure and of pricing, in which we are very much interested. On the first occasion we went through the draft Bill for the Nationalisation of the Coal Mines.[20] It is drafted very much on the lines

[18] MacDougall's 'Some Random Notes on the Reparations Discussion in Berlin, September-November 1945', was circulated in the Section as EC(S)(45)44, 29 November 1945 (T230/19 and 75). On MacDougall's mission see Donald MacDougall, *Don and Mandarin, Memoirs of an Economist*. London: John Murray, 1987, pp. 55–9, and also Alec Cairncross, *The Price of War*. Oxford: Basil Blackwell, 1986, Chapter 5.

[19] Meade to Bridges, 6 December 1945 (enclosing EC(S)(45)46 Revise, 'Economic Survey for 1946, Report by the Economic Survey Working Party', 6 December 1945), T230/55. The Section meeting was on 4 December, and the draft had been sent out on 30 November 1945 (T230/54). For the meeting of the Steering Committee on 18 December see below, pp. 190–1.

[20] SI(0)(45) 2nd Meeting, 5 December 1945, CAB124/918; Draft of Coal Industry Nationalisation Bill, 5 December 1945, T230/106.

of requiring the industry always (i) to cover its current costs, including presumably overheads such as its contribution to the Treasury to meet the service of the compensation stock, and (ii) to pay over to the Treasury just enough to meet this charge. Everything else is by way of exception. I asked (a) whether the Minister would have power under the Act to determine the principles of price policy for the industry, and (b) whether it was possible for this to be allowed to lead to a permanent or temporary profit or loss. Philip Chantler and I have been briefing the Lord President on this as the draft has been before the Lord President's Committee of Ministers and then before the Cabinet.[21] In the result a little more flexibility has been introduced into the financial provisions of the Bill, although the main conception remains unchanged – namely of the fixing of prices year in year out just at a level to cover average costs including the annual service of the compensation money.

At the second meeting of Gilbert's committee, at the end of a long meeting on other matters, I was called on to talk on our complicated and abstract paper on price fixing in socialised industries. The tired and overworked permanent secretaries around me were already yawning and looking at their watches before we came to this point! I therefore confined myself to saying that in order to retain freedom to adopt price policies on the lines which we had advocated it was essential to avoid the idea that socialised industries must never permanently or temporarily make a profit or loss over and above the cost of the compensation money. For this reason the Economic Section not only agreed with the decision which the Committee had just reached (namely that socialised industries should always be financed on Govt credit and not on stock secured on their own equity, since otherwise one would have equity owners in a business over which they had no power of control at all), but would wish to go further and argue that socialised industries should always be financed by the issue of ordinary Govt Stock as opposed to Govt guaranteed stock tied to the earnings of the particular socialised industry. Then the Govt could give each industry directions about its price policy; each industry could pay its resulting profits into an extra-budgetary fund from which the service of the compensation money for all industries would be met; the profits of some industries (or of some years) could be set against the losses of other industries (or of other years) and the Treasury would have to meet or to enjoy any balance of loss or profit. I found myself in a minority of one; but I shall try to pursue this point.[22]

Philip Chantler and I went to lunch in Peggy Joseph's flat to discuss the principles upon which the price and output of coal should be determined after socialisation. She is the economist at the Ministry of Fuel and Power; and we met there Quirk, de Peyer and Hemming from the Ministry. I gave

[21] Chantler to Lord President, 'Coal Mining Industry (Nationalisation) Bill, Memorandum by the Minister of Fuel and Power (LP(45)238)', 22 November 1945 and 'Coal Mining (Nationalisation) Bill, Revised Draft, Dated 5th December 1945', 6 December 1945, CAB21/2207. The Lord President's Committee discussed the draft Bill on 9 and 23 November, the Cabinet on 13 December (LP(45) 42nd and 44th Meetings, CAB71/19; CM(45) 62nd Conclusions, CAB128/2).

[22] SI(0)(45) 2nd Meeting, 5 December 1945, CAB124/918; see below p. 197.

them a detailed argument of the way in which our ideas might be applied in the case of coal by setting up a selling organisation which would fix prices for each quality of coal in each district and would adjust these prices from time to time to keep the demand and supply for each particular quality of coal in each district in balance, and by requiring the producers in each production unit on the basis of these fixed prices to maximise profits. The long-term development plans of the industry might, of course, quite consistently with this be worked out centrally on the basis of information about costs provided from the different production units. We argued hard and maintained our point of view; but I cannot say that I think that we have yet made very much impression.[23]

Meanwhile I have been reading the Heyworth report on the Gas Industry, which recommends socialisation in the form of a number of independent regional boards financed on Government credit but definitely with the idea that each region should just cover average costs.[24]

An official committee under the chairmanship of Max Nicholson has been set up to consider the future of the Economic Controls, and I attended its first meeting. The Lord President under his own steam has promoted the idea that we ought to go carefully through all the controls in order to make sure that all except those that were really essential were relaxed or abolished. I consider this general anti-control feeling to be very healthy (particularly in a Socialist Lord President). At Nicholson's meeting all the main departments made a short statement about what they thought the immediate outlook to be for their controls; and they are now each to submit a short paper stating the position as regards their own department. I made the point that I did not see how the problem of controls could be intelligently discussed quite out of relation to such problems as wage policy and tax policy. For example, the problem of getting labour into the right occupations could be tackled either through wage inducements which attracted them there, or by labour direction. Moreover the degree of control over consumption required depended upon the size of the inflationary gap between spendable incomes and supplies and this depended upon tax policy. For example, to some extent purchase tax on new cars or the present licensing of purchases of new cars were alternatives.[25]

Nicholson has started a series of very informal meetings in his room each week of officials on problems of internal and external planning. He is more interested in the structure of administrative machinery for planning than in economic policy itself, which is useful. At one of these meetings we discussed the same problem of the relation between the work to be done by the official Committee on Controls and the work to be done by the Steering Committee both in estimating the size of any future inflationary or deflationary gap and in discussing the ways of filling the gap. We also had another of these informal meetings discussing the structure of planning

[23] For an indication of Joseph's views see 'The Coal Minining Industry: Basic Economic Principles, Memorandum by Miss Joseph', September 1943, T230/106.

[24] *The Gas Industry, Report of the Committee of Enquiry*, Cmd. 6699, December 1945.

[25] DC(45) 1st meeting, 10 December 1945, CAB132/58.

for the supplies of goods to foreign countries (e.g. for relief, for Germany etc.).

I have held a staff meeting of the Economic Section in order to discuss the future work of the Section. I circulated a short paper suggesting that there were the following four essential problems which we must discuss:-[26] (i) How to control the various items of national expenditure. We have now got Whitehall setting a target national income and forecasting the future of the main categories of national expenditure. We must now go full steam ahead on the problems [of] how to control such expenditure. I have set Shackle to work on a paper on how to control Public and Private Investment; J. C. R. Dow who has just joined the Section on working on the subject of how variations in Income Tax might be made compatible with Pay As You Earn, so that, if necessary, frequent and rapid changes in taxation on wage-earners could be used to influence their consumption expenditure. (At present, PAYE means that one has to decide in September 1945 on the rate of tax to rule from April 1946 to March 1947.) (ii) How to apply our general principles of pricing in socialised industry to particular industries. Chantler is preparing a paper on coal mining. (iii) How to devise a wages policy which will attract labour into the industries in which demand exceeds supply without leading to inflation. (iv) How to tackle restrictive practices in the unsocialised sector of industry. Dennison is going to prepare papers on (iii) and (iv).[27]

We have also held a staff meeting on a paper of John Wood on the Distribution of Industry. This is a good but extreme paper.[28] It argues that the present policy of bringing work to the workers by pushing new firms into the development areas is both wrong and ineffective. It is very negative in tone. I cannot believe that it is right either intellectually or politically for the Section to put this out in this form. In a completely free pricing system wage-rates would fall to extremely low levels in depressed areas and this cheapness of labour would in fact attract new enterprise into the district as well as forcing labour out of the district. Since we interfere with the wage system we must take special steps both to help labour out and to encourage [industry] in. The right policy is a combination of the two; and the Section should say so, thereby drawing attention to the fact that the present government are not giving sufficient emphasis to labour mobility. I had a great argument about this with Wood and with Stanley Dennison, who is Wood's patron in this matter. I must talk to them again in private and see what future course of action can be arranged.

The problem of variations in social security contributions as a means of preserving consumers' buying power is coming up for discussion again.[29]

[26] EC(S)(45)43, 'Future Work of the Section', 27 November 1945, T230/19.

[27] Shackle's paper, 'The Means and Possibilities of Investment Policy, Part I' was circulated on 14 February and a postscript on 22 February (EC(S)(46)11 and 13, T230/20); Dow's paper, 'Variations of Income Tax as a Short-run Instrument for National Income Stabilisation', was circulated on 15 February 1946 (EC(S)(46)12, T230/20); and Chantler's paper was circulated on 23 March 1946 ('An economic policy for the socialised coal industry', EC(S)(46)17 Revise, T230/21). Papers by Dennison have not been located.

[28] 'The Distribution of Industry Policy', 24 October 1945, EC(S)(45)35, T230/18.

[29] Meade had put forward this proposal in 1942 (see T230/101 and *The Collected Papers of James Meade*, Vol. I, Chapters 12 and 13). Such a scheme was included as Appendix II of the 1944 White Paper on *Employment Policy* (Cmd. 6527).

The Bill for Social Services is now in draft and I briefed the Lord President to the effect that if we did not get the power to vary contributions in the present Bill we might be too late to use it as an effective instrument when the post-transitional period slump threatened. The Lord President made a fuss about the point at the Cabinet. Both Gilbert at the Treasury, who admits that in any case he dislikes the whole idea, and the officials at the Ministry of National Insurance are of the opinion that it is wholly impracticable to take the powers in the present Bill. The cat is among the pigeons. I shall try to use this as an opportunity to get the whole problem of the control of consumers' expenditure in times of slump thoroughly reviewed.[30]

There have been four solid days of meetings, morning and afternoon, in this fortnight to take evidence for the Census of Distribution Committee. I attended three sessions. At the first the representatives of the small grocers gave evidence against a Census. At the second [Henry] Clay, E. A. G. Robinson, and Hugh Weeks gave evidence for a Census. At the third representatives of the Town Planning Institute and the Birmingham City Engineer gave evidence of how information about numbers of shops etc. would be useful to Town Planners.[31]

In external affairs this week has been a decisive one as far as the Washington conversations are concerned. There were a series of Cabinet Meetings at the beginning of the fortnight considering Bridges' report from Washington.[32] In the end the difference boiled down to two points. The American draft loan agreement seemed to deprive us of our rights to discriminate against American goods even if the dollar was scarce in the terms of Article VII of the [International] Monetary Fund; and it deprived us of the transitional period rights under Article XIV of the Fund. The Americans gave way on the first, which would have been an outrageous demand. We had to give way on the second, which was much more reasonable since the Americans could argue that they were giving us sufficient dollars to make the distinction between dollars and other currencies indifferent to us so far as current payments during the transitional period were concerned. So at long last the White Papers were issued; the PM made his (and what was planned to be Cripps') statement in the House; the great debate took place; the resolution approving the agreements and the Bretton Woods Act was passed in the House of Commons.[33]

30 CP(45)315, 'Report by the Social Services Committee on the National Insurance Scheme, Memorandum by the Lord Privy Seal', 1 December 1945, CAB129/5; Meade to Lord President, 'Report by the Social Services Committee on the National Insurance Scheme (CP(45)315)', 5 December 1945, T230/105; CM(45)60th conclusions, 6 December 1945, CAB128/2; and see below, pp. 189–90.

31 For the scanty records of these meetings, the last of which took place on 14 December, see BT70/99.

32 CM(45) 58th and 59th Conclusions, 3 and 5 December 1945, CAB128/4; cables NABOB 446, Bridges to Prime Minister, 3 December, and NABOB 458, Bridges to Eady, 4 December 1945, T236/442.

33 *Statistical Material Presented during the Washington Negotiations*, Cmd. 6707; *Financial Agreement between the Governments of the United States and the United Kingdom*, Cmd. 6708; *Proposals for Consideration by an International Conference on Trade and Employment*, Cmd. 6709; *House of Commons Debates*, Vol. 416, 6 December 1945, cols. 2662–70 (Attlee's statement) and Vol. 417, 12 and 13 December 1945, cols. 421–558 and 641–747 (the great debate).

At this point I cannot refrain from recording something which has given me infinite pleasure, namely the following personal cable for me from Liesching in Washington: 'We have finished the job in spite of everything. When we record the Commercial Policy Agreement tomorrow I shall be thinking very specially of you as the architect and founder and shall be wishing you were with us. All good wishes.' Moreover, on the Saturday after the publication of the White Papers Margaret and I went to the wedding of Harry Hawkins' daughter. He had just come back in time from taking part in the American side in the Washington conversations. He said to me that just before he left Washington, Liesching was trying to arrange that my name should be officially recorded at the last plenary meeting on Commercial Policy; and, Hawkins added, it was certainly fully deserved.

Early in the fortnight before the White Papers were issued I had lunch in the House of Commons with Hugh Gaitskell and Rosenstein-Rodan. The discussion was on the Washington talks. I spoke a bit in support of the Bretton Woods agreement, but as nothing was published I found it embarrassing to talk on the commercial policy side, when Gaitskell led the conversation to that topic. The week-end after the publication of the White Papers Patrick Gordon-Walker came round for the evening and I pointed out to him some of the salient features. He made some of these points when he spoke in the debate in the House.[34] On the first day of the debate I had lunch in the House of Commons with Evan Durbin and spoke on these subjects with him. I observed Kaldor lunching with Robert Boothby. Also Balogh was lunching there. Afterwards I left with Balogh, who told me that the opposition's tactics would now be to wreck the projected trade conference by getting our delegation sent with wrecking instructions (it is useful that he should blab so freely!), and who gave me a great lecture on the ethics of what had been done. He asserted that the opposition had been hustled and rushed, that it would lead to Fascism if there could not be prolonged democratic deliberation on these issues, and that ordinary Members of Parliament must have access to the civil service experts in order to inform themselves on these technical issues. He seemed to hold me personally responsible for these evils! But I fear that the day was one of bitter defeat for him.

Margaret and I had dinner earlier in the week with Jenks (the Legal Adviser of the ILO) and Plumptre (one of the Canadian delegates to the Preparatory Commission of the United Nations Organisation now meeting in London)[35] and Perez Guerrero (a Venezuelan who was a colleague of mine in the League [of Nations] at Geneva and is now Venezuelan delegate to the Preparatory Commission). It was most illuminating to me to see from what they all said how the whole world was waiting for a successful outcome to the Washington talks, since the absence or presence of Anglo-American agreement on economic and financial matters was likely to make the difference between chaos or co-operation in a very extended international field.

What a nice man, incidentally, Clay is. He wrote a letter to *The Times*

[34] See *House of Commons Debates*, Vol. 417, 13 December 1945, cols. 685–90.
[35] From 24 November to 23 December 1945.

against these agreements in which he made an error of fact about the computation of the prospective gap in our balance of payments. I sent him a note pointing this out and he corrected it at once in *The Times* and sent me a most charming note making no excuses for his error. If only everyone could conduct a controversy like this.[36]

Douglas Jay called on me to discuss what we could and what we could not now do under the agreements. He was very worried with our undertaking to do without the Bretton Woods transitional period freedom. He argued that a country which was making use of that freedom could block its own currency which it paid for our exports and demand dollars for all our imports from it. I pointed out that the evil was confined to those countries other than the USA, Canada and the Sterling Area (for whom special arrangements were contemplated) and other than countries not members of the Fund (in the case of which we could still block balances). In the case of a country which was a member of the Fund and which behaved as Jay feared, we could insist that it paid for its purchases from us in terms of sterling and not in terms of its own currency. There was nothing in any agreement against this; and indeed Article VI of the IMF gave us express permission to take measures to prevent an export of capital. The evil was, therefore, confined to our excess of imports over exports with this very limited range of countries. It is most important to coax Jay, who has never been very positively in favour of these agreements, into at least continued acquiesence with them.[37]

Well, the first great step has been taken. It has, however, occurred in a form which has one great disadvantage. I would myself argue that the scarce currency clause of the IMF; the exchange alteration clause which would allow us to depreciate if we needed without allowing the USA or other countries to follow us with unnecessary competitive depreciation; the fact that a country with an unfavourable balance of payments could limit imports while our customers without an unfavourable balance could not do so; made the Bretton Woods and the Commercial Policy agreements positively advantageous on their own merits. They have, however, now inevitably come psychologically to appear as unpleasant prices which we have been forced to pay for American money.

Eady has held a second meeting of his Working Party on the Balance of Payments to discuss the change brought about by the Washington loan agreement. There seemed little point in the meeting which reached no conclusions; but it was interesting to observe the minds of officials gradually adjusting themselves from the view that the great thing was to save dollars to the new view that the great thing is to get our balance of payments with the rest of the world as a whole right. I made a great plea for the view that we should from now on do everything to buy in the cheapest market; and that we should do all we can to get this principle accepted (rather than purchases on the basis of trade in a previous representative period) as the basis for the definition of non-discrimination in import

[36] Clay's two letters on 'The American Loan' were published in *The Times* on 13 and 15 December 1945.

[37] For Jay's views see also Jay to Meade, 17 December 1945, T230/142.

quotas and in state trading. Not only would this keep the value of our exports down, but it would enable us to undercut and drive out our competitors in export markets into which the total volume of imports was controlled by the importing country. After the meeting I wrote to Helmore about this, sending him copies of the letters which I had already sent to R. F. Kahn at the Board of Trade in favour of auctioning import licences when goods were subject to import quotas.[38]

The question of Civil Aviation has been up to Ministers in the form of a draft White Paper about the socialisation of Civil Aviation. This started off with an introduction about our international civil aviation policy and how it was based on the principle that each country should have a quota of the traffic on each route based on the traffic originating in its own territory. I briefed the Lord President strongly against this. I said that we must have a Civil Aviation policy which was consistent with our shipping policy, in the case of which it would be disastrous to allow the Americans to adopt such a principle. We must be free to take shipping traffic from the Americans. I argued that we should have the principle both in Shipping and Civil Aviation of allowing the cheapest source of the service to take the traffic; but that both in Shipping and Civil Aviation we might have transitional period arrangements which would be perfectly in line with the Commercial Policy proposals and would allow us time to re-build our civil aviation and the Americans time to contract their shipping. Hurcomb saw my minute before the meeting. As a result of this and the opposition of War Transport, the offending paragraph was removed from the White Paper. It is, however, quite another thing to get the policy changed, and I understand that Cripps at the meeting said that we were inevitably committed. I have written to Helmore on this, hoping that he will show my letter to Cripps and that a last-minute alliance between the Board of Trade and the Ministry of War Transport will get the policy changed.[39]

There has been a meeting between Murrie, Eastwood (our new Under secretary at the Cabinet Office), Campion and myself, as a result of which I believe that at long last the notice will be sent out actually setting up the official committee on External Economic Intelligence.[40]

I have spent a long time this fortnight making arrangements for all the rooms in the Section to be redistributed and to get more clerical assistance for members of the Section. A weary time-absorbing job.

I had lunch with J. V. Wilson (who was at the League at Geneva and is now the New Zealand delegate to the Preparatory Commission of the United Nations), Turner, one of his colleagues, and A. G. B. Fisher. We talked mainly on the problem of the future site of the United Nations, and I developed my personal views against its being in the territory of any one of the great powers.

[38] The minutes of the meeting, on 11 December, are on T236/1088; Meade's letters to Kahn and Helmore, of 3 and 14 December respectively, are on T230/9.

[39] 'Socialisation Aspects of British Civil Aviation Policy', GEN98/7, 7 December 1945, CAB78/39; Meade to Lord President, 'Socialisation Aspects of Civil Aviation', 11 December 1945, T230/3; GEN98/ 2nd meeting, 11 December 1945, CAB78/39; Meade to Helmore, 15 December 1945, T230/106. The White Paper, *British Air Services*, Cmd. 6712, was published on 20 December 1945.

[40] See above, p. 155.

Margaret and I went one evening to a reception at Chatham House to meet delegates to the Preparatory Commission. We met a few delegates (mainly English-speaking) and many friends; and I was able to introduce Margaret to a few of my Whitehall colleagues. There was a terrific crush.

Received a visit at the Office in the course of the week from a M. Perroux who is head of a Conjuncture Institute in Paris. He is stone deaf and not able to speak English well, and he asked me to explain to him in precise detail how the Economic Section worked and what were its relations with the various ministers, departments and Cabinet! Luckily he brought another Frenchman with him to whom I spoke in English and who then bawled my remarks (or a version of them) at Perroux in French.

## 23 December 1945

I have spent some time this week trying to work up a campaign to get powers taken in the National Insurance Bill to introduce at a later stage a scheme for varying the National Insurance contributions as a means of stabilising consumers' expenditure. I called on Bridges as a result of my conversation with Gilbert last week and explained my fears that we should not be ready with any effective device to prevent a decline in consumers' expenditure in time for the first post-war depression, if income tax remained inflexible under present pay-as-you-earn arrangements and if we had not taken the powers and set up the necessary machinery in time for the variation of national insurance contributions. Then Chester and I went to call on Hancock, the official at the Ministry of National Insurance primarily in charge of the Bill. It was really a rather encouraging interview, because it became clear that, although the Ministry of National Insurance would naturally find the scheme a nuisance and a mere complicating intrusion into their scheme for national insurance, and although the legislative time table was so close that it would be very difficult for them to get the necessary ministerial approval and to do the necessary drafting before the Bill must be introduced into the House, yet Hancock did not discuss the suggestion as in any way impracticable. Their two objections to it were, first, that people had in any case to get used to the idea of much higher contributions and that the task of getting the Bill through Parliament would be made much more difficult if this extraneous complication were introduced, and, secondly, that there were considerable legislative and administrative difficulties in the way of taking the proposed course. After this interview I wrote a considerable minute on the subject to the Lord President, who is as keen as mustard on the idea and wants to get the necessary powers introduced into the present Bill.[41] Later in the week I drafted a paper which the Lord President is going to circulate to the Cabinet urging this course; and Max Nicholson and I called on the Lord President to discuss it with him. As a result the paper is to be circulated to the Cabinet, and the Lord President is writing letters to the Chancellor of the Exchequer and the President of the Board of Trade

[41] Meade to Lord President, 18 December 1945, T230/105. On the Bill see above pp. 184–5.

enlisting their support. Unfortunately the Lord President will be away in Canada for the next month during which these decisions will be taken, and we shall have to conduct this campaign without the presence of the leading protagonist.[42] If it were not for the opposition of Sir Bernard Gilbert, I believe that we should win without the Lord President's presence; but these two factors combined are not promising.

There have been two meetings of the Steering Committee on the Economic Plan this week. At the first we went through our Economic Survey for 1946.[43] Relatively few changes were made. At the suggestion of Douglas Jay (who is rapidly constituting himself unofficial Minister for the Development Areas!) some reference was inserted to the need for taking work into these Areas – though we managed to take the opportunity of inserting some reference at the same time to the desirability of increasing labour mobility out of the Areas! Ince sent us some words to meet this point. At Eady's suggestion I consulted with R. W. B. Clarke to make some changes in the draft on the inflationary gap, which have – I think – much improved the draft in distinguishing more clearly between, on the one hand, measures (such as increased taxation) which reduce the demand for goods and services and thereby reduce both the pressure of inflation and the gap between total resources and the planned use of resources and, on the other hand, measures (such as the licensing of the production of inessentials) which reduce the supplies available and thereby increase the inflationary pressure at the same time that they reduce the gap between the total supply of economic resources and the planned use of them. At this same meeting of the Steering Committee it was decided to send the Survey forward with a covering note from the Committee to Ministers; and at Bridges' instigation this note took the precise and definite line that the situation showed that we could not both carry on the military sector at the level proposed and reconvert to peace simultaneously, and drew the courageous and definite conclusion that we must cut the Armed Forces plus Munitions demands by 1,000,000 men or so for 1946. Another feature of this covering note, which was approved at a second meeting of the Steering Committee,[44] was that it made the definite proposals that the Survey should be kept under continuous review and that the next number should give quarterly information for the following twelve months and should also give estimates not only for a year in advance but for a number of years ahead. This will enable one to consider (a) the rate of change which is expected over the next twelve months and (b) the sort of more ultimate goal towards which the economy should be adjusting itself. The Steering Committee has also approved for circulation to Ministers the detailed

[42] The draft paper and letters are enclosed with Meade to Christie, 21 December 1945, T230/105. Morrison embarked on the *Mauritania* on 27 December for Halifax, Nova Scotia, to give speeches and meet politicians and trade unionists in Ottawa, Montreal, Quebec, Toronto, New York and Washington (Donoughue and Jones, *Herbert Morrison*, pp. 377–9 and CP(46)77, 'Visit to Canada and United States, January 1946, Memorandum by the Lord President of the Council', CAB129/7).

[43] ED(45) 2nd meeting, 18 December, which discussed ED(45)5 and 6, 'Economic Survey for 1945', 12 and 17 December 1945, T228/20 and CAB134/186.

[44] ED(45) 3rd meeting, 21 December 1945, T228/20 and CAB134/186.

document which the Central Statistical Office has prepared with all the departments concerned showing the statistics which it will be necessary to collect for Employment Policy.[45] We certainly make progress on this front under Bridges' leadership.

Philip Chantler and I attended another lunch in Peggy Joseph's flat with Quirk, de Peyer and Hemming from the Ministry of Fuel and Power to continue our informal discussions on how the prices and output policy should be determined in the nationalised Coal Mines. Chantler had prepared some notes; but these were not very detailed and did not add much to my knowledge of the practical issues involved in applying our ideas about pricing to the actual conditions of the Coal Mines. The discussion at the lunch continued on the old lines. The officials at Fuel and Power did not seem to have changed their attitude of believing that our ideas were both impractical and unnecessary; and they did not shift me from my belief that they were not only practical but very necessary if considerable economic wastes are to be avoided. After the Christmas holidays I must persuade Chantler to fill out his paper rather more concretely.[46] We must peg away at this.

Sir John Woods, Permanent Secretary of the Board of Trade, has held the first meeting of the official committee which has been set up under his chairmanship to consider the problem of Bulk Purchases of Imports. Marcus Fleming is to be our representative; but as he was unable to go, I attended. I think that this is to be an important committee. The problem raises many issues: the meaning and practice of non-discrimination under the proposed commercial policy arrangements; the social utility of organised commodity markets with their speculative operations in futures; the social loss or gain in stabilising prices by long-term contracts; the administrative problems of carrying out a policy of stabilising the cost of living or of paying guaranteed prices to farmers in the absence of monopoly purchase and sale of imports and home production of foodstuffs by the state. The Committee is to proceed, very sensibly, by the simultaneous preparation of studies of particular commodities and of short papers on general principles.[47]

On my way to this meeting I looked in on Liesching to congratulate him on the Commercial Policy success in Washington. I also took the opportunity of warning him that a number of people, including Douglas Jay, were suggesting to Brook and Bridges that there should be an official committee with someone other than a Board of Trade official in the chair to deal with the preparations for the coming conference on Trade and Employment. I told him that I had advised Brook that the right way was, of course, for Liesching to organise a working party of officials for this purpose. Liesching saw the red light. There is, of course, some danger of

[45] ED(45)4, 'Report of the Working Party on Statistics for Employment Policy', 10 December 1945, CAB134/186.

[46] See above, pp. 182–4.

[47] The committee had been set up by the Lord President's Committee in October 1945 to 'submit a report to the Committee on the subject of bulk purchase and other forms of long-term control of commodities other than food'. The first meeting which Meade attended was on 20 December 1945, T236/56. For the second meeting see below, p. 198.

an organised attempt to get the delegation sent to the coming trade conference with instructions which as nearly as possible amount to wrecking instructions.

A. J. Brown is getting ahead with our first Overseas Economic Survey, and we have had a full Staff Meeting to discuss his first draft.[48] After a general discussion I have delegated to a little sub-Staff meeting under Fleming, consisting of the members of the Section mainly concerned with external problems, the responsibility of going through this draft in detail.

Max Nicholson held another of his informal official meetings, to which I took Marcus Fleming, for the purpose of discussing what internal organisation is required in Whitehall for co-ordinating departmental policies so far as the activities of the new international bodies is concerned (International Labour Office, Bank, Fund, Trade Organisation, Economic and Social Council). We had an interesting discussion, but did not reach any very definite conclusions, except (i) that the problems of inter-departmental discussions for the purpose of constitution-building were quite different from those of determining the substantive policies to be urged on the bodies when they were set up, and (ii) that the greatest lacuna in the interdepartmental machinery was that dealing with commodity policy which, after its brave start with Keynes' paper on Buffer Stocks,[49] has fizzled out, largely because it has had no central departmental focus.

[48] EC(S)(45)41 and 47, 'Draft of first part of Overseas Economic Survey' and 'Draft of second part of Overseas Economic Survey', 23 November and 15 December 1945, T230/19.

[49] The first surviving draft, 'International Control of Raw Materials', 14 April 1942, is reprinted in *The Collected Writings of John Maynard Keynes*, Vol. 27, pp. 112–34. For discussions of earlier drafts see T247/9.

# 15

## January 1946

### *13 January 1946*

In the course of this fortnight I have written and sent off to Bridges a minute on the future work which needs to be done in respect of the Economic Plan. My suggestions fall into two main parts:- *First*, the development of the Economic Survey by (i) doing our forecasts for the next year in advance by quarters or by half years so as to show the expected trends and (ii) doing the target national income and the forecasts of probable national expenditure for a more distant year (e.g. 1950) in order to consider the longer-distance goal towards which we should be moving. *Secondly*, the consideration of the means whereby we intend to control the main items of national expenditure. We have now put in motion the setting of a target national income and the forecasting of the probable trends of national expenditure; and we have asked Ministers what parts of the national expenditure they want reduced to close the gap. But how are we going to make sure that we can both restrict and stimulate national expenditure in the desired way? I have suggested to Bridges that (i) steps should now be taken to build up a reserve of public investment projects and to get them all through their preliminary stages; (ii) a review should be made of the short-run and long-run direct and indirect controls and inducements whereby (a) investment and (b) personal consumption might be influenced; and (iii) a review should be made of wages policy in order to see how wages might be varied so as to induce labour to move into the expanding, and out of the contracting, areas, occupations and industries. This minute I discussed with Tress and Stafford. I also sent a copy of the first draft to Max Nicholson. This started an amusing train of events! Nicholson clearly thinks that while the Economic Section are responsible for doing the Survey and forecast his 'Office of the Lord President' is responsible for seeing to the 'implementation' of any economic plan which may be reached on the basis of Ministers' decisions. If this means that it is their business rather than ours to advise on whether a decision to restrict expenditure is best 'implemented' through (e.g.) a rise in income tax or a greater stringency of certain direct controls, this is, of course, quite unacceptable. If it means that Nicholson is interested in seeing that Departments carry out the more detailed decisions, well and good. My draft minute was answered by a set of notes by Campbell Secord, who has joined Nicholson's Office, on the 'implementation of economic planning' which really was a purely economic analysis of general methods of economic control over expenditure – a typical Economic Section paper. Nicholson asked us (myself, Sayers and Fleming) to discuss this with himself, Secord, Flett and Johnston. We went; but politely insisted on discussing my draft minute to Bridges rather than Secord's notes![1]

On the subject of variations in national insurance contributions I believe that we have carried the day, although in a second-best form. I rang up John Henry Woods, Permanent Secretary of the Board of Trade, and spoke to Austin Robinson about it, as a result of which I hear that Cripps (to whom Morrison had written enlisting his support before going to Canada) is now in favour of the inclusion in the present Bill of a clause giving the Chancellor power to introduce a scheme for varying national insurance contributions at a later stage. Max Nicholson and I called on Bridges with Gilbert there, and Nicholson and I argued hard on the one side that the necessary power should be taken in the present Bill, while Gilbert argued hard on the other side. As a result of this Bridges asked Gilbert to find out from the Parliamentary Counsel what the introduction of the necessary clause would involve in the way of redrafting the Bill, and after this to arrange a ministerial meeting to decide the issue. I then got on to Keynes, who wrote a minute to the Chancellor of the Exchequer supporting the inclusion of the clause in the present Bill. The outcome was a paper by the Chancellor of the Exchequer saying that we favoured the inclusion in the present Bill of a clause giving him power to vary national insurance contribution on grounds of unemployment, but the variations not to be automatically linked to the unemployment percentage.[2] It is a great pity to lose this automatic link, since it will inevitbly mean that variations are less prompt (I can imagine the comings and goings in Whitehall before any Chancellor takes the plunge of varying the contribution) and that upward variations are very rare. The Chancellor is scared stiff of the political implications of choosing any 'standard' rate of unemployment around which a scale of automatic variations would have to centre. It is amusing to think that the result of the efforts of a Treasury official like Gilbert to scare the Chancellor out of the scheme altogether has been merely to scare him out of the automation of the scheme – which was the greatest safeguard that the Treasury had that the scheme might not make a net loss over the years. Now there is much greater likelihood that the contributions will be reduced but not raised.

We have received a draft paper from the Treasury on the future of the Stabilisation Policy and with some reference to Wages Policy. This refers back to a request by the Lord President's Committee as far back as September of last year (resulting from the committee's discussion of our

[1] Meade to Bridges, 'Future Work on Economic Planning', 10 January 1946, T230/58. A copy of the first draft is on T230/20 (EC(S)(46)1, 'Draft Minute to Sir Edward Bridges, Future Work on Economic Planning', 2 January 1946). Secord's notes have not been located.

[2] GEN113/1st meeting, 14 January, Meade to Keynes, 7 January, Keynes, 'Employment Policy and the National Insurance Bill', 7 January, and 'Employment Policy and the National Insurance Bill: Memorandum by the Chancellor of the Exchequer', 9 January 1946, T230/105. For the beginning of Meade's campaign see above, pp. 184–5 and 189–90.

Economic Survey of that date) for a paper by the Treasury on the future of the stabilisation policy. Since then the Chancellor has announced at the time of his autumn Budget that the cost-of-living index will be stabilised without qualification for a year or so ahead, so the immediate issue is really already decided.[3] Partly for this reason the Treasury paper was a rather uninteresting and not very useful contribution. Tress and Sayers (who has now joined the Section to deal with some of these internal problems) and I discussed the issue; and Sayers produced a good paper marshalling the arguments against a permanent stabilisation of the cost of living (the unlimited budgetary liability; the increasing distortion of consumption since it was administratively possible to subsidise only a limited range of articles; the fact that in the subsidised industries wage-earners are positively encouraged to ask for higher wages in the knowledge that the price to consumers of their product will not be allowed to rise further, and a large part of the incentive to efficiency on the part of the producers is removed since increased costs will be met by increased subsidies; and the evidence that wage-rates during the war went up almost as rapidly after the cost of living had been stabilised as they did before) and setting out briefly the need for a wages policy in the future which divorced wage-rates from the cost of living and made them depend again upon the supply-demand relationships in the various occupations. This paper we circulated; and Tress and Sayers attended a meeting held by Proctor on the subject. The Treasury paper is to be withdrawn but Proctor's meeting is to become a permanent working party to watch the subject.[4]

Nicholson has held another of his informal meetings of officials to discuss on this occasion the general problems of implementing the decisions of Ministers and giving them the proper degree of publicity. I gave a general lecture on the nature of the post-war economy. It would not be *laissez-faire*, but it would also not be authoritarian (in the manner of the war economy). People must be induced (e.g. through tax policy, wage policy, etc.) to do what they ought to do for the good of society. This led to an interesting discussion on wages policy. Emmerson of the Ministry of Labour was present. He made some interesting remarks about the difficulties of wages policy, particularly in view of the extent to which different groups of workers considered that their wage-rates ought to bear certain historical relationships to each other. (e.g. It would be difficult for the Trade Union concerned to fight for an advance in the wages of laundry workers – where an increase is desirable in order to attract workers – without asking for a similar increase in the wages of the other occupations covered by the same union.) Incidentally I believe it came as quite a new idea to Emmerson that the wages of unpleasant work ought actually to be higher, and possibly many times higher, than the wages of pleasant work, if that were necessary to attract workers to these jobs.

3 'Draft Report on Stabilisation Policy and the Control of Prices', 28 December 1945, T161/1299/S53992; LP(45) 31st meeting, 7 September 1945, CAB71/19 (see above, pp. 128–9); *House of Commons Debates*, Vol. 415, 23 October 1945, cols. 1877–8.

4 Sayers, 'Comments on Stabilisation Policy and the Control of Prices', 9 January 1946, EC(S)(46)5, T230/20 and T161/1229/S53992. Proctor's meeting was on 10 January 1946 (SWP/46/1st meeting, T161/1299/S53992.

This week the Chancellor of the Exchequer sent for me and tried out some of his ideas about taxation for the next Budget. I gave him a lecture about the general position. The year 1946/47 was undoubtedly going to be one of extreme inflationary pressure in the markets for consumption goods. It should be a year in which any tax adjustments which might have the effect of increasing the pressure of demand should be kept to a very minimum. At the same time I would not be so confident as some people in Whitehall that the change from an excess to a deficient level of demand might not come sooner after 1946/47 than was allowed for. If I was Chancellor the thing I would be most anxious about was whether I have sufficient flexible tax adjustments in hand to meet a deficient demand if it rather suddenly and unexpectedly developed – particularly in view of the rigidity which PAYE had introduced into the income tax. The Chancellor had a sensible scheme in mind for the repayment of income-tax credits with this sort of purpose in view.[5] He was, however, smitten with the idea that there might be some immediate danger of deficient demand because consumption goods will now begin to pour onto the market at a time when, with reduction of overtime, women going out of industry etc., there would be a decline in total demand. I assured him that the figures which we had worked out for our Economic Survey for 1946 made it quite certain that this would not happen. Keynes, however, is on a similar tack. He has written a minute to Proctor on our Survey for 1946 criticising our estimated wages-bill as being much too large.[6] It is very important from every point of view to make sure that Keynes sees that the national income forecasts, in the absence of Stone, are nevertheless sensible and reliable, and that we do not allow any credence to be given to the idea that the forthcoming financial year is anything but an inflationary year. I have got Tress and Stafford working away hard on this topic to brief me fully on our estimates before next Wednesday [16 January] when there is a Budget Committee and when these ideas are likely to come up.

In the course of his conversation the Chancellor told me that I must take the initiative and brief him or visit him whenever I thought that there was anything on which I should advise him. This raises very difficult issues for me (a) as regards the Lord President, since it may be awkward to be briefing both these Ministers simultaneously on the same issue, and (b) more particularly, as regards the Treasury officials, since my relations with them might become very difficult if I was briefing the Chancellor independently on their subjects without being a part of the Treasury machine. I managed to maintain a non-committal attitude, and went and reported on this to Bridges the next morning. He said that Dalton was now feeling politically a little stronger and that this was the reason for his request that the Section should brief him as well as Morrison. He said that the best thing was to avoid laying down any hard and fast or too precise formula. I am inclined to believe that, however attractive is the immediate prospect of briefing the Chancellor when one wants to do so, in the long

5 Dalton recorded his ideas in a note to Bridges, 'Next Year's Budget', 17 November 1945, T171/386. On the post-war credits scheme see T171/388, section 2.

6 Keynes, 'Economic Survey for 1946, Estimate of Net National Income', 2 January 1946, T230/55. See also below, p. 204.

run the influence of the Section in the Treasury depends rather upon relations with Treasury officials than with the Chancellor.

There have been a few developments on the socialisation front this fortnight. There has been no further meeting of Gilbert's official Committee on Socialisation; but a report is in draft and a meeting is to be held next week. I have, accordingly, taken the precaution of drafting a section to go into the report (probably expressing a minority of one) arguing that the compensation stock should take the form of Govt debt and should not be secured on the earnings of the socialised industries (even with a Govt guarantee of the stock), with the object which we have been developing in the Economic Section of enabling the Govt thereafter to adopt a price policy in each industry which would equate prices to marginal costs without too much regard to the total earnings of the industry.[7]

Gilbert Ponsonby, who has gone back from the Ministry of War Transport to lecture at the London School of Economics on transport problems, came to call on me, having first sent me a paper which he had written on the co-ordination of transport.[8] This we discussed together with Philip Chantler and Sayers. Ponsonby's thesis, with which of course we all agreed, was simply that the best method of obtaining proper co-ordination was to set prices for the various forms of transport which measured their costs and then let the consumers of transport choose those means which best met their needs at the given costs. This is, however, totally at variance with the ideas of the Ministry of War Transport officials who apparently believe that the way to get an orderly co-ordination of transportation is to charge the same price (presumably regardless of cost) for the same transport facility whatever means it is provided by. (This, I was told by Philip Chantler, was borne out by a visit which he and Alec Johnston of the Lord President's Office paid to my brother-in-law Stephen Wilson at the Ministry of War Transport to discuss their plans for nationalising transport. Their view is to get just such a co-ordinated structure of transport rates as will involve the same rate being charged by each source of transport.) Clearly we have here a simple economic battle to fight of basic importance. But when we came on to ask Ponsonby whether he meant that average or marginal costs must be covered by each price, he seemed to favour some form of average cost and we no longer agreed together!

I have held a meeting with Sayers and Chantler to discuss the first draft of a paper which Chantler is preparing to show how the general ideas which the Section has put forward on the Socialisation of Industries might be applied in the case of Coal. I found this draft a little disappointing. What I am sure is wanted is a paper showing in a wealth of factual detail the need for some sort of mechanism such as we had suggested and the practical

[7] SI(0)(46) 1st meeting, 17 January 1946, T228/269; Meade to Economic Section, 'Socialisation', 2 January, and Meade to Gilbert, 14 January 1946, T230/107. See also Chester, *The Nationalisation of British Industry 1945–51*, pp. 564–7, and below, p. 206.

[8] Not located.

means by which the mechanism might be applied under the present Coal Bill. Chantler is to redraft his paper.[9]

We have now received a copy of the Iron and Steel Industry's Report on what should be done with itself.[10] This we must now study very carefully, but the problem of inadequate staff is becoming really acute.

In the course of the fortnight I lunched with Proctor and had a very fruitful talk with him on the problems of the future of the Economic Plan, the Stabilisation of Prices, the Control of Investment (on which subject Shackle in our Section is preparing a paper in full co-operation with Vinter of Proctor's section in the Treasury), etc. I also went to call on Keynes for the first time since his return from Washington [on 18 December]. We had a general discussion about the Washington negotiations, variations in National Insurance Contributions, the Economic Plan, problems of Socialisation, etc.

As Marcus Fleming was away in bed with the 'flu, I attended on his behalf a meeting in Hutchinson's room in the Ministry of Supply of the Working Party on Bulk Purchases of Raw Cotton. Should the Liverpool Cotton market be restored or should Govt bulk purchasing continue? I am pretty sure that this is not the sort of market where it is most fruitful to make the socialistic experiments. Let monopolistic industries be socialised; but let an organised produce market where there has been something approaching a 'perfect market' and where indirect advantages to our balance of payments of a substantial amount have been gained, continue competitively. R. F. Bretherton of the Ministry of Supply had drafted a rather tendentious report which was really an argument for continuing a state monopoly of the import of cotton. Thompson-McCausland of the Bank was on the side of a free market. R. W. B. Clarke of the Treasury would obviously temperamentally be in favour of state purchase; but I gathered from his silence that the Treasury had not yet decided to give up the possible contribution to our balance of payments of a free cotton market.[11]

After Marcus' return we held a staff meeting at which Marcus generally consulted with the members of the Section about the subject. Marcus has also written a paper on Buffer Stocks and Quantitative Export Restrictions for dealing internationally with primary products which are in over-supply.[12] It is an ingenious and rather elaborate scheme which combines national buffer stocks with international regulation by export quotas – a scheme which I confess I do not yet properly understand even after a Staff Meeting on the subject. But this is due to the fact that I have not been able to give the time which it deserves to its study, and I must try to do this next week.

I have sent Helmore at the Board of Trade a letter about the application to State Trading of the balance of payments let-out for import quotas, raising a point which P. W. Martin of the Ministry of Food has brought to

[9] The paper became 'An Economic Policy for the Socialised Coal Industry', 23 March 1946, EC(S)(46)17 Revise, T230/21.

[10] Se below p. 208.

[11] On the committee see above p. 191. Only the minutes of the first meeting are on T236/56.

[12] EC(S)(46)3, 'A Buffer-Stock-cum-Quota Commodity Regulation Scheme', 4 January 1946, T230/20.

my attention. In the Washington proposals the let-out for import quotas on balance of payments grounds is said to apply to state trading. But does it also relieve the state trading import authority from observing the maximum protective margins between import prices and selling price at home which will have been set as part of the tariff bargain? Clearly it should do so, since the whole idea is to make it possible to do by state trading what can be done by private trading. A quota restriction on private imports would raise the domestic price of such imports above the world price by more than any existing tariff. If there is no exemption from the state trading protective margins on balance of payments grounds, then it would not be possible to restrict on balance of payments grounds any commodity which was state-imported and which could not be price controlled – unless a gratuitous profit to the first purchaser of the commodity from the state is the answer. We must insist in the final draft that balance of payments restrictions on quantities relieve a state-importer from the limits set to protective margins.[13]

Liesching held a meeting in the Board of Trade which I attended to discuss the possible place in this country for the meeting of the nuclear states for the preliminary trade negotiations in the summer of this year. After discussing many possible alternatives, Brighton or Eastbourne seemed to live. The Ministry of Works is now making enquiries.[14]

I had lunch at the Café Royal with Bertram Pickard (of the secretariat of the United Nations Organisation) and Miss Midwinter (of the Foreign Office) in order to meet a Czech called Kunosi. We talked to him about the part which the Economic and Social Council might play in the brave new world. He took a purely Russian point of view. He explained the Russian dislike of the ILO so long as it contained tripartite representation (a dislike which I frankly share, as I do not believe that the encouragement of monopolies of workers and of employers is at all a good thing). He expressed great cynicism about the Washington commercial policy proposals. Rather a depressing lunch. Practically every topic one touched upon bristled with possible conflict of opinion between the Russian and the Anglo-American way of doing things. I suppose *the* great question of the next years is whether a *modus vivendi* can be found between these two ways of life. The Czechs with their obvious intentions to go along with the Russians but with their equally obvious interest in the ways of the liberal West provide one of the few intellectual bridges.

I spent yesterday morning delivering a lecture at Chatham House on Economic Planning (with Max Nicholson in the chair) to a large audience of Naval and RAF educational officers. I spoke about the problems of forecasting a large total national income and then so controlling the national expenditure as to reach this target. Nicholson stressed the need to keep contact between the ideas which we were trying to apply at the centre in Whitehall and the ideas which were presented to the people as a whole on these subjects. I have no doubt that educational talks of this kind,

[13] See below, p. 218.
[14] The meetings were eventually held in Church House in London from 15 October 1946.

and of the kind which I gave last summer on similar sessions at Oxford to members of the Foreign Service,[15] are well worthwhile in the long run.

The fortnight has been quite busy in Establishment matters. I have now formally become Director of the Section. Sayers has joined the Section. Tom Wilson has, unfortunately, decided to leave the Section. I have been having a battle royal to get David Bensusan Butt for the Section, the other claimant being Douglas Jay who wants an assistant to help him at No. 10. This has involved calling on, and minuting, Bridges. I thought at one moment that I had lost; but I believe I may yet win! Certainly with all the present work I must try to get rather more staff. Norman Brook and I went to a meeting in the Treasury with Wilson-Smith (head of the Treasury Establishments) and Helsby to discuss two Establishment matters. Should our junior members all have to come in as 'career' civil servants or should all or some come in on definite short contracts? Should the senior members of the Section, as at present, all cover one large grade (covering Principals and Assistant Secretaries) or should they fall into the two normal grades? In neither of these did we reach any conclusions.[16]

The first week of the fortnight was complicated by the fact that poor Margaret was smitten down with 'flu. As a result I had to get the children up, get the breakfast, do the fire, do the hot-water bottle and the thermometer before going to the office, and put the children to bed, get the supper, do the fire, hot-water bottles and thermometer on getting back from the office. Little does the office-worker realise, until such a catastrophe overtakes him, how much he owes to his wife!

## 27 January 1946

Ministers have decided to include in the present National Insurance Bill the power to vary National Insurance contributions as a means of maintaining total purchasing power and so employment. The Bill has now been published with a clause to this effect included. There was a ministerial meeting held in the Chancellor's room to discuss the matter. The Chancellor of the Exchequer was in the chair. The others present were: the Lord Chancellor, the Lord Privy Seal, the Minister of Labour, the Minister of National Insurance (accompanied by his Permanent Secretary Phillips), Palmer (representing the President of the Board of Trade), Nicholson (representing the Lord President), Bridges, Gilbert, Murrie and myself. All Ministers agreed that the power must be included. The question arose whether the variations should be on an automatic sliding scale or at the discretion of the Chancellor. The Chancellor argued for the second because he did not want to have to fix a 'normal' level of unemployment, which certainly does raise big political difficulties. The Lord Chancellor rather favoured an automatic scale. Nicholson speaking for the Lord President who was still away in Canada was able to get it agreed that the power should be taken in a form which, when the time

[15] See above, p. 109.
[16] On 9 January: see Helsby, 'Economic Section', 9 January 1946, T217/1.

came, would allow the Chancellor to introduce either an automatic sliding scale or *ad hoc* changes in contribution. The problem arose whether the new scales of contribution would be introduced soon enough to enable variations in them to be used in time to influence demand during the first post-war recession. The Minister of National Insurance suggested that the new rates would probably be introduced by the beginning of 1948. At the request of the Chancellor I said that I thought that this would be soon enough, but that it would be rash to rely upon a general recession in demand not occurring until some time after that date. We must be ready by the beginning of 1948; PAYE made Income Tax very inflexible; the timing of the repayment of deferred income-tax credits might be useful, but individuals might treat them not as supplements to income but as accumulated savings, which might mean that they would not have any very great effect upon the demand for consumption goods. After the meeting I briefed the Lord President to the effect that the Chancellor's desire to avoid an automatic sliding scale was dangerous for two reasons: first, because it would make it politically much more difficult ever to raise rates of contribution, so that the long-term balance of the fund would be so much the more endangered; and, secondly, because it would increase the delay between a change in unemployment and the consequent change in the rate of contribution because there would on each occasion have to be an *ad hoc* decision resting upon official and Ministerial meetings, special printing of new stamps etc. I advised him to make sure that the clause in the Bill did allow for the alternative of an automatic sliding scale when the time came.[17]

This fortnight has also shown considerable development on the Economic Planning front. The four Ministers primarily responsible for the Economic Plan (the Lord President, the Chancellor of the Exchequer, the President of the Board of Trade and the Minister of Labour) have met to consider our Economic Survey for 1946. In preparation for this meeting Bridges, Gilbert, Nicholson, Flett and I met to consider the way in which we should advise ministers on this question. We were agreed that quite the outstanding thing was that if we were to be able to carry on the reconversion to peace in any way on the scale contemplated in the Survey there must be a radical cut in the manpower and other resources allocated to the Armed Forces and their Supply. The Defence Committee was about to meet and to hear from the Prime Minister that they must plan for the employment in the Armed Forces and their Supply of only 1,800,000 instead of 2,600,000 by the end of 1946. (This meeting has since taken place with the result that the Chiefs of Staff are to examine the implications of such a cut and that the Manpower Committee is to reconsider the re-allocation of manpower among the other civilian uses on the assumption that this cut takes place.) We agreed further that Ministerial approval should be sought for us (a) to revise the Survey for 1946, to project it into 1947 and to do all this, as far as possible, by quarters or by half-years and (b) to examine the problems which would be involved in preparing an Economic Survey for 1950.

[17] GEN113/1st meeting, 14 January, and Meade to Lord President, 17 January 1946, T230/105. The National Insurance Bill was published on 25 January 1946.

After this meeting Douglas Jay in conversation with me suggested that there should also be some Ministerial decision to ensure that all projects for domestic investment were very carefully scrutinised, as there would be a considerable 'inflationary gap' during 1946 whatever happened to the decision on manpower for the Services, which in any case related to closing the gap at the end of 1946 and not during 1946. I fully agreed with this. Investment which was not going to be of immediate help to the export industries or which was not in the development regions should on general Employment Policy principles be postponed in present circumstances if it could be postponed without catastrophe. I spoke to Nicholson about this. Before the Ministerial meeting Tress, Nicholson, Flett and I went to see the Lord President to speak to him on these lines. The Ministerial meeting went off quite well. The discussion was a bit desultory. I managed to get an opportunity to say my piece about the need to postpone investment wherever possible. Ministers were fortified in the need to take a strong line on the subject of manpower for the Armed Forces and their Supply at the Defence Committee which was meeting later the same day. There was a useful and illuminating discussion about wages policy, in which Cripps (no doubt primed by Austin Robinson) took the lead in arguing that there was no point in having a plan for the use of our resources including manpower unless we had some way of attracting manpower without direct labour controls (i.e. by a wages policy) to the occupations where it was wanted. Cripps also talked a lot about the need for an Economic Plan and emphasised that the Survey was not a Plan. In this, of course, he was quite right. The Survey merely shows what demands are likely to be made on the community's resources on the basis of current programmes and policies. It does not become a Plan until Ministers have taken decisions as to how these demands should be adjusted so as to fit in with the total resources available. But I fear that Cripps (in this also no doubt primed by Austin Robinson) wants a detailed Economic Plan in the sense of a statement of exactly how many shirts, how many pairs of boots and shoes etc. we should produce over each of the next five years. This, I believe, if taken seriously would lead to the sacrifice of all the flexibility which a proper use of the pricing and costing system demands. The outcome was that the Lord President was authorised to draft a covering note for him to attach to the Survey in submitting it to the Cabinet.[18] Nicholson and I, in consultation with Bridges, have drafted such a note covering the following points:- (a) the need to cut the manpower for the Armed Forces and their Supply; (b) the need to screen carefully all Investment Projects in 1946; (c) the need for a Wages Policy to attract labour where it is wanted from where it is not wanted (e.g. the distributive trades); (d) the need to arrange for some suitable publicity about the major economic problems of 1946 (on this subject there is great sparring between the Chancellor of the Exchequer and the Lord President and I have left the subject severely alone for Nicholson and Bridges to deal with); and (e) the fact that the four Ministers have authorised us to revise the Survey for 1946, to project it

[18] MEP(46) 1st meeting, 21 January 1946, CAB134/503; DC(46) 3rd meeting, 21 January 1946, CAB131/1.

into 1947, to do 1946 and 1947 as far as possible by quarters or by half years, and to examine the problems involved in doing a Survey for 1950[19]

I have now got Bridges' approval to call meetings of my Economic Survey Working Party in order to prepare a report for the Steering Committee on the problems which would be involved in doing an Economic Survey for 1950. I am glad that this is so. Early this fortnight Austin Robinson who is so keen on doing a Survey for 1950 in order to know on what scale to plan particular industries had written a note on how to set about planning for 1950. At the end of this note he had a whole series of suggestions as to how the different parts of the work should be done – some of it by working parties which excluded the Economic Section. This he had sent to Proctor in the Treasury as well as to myself with the suggestion that Proctor as secretary of the Steering Committee should organise the work. I told Proctor, who immediately agreed with me, that I thought that this was obviously a job for my Economic Survey Working Party. I have got Tress, Saunders of the Ministry of Labour and Stafford of the Central Statistical Office all to write papers on how to do a Survey for 1950. Now I shall be free to hold a meeting of all the departments to which all these papers as well as Austin Robinson's are circulated and the problem of the 1950 Survey will become fairly and squarely again the primary responsibility of the Economic Section.[20] Austin's paper almost entirely related the Survey for 1950 to the problem of seeing what was likely to be the desired scale of different industries after the transitional period, so that the Board of Trade and other similar departments can go about their present plans for particular industries with a better knowledge of the size which they should ultimately be. This is all very proper and useful so long as it is used for such purposes as improving the knowledge of the future in the framework of which present investment plans are drawn up. It will be very undesirable if it is used to draw up detailed rigid plans for particular industries which fix their scale of production now firmly for the next five years. We in the Economic Section also want the Survey for 1950 to examine the overall balance between total demand and the total available resources so that it will be useful to determine whether there is likely to be a general 'deflationary' or 'inflationary' gap in 1950. We must clearly devise a Survey which is useful for both purposes.

Sir Donald Fergusson, Permanent Secretary of the Ministry of Fuel and Power, has written a letter to Bridges complaining that our Economic Survey for 1946 did not lay enough stress on the basic industries (such as Fuel and Power, Transport, etc.) without which we cannot achieve any of our programmes (e.g. for export, for housing, etc.). We have drawn up points for a reply on the lines that our Survey was in terms of the final uses of resources (e.g. for personal consumption, Defence, Housing, Industrial

[19] Nicholson to Lord President, 22 January 1946, and 'Economic Survey for 1946, Memorandum by the Lord President', T230/55.

[20] Robinson, 'Long-term planning', 15 January, and Robinson to Meade, 16 January 1946, T230/61 and CAB139/168; Tress, 'Notes on the problems involved in an Economic Survey for 1950', Saunders, 'Notes on long-term planning', and Stafford, 'An Economic Plan for 1950', CAB139/168. Meade's meeting took place on 1 and 5 February (see below, pp. 210–12).

Investment, Foreign Balance) and did not, therefore, make reference to specific industries such as Fuel and Power the use of which was common to all these final uses. We assumed that when Ministers had decided on the final uses, these industries would make their claims on resources as necessary to achieve the agreed final results. But we admitted that our Survey might properly have been developed more on the side of seeing what were the implications for particular industries.[21] Clearly this general question is going to be of great importance to us in the future. We must satisfy the legitimate interest in the future development of particular industries without encouraging a rigid plan for output industry by industry.

Keynes has been making a nuisance of himself again about our Survey for 1946. He sent me a minute in which he criticised the statistics of our national expenditure forecasts for 1946. These points were easily met. He himself had made a statistical howler about building labour; and on the question of investment in working capital by private industry and disinvestment in working capital by the state during the transition from the war economy to the peace economy he accused us of making a number of howlers which we had not made. He then went on to accuse us of a 'logical absurdity' in showing a gap between total national expenditure and the target national income. I wrote him a spirited reply. As for the logic of the gap, I explained that we all agreed that *ex post* expenditure must equal income. But why was there any absurdity in saying that the value (at current prices) of the goods and services which people *ex ante* were planning to purchase was greater than the value (at current prices) of the goods and services which could in fact be produced? This exactly described the actual situation. It is a pity that Keynes should take this line. I can't help feeling that as Stone is now gone he feels that his successors must be making asses of themselves. Stafford is carrying on quietly a correspondence with Keynes on the size of the 1946 national income.[22] [I] hope that by degrees the new firm will gain his confidence.

Nicholson has held another of his informal discussion groups on internal economic problems. We discussed in the main Investment Policy and Wages Policy. On Investment I raised the issue whether we did not need some official machinery now to screen all major investment projects during 1946 at least, during which there was going to be such an excess of demand over available supply of our resources. Proctor explained how the Investment Working Party was going to come to life again soon and how they were likely to start off by examining the general programme of investment of the various departments. (Incidentally I have seen a draft paper by Vinter which Proctor is sending up to Gilbert in the Treasury to send round to start off the work of the Investment Working Party again. It is on the whole a good and helpful paper. It deals, however, almost exclusively with the non-financial aspects of investment – e.g. what are the obstacles which prevent rapid action between deciding to undertake a particular project and actually spending the money on it, what is the action

[21] Meade to Bridges, 23 January 1946, T230/55. Fergusson's letter has not been located.

[22] Keynes to Meade, 'Economic Survey of 1946', 15 January, and Meade to Keynes, 18 January 1946, T230/55. The correspondence between Stafford and Keynes is on T230/55 and CAB139/163.

which it is necessary to take to get a large shelf of public investment projects ready for initiation when a slump comes. But the paper expressly does not deal at all with the financial inducements – rate of interest, variable grants-in-aid, taxes and subsidies – which may be necessary actually to get investment undertaken at the correct time. Tress and Shackle are disturbed at this fact. Of course, logically, it is rather ridiculous. But on tactical grounds I am sure that we should accept this for the time being, and get the Treasury to go as far as possible on the non-financial aspects of investment policy. We can take up the financial aspects as occasion arises (e.g. at the Budget Committee) and postpone any frontal attack on this until the other stages are further on.) One cannot hope to do everything at once.[23]

On Wages Policy I am glad to hear that Bridges has now approved the setting up of a working party under Nicholson to consider the whole problem of a wages policy.[24] The Ministry of Labour meanwhile have submitted to the Manpower Committee a paper which was based largely on the rather absurd view that if wages are equal in occupations A and B, then it isn't wages but conditions of work which are at fault if unpleasant job A cannot attract labour from pleasant job B. There seems to be no comprehension in that Ministry that higher wages should be paid in unpleasant jobs in order to man them up. I got in touch with Dennison (the Secretary of the Manpower Committee) and Austin Robinson (who briefs Cripps who goes to the Manpower Committee) to try to get this paper referred to Nicholson's working party. I am not sure what the outcome was.[25] Meanwhile a paper has come before the Lord President's Committee on the Agricultural Minimum Wage. This presented an exquisite problem to the social scientist! The Government has decided not to withdraw the Essential Works Order from agriculture because it is afraid that it could not man up agriculture if the agricultural workers were free to leave the industry; the Agricultural Wages Board has refused the workers' demand for higher wages, so that workers are held by force in an industry in which a rise in wages sufficient to attract the workers is (so the workers assert) refused; and it is in an industry in which if there were a rise in wage costs because of the stabilisation of the cost of living there would have to be a rise in the Government's subsidy to the industry rather than a rise in prices of the product to the consumer to meet the higher costs, with the result that the employers have a relatively small incentive to resist wage demands. In these conditions the workers ask the Government to exert some pressure on the independent members of the Wages Board in

[23] Vinter to Meade, 18 January 1946, enclosing 'Treasury: Investment Working Party', Shackle to Meade, 'The Treasury Paper for the Investment Working Party', 23 January, Tress to Meade, 20 January, and Meade to Shackle and Tress, 24 January 1946, T230/85.

[24] Nicholson to Bridges, 9 January 1946 (approved by Bridges on 16 January 1946), CAB124/783; see above, p. 161.

[25] MP(46)4, 'Problem of Recruiting Labour in Unattractive Industries: Memorandum by the Minister of Labour', 17 January 1946, CAB134/509; Meade to Dennison, 19 January, and Robinson to Meade, 21 January 1946, T230/111. Robinson agreed with Meade that it was 'a wicked and preposterous paper', and briefed Cripps accordingly. The paper was referred to Nicholson's working party: MP(46) 2nd meeting, 22 January 1946, CAB134/509.

order to get the ruling reversed. But it is the Government's declared policy not to interfere with the ordinary machinery of wage negotiation. Sayers wrote a very good minute on all this for the Lord President. It shows (a) the difficulties of the Government washing its hands of wages policy in a world in which the labour controls are disappearing and in which the only way of manning up an undermanned industry in conditions of full employment is by attractive wage-rates and (b) the adverse effects of a rigid policy of not allowing the cost of living to rise at all. In the result the Lord President's Committee (probably wisely) decided not to intervene to upset the decision of the Agricultural Wages Board.[26] But these incidents together with Sayers' minute will gradually make it clear that a Wages Policy is necessary.

There have been two meetings of Gilbert's official Committee on Socialisation which I attended. On both occasions I was fully primed to defend our view that compensation should take the form of untied Government debt so that the particular socialised industries would be relatively free to make profits or losses and to argue for the inclusion of the reasons for this view in the report. On the first occasion we did not reach this section in our discussion of the draft report. On the second occasion we reached this section, whereupon Gilbert suggested that we should exclude all discussion of the question whether stock should be tied or not from this report and should then go on later to study in a separate report the whole question of the price policy of socialised industry.[27] So the day is still further postponed when this question will really begin to be discussed by officials or by Ministers.

There have been two meetings of the Budget Committee this fortnight, which have raised very important issues and on which I have spent much of my time.[28]

Two whole days have been taken up with the Census of Distribution Committee in which Sir Richard Hopkins, our chairman, went through point after point getting the Committee to agree on their general decisions before the Secretary sat down to draft the report.[29] There was a certain amount of uneasiness shown by our two representatives of the small shopkeepers; but it is now pretty clear that we are going to recommend unanimously that a Census of Distribution should be taken. The only

[26] LP(46)15, 'Agricultural Minimum Wage, Memorandum by Minister of Agriculture and Fisheries', 22 January 1946, CAB132/2; LP(46) 3rd meeting, 25 January 1946, CAB132/1. Sayers' minute has not been found.

[27] SI(0)(46), 1st and 2nd meetings, 17 and 21 January 1946, T228/269; and see above, p. 197. The committee's second report was not completed until May 1946; see below, p. 261.

[28] These meetings took place on 16 and 23 January; the important issues raised at both (and subsequent) meetings included the reform of death duties which Dalton hoped to carry out (see his 'Next Year's Budget', 17 November 1945, T171/386). At the second meeting Meade put forward his own suggestions which he elaborated in a memorandum considered by the Budget Committee later in January and discussed with Dalton in February (Meade to Bridges, 24 January 1946, Bridges to Chancellor, 16 February 1946, T171/388; and see below, pp. 214 and 223). When Meade left the Cabinet Offices in 1947 he wished, but was not permitted, to keep a copy of his memorandum (Norman Brook to Meade, 29 August 1947, Meade Papers 3/10).

[29] No minutes of this meeting are on BT70/99.

question is how much detail should be included in the questions. (An attempt on my part to recommend a full enquiry into the break-down of costs and into profits was generally resisted.) It is also clear that the questions asked of the small shopkeepers will have to be much simpler than those which can be asked of the large shops.

We have continued our general series of briefs to the Lord President for his committees. Miss Watts has done one on Shipbuilding and one on Civil Aviation.[30] I have held a meeting of Sayers, Dennison, Wood, Tress and Chantler to discuss the general lines to be taken on a series of papers which are coming up next week on the present Unemployment Situation, the problem of determining what firms if any should be allowed to set up or to expand in London, and the problem of getting the Ministry of Food to toe the line in the general policy already agreed on by which raw material allocations are to be given preferentially to firms situated in the development areas where there are local pockets of unemployed labour to be absorbed.[31]

I have made arrangements, after discussion with Brook, Murrie and Alec Johnston that Chantler in our section should give the Lord President briefs on the general economic background of Housing policy when the Lord President attends the Prime Minister's meetings which are now held to examine the progress of the Housing programme.[32]

There has not been so much on in the external field this fortnight. One possibility of early action is, however, the result of the talks now going on at Bermuda with the Americans on Civil Aviation. We are still stupidly taking the line that in Civil Aviation we must be free to reserve to ourselves a proportion of the traffic coming to and from this country – a policy which, if applied by the Americans to shipping, would be disastrous to us. Shipping is much more important to our balance of payments than civil aviation. We have always argued that we should have a general set of principles *à la* Article VII for international transport, under which there would be special transitional arrangements whereby we could for a period support our civil aviation and the Americans their shipping, but that thereafter subsidies and quotas should be avoided and the traffic should go to the cheapest carrier. Shackle in the Board of Trade and Gorell Barnes in the Treasury are

30 'Shipbuilding Industry: Memorandum by the First Lord of the Admiralty and the Minister of War Transport LP(46)17', 23 January 1946, CAB124/208; 'British Air Services', 24 January 1946, T230/3.

31 The resulting section briefs on the first and third topics were: Tress, 'The Employment and the Unemployment Situation, Memorandum by the Minister of Labour and National Service (LP(I)(46)6)', 30 January, and Chantler, 'Allocation of Raw Materials in Development Areas: Memorandum by the Minister of Labour and National Service, the President of the Board of Trade and the Secretary of State for Scotland (LP(I)(46)2, 7, 8 and 9)', 29 January 1946, CAB124/218. The LPC discussed a memorandum by the Minister of Town and Country Planning on 'Greater London Planning' on 15 February 1946 (LP(46)32, CAB132/2; LP(46) 6th meeting, CAB132/1).

32 The minutes of the PM's meetings, 'to review the progress of the housing programmes and to deal with any major questions that might arise', in 1945 and 1946 are on CAB134/320. Briefs to Morrison from Chantler can be found on CAB124/450 and 451.

with us on this. I have told Fleming and Miss Watts to be prepared to come into very early action on this.[33]

The problem has arisen of the UK representation on the Commissions and their Committees of the Economic and Social Council of the United Nations Organisation. The Economic Section ought to be closely connected with any delegations or representatives sent from the UK on the Economic and Employment Commission and its Committees on Employment, the Balance of Payments and Economic Development. Where it is a question of appointment of technical experts in their personal capacity, there should be no bar to the actual appointment of members of the Economic Section. I have minuted Brook on this and he has promised to send my minute on to Bridges.[34]

Fleming has written a revised version of his paper on Buffer Stocks (in the intervals of his work for the UK delegation to the Economic and Social Council which the first Assembly of the United Nations Organisation meeting here in London has just set up). Dow has prepared for him a very good analysis of all the earlier discussions in Whitehall in 1941–1943 on Buffer Stocks.[35]

I have had a busy fortnight on Establishments. Butt has unfortunately been allotted to Jay.[36] Meanwhile I have been making efforts to get an early Class B release from the Air Force for Jefferies who is coming to work in the Economic Section. I have also put in an application to get Brian Hopkin, at present secretary of the statistical committee of the Royal Commission on Population, to be seconded to the Economic Section for two years from June of this year when his present work is likely to come to an end. Apart from his being generally a good economist, I think that it will be useful for the Economic Section to have him when Population Policy is put on the map, as it will be by the Report of the Royal Commission which will probably be ready by the end of the year.[37] I have also been engaged in trying to re-allocate the subjects among the various members of the section. For example, I have asked Tress to take on Manpower and the Distribution of Industry in addition to the National Income and Expenditure work which he does for the Economic Survey. Sayers I have asked to write a brief on the Report which has come in from the Iron and Steel Federation on the Iron and Steel Industry. (Incidentally I have read this report which is very well done, but it avoids skilfully all reference to relative costs of iron and steel here and abroad and the relevance of this to our import programme.)[38]

[33] Shackle to Meade, 15 and 26 January, and Gorell Barnes to Meade, 26 January 1946, T230/3; see also below p. 217. The Bermuda talks had started on 15 January and they would continue until 11 February.

[34] Not located.

[35] EC(S)(46)3 Revise, 'A Buffer-Stock-cum-Quota Commodity Regulation Scheme', 26 January 1946, T230/20 and 'A summary of previous discussions of commodity policy, Note by the Economic Section', EC(S)(46)8, T230/20. The UNO meetings were in London 23 January–18 February 1946.

[36] See above, p. 200.

[37] It reported in June 1949 (Cmd. 7695).

[38] Sayers, 'The Iron and Steel Modernisation Plan', 23 January 1946, EC(S)(46)7, T230/20; British Iron and Steel Federation, Report to the Ministry of Supply and on Iron and Steel Industry, December 1945, T230/87. See also below, p. 234 on the further developments on this issue.

I have now managed to launch the idea that there should be a real library for the Economic Section of economic books and periodicals. Brook held a meeting of all the various sections in the Cabinet Offices which might be interested in library facilities:- Campion for the statisticians, myself for the economists, Jacob for military, Topham for the historians. We agreed finally on the idea that we should ask the Treasury to join with us in a joint library with a properly trained librarian.

In the course of the fortnight I have lunched with Paul Cadbury (a fellow member of the Census of Distribution Committee) and Tinbergen who is here as part of the Dutch delegation to the United Nations Organisation. Margaret and I went to supper with the Jays. Mrs Jay who is a member of the Royal Commission on Population explained that she is alone preparing a minority report to say that taking fees for education should be illegal, i.e. that the middle classes should be forced into free state education and thereby give up the expensive educational competition among themselves for their children which made the cost of a large family so prohibitively expensive for them. Query: is this compatible with individual liberty and with experimentation in educational methods? Certainly it is desirable that this expensive snobbish rivalry in education for the middle class children should stop. I certainly would not mind Tom missing a Public School if I did not feel that many of his friends would go to Public Schools and thus get a better chance in life than he. We have also had to lunch here Rasminsky of the Canadian Foreign Exchange Control and Hiss of the US State Department (who was executive secretary of the San Francisco Conference) who are part of the Canadian and American delegations to the Assembly of the United Nations Organisation.

# 16

## February 1946

### *10 February 1946*

Since Ministers looked at our Economic Survey for 1946 and, *inter alia*, decided that we should attempt (i) to do it by quarters for 1946, (ii) to do 1947 and (iii) to report on the problems which would be involved in doing a survey for 1950, I have spent some time (and have incurred a great deal of trouble) in trying to carry out this instruction.[1] The real trouble has been caused by the little group of Cambridge economists in the Board of Trade (E. A. G. Robinson, R. F. Kahn and W. B. Reddaway) who strongly hold two views: (i) that for 1946 one should now try to do, not a forecast of departmental requirements and a comparison of this with available supplies, but rather an actual forecast of what is likely to happen in the absence of any further ministerial decisions about how the gap between requirements and availabilities should be closed; and (ii) that the greatest priority should now be given to doing a Survey for 1950 rather than revised Surveys for 1946 and 1947. For (i) they argue that the best way to bring Ministers up against the hard facts of life is to show them what is actually likely to happen to (e.g.) the volume of exports or the clothing ration in the present state of pressure on resources, rather than to show a nice clothing requirement and an export target which together with other requirements add up to more than the available supplies. Against this I have been adamant on the grounds (which Bridges has told me that I am quite right in maintaining) that the procedure suggested by the Board of Trade economists would mean that the Economic Survey Working Party (i.e. the Economic Section and the Central Statistical Office in consultation with the Treasury, Board of Trade, and Ministry of Labour) would, in forecasting what amounts of labour various departments were in fact likely to obtain, certainly give the impression that it was allocating the available resources among the various departments, which it would be most undesirable for the Economic Section to do. In fact the facts of the situation can just as clearly be shown for demonstrating the gap between requirements and availabilities and allowing the departments to put in papers and generally to raise a scream to underline what is likely to happen to their interests in the absence of Ministerial action to close the gap. For (ii) the Board of Trade economists argue that there are many decisions

[1] See above, pp. 201–3.

which have to be taken now (e.g. training of labour for different occupations, investment decisions, etc.) which vitally affect or depend upon what the situation is likely to be in 1950. We are inclined to agree with them that it is worth having a shot at 1950, but we would certainly put much more stress on the uncertainties that are likely to surround our answers.

I had discussions with Tress, Campion, Stafford, E. A. G. Robinson and others about the way to organise this work. Four papers on the problems involved in doing a survey for 1950 were circulated: by E. A. G. Robinson, Tress, Stafford and Saunders of the Ministry of Labour. I held a staff meeting in the Section (to which Stafford of the Central Statistical Office and Campbell Secord of the Lord President's Office were invited) to discuss the issues. We then held an Economic Survey Working Party meeting to discuss the Survey for 1950. At the beginning of this meeting I tried to clear off the problem of revising the Survey for 1946 and doing it by quarters. We were then treated to a disgraceful and clearly prepared filibuster by the three Board of Trade economists, Robinson, Kahn and Reddaway which lasted two hours, prevented us doing any other business and was confined to the argument that in the revision of the 1946 Survey we must do forecasts of probable actual outcomes and not of requirements. Both Proctor of the Treasury and Douglas Jay rang me up afterwards to say what a disgraceful show it was . . . At the end of the two hours, however, we gained the point which we had hoped to clear up in five minutes. A few days later I held a second meeting of the Economic Survey Working Party on the problem of a survey for 1950. This went quite well. The Board of Trade economists were, I think, a little contrite. We decided: (a) to prepare a report for Bridges on the purposes of doing a survey for 1950 (which are twofold: first, to see how soon an inflationary overall pressure on resources may give place to a deflationary gap, and secondly to see what is likely to be the fortunes of particular industries etc. in order to base decisions which may be required now for such industries on better information) and (b) to set up a small working group to see how much of a survey for 1950 we can do without bothering departments outside the Treasury, Ministry of Labour and the Board of Trade for detailed information.[2] (Bridges is *most* insistent that we should not go bothering departments for information about 1950 yet.) We can certainly have a shot at doing the target national income for 1950; [make] guesses about productivity and wage-rates and hence about prices; turn the national income into personal incomes after payments of taxes; guess how much people will spend on consumption out of these incomes. On the other

[2] The four papers were: Robinson, 'Long-term planning', 15 January, Tress, 'Notes on the problems involved in an economic survey for 1950', Stafford, 'An economic plan for 1950', and Saunders, 'Notes on long-term planning', circulated on 28 January as EC(S)(46)9 (T230/20). The Working Party meetings were held on 1 and 5 February 1946: see Meade to Campion, 29 January 1946, CAB127/168, and Meade, 'Economic Survey Working Party', 2 February 1946, CAB139/168. Of the first meeting Robinson later wrote to Reddaway: 'I hope . . . the long tiresome meeting at which you, Kahn and I, plus Otto Clarke, fought the combined stupidities of the Cabinet Office and the Central [Statistical] Office was [not] all time entirely wasted.' (Robinson to Reddaway, 19 February 1946, ROBN5/1, Robinson Papers, Churchill College, Cambridge).

hand, it may be difficult to do Government expenditure, or public or private investment without worrying departments. We have then to consider the foreign balance, and then to construct various alternative Plans (e.g. by tax reduction to stimulate consumption or by public investment programmes) to fill any 'gap' which may otherwise be disclosed. On this basis we can then proceed to consider the probable future fortunes of particular industries. The tenuous and insubstantial nature of all these calculations relating to particular industries is obvious, and becomes still more obvious when account is taken of the fact that one has got to do a Balance of Payments forecast for 1950 which will enable one to subtract imports and add exports to domestic demand for each of the particular products considered.

This Balance of Payments forecast is being undertaken by R. W. B. Clarke of the Treasury in a small group working for the Balance of Payments Working Party (of which more below).[3] It is in this connection that the Economic Section is obviously going to have the most unpopular role to play. It is Clarke's belief apparently that one can just go through our exports and our imports and say what is likely to happen, regardless of the level of prices and costs here and abroad. It will be our task to ask at every point what elasticity of demand is being assumed at home and abroad for each commodity and what level of relative prices and costs and exchange rates is being assumed. I have already discussed with A. J. Brown the possibility of our doing a little econometric research to consider the elasticity of demand for our imports and exports.[4]

Meanwhile the survey for [1946] has gone to the Cabinet with a covering note by the Lord President. We also prepared (Stafford and Tress) a paper which the Lord President circulated at the same time to the Cabinet explaining how the decisions which Ministers had taken on cutting the Armed Forces and the manpower to be available for their supply by the end of 1946 affected the position in terms of the monetary gap during 1946. Our main points were (i) that the position was really a good deal worse than we had shown in our Survey in that the Supply departments started 1946 with a labour force some 450,000 greater than their programme on which our Survey was based; (ii) that the cuts in manpower related to end 1946 and if, as was probable, they were concentrated in the last months of 1946 they would not very greatly affect the overall strain during 1946; and (iii) that as the demobilised men had leave and then took time to produce final consumption goods, but on the other hand had demobilisation clothing, gratuities, pay, etc. the inflationary strain was *pro tanto* increased. We also briefed the Lord President on all this for the Cabinet meeting. The result was good. The manpower cuts were all confirmed and indeed, as far as the Munitions manpower was concerned, there was serious talk of increasing it and of getting it early rather than late. The Cabinet also, on our instigation and that of Douglas Jay, decided that all projects for expenditure on investment should be most carefully screened

[3] pp. 215–16.
[4] See below, pp. 245–6.

and pruned during 1946.[5] Early next week, so it happens, there is to be a meeting of Gilbert's Investment Working Party, at which no doubt this problem of reducing investment projects for 1946 will be a main item of discussion. I am taking Sayers to this Investment Working Party, and hope to make him our Investment expert. I have discussed the papers for next week's meeting with him and Shackle, who is preparing a paper on the subject.[6]

A good deal of time has been spent this fortnight in discussing with Nicholson, Tress, Bridges the draft which Nicholson is preparing of a public statement which the Lord President is to make on the Economic Plan or rather – so as not to promote too definite demands that 'The Plan' should be published – on the economic situation in 1946, a statement which will show that there is something like an Economic Plan going on.[7] I have also prepared for the Chancellor of the Exchequer a passage for his speech on the second reading of the Control of Investment Bill, explaining the capital issues control and the guarantee of new issues which that Bill contains as part of the larger planning machinery. But in the event the Chancellor's speech contained none of my nicely balanced exposition![8]

In the course of conversations with Keynes on other matters he has referred again to our estimates of national income for 1946; he is certainly in a much subdued mood and even goes so far as to admit that we have established a number of our points! His minute in which he generally condemned our estimates for 1946 and our methods of making those estimates was framed in almost exactly the same words which Kahn used of us in criticising us at the first Economic Survey Working Party referred to above that I suspect some collusion among the economists at King's College Cambridge! . . .[9]

There has been another meeting of Gilbert's official committee on Socialisation problems. We have once more been through a draft report, which becomes more and more risible. The draft started with some attempt to lay down some general principles for socialisation schemes. The procedure of the Committee is to go through this draft paragraph by paragraph and to delete every expression of view with which either Fergusson (representing Coal, Gas and Electricity) and Hurcomb (representing Transport) cannot agree. The result is a report which says practically nothing at all.[10]

[5] CP(46)32, 'Economic Survey for 1946, Memorandum by the Lord President', 30 January 1946, CAB129/6; CP(46)40, 'Economic Survey for 1946, Note by the Lord President of the Council', 5 February 1946, CAB129/6 and T230/55; Tress to Lord President, 'Economic Survey for 1946 (CP(46)32 and CP(46)40) and Report by the Manpower Committee on the Man-Power controls during 1946 (CP(46)35)', 6 February 1946, T230/55; CM(46) 13th conclusions, 7 February 1946, CAB128/5.

[6] Gilbert's meeting was on 11 February (Gilbert to Meade, 13 February 1946, T230/85); the papers are on T230/85 and 86. Shackle's paper, 'The Means and Possibilities of Investment Policy', 14 February 1946, EC(S)(46)11, is on T230/20 and 85.

[7] See below, p. 220.

[8] 'Investment Bill, Speech in H. of C. in support of Second Reading (Draft)', T233/26; *House of Commons Debates*, 5 February 1946, vol. 418, cols. 1552–668 and 1677–90.

[9] See above, pp. 196 and 211.

[10] SI(0)(46) 3rd meeting, 7 February 1946, T228/269; SI(0)(46)12, 'Official Committee on the Socialisation of Industries, First Report', 21 February 1946, CAB124/919, T234/1.

We were also to have discussed a paper by the Ministry of Labour on wage-fixing machinery in socialised industries, which says more or less *simpliciter* that the ordinary machinery for independent wage negotiations should be carried over to socialised industries. The line which I was intending to take on this was that one could not really take a line on this until one knew more about the future of Governmental wage policy (if any), on which Nicholson's working party is due to start work shortly. If the Government should decide to take a more positive line in affecting relative wage-rates so as to help man up the undermanned industries and reduce the supply of labour in the overmanned industries, it might be desirable to have a rather different wage-fixing machinery in socialised industries. (Incidentally, on wages policy Peggy Joseph of the Ministry of Fuel and Power has sent us a rather interesting paper in which she suggests a grand annual review to determine how much wage-rates can go up over the whole of industry in such a way as not to cause an undue upward inflation of prices, and then a grand centrally agreed apportionment of this cake among the occupations which need increased wage-rates most to man them up.)[11]

Next week there is to be a meeting of the Socialisation Committee to discuss Price Policy and I have sent in a short draft to Gilbert to be circulated giving my reasons for believing that prices should not always be such as just to cover long-term costs (including the annual service of the industry's compensation stock).[12]

There have been two more Budget Committees this fortnight.[13]

In addition there have been a wide range of other matters to deal with on the domestic front. The Lord President sent to see me about the 40-hour week. There is Trade Union pressure for the introduction of a 40-hour week; but I had no difficulty in explaining to the Lord President how out of the question it is in present circumstances, when the reduction in production which it would involve would immensely increase the already gaping discrepancy between demands on the community's resources and the available resources themselves. Or if, on the other hand, the normal hours of work were reduced to 40 but people still worked 47, costs of production would be raised with effects on exports, on the cost of living or on the subsidies required to prevent a rise in the cost of living. Tress is doing a note for the Lord President on this.[14]

We have had a Staff Meeting to discuss a paper by Sayers on the future of the Iron and Steel industry.[15] This is rather an interesting exercise in the problem of programming investment.

11 SI(0)(46)5, 'Wages and Working Conditions in Socialised Industries: Note by the Minister of Labour and National Service', CAB124/918; Joseph, 'General Wages Policy', 6 February 1946, T230/111.

12 SI(0)(46) 4th meeting, 14 February 1946, and SI(0)(46)8, 'Price Policy and the Financial Structure of Socialised Industries, Memorandum by the Economic Section', T228/269.

13 These two meetings, on 30 January and 6 February 1946, continued the discussion of Dalton's and Meade's ideas on the reform of death duties begun at the previous two Budget Committee meetings mentioned above, p. 206. For the outcome see below, pp. 223 and 259–60.

14 See below, pp. 232–3.

15 A revised version of the paper was circulated on 13 March: EC(S)(46)16 Revise, 'Capital Development and Future Organisation of the Iron and Steel Industry', T230/21 and 107; see below p. 234.

We have been asked to prepare notes (which Tress has done) for the Prime Minister for his speech on the second reading debate on the National Insurance Bill.[16]

We have written many briefs for the Lord President for the Cabinet, Lord President's Committee or its Industrial sub-Committee on various topics, including shipbuilding, location of industry in London, disposal of surplus stores, clearance of factor space, removal of slum factories, etc.[17]

In the external field the main development has been in the programming of imports and in the forecasting of the balance of payments in general. Eady has held a meeting of his Balance of Payments Working Party to discuss a document prepared by R. W. B. Clarke on the Import Programmes for 1946.[18] This is a very considerable advance, as the whole import programme is surveyed in a rational manner from the point of view of foreign exchange requirements. Fleming, Chantler, Miss Watts and I discussed the document before the meeting. We suggested some improvements in the document: for example, petrol imports and expenditure on films were not shown and should be shown before one can properly discuss how much to let up on food supplies as opposed to other 'easements'. (A popular row which there has been this week as a result of the Ministry of Food's decision not to put Dried Eggs on the market for a time underlined this.)[19] We also argued that the imports should be shown in comparison with imports for previous years and with changes in stocks to show the domestic consumption of the imported supplies. But generally speaking this has been a very good development.

At the end of the Working Party Meeting Eady proposed, and it was agreed, that Clarke should have a small working group of the Treasury, the Economic Section and the Board of Trade to do a balance of payments estimate for 1950 in the course of the next six weeks. Clarke actually said that the purpose of doing this was to show that we certainly could not expand our exports sufficiently to put our balance of payments in order without import restriction and that in view of this we should, of course, have to go into the International Trade Conference with a view to accepting no restriction [on control] of imports. At this I exploded. We had, I pointed out, already committed ourselves to support the American trade proposals and we could not back out of them in good faith; and in any case the import restriction rules were carefully framed so that we could restrict imports in 1950 if that were necessary and would not be allowed to do so if that were not necessary. So I could not see that the result of the 1950 Balance of Payments enquiry could make any different to our policy at all. In this Helmore of the Board of Trade supported me. We are clearly in for a difficult time on this subject. Our imports and exports in 1950 are clearly the most uncertain of all the uncertain items in our general

[16] 'Economic Aspects of the National Insurance Scheme', 2 February 1946, T230/105.

[17] These topics came up as papers by the Admiralty and Minister of War Transport on shipbuilding, by the Minister of Town and Country Planning on Greater London planning, by the Home Secretary on clearance of storage space (LP(46)7, 32 and 11, CAB132/2).

[18] On 28 January (T230/10) to discuss 'The 1946 Import Programme: A Note by the Treasury' (T230/11).

[19] See below, p. 216.

economic position. The attempt will be made to make estimates for these quantities with no reference to relative prices and costs and elasticities of demand. It will be the function of the Economic Section to insist on talking about elasticities of demand and supply, relative prices and costs, exchange rates, effects of a more liberal commercial policy elsewhere, etc. as means of balancing a disordered balance of payments. I have asked A. J. Brown to consider the possibility of measuring some of these elasticities.[20]

The great world food crisis has broken this week. Philip Chantler has been working on this for us and has briefed the Lord President on some aspects of it and on the related shipping problems. Unfortunately at the same time that the British housewife has heard of the raising of the extraction ratio for wheat and the cutting of the fat ration (which are the direct outcome of the world food shortage), she has been informed of the cutting off of supplies of Dried Eggs which is a quite unrelated dollar exchange problem, the Ministry of Food having decided months ago to cut off supplies for a time while shell eggs are more plentiful.[21] The Dried Eggs crisis (having led to popular demands that dollar expenditure should be cut down on tobacco or films rather than on dried eggs) has brought the whole problem of our balance of payments to the Cabinet. The report of the Balance of Payments Working Party together with a hair-raising paper by Keynes on our overseas financial commitments has been rushed to the Cabinet. I hope it may lead to really drastic action in reducing our overseas expenditure. Fleming and Chantler have briefed the Lord President on the report of the Balance of Payments Working Party and the Dried Eggs crisis respectively.[22]

In talking with Keynes he told me of the papers which were being prepared and the meetings which were being held on the problem of the

[20] See below, pp. 245–6 and 249–50.

[21] Paul Addison (*Now the War is Over*, London: BBC and Cape, 1985), described the problem as follows:- 'Early in 1946 the food experts in Washington began to predict a world wheat shortage, aggravated by a shortage of rice. Famine threatened Germany, where Britain was now one of the occupying powers, and Asia, where Britain was still directly responsible for the welfare of India, Burma, Ceylon, Malaya and Singapore. To meet its own requirements as well as those of dependent peoples, Britain had to import grain from the United States, a land of abundance free of rationing. In February, Smith [the Minister of Food] shouldered the White Man's Burden and announced that in order to divert supplies to the threatened areas the British government would henceforth reduce its imports of wheat for consumption in Britain. To conserve grain stocks, the extraction rate of flour from wheat would be increased to 85 per cent, darkening the colour of a loaf that was already grey, reducing the volume of animal feeding stuffs, and restricting livestock production. . . . Smith also stirred up a housewives' revolt by threatening to discontinue supplies of dried eggs – the lifebuoy of many a drowning cook.' (Supplies of dried eggs, which were a 'ship-saving' contrivance begun in June 1942, mostly came from the USA under Lend-Leade and were discontinued on 2 February 1946.)

[22] Chancellor of Exchequer, 'Balance of Payments for 1946', CP(46)53, Keynes' 'Political and Military Expenditure Overseas', 8 January 1946, circulated under a covering memorandum from the Chancellor entitled 'The Overseas Deficit', CP(46)58, CAB129/7; Fleming to Lord President, 'Balance of Payments for 1946: Memorandum by the Chancellor of the Exchequer CP(46)53', 9 February 1946, CAB124/1043, Chantler to Lord President, 'Dried Eggs', 9 February 1946, CAB21/298, and CAB124/960; above, pp. 212–13, pp. 2–4; see also below, p. 225.

forthcoming Sterling Area Negotiations. I went to Bridges and asked whether I could be brought in. As a result I have been sent the papers and am to go to the meetings in the Treasury. I have spent some time studying these papers.[23]

We have held a Staff Meeting to discuss a draft by A. J. Brown of a concluding section for his Overseas Economic Survey. This part dealt with the conclusions to be drawn from the Survey for our own economy. I hope now that we shall very soon be able to get a draft round to Helmore and his official committee [on Overseas Economic Information], as we have already spent too much time on this.[24]

Miss Watts, in close consultation with Gorell Barnes in the Treasury, has been briefing the Lord President on the Civil Aviation discussions which have been taking place in Bermuda with the Americans.[25] The contest has been a very exciting one and in some ways reminiscent of the Washington financial discussions. A compromise draft agreement has been reached; but our tough boys (the Ministry of Civil Aviation), who wish to deny the Americans all 'Fifth Freedom' rights of picking up traffic in this country to take on to other destinations and who wish to have rigid quantitative regulations of the amount of traffic which the Americans may carry to this country, have tried to prevent any agreement, while those (including now the Treasury!) who wish to see the financial agreement go through Congress and who realise the fateful consequences to our shipping earnings (which are so many times more important to our balance of payments than our civil aviation earnings) which the application of similar 'anti-Article VII' principles by the Americans to their shipping would have, have tried to press for agreement. The issue is still not decided.

Fleming and I called on Liesching and Shackle at the Board of Trade to discuss the treatment of International Employment Policy. We wished to urge that the Economic and Social Council, which as the international co-ordinating body should have the ultimate responsibility for international employment policy, should be given some real responsibility in preparing the employment policy part of the agenda for the forthcoming international conference on trade and employment, even though (so as not to spoil the chances of success in the tough pressure which will be needed to get the trade proposals accepted) the Council should be given nothing but nominal responsibility on the commercial policy side. Liesching seemed quite amenable to this idea. We also discussed with him the internal organisation required in Whitehall to deal with such problems as international employment policy, and in particular to prepare instructions for UK delegations to the Economic and Social Council and the other Specialised International Agencies in the economic and financial fields. We discussed the possibility of an interdepartmental official Committee

23 'The U.S. Financial Agreement as it Affects Relations with the Sterling Area', SAN(46)1, Keynes, 'Notes on Sterling Area Negotiations', 23 January 1946, SAN(46)2, and SAN(46) 1st meeting, 30 January 1946, T236/159.

24 EC(S)(46)5, Draft of Concluding Section for Overseas Economic Survey, circulated 18 January 1946, T230/20; see also below, pp. 226, 237.

25 Watts, 'The Bermuda Conference', 2 February, Watts to Lord President, 'Anglo-American Civil Aviation Discussions at Bermuda', 2 and 6 February 1946, T230/3.

under Foreign Office chairmanship. Liesching suggested that I might talk to Bridges on this. As I knew that Norman Brook was preparing a paper on these lines for the PM, envisaging such an official steering committee under Foreign Office chairmanship and with a mixed Foreign Office-Cabinet Office secretariat, I went to see him. He has sent a draft of his paper (to which Fleming and I made a few alterations) to Liesching who has told me that he fully agrees with it.[26]

Incidentally Stinebower of the USA delegation to the United Nations has said to Fleming that he very much hopes that we shall press for an Englishman to be the head of the Economic side of the United Nations secretariat, and said why not Richard Law. I think this is a very good idea. I have mentioned it to Norman Brook who is going to pass it on to Bridges. I hope that something comes of it.

I have seen a number of letters by John Wall of the Ministry of Food on the problem of applying the American trade proposals to state trading. Poor Wall seems to find it impossible to realise that the state trading protective margin is in all relevant respects the same as a private trade tariff. Mrs Hollond of the Ministry of Agriculture has written a paper to show this to be the case. Mrs Hollond wishes to bring us in on an attempt to convince Wall that he is making a lot of imaginary difficulties. I have passed all these papers, together with the ones which I have already acquired or written in the process of correspondence with Helmore and P. W. Martin on the problem of applying the balance of payments import restrictions let-out to state trading, on to Fleming. I think that he must become in future our expert on the minutiae of the commercial policy agreement.[27]

## 23 February 1946

We have now held a first meeting of the small group of officials to work on the problem of the Economic Survey for 1950. The meeting went very well. We have started on the consideration of the 'target' national income for 1950, and have farmed out two main projects of work. Saunders of the Ministry of Labour is to consider the future size of the working population, movements in hours of work, movements in wage-rates and the minimum level of unavoidable unemployment. E. A. G. Robinson of the Board of Trade is to consider movements in productivity (i.e. output per man). An attempt is to be made to consider movements in wage-rates and movements in productivity as far as possible by groups of occupations (e.g. textiles, agriculture, engineering, etc.). If this is done (with some assumptions about profit margins) we should be able to construct

[26] The upshot was the official Steering Committee on International Negotiations which began meeting in June 1946. It had the functions 'of securing co-ordination between Departments in respect of relations between various international bodies and resolving, subject to Ministers, such inconsistencies as may arise in the objectives sought by different Departments in their dealings with different international bodies' (CAB134/377).

[27] These papers have not been located. On the issues involved see also below, pp. 238 and 257.

(unsubsidised) price indices for separate sections of the economy. After this stage, we shall be in a position to forecast the level of the main items of national expenditure and compare this with the 'target' national income.[28]

Keynes has held a meeting which I attended with Stafford and Jackson of the Central Statistical Office on this year's Budget White Paper. He is just off to the United States to take part in the conference which is setting up the International Monetary Fund and the International Bank; and he was clearly anxious about the prospects of this year's White Paper now that Stone is not concerned with it.[29] I was a little dreading the meeting; but in the event it went very well. There was some discussion on some relatively minor technical points: we agreed that the $650 million borrowed under the recent Washington financial talks for clearing up the Lend-Lease pipeline etc. must be added to Government Expenditure and to Overseas Disinvestment in 1945; and there was some discussion as to whether the 56 days paid leave which the Forces enjoy on demobilisation should be included in the Pay of the Armed Forces or (like the demobilisation gratuities) treated as Transfer Payments. Stafford and Jackson produced the good idea that there should be a new break-down of the national income into that generated in the private sector (e.g. unsocialised industry) and that generated in the public sector (e.g. armed forces, police, socialised industry). Keynes opposed the inclusion of such a novelty until it had been worked out and examined in Whitehall. In this he may have been wise, but I strongly supported, as of great interest in an economy which was likely to be semi-socialised and semi-private enterprise, that such a break-down should be made. One could do a similar breakdown of expenditure between private (e.g. personal consumption) and Government (e.g. pay of the armed forces); and one would be able then to judge how far we had gone in socialising (a) the management of the economy (on the national income side) and (b) consumption (on the expenditure side). In order to make the split more meaningful I suggested a threefold division on the national income side into: (i) private enterprise, (ii) public corporations and socialised industrial activities, and (iii) governmental non-commercial activities.

Incidentally, Stone is now back from the United States where he has been preparing at Princeton for Loveday a long report on the problems involved in doing national income and expenditure estimates. I had lunch with him at the Reform Club and discussed his Princeton work, the Budget White Paper and the state of his investigation for the inter-war years of the national income and expenditure. I was hoping to get from this latter a 'propensity to consume' function which would help with our 1950 estimate; but unfortunately it is clear that this will not be ready for a year's

[28] The meeting was on 12 February; drafts of Saunders' study are on CAB139/168. On the Board of Trade work see below, pp. 231–2.

[29] See Keynes to Brittain, 'Budget White Paper', Keynes to Stafford, 15 February 1946, and related correspondence on CAB139/30; see also below, p. 240. Keynes embarked from Southampton on the *Queen Mary* on 25 February for the inaugural meetings of the International Monetary Fund and World Bank in Savannah, Georgia, which began on 9 March 1946.

time.[30] On Stone's initiative the National Institute of Economic and Social Research have organised some meetings between economists and Chartered Accountants to consider questions of the use of such concepts as income, profit, investment in stocks, savings, etc. which are common to both professions; and I have been persuaded to serve with Stone and Hicks on a small committee for this purpose.[31] I am myself very keen that this excellent idea should be extended to the examination between economists and cost accountants of such concepts as marginal and average costs, variable and fixed costs, etc. It seems to me that with the socialisation of industries, price control, etc. looming more importantly in the future it is most important to get the cost accountants in the habit of measuring costs in a way which has the maximum economic significance.

Ministers are about to open a great publicity campaign on the economic position of 1946. The Lord President has already seen the FBI [Federation of British Industries]. A White Paper is about to be issued on the cuts in the manpower for the Armed Forces. Conferences are about to be held with the Trade Unions [on 6 March]. The idea is to stimulate output for this year and to explain why things must remain tight this year. As part of this campaign the Prime Minister is to make a speech in Parliament which will incorporate the matter which was contained in the draft prepared by Nicholson for the Lord President.[32] Jay has been commissioned by the PM to do a draft of this speech. I have urged him to put in it some reference to our technique of planning: measurement of a 'target' national income; forecast of the main items of national expenditure; comparison and adjustment of expenditure with 'target' income. It is becoming increasingly embarrassing that no public pronouncement has been made on these lines. We ought to be discussing the ideas with other economists not only in this country but all over the world, and we could make the ideas travel round the globe if we would do so. This week, for example, I have had a visit from a Czech economist (Hardraba) who is attached to the Czech embassy here but represents the Planning organisation in Prague. I was able to tell him very little. What a difference it would have made if I could have explained to a Czech (and Czechoslovakia is the one hopeful bridge between us and the Russians in ideas) the type of liberal-socialist planning which we were undertaking.

[30] Stone was chairman of the sub-committee on national income statistics of the League of Nations Committee of Statistical Experts, which met at Princeton, NJ, 17-20 December 1945. Stone's preparatory memorandum on 'Definition and measurement of the national income and related totals' formed the basis of discussion and the bulk of the sub-committee's report on *Measurement of National Income and the Construction of Social Accounts*. Geneva: United Nations, 1947. The first volume of Stone's inter-war study was published in 1953 (*The Measurement of Consumers' Expenditure and Behaviour in the United Kingdom, 1920–1938*, vol. 1. Cambridge: Cambridge University Press).

[31] The Committee was the result of a meeting of a 'Joint Exploratory Committee on Co-operation in Research between Accountants and Economists' at the Institute of Chartered Accountants on 11 July 1945, which discussed a set of proposals by Stone. Meade was invited to serve on the Joint Research Committee on 18 February 1946 (Meade Papers 3/12). See below, p. 277.

[32] *Statement Relating to Defence*, Cmd. 6743, February 1946; *House of Commons Debates*, Vol. 419, 27 February 1946, cols. 1951–65; see above, p. 213.

We have done a good deal of work this fortnight on the control of Investment from the point of view of the Economic Plan. Gilbert's Investment Working Party is coming into action again: – the immediate purpose being to see how Investment can be restrained in the months immediately ahead as a means of closing the gap, and the longer-term purpose being to see (through the means of a sub-group of the Investment Working Party which Proctor is going to run) how the administrative and similar difficulties (acquisition of land, preparation of plans, etc.) can be overcome which stand in the way of a rapid turning on or off of the public investment tap. Meanwhile the Economic Section are drafting a paper (by G. L. S. Shackle) on the problems of investment. This paper we are dividing into two parts:- the first on the 'physical' and the second on the 'financial' aspects of investment. The first part is now in draft and deals with the programming of public and private investment; an analysis of the amount of investment which is controlled by various types of authority (e.g. central government, local authority, socialised industries, private enterprise); an analysis of the various negative controls (e.g. financial restriction through capital issues control or local authority loan sanctions, or 'real' restriction through building licences or machinery licensing); and a discussion of the various 'real' obstacles which may stand in the way of turning on the investment tap promptly (e.g. land acquisition etc.). During this fortnight Gilbert has held a small preliminary meeting (which Sayers and I attended) to discuss the agenda for the first formal full meeting of the Investment Working Party (which I attended); and we have had two staff meetings to discuss Shackle's paper on investment.[33]

The main issue which we have had to discuss in all this is the way in which investment expenditure should be controlled in the months immediately ahead. I came out at the Investment Working Party as the protagonist of the idea that, as in the case of the Import Programme, each department should be given a value 'ration' or 'allocation' limiting globally the total investment which they, or the public or private agencies which they sponsored, should be allowed to undertake in a given period. This would greatly decentralise the responsibility for fixing investment priorities. Each department would have to determine the priorities within its own sphere. The central body would only have to allocate the global rations; and as I pointed out to Gilbert in a letter which I sent him after the meeting, six departments would cover ⅞ of total investment.[34] The problem of controlling this ration would, however, be a serious one. As far as building was concerned, the present building licensing system would be used to enforce a departmental allocation. Licences could be issued, whether to private enterprise or to public bodies, only in so far as the sponsoring department approved the scheme and the scheme fell within the department's allocation. But for machinery the problem is a much more difficult one, since the present machinery licensing gives a permit to the

[33] Shackle, 'The Means and Possibilities of Investment Policy, Part I', 14 February 1946, EC(S)(46)11, T230/20 and 85; 'Note of an Informal Meeting [on 11 February] to discuss IWP/46/1–3', 14 February 1946, T161/1296/S53555/1. The Investment Working Party met on 19 February (Meade to Gilbert, 20 February 1946, T230/85).

[34] Meade to Gilbert, 20 February 1946, T230/85.

machinery producer to produce a certain amount of machinery (on condition that it is of a certain kind and that a certain proportion goes to export). Thus there is no direct control over the purchase of machinery, and it is a little difficult to see how a departmental ration could be made to work.

After the meeting on the Investment Working Party I had a discussion on the subject with Jay and Vinter of the Treasury.[35] Jay took the opposite view of the type of control which was necessary, namely that there should be some central screening of investment projects – project by project – and not a general departmental global ration. He is, as always, very much moved by the regional problems of encouraging projects where labour is in surplus supply and restraining only in areas of labour scarcity; and he argues, with some force, that a global departmental ration will not meet this point, since it does nothing to prevent a departmental scramble (well within the global allocations) for resources within an area of acute labour shortage with the result that within that area projects of low priority may oust projects of high priority. The sort of compromise which seems to be emerging is a global departmental allocation which the departments will do their best to stick to with the present system of controls *plus* some special machinery for screening all large projects of say £1 m. or £½ m. and upwards in areas of special stringency.

Dow has finished a draft of his paper on PAYE and the possibility of varying income tax as a means of maintaining consumers' expenditure. He is now going on to examine national insurance contributions, the repayment of post-war tax credits and variations in indirect taxation (e.g. purchase tax) from the same point of view.[36] These investigations together with the second part of Shackle's paper on investment (in which he will discuss variations in the rate of interest or variations in taxes and subsidies as a means of stimulating or discouraging investment) will form our ammunition in the great campaign which we must open sooner or later to persuade Whitehall that monetary policy (rate of interest), fiscal policy (rates of taxation and subsidy) and wages policy (rates of rewards to factors) must be the liberal-socialist instruments for economic planning.

As far as wages policy is concerned, this fortnight has been quite a busy one. There has been a first meeting of Max Nicholson's working party on Wages Policy, at which Emmerson of the Ministry of Labour spoke to a paper by the Ministry of Labour in which it was argued that nothing should be done to disturb the present system of collective bargaining.[37] We (i.e. Sayers and myself) did not deliver a head-on attack on this system; but we argued that it must be modified to take account of the new conditions which would arise in conditions of Full Employment in which (a) relative wage-rates must be varied to attract men into undermanned, and out of

[35] Recorded in Meade to Sayers, 21 February 1946, T230/85.

[36] 'Variations of income tax as a short-term instrument for national income stabilisation', 15 February 1946, EC(S)(46)12, T230/20, and 'Variations of national insurance contributions as a short-term instrument of national income stabilisation', 2 May 1946, EC(5)(46)21, T230/21. See below, p. 248.

[37] WP(46) 1st meeting, 14 February 1946, and WP(46)2, 'Wages Policy, Memorandum by Minister of Labour and National Service', 9 February 1946, CAB132/88.

overmanned, occupations and (b) the total increase in wages must be limited, or nearly limited, to the increase which would be possible without any increase in prices and costs, i.e. to the increase made possible by (i) increased productivity, (ii) an improvement in the terms of international trade, and (iii) any squeezability of profits. We suggested that three types of Governmental statement might be made: (a) a general White Paper and/or a series of Ministerial speeches explaining these issues; (b) a periodic statement to the Trade Unions as a whole (the TUC) explaining the limits set by (i), (ii) and (iii) above and stating what is the total wage increase which the workers as a whole have to divide among themselves in, say, the coming year without any increase in prices and costs; and (c) particular pronouncements about particular wage negotiations pointing out the extent to which the occupation in question was over- or under-manned. Sayers has prepared an Economic Section paper on this subject which is to be taken by the Wages Policy working party next week. In this paper we have also pointed out that all this involves a decision on Price Stabilisation policy. We have argued that, while Price Stabilisation obviously restrains wage increases which are tied to the Cost of Living and has a similar indirect effect in other cases, it may become a really dangerous feature if workers (who do not fully appreciate the fact that increased cost-of-living subsidies mean increased taxation) feel that they can press for higher wage-rates without any effects on the cost of living.[38] (Incidentally, Keynes tells me that in a conversation with the Chancellor on this year's Budget, the Chancellor was moved somewhat off his previous ground in which he gave such definite assurance that the cost of living would not be allowed to rise for a year. If this is so, it will help us with this Wages Policy.)

There has been another Budget Committee. I have also been to see the Chancellor this week on this question, and Keynes has reported to me the result of a three-hour interview which he and Bridges had with the Chancellor. The result seems to be not too bad.[39]

Gilbert has had another meeting of his Socialisation Committee, at which a paper by the Ministry of Labour was presented by Emmerson and agreed by the Committee on the problem of wages policy in socialised industries. I felt rather unhappy about it. The thesis was that there should be ordinary collective bargaining between the Trade Unions and the Boards of the socialised industries. The implication was that, since these Boards would be independent of the state, the state had no wages policy for socialised industry. Such problems, for example, as whether there should be regional differences in wage-rates are to be the concern of the Trade Unions and the Boards and not of the state. For the first time I fully realised the implications of socialisation in the form of public boards instead of by departments. We eliminate the 'maximisation of profits' as the motive force and we substitute – what? Not the equating of marginal

[38] 'Wages Policy: Memorandum by the Economic Section', 25 February 1946, W(46)3, CAB132/88, and EC(S)(46)14, T230/20.

[39] Meade discussed the reform of death duties with Dalton (Trend to Dalton, 16 February 1946, T171/388). Keynes' interview took place on 20 February; Dalton's private secretary's notes of this meeting record the decisions taken then in the light of the Budget Committee meeting (Trend to Chancellor, 'Budget', 20 February 1946, T171/386).

cost and price, certainly. Merely the arbitrary decision of a public Board which is responsible to no one and has no financial interest in the outcome, to do just what it considers right within a certain framework (e.g. covering its total costs over a period of years). I feel more and more the need for making a reality of the general powers which the Minister of Fuel and Power retains; for example, in the Coal Bill of giving general directives about policy to the Board. We then had a hurried discussion on the note which I had put in on the thesis that the price policy of a socialised industry should not be merely to cover its total costs (in the sense of the annual service of its compensation stock) year in year out. The Government should hold, as it were, the equity in return for fixed stock issued to the previous owners. Certain pricing principles should then be laid down for the managers of socialised industries and the Treasury should take resulting profit or loss. All this appeared rather lunatic to most of the members of the Committee. Gilbert is now in the process of drafting a report to Ministers on this subject. It will be amusing to see what he makes of it.[40]

A ministerial committee has been set up under the Lord Privy Seal to consider the employment of foreign labour in this country.[41] Norman Brook is keen that something should come of it. So is Douglas Jay. Tress and Miss Watts are going to help on work for this committee (the former on the present acute shortage of manpower, the latter on the longer-term demographic position which certainly suggests that we need immigration rather than emigration). Here at last is a real opportunity to do something to shift the Home Office, whose anti-foreign bias is unbelievable. I had a long talk on this with Jay and Drew (who is to be secretary of the Committee). There are, to begin with, the Poles in the Polish Army, Italian prisoners of war on farms, and other special classes of foreign labour to consider.

An immense amount of activity is taking place in Whitehall on the world food crisis, with Ministerial meetings with the PM in the chair every week and with official meetings under Norman Brook. Somehow, in spite of efforts on my part, it did not seem that Philip Chantler who covers this work for the Section was being used at all. The Lord President was being briefed by Nicholson without us; and Brook was holding his meetings without Chantler being present. I think I have at last fixed things up. The position is appalling. We know that millions of people in India will starve in this year in which a supreme effort is to be made to reach a friendly and final political settlement, unless 2 million tons of grain are imported. This is only 2 per cent of the grain fed to animals in the USA. How much is it of our consumption of grain? How much would be released (a) if we went down to present European standards, (b) if European livestock were slaughtered, (c) if Canada and Australia raised their extraction ratios? I have urged

[40] SI(0)(46) 4th meeting, 14 February 1946; SI(0)(46)5, 'Wages and Working Conditions in Socialised Industries, Memorandum by the Minister of Labour and National Service' and SI(0)(46)8, 'Price Policy and the Financial Structure of Socialised Industries, Memorandum by the Economic Section', T228/269; SI(M)(46)18, 'Official Committee on the Socialisation of Industries, Second Report', 10 May 1946, T234/1; see below, p. 248.

[41] For the relevant papers see CAB124/301. The Committee was set up on 14 February 1946.

Chantler to urge Nicholson and, with him, the Lord President to submit a short paper saying here is this appalling catastrophe; it is economically perfectly soluble on the following alternative lines (giving the main orders of magnitude of the possible alternative grain economies); it is now up to the politicians to decide.[42]

When I came into the office on Monday morning at the beginning of this fortnight, I found a hectic message from the Lord President's secretary for a short brief on the paper by Keynes which the Chancellor had just submitted together with the import programmes for 1946 for discussion by the Cabinet that morning.[43] The paper drew a very grim (and justifiably so) picture of our overseas financial position if we went ahead at the present rate of expenditure on overseas military forces, loans to allies, relief aid, support of a bankrupt Germany, etc. The Lord President who, like most Labour Ministers, cannot forget 1931 was in a great concern whether we were not in for another external financial crash, and also (shades of the May report!) wished to know whether there should not be a similar general survey of our internal expenditure to see whether we were not overdoing things there as well. I scribbled a short MS brief for him saying (a) that I thought that Keynes was certainly right in his main contention that we must greatly restrict our overseas commitments, but (b) that the Economic Survey for 1946 (which the Cabinet had just considered and on the basis of which great cuts were to be made in the Armed Forces and Munitions) in fact constituted just such a review of our internal resources and the claims on them which did ensure that we cut our domestic coat according to our domestic cloth. What was wanted was some similar external machinery to ensure that we cut our external coat according to our external cloth. A. J. Brown, in consultation with a group of other members of the Section organised by Fleming, is writing a general brief for the Lord President on Keynes' paper.[44] There is also coming up for Cabinet consideration in the near future a paper on the future level of German industry on which A. J. Brown is also preparing a brief for the Lord President. Shall we, for the purpose of maintaining quadripartite unity in control of Germany, agree to such a reduction in the level of German industry as may cripple the Ruhr (i.e. just that part of Germany for which we are responsible) so that we shall have to finance the import of food and other necessities into our zone in Germany without getting any payment for them in the form of German manufactured exports?[45]

42 For the Ministerial Committee see CAB134/729, and for the official meetings see CAB124/961. Up to 19 February the Economic Section was not on the circulation list of papers going to officials. The Lord President sent Chantler's paper, 'World Food Supplies: Possible Measures to Economise Wheat in the U.K.', 1 March, to the Prime Minister, and forwarded it to the Ministers of Food and Agriculture for comment (Graham Harrison to Pimlott, 2 March 1946, CAB129/962). The Lord President did not, however, submit a paper to the Ministerial Committee. See also below, p. 244.

43 See page 216, note 22.

44 Meade to Lord President, 'The Overseas Deficit CP(46)58', 11 February 1946, CAB124/1043. The May Report was the Report of the Committee on National Expenditure which appeared in July 1931 (Cmd. 3920) recommending substantial cuts in government expenditure, especially on unemployment insurance.

45 Memoranda on the level of German industry by the Chancellor of the Duchy of Lancaster and the Foreign Secretary were to be discussed at Cabinet on 18 March (CP(46)114 and 115, 12 and 17 March 1946, CAB129/8; CM(46) 25th Conclusions, CAB128/5): see below, p. 237.

R. W. B. Clarke is now starting on his survey of the balance of payments of this country for 1950. I have suggested that Tress and Miss Watts should represent us, the former to keep in line with the general survey for 1950 and the latter to deal with balance of payments figures. Our line must be to co-operate; but we must not countenance the doctrine that exports (or imports) can be at all accurately forecast for 1950 when we don't know the scope or the effects of any clearance of tariff and similar obstacles to our exports, of any reduction in German exports on our competing products, or of any changes in relative prices, costs and exchange rates. It will be one of our functions to insist that the level of our exports can be determined by such factors as these, and that we need not submit to the fatalistic view that a certain level of our exports is pre-ordained perhaps on a scale insufficient to finance our desired imports.[46]

A. J. Brown has now finished a draft of his Overseas Survey. It was good, but immensely long. He is now rewriting it in order to cut it substantially in length.[47]

There has been a meeting in the Treasury with Bridges in the chair of the Treasury (Keynes, Waley and Rowe-Dutton) and the Bank of England (Siepmann, Thompson-McCausland and Kershaw) to discuss the negotiations with the Sterling Area countries. The discussion was on a draft by the Bank.[48] Keynes was very good in arguing that countries such as India, Egypt, Palestine and possibly some of the colonies were in the position of having enormously inflated price levels in relation to their exchange rates and/or enormously inflated note circulations in relation to their price levels; they would, therefore, be a sink for imports and would be able to export little or nothing; so long as they thought that they could finance other imports with their swollen sterling balances, they would have little incentive to restrict imports effectively by import control (and in any case import control in countries of this kind when there would be such gigantic profits to be made on imports would be relatively ineffective) or to devalue their currencies. I joined Keynes strongly in support of the view that devaluation was the only answer when there was such price disequilibrium, and devaluation would, incidentally, produce profits for these countries in respect of their sterling balances which would provide the easiest form for the cancellation of a part of the sterling balances which is mentioned in the Washington financial settlement. Keynes was using this argument to argue that something more drastic in the way of blocking of sterling balances was desirable than the ingenious proposals of the Bank that there should be a 'statistical blocking' in the sense that part of the agreement with each sterling area country should be that it should not run down its balances by more than a certain amount in each period, and a statistical review would be made to see that the agreement had been kept. If it had not, the country in question might be called on to replenish its balances

46 See Clarke to Meade, 19 February, Meade to Tress, 21 February, and Meade to Clarke, 21 February 1946, T230/276, and below, p. 245.

47 'Draft of Overseas Economic Survey', 13 February 1946, EC(S)(46)10, T230/20; the revised draft (EC(S)(46)15, 4 March 1946, T230/21) was half the length.

48 SAN(46) 2nd Meeting, 12 February 1946, SAN(46)4, 'The U.S. Financial Agreement as it Affects Relations with the Sterling Area', 8 February 1946, T236/1659.

(e.g. by using its resources with the International Monetary Fund) or in the last recourse its balances might be actually blocked. I felt very sympathetic to the Bank's suggestions on this head, but Keynes wanted to bring these countries more brutally up against the need for them either to devalue or to restrict imports by simply blocking a large part of their balances which constituted their foreign liquid reserves. There was also some discussion of the measurement of the balances in respect of which the various countries should be asked to make a sacrifice. The Bank wished to restrict it to the growth in the officially held balances (i.e. by Treasuries or Central Banks or similar institutions). I supported Keynes' view that we should bring into account the total improvement in each country's foreign exchange position since the beginning of the war – i.e. not only the increase in official balances but also the increase in gold holdings or repatriation of securities etc. and the increase in the privately owned balances. The sacrifice asked of each member of the Sterling Area should be related to this.

Liesching has held a general interdepartmental committee meeting to consider preparations for the coming international conference on trade and employment; and R. J. Shackle has started a series of sub-committee meetings to discuss the non-tariff provisions in the commercial policy discussions. He has held one already on state trading and the definition of the protective margins which would be permitted under state trading. Marcus Fleming has represented us at both these meetings.[49]

The Lord President called for Miss Watts, accompanied by myself, to go to see him to explain to him the technical terms (such as 'fifth freedom', cabotage, etc.) which she has been using in her briefs to him on the international aspects of Civil Aviation. She gave a very lucid explanation and has now sent to the Lord President a little list of such terms and their meaning.[50]

I went to lunch in the House of Commons with Noel-Baker and found Hall-Patch and Keynes there as the other guests. The purpose of the lunch was to indoctrinate Keynes with the correct views on the problems of co-ordination of the work of the International Monetary Fund and the International Bank with that of the Economic and Social Council, before he left for the United States [on 25 February] for the conference to set up the Fund and the Bank. To our horror we discovered that the Treasury had not even briefed Keynes on the set-up (which is now more or less crystallised) under the Economic and Social Council. He did not know whether the Council itself would have ministerial or expert representatives; he had not heard of the Economic and Employment Commission of the Council, nor of its three sub-committees on Employment, Balances of Payments and Economic Development. Yet he was not ill-disposed towards such an opportunity of arranging for common action by the main 'specialised agencies' in the economic field. The main real issue (and we spent some time discussing it without arriving at any very clear conclusion)

[49] TN(46) 1st Meeting, 19 February 1946, CAB134/711; TN(N)(46) 1st Meeting, 22 February 1946, CAB134/715.

[50] Watts to Lord President, 'Civil Aviation', 22 February 1946, T230/3.

is the question of exchange devaluation. Keynes agreed that in general employment policy (whether the Bank and the Fund should adopt an expansive or contractionist policy at any given time) there was nothing to be said against full and even public common discussion on, say, the Economic and Employment Commission. But, he argued – and with justification – exchange devaluations must take place in an atmosphere of extreme secrecy because of the speculative forces which would otherwise be released. But what, I asked, about those balance of payments questions in which commercial policy import restrictions *versus* exchange rate adjustments might be the main issue? Could these never be discussed in common? I don't believe that we found an answer.

I had lunch with Rasminsky and Hume Wrong of the Canadian delegation to the UNO, together with Lionel Robbins. We had a pleasant gossip about persons. Margaret and I went out to dinner with Mr and Mrs Jussiant, of the Belgian Embassy, and met there a Baron Kervyn (also a Belgian economist now attached to the Embassy who had been a resistance leader and condemned to death by the Germans when he was in Dachau), a Mr and Mrs Boyle from the Ministry of War Transport, and a Belgian girl, daughter of the permanent secretary of the Belgian Foreign Office. These people exude in an almost embarrassing way a love of everything English (or should I say British?). Here, for example, is the easiest seed-bed in the world for our ideas on liberal-socialism. They don't want Russian Communism nor American Capitalism, and they start with a profound love of all that is English.

# 17

## March 1946

*17 March 1946*

After ten days holiday with Margaret at Brighton I have returned for a fortnight's work with the Economic Section. There has been much activity with the Economic Plan, in particular with the problem of investment. We have in fact succeeded in selling the idea to the Treasury that there should be a departmental value allocation for investment expenditure so long as the need is to restrict investment, i.e. that there should be some decision as to what, in view of the available resources and the other demands on resources, is the total value of investment which can be permitted for the forthcoming period and that departments should put in global value requirements covering all investment sponsored by each department and that those departmental requirements should then be centrally pruned until they are reduced to the total permissible sum. The main question has been how these departmental allocations should be carried out with the existing mechanism of controls. The relevant controls are (i) those over building and (ii) those over machinery. But as for (i) the actual allocation of resources to departments and its policing are carried out in terms of allocations of building labour and the differences in total value produced per head of building labour vary so greatly according to the different uses of building labour (e.g. for new housing where much equipment goes into the house the gross value for building labour employed is much higher than for minor repairs) that it is impossible to translate a building labour allocation into a building investment value within the degree of fineness required to work departmental value investment allocations even for building alone with any degree of accuracy. As for (ii) at present the machinery control has been so relaxed that all that happens now is that the producers (*not* the users) of machinery are given general freedom to produce machinery provided a certain proportion goes to export. This means that there is no control over machinery purchases by users except in so far as it is necessary to obtain a licence to install the machinery. There have been meetings of Gilbert's Investment Working Party to discuss these issues and I have held a number of meetings in the Section with Sayers, Tress, Shackle and Stafford to discuss the issues. The outcome has been a report by the Investment Working Party to Bridges' Steering Committee which has taken the following line:- (a) the present stringency is not likely to last very long so that we should not consider a total overhaul of the control machinery but should do our best over the next year or so to implement a departmental investment ration by means of the existing control over building and (b) as for the degree of cut required in investment as a whole for 1946/47 Ministers should await the revised Survey for 1946/47 (which the Economic Survey Working Party – alias the Economic Section and the Central Statistical Office – is under an obligation to produce by the end of the month) in order to see just what percentage cut on existing departmental investment programmes is required.[1] On this the Section have expressed hesitations. As to (a) we should not be too sure that excess investment pressure will not last for a very considerable time. If the Government in fact carries out a very big housing programme and sees that by hook or by crook there are very big programmes of capital re-equipment in, say, iron and steel, railways, gas, electricity, coal, cotton, etc., the pressure may last a long time. If we do not deal with this by a rise in the rate of interest, we may need negative restrictive controls for a number of years, and in this case there would be a case for a revision of the existing method of control which really is a very inadequate makeshift. As to (b) it would be giving Ministers a totally false impression if they thought that the instrument of control at present available for use could be employed with a degree of fineness to which the revision of the Survey would have anything to contribute, i.e. the idea that it is worth waiting to see whether investment demand should be cut by, say, 7½ per cent instead of by 10 per cent is ridiculous when you only have a blind instrument of control the effect of which you cannot estimate within, say, 20 per cent.

All this leaves me with a sense of vague disquiet and uncertainty. The present control is quite inadequate for this purpose; but do we really want to impose a new and more rigid control over the total amount which anyone and everyone may spend on investment with all the arbitrariness of any central licensing system which has got to judge between claimant A and claimant B? How do we wish to control investment in the long run? Could some permanent system be devised for fixing the total value of investment for each future period and then auctioning the licences to invest up to this amount (if necessary at a negative price, i.e. at a subsidy to keep investment up to the required figure)? This would combine the use of the price system to determine who should invest with a complete central control over the total amount to invest. Campbell Secord has suggested to me a variant of this: the licences to invest would be put on sale on tap for each future allocation period, and the tap prices would be adjusted from time to time (if necessary to a negative level) to ensure that just the right amount was undertaken in each period. Would these schemes be workable? If so, one might now argue strongly for moving towards them by instituting an overall control of investment expenditure through the issue of licences to purchase given values of building and machinery.

[1] ED(46)3, First Report of the Investment Working Party, INVWP(46)4 Revise, 13 March 1946, CAB134/188. Drafts of the report, discussed at Working Party meetings on 4 and 8 March, are on T161/1296/S53555/1 and T230/8. On the Economic Section's discussion see notes on T230/85.

Meanwhile I have been making some revisions to Shackle's paper which we are preparing for the Investment Working Party on Investment Problems; but in this paper we are not going into any length on this central issue.[2]

The meeting of Bridges' Steering Committee which discussed the report of the Investment Working Party also discussed a paper on the statistics required for Employment Policy (suggesting the ways in which the necessary legal powers to collect these statistics should be obtained) and a paper on the question of the publicity to be given to the Economic Plan. On this latter there was a very lively and interesting discussion ending in what I am sure is the correct decision, namely that we should publish soon for 1946/47 both manpower and national income-national expenditure tables, showing the total resources and the uses to be made of them. I argued strongly that if this were done the tables must be in a balanced form: i.e. they should only be published when Ministers have turned the Survey (which shows a gap between claims on resources and total resources) into a Plan (in which claims have been adjusted to add up to total resources). Otherwise one would be advertising the fact that a boom or a slump was expected. Oliver Franks made a very moving appeal for publication. He stated that in the sort of democratic community in which we were operating we should have to publish in the end, and the desired results would be obtained only by frankly disclosing objectives and inviting co-operation to meet them. There was at first a general tendency to suggest that the manpower tables should be published but not the national income-national expenditure tables, on the grounds that the latter involved making assumptions about productivity, hours of work, taxation, prices and wages which the former did not. I argued that apart from prices and wages (and the national income and expenditure could be done purely in 'accounting' wage-rates, e.g. at 1945 wage-rates, so as to avoid forecasting the actual movements of wage-rates) the demand for manpower depended as much on productivity etc. as did the national expenditure figures. I also pointed out how we had a stream of foreign visitors (e.g. the Czech Hardraba from their planning office) [see above, p. 220] wanting to know how we did things and that it was most desirable to be able to tell them how we did it in terms of the national income and expenditure. In the end it was decided to set up a small working party to prepare a report to show Ministers what the publication of all the summary tables would involve.[3]

We have had another meeting of the small group to discuss the Survey for 1950. At this meeting Saunders reported on what he had done in the Ministry of Labour in the way of preparing forecasts on Working Population, hours of work, unemployment, etc. The sting was a bit taken out of the urgency of the past pleas by the Board of Trade (E. A. G. Robinson in particular) by the fact that at this meeting they had to confess

[2] See page 221, note 33 and papers on T230/85.

[3] ED(46) 1st meeting, 15 March 1946, T228/20 and CAB134/187; ED(46)2, Report of Working Party on Statistics for Employment Policy, and ED(46)4, 'Publicity for Planning Estimates, Note by the Secretaries', 13 March 1946, CAB134/188.

that they had so far made no progress at all on their part of the subject (forecast of productivity, industrial investment, etc.).[4]

During our holiday in Brighton there had been the great manpower debate in the House of Commons in which the Prime Minister, Lord President and other Ministers had made some veiled references to the Economic Plan.[5] I was gratified, I must admit, by the very enthusiastic praise which the Lord President gave to the Economic Section in his speech; but I am not sure that it does the Section much good. It may make the ordinary department a bit suspicious and even jealous of our position.

Also, during my holiday the Working Party on Wages under Nicholson had met. I understand from Sayers that the Ministry of Labour remained quite unmoved. They want to preserve the status quo more or less exactly on the grounds (which are no doubt very strong) that the existing machinery of wage negotiation is very successful in avoiding labour disputes, and that one might lose more by strikes than by getting a more theoretically satisfactory set of relative wage-rates by other means. Meanwhile, the Cabinet have demanded and the Lord President has agreed that the Wages Policy Working Party shall report in the next fortnight. So now Sayers has done a short redraft of our paper on wages making every concession possible to the Ministry of Labour point of view but insisting that in conditions of full employment some additional restraint on wage increases in industries which are not really undermanned must be necessary. We are to meet next week.[6] Nicholson has an idea, which the Ministry of Labour is I believe ready to accept, that there should be some central Industrial Commission of workers and employers which would give a means of the Government giving to both sides of industry the necessary factual information from which it could be seen (a) how much total wages increases are possible in the near future and (b) how far different industries require changes in relative wage-rates to prevent over- or under-manning. A most important point in all this is, however, the future of the stabilisation of the cost of living. I feel strongly that it should now be stated that rather than holding the cost of living exactly where it is, the total cost of the subsidies should have an upper limit set to them. Workers would then know that if as a whole they pressed for wage increases beyond the margin of increased productivity, improvement in international terms of trade or squeezability of profits, the average real wage would not increase. I have talked to Bridges about this who agrees that I might talk to the Chancellor about it before his Budget speech.[7]

During my holiday there was some trouble, I fear, with the Ministry of Labour over a paper written by Tress for the Lord President on the 40-hour week. In this (which the LP had asked for in order to clear his mind

[4] See above, p. 218.

[5] *House of Commons Debates*, Vol. 419, 27 February 1946, cols. 1951–65 (Attlee), 28 February 1946, cols. 2113–35 (Morrison), 2207–16 (Cripps). For Morrison's praise of the Section see cols. 2129–30.

[6] W(46) 2nd meeting, 28 February 1946, CAB132/88; CM(46) 24th Conclusions, 14 March 1946, CAB128/5; W(46)3, 'Wages Policy, Memorandum by the Economic Section', CAB132/88; below, p. 243.

[7] On the pre-Budget discussions on the stabilisation of the cost of living see T171/386 (Section 3).

before talking to his political associates on the subject) Tress had shown how the 40-hour week in present conditions of scarcity would be an intolerable reduction in our resources and our output. The Lord President circulated this paper to Dalton, Cripps, Shinwell and Isaacs suggesting that it should go to the Labour Party Executive. All agreed (Shinwell in particular emphasising that in the present conditions anything which reduced output in the coal mines would be intolerable) except Isaacs who wrote a most condemnatory letter saying that our paper completely overlooked the fact that decreased hours of work might increase the productivity of labour (a matter which we had not sufficiently stressed, but which the M. of Labour grossly overstated) and that we had left out of account the human factor. Ince, Permanent Secretary of the Ministry of Labour, was the person who was really upset by the Economic Section preparing a paper which was circulated to Ministers on a M. of Labour subject without having first consulted the M. of Labour. (The fact that the Lord President had without our knowledge circulated the paper was certainly unfortunate.) Ince had rung up Bridges to complain of our behaviour. All this is very regrettable and shows how circumspectly the Section must move.[8]

A lot has been happening on the Socialisation front. There have been two meetings of Gilbert's committee on Socialisation (which by the way Barlow of the Treasury seems to have taken over). The two main points at issue have been (i) the problem of compensating the employees of private industry for disturbance caused by socialisation (which has been a battle between Fergusson with his eye on the coal miners who wishes to restrict all rights of compensation to the mere duty of the Coal Board to take over existing legal contracts and Hurcomb who has his eye on all the previous precedents in public utilities and wishes to keep the goodwill of the higher executive and technical officers in gas, electricity, railways, etc.) and (ii) the question of the regional organisation of the electricity industry. The Ministry of Fuel and Power had suggested to the Lord President's Committee on Socialisation that the organisation of the electricity (distribution, *not* generation) industry should be on a regional basis. The LP had got it referred back to the official committee because he wants the postalisation of electricity charges throughout the country. The Ministry of Fuel and Power are against this. I supported them strongly on the grounds that to charge the same price though the cost might be very different would lead to great diseconomies. Hurcomb supported this view. So Ministers are to get the case against postalisation given to them.[9]

The Lord President's Ministerial Committee on Socialisation has had before it the Ministry of War Transport's paper on the socialisation of transport and papers by the Minister of Supply recommending the socialisation of Iron and Steel. On the former Chantler briefed the Lord President emphasising that the economic method of co-ordinating transport was to ensure that each form of transport was offered freely to

[8] Unfortunately, this paper has not been found. Papers by Tress on the 40-hour week, of 18 February and 1 March, are referred to in Sayers to Lord President, 'Prosperity Campaign (CP(46)122)', 3 April 1946, T230/111 and CAB124/904.

[9] SI(0)(46) 5th and 6th meetings, 4 and 8 March 1946, T228/269.

the consumer of transport at a price equal to its cost of production and to allow consumers freedom to choose which form of transport they would use having due regard to convenience, speed, certainty, and cost. The brief accordingly attacked the ideas in the paper of co-ordinating transport in the sense of having a common price per ton-mile for each form of transport and of restricting very severely the use of road transport outside the state monopoly. The Lord President sent for Chantler and exclaimed, after Chantler had explained how we thought that a socialised industry should be run, 'But that is not socialisation, it is competition!' I must confess that we have not yet made much progress in our ideas on 'socialist competition' and on how to set the prices of socialised industries.[10]

The Iron and Steel issue has come up now that the Iron and Steel Industry have put in their report on the programme of development which they wish to carry out in the industry and the officials of the Ministry of Supply have reported (favourably) on it. The Minister of Supply has concluded that the industry should be socialised, and the Lord President's Ministerial Committee has agreed with this verdict. Sayers wrote a long paper for the Lord President on this subject.[11] We agreed that on the grounds of the inevitability of monopoly there was much to be said on economic grounds for the socialisation of iron and steel, though administratively it would be a terribly complex job. On the investment programme we advised (i) that its timing should be reconsidered because in the general interests of employment policy less expenditure was required in the early years and more in the later; (ii) that its composition should be reconsidered because, in view of the large rise in coal costs, it was the finishing end rather than the early end (pig iron) in which we were likely to be in least disadvantage with the foreigner; and (iii) that developments (e.g. in foreign trade) were very uncertain, so that the total plan should not be rigidly pre-determined. All this led us to conclude that certain outstanding projects which would be needed practically whatever happened should be selected, and that these should be started while the rest was kept very much in a flexible reserve until conditions became rather more certain.

Ministers have also decided that the Government import monopoly for raw cotton should be continued, in spite of the fact that John Henry Woods' official committee on the subject (of which Marcus Fleming was a member) reported that the balance of advantage was on the other side. Marcus

[10] SI(M)(46) 3rd, 4th and 5th meetings, 8, 14 and 15 March 1946, SI(M)(46)4. 'Nationalisation of Transport, Memorandum by the Minister of War Transport', 23 February 1946, CAB134/687; LP(46)52, 'Future of the Iron and Steel Industry, Memorandum by the Minister of Supply and Aircraft Production', 4 March 1946, T228/74; SI(M)(46)8, 'Future of the Iron and Steel Industry, Memorandum by the Minister of Supply and Aircraft Production', 13 March 1946, CAB134/687; Chantler to Lord President, 6 March 1946, T230/107. On these meetings and memoranda see also Chester, *The Nationalisation of British Industry 1945–51*, pp. 123–4 and 152–4. See also below, p. 241.

[11] British Iron and Steel Federation, Report to the Ministry of Supply on the Iron and Steel Industry, December 1945, and 'Memorandum by the Ministry of Supply, Iron and Steel', both attached to Sayers, 'Capital Development and Future Organisation of the Iron and Steel Industry', 13 March 1946, EC(5)(46)16 Revise, T230/21, 87 and 107. See also Chester, *The Nationalisation of British Industry 1945–51*, pp. 150–1.

Fleming briefed the Lord President on the report of the official committee. I added a brief stating that if the Government wished to run a mixed economy successfully they should have some criterion to distinguish between industries which should and those which should not be socialised; that natural monopolies like railways, gas, electricity were the true candidates for socialisation; and that the cotton market with a large number of sellers, a large number of buyers, an organised market, and a standardised commodity presented the classical features of the case in which competition might be expected to work in the social interest. But Cripps, Dalton and Shinwell pressed for socialisation on purely political grounds, and so the issue was decided.[12] This saddens me considerably in my hope that we might achieve a society with rigorous and untrammelled competition where the conditions for competition are favourable and socialisation where monopoly is inevitable. This philosophy has not yet, I fear, made great headway.

The Census of Distribution Committee has at last, thank goodness, finished its labours. After another two days of meetings (including an official lunch at the Savoy given by the Board of Trade to the members of the Committee with Belcher, the Parliamentary Secretary to the Board of Trade, presiding) we have managed to produce a unanimous report, signed by everyone including the two representatives of the small retailers, recommending that a Census of Distribution should be taken. The recommendations have already been to the Lord President's Committee (I briefed him on the subject); and Ministers have decided that Census should be taken.[13] So that is that.

We have meanwhile been briefing the Lord President on a host of topics as they have come up to his committees or to the Cabinet. In addition to the subjects mentioned above, we have, for example, this week covered the Film Industry, the Herring Board, the Institute for Industrial Management, the Employment and Unemployment Situation, Special Areas in Scotland, whether import duties should be re-imposed on the importation of Fish, and the Civil Aviation Bill.[14] Films and Herrings are interesting in that consideration of both of them has led to the constitution of official committees (on which, I presume, the Section will be represented) to consider problems connected with Restrictive Practices. Films raised the problem of seeing how the independent producers of

[12] 'Central Purchase of Cotton, Report by the Official Committee', appendix to LP(46)55, 'Bulk Purchase of Cotton, Memorandum by the President of the Board of Trade', 3 March 1946, CAB132/2; Fleming to Lord President, 'Bulk Purchase of Cotton. Memorandum by the President of the Board of Trade LP(46)55', 6 March 1946, and Meade to Lord President, 'Bulk Purchase of Cotton (LP(46)55)', 7 March 1946, CAB124/337; LP(46) 9th meeting, 8 March 1946, CAB132/1.

[13] See BT70/99 for the drafting of the report; LP(46) 10th meeting, 15 March 1946, CAB132/1.

[14] Most of these topics were raised in LPC memoranda: LP(46)47 (herring industry), 57 (future film policy), 58 and 60 (Scottish development areas), 61 (import duties on foreign fish), CAB132/2. On the Institute for Industrial Management see T228/624. Tress to Lord President, 'Employment and Unemployment, Memorandum by the Minister of Labour and National Service on the Employment and Unemployment Situation (LP(I)(46)19), and Note by the President of the Board of Trade on the Improvement of Basic Services in the Development Areas LP(I)(46)17)', 19 March 1946, CAB124/219; Watts to Lord President, 'Civil Aviation Bill', 16 March 1946, T230/3.

films could acquire screen time for their products, when all the cinema houses were under the control of the monopoly producers of films. The Herring Board raised the problem of the starting up of the activities of a Statutory Board, one of whose main functions might be to lead to the restriction of supplies and the maintenance of the prices of the commodity in question. On our instigation the Lord President suggested, and it has been agreed, that a committee under Board of Trade chairmanship should be set up to investigate the future of all such statutory boards.[15] This is a great opportunity.

Meanwhile, the really great economic problem is the World Food Crisis.[16] The immediate issue is the meeting of the Combined Food Board in Washington at which the Minister of Food (without in my opinion a hope) is attempting to ensure that allocations of wheat to the United Kingdom and to India are not cut. Meanwhile the time approaches when millions will starve in Germany and India. The real solution is a very small cut in the amount of grain consumed by animals (other than human) in the USA. But our standards, while greatly below the American, are much above the European and immensely above the Indian. We simply shall have to cut. Chantler has briefed the Lord President to show how much we could have (a) with and (b) without bread rationing. All this is in a state of suspended animation until the telegram arrives (as I am sure that it will) from Washington saying that we cannot get our full allocation. Then Ministers will at last have to face the hard facts and decide how we shall best cut our consumption.[17] The other outstanding food problem is that of cereal supplies for 1946/7. There seems to be the probability (with excess stocks all used up) of very inadequate supplies from North America; and unless something can be done to encourage an increased acreage in North America or the reduction of feeding of cereals to the beasts, the position may be worse next year than this. One gets an acute feeling of impotence and frustration when one realises that the hopes of literally millions of people for the barest subsistence, for the avoidance of actual famine and starvation, depends upon the politics of the American Congress and the Farm Block and the difficulty of rigging prices over there so that it pays to produce less animals and more cereals for human consumption.

Meanwhile the annual review of agricultural prices for UK farmers has been up before Ministers. I had hoped that by this time one might have been able to get some general downward adjustment of UK farm prices. But in view of the acute food crisis cereal prices have (inevitably and rightly) been raised in order to encourage production.[18]

[15] LP(46)64, 'Herring Industry, Note by Lord President of the Council', 13 March 1946, CAB132/12; LP(46) 10th Meeting, 15 March 1946, CAB132/1; for the proceedings of the committee see BT64/306.

[16] See above, pp. 216 and 224–5.

[17] WFS(46) 5th Meeting, 5 March 1946, Conclusion 1, CAB134/729; Chantler to Lord President, 'Food Supplies: Wheat Allocations, Instructions for the U.K. Representatives on the Combined Food Board: Memorandum by the Secretary WFS(46)50; The Situation in Germany and Austria: Memorandum by the Chancellor of the Duchy of Lancaster WFS(46)49', 4 March 1946, CAB124/962; see below, p. 244.

[18] LP(46)54, 'Review of Agricultural Prices, February 1946, Joint Memorandum by Minister of Agriculture, Secretary of State for Scotland and Home Secretary', 5 March 1946, CAB132/2; LP(46) 9th Meeting, 8 March 1946, CAB132/1.

A. J. Brown has now produced a revised and shortened version of his Overseas Economic Survey, which I have sent to Helmore of the Board of Trade asking him to circulate it to his official committee on overseas economic intelligence. At the same time I have sent to Helmore a copy of a note by Marcus Fleming on the sort of overseas economic intelligence which we ought to be getting our representatives overseas to collect. I hope that this will get the work of that Committee started;[19] but I don't myself expect that we shall get much going so long as the Board of Trade are so overburdened with work in preparation for the international conference on trade and employment.

A. J. Brown is now also helping the Ministry of Information and the Board of Trade to prepare an information pamphlet for Consuls etc. overseas about our trading position in the inter-war years. It is useful for the Section to play a part in these economic intelligence projects, though I confess that it is not the aspect of the Section's work which most appeals to me.[20]

We have also been asked for help by Chegwidden who has gone as director of civilian studies to the Imperial Defence College. There they are just about to start courses for staff officers on the problem of the conditions which are necessary for the economic prosperity and security of the British Commonwealth. I have asked A. J. Brown to help Chegwidden on this little topic!

Ministers are also giving attention to the problem of the future of the Ruhr and of German Industry in general. This problem raises acute political issues. But there are also problems of first-rate importance to us. If that part of Germany which we have to feed and which is mainly industrial is bereft of all industrial output, how will it finance its imports? May not its feeding etc. constitute a direct drain on our already strained balance of payments? This would indeed be a mockery of reparations! A. J. Brown is briefing the Lord President on this issue.[21]

Marcus Fleming has been preparing some notes for the interdepartmental conversations in preparation for the international conference on trade and employment. The first which is finished and which we have sent to the Board of Trade and the Treasury is on the test on which import restrictions should be permitted in order to defend an unbalanced balance of payments. The test which we now propose relates mainly to monetary reserves, i.e. that countries can employ import restrictions only to the extent necessary to put a stop to a serious fall in reserves or to keep reserves above the danger line, and that while they are doing so they should do everything reasonable to prevent capital exports and should not put any unreasonable obstacle in the way of capital imports.[22]

[19] EC(S)(46)15, 4 March 1946, T230/21; Meade to Helmore, 14 March 1946, CAB21/2206; below p. 246.

[20] Correspondence about this task can be found on ROBN5/1, Robinson Papers, Churchill College, Cambridge.

[21] CM(46) 25th Conclusions, 18 March 1946, CAB128/5; Brown to Lord President, 'The Future of Germany and the Ruhr', 27 March 1946, T230/75.

[22] Fleming, 'Import Restrictions on Balance of Payments Grounds', sent by Meade to Shackle, 14 March 1946, T230/9.

The second note on which he is working presents more difficulty.[23] When import restrictions are imposed on balance of payments grounds or on other grounds, what happens to the margin between the foreign selling price of the commodity and the domestic scarcity price? Similarly when imports are restricted on balance of payments grounds by a state trading monopoly below the level which would otherwise be permitted, what happens to this margin of price difference which would *ex definitione* be greater than the permitted protective margin? I argue, and Marcus agrees with me, that we must in both cases be permitted to absorb the increased margin by a fee on the import licence or, in the case of state trading, by charging a higher protective margin. This [is] for a number of reasons. (i) Otherwise we could not auction import licences, which I regard as the true way of combining a quantitative import restriction with the continued working of the price system. (ii) Otherwise either the margin would accrue to the foreign supplier (which would be absurd, since the idea is on balance of payments grounds to save foreign exchange and it would be silly to pay foreigners a higher price for a smaller supply), or else a quite arbitrary profit will accrue to the private trader or individual who happens to be the lucky person who first gets hold of the supplies, or else the supplies must be price controlled and either rationed or liable to shop-shortages and queues. (iii) Otherwise it will not be possible to adopt for import licences a principle of non-discrimination other than that based on the basis of trade in a previous period. If licences could be auctioned or a fee charged roughly to equate supply and demand, we should automatically purchase in the cheapest foreign market which would both be good for our balance of payments and also is the true principle of non-discrimination. But, strange as it may seem, this problem does not seem to have been discussed at Washington. Shackle of the Board of Trade seems to think that the Americans might consider that we were going back on our undertakings if we said that state trading bodies should be able to exceed the permitted protective margins in these cases. The alternative is to put a tax on the home production as well as on the importation of the commodity whose importation is being restricted, since this is thought to be permissible (since it gives national treatment in the matter of taxation). But this would in effect mean that we could dispense with American cars only in so far as we were prepared to purchase less cars whether home produced or imported, and I cannot believe that this is either sensible as a means of dealing with a shortage of *external* purchasing power or practical politics. This is going to be a difficult nut to crack.

The International Monetary Fund and Bank are, I hear, to be located in Washington! The Americans were strongly against New York (which would have been unacceptable to Congress as being too much bound up with 'international bankers') and had decided on Washington. We ought to have fought tooth and nail for the Canadian counter-proposal that the Fund and the Bank should go to the site of the headquarters of UNO.[24]

[23] This became 'Protective Aspects of Quantitative Restrictions of Imports', 27 March 1946 (T230/9); see below, p. 245.

[24] See *The Collected Writings of John Maynard Keynes*, Vol. 26, pp. 211–12, 218.

But the Treasury gave in without, so much as I know, lifting a finger in support of this. I briefed Bridges strongly on it, but I fear too late in any case. This all serves to show how very little importance the Treasury really places on the Economic and Social Council and its Commissions. Of course, the Bank, the Fund, the Trade Organisation and the rest should all be in the same place as the main economic co-ordinating agency.

Norman Brook and I have now had another meeting with Wilson-Smith and Helsby of the Treasury to fix up the normal method of recruitment to the Economic Section.[25] Economic Assistants are to be recruited on a career basis on the same conditions as Assistant Principals, but pensioned under the FSSU and thus encouraged to resign and return to academic life. Economic Advisers are to be recruited at a more mature age for strictly limited appointments of five years. In no case is the Section to be required to keep anyone on for more than five years.

I went out to lunch at the Senate House of the University of London to meet M. Perroux the French economist who has been giving a series of lectures on nationalisation problems in the University of London. He has apparently been making considerable reference to the *Economic Journal* symposium by Fleming and myself on Price and Output Policy in Socialised Industries![26] There were present Carr-Saunders, Lionel Robbins, Plant, Hayek and Benham of the London School [of Economics]; Miss Jebb of Bedford College; Professor Neale of University College; and the Vice-Chancellor of the University.

We have held a dinner of members of the Section to say good-bye to Lionel Robbins. We were hoping that John Jewkes would come as well so that both the past directors of the Section would be there to give their reminiscences, but unfortunately at the last minute he was kept in Manchester by a meeting of the Cotton Working Party.[27] Lionel made a delightful speech of reminiscences of our early days in the New Police Building when we slept with the Scotland Yard detectives in the cellars of Scotland Yard through the 1940 Blitz, and during the day under Arthur Greenwood and Francis Hemming paced the corridors saying that we would resign because we were given nothing to do![28] Times have changed since then.

## 31 March 1946

We have been active this week revising our Economic Survey for 1946, which is now becoming an Economic Survey for the financial year 1946/47, the estimates of labour supplies and of the target national income on the

[25] See Helsby to Brook, 18 March 1946, T217/1.

[26] 'Price and Output Policy of State Enterprise: A Symposium', *Economic Journal*, Vol. 54 (December 1944), pp. 321–39 (reprinted in *The Collected Papers of James Meade*, Vol. II, Chapter 3). For Perroux's views on nationalisation see his pamphlets *Economie organisée et économie socialisée* and *Les Nationalisations* (Paris: Editions Donat Montchretien, 1945), and see below p. 243.

[27] On the Cotton Working Party see below, p. 274.

[28] Cf. Lionel Robbins, *Autobiography of an Economist*. London: Macmillan, 1971, pp. 169–72.

one hand and of labour requirements and of the programmed levels of national expenditure on the other hand being done quarterly in order to show the movement over this year of very rapid transitional change. After a meeting of my Economic Survey Working Party and innumerable consultations with Tress, Stafford, Campion and various officials in various departments, we now have a draft which we hope to get finally to Bridges in the middle of next week.[29] We are doing the survey on this occasion in two parts. The present part, as on the last occasion, compares the total demands made on the community's resources (in terms of manpower and of national expenditure) with the total available resources. It shows some, but a very much smaller, 'gap' than last time, since in the meantime all the far-reaching decisions have been taken about cutting down the Armed Forces and the munitions industries. The second part will attempt to survey some of the possibilities of getting factors of production in fact into different uses: for example, it will consider whether it is possible to get sufficient labour into the industries producing building materials in order to make it possible to fulfill the building programme or whether it would not be more realistic to reduce the building programme itself to avoid unemployment among bricklayers. (The preparation of this Survey has been a frightful task, particularly for the Central Statistical Office, which have the preparation of the Budget White Paper on hand at the same time. The Budget White Paper will this year be a very good product, I think, in spite of the absence of Stone.[30] The Central Statistical Office have certainly come up to scratch on this.)

Meanwhile Proctor has held two meetings on the subject of the preparation for Ministers of a draft White Paper publishing The Plan, i.e. forecasts of the available supplies of manpower and of the target national income over the coming year and of the planned distribution of manpower among the various industrial groups and of the 'target' levels of national expenditure on the various main categories. This will in fact be the summary tables in our revised Economic Survey for 1946 *after Ministers have taken decisions as to how the various demands on resources should be adjusted so as to make them add up to the total resources available*, i.e. our Survey after the 'gap' has been removed by making all the various departmental targets consistent with each other. Proctor has now prepared a very good draft White Paper and draft covering note for Ministers.[31]

The discussion of this published Plan has brought to the front an issue of supreme importance. Should the Plan be published in terms of a calendar year or of a Financial Year? I feel very strongly that it should be on the basis of a financial year for the following reasons. The Budget must be regarded as the main instrument for implementing the Plan. In a Liberal-Socialist economy it is fiscal policy, *par excellence*, which must

[29] EC(S)(46)20, 'Draft of Economic Survey for 1946/47 Interim Report as circulated to the E.S.W.P.', 1 April 1946, T230/58; see below, p. 247.

[30] *National Income and Expenditure of the United Kingdom 1938 to 1945*, Cmd. 6784, April 1946.

[31] ED(46)9, 'Draft White Paper on Economic Survey for 1946–47', 3 April 1946, CAB134/188.

be used in order to ensure that the level of personal expenditure, investment etc. is right. Success or failure depends, in my opinion, on whether or not we manage to get this the accepted Treasury doctrine. What we want is (i) to prepare a Survey of Resources and requirements at the end of each calendar year covering the next financial year, (ii) to spend January and February getting Ministers to take the necessary decisions to close any 'gap' revealed in such a Survey between overall supply of and demand for resources, (iii) to get the resulting 'Plan' published before the Budget (beginning of March), (iv) to get the Budget decisions and the Budget speech largely directed to carrying out this Plan. Clearly this marriage between the Plan and the Budget will be more easily consummated if the Plan is in terms of the Financial Year. I have managed to sell this idea to Proctor in the Treasury, to Austin Robinson in the Board of Trade and to Secord in the Lord President's Office. But there is opposition from Campion in the Central Statistical Office on the grounds that the Budget White Paper publishes the back figures of National Income and Expenditure on a calendar year basis and that the comparison of the results with the planned forecasts will therefore be impossible unless the Plan is also based on a calendar year basis. The answer to this is that the main national income and expenditure figures for past periods should be published also on a financial year basis. The other opposition comes from Nicholson who argues that for educational and publicity purposes the Plan must be published on a calendar year basis. He admits my arguments and has the bright, but I confess I think the utterly silly, idea that we should have two planning years – one a financial year for internal administrative purposes and the other a calendar year for external publicity purposes! Luckily the Plan this year must be published on a financial year basis, because we shall be half-way through the calendar year when it is published this time and we have done all our work for the revised Survey (on which the publication must be based) on a financial year basis. I intend to fight to the limit on this issue.

I have had lunch with Marjolin who is secretary in Paris of the French Commissariat du Plan. He told me something of what the French Plan is like. It appears to be rather less liberal than ours, being based more on the quantitative outputs of particular industries. They started thinking about the needs for re-equipment and modernisation of particular industries and were led from that to investigations of the overall economic situation. He discussed with me the overall fiscal measures that may be taken to influence total demand; but he said that he thought that they were more likely than us to maintain certain particular controls (i.e. the allocation of particular raw materials) which would mean that their plan would be less 'liberal' than ours.

A lot has happened on the Socialisation front. After the Lord President's Socialisation Committee had (in spite of our brief to the Lord President [above, p. 233]) twice blessed the Minister of War Transport's Scheme for Transport Nationalisation, including the most illiberal proposals for dealing with Road Transport which would have prevented manufacturers from carrying their own goods in their own vehicles above a certain distance, there has – thank goodness – been an intervention which has thrown the whole issue into the melting pot again. Jay briefed the PM on the lines that (i) C licensees should be free to carry their own goods without limit and (ii) A and B licensees should be free to carry other people's goods without limit within a distance limit from their base which would be much greater than that proposed in the Minister of War Transport's paper. The PM sent for the LP. They decided that Jay and I should prepare a joint paper on this subject. After discussion with me Jay prepared such a paper, which the LP then decided should be circulated to his Ministerial Committee on Socialisation. I managed to make sure after consultation with Alec Johnston of the Lord President's Office and with Norman Brook that the paper when circulated to Ministers should appear to come wholly from the Prime Minister's Office and not from the Economic Section. It would never do for the Section to circulate papers to Ministerial meetings taking a line opposed to that of the Lord President, particularly when Hurcomb is head of the Ministry of Transport and takes a most severe view of official proprieties. The Board of Trade and Ministry of Supply have taken our line; but the discussion at the Lord President's meeting was quite inconclusive. The matter will now go to the Cabinet. I took the opportunity of briefing the Lord President in the sense that I thought that if a limit of distance was set to the loads which could be done by A and B licensees the opportunity should be taken of removing all restriction on the number of A and B licensees, a restriction which I castigated as being a typical example of an inter-war statutory restrictive practice which was based on the idea of making us all wealthy by forbidding us to produce useful goods and services.[32]

We (in the person of Miss Watts) have briefed the Lord President on a somewhat similar point in connection with Civil Aviation.[33] In this case the proposal is that while regular air lines should be nationalised, charter services should be kept free. But the Minister of Civil Aviation wishes to

[32] Jay to Meade, 25 March 1946, SI(M)(46)11, 'The Position of Road Haulage in a Nationalised Transport System, Note by the Lord President of the Council', 26 March 1946, T230/107; SI(M)(46) 6th meeting, 29 March 1946, CAB134/687; Meade to Lord President, 28 March 1946, T230/107. cf. Chester, *The Nationalisation of British Industry 1945–51*, pp. 124–8, where Jay's paper and the ensuing Ministerial discussion are described at length. As Chester points out (pp. 117–18), 'In order to understand the course of the arguments and the nature of the various proposals it is necessary to know something about the classes of licence introduced by the Road and Rail Traffic Act, 1933. An "A" licence entitled the licensee to carry anywhere, for hire or reward, goods other than his own. He was prohibited from carrying his own goods, except those needed in his trade as a carrier. The contract "A" licence was issued to public carriers and entitled them to hire vehicles for the exclusive use of persons or firms specified in the contract. . . . A "B" licence entitled the holder to carry both his own goods and, subject to any conditions that might be attached to the licence, the goods of others for hire or reward. The holder of a "C" licence was entitled to carry for himself alone, in other words, to carry only his own goods. All licences were issued by the Licensing Authority for the region and appeal against their decisions lay to a Road and Rail Traffic Tribunal. Persons seeking only to carry their own goods in their own vehicles were given "C" licences on application. . . .

The licensing scheme was suspended at the beginning of the war and a system of wartime control introduced. . . . In 1938 there had been some 27,000 operators with "A" or "A" contract licences, 34,000 with "B" licences and 178,000 with "C" licences, but during the war there was a substantial decline in all three groups.'

[33] Watts to Lord President, 'Civil Aviation Bill', 28 March 1946, T230/3.

interpret charter services so narrowly as to exclude virtually all competition with the national system. Both in the case of land and of air transport we have preached the doctrine that the national system should not fear competition unless either it expects to be less efficient than its private competitors or it intends to discriminate in its charges against certain users of transport in order to subsidise other users.

Marcus Fleming and I had lunch with the French economist Perroux and afterwards had some considerable discussion with him about problems of nationalisation, on which he has been lecturing in London. He had studied our *Economic Journal* articles on the Price and Output policies of socialised industries but did not consider these problems as important as the problems of Rationalisation and Investment Programmes which depended upon central decisions.[34] Marcus and I agreed with him that these questions which involved the closing or opening of new plants and 'lumpy' investment could not be taken on a decentralised basis on the calculation of marginal costs and prices.

There have been one or two more meetings of Nicholson's Working Party on Wages Policy and a report has now been sent to and approved by the Lord President's Committee. We have established the point that in conditions of full employment special measures will be necessary to restrain increases in wage-rates in industries which are not seriously undermanned (i) to allow increased wages in the undermanned industries to have their full effect in attracting labour to those industries, (ii) to prevent an overall wage and price inflation with adverse effects on our export position, and (iii) to prevent increased labour costs and so localised unemployment in fully manned industries. We recommend no revolutionary change in the existing machinery for wage fixation but that there should be a National Industrial Conference of Employers, Workers and Government to explain to both sides of industry the national needs of a wages policy. Sayers and I took the opportunity of attacking the policy of stabilising the cost of living by price subsidies, at any rate as a long-term policy; and I briefed the Lord President when the report went to his Committee in this sense, warning him that he should make sure that the Chancellor in his forthcoming Budget speech should not commit the Government too far in maintaining the stabilisation policy.[35]

Sayers has briefed the Lord President on the Miners' Charter, in which the miners demand every kind of improvement in their conditions. We allow that, on the principles of wages policy outlined above, coal mining is one of the industries in which an improvement of wages is probably required in order to attract labour; but argue against too great a readiness to reduce hours of work, since this would reduce output unless there was a more than corresponding increase either in productivity or in the amount of labour attracted to the mines.[36]

[34] See page 239, note 26.

[35] W(46) 3rd and 4th meetings, 20 and 25 March 1946, CAB132/88; LP(46)71, First Report of Official Working Party on Wages Policy, 26 March 1946, CAB132/3; LP(46) 11th meeting, 29 March 1946, CAB132/1; Meade to Lord President, 'Wages Policy (LP(46)71)', 27 March 1946, CAB124/783.

[36] Sayers to Lord President, 'The "Coal-Miners' Charter" (CP(46)116)', 28 March 1946, T230/107.

Patrick Jefferies has now joined the Section as an Economic Assistant and Sayers and I are going to start him off on an investigation of changes in relative wage-rates and in supplies of labour.[37]

There have been a series of interdepartmental meetings on the World Food position. As Philip Chantler, who usually represents us on this, has been away on leave for a fortnight I have found myself heavily engaged. The Minister of Food has come back from Washington with our wheat allocation cut no more below what we went to claim, while India (although with our support she receives very much more than at the previous allocation in spite of American opposition) is to receive so limited [an] amount that widespread starvation is almost inevitable, and Germany is to live on only 1000 calories [per day]. I cannot myself believe that it is right that we should not take a serious cut, much less should take no cut at all. There has been a meeting of Norman Brook's official committee to discuss the situation and then a series of meetings under Francis Williams (the Public Relations officer at No. 10 Downing Street) to discuss the draft of a White Paper on the World Food situation. I prepared a brief on the subject for the Lord President making clear my feeling of unease on this subject. In my first draft I suggested flat-footedly that we should sacrifice some of our allocation to the Indians. I had a long argument about this with Nicholson, who took a poor line in my view – there were too many difficulties in the way of assuring that the supplies got to the starving people in India, that it was politically most important that people in this country should be strong and contented, etc., etc. I told him that I was unconvinced and still thought that there was a fairly straight moral issue. But rightly or wrongly I compromised in my minute to the Lord President and merely suggested that, while we should accept our total allocation, we should regard a certain part of it as an insurance fund from which we must be prepared to advance particular cargoes to avert particular local disasters in India or on the Continent if and when this became necessary. Nicholson agreed to back this idea; and Jay, to whom I sent a copy of this minute, said that he thought it a good idea because it had a chance of acceptance by Ministers. Jay himself has been first-class throughout this issue and really has done more than anyone else in Whitehall to save us from the moral catastrophe of having made no really great sacrifice to save Europe and India from disaster.[38]

Liesching has held a meeting of his full official committee to discuss preparations for the forthcoming conference on trade and employment. The subject of discussion was a public announcement to be made to ask industry to send in its views about tariffs, preferences, etc. The draft contained no reference to Employment Policy. The representative of the Minister of Labour wished to insert such a reference, but proposed it in the form of a statement that we hoped to achieve such a reduction in tariffs and other trade barriers as would lead to full employment. I argued strongly that this got the emphasis all wrong. We did not want to encourage

[37] See below, p. 248.

[38] Meade to Lord President, 'Rice and Wheat Allocation', 21 March 1946, CAB124/964. On Jay's role see also his autobiography, *Change and Fortune*, pp. 140–2.

the American view that a reduction of trade barriers was all that was necessary to preserve full employment, but rather our view that domestic policies were necessary to ensure full employment and that an effective application of such policies was almost a necessary condition for the successful carrying out of a policy of reduction of tariffs and other trade barriers.[39]

Marcus Fleming has now finished an admirable paper on the protective aspects of quantitative restrictions and of state trading restrictions, which I have sent on to Shackle in the Board of Trade with the suggestion that it should be circulated to his sub-committee on Non-Tariff Aspects of the forthcoming trade conference.[40] Our view is that when a state has the right to impose quantitative restrictions (e.g. on balance of payments grounds) this will cause a divergence between the price at which the goods are bought from the foreigner and the scarcity price in the domestic market. This we must be free to fill by a special levy (e.g. a higher import duty, a special licence fee or by the auctioning of import licenses, or in the similar case of restrictions imposed by state trading monopolies by a higher protective margin between foreign and domestic price). If we filled the gap by a higher price to the foreign supplier, the point of the restrictions as a means of saving foreign exchange would be lost; if by reducing the price to the domestic consumer, shop shortages or rationing would result; if by neither, then some middleman makes a huge and unnecessary profit. Another way to fill the gap would be to impose an indirect tax both on imports and on home supplies. But this would mean that we could only save foreign exchange by restricting imports of particular goods, if we were prepared to restrict the home production of the same goods, i.e. we could protect our balance of payments by reducing our total consumption of the type of goods which we import but not by producing at home instead of importing. The question is what is compatible with the American proposals which we are committed to support. As the only way of combining the price mechanisms with quantitative controls is to allow charges of this kind, I hope that we can persuade the Americans of their reasonableness.

The Treasury have now sent in a draft of their ideas of the conditions in which it would be permissible to impose quantitative restrictions on balance of payments grounds. It seems to take over many of the ideas in our draft.[41] I must get Marcus Fleming, who has been on leave this week, to study it next week.

We have had a Staff Meeting to discuss a paper by A. J. Brown on the size of the elasticity of demand for UK exports and the implications of this for such matters as the effect of currency depreciation on our balance of payments. It was a very ingenious analysis based on the elasticity of substitution between British and other goods in foreign markets, measured from data in a League of Nations publication on changes in the ratios between our manufactured exports and total manufactured exports and between our prices and world prices for the same. All this is very

[39] TN(46) 2nd Meeting, 30 March 1946, CAB134/711.

[40] 'Protective Aspects of Quantitative Restriction of Imports, Note by the Economic Section', 27 March 1946, T230/9; see also below, p. 256.

[41] Waley to Shackle, 23 March 1946, T230/9.

relevant because we have just had a letter from R. W. B. Clarke explaining how he intends to carry out his working party on the subject of our balance of payments in 1950. In this letter he deals fully with the primary question of the level of total world activity and of the difference in the demand for our exports which will be brought about in different products and in different markets by a high or a low level of economic activity and so of demand in the United States and in other countries. But he does not deal at all with changes in prices and costs and the consequential substitution of our exports for the exports of other countries, which is just the subject of Brown's paper.[42]

A. J. Brown's first draft of the Overseas Economic Survey has at last been circulated. I went to call on Helmore at the Board of Trade who is chairman of the official committee on External Economic Intelligence. The paper is now circulated; a meeting is to be called; this matter seems at last to be launched![43] Brown has also been discussing with Chegwidden the work which the latter, as director of civilian studies, has been preparing for the Imperial Defence College on the economic factors necessary to preserve the prosperity and strategic strength of the British Commonwealth. Brown is also rewriting for the Board of Trade a paper which has been prepared in the Ministry of Information on our external trade in the inter-war period. The idea is to send this out to our overseas commercial representatives very shortly as a background paper before the forthcoming trade conference. Brown has also been briefing the Lord President on the economic effects of separating the Ruhr from Germany.[44]

I had lunch with Rosenstein-Rodan of University College [London]. He has made the suggestion that some members of the Economic Section might in the next academic year give a course of lectures on questions of applied economics at University College. This raises obvious difficulties about official secrets; but it is clearly an admirable way of maintaining contact between the Section and the academic world. I must talk to Norman Brook about this. It might appeal to him, as he is so keen on encouraging the conditions in which members of the Section might return to academic life after a period in the Economic Section.[45]

[42] EC(S)(46)18 (Second revise), 'Some fundamental elasticities in British external trade: a preliminary note', 3 March 1946, T230/21 and Meade Papers 3/9; League of Nations, *Review of World Trade 1938*; Clarke to Robinson, 18 March 1946, T230/276.

[43] See above, p. 237. The meeting of Helmore's Committee on Overseas Economic Information was to be held on 15 April (CAB134/204).

[44] See above, p. 237.

[45] See below, p. 258.

# 18

## April 1946

*6 April 1946*

This week we (i.e. Economic Section and Central Statistical Office in the persons of Tress and Stafford) have finished our revised Survey for 1946/47 and have sent it to Bridges.[1] With the revised departmental programmes the 'gap' between requirements and total available resources is now much reduced. Indeed we are recommending that there should probably not be any further conscious cutting of departmental programmes merely to close the gap, because (i) there are statistical uncertainties, (ii) certain programmes may in any case be impossible to reach (e.g. the target for building labour if achieved looks like causing merely unemployment among bricklayers because of the lack of labour in brickmaking) and (iii) the fineness of governmental controls is not such as to make it possible by planning to carry out very fine adjustments. It is best to err on the safe side by allowing for some inflationary pressure. It would indeed be absurd so to prune departmental programmes that one actually caused deflation and unemployment in this period of acute shortage. This is a point on which Keynes, with whom I discussed these matters, is laying great stress. We have promised to follow up our revised Survey with a further report on the possibilities of fulfilling particular programmes. (e.g. Can one prevent too many people going into transport? Will there be enough building materials for the builders to use? Will there be enough coal to keep industry going? and so on.)

I have continued my campaign (in discussions with Oliver Franks, Douglas Jay and Keynes) for our timing our plan to the Financial Year, in order to ensure that the Budget shall be regarded as the main instrument of carrying out the Plan, rather than to the calendar year. Franks and Jay are fully sold on the idea, I think. I did not get so far with Keynes who would all the time talk about whether the Plan should be published or not. But of course basically he favours the idea of linking up fiscal policy with our overall Survey of national expenditure.

With Sayers I attended a meeting of Nicholson's Wages Policy working party to discuss the methods of determining agricultural wages. There was

[1] Meade to Bridges, 4 April 1946, T230/58; 'ESWP/31 46 (Final), Economic Survey for 1946/47, Interim Report by the Economic Survey Working Party', 5 April 1946, EC(S)(46)21, T230/21.

a duel between the Ministry of Agriculture (who are dimly aware of the fact that when the state sets agricultural quantitative output targets and tacitly says that it will guarantee to the farmers whatever price is necessary to cover their costs – including wages – on that output, the state cannot avoid being implicated in wages policy) and the Minstry of Labour, who just want in agriculture as everywhere else there to be a joint negotiation between workers and employers with the state completely washing its hands of the result. Sayers and I pegged away at the point that if our agricultural policy could take the form of guaranteeing certain prices to the farmers as opposed to giving them a tacit guarantee that prices will be adjusted so as to bring forth a given output, the farmers just like any other employer will have a full incentive to resist wage increases which were not necessary to attract the desired number of workers to the work. This of course might be a sensible post-war agricultural policy where prices could be fixed in some sort of relation to world prices and without too much regard to home output; but at the moment with the world food crisis quantitative targets must be set. The meeting reached no conclusions![2]

There has been another meeting of Gilbert's Official Committee on Socialisation at which we strengthened the report to be sent to Ministers in favour of a regional as opposed to a national organisation for electricity distribution. The meeting then went on to discuss a draft report to Ministers on Price Policy in Socialised Industries in which the majority more or less say that each Board should independently decide what prices to fix, but that these prices should more or less cover total costs. On the other hand, 'one of us' (i.e. myself) dissents and says that, for many reasons (recorded in an earlier entry), the mere covering of total costs as an invariable rule would lead to many grave disadvantages. I fear that there is an impasse. None of the official members of the committee have really begun to see the part which prices and marginal costs should play in socialised industries.[3]

The main work which I have done this week is to hold a series of meetings in my room ranging from full staff meetings to personal discussions with individual members of the Section to get rather more organised all the various enquiries which we have in hand. Thus Jefferies is now working on comparing pre-war and present figures of (a) the numbers of people and (b) average earnings in various industrial groups in order to see how movements in relative wages have accorded with movements in the relative demands for different types or uses of labour.[4] I have discussed with Dow the work which he is doing on variations in various forms of tax and similar factors (e.g. income tax payments under PAYE, national insurance contributions, purchase tax, repayment of income tax post-war credits) as a means of controlling total expenditure on personal consumption.[5] We have had extensive discussions on a draft of a study which Chantler is preparing on the Coal Industry as an exercise

[2] W(46) 5th Meeting, 1 April 1946, CAB132/88.

[3] SI(0)(46) 7th meeting, 1 April 1946, T228/269; above, pp. 214 and 224.

[4] Papers by Jefferies, 'Notes on Regional Differences in Wages in the Interwar Period', and 'Wage Policy and Undermanned Industries', are on T230/111.

[5] See above, p. 222.

in the way in which our principles about prices and marginal costs might be applied in a particular socialised industry.[6] John Wood has been started off to prepare notes on all the pre-war statutory restrictive schemes (e.g. the Herring Board, the Agricultural Marketing Boards, Licensing of road vehicles etc.) so that we shall be prepared for meetings of the Committee of officials which the Board of Trade is to organise in order to advise Ministers on what should be their general line of policy in this field. I hope that this will provide an opportunity for making an attack on discouragements to competition in that sector of the economy which is to be left to private enterprise.[7] I have had considerable discussion with George Shackle to guide him in the enquiry which he is now doing on investment in housing in order to see how sensitive such investment would be to influence through variations in the rate of interest or in the rate of subsidy.[8]

I have, by the way, conceived the idea that we should get rid of the subsidies to the cost of living and to housing (and should modify rent restriction so as to let rents rise to a level which would cover the costs of housing) and should use the funds to pay increased family allowances. If my arithmetic is correct this should allow us to pay allowances of about £2 10*s* 0*d* [£2.50] instead of 5/- [25p] a child after the first child! (And if these allowances were paid free of tax, it would represent an income of some £6,000 a year per child to a man who pays 19*s* 6*d* [97½p] in the £ on his marginal income!) There is no doubt that the population problem is soluble if we like to remove such advantages as those of cheap food and houses which are given to everyone and concentrate the resources on family allowances. When the Jays were at supper here the other day, Peggy Jay told me that the Royal Commission on Population was not going to recommend 'buying children'.[9] When I asked her why, she said that it was because it would be too costly. I think that I must point out this arithmetic to her. I have asked Miss Watts to work out the correct sums.

I have held a meeting of Marcus Fleming, A. J. Brown, Tress and Miss Watts to discuss the line which we should take at the Working Party which R. W. B. Clarke is organising in the Treasury to forecast our Balance of Payments position in 1950. Clarke has sent a letter to Austin Robinson in the Board of Trade outlining the way which they intend to go about it. This is all concerned with the income effects upon the demand for our exports of large variations in the level of demand in the United States and elsewhere. This is all right so far as it goes; but it utterly fails to take account of the possibility of our expanding our exports because our prices and costs (whether because of changes in wage-rates, in productivity or in exchange rates) are low relative to those of others who produce competing goods. A. J. Brown has produced a revised version of his paper on the elasticity of demand for our exports which suggests that a 10 per cent depreciation of sterling might fill 30 per cent out of the 75 per cent increase in our exports required over the pre-war level to put our balance of payments right. I am very keen that we should circulate a comment on Clarke's letter to

[6] See below, p. 253.
[7] See above, p. 23 and below, p. 253.
[8] Shackle, 'Housing and Investment Policy', 11 June 1946, EC(S)(46) 28, T230/22.
[9] See Royal Commission on Population, *Report*, Cmd. 7695, June 1949.

Austin Robinson and a copy of Brown's paper before Clarke's working party starts meeting in order that we may prevent the importance of relative prices and costs from being neglected. Marcus Fleming is going to hold a series of meetings to get a draft letter to Clarke and a redraft of Brown's paper ready.[10]

I had lunch with Austin Robinson and a man called McDougall from Washington, who is concerned with the new proposal that a joint Anglo-American group should be continued in the post-war world at the Department of Commerce in Washington for the exchange of economic information between the Administration and the UK Government. They wanted to know whether the Economic Section could help, possibly by preparing a regular report on economic events etc. here for submission to the Americans. Yet one more possible job!

## *27 April 1946*

For me these three weeks have been completely overcast by the death of Keynes, to whom I certainly owed more than to any other single man. He cast a spell over me in 1930 when I went to spend a year at Cambridge and the magic has never left. It is very sad that the last time I met him was an occasion on which we sharply disagreed and not one of those charming occasions when his witty friendship rather than his petulance was brought into play. It happened this way. On his return from Savannah, where the Bank and the Fund were set up, he read our revised Economic Survey for 1946/47 and the draft White Paper showing how this might be published. He developed a very strong feeling not only that this should not be published (with which I had much sympathy) but also that this sort of work should not really be continued at all in its present form (with which I had no sympathy at all). His feeling was that the forecast estimates which we were making were so uncertain as to be quite unreliable; that the forecasts of investment plans, for example, would also be greater than the amount which the investing agencies could in fact carry out, so that we should always have a deflationary bias in our advice. (There is, of course, much substance in this, and we must beware always to allow some margin of shortfall on this account.) But I believe that subconsciously Keynes may have been moved by his distrust of Campion and of the CSO without Stone. He would never believe that in these circumstances the work would be well done. He also argued strongly for doing the forecasts in terms of the calendar year rather than the financial year, largely because if they were to be published in, say, March this would involve looking less far ahead and would therefore be subject to less error, but partly, I think, because he positively disliked the idea that the figures of our estimates should be directly comparable with the budgetary estimates of revenue since this left less work for the 'intuitive hunch' method of dealing with budgetary policy. Keynes expressed his fears to Bridges and persuaded Bridges that it would be unwise to publish this year. Bridges discussed this with me and I agreed.

[10] See above, p. 245 and below, p. 255.

At a meeting of the Steering Committee it was agreed accordingly to send the draft White Paper forward to Ministers with the recommendation that it should not be published at any rate this year.[11]

I subsequently had a long talk with Bridges on all this. It is quite clear that Bridges was in no doubt at all about the desirability of our continuing with this sort of forecasting work on the lines on which we had embarked. He promised to back me up 100 per cent in any insistence that we should go on preparing the forecast tables of Manpower, Balance of Payments and National Income and Expenditure as before. We discussed, however, certain ways in which we might modify the work (e.g. by abandoning the quarterly estimates, by relegating all the Tables to an Appendix and making the main body of the text of the Survey more of a chat about the general position and prospects). All these possibilities I subsequently discussed with Stafford and Tress, and we were laying plans to meet these points. Meanwhile I had called on Eady in the Treasury to try to persuade him that the planning and forecasting should be done in terms of the financial year. I seemed to be making good progress on this head and Eady and I arranged to call together next day on Keynes to persuade him. We did so. This was the last time I ever saw Keynes. I soon discovered, however, that it was not a question of whether the Survey should be done in terms of a financial or calendar year that was at issue but, in effect, whether a Survey should be done at all and that Keynes had been sowing the seeds of great doubt in Eady's mind on the whole subject. It was a painful and distressing interview, in which I had to meet the whole battery of Keynes' wit, petulance, rudeness and quick unscrupulousness in argument. I was actually reduced to tears! After the meeting I called on Eady and for a long time tried to reassure him in the faith. Incidentally I explained to him that I was not utterly incompetent in these matters and related to him the early history of the Budget White Papers, – how in June and July 1940 I first drew up outline tables of national income and expenditure, how in September 1940 Stone came as my assistant to do the statistical work on them and how in December 1940 we showed to Keynes a first draft of what later became the first White Paper on the National Income and Expenditure. Eady is influenced by anything rather than pure reason and this account of historical origins had much effect upon him.[12]

And then Maynard died.[13] How beastly and petty all these little worries then appeared. He was the greatest genius I have ever met. His personal magnetism for young men, including myself, was unequalled. His charm, artistry and personality are such as I have never met in anyone else. He combined the scientist, artist and humane moralist and man of affairs in a unique manner.

11 ED(46) 2nd meeting, 9 April 1946, T228/20.

12 Eady to Meade, 23 April 1946, T230/58. On the history of national accounting see T230/96 and Richard Stone, 'The development and use of national income and expenditure estimates' in Chester, *Lessons of the British War Economy*, pp. 83–101. Meade's original memorandum is in Meade Papers 3/1, reprinted in *The Collected Papers of James Meade*, Vol. I, chapter 7.

13 On Easter Sunday, 21 April 1946, at Tilton, his country home in Sussex.

Now the question arises in Whitehall of what the Treasury should do without him. Norman Brook spoke to me about this and subsequently spoke to Bridges. They both of them, I believe, would favour the idea that Maynard is irreplaceable, that an entirely new era must open, and that the Economic Section as a whole should be used to give advice to the Treasury on economic matters.

There has been a meeting of the 'Nuclear Ministers' – Morrison, Dalton and Isaacs (Cripps being absent in India) – to discuss the report of the Investment Working Party and the report on Statistics required for Employment Policy. Bridges, Gilbert, Campion and I attended. Little of importance came out of this. As far as investment was concerned it was agreed to continue to rely on the control of building as the main form of investment control; and there was a discussion as to the legal procedure to be adopted to collect the necessary statistics (e.g. should there be a separate Census of Distribution Act or should this form Part II of a general Statistics for Employment Policy Act?)[14]

I have sent two papers on Investment to Proctor (arising out of the paper which Shackle has been preparing for the Section on Investment [above pp. 221–2]): the first outlining some of the difficulties involved in interpreting as a forecast of total private investment the results of any sample of large existing firms of their future investment plans; the second a more general paper raising the issue whether or not a restrictive control of investment will be required for a long enough period to make it desirable to alter and refine the existing control through licences of total investment.[15]

We have had a staff meeting to discuss a very good paper by Dow on the possibility under existing PAYE of varying income tax promptly to influence consumers' expenditure. We have reached the provisional conclusion that, without quite substantial alterations of the existing mechanism, it is not possible to do anything which cannot be better done through variations in National Insurance Contributions. The sort of change which would be necessary would be on the lines proposed in a recent article in *The Economist*, whereby all incomes would be taxed at a flat rate (except for a sur-tax on incomes above, say, £500) and allowances would take the form of the repayment of the first £*x* of tax paid rather than the form of exemption from tax on the first £*y* of income. In this case the rate of tax charged could presumably be easily and frequently varied.[16] I have asked Dow to work out tables on this basis to see how nearly the rates of progression could be made to approximate to existing rates.

Dow is also preparing a note for the Lord President on the implications of the recent Budget from the point of view of the Economic Plan (i.e. the balance between total demand and supply of resources).

I have delivered a lecture to a party of Principals newly admitted to the Civil Service on the general subject of Employment Policy and how it is being tackled in Whitehall, i.e. on our machinery for making Economic

[14] MEP(46) 2nd meeting, 16 April 1946, CAB134/503; on the outcome see BT70/134.

[15] Meade to Proctor, 9 April 1946, sending 'Notes on Investment Policy, Memorandum by the Economic Section' and 'Forecasting Investment by Private Enterprise, Note by the Economic Section', T230/85.

[16] See above, p. 222, 'Taxes and Incentive', *The Economist*, 6 April 1946, pp. 545–6.

Surveys of the balance between total demand and supply of resources and on the work of the Steering Committee.

Lord Pakenham is to speak for the Government soon in the House of Lords on a motion raised by Lord Cherwell about the general economic position. Bridges has put him on to us to co-ordinate the general brief to which he should speak. This means our discussing with the Ministry of Labour, Board of Trade and Treasury the general problem of what may and what may not be said. Tress and I have had a talk with Pakenham and E. A. G. Robinson of the Board of Trade on the subject.[17]

On the Socialisation front there has been a meeting of Gilbert's official committee at which we discussed the principles of compensation for individual employees who are disturbed by socialisation schemes, the organisation whereby workers will be able to consult with the management so as to have a chance of making their suggestions about improvements and changes in management, and import and export policy. On the last subject we merely propose to report at this stage to Ministers to the effect that socialisation should not give any immediate changes to import-export policy and that the committee should report later on particular problems which come up.[18]

I have had some further correspondence with Gilbert on Price Policy in Socialised Industries, and we have now got a draft report which commits the whole committee to the view that to insist on covering costs in the short run would be a mistake as making socialised industries much more rigid than unsocialised industries in price policy. I am left with a minority view of one explaining the reasons for the view that even in the long run socialised industries should not necessarily just cover the annual service of the compensation stocks.[19]

Philip Chantler has now written and revised a very excellent paper on price policy in a socialised coal industry. To my horror Fergusson told me that they have it in mind to fix uniform pit-head prices throughout the country for the various grades of coal. Chantler's paper, with a great wealth of factual detail, makes it clear why – to obtain the real economies which are possible – a flexible price system for coal must be adopted which depends upon supply-demand relationships for various grades of coal in various regions and markets. This paper has now gone to Quirk, de Peyer and Peggy Joseph in the Ministry of Fuel and Power. Later I shall send it to Fergusson.[20]

I have had a correspondence with E. A. G. Robinson on the distinction between the state running certain undertakings and the state setting up a monopoly. We are agreed that in certain cases (iron and steel, road transport) there may be a strong case for the state running certain undertakings without necessarily setting up a monopoly.[21]

[17] See below, p. 261.

[18] SI(0)(46) 8th meeting, 8 April 1946, T228/269.

[19] Gilbert to Meade, 5 April, and Meade to Gilbert, 9 April 1946, T230/10; SI(M)(46)18, Official Committee on the Socialisation of Industries, Second Report, T234/1.

[20] 'An Economic Policy for the Socialised Coal Industry', 23 March 1946, EC(S)(46)17 (Revise), T230/21.

[21] Robinson to Meade, 5 April, and Meade to Robinson, 8 April 1946, T230/107 and ROBN5/1, Robinson Papers, Churchill College, Cambridge.

I sought an interview with the Lord President to remonstrate with him on some of these problems of socialisation. I started on the problem of transport. The first part of the argument was rather heated! The Lord President attacked, and I defended, the argument in a recent minute of Philip Chantler that true co-ordination between rail and road transport meant fixing road and rail charges at levels equal to marginal cost and then letting the users of transport choose what types of transport they would use. The Lord President said this was competition, not co-ordination. We agreed that we were arguing about words. In the end I tried the argument from industrial efficiency. I said that there would be a straightforward waste of labour if goods were taken on a system on which the marginal cost was higher instead of on one where the marginal cost was lower. This, I said, involved just as much an avoidable reduction in output per head as did the existence of straightforward technical inefficiency in any industry. This began to make some impression. I said that prices could be kept equal to marginal cost by means of any necessary adjustments in railway rates and/or in road taxation. The Lord President asked me to write him a minute on this, which I have now done, ending it up by suggesting as an immediate policy: (i) that the railways should be nationalised; (ii) that the state should have the power to acquire and run any road transport it likes, passenger or [freight]; (iii) that private enterprise should be allowed to run any road transport it likes in competition with the state; and (iv) that there should be an examination of railway and road costs and prices to see whether any subsequent adjustment of railway rates or of road taxation should take place. The very restrictive proposals of the Ministry of Transport on this subject have now been discussed by the Cabinet (the Lord President being briefed on similar lines by Chantler) and have been referred back to the Lord President's Ministerial Committee on Socialisation Problems for reconsideration of the position of the C licensee.[22] So there is some hope that a substantial improvement to the suggestions may be made.

On wages policy Sayers has prepared a note on regional wage differences in which he argues the case for preserving and developing regional differences in wage-rates as a means of bringing the supply and demand for labour into proper relationship in different regions. We are waiting for Jefferies to do a piece of realistic work on existing regional wage differences to append to it, and shall then circulate it to Nicholson's working party on wages policy.[23]

Meanwhile, there has been another meeting of Nicholson's working party to consider the constitution of the proposed National Industrial Conference, the body (which has now received general Cabinet approval) which is to serve for the link between the Government and the Trade

[22] Chantler to Lord President, 'Nationalisation of Transport, Memorandum by the Minister of Transport', 12 April, and Meade to Lord President, 'Economic Efficiency and the Nationalisation of Transport', 26 April 1946, T230/107; CM(46) 35th Conclusions, 15 April 1946, CAB128/5.

[23] 'Regional differences in wage-rates', circulated in the Section as EC(S)(46)22, 2 May 1946, T230/21. Drafts are on T230/111. See also below, pp. 262–3.

Unions and Employers' Federation to discuss general wage principles and problems in the light of current economic conditions.[24]

I have written Jay a letter to urge that cost-of-living subsidies should be reduced or abolished and the proceeds used to pay increased family allowances, thus making a better use of the money from the point of view of the distribution of the national income and also being in line with what is wanted in the way of a population policy. (I have also tried out the idea in conversation with Patrick Gordon-Walker, one of the new Labour MPs, who was a friend of ours in Oxford and now lives near us; and he seemed to think it a good idea politically.) Jay came to supper with us and he seemed to support the idea. But unfortunately Jay seems much more inclined than I would be to attempt to affect the distribution of real income by subsidising essential commodities and services (housing, food etc.) and taxing luxuries rather than by taxing high incomes and paying allowances to the poor (e.g. family allowances). The second is much the more liberal and efficient method. It leaves free choice to consumers and does not involve giving subsidised food to millionaires without dependents. (It is incidentally, because of this predilection for subsidising and taxing particular things that Jay supports me on Gilbert's Socialisation committee in my argument in favour of long-term profits or losses for certain socialist industries. I find this support embarrassing! I want long-term profits or losses because I believe that long-term marginal costs may be above or below average costs and because I want to avoid subsidising or taxing marginal costs.)

There has been another meeting of the Balance of Payments Working Party under Eady's chairmanship, which Marcus Fleming and I attended. The main purpose of the meeting was to approve departmental import programmes for the second half of 1946 and first half of 1947. Exports having made a considerably better showing in recovery than had been expected, the total deficit on our Balance of Payments for 1946 is likely to be considerably less than had at one time been anticipated. Keynes, at the same time that he had delivered his broadside on our Economic Survey, delivered a similar broadside in the form of a minute which he sent to Bridges severely criticising the form in which R. W. B. Clarke in the Treasury was drawing up the Balance of Payments accounts. He wanted imports cif and not fob; he wanted oil to be treated in a way which showed the value of our total oil imports as an import instead of giving a net figure after allowing for profits made by overseas oil companies etc.; he wanted some of our overseas expenditures which are later recoverable (e.g. expenditure on relief of Germany) not to appear as current payments, but to be treated as overseas lending. There was much good sense in his criticisms. I suggested at the Balance of Payments Working Party that a sub-group should be set up to consider generally the question of the form of presentation of Balance of Payments accounts. This was agreed. Meanwhile R. W. B. Clarke has started his working party to consider the 1950 Balance of Payments. Brown and Tress have attended for us.[25]

[24] W(46) 6th meeting, 15 April 1946, CAB132/88.

[25] BPWP(46) 4th Meeting, 18 April 1946, T236/1088; BPWP/5/46 'Import Programmes for Mid-1946 to Mid-1947: A Note by the Treasury', 11 April 1946, T230/11; Keynes,

I must make sure that they ensure that any report which appears gives adequate emphasis to the importance of relative prices and costs, exchange rates etc. in determining the volume of our imports and exports.

Marcus Fleming and I have had some discussions in preparation for the forthcoming commercial policy conferences with Shackle in the Board of Trade. First, we had a long meeting in Shackle's room to consider the line to be taken in answer to a letter from Waley in the Treasury enclosing a Treasury redraft of the criteria on which import restrictions should be permitted on Balance of Payments grounds. The main point is that the Treasury seems to regard the use of quantitative import restrictions on these grounds as a thing which will and should be more or less permanently used. They have removed the clause from the draft which states that if such restrictions go on for a number of years there should be some special enquiry to see if there is no better way of meeting the Balance of Payments problem. We and Shackle insist that this should go back into the draft. A second interesting point has arisen. To what extent should country A be able to employ discriminatory import restrictions against other countries in order to make use of the blocked currency of B? Clearly if this right is unlimited, it puts a great premium on B blocking its currency and thus obtaining discrimination in its favour from A. But if A cannot do this, what can it do? Can it let B's blocked currency depreciate and find its own level? Apparently under the International Monetary Fund rules, only if A buys and sells gold freely. Can it discriminate against B by restricting its exports to B? Can it under the IMF demand payment for its exports to B in its (A's) own currency? We have written a letter raising these points.[26]

They are closely connected with the general question of the relations of countries which are members of Bretton Woods and of the contemplated trade organisation with non-members. This has been raised in an acute form in a letter from Coulson of the Foreign Office to Welch at the Board of Trade about getting trade going with the Balkan and Eastern European countries which are used to compensation and barter deals and which are now very much in the Russian sphere. The FO want to expand trade with them. Marcus Fleming and I attended a meeting in the FO under Coulson's chairmanship to discuss the point.[27] If these countries have overvalued currencies (as they seem to do) it is very difficult to think of any means of trading which does not involve the profits on our exports to them being used to recoup the losses on our imports from them. Yet any measures of this kind would appear to offend either against Bretton Woods (multiple-currency practices) or the trade proposals (discriminatory subsidies on imports). One possibility is to attempt to get an adjustment of exchange rates. Another is to set up a number of barter companies which would buy goods here, sell them in these countries, buy their goods there and bring them back for sale here. (This would not, of course, work if there were a payments agreement which permitted importers in the countries in question to obtain the sterling to buy goods directly from here without any transaction in the opposite direction.)

'Notes on the form of the Balance of Trade and Balance of Payments Statistics', 12 April 1946, and Note of Meeting of 25 and 26 April re ' "1950" Balance of Payments', T230/276.

26 Waley to Shackle, 23 March, and Meade to Shackle, 25 April 1946, T230/9.

27 Coulson to Welch, 17 April 1946, and Minutes of a Meeting of 15 April, T230/137.

A second problem which Marcus Fleming and I have been discussing with Shackle in the Board of Trade is what will happen to the protective margins under state trading or to the profit margin which will presumably be reaped by traders when goods are subject to quantitative import restrictions on balance of payments grounds. We have always taken the line that in such cases the state should be able to skim off the extra profit by raising the protective margin under state trading or by selling or auctioning the import licences for a fee.[28] We have, however, compromised with Shackle who is of the opinion that the abandonment of the protective margins set under state trading would be totally unacceptable to the Americans. We have agreed that he should continue with the report which he is preparing on state trading on the assumption that the protective margins cannot be raised when imports have to be restricted on balance of payments grounds, but we have reserved our right without prejudice to argue that it should be feasible to charge an import licence fee when quantitative restrictions have to be imposed on private trade on balance of payments grounds.

Sir John Orr, Director of the Food and Agriculture Organisation, asked me to lunch with him at the Athenaeum to discuss his plans for FAO. He made my hair stand on end! He has fantastic grandiose ideas whereby the organisation shall draw up a world food budget, shall set up a world food council, shall institute a world food fund, etc. whereby every farmer shall have a guaranteed price for everything which he produces and every consumer, on a world plan, shall be given exactly the food which he needs nutritionally. All this, involving most of the functions of the International Monetary Fund, the Bank, the Trade Organisation and the Economic and Social Council, he seems to wish to bring into operation this summer! He is clearly riding for a stupendous fall. Moreover, he belittles the really good work which the organisation could do in the way of spreading the best technical knowledge and practice in agricultural production and in instruction and in collecting facts and statistics. I spoke to Broadley of the Ministry of Food about this later, and he seems to be equally alarmed. He asked whether I could speak to Norman Brook about the need for Orr having a really good British official at his side to help him set up a proper organisation, which I have done. Meanwhile, FAO is to have a conference in May to consider the prospects of the world demand and supply of food next year (a very right and proper thing for it to do, in my opinion) and Broadley is trying to persuade me to go out with him as part of his delegation to this conference in case Orr's wilder ideas should be brought up. It is an attractive idea to go to Washington for a week or so![29]

I have had visits from a Canadian called Hackett, who is economic adviser to some bank in Canada, and an American called Meehan from the Department of Commerce, who both seemed to want to talk about our export prospects. There is really little to say but 'Wait and see; and if we don't reach our target, we shall have to depreciate the exchange'. But in my present official position it is difficult to say just this, as one must not engender distrust in sterling.

[28] See above, pp. 238 and 245.

[29] The conference was to begin on 20 May. Meade did not attend.

I have been busy on a lot of establishments work, which comes in fits and starts. Among other things, Rosenstein-Rodan with whom I lunched recently [above, p. 246] has an idea that some of the Economic Section members should deliver some lectures next academic year at University College [London]. This is a good idea in many ways, as it is good to keep members of the section in touch with academic life. I have the general approval of Brook and Bridges to go ahead with the experiment.

Norman Brook raised with me the question of what the Treasury could and should do to replace Keynes. He is clearly of the opinion that they should make more and more use of the Economic Section. He has spoken on this with Bridges, who is, I believe, of the same opinion.

During this period the Budget has been made public. In the discussions of the Budget Committee I made a strong plea for as little remission of taxation as possible, on the grounds (well illustrated by our Economic Survey) that this year would be one in which the pressure of demand would greatly exceed available supplies. Even the decisions greatly to reduce the size of the Armed Forces and the Munitions industries which were taken as a result of our first Survey early in 1946 did not change this, because the cuts would become fully operative only late in the financial year and the granting of paid leave would mean that there was not a corresponding increase in civilian production, much of which would in any case be additions to work in progress which would not reach the final markets until 1947/48. Moreover, the payment of gratuities etc. to the demobilised would increase purchasing power. In the event I think that the Budget was very moderate in the reliefs which it gave.[30]

One of the great issues this year was the future of profits taxation. Everyone, including the Chancellor, was agreed that EPT [Excess Profits Tax] was a thoroughly bad tax from the point of view of incentives and that it should go as soon as possible. The decision to abolish it does not reduce the revenue this year, but will greatly improve economic incentives. The question arose whether it should be replaced. The Chancellor much wanted either an increase in NDC [National Defence Contribution] (or some similar flat rate tax on company profits) or a tax on excess dividends as opposed to excess profits. The first has the disadvantage that it falls entirely on equity capital and on equity capital even where no excess profits are made; the second proved administratively impossible and a poor revenue yielder. (I personally was not altogether opposed to these ideas as short-term increases. They combined improved incentives with less loss of revenue. But I think that the final decision not to go for them was right.) Keynes, Hopkins and I all argued that if an alternative revenue-raiser must be found we should examine the possibility of an annual capital tax. This idea, in spite of considerable hesitation from the Board of Inland Revenue, was eventually sold to the Chancellor.[31]

[30] *House of Commons Debates*, Vol. 421, 9 April 1946, cols. 1803–40; above, pp. 196, 201 and 212–13.

[31] On the profits taxation discussion see T171/388, section 7, and also Trend, 'Budget', 20 January 1946, T171/386. The National Defence Contribution was first introduced by Chancellor of the Exchequer Neville Chamberlain in his last budget in April 1937, as a

Another great issue was raised by the Chancellor's desire to do something very radical with the Death Duties. His first wish was to introduce high progression into the Legacy and Succession Duties, together with his substitute Rignano scheme (as put by him to the Colwyn Committee) that all inheritance above a certain figure should be changed into a terminable annuity. I believed that the Chancellor was on to a really good idea in attempting to get a greater diffusion of inherited wealth. The idea met with very great opposition, particularly in the case of the limitation of inheritance above a certain figure, largely on the grounds that it would raise little or no revenue but would cause a political stink and rumpus in a year when such should particularly be avoided. The overwhelming difficulties were, however, administrative. The thing could be made to work for direct bequests from A to B; but when A leaves to B for life with remainder to C, C's as well as B's value of the inheritance would have to be valued for a prospective duty at the time of A's death. Even more difficult problems arise in the case of indeterminate bequests, when A leaves in trust to B to be subsequently distributed in at present indeterminate ways between C, D, E and F. Could, therefore, the Chancellor's ideas be put into practice without some alteration in the laws of inheritance of property? At the back of all this there lies also, of course, the problem of dealing with gifts *inter vivos*. I tried to introduce a different form of the tax: namely, the principle that each person would be taxed progressively on the total sum which he had received by way of inheritance up to date. This would not involve valuing any individual's inheritance until he actually received it; but on the other hand, it would involve keeping, as it were, a 'Doomsday book' of inheritances up to date for each person. It would have the advantage of taxing people really in accordance with the advantage which they obtained from inherited wealth. This was laughed out of court at first. But with persistence I obtained some support from Hopkins and Keynes and in the end the Chancellor showed some interest in it as a possible future change.[32]

Another point which Keynes and I both had very much at heart was that the cost-of-living subsidies should be tapered off as soon as possible. We managed to get some considerable improvement in the Budget speech in this respect.[33] The undertaking now given about the cost-of-living is not too inflexible.

Towards the end I had a considerable talk alone with the Chancellor in which I attempted to sell him my idea for the treatment of inheritance.[34] I urged him to go this year merely for some modification of the existing

complicated tax on the growth of profits above a fixed amount: in face of considerable criticism it was amended to a 5 per cent tax on profits by Chamberlain's successor, Sir John Simon, in June 1937 (B. E. V. Sabine, *British Budgets in Peace and War 1932–1945*. London: Allen & Unwin, 1970, chapter V). It was renamed Profits Tax in the 1946 Finance Act.

32 See above, pp. 206, 213, 223; (Colwyn) Committee on National Debt and Taxation, *Report*, Cmd. 2800 (London: HMSO, 1927), paras. 929–934; B(46)11, Meade to Bridges, 24 January 1946 and related correspondence on T171/388.

33 See T171/386, section 3.

34 Above, p. 223.

Estate Duties but to set up a committee to enquire into my idea for inheritance together with some special reference to (a) gifts *inter vivos* and (b) the laws of settlement. I also urged him to give up the idea of a substitute tax on profits this year for EPT but to set up an enquiry on the possibility of an annual capital tax.

I have now written a minute to Bridges (though I have not yet sent it, as I do not know whether I might not be appearing too eager to step into Keynes' shoes) on five problems which seem to me to require detailed examination before the next Budget Committee begins. (i) The annual capital tax. (ii) My idea about an inheritance tax. (iii) The treatment of post-war credits. In this respect, I maintain, there are two essentially different ways of treating them. (a) One can try to get them paid off in such a way that the recipients will treat them as capital and will save as much as possible of them. In this case there is much to be said for paying them off as soon as possible in a single large sum in the form of securities or savings deposits, while consumption goods are still rationed, price-controlled, licensed, etc. The shortage of supplies might cause much of the repayments to find their way into permanent savings. (b) One could try to repay them in such a way that they would be treated as much as possible by the recipients as spendable income, and the repayment would then be delayed and varied as a means of preventing general depressions of purchasing power. In this case I suggest that the sums should be paid over at once into blocked interest-bearing savings deposits and that the monthly rate at which they could be withdrawn should be regulated so as to regulate the rate of consumers' expenditure. (iv) The future of the cost-of-living subsidies. Here I make my suggestion that as they are tailed off some part of the savings should be used to increase children's allowances, both in the interests of population policy and also in order to sweeten the pill of their abolition. (vi) The balance of revenue and expenditure in 1950. There are a number of issues (for example, whether one should try to find a substitute such as an annual capital tax for EPT) which depend upon an idea of what the revenue and expenditure are likely to look like after the transitional period special expenditures are over but when the new social services etc. are in full operation. I suggest that approximate estimates should be prepared.[35]

On Budget Day I attended a cocktail party given by the Chancellor and Mrs Dalton in No. 11 Downing Street. There were present all the officials responsible for the Budget. Bridges, Hopkins, Eady, Gilbert, Brittain, Gregg, Carter, and Rowlatt (the Parliamentary draftsman). Also Catto and Cobbold from the Bank of England. Also Evan Durbin. It was amusing to see the Chancellor in an inflated mood moving in rather a patronising way among his advisers telling them that they were a good lot!

[35] 'Note by Mr Meade', 25 April 1946, T171/389; and see below, pp. 271–2.

# 19

## May 1946

### *12 May 1946*

As far as the Economic Plan is concerned I have not been very active myself this fortnight. Tress has been working hard with Stafford in the Central Statistical Office and with officials in the other departments to produce a revised version of our Survey for 1946/47. Tress has also done a good deal of work in preparing a brief for the speech on the general economic situation which Lord Pakenham has made on behalf of the Government in a debate on this subject in the House of Lords.[1]

On the socialisation front there has been a meeting of Gilbert's official committee which, in addition to completing their report for Ministers on the compensation to be given in socialised industries on account of loss of office, has also agreed the report for Ministers on Price Policy in socialised industries. I have got the committee to put forward the unanimous view that in the short run socialised industries should not be expected to cover their average costs year in year out, but should be free to make profits in good years and losses in bad years. This is something, because otherwise socialisation might have made industries increase the variations in their output in face of variations in demand in a shockingly uneconomic manner. But I still express a minority of one view that to cover total costs should not be the main underlying long-period criterion.[2]

There has been some activity on the Wages Policy front. A meeting of Nicholson's Wages Policy Committee has been held in order to discuss the problem of Agricultural Wages. There are three real issues here: First, what type of machinery there should be for fixing agricultural wages in circumstances like the present when it is implicitly understood (because of the world food shortage combined with the policy of stabilising the cost of living) that the Government will allow any increases in prices to the farmers necessary to induce them to produce the target domestic output but without allowing this increase in prices to fall on the consumer at all. Secondly, what measures if any the Government should take to prevent the recent increases in the agricultural minimum wage from leading to

[1] Meade to Bridges, May 1946, sending 'completely revised version of our Economic Survey for 1946-47', T230/58; above, p. 419 and *House of Lords Debates*, Vol. 141, 8 May 1946, cols. 96–112.

[2] SI(0)(46) 9th meeting, 1 May 1946, T228/269; SI(M)(46)18, Official Committee on the Socialisation of Industries, Second Report, 10 May 1946, T234/1.

sympathetic increases in other competing rural occupations (such as roadmaking) and thereby largely stultifying their main purpose of helping to man-up agriculture. Thirdly (an issue which we have tried to star but which Nicholson has done his utmost to soft-pedal), whether or not emphasis should be put upon the reintroduction and maintenance of regional differences in agricultural wage-rates. On the first, we have taken the line that we have got to muddle through the present transitional difficulties as well as may be, but there is an essential long-term moral; namely, that long-term agricultural policy which (as has been decided) gives the farmers a stable guaranteed price for the products which they produce must in no way be suggested to imply that these guaranteed prices will be automatically adjusted to take account of changes in wage-rates or other costs. They would, of course, be adjusted from time to time, taking into account the prices of competing imports and the scale of domestic agriculture, in order to decide how much protection to give to agriculture. But the farmers must just be told to go ahead and produce as much as they can at these prices, and *there must be no rigid quantitative plan for domestic agricultural output*. In these circumstances the farmers would have a real incentive to bargain with their wage-earners, to pay them on the one hand enough to attract the labour but on the other hand not to pay so much as to bring their costs out of line with the guaranteed prices. On the second issue, we have backed the Ministry of Agriculture against the Ministry of Labour in the view that something should be done to discourage sympathetic wage increases in other rural occupations which would remove the greater part of the attractive power of the increased agricultural wages. The Ministry of Labour are scared to death at any interference with the independent wage negotiating organisations. We have taken the line that the proposed National Industrial Conference (the whole purpose of which was to persuade both sides of industry to get relative wages right) should at least be permitted to take up this sort of problem, although it would not itself, of course, be responsible for making any concrete proposals about any particular wage-rates. On the third issue, we have made a great song and dance on the grounds that if you have national wage-rates you have no 'liberal' means of attracting the work to the over-manned, and the workers to the under-manned, regions. I wrote minutes to the Lord President on all these three issues. At the Cabinet meeting doubts were expressed as to whether we were not in danger of running into an upward spiral of wages and costs, and it was decided to ask the Steering Committee under Bridges to organise an enquiry into the probable course of future wages, costs and prices.[3]

We have also had a Staff Meeting to discuss the problem of regional wage differences (on which subject Sayers has written an analytical paper and Jefferies is engaged in doing some realistic study)[4] and also on the problem of a national minimum wage. Sayers and Tress, largely as a means of breaking the connection between the cost of living and the money wage-

[3] W(46) 7th meeting, 6 May 1946, CAB132/88; CM(46) 42nd Conclusions, 6 May 1946, CAB128/5. On the enquiry into wages etc. see below, p. 283.

[4] See above, pp. 248, 254.

rate, are in favour of fixing a national minimum wage-rate (about equal to the rate of unemployment benefit) which would vary directly with a cost-of-living index specially devised to measure the cost of the goods and services included in a minimum subsistence. The idea would be that unemployment benefit and the national minimum wage portion of wages would be directly linked to this subsistence cost of living, and that in return the rest of wages should be made completely independent of the cost of living. Marcus Fleming resists this proposal on the grounds (with which I much sympathise) that all one's weight should be thrown into reducing the link between money benefits, wage-rates etc. and the cost of living and that this proposal would in effect increase the link.

I am very glad to record that a letter has now been sent out by Woods of the Board of Trade announcing the setting up of a Committee under the chairmanship of Miss Kilroy to consider (as a result of an earlier decision of the Lord President's Committee taken in connection with a discussion of the future of the Herring Board) the broad lines of policy which the Government should adopt towards supervisory boards which are set up to regulate particular industries (e.g. Herring Board, Agricultural Marketing Boards, etc.).[5] Woods' letter, I am glad to say, draws the terms of reference of the Committee rather broadly, referring to the general principles to be adopted in the matter of restrictive practices. I have suggested that I should myself represent the Economic Section on this Committee. I hope that this may really activate the whole question of preventing restrictive practices in the unsocialised sector of industry – a feature which at the moment is, in my opinion, the most serious deficiency in the Government's domestic policy. Whether or not we shall be able to drag in A, B and C traffic licensing (that most controversial of issues!)[6] in the unsocialised sector of transport I much doubt! I have held a meeting of Sayers, Chantler and Wood in the Section to start preparations for this Committee.

Most of my time this fortnight has, however, been spent on external economic issues. In connection with R. W. B. Clarke's working party which is forecasting the 1950 balance of payments E. A. G. Robinson has sent round a rather ridiculous Gallup Poll to various officials in various departments asking for personal estimates of the extent to which the 1950 demand for manufactured imports in the different parts of the world is likely to exceed the 1937 demand on certain 'optimistic' assumptions (i.e. that there is a high level of domestic demand in each country and that there is the sort of degree of liberalisation of their trade barriers as is contemplated in the ITO proposals). He has himself circulated a Board of Trade estimate of the demand on the corresponding 'pessimistic' assumptions. The idea is on the basis of these 'pessimistic' and 'optimistic' assumptions of the level of world demand for manufactured exports to estimate a 'pessimistic' and 'optimistic' forecast of the demand for *UK* manufactured exports. I dissuaded individual members of the Section from taking part in this Gallup Poll, but took the opportunity of doing a

[5] See above, p. 235; for the Committee's terms of reference and proceedings see BT64/306.
[6] Above, pp. 241–2 and 254.

really thorough Economic Section piece of work. Brown has revised his paper on the elasticity of demand for UK exports and on the other elasticities affecting UK trade. On the basis of this and of assumptions which Brown has made about the level of demand for manufactured imports in the various countries, we have produced figures which combine the two great factors: level of external demand and the relationship between our prices and costs. We have claimed to show that our manufactured exports may vary from a reduction of 25 per cent below 1937 on the assumption of a 'pessimistic' level of external demand combined with a 20 per cent movement of relative prices and costs against us to an increase of 200 per cent above pre-war on the assumption of an 'optimistic' level of external demand combined with a 20 per cent movement of prices and costs in our favour. Also that we could get an 80 per cent increase in our manufactured exports *either* on the optimistic level of demand with no adjustment of relative costs *or* on the pessimistic assumption with a 20 per cent adjustment of costs. I wrote all this up into a letter to E. A. G. Robinson last Saturday morning in bed. We have now discussed it in the Section and sent it off with a copy of Brown's revised paper attached.[7] We draw two morals: first, that we must pay attention to relative prices as much as to the level of external demand; and secondly that we can if we want put our balance of payments right without permanent severe import restrictions and that the real questions are how much adjustment of prices and costs, if any, is required for this purpose and whether one can get that adjustment without exchange depreciation.

I have had a meeting with Marcus Fleming and Tress to discuss the problem of the way in which our Balance of Payments accounts should be presented, in connection with the sub-working party of the Balance of Payments Working Party which is to study this question.[8] The following points arise: (i) The distinction between current and capital payments, the latter presumably being those in respect of which we genuinely expect repayment some time. (ii) The different distinction between payments, whether current or capital on the above definition, which are special to the clearing up of the war and are non-recurrent. (For example, payments to feed Germany are non-recurrent, but whether they are capital payments or not depends largely upon whether we expect them to be repaid.) (iii) Should figures be recorded on a payments or a transactions basis? (e.g. Should the value of goods exported be recorded or the payments made for exports?) My view is that transactions should be recorded, the difference between this and payments being a capital item. (iv) Should imports be recorded fob or cif? I used to think that cif was clearly right. But I begin to doubt it, as a result of arguments put forward by R. W. B. Clarke. (a) After all, fob does really represent our payments for the imported goods, and it is reasonable to show a net shipping balance. Why should we count as an

[7] Robinson, 'Forecasting British Exports of Manufactures in 1950', April 1946, T230/134; Meade to Robinson, 10 May 1946, T230/276 and Meade Papers 3/2; Brown, 'Some fundamental elasticities in British external trade: a preliminary note', T236/1103 and Meade Papers 3/9. On Robinson's Gallup Poll see also ROBN5/1, Robinson Papers, Churchill College, Cambridge.

[8] See Meade to Fleming, 18 April 1946, T230/276, and see below, pp. 326–7.

expenditure and receipt what we pay ourselves for carrying the goods? (b) If all imports were recorded fob world import and export figures could be compared. (c) Canada and the USA record their imports fob. They are very unlikely to change. If we changed to their practice, we might go a long way to getting world uniformity on their basis. (v) Whether or not we should give, as is done in the present Bank of England figures, a net figure for oil transactions or should show all our oil imports as imports. Here I am sure that we should do the second. (vi) The connection of all this with the figures of total national expenditure. Whether, for example, payments to feed Germany are treated as capital or current items in the balance of payments must also determine whether they are treated as items of current expenditure in Govt expenditure on goods and services. Otherwise the total national expenditure and total national income will not balance properly. (vii) We have also to bear in mind whether the accounts are being drawn up in a way which will fit in with the waiver clause under the American Loan Agreement.

There has been a meeting of the Trade Negotiations Committee to discuss the timetable of the coming commercial policy negotiations. The Americans now wish to put off the meeting of the Nuclear countries till March 1947, because of the delay of the passage of the Loan Agreement. The reason is that under their Trade Agreements Act they have to give 90 days' public notice of all the tariff items which they may negotiate. This notice they wouldn't give before the Loan Agreement was through Congress and now they don't want to give until after their November elections. But they wanted meanwhile to have a series of almost perpetual meetings of the Preparatory Committee set up by the Economic and Social Council to prepare for the final world trade conference and of sub-committees to draft all the non-tariff parts of the convention. We are going to resist this on two main grounds: first, that we simply haven't got the high-level skilled personnel to be in permanent session on all this; and secondly, that the tariff negotiations must not be separated from the non-tariff matters, or the whole thing will collapse, because none of the other countries will take it seriously until they really see the American tariff coming down. Our proposal is to have a Dominions conference about the non-tariff matters in July in London, to have a general educative meeting of the Preparatory Committee in October and the meeting of the Nuclear countries next March to get commitments on tariffs and non-tariff matters. I agreed with this but I urged strongly (and later briefed the Lord President to this effect) that the Dominions meeting for July should be put off if the American Congress rejected the Loan Agreement.[9] I could see nothing but confusion from an Empire meeting on Commercial Policy discussing what to do if the loan were rejected before an exhaustive examination of all the issues by officials and Ministers in London. (This problem has all subsequently become more academic, I am glad to say, since today brings the news that the Senate has passed the Loan Agreement [on 10 May].)

A special problem has arisen in this connection, on which we had a special meeting in Liesching's room (Liesching, Helmore, Shackle and

[9] TN(46) 3rd Meeting, 3 May 1946, CAB134/711.

Young; Snelling; Coulson; myself and Fleming), namely whether or not at the meeting of the Economic and Social Council which opens in New York this month we should try to prevent the Economic and Employment Commission of the Council from being set to work to prepare for the Employment Policy part of the Agenda of the Trade Conference.[10] The point is that in view of the delicate situation about timing outlined above and also in view of the fact that Australia, who is so vitally keen on international employment policy, is not a member of the Economic and Social Council but is a member of the Nuclear countries to negotiate ITO, we want the forthcoming meeting of the Economic and Social Council to make as little reference as possible to the Trade Conference. On the other hand, Fleming and I are very keen that the Economic and Employment Commission should as soon as possible start substantive work on its central problem of international employment policy. The general conclusion was that we should aim at getting it to start a study on this subject for the Council, but not that it should start to prepare the agenda on this topic for the Trade Conference. The Council could, of course, make any study available to the Trade Conference. Marcus Fleming, who is going to the Economic and Social Council and the Trade Conference! It is nice to see the Economic Section making itself useful.
the Specialised Agencies and UNO, is now also to be briefed by the Board of Trade (who in present circumstances find it almost impossible to send a representative) on the whole subject of the relationship between the Economic and Social Council and the Trade Conference£ It is nice to see the Economic Section making itself useful.

Actually Marcus Fleming will have another duty while in New York. There is at the same time to be a meeting in Washington of the Food and Agriculture Organisation to discuss the prospects of food supplies next year. It is feared that John Orr may try to raise the whole question of his fantastic and extravagant World Food Plan which I have recorded in an earlier entry. Broadley of the Ministry of Food tried to persuade me to go to Washington on the UK delegation in case this should happen; but with all that there is on and with Fleming in New York, it did not seem desirable.[11] We have arranged that Marcus Fleming should be available for consultation by the UK FAO delegation. We have also provided them with a short brief, drafted by Philip Chantler, explaining how the proper use of all the existing and projected international agencies (the Fund, Bank, Economic and Social Council, and Trade Organisation) would really bring abour Orr's beloved food plan, by maintaining demand in backward and other countries, by freeing the channels of world trade and by devising an unrestrictive commodity policy, leaving for FAO the very important and proper, if limited, task of taking measures to improve nutritional policies and agricultural techniques throughout the world. (Incidentally, I have had lunch with Enfield of the Ministry of Agriculture and took the opportunity of raising these points with him as well as

[10] Summary of meetings in Liesching's room, 9 May 1946, T236/702. The UNESCO meeting took place 25 May-1 June 1946.

[11] Above, p. 257.

discussing the importance of preserving regional differences in agricultural wage-rates, of which I have written above.)[12]

Rowe-Dutton of the Treasury has written to ask us to give the economic argument in favour of the Interpretative Declaration which we are putting forward at the International Monetary Fund to the effect that we must be counted as having a 'fundamental disequilibrium' (and thus the right to depreciate) if we have 'persistent and chronic' unemployment arising from pressure on our balance of payments. They wish to brief Bolton as to the lines on which we should support this. I gave an argument on the following lines: 'Basically we believe a fundamental disequilibrium to mean an adverse balance of payments. If a country (assuming that it is not unreasonably restricting normal capital imports or failing to restrict abnormal capital exports) is chronically and persistently losing reserves, then it should have the option of depreciating. Our declaration is a gloss on this. A country may have heavy general unemployment at home and an equilibrium in its balance of payments, which would be upset if it expanded domestically to create employment. In these circumstances it should be able to expand domestically and to depreciate in order to deal with the consequential upset of its balance of payments.' Rowe-Dutton has sent my argument forward in the Treasury just as it stands.[13] This is grand because it covers the wider issue of what is meant by a fundamental disequilibrium itself. We shall now get that linked directly to the Balance of Payments and not to any absurd idea of the level of prices and costs etc. Rowe-Dutton's suggestion is that Bolton should be instructed to get my argument officially recorded *verbatim*. I hold my breath to see what will happen!

I have written a letter to Coulson in the Foreign Office on the problem of organising trade with the countries of South-East Europe.[14] The main theme of my letter is that if the difficulties of trade with these countries is that their currencies are overvalued we should do all we can to get their currencies adjusted: (i) if they wish to become members of the IMF, by insisting on a reasonable initial par value for their currency; (ii) if they are members of the IMF, by getting them to apply for depreciation under Article IV; (iii) if they are not members of the IMF, by trying to persuade them to depreciate and, if they won't do so, by allowing our exporters to sell blocked balances of their currency in the London money market for what they will fetch, i.e. at a depreciated rate (a thing which we are not allowed to do if they are members of IMF). I am quite sure that in the international sphere the fundamental condition on which one can hope to get reasonably liberal arrangements is to get exchange rates suitably adjusted. Otherwise one is bound to have quantitative regulation of trade, compensation or barter deals, etc., etc.

We have had a staff meeting at which Fleming gave us a very interesting account of the structure and growth of the Economic and Social Council and its subsidiary organs from Dumbarton Oaks[15] to the present day.

12 pp. 261–2.

13 Rowe-Dutton to Meade, 2 May, Meade to Rowe-Dutton, 7 and 8 May, and Rowe-Dutton to Meade, 10 May 1946, T230/83.

14 Meade to Coulson, 9 May 1946, T230/137.

15 The preliminary meeting to set up the United Nations Organisation held in Washington DC in 1944.

I have had a strange interview with Eady who sent for me. He started by saying how important it was, since the death of Keynes, that we should co-operate on all the external financial stuff and gave an almost perfect account of what the ideal relationship between the Treasury and the Economic Section should be. He then went on to say that the sort of work in which they wanted most help now that Keynes was dead was in the general economic interpretation of the Balance of Payments figures. I naturally thought that he was going to add that he hoped the Economic Section would help them over this. But not a bit of it. What he added was that as Edgar Jones was going to be sent to Washington he wondered whether the Section would release a junior person to replace Edgar Jones in the Treasury. The man is truly unaccountable.

I attended the first of a course of lectures which Viner is giving at the London School of Economics on international economic and financial relations. It was a good eloquent plea for the philosophy behind Article VII, Bretton Woods, ITO and all that. Not very much in the way of economic analysis or argument (perhaps that will come in his later lectures) but something which warms the heart of one who has striven hard for this philosophy in this country during a period of years in which all the economists in favour of it have been in Government service and therefore muzzled.[16]

I have had lunch with Coombs the Australian who runs a Department not unlike the Economic Section in Canberra. I explained to him how our organisation works. He wants to send one of his men to work for a year in the Economic Section. I like this idea, provided one could be sure that he would act as a *UK* official and not reveal anything to the Australians. I have spoken to Norman Brook about this who takes the same line.[17]

I attended a cocktail party given by Norman Brook to entertain the officials who have accompanied the Dominions Prime Ministers on their present talks.[18]

Rosenstein-Rodan lunched with me at the Reform Club to discuss details of the idea that some members of the Economic Section should give some lectures at University College next academic year. This now has official approval.[19] The next step is for me tentatively to approach some of the Economic Section people to see if they would welcome invitations.

Margaret and I attended the memorial service for Lord Keynes in Westminster Abbey.[20] It was a most impressive ceremony. Although I do not believe in all the Christian theology and dogma which lies behind it (and I am sure Keynes did not), it was certainly very, very moving and somehow or another very fitting. 'Let us now praise famous men . . .' and 'I will not cease from mental strife . . . until we have built Jerusalem in England's green and pleasant land' are somehow exactly right for Keynes.

[16] Viner's lectures were not published, but his views are recorded in his 'International finance in the post-war world', *Lloyds Bank Review*, no. 2, October 1946, pp. 3–17, reprinted in his *International Economics*. Glencoe, Ill.: Free Press, 1951.

[17] Trevor Swan was seconded to the Section August 1947–December 1948.

[18] Taking place 23 April–23 May 1946.

[19] See above, pp. 246 and 258.

[20] On 2 May 1946. There is a copy of the order of service in Meade Papers 3/9.

Most of the Cabinet were there; the City; the Civil Service; the academic world; and the artistic world. And Keynes' old father (aged 93) and his mother were with Lydia among the small family group. Poor Lydia looked truly heartbroken.

# 20

## June 1946

*7 June 1946*

After much discussion and after a full meeting of the Economic Survey Working Party we have now completed and sent to Bridges our final version of the Economic Survey for 1946/7.[1] Our general conclusions are: (i) As far as the gap between global demand and supply is concerned, on the basis of current departmental programmes and policy (particularly after the severe cuts in the programmes for the Armed Forces and their Supplies which resulted from our previous Survey)[2] the position is probably manageable. (ii) This does not, however, of course mean that there is not an acute continuing inflationary pressure. If demand were not vigorously controlled, there would be a wild rise in prices. It merely means that current departmental programmes and aspirations are now nearly self-consistent. (iii) The indications are that the excess of global demand over supply is likely to continue in, and possibly get worse in, 1947, when the release of factors from demobilisation will be over, but the development of civilian programmes for personal consumption and for export etc. will be developing. We suggest that we should straightaway put in hand a Survey for 1947/48. (iv) The main immediate problem is, however, the problem of getting resources into the right occupations. The difficulty of our manning-up coal-mining, for example, may lead to a lack of coal which will paralyse industry next winter. Similar particular 'bottlenecks' exist in textiles, building materials and agriculture. (v) The one possibility of increasing the supply of labour considerably is through the use of foreign labour. (vi) We raise the problem of how to control the situation. Direct controls over labour are more or less gone. To get the right things produced on the right scale must depend more and more upon the price mechanism, e.g. getting more textiles produced by making the prices and wages in textiles more attractive to producers. But so long as we have an excessive total demand over supply, in the interests of anti-inflationary action we may be unable to allow any let-up on the general control of prices, in case any small relaxation of the anti-inflationary dam should let loose the whole flood.

[1] EC(S)(46)24 (Revise), 'Economic Survey for 1946/47, Report by the Economic Survey Working Party', June 1946, T230/21. The draft report, excluding the final section, had been circulated for discussion in the Section on 17 May, the conclusions on 22 May (EC(S)(46)24 and ESWP/5/46, T230/58).

[2] See above, p. 212.

Now that the Survey for 1946/47 is out of the way, we have started again to think a bit about the problem of a Survey for 1950. Saunders of the Ministry of Labour has put in useful papers on the working population and the probable level of minimum unemployment. I have arranged that Shackle in the Economic Section should be available to work on this subject. Tress has held a meeting of the working statisticians from the CSO, Board of Trade, Treasury, and Ministry of Labour to get a new start on it.[3]

We have had a visit from Dr Firestone of the department of reconstruction in Ottawa. He has shown us the general forecasts of national income and expenditure which they have done, which are very much on the lines of our own. I got Bridges' permission to let him read our two Surveys. Firestone has proposed a joint meeting of the Canadians, the Americans and ourselves for this autumn in Ottawa to discuss techniques. We have agreed in principle. It is, of course, very encouraging to see this possibility of joint UK-North American action on methods of preserving a high and stable level of total demand.[4]

A most fundamental and important development has taken place in all this Economic Planning. Bridges circulated to the Budget Committee the minute which I sent him a few weeks ago [above, p. 260] on future budgetary problems, in which I suggested (i) an examination into the possibility of an annual capital tax as a new source of revenue, (ii) an examination into the possibility of a progressive tax on inheritances (as opposed to estates) and in particular of my suggestion that the progression should relate to the total amount which each person had inherited up to date, (iii) a consideration of the way in which income tax post-war credits should be handled, particularly from the point of view of controlling total consumption expenditure, (iv) the problem of tapering off the cost-of-living subsidies and (v) the idea that we should consider the balance of revenue and expenditure for, say, 1950 in order to see whether any new important source of revenue was necessary. The Budget Committee went through this.[5] They are going to suggest an enquiry into (i). The enquiry into (ii) should be postponed, because we cannot do everything at once and I agreed that this particular reform could be done later just as well as now. On (iii) they decided to go (in the interests of anti-inflation policy) for the longest possible postponement of repayment. On (iv) they are taking a drastic line. With increased agricultural wage-rates and with rising overseas prices of wheat the position is getting out of hand. The annual cost of the subsidies which was reckoned at £335m. for 1946/47 is expected to be running at £415m. by the end of the year. A draft report has been prepared by the Budget Committee for the Chancellor on this in order to

[3] ESWP(46)7 and 8, 'The Working Population of Great Britain 1945–1950, Provisional Estimates by the Ministry of Labour', 31 May, and 'Normal Level of Unemployment: 1946–50 Provisional Estimates by the Ministry of Labour', T230/61. Tress's meeting took place on 6 June (CAB139/168).

[4] Meade recorded the meeting, between Firestone, Meade, Tress and Stafford on 21 May 1946, in Meade to Brook and Bridges, 22 May 1946, CAB139/162. Tress went to North America to discuss economic forecasting in August 1946 (below, p. 311).

[5] At 'a small informal meeting' on 29 May: Bridges to Trend, 27 May 1946, T171/389.

bring him up against the fact that the position is really serious.[6] The tapering-off must start. (Incidentally, on commenting later on this draft I raised the point that we should aim for 1947/48 not merely at a balanced budget, but at a budget surplus, if we were to pay more than lip-service to the idea that surpluses should be raised when we are fighting inflation in order to allow deficits to be made when we are fighting deflation.) On (v) some investigation of a more long-period balance should be made in the autumn.

But the great event, for which I have been long waiting, was that the Economic Section were asked to prepare for the Budget Committee a full dress paper on the control of inflation.[7] I had an uncanny feeling of having stepped into Keynes' shoes. At last we can really link up the Economic Plan and Budgetary Policy. If we can pull this off, it will be a really important gain for effective Liberal-Socialism. We shall be on the road to control the economic system not by an infinite series of *ad hoc* and illiberal controls but by a general financial policy for the control of the main lines of national expenditure.

I have mobilised all forces for the supreme test! Dow is writing a passage on the relation between the demand for and supply of consumption goods in 1946/47 and 1947/48, although the 1947/48 position is bound to remain very uncertain until we have done a proper Survey for 1947/48. (Incidentally, it was agreed at the Budget Committee that the correct procedure was to do an Economic Survey for 1947/48 for the Steering Committee, which would deal, as usual, with the general problem of the use of our resources, and on the basis of this to write a special report for the Budget Committee on the problem of inflation. This is absolutely right.) Miss Watts is doing a lot of work on the Cost-of-Living Index and problems connected with it.[8] I have had discussions with Proctor and Tress. I am going to call on Gould in the Ministry of Labour next week on certain problems of wage-rates and the cost of living.

Meanwhile I have completed a first outline of the paper which falls into the following sections. I. I distinguish between two methods of controlling inflation: the first, Direct Control (price control, rationing, etc.) which means that people cannot spend all their incomes because there is an excess demand which, coming up against price control, results in shop shortages and forced savings; and secondly, Financial Control which cuts off excess spending power (e.g. by taxation) so that there is a more equal balance between demand and supply. I deploy three arguments in favour of shifting the emphasis more on to Financial Control: first, that Direct Control reduces the incentive to work (for example, voluntary absenteeism among miners is largely due to the fact that in a small number of days' work miners can earn all that they can spend at present controlled prices); second, that it paralyses all effective 'Planning in a Free Society' (i.e. the use of relative prices and wages to get the right things produced) because the fact that

[6] 'Cost of Living Subsidies, Draft Report by the Budget Committee', 3 June 1946, T161/1299/S53992/7.

[7] 'Control of Inflation', [June 1946], T171/389 and Meade Papers 3/10, reprinted in *The Collected Papers of James Meade*, Vol. I, chapter 17; see below, pp. 281–2.

[8] See below p. 281.

there is a potential excess inflationary demand in every market means that fears of letting loose the inflationary flood inhibit one from allowing increases in prices and wage rates in the 'bottleneck' sectors of the economy; and, third, that the use of Direct Control is costly in administrative manpower and leads to petty bureaucratic annoyance. II. A quantitative analysis between the potential monetary demand for goods and services (a) in consumption markets and (b) in investment markets in 1946/47 and 1947/48. III. A section on the problem of wage-rates and the cost of living. The cost-of-living subsidies are very inflationary in the sense that, if they are financed by an increased budget deficit or a reduced budget surplus, they increase by so much the excess of global demand over supply. Would, however, their removal and the consequential increase in the cost of living lead to an inflation of wage-rates? I cast some doubt on the closeness of the connection by reference to the fact that wage-rates have risen during the war at much the same rate after the stabilisation of the cost of living as before the stabilisation policy. I suggest four possible lines of 'bargain' with the Trade Union movement over this: first, introduce the new cost-of-living index, containing drink, tobacco and entertainments, and then reduce these indirect taxes somewhat as the subsidies are tapered off. The index will rise less than the old one (in which subsidised foods had a very heavy weight and there was no weight for drink, tobacco and entertainments). Second, consider the possibility of introducing some idea of a subsistence legal minimum wage (equal, say, to what the worker could get in unemployment benefit) closely tied to a cost-of-living index on condition that all the other part of wages was in fact untied. This would almost certainly involve tying all social security benefits closely to the cost-of-living index and the removal of the subsidies would therefore cost a good deal in extra social security benefits. Third, consider the possibility of some increase in children's allowances when the subsidies are removed so that one is concentrating on those who need it (i.e. large families with small means) the help which was previously being given indiscriminately by reducing the price of foodstuffs to everyone (including the millionaires with no dependents). Fourthly, use the net savings on the cost-of-living subsidies to finance the Employment Stabilisation Fund mentioned in the next section. IV. If we are to make a reality of a budgetary policy which raises a surplus when there are inflationary tendencies to offset and incurs deficits when there is deflation to fight, we must have a surplus next year. But we must be prepared to have a deficit in the near future. Increased productivity may so increase the total output of goods and services that within a comparatively few years' time we may need to be stimulating expenditure. Here I make two suggestions. First, post-war tax credits should be repaid by paying the whole lot over now into special savings accounts bearing interest at, say, 2½ per cent; but these accounts should be blocked, and it should only be possible to draw on them later (in frequent – e.g. monthly – amounts so as to make them approximate as closely as possible to spendable income rather than to capital receipts) at a date and at a rate which is desired expressly to maintain consumers' expenditure. Secondly, institute an annual payment of £200m. from the budget into an Employment Stabilisation Fund. This will correspond to a

Sinking Fund in times of inflation. In times of deflation payments will be made out of the Fund for the various purposes (e.g. repayment of tax credits, balancing of the National Insurance Fund when National Insurance Contributions are reduced) of maintaining total demand. The ordinary orthodox principles of budget balancing can then be applied to the ordinary budget.

There has been a meeting of the Investment Working Party which Sayers and I attended. First, they discussed the problem of bringing under the review of the Working Party all large projects of capital investment costing £500,000 or more. Secondly, they discussed our general paper on the control of investment.[9] I said that its purpose was to express unease on two points:- (i) that we might be in for a longish period of excess pressure of demand in the market for investment goods, and all we had to deal with it was building licensing. Might we not need some more generalised control (e.g. an expenditure ration for investment) which covered machinery as well as building? (ii) Secondly, the number of hoops which a wretched investor had to go through now in order to be permitted to raise the money for investment, to satisfy the planning and location of industry considerations, and to obtain the necessary building licence was formidable. Might we not run the risk of so clogging the machine that we could not let up on investment sufficiently quickly if we found we had to offset a deflationary pressure? The plan was in general for a more simplified and generalised method of controlling investment.

Incidentally, the present policy of ultra-cheap money[10] in a period of great stringency as far as real resources is concerned is having a peculiar effect. Every industry is going round making plans for investment on the assumption that 3 per cent or even 2½ per cent represents the true 'opportunity cost' for capital. Then a little man in a bowler hat with an application form for a building licence to be filled in in triplicate runs round to start the process of scaling all the demands down – not in the economic way of asking everyone to do their calculations on a 10 per cent basis but on some mystical principle of social priorities. Of course, there are serious disadvantages in raising the rate of interest, particularly in the burden which the increased interest on the national debt would put on the budget and in the difficulties which might arise later in bringing the rate down again when the stringency is over. What attracts me at the moment is a tax on capital goods (building and machinery) which corresponds in its effect to a higher rate of interest for new investment without affecting the terms of existing indebtedness. Meanwhile the passion for investment continues. Even at a 2½ per cent rate of interest and comparing total costs on the new plant with *total* (instead of prime) costs on the old plant, the Cotton Working Party Report which I am just reading can show hardly any saving through new investment, but recommends a huge programme.[11] It is,

[9] INV.WP(46)6, Minutes of the Meeting of the Working Party on 28 May 1946, and IWP(46)7, 'Direct Controls on Investment and the Preliminaries to Investment, Note by the Economic Section', 1 May 1946, T230/86.

[10] Chancellor of the Exchequer Hugh Dalton's policy of trying to reduce interest rates on government debt to 2½ per cent from 3 per cent for long-term bonds; in June 1946 a 20-year bond at 2½ per cent was currently on offer.

[11] Tripartite working parties for the cotton, furniture, hosiery and footwear, and pottery industries had been set up by Cripps in 1945 'to examine and inquire into the various

however, fair to add that they have done their sums on the basis of current wage-rates in the textile industries, while to attract the labour force which would be necessary with the old-fashioned machinery to produce the needed output of textiles might require a much higher wage-rate. If one did the sums on the basis of this higher wage-rate, the balance would come out more favourably to investment.

I have delivered my old, old lecture on Full Employment and how we are setting about it twice more. First, to the assembled generals, admirals and air-marshals of the Imperial Defence College with General Sir William Slim in the chair; and secondly to one of the training courses for a batch of assistant principals who have just been admitted to the Civil Service.

Miss Kilroy has had a meeting of her Board of Trade interdepartmental committee on the principles which should govern the operations of statutory boards set up to supervise industries, in order to ensure that they do not indulge in restrictive practices. There was a very feeble Board of Trade paper before us. It had some good sentiments, but there were so many let-outs that all the assembled representatives of all the agricultural and other departments which were watching the interests of their organised monopolies were able to agree. I fear that I made a nuisance of myself and argued that we must be much more stringent in our attitude. We are now drafting a full dress Economic Section paper on the subject. John Wood has been collecting together a good deal of factual information about the agricultural marketing boards in the past; Sayers has written an analytical note on the subject; and Chantler is now engaged in preparing a draft paper. We shall take the line that as we are now going to have full employment the case for restrictive boards, which was never strong, is now non-existent; that boards made up of organised producers as opposed to outsiders are very dangerous; that there are some fairly innocuous activities (such as a levy for a central research organisation, or the grading of qualities of the product); that some marketing functions, such as co-operative marketing to take advantage of economies in large-scale marketing or to by-pass monopolistic middlemen, may be permissible, though they should always be safeguarded by the twofold rule that the organisation should be required to take and to market any amount of the product which any producer may wish to produce; that organised schemes for the stabilisation of prices received by producers either by buffer stock schemes or by price insurance schemes (e.g. a levy on sales in times of high price to subsidise sales in times of low price) may be desirable (Incidentally a report by a working party on Colonial Products under Caine in the Colonial Office, and which Marcus Fleming has attended for us, suggests dealing with colonial primary products by price insurance schemes. This is an enormous improvement in principle over the pre-war quantitative restriction schemes which were fashionable for primary products

schemes and suggestions put forward for improvements of organisation, production and distribution methods and processes in the industry, and to report on the steps which should be taken in the national interest to strengthen the industry and to render it more stable and more capable of meeting competition in the home and foreign markets'. The Cotton Industry Working Party Report was discussed by the LPC on 31 May 1946 (LP(46) 19th meeting, CAB132/1) and subsequently published (London: HMSO).

domestically and internationally); that schemes to maintain minimum prices to consumers, limitation of output, limitation of new entry or of capacity should never be allowed; that if a depression of a particular industry leads to the necessity for temporary help this help should take the form of a temporary and tapering subsidy; and that if, in spite of this, it is decided to allow output restriction and price maintenance occasionally in these special circumstances, such schemes should be (a) temporary, (b) on a definite predetermined schedule of tapering off, and (c) never administered by the organised producers.[12] I wonder what will be the outcome of this!

The question has arisen of the way in which the prospective rise in agricultural wages should be dealt with. The Chancellor has argued, in order to avoid on the one hand increased subsidies and on the other hand allowing the cost of living to rise, that some pooling arrangement should be worked out whereby the increased labour costs should be offset for the marginal producer without giving increased profits to the intra-marginal producer. Vandepeer at the Ministry of Agriculture held a meeting which Chantler and I attended. I suggested that a theoretical and administrative possibility might be to raise the price to all farmers and to finance the increased subsidies by a levy on all farm profits; but I did not think that at this period of food crisis when EPT [Excess Profits Tax] was generally being abolished, it would be possible to institute, as it were, a special profits tax for agriculture. The only other possibility which came out of the meeting was to extend the use of the acreage payment as opposed to a straight increase of price, since the former would help more the farmer on land where the output per acre is low. Too much reliance on this would, however, mean that farmers did not farm up to the intensive margin and would also put a premium on inefficient farming.[13]

I wrote the Chancellor of the Exchequer a minute on the problem of New Towns commenting on a paper on the subject by Douglas Jay which he had circulated.[14] Jay had suggested that building in New Towns should start first in the development areas where there is not quite so severe a stringency of labour and other factors required for building. I argued that this was foolish. The development areas were places where there was a superfluity on the whole of social capital (housing, drainage etc.), but a great lack of suitable new factories. Build factories, not new towns in these areas. If people are to be moved from their homes and new social capital constructed for them, do not choose the development areas, but those areas where development is most economical. Jay had also referred to the danger that new towns not in the development areas might suck industry

[12] Minutes of first meeting, 24 May 1946; SBC1, 'Supervisory Boards Committee: Memorandum by the Board of Trade', BT64/306; SBC2, 'Supervisory Boards and Restrictive Practices, Memorandum by the Economic Section', 18 June 1946, T230/22 and BT64/306; 'Working Party on Colonial Products, Interim Report', 21 May 1946, BT64/306; see below p. 286.

[13] LP(46)129, 'Agricultural Prices and Wages', Memorandum by the Chancellor of the Exchequer, 7 June 1946, CAB132/3. No record of Vandepeer's meeting has been found.

[14] LP(DI)(46)17, 'New Towns: Note by the Chancellor of the Exchequer', 21 May 1945, covering Jay's 'New Towns and the Distribution of Industry', CAB124/789. Meade's minute has not been found.

and population from the development areas. I said that I agreed that it was in principle desirable to ensure that the new towns built (e.g. near London) to deal with congested areas should draw their industry from the areas to be de-congested rather than attracting new industry away from the development areas. But why be upset if some population is drawn from the development areas? Surely the sensible policy is to bring some new industry into the development areas and to combine this with the transfer of some mobile labour out of the development areas.

This latter point I have taken up in a letter to Sir John Woods at the Board of Trade. A personal report by Dennison and Wood on Reconstruction in the various Regions which criticised the development area policy on the grounds that mobile labour should be transferred out of these areas, drew from Woods the remark that one had to choose between either bringing industry into these regions or transferring labour wholesale out of them. I wrote to say that I couldn't see why one shouldn't combine bringing the work to the men and the men to the work.[15]

There have been two lunch meetings at the National Institute of Economic and Social Research of the informal group of Economists (Stone, Hicks and myself) and Accountants (Rees, Sewell Bray, Norris) to discuss common problems (e.g. definition and measurement of income, profit, etc.).[16] It looks as if these are going to be profitable meetings. Two new ideas at least have already occurred to me as a result of them. (i) Ask firms at the Census of Production to give figures of their stocks at the beginning and end of the year valued as for income tax and balance-sheet purposes and also valuing at the end of the year each item of stock at the price used for the valuation of that item for income-tax purposes at the beginning of the year. One would then be able to get an idea of the value (at beginning-period prices) of the increase in stock and to correct any profit figures for the differences between this and the increase in stocks as valued for income-tax purposes. (ii) Get the Census of Production and the Inland Revenue Schedule D figures tabulated in such a way as to show for each industry separately those companies which closed their books in the 1st quarter, those in the 2nd quarter etc. This would enable one to have a quarterly chain series. At present these periods are all jumbled up in both cases.

In the international sphere I have spent a great deal of time drafting, holding staff meetings etc. in order to prepare an Economic Section paper on International Employment Policy. I think that it is important that at the forthcoming conference on Trade and Employment the UK should be among the countries which will stress the Employment as well as the Trade part of the conference. On its merits we shall in fact be able to maintain liberal commercial policies only if the worst world depressions are avoided; and we want to resist any tendency which may show itself on the American side to suggest that freer trade itself gives greater employment. It does nothing of the kind. It gives a more economical use of resources,

15 EC(S)(46)23, Dennison and Wood, 'Reconversion in the Regions', 13 May 1946, T230/21 and CAB124/640. Meade's letter is on the latter file.

16 See above, p. 220. The meetings were held on 24 May and 3 June 1946. Minutes of the meetings, and copies of the papers discussed, are in Meade Papers 3/12.

but measures to maintain total demand are necessary to give full employment. Politically it is also important that we should use the popular 'full employment' tool to help build the less fashionable structure of liberal trade; and thus we must make it clear that we take the Employment part of the conference seriously. Before he went to New York for the Economic and Social Council Marcus Fleming left a draft paper on this subject on the basis of which I wrote a paper which I have sent to Shackle and Liesching in the Board of Trade. In this we have argued (i) that domestic full employment policies are essential and that countries should recognise their international as well as their national duty to maintain total demand internally; (ii) that there are a number of possibilities through the new international organisations of getting some direct international control over total demand, in particular through (a) the organisation of international buffer stock schemes for primary products, (b) the planning and timing of capital works financed through the International Bank [for Reconstruction and Development] or of international projects of development supervised by the Economic Development sub-committee of the Economic and Employment Commission of the Economic and Social Council, (c) the movement of capital funds to countries which are having an adverse balance of payments because they have internal policies of expansion in conditions of world depression, which help to sustain total world demand but at the temporary expense of their balance of payments, and (d) concerted action through the International Monetary Fund for expanding the supply of, and reducing the cost of, credit; (iii) that countries which maintain domestic demand successfully and which thereby get into balance of payments difficulties in a world of depression should have adequate means (through exchange rate adjustment, restriction of imports and/or the discriminatory restriction of imports from a 'scarce currency' country) of protecting their balance of payments; and (iv) that there should be a general international convention to establish these principles and to give the Economic and Social Council the job of co-ordinating all the necessary action.[17]

Generally my draft differs from Marcus Fleming's in two respects. Both are reducible to a common factor: I have confined myself to what could be done in terms of the international organisations as they already exist or are contemplated; Marcus produced a more utopian scheme in two respects. First, he laid down the principle that the International Monetary Fund should lend without any limit to any country which maintained employment at home in a world slump and thereby had a balance of payments difficulty, provided only that the Fund could ask this country to depreciate if its currency were overvalued from a long-term point of view. Indeed Marcus went further than this and rather suggested that countries would be obliged to maintain employment by domestic expansion and to 'import unemployment' from unemployment countries and should not be permitted to protect their balances of payments by import restrictions or by

[17] Fleming, 'Note on International Full Employment Policy', 13 May 1946, circulated by Meade on 20 May as EC(S)(46)25, T230/21; Meade, 'International Employment Policy', sent to Liesching on 24 May 1946, T236/702.

exchange depreciation unless their exchanges were overvalued for the long-term point of view. In other words, if the Americans have a slump we must face the adverse balance, borrow from the Fund and expand at home. The argument is that internationally by spreading the problem of counteracting the particular force of deflation at work in the United States throughout all the different countries, the deflation becomes more manageable. Secondly, he suggested that instead of a country in balance of payments difficulties being permitted to impose non-discriminatory restrictions on imports, the other countries should rather give discriminatory advantages to their imports from it. There is much to be said for this theoretically. But both points are so far removed from the general settlement as contemplated that I suppressed them. I had sent my paper to the Board of Trade before I heard that the talks with the Dominions on these subjects are not likely to be until September or October.[18] But now there will probably be an opportunity of having considerable discussion on this with Marcus before carrying it much further interdepartmentally.

There has been some further activity on the problem of the conditions in which it should be permissible to impose quantitative restrictions on imports in order to preserve a country's balance of payments. Coombs of Australia has produced a most infernally elaborate and complicated arithmetical formula based on movements in reserves etc. to determine whether a country should be permitted to restrict imports. The following thought occurred to me. A general formula will not do because what suits one country's conditions does not suit another. But when we gave up a general formula for all tariffs (e.g. a tariff ceiling, or a 50 per cent cut in every tariff) we turned, not to a few vague aspirations (we undertake only to have moderate tariffs) but to the great precision of hard-headed bilateral negotiations of all tariff rates. Why not do the same in this case? Let every country have its own precise formula as to the conditions in which it will impose import restrictions, each formula suited to the conditions of each country; but let there be a grand bilateral-multilateral bargain in which each country says 'I will make my formula tighter in this particular respect if you will make your formula tighter in that particular respect'. I sent this idea to Shackle in the Board of Trade and Waley in the Treasury. As might have been expected, the former liked it and the latter did not![19]

We have now had a meeting in Waley's room in the Treasury with the Board of Trade, Bank of England and Economic Section. We got a more or less agreed draft with the following important points of disagreement which will have to go to Ministers: (i) The Board of Trade and we would like to encourage this idea of a separate arithmetical test suitable for each country; the Treasury and Bank won't look at it. (ii) Most important of all, the Treasury and the Bank of England won't have any reference to the fact that a country should undertake not to permit capital exports which might have reasonably been prevented nor to interfere unreasonably with capital imports when they are appealing to the state of their reserves as

[18] They took place on 15 October–26 November 1946.

[19] See Shackle to Meade, 30 April and Meade to Shackle, 13 May 1946, T230/9, and Meade to Waley, 21 May 1946, T236/697.

justifying the use of import restrictions. Shackle of the Board of Trade and I, both at the meeting and in subsequent letters, have argued with as much force as possible that the absence of any such clause would enable any country at any time by encouraging a sufficient net export of capital to justify any import restrictions which it might want to impose on protective grounds. (iii) The Bank are most anxious to have an almost unlimited provision which would allow a country to discriminate in favour of a country of whose currency the former holds a blocked balance. But this might put a frightful premium on having an inconvertible currency; and might lead to more or less permanent bilateral trade arrangements. I am glad to say that Waley did not support Thompson-McCausland of the Bank of England over this. On the other hand, we did have some success in getting the Treasury and the Bank of England to accept a clause which envisaged that if import restrictions on balance of payments grounds went on for two years or more an investigation could be organised to see whether there were not other ways of dealing with the situation.[20]

Shackle in the Board of Trade has had an interdepartmental meeting to consider his draft report on the application of the State Trading principles contained in the Trade Proposals. Some interesting points arose: (i) It is becoming clear to me that the simple way of dealing with discrimination and protection under State Trading, which covers the case where there are differences in the qualities of the imports from various sources is as follows: The same percentage 'protective margin' (i.e. excess of selling price in domestic market over purchase price from foreign supplier) must be levied on every source of supply and the domestic consumers' demands for each source of supply must be fully met. In these circumstances there is no discrimination and a limit to protection. (ii) There was a terrific coming and going over the point that the limitation of the 'protective margin' might mean that we should have to abandon our policy of price stabilisation in this country in those cases in which the foreign price fell below our domestic stabilised price by more than the protective margin. If so, good riddance to bad rubbish, say I. I was asked to redraft this passage of the report in co-operation with Mrs Hollond. I have done my bit in the sense that a mountain is being made out of a molehill. (iii) The old problem arose whether, when import restrictions were being imposed on balance of payments grounds, it should be obligatory to observe the 'protective margins' (it clearly couldn't be obligatory any longer to maintain the obligation to satisfy the full domestic demand). I said that I would much prefer that both obligations should lapse. But I was prepared not to insist, provided that it in no way begged the question whether we should be free to auction import licences or to charge special licence fees when we were dealing with import restrictions by quotas in private trade.[21]

At last our first Overseas Survey is finished. Helmore, A. J. Brown and I called on Norman Brook and we have agreed that it should be circulated to the Lord President's Committee as the work of the Economic Section,

20 'Note of a Meeting in Sir David Waley's room on Thursday, 23rd May 1946, to consider a paper on restrictions to safeguard the Balance of Payments', T230/9; Shackle to Meade, 27 May 1946, T230/137; Meade to Waley, 23 May 1946, T236/697.

21 The minutes of the meeting, on 16 May 1946, and drafts of the report are on T230/176.

undertaken in consultation with the departments on Helmore's official committee on overseas economic intelligence.[22]

The Board of Trade are preparing a film on World Trade to propagate the ideas behind the Trade Proposals. I went to a showing at the Air Ministry of a number of documentary and educational films to show how similar things had been done in the past. One on the Statistical White Paper on the UK war effort. One on Food problems before, during and after the war. The third was Polanyi's very ingenious diagrammatic film about the Trade Cycle. (I feel that there is something fishy about the treatment of money coming into and out of the banks in this film.) Well, I wish the publicity experts luck. I would not be much good at doing a film on the virtues of Free Trade![23]

I had lunch with Thompson-McCausland of the Bank of England when we agreed about the questionableness of maintaining ultra-cheap money in a period of considerable inflationary pressure and disagreed (a) on the desirability of having ultra-cheap money, in spite of the fact that it might be accompanied by very great liquidity, when it was necessary to offset deflation and (b) on the propriety of adjusting one's balance of payments through adjusting one's rate of exchange.

## 30 June 1946

My paper on the Control of Inflation has now been sent forward to the Chancellor.[24] It concludes with five recommendations. I. There should be a shift of emphasis from controlling inflation by means of price controls etc. to a fiscal policy which more nearly adjusts total spendable incomes to the total supplies of goods and services available to be bought. II. In the interests of inflation policy some attention should be given to the possibility of easing off the rate of domestic investment and even of the restoration of the balance of payments in order to increase supplies of goods and services available for consumption. III. A scheme should be devised for the repayment of post-war credits whereby they are all paid into special savings deposits earning interest, but are blocked and only released later as required to influence the total demand for goods and services. IV. The cost-of-living subsidies should be rapidly tapered off, and the process should be eased (i) by the introduction of a new cost-of-living index based on the 1937/8 family budgets, preferably excluding such highly taxed commodities as beer, tobacco and entertainments on the ground that variations in the prices of such commodities merely reflect conscious tax policy. (Nita Watts has done some calculations on this subject which suggest that such an index would now stand at about the same level as the existing official index in relation to September 1939,

22 'Survey of the Overseas Economic Position as how it affects the United Kingdom', 14 June 1946, circulated as EC(S)(46)29 and LP(46)149 (T230/22 and CAB132/3).

23 The White Paper was *Statistics relating to the War Effort of the United Kingdom*, Cmd. 6564, November 1944; Polanyi's film was *Money and Unemployment* (1939).

24 'Control of Inflation', sent to the Chancellor on 17 June 1946, T171/389 and Meade Papers 3/10; see also above pp. 272–4 and below, pp. 292–3.

namely at 132, but that the removal of the cost-of-living subsidies would raise the new index only to 144 and the old index to 153. She has written a paper on this which we are sending to the Ministry of Labour, the Ministry of Food and the Treasury for confirmation. If the calculation is correct, the argument for an early introduction of this new index is very strong. I have spoken to Gould, the chief industrial commissioner at the Ministry of Labour about this, and he is very keen on the idea.)[25]; (ii) by using some of the net savings on cost-of-living subsidies for the purpose of making special concessions on other taxation or expenditure and, in particular, on increasing expenditure on children's allowances; and (iii) by allocating the remainder of the net saving to the Employment Stabilisation Fund mentioned below. V. An Employment Stabilisation Fund should be set up into which a payment of £200m. should be made each year and out of which special payments should be made when the need arises later to stimulate employment. I argue this case on the grounds that next year, if ever, a surplus is required in the interests of stabilisation and employment policy, and that this is a way of making the thing a possible starter politically. (I believe, however, that I have made an error in suggesting that £200m. should be paid into this Fund every year and that the Budget should then be balanced on ordinary orthodox principles. I believe that it would be better to say that in any year in which a surplus is required in the interests of anti-inflation policy this surplus should be paid into the Employment Stabilisation Fund, and that in any year in which a deficit (due either to reduction in taxation or to special expenditure) is required to prevent deflation, the money should be found from the Employment Stabilisation Fund – which would, of course, have the power to borrow. This Fund would then be a mere accounting device to see whether over a period employment policy had led to a net surplus or deficit. If one has a fixed contribution from the budget to the ES Fund of, say, £200m., then the position will break even only when £200m. a year is being paid out of the ES Fund.)

The Steering Committee has now met to consider our Economic Survey for 1946/47.[26] The Committee went through our paper carefully and a number of changes were suggested – all, I think, of relatively minor importance except one which I very much welcomed. This was that we should very considerably expand the passage in our Survey on the threat of inflation. Up to now we have considered the Survey almost solely in terms of the available real resources and the amount of demand which departments upon the basis of current programmes wish to put upon them; we have not considered the magnitude of the 'true requirements', i.e. of what people might try to buy in the absence of price controls, rationing, etc. This latter magnitude we are now discussing, in the same way as it is discussed in my paper for the Budget Committee on the control of inflation. This has the great advantage of linking up more closely our work for the Steering Committee and Economic Planning with budgetary policy.

25 Watts, 'The Cost of Living Index', 16 August 1946, EC(S)(46)31 Revise, T230/22. The new cost-of-living index was introduced in June 1947.

26 ED(46) 3rd meeting, 25 June 1946, T228/20 and CAB134/87.

We have also developed in the same section the possible threat of inflation from increased costs by way of increased wage-rates and have introduced some figures showing the rate at which wage-rates have risen during the war and are still continuing to rise. When one compares this rate of increase with the possible 1½ per cent per annum increase in productivity it becomes clear that unless something radical can be done about it our costs and prices are bound to go on rising appreciably with great detriment to our external competitive position unless either costs and prices rise equally rapidly in other countries or else we are prepared to contemplate a more or less continuous depreciation of the exchange.

There has been another meeting of Gould's working party on wages at the Ministry of Labour to discuss a first draft of a report.[27] I criticised this on the grounds that it was too optimistic about this central problem of wage inflation. Gould was suggesting that the recent round of wage increases marked the attainment of a new post-war settlement, and that we might expect no further considerable change in the next twelve months. I persuaded them to insert a table showing the rate at which wage-rates have increased during the war years and subsequently, which showed what a miracle this sudden reversal of trend (in continuing conditions of excess demand for labour) would be; and I also called attention to the fact that our task was not even the difficult one of stopping all wage increases, it was the more difficult one of permitting wage increases in those vital industries which were undermanned without allowing sympathetic wage increases elsewhere.

There has been a meeting of the Lord President's Ministerial Committee on Economic Planning with the Chancellor of the Exchequer, the Minister of Labour, John Henry Woods (representing the Board of Trade in Cripps' absence in India), Bridges, Gilbert, Jay, Nicholson, Francis Williams and myself. The purpose of the meeting was to discuss the Draft White Paper which had been prepared to show what it would look like if the Economic Survey were published. As recommended by the Steering Committee, it was decided to postpone publication until next year. This, however, raised the question whether the Survey when published should cover the calendar or financial year. On this the Chancellor of the Exchequer argued that he was in favour of the Survey for the calendar year being published and debated in, say, November of the previous year. He was clearly thinking very much in terms of a division of labour between himself and the Lord President, he having his publicity in April on Central Government finance and the Lord President having his innings on the Economic Plan in November. To one who like myself believes that the main instrument in a Liberal-Socialist state for carrying out any plan must be fiscal policy, and who therefore believes that budgetary policy and the economic plan must be as closely linked as possible, this was terrifying. Greatly daring, I intervened in the discussion and argued: (i) that much of our Survey

[27] This is the 'enquiry into the probable course of future wages, costs and prices' sought by the Cabinet in May 1946 (see above, p. 262). Its report, 'Official Working Party on the Trend of Wages Costs and Prices', 22 July 1946, was circulated in July to the Steering Committee on Economic Development and to the LPC (ED(46)21, 26 July 1946, CAB134/188; LP(46)192, 24 July 1946, CAB132/4); see below, pp. 295–6.

material (e.g. the whole of Central Government expenditure and the vast majority of public investment) related to the financial year, and that for this reason forecasts relating to the financial year were likely to be more accurate than those relating to the calendar year and that we could not afford to sacrifice accuracy; and (ii) that as tax policy must be related very closely with the carrying out of the economic plan the two must be closely related. I suggested therefore that we should prepare by November or December each year a first draft of a Survey for the following calendar year, that during January to March this would be available for the Chancellor to consider in connection with his Budget and for the Steering Committee and the Lord President in connection with the general aspects of economic policy, and that after the Budget a final Survey should be prepared without any gaps between demands and supplies and should be published for a general debate on economic affairs in the light of the Budget and of the other decisions which had been taken. The Chancellor misunderstood me to be suggesting that he should discuss his Budget secrets with the Lord President etc. and took me severely to task. I attempted to explain that this had not been my intention at all. It is now left that the Steering Committee should prepare a paper on this issue and Proctor is about to summon a working party for that purpose. Meanwhile the Steering Committee have instructed us provisionally to proceed with the preparation of a Survey for the financial year 1947/8.[28]

At the end of this Ministerial meeting the Lord President suggested that the Steering Committee should set in hand enquiries into (i) the domestic measures which we could adopt for the purposes of offsetting a slump and (ii) the measures which we could take to protect our balance of payments if there were a world slump. After discussion with Proctor and R. W. B. Clarke of the Treasury and John Henry Woods and Helmore of the Board of Trade I wrote a minute to Bridges on how these enquiries might be carried out, suggesting: (i) that the Economic Survey Working Party might prepare a general quantitative estimate of the problem – how much decline in national expenditure by way of a primary decline in investment or in our export trade or of a secondary decline in consumers' expenditure might we have to be prepared to offset; (ii) that Proctor's panels under the Investment Working Party should carry on with their investigation into the extent to which it will be possible to vary the rate at which Public Investment is undertaken; (On this subject Proctor had just previously had a meeting of the Treasury, Board of Trade, Ministry of Health and ourselves to initiate this sort of enquiry. We have split the problem into three questions: (a) how to forecast and measure the amount of public investment that there was ready to be done (in this connection we have already sent out the circulars to and received replies from the local authorities and public utilities and we now wait on the Board of Trade to propose how we shall obtain by sample some indication of the future investment programmes of private enterprise) (b) how to measure the time-lag which may occur between the decision to initiate investment

[28] MEP(46) 3rd meeting, 17 June 1946, discussing MEP(46)3, CAB134/503; ED(46) 3rd meeting, 25 June 1946, T228/20 and CAB134/187.

expenditure and the actual undertaking of the expenditure, and how to reduce those time-lags to a minimum; and (c) a survey of the existing control or influence which the Central Government can exercise over the various investment agencies); (iii) that the Economic Section should put together, and submit to Bridges for his consideration as to the best way of handling the problem, what work it has already done on such fiscal measures as the variation in National Insurance Contributions, timing of repayment of tax credits, variations in direct and indirect taxation, fiscal measures to regulate the extent to which companies will distribute their profits or undertake investment projects; (iv) that the Board of Trade should organise a small group together with the Treasury and the Economic Section to discuss what can be done within the framework of Bretton Woods, ITO, etc. to protect our balance of payments in times of world depression; and (v) that this last enquiry is very closely connected with the line which we should take on International Employment Policy at the forthcoming Conference on Trade and Employment and that the Board of Trade in preparing a brief on this subject should submit it at the same time to Bridges' Steering Committee.[29] (This has proved a very good opportunity for launching our paper on International Employment Policy. The Board of Trade have agreed that we should first discuss it in a huddle with them and the Treasury and I have now sent six copies to Waley, who is sending some out to Grigg and others at the Bank and the Fund in Washington for their observations. The need for some real lead on this subject was well illustrated to my mind at a meeting to which Helmore of the Board of Trade took me with Walter Nash, the New Zealand deputy Prime Minister, to discuss the Employment Policy chapter of the American trade proposals. The whole meeting was at sixes and sevens. A South African representative did nothing but argue that imperial preference gave employment, and everyone argued on the assumption that if you started up an industry by means of protection you produced more wealth – quite regardless of the fact that you might have produced something else even more valuable.)[30]

There have been two more interesting meetings of the group of economists and accountants, at which [Sewell] Bray and Norris argued with Rees in favour of the central registration – not necessarily with public disclosure – of all company accounts in a standard form, so that one could get as much information as possible from the reliable and basic audited accounts rather than from statistical estimates such as those prepared for Census purposes. The economists – i.e. Stone and I – lay back and listened

[29] Meade to Bridges, 21 June 1946, T161/1295/S53261/4. On Proctor's meeting see 'Notes taken at an Informal Meeting in Mr Proctor's room on Tuesday, 18th June, 1946, to discuss INVESTMENT', T161/1297/S53555/01. The enquiries continued intermittently for three years (see T230/214); the Section's first contribution was EC(5)(46)36 Revise, Dow, 'The Possible Magnitude of a Future Depression', 6 November 1946, which Meade sent to Gilbert on 8 November (T230/22, 23 and 24). See also below, pp. 299 and 321–2.

[30] Helmore to Meade, 21 June, and Meade to Waley, 24 June 1946, T236/702; and see below, p. 302. Meade also included a copy of 'International Employment Policy' with his minute to Bridges (see note 29). The meeting to which Helmore took Meade was on 17 June 1946 (T236/702).

with fascination to the two accountants trying to convince their colleague of this admirable idea![31]

Oliver Franks came to supper with us the other day. He spent most of the time arguing about the efficacy of all the work which we were doing on the Steering Committee. Would Ministers when the time came really have the will to act quickly and extensively enough in stimulating total demand so as effectively to avoid a major depression? Were they not more likely to do too little and too late and then to deal with the trouble piecemeal, by particular 'planning' interventions for each industry and region, so that our hopes of anything 'liberal' in the solution were slender? A salutary dose of cold water, but I have not as a result changed my general attempts to set the stage for a 'liberal-socialist' solution.

We have now finished and sent to Miss Kilroy in the Board of Trade our Economic Section paper on Statutory Boards and Restrictive Practices. On the basis of a general analytical paper by Sayers and of factual notes by Wood, Chantler has written an admirable final document of which 36 copies have now been circulated in the Departments.[32] We attempt to outlaw such practices as Quotas fixing maximum output on sales, Minimum Prices, Restriction on Entry or Discrimination in Prices. We argue rather for the development, where appropriate, of co-operative marketing, perhaps on a compulsory basis, given the essential safeguard that the co-operative marketing organisation must be under an obligation to purchase all supplies forthcoming at the price which it quotes and to sell the whole of these supplies sooner or later. Such an arrangement would permit: (a) the short-circuiting of the middlemen where the middlemen had through their monopsonistic power been able to exploit the producers. (Incidentally we point out that an appropriate way to deal with this particular issue is to break the middleman's monopoly or to restrain it by fixing *maximum* – not as in the case of the Milk Marketing Board *minimum* – retail and wholesale margins.); (b) the enjoyment of the advantages of large-scale marketing; and (c) obtaining greater stability of prices for the producers either by a buffer stock arrangement or by charging higher prices to consumers than those paid to producers in times of high demand or low supplies in order to finance the opposite arrangement in the opposite conditions. This, combined with some general subsidy or some degree of protection against imports, should enable us to carry out our agricultural policy without resorting to any of the objectionable restrictive practices noted above. We now wait to see what is the reaction in departments.

The problem of the immediate output of coal next winter which is one of the main themes of our Economic Survey has been brought to a head, momentarily, by the proposal for a five-day week in the coal mines. We wrote a very strong minute to the Lord President warning him of the dangers in the coming winter if this problem is not put right – people cold in their homes and unemployed because of the shortage of fuel in their

31 On 12 and 21 June: minutes in Meade Papers 3/12.

32 'Supervisory Boards and Restrictive Practices, Memorandum by the Economic Section', EC(S)(46)30, T230/22, BT64/306 and Meade Papers 3/2. On its preparation see above, pp. 275–6.

factories on top of bread rationing and the shortage of food. We suggested that it should be a hard-and-fast condition of granting the five-day week to the miners that they should accept the large-scale introduction of foreign labour (and particularly of Poles) into the pits. I went with Douglas Jay and Max Nicholson to urge this on the Lord President, and xenophobe though he is, he fully agreed. Yet in the result, I fear, the Minister of Fuel and Power has got away with approval of the five-day week without any precise condition about the introduction of foreign labour.[33]

The problem of compensation and betterment has come up again as the draft bill is now before Ministers. I briefed the Lord President on the old lines that we fear that the present proposals may gravely hold up development, since the owner of land with development value will in effect own the existing use of the land without owning the development value. If the proposed Land Commission charges a Betterment (i.e. really a Development) charge on the land which is equal to the greater part of its development value (and it must do this if it is to be sure of collecting in this way the greater part of the funds to finance compensation), then the existing landowner will have little or no incentive to develop. The wretched developer will now have to deal (a) with the planning authority to get his development approved, (b) with the Land Commission to get the development value of the land and (c) with the existing landowner to get the land itself, this last person having no incentive to sell. We shall have to rely more and more, I expect, on compulsory purchase by the Land Commission, a power which has now been introduced as a result of our earlier representations to the Lord President [above, pp. 170–1]. The whole subject has, however, been simplified, but made in my opinion pretty unfair, by a proposal of the Minister of Town and Country Planning that when development rights are acquired compensation should be paid to the previous owners only in so far as they are out of pocket, i.e. only in so far as they have paid down cash for development rights or have spent money on the initial stages of development which they will now not be permitted to complete. This means that a person who bought land at a high price in relation to its existing yield on the expectation that it would be worth more later on will now get nothing for this element of development value. This is perhaps only in degree more unfair than the remarkable ideas about floating value, i.e. that if you pay people 25 per cent of the admitted market value of their property you are being quite fair. If it would greatly reduce the cost of compensation, then presumably the Land Commission's Charge on Development (so called for Betterment) could be reduced and some considerable incentive to develop permitted.[34]

[33] Meade to Lord President, 'Output, Recruitment and Conditions of Employment in the Coal-Mining Industry, Memorandum by the Ministry of Fuel and Power CP(46)232', 19 June 1946 covering a note by Chantler and Tress of the same title, CAB124/706. The Ministry of Fuel's paper was discussed at the Lord Presisent's Committee on 21 June: LP(46) 22nd meeting, CAB132/1. See also Jay, *Change and Fortune*, pp. 142–9.

[34] CB(46)3, Development Rights Bill, discussed at CB(46) 1st and 2nd Meetings, 24 and 25 June 1946, Meade to Lord President, 'Compensation and Betterment (CB(46)3 and 4)', 21 June 1946, CAB124/385; CB(46)4, 'Town and Country Planning (Development Rights) Bill, Memorandum by the Minister of Town and Country Planning', 20 June 1946, CAB124/386.

I have sent the Lord President's private secretary a minute and a long memorandum which the Economic Section did in 1944 on Nutrition and Agriculture, the thesis being that our policies of Full Employment, Social Security, Redistribution of Income, to say nothing of such direct nutritional schemes as Milk and Meals in Schools, were in fact an adequate expansionist agricultural policy in themselves, since they would lead to the expansion of demand for just those agricultural products which this country could best produce.[35] This was in connection with a public speech which the Lord President was to make at a Farm Week on the connection between food and agriculture. He made a few of these observations, but in a very minor key.

There has been a good deal to do on the external side these three weeks. I attended with A. J. Brown a meeting in the Foreign Office to consider the draft of a report on the possibility of our trading with South East Europe [on 12 June]. The position is truly ridiculous. We have, apparently, gone round fixing up a series of monetary and payments agreements with these various countries with very overvalued exchange rates, which we now have to stick to. At the same time we refuse (quite rightly) to give them any extensive credits. They can only buy from us when they get sterling from their sales to us, but having a very overvalued currency no one in this country buys anything from them – a system which is almost ideally devised to prevent any trade at all from ever taking place. At the same time it is not compatible with our payments or monetary agreements to promote private barter or compensation deals whereby some exporter in this country sends out goods and swaps them for goods which it is profitable to bring back here – financing the nominal loss on his imports by the nominal profit on his exports. I kicked up a great fuss at the meeting to say that we must explain in the report that *either* we must take steps to get the exchange rates set at a level where two-way trade could take place *or* we must do without payments and monetary agreements and promote private barter agreements. We were in the end commissioned to redraft the central sections of the report and A. J. Brown has now done so. We shall discuss it next week.[36]

There has been a meeting in the Treasury under Eady with Waley, Frank Lee and Brooks from the Treasury, Hall-Patch from the Foreign Office, Cobbold from the Bank of England and myself to discuss with George Bolton, late of the Bank of England and now our Executive Director at the International Monetary Fund, the future of the International Monetary Fund and Bank. First there was a long discussion about the staffing problems of these institutions. The point which interested me most was the reaction of Eady to the unanimous proposal of all the Executive Directors of the Fund that Lionel Robbins should be asked to be the Director of Research etc. at the Fund. Eady obviously wanted to suppress this invitation, which he successfully did. However, later Lionel came to hear of the invitation through an American journalist and kicked up a fuss

[35] Neither Meade's minute nor the Section memorandum have been located.

[36] The draft report and the redraft of paragraphs 19–30 by A. J. Brown are on T230/137. The next meeting was on 5 July (see below, p. 303).

about it – as he well might, the salary being very attractive, the post very influential, and the suppression of the invitation giving the impression that Whitehall no longer had any use for him. A more foolish act than Eady's I cannot conceive. We have very few really good people in these new institutions; Lionel would have been perfect for the job; and he would not even have left a gap in Whitehall.

Secondly, there was a discussion about the initial exchange rates which would be set under the Fund. Bolton warned us that for prestige reasons the countries, for example, of South-Eastern Europe would probably wish to start off with their existing rates as the initial par rates. Eady's view seemed to be that HMG should not instruct their Executive Director on this subject in order that the Chancellor should be able to swear honestly that we had not tried to put pressure on these countries to depreciate, and that the fixation of initial rates must be a thing which was the real responsibility of the Fund. On the other hand, it appears to me that to get these initial rates right is a matter of great importance. Incorrect rates of exchange are the greatest enemy of Liberal-Socialist arrangements in the international sphere. They mean that you cannot use the price mechanism to determine the volume or direction of trade. The problem of starting up our trade with South East Europe, to which reference is made above, is a very good case in point.

Thirdly, Cobbold of the Bank of England raised the possibility of getting the location of the Fund and the Bank moved from Washington. He had in mind somewhere like Philadelphia, on the assumption that New York would be in any case out of the question. To my great surprise I found myself for once in agreement with this central banker! I supported him in his view that it was a very great pity to have these institutions so closely tied up with American politics. But there I found the agreement abruptly ended. I wanted to use the opportunity, if there really was one, to get the Fund and the Bank together with the International Trade Organisation at the same place as the headquarters of UNO; but I found that Cobbold was unable to decide whether he disliked this or Washington most!

Fourthly, the question arose of the relationship of the Fund and the Bank with the Economic and Social Council. It appeared that the Economic and Social Council had drawn up a draft relationship agreement which (when I subsequently read it) seemed to be full of all the safeguards necessary for the Fund and the Bank but which sent cold shivers down the backs of Bolton and Cobbold, who had got the impression that the Economic and Social Council were wanting to dictate the whole of their operations to these institutions. Clearly these financial bodies, just like central banks, are going to be very difficult to bring into the general picture for the purpose of determining a coherent international economic policy. For example, they were most excited by the possibility that the proposed sub-Commission of the E. & S. Council on the balance of payments would interfere with a question which the Fund considers to be exclusively its own. Yet, of course, there may be a frightful clash of policy on this subject between the Fund which is likely to resist exchange-rate variations and to say that a balance of payments problem should be dealt with by import restrictions and the International Trade Organisation which should, at least, resist this and at least demand that if import restrictions look like becoming semi-permanent there should be variations in exchange rates. This is, of course, a difficult question because particular exchange-rate variations are not things which can be discussed openly in advance; nevertheless, this is clearly a case in which some central clearing-house for general principles is necessary.[37]

The next day at the first meeting of Hall-Patch's new interdepartmental committee [the Steering Committee on International Negotiations] which is intended to obtain a coherent policy for our delegates at all the various international organisations Waley raised this general issue. At the end of the meeting he showed Hall-Patch and myself a draft telegram which he wished to send to Washington very much on the lines that the Fund and the Bank could not accept the type of relationship agreement at present contemplated. This was intended to represent a coherent and well co-ordinated policy for our delegates at the Fund and the Bank on the one hand and at the Economic and Social Council on the other; but as our delegation at the Economic and Social Council (led by Noel-Baker and briefed by Marcus Fleming) were officially taking exactly the opposite line it could hardly have had the desired effect. I wrote to Waley suggesting that he should redraft his telegram to show in detail which particular clause of the draft agreement between the Fund and UNO required what particular amendations. I subsequently heard that the question of this draft agreement was not coming up to the Economic and Social Council until the autumn and advised Waley to put off any telegram until our delegation was back from the present meeting of the Economic and Social Council in New York. To this Waley agreed.[38]

Bridges has had another meeting of his committee on the Sterling Area Negotiations.[39] I was dreadfully uneasy at this meeting. There seems to be a reckless move on foot, led by Cobbold of the Bank of England and supported strongly at the moment by Alec Grant in the Treasury, to lead us into a super-bankers'-bluff and so into a super-1931 [financial crisis]. According to this theory we don't cancel anything very much of our sterling balances and we don't really block any of them at all. We don't even have any definite agreements with them about any running down of their balances at certain predetermined rates. The idea is that if you tell them all that sterling is as good as gold no one will ever want to remove any of it! This (a) entirely ignores our obligation to the Americans under the Loan Agreement to cancel part of our sterling balances and to 'block' another part, (b) entirely ignores the fact that countries like India with very overvalued currencies will happily remain a sink for imports which they will finance with their sterling balances and (c) gives no indication of how we are going to avoid another foreign-exchange crisis by comparison with which 1931 won't be in the picture, if and when some crisis occurs which

37 'International Monetary Fund, International Reconstruction Bank, Note of a meeting at the Treasury on 11 June 1946', T230/1168. (The draft relationship agreement, which was sent to London by Isaiah Berlin on 23 May 1946, is also on the same file.)

38 IOC(46) 1st Meeting 13 June 1946, CAB134/377; Meade to Waley, 14 June, and Waley to Meade, 15 June 1946, T236/1168.

39 On 17 June 1946. The minutes are on T236/1660.

makes people begin to call the London bankers' bluff. But Cobbold with Bridges raced us through each one of the sterling area countries explaining why in each case we should or could not do anything. Poor Keynes must have turned in his grave.

A day or two later a dinner was given in the University of London in honour of Viner before his return to the United States [above, p. 268]. (Present: Niemeyer, Carr-Saunders, Robbins, Plant, Benham, Tawney, Ashton, Raisman, Bridges, Hall-Patch, Waley and myself.) At one point Lionel Robbins and I were able to get Waley alone and tried to put the fear of God into him about the folly of this procedure. I think this has had some temporary effect.[40]

Waley has since had an interdepartmental meeting of the Colonial Office, Dominions Office, Board of Trade, Treasury and ourselves to discuss the treatment of the Colonial balances.[41] I am glad to see that we had there swung back in favour of a definite agreement at least to insist on the maintenance of minimum balances.

After the dinner at the University of London I went up to Benham's flat with Viner, Robbins and Plant and tried to explain the principles of Liberal-Socialism. The state should (a) take measures (e.g. through tax policy) to maintain total demand, (b) should behind this promote real competition among private enterprise except (c) where competition was not technically possible, in which case it should socialise and consciously make prices equal to marginal cost, and (d) should take steps through progressive taxation of income and property [and] through social security to redistribute income in favour of the poor. All seemed to be agreed except on (c) where I was much attacked. Lionel supported me, and I think Viner too, on (a), but I am not sure that Plant or Benham really even believe in that.

Another evening Margaret and I went to the Robbins' house after supper to meet Viner, together with Mr and Mrs Richard Law and Mr and Mrs Alec Spearman. It was interesting to meet this group of disappointed Conservatives. Spearman is very nearly a Liberal-Socialist. But I was really surprised to find, as in the case of Mrs Spearman and to a lesser extent of Dick Law, how evil some people were able to consider the present Government to be.

Have lunched with both Roy Harrod and Richard Kahn mainly in order to explain to them what we are doing to staff the Section in the future.

40 Waley reported his meeting to Eady the following day: Waley to Eady, 19 June 1946, T273/368.

41 Working Party on Colonial Sterling Balances, 2nd meeting, 27 June 1946, T236/2683.

# 21

## July 1946

*27 July 1946*

This has been an extremely busy month with an abnormal amount of work and a staff largely depleted by Sayers being in hospital and others being on leave.

The paper which I wrote on the control of inflation has now been discussed by the Budget Committee after it had been seen by the Chancellor of the Exchequer.[1] The Committee decided that we should call on the Chancellor to discuss the various points. There was general agreement with the suggestions which I had made, subject to two provisos: first, it was thought that the cost-of-living subsidies should not be dramatically and suddenly removed with some dramatic bargain (e.g. for certain increases in expenditure on social security) but should gradually and quietly be tapered off with as little noise as possible; and, secondly, Hoppy [Sir Richard Hopkins] opposed my idea of a fixed annual contribution from the Budget to the Employment Stabilisation Fund of £200m. on the grounds that no fixed sinking Fund had ever in fact been maintained in the past. He argued rather for an annual statement with the Budget Financial Statement of what was the cumulative budget surplus or deficit over, say, a ten-year period, in order to concentrate attention on the Budget surplus or deficit over a period of years rather than year by year. I am disposed to agree that my proposal for a *fixed* annual contribution to the proposed Employment Stabilisation Fund would be wrong, on the grounds that in order to 'break even' from the point of view of the effect of the budget on overall inflation or deflation one would have to find £200m. of extra expenditure from the Employment Stabilisation Fund, whereas the sensible thing as often as not would be merely to reduce taxation and get rid of the £200m. budgetary surplus. After a meeting of Ministers at No. 11, which I was attending on another subject,[2] the Chancellor button-holed me and we had a long talk on my paper. He was, I am glad to say, clearly very attracted by the general lines of it. He was particularly attracted by the idea of introducing the new cost-of-living index, which would be less sensitive to tapering off of the subsidies, and of devoting some part of the saving in cost-of-living subsidies to increased

[1] Above, pp. 272–3.

[2] MEP(46) 4th meeting, 12 July 1946, which discussed a memorandum by Dalton on 'US Dollar Expenditure', 11 July 1946 (CAB134/503).

payments for social security. He seems very much to have taken the point that the repayment of post-war tax credits must be postponed and used later to stimulate consumption when they will be needed for this purpose. He was also attracted by the idea of putting aside the resulting budget surplus into an Employment Stabilisation Fund. Later Bridges, Hoppy, Gilbert, Bamford (who has taken Brittain's place) and I called on the Chancellor. As a result of a meeting of the Lord President's Committee which had rather frowned on the action of the Minister of Labour in setting up his advisory committee on a revised cost-of-living index, the Chancellor had somewhat receded in his preparedness to face the tapering off of the cost-of-living subsidies. But the Budget Committee has been commissioned to put up to him alternative schemes: first, for a dramatic reduction of subsidies (rather on the lines of my suggestion) and, secondly, for a gradual and very quiet tapering off.[3]

There has been very considerable activity on the 'Economic Plan' front. There have been two more meetings of Bridges' Steering Committee on our Survey for 1946/47 which have resulted in the preparation of a covering note, which – together with our Survey – has gone to the Lord President's Committee and has been discussed by Ministers.[4] As a result of these meetings of the Steering Committee two immediate and special, and one longer-term and more general, issues were brought out. The two specific issues were building labour and coal. In view of the continuing excess pressure on our resources and of the shortage of building materials (timber and steel), we recommended that the labour force in building, which is running at more than 100,000 below the planned level, should be allowed to continue to run at 100,000 below the planned target of 1,400,000 for the end of 1946. On coal we had great struggles with Fergusson of the Ministry of Fuel and Power, who won't hear of introducing foreign labour into the pits on any scale for fear of disturbing the National Union of Mineworkers and who rely solely upon inducing a better spirit among the existing workers and so increasing productivity. In the result the Steering Committee's covering note called attention to the gravity of the coal situation and instanced it as a case of the limitations of economic planning, anyhow as a means of adjusting quickly a situation which was seen to be wrong, but had no definite proposals for further action. (The outlook is indeed grim; and on this subject of recruitment to the coal industry coming up recently to the Lord President's Committee, we briefed the Lord President to the effect that he had better accept as inevitable a serious shortage next winter and turn all the heat on to considering the best means of ensuring that the available coal was allocated in proper proportions to the most essential uses.)[5]

[3] Note by Trend, [July 1946], T171/389; LP(46) 26th meeting, 17 July 1946, CAB132/1.

[4] ED(46) 4th and 5th meetings, 4 and 11 July 1946, which discussed ED(46)16, 'Economic Survey for 1946-47, Draft report by the Economic Survey Working Party', 2 July 1946, and ED(46)17 and 18 (drafts of covering note), CAB134/187 and 188; LP(46) 28th meeting, 28 July 1946, which discussed MEP(46)5, 'Economic Survey for 1946/47', CAB132/1; below p. 295.

[5] LP(46) 27th meeting, 19 July 1946, CAB132/1; Tress to Lord President, 10 July 1946, CAB124/707.

The general issue which has now come up is how to implement any general economic plan. It has arisen in connection with the relative sizes of the industries producing investment goods and the industries producing consumption goods. The former are too big, it is argued by those who (like myself) believe that we should now increase the supply of goods and services for consumption in order (i) to diminish the inflationary pressure in the market for consumption goods, (ii) by removing shop shortages to increase the incentives to produce and to earn income, which at the moment cannot be fully used, and (iii) not to have too large an investment sector, since we should postpone much investment until a later date when it may be positively needed to help maintain full employment. But the question arose, how are we to bring about any change? We no longer have labour direction. The determination of wage-rates, and so of the relative attractiveness of different jobs, is left to the uncontrolled chances of wage negotiations between monopolies of employers and monopolies of workers. The Ministry of Labour in the person of Ince was really defeatist about this, and showed it by arguing that the present distribution of labour was just what was wanted. The Board of Trade, in the person of Woods, argued that they did not like the present distribution of labour, but they were really unable to see what one could do to alter it, at any rate at all quickly.

In fact, the crux of the issue is now reached. We have devised a reasonably satisfactory technique for drawing up a paper plan. Can it be implemented in a free society? In the longer run I am sure that this can be done primarily by fiscal policy. In present circumstances it must be done by a judicious mixture of fiscal inducements and direct controls. We briefed the Lord President on this issue (both in connection with the Economic Survey and also in connection with a paper by the Minister of Labour arguing why he couldn't really do anything to divert labour from the less to the more essential jobs) on the following lines.[6] There are the following seven ingredients in any composite policy for this purpose:- (i) what raw material controls exist (e.g. the steel allocation which must certainly be continued now that a serious shortage of steel threatens) must be used consciously to get resources into the most desired uses; (ii) the investment controls and programmes must be used selectively in order to get investment increased where it is most wanted (e.g. cotton spinning); (iii) we must consider the possibility of adjusting relative prices and profit margins, where these are under control, so as to make more profitable the production of those things of which we want greater supplies; (iv) similarly the problem of relative wage-rates is acute, and something must be done to encourage increases in relative wage-rates where such increases are wanted in order to man-up an industry without wage increases elsewhere; (v) we must consider further the rules for disallowing unemployment benefit, in order to make sure that no unemployed man can reasonably refuse work in any essential industry; (vi) we must consider the possibility

[6] LP(46)175, 'Diversion of Labour to Industries of National Importance, Memorandum by the Minister of Labour and National Service', 8 July 1946, CAB132/4; Meade to Lord President, 'Wages Policy', 27 July 1946, CAB124/783.

of various means of putting a stop or limit on employment in those occupations which are less essential (The usual argument against this is that this is deliberately to create unemployment and must therefore be avoided at all costs; but in fact we shall never achieve any economic plan, unless we are prepared to operate from both ends, making opportunities less in the overexpanded jobs as well as increasing the powers of attraction in the undermanned jobs); and (vii) finally there is fiscal policy, which falls into two parts. (a) Particular taxes and subsidies can clearly be used to induce resources to leave one type of employment and to enter another. (b) But it is equally important to achieve an overall level of taxation which is high enough to avoid a general excess of potential demand over supply (as well, of course, as being low enough to avoid overall deflation). Attempts to get relative prices and wages right will be much more successful in the absence of a general excess inflationary pressure, the presence of which is apt to lead to a policy of clamping down rigidly on all price increases; and it will, moreover, mean that while there is an excess of demand over supply in the relatively undermanned industries, there is some excess of supply over demand elsewhere. This will be much more conducive to a redistribution of the factors of production than an all-pervasive excess of demand.

These papers have now all been taken by the Lord President's Committee. It was a very good meeting. The discussion was very intelligent and Ministers showed great awareness of the fact that we had now reached the stage at which we must consider how we could implement any plan. This point was well brought out by the President of the Board of Trade (briefed, I have no doubt, by Austin Robinson and Richard Kahn); and I was able to say something about it, as the Lord President asked for any views which I would like to express. In the result we got just what I had hoped for, namely a request to Bridges' Steering Committee to carry out a general enquiry into the various possibilities of implementing the plan.[7]

At this same Ministerial Committee there came up for discussion the report of Gould's Working Party on the Trend of Wages, Prices and Costs. There have been three more meetings of this Working Party this month and in the end we have produced what is, I think, a very good report.[8] Gould, representing the Ministry of Labour view, started off on the line that all the recent heavy wage increases represented more or less permanent post-war wage settlements and that there was accordingly little or no cause for anxiety and that there would be more or less complete stability of wages over the next twelve months. We carefully examined all the recent wage settlements and it became clear to me that there was much more in this point of view than I had at first realised. On the other hand, I think that we managed to shake Gould's complacency a bit on the following three grounds:- (i) We have never before experienced wage stability in a period of full employment and acute labour shortage. Even after the cost of living was stabilised in April 1941 wage-rates continued to rise by about

[7] LP(46) 28th meeting, 26 July 1946, CAB132/1.

[8] LP(46)192, 'Official Working Party on the Trend of Wages, Costs and Prices', 22 July 1946, CAB132/4; see also above, p. 283.

5 per cent per annum. Could we really rely on wage stability, whatever the form of agreements might be, in conditions in which there was an acute and all-pervasive shortage of labour? (ii) At the working party we examined the relationship between wages and earnings on the one hand and prices on the other. Wage costs are clearly up much more than prices, – much more than would be accounted for by any conceivable increase in productivity. This gap is largely filled for the time being by subsidies to the cost of living. But sooner or later these must be tapered off, and meanwhile the course of world prices was markedly upwards. As the adjustment took place, could we expect wage stability as prices rise? (iii) In a free society we were no longer able to direct labour from one job to another. This means that we must be able to use variations in relative wage-rates to man-up the vital undermanned industries. What prospects were there of allowing or encouraging upward movements of wage-rates in certain undermanned industries without provoking sympathetic wage demands in a whole range of other industries?

The difficulties in this last question are illustrated by the recent increase in the wages of County Council Roadmen, a problem to which the first half of the Report of the Working Party was devoted. The agricultural workers having received an increase in their minimum wage of 10/- [50p], the County Council Roadmen, as a purely sympathetic move, obtained an increase of 12/- [60p], thus *more* than replacing the previous wage differential, which it is desirable to diminish in the interests of manning-up agriculture. Ministers were very moved by these events, as well they might be; and from their previous attitude of believing that there should be no government interference with wage-fixing except by giving both sides of industry a general picture of the general economic background through the proposed National Industrial Conference, they have moved to a serious consideration of a much more extensive intervention in wage-fixing. Shinwell, the Minister of Fuel and Power, who has for long advocated a policy of a Minimum National Wage plus government intervention in fixing wage-rates over and above this, is to put in a paper on it and Cripps suggested that he should consider the fixation of profit margins at the same time.

This all gives pause for thought. But after all the Trade Unions and Employers' Federations are vast monopolies and monopsonies, and the way in such circumstances to make private enterprise produce the right results is to fix wages and (if the producers are also monopolists) prices so that the monopsonistic and monopolistic powers disappear. This would also prevent inflation in spite of full employment and would enable relative prices and wages to be used to carry out any economic plan. State intervention to fix factor and product prices, adjusting these to bring supplies into balance with demands, is theoretically a sound form of liberal-socialism. It is much preferable to quantitative restrictions, labour direction, etc. It will be exciting to see how far this new move goes and, if it goes any distance, how well it succeeds.

We have had a meeting of Proctor's Investment Working Party Panels, representing all the departments which are important from the point of view of actually influencing the planning and timing of investment.[9] There was an interesting general discussion of the actual problems which make difficult a prompt turning on of the investment tap, such as the failure to have acquired land, to have made plans in advance, etc. Two groups are to be set up:- one to consider the problem of inducing the local authorities to have ready a real shelf of works, i.e. to have the plans ready, land acquired, etc. and then to wait for the signal to go ahead; the other to consider the formulation and control of investment programmes by the socialised industries.

This last point has been much brought to the front by a paper by Hitchman of the Ministry of Labour, which has been submitted to Proctor's Investment Working Party Panels after a preliminary draft had been discussed between Hitchman, Proctor, Tress, Vinter, Stafford and myself.[10] The general thesis is that the United Kingdom economy after the war is going to depend much more upon the metal industries, i.e. the investment industries, both for export and for large-scale domestic investment. But this makes us very vulnerable, because exports and private investment are the two parts of the national expenditure which it is most difficult to control. Moreover, it not only makes us generally more vulnerable to depressions; it also means that any measures taken to offset a depression will have to be designed to stimulate demand for the products of these industries, which during a general depression will be subject to special 'structural' depression. We pointed out (a) that to some extent, since the products of engineering could be used for home investment or personal consumption as well as for export, concentration of exports on these products rather than on coal, textiles, shipbuilding, etc. might make it easier for us to offset an external slump by domestic action and (b) that the extension of socialisation made it easier to control investment in plant and machinery. These factors serve to underline the importance of making sure that as much or more attention is given to the planning and timing of investment projects by socialised industries as by local authorities, which are concentrated much more on building and civil engineering. (I have had a talk with Frank Lee and Lindsell of the Ministry of Supply who are dealing with steel to explain the general Economic Planning machinery with particular reference to the steel investment programme.)

There has also been a meeting of Sir Bernard Gilbert's full Investment Working Party. It is now ruled that, in addition to general total investment programmes (in £ *s. d.*) being put up by departments to the Investment Working Party, all individual projects costing £500,000 or more must be put up for individual approval. This was the first meeting to go through all the individual 'cases', on this occasion mainly waterworks and sewage works of various kinds. We spent the meeting saying No to the great majority, in spite of the fact that they all had strong cases (as everything

[9] This took place on 23 July: 'Future Work on the Investment Panels, Note by the Treasury', 16 July 1946, T161/1297/S53555/01.

[10] Hitchman, 'Investment Working Party: Distribution of Manpower between the end of the Transitional Stage and 1951, and its Relation to Investment Programmes', sent to Meade on 12 June 1946, T230/85; see also Meade to Hitchman, 24 June, and Hitchman to Meade, 25 June, on same file.

has these days) to be allowed to go ahead. I had a feeling that one more definite step had been taken and here was a policy for postponing expenditure in times of overall pressure actually in operation.[11]

We have similarly briefed the Lord President on a proposition put up by the Ministry of Transport to sanction legislation to start great schemes of motorways.[12] I argued that this should be postponed, but that it was not sufficient merely to postpone the issue. Ministers should decide whether or not in the longer run they thought these motorways were worth having. If so, since land acquisition, surveys, planning, etc. involved two years delay in road schemes, they should positively encourage the Ministry of Transport to go ahead now with these preliminaries, but without any undertaking as to the time when the expenditure could actually be started.

As chairman of the Economic Survey Working Party, I have held a meeting of our 'nuclear' group – Treasury, Board of Trade, Ministry of Labour and Central Statistical Office – to consider how we should go ahead on the Survey for 1947/48 which we have been commissioned to do.[13] There are three main points:- (1) We are going to ask departments to make all their estimates on the basis of current wage-rates adjusted for any known changes in wage-rates, current import prices similarly adjusted, and present levels of productivity, their prices to be consistent with these assumptions. Then we shall modify these by discussing with the various departments what they (and we) think are likely to be further changes in costs and prices. (2) This year, in the market for consumption goods, we are going to try to get away from the rather bogus idea of the supplies of consumption goods which departments would sponsor to the fundamental propensity to consume idea of what consumers, given their incomes, tax payments, accumulated savings, etc. would wish to spend on consumption goods and services. With definitely rationed supplies (main foods and clothing) we shall, of course, ask what supplies the departments wish to sponsor. But for the rest we shall this year make the radical change of starting the calculation from the centre; i.e. we shall calculate personal incomes after tax; bearing in mind pre-war experience and the probable effects of war-time backlogs and war-time accumulations of savings we shall estimate total desired expenditure on consumption; we shall examine this from two points of view – first, in conjunction with government expenditure, the foreign balance and domestic investment in order to compare the total demand on resources with the 'target' national income, and, secondly, in order to break it down into demand for the main categories of goods such as drink, tobacco, food, etc.; we shall then in conjunction with the various departments and the Ministry of Labour have to consider whether the specific difficulties are such that these particular demands cannot be met. Heaven help us in doing all this – it will mostly be pure guesswork on this occasion. (3) The third question is the old one

[11] INV.WP(46) 3rd meeting, 8 July 1946, T161/1297/S53555/02.

[12] LP(46)191, 'Motorways Bill, Memorandum by the Minister of Transport', CAB132/4; Meade to Lord President, 'Motor-ways: Memorandum by the Minister of Transport LP(46)191', 24 July 1946, CAB124/619.

[13] On 26 July: see ESWP(46)12, Tress, 'Economic Survey for 1947–48', 23 July 1946, T230/56.

whether we should do the Survey for the financial year 1947/48 or the calendar year. We have decided to ask for both in effect.

This last issue has been discussed again, at the group under Proctor which is to prepare a report for the Steering Committee on the issue. We had a fine old tussle. I argued strongly for the financial year plus publication of the Survey after the Budget next May or June. The Central Statistical Office (because they are frightened of a demand that their back figures of national income will all have to be adjusted on to a financial year basis) and the Lord President's Office (because of Max Nicholson's absurd belief that the calendar year basis is necessary for publicity purposes and because of a perverse desire, I suspect, to make the Budget and the financial year less important) favour publication in March on a calendar year basis. I remain fundamentally convinced (a) that it must be on a financial year basis in order that the Economic Plan and the Budget may be considered concurrently and in relation to the same facts and (b) that publication should be after the Budget, because it is really not possible to say how any prospective gap is likely in effect to be closed until the Budget decisions can be taken into account, and the budgetary 'means' are so important here that one cannot determine the 'ends' without simultaneously considering the means. For example, the question should one go for high investment and low consumption, might be differently answered in ignorance, and in knowledge, of the rates of taxation which the policy of austerity involved. But I confess that I was a little shaken after the meeting by Campion and Secord who said that my present frontal attack on this problem of the connection between the Budget and the Plan was liable unduly to scare the Treasury. It would be much more sensible to allow a general Plan for the calendar year to be published in March, since, though this would enable the connection between the two not to be so directly obvious, it would soon become manifest that the Chancellor would have to address his Budgets to carrying out the Plan. It would only be necessary for him to fail to do so on one occasion, and the outcry would be such as to ensure the connection in the future.

At one of the meetings of the Steering Committee the Lord President's remit for an enquiry on how to deal with a slump was discussed. The Board of Trade have, as I suggested, been asked to organise an answer to the question how we could react to a world slump, and to link this up with the preparation of a brief on International Employment Policy for the UK delegation to the forthcoming conference on Trade and Employment. The Economic Survey Working Party has been asked to do a study on the quantitative aspects of the next slump, e.g. by how much can we expect exports, home investment and consumption to decline; and Dow is now preparing a draft of this paper. No one has as yet been asked to prepare any paper on the actual weapons to be used in these conditions, but this will come. And we already have a number of notes in draft on variations in national insurance contributions, variations in income tax and in indirect taxation, and the timing of the repayment of post-war tax credits.[14]

[14] ED(46) 4th meeting, 4 July 1946, CAB134/187 and T228/20; and see above, pp. 284–5.

The Lord President asked me to lunch tête-à-tête, and I gave him a good lecture on anti-slump policies and on the need to take measures against restrictive practices and to make the unsocialised sector of the economy really compete. I painted to him the picture of a world in which we taught the Americans the necessity for a global control over total national expenditure, but learnt from them (for our unsocialised sector) the lessons of policy against monopolistic devices.[15]

I have had a visit from a Nawab from Hyderabad, sent to me by the Chancellor, to explain to him the organisation and work of the Economic Section. He is hoping to start a similar body in Hyderabad.

I went out to dinner with Campion and Max Nicholson with an American journalist (a socialist who stays at the Ritz) called Alsop. He had an utterly childish belief in everything which we were doing in this country and Max Nicholson spoke more nonsensical generalisations about the need for planning without any explanation of what was meant by planning. I tried to tell him something of what we were actually [to] do in the control of total demand, but I don't know that it got very far.

I have delivered my old lecture on Employment Policy yet once more to a new group of Principals who have just joined the Civil Service.

There have been two more lunches with the accountants, in the course of which we have gone through the system of accounts which Stone is going to publish shortly in the report which he has done for the League of Nations.[16] The accountants are playing up marvellously and are translating all their company accounts into Stone's system. At the last meeting we got on to the interesting point of cost accounting, and of marginal and average costs. I argued, however, that there were two distinct chapters in Economic Theory, the first dealing with the global balance of accounts for the whole community – i.e. total profits, wages etc. and total expenditures on consumption, investment, etc. – and the second dealing with relative prices and costs. It was in connection with the second that we ought to discuss cost accounting. I hoped that we should do the second very much, because it was very important to discover what was practicable and what was not in measuring marginal costs etc. But I thought that we had better finish the former first.

Some correspondence has passed (largely as a result of our briefs on Transport Nationalisation) between the Lord President and the Minister of Transport in which the Lord President expressed the need for a general enquiry into the rate structure in transport. As a result Alec Johnston of the Lord President's Office and I went to call on Stephen Wilson at the Ministry of Transport. They are thinking in terms of asking the Transport Commission when Transport has been nationalised to put forward its views and then to discuss them at some more general body. I argued against this and said that there should first be an independent, sort of Royal Commission, enquiry and a Government decision about the principles on which rates should be set (e.g. that they should be in relation to the

[15] It was probably after this meeting that Meade sent the Lord President 'a reading list on Employment Policy': Meade to Pimlott, 19 July 1946, CAB124/220.

[16] On 9 and 24 July 1946: Meade Papers 3/12. For Stone's report see pp. 219–20.

marginal costs of producing the different types of transport) and that only then should the producing body suggest how it was going to apply the chosen principle. The outcome is, I think, that an official working party is to be set up this autumn to keep in close touch with the Transport Commission and to be in a position to convey to it the views of Ministers as it formulates its ideas on rate structure.[17] This is better than nothing.

I have been to see Miss Kilroy and G. H. Andrew in the Board of Trade on the future work of their Committee on Supervisory Boards and Restrictive Practices. Our vast paper on this subject has somewhat alarmed them.[18] The unfortunate fact is that the President of the Board of Trade is not very sound on this. The official line is that restrictive practices are not necessarily good or bad, but must be looked at to see that they are not misused. Our paper took the line that restrictive practices were rather more than *prima facie* bad and should in the brave new world be avoided like the devil except in very exceptional circumstances. Miss Kilroy has very limited terms of reference which are really no more than to see how the Board of Trade's general policy in regard to restrictive practices in industry (which is merely that each one should be looked at and judged on its merits) can be applied to statutory boards. She is, however, prepared to go so far as to recommend that certain named restrictive practices (such as minimum prices, maximum quotas of production, limitation on new entry) should not be employed unless there has been a clear examination to see whether means which do not involve restriction (e.g. levy-subsidies, buffer stocks) could not serve the purpose, and in any case should only be used under very strict conditions.

The question of paying part of the present agricultural subsidies in the form of subsidies to marginal production, thus economising on the subsidies to intra-marginal production, has been up to Ministers. A rise in the price paid to farmers combined with a special levy on all farm profits would do the trick satisfactorily, but is not a political starter at a time when farmers have to be induced to give maximum production while EPT [Excess Profits Tax] is being removed from industry. An extension of acreage payments (on the general presumption that the most costly production is where yield per acre is low) is the only practicable approximation. But an acreage payment, unlike an increased price for the product, gives less incentive (a) to be efficient or (b) to cultivate intensively so as to raise output per acre and (c) not to retain cereals on the farm for animal rather than human consumption. I briefed the Lord [President] on these lines.[19]

17 Meade to Lord President, 'Economic Efficiency and the Nationalisation of Transport', 26 April, Morrison to Barnes, 22 May, and Johnston to Meade, 27 June 1946, CAB21/2345. Johnston and Meade called on Wilson on 1 July. The resulting Working Party on Transport Charges first met on 24 February 1947.

18 See above, p. 286.

19 LP(46)163, 'Marginal Production in Agriculture, Memorandum by Minister of Agriculture and Fisheries, Secretary of State for Scotland and Home Secretary', 1 July 1946, CAB132/4; Meade to Lord President, 'Marginal Production in Agriculture (LP(46)163), Special Review of Agricultural Prices (LP(46)164), Memoranda by the Minister of Agriculture and Fisheries, the Secretary of State for Scotland and the Secretary of State for the Home Department', 3 July 1946, CAB124/570.

A paper has also been put up to the Lord President's Committee for an extension of the subsidies to farmers on liming and water drainage. This raises the interesting issue why you should not subsidise the finished product (which is what is wanted) rather than certain factors of production and thus get the factors used in uneconomic combinations. The possible arguments in favour of subsidies to these particular factors did not seem very strong to us. The President of the Board of Trade had written to the Lord President to suggest that these things should not be taken piecemeal but that the Agricultural Ministers should put up a total budget for the support which they needed. We backed this. But in the event the proposal seems to have gone through unchallenged.[20]

Sir John Woods has held a meeting which Fleming and I attended to discuss our paper on International Employment Policy both as a possible basis for a brief for the UK delegation to the conference on Trade and Employment and also as a starting point for an answer to the Lord President's request for a report on how we should deal with an external slump. Some quite useful points came from Austin Robinson of the Board of Trade: first, that our document was over-optimistic in not recognising the structural unemployment which would be caused in this country from a decline in our exports, and secondly, that we should use this as an argument for persuading Ministers of the desirability of getting an international policy for employment, since if all countries pulled together, none need suffer from such inevitable structural unemployment. The Treasury (in the persons of Sir David Waley and Otto Clarke) said very little. They had sent copies of our paper to Grigg and Bolton, our representatives on the International Monetary Fund and International Bank. Their replies had not come. But they came the next day. They were hysterical in their reactionary condemnation that any attempt should be made to use the Fund or the Bank for these silly schemes for stabilising total demand! We had been asked to redraft our paper, which we shall now do. The next battle will come at the next round.[21]

I attended a meeting of Ministers to discuss what should be done, now that the American Loan is past Congress, in the way of letting up on our import programme. A little on variety foodstuffs and a bit on petrol seemed to be the very sensible answer. It is quite clear that Ministers are not going to let up on the export drive merely because the loan is through. It is also clear that if there is to be any letting up they will make sure that it is on imports and not on exports, on the grounds that we need now to make our export contacts if we are successfully to invade new markets,

[20] LP(46)194, 'Continuation of Grants for Agricultural Lime in the United Kingdom and Field Drainage and Farm Supplies in England and Wales, Memorandum by the Minister of Agriculture, the Secretary of State for Scotland and the Home Secretary', 23 July 1946, CAB132/4; Nicholson to Lord President, 'LP(46)194, Note from Sir Stafford Cripps', 26 July, and Chantler to Lord President, 'Continuation of Grants for Agricultural Lime, Field Drainage and Farm Water Supplies. Memorandum by the Minister of Agriculture and Fisheries, the Secretary of State for Scotland and the Home Secretary (LP(46)194)', 25 July 1946, CAB124/570.

[21] 'International Employment Policy, Note of a Meeting held in the Secretary's Room on 15 July', T236/702; above, pp. 277–9; Grigg to Waley, 11 July, and Bolton to Waley, 15 July 1946, T236/702. See below pp. 309 and 330.

whereas we can dispense later with imports more easily. Indeed this was a definite conclusion at the meeting of Ministers which discussed our Economic Survey for 1946/47.[22] All this is very sound.

A. J. Brown and I attended another meeting of the Committee in the Foreign Office on the possibilities of trade with South East Europe. They accepted our redraft of the central section of the document to the effect that payments and monetary agreements were all very well if exchange rates were so adjusted that trade could profitably flow in both direction, but simply meant that there would be no trade with a South Eastern country with an overvalued currency because, since our importers would never find it profitable to buy any of [their] goods, their importers would never have any sterling to spend on our goods. They also modified the conclusions somewhat to meet us, and did not assert quite as roundly as before that we must just grin and bear the absence of trade.[23] I am intending to write to Waley in the Treasury on this as ammunition for the view that when the International Monetary Fund comes to fix initial par rates of exchange our representatives should be briefed as to the importance of getting these currencies properly adjusted.

Waley has had a series of three meetings in the Treasury on the problem of the treatment of Sterling Balances. The first two were concerned solely with the colonial sterling balances, on which subject a paper is being prepared for Ministers.[24] There was a considerable clash between the Treasury and the Colonial Office as to whether any of the colonial balances should be cancelled. Certainly they should, from the point of view of the general settlement of our external financial position; but I had considerable sympathy with the Colonial Office argument that it was hard to combine cancellation with our general policy of providing funds for Colonial Development. The point on which I kept insisting was that we must have firm and precise Minimum Balance Agreements, i.e. a firm understanding with all our creditors including the colonies that they can not draw down their balances below a certain figure at any given date. This is quite essential if we are to avoid the position that we may be subject to a quite unmanageable run on our reserves. There should be sanctions against those who go below these figures and we should be prepared with schemes (however difficult) for blocking the balances of those who did not carry out these agreements. If any one of our creditors was in need of special assistance beyond this, we should not normally give it by allowing a further drawing down of their balances, even if we could afford it. Rather we should give additional support in the form of loans, because (a) we could get interest on these loans higher than that which we paid on the balances, (b) it would maintain the general proposition that these Minimum Balances must be adhered to, and (c) while under the Loan

[22] MEP(46) 4th meeting, 12 July 1946, CAB134/503; LP(46) 28th meeting, 26 July 1946, CAB132/1.

[23] See above, p. 288. The meeting was on 5 July (T230/137). Subsequent correspondence and a further draft, circulated 15 July, are on T230/138.

[24] Minutes of the Working Party on Colonial Sterling Balances are on T236/2683. The paper for ministers was SAN(46)8, 'The U.S. Financial Agreement as it Affects Relations with the Sterling Area', 19 July 1946 (T236/1660).

Agreement we could not tie the sterling balances when we released them there was nothing to prevent us using the same freedom as the Americans to tie any loans which we extended. In the third of Waley's meetings I attacked the silly proposition of the Bank that the amounts which we released from the sterling balances should be non-cumulative, i.e. that a country should not be able to use next year that part of its balances which was freed last year. I said that I could not think of anything which was more likely to reduce the willingness to hold sterling than this mousetrap arrangement for foreigners' money. The only way to square the circle (i.e. really to safeguard ourselves against an unbearable foreign drain and at the same time to make our money as acceptable as possible to foreigners) was to draw a formal line, and to say below this amount we cannot let you draw freely but every penny above it (no matter when or how you acquired it) is as good as gold.

The Chancellor has sent us a message asking us to give him an appreciation of the recent revaluations of the Canadian and Swedish currencies, their effect upon us and an opinion on whether we should consider similar action. Miss Watts has drafted a note which, after discussing a few changes with her, I have sent to Bridges and Waley in the Treasury for their opinion. The note is, I think, a very good one.[25] On the basis of the information given in our Overseas Economic Survey, brought up to date by price changes in the United States and by their currency revaluations, we have tried to assess our cost and price position vis-à-vis other countries. We show the extent to which these recent changes have improved our relative position. We argue that in the short run, so long as our imports are quantitatively controlled by us or by the scarcity of foreign supplies and our exports can be sold in the same volume (which depends upon what we can make available) regardless of price, a revaluation of the pound would not only make the cost-of-living stabilisation policy easier to maintain but would also improve our balance of trade by turning the terms of trade in our favour without affecting the volume of trade. Nevertheless on longer-run grounds we would decisively advise against any revaluation unless there is a catastrophic rise in foreign prices on three grounds: (1) The future course of American prices and costs is uncertain. There may be a slump. If we revalue now, Bretton Woods may make it difficult to devalue again later. (2) We believe that there is evidence that in more normal conditions the demand for our exports is very elastic so that a revaluation of our currency worsens our balance of trade. We believe that, as we have to get a much bigger share than pre-war of total export trade, we shall need to have an undervalued currency as compared with pre-war. We should wait and see how our balance of payments goes in the next year or two before thinking of revaluation of the currency. (3) Finally, the adjustment of relative wages and the tapering off of cost-of-living subsidies will almost certainly involve some general rise in wage-rates in this country. We need a field for manoeuvre internally and if the present upward trend of foreign prices gives us this elbow room we should not dissipate it in a revaluation of the currency.

[25] Not found. The revaluation of the Canadian dollar from US 90c to US $1 was announced on 5 July; the Swedish Krona was revalued by 17.7 per cent on 13 July.

I have had some correspondence with Shackle in the Board of Trade on the paper which is at last going into the Trade Negotiations Committee about the formula which should be used to decide whether a country is justified in imposing import restrictions on balance of payments grounds.[26] A draft, agreed between the Treasury, Board of Trade and Economic Section, will now go forward except on two points on which the Board of Trade and the Economic Section oppose the Treasury. First, we believe that the test which is based on the movements in a country's reserves must have some reference to the duty of avoiding abnormal capital exports; otherwise any country could manipulate its reserves so as to qualify for import restrictions. Secondly, we believe that it would be preferable to aim at getting more precise arithmetical definitions for each country about the safety level of its reserves and the speed at which they should be falling to justify the use of import restrictions.

Shackle has held a small meeting of Board of Trade, Ministry of Food, Colonial Office and ourselves to discuss the application of the state trading rules under the Trade Proposals to export, as opposed to import, trade.[27] Two points of interest arose. First, the Ministry of Fuel and Power are apparently trying to obtain *carte blanche* for subsidising exports of coal under the socialised board by arguing that it is a commercial practice in coal to export at a lower price than on the home market. Shackle had quietly incorporated all their nonsense in his draft. Clearly a state monopoly would have an unlimited right of export subsidy in this argument. The only sensible thing is to say that, to avoid unjust subsidies, a state selling organisation must sell at home at the same price as abroad. The second point was to permit some element of averaging over good and bad years in order to allow genuine price stabilisation schemes. For example, the Colonial Office wish to have 'price insurance' schemes for their exports whereby they will purchase the primary products from the natives at a fairly stable price and sell at the world market, as the world price goes up or down, sometimes above and sometimes below this price. Theoretically under the Trade Proposals they could do this provided that the price to the domestic consumer in the colony went up and down with the world price, but this might be utterly impracticable administratively. These 'price insurance' schemes are such an advance on the only quantitative restriction schemes which are usually proposed for primary products that they deserve every encouragement; and indeed they have a lot to be said for them on their own merits. To bring them within the scope of the Trade Proposals some form of averaging over the years would be necessary. (Incidentally, this is not merely a state trading point. The Colonial Office in some cases might wish to work a price insurance scheme not through state purchase for export, but by imposing a levy on exports in years of high export prices in order to pay a subsidy on exports in years of low export prices. Such levies and subsidies, if they balanced over the years, would have to be considered as not offending against rules inviting export taxes and subsidies.)

26 Shackle to Meade, 'Import Restrictions on Balance of Payments Grounds', 18 July, and Meade to Shackle, 'Import restrictions on balance of payment grounds', 22 July 1946, T230/9. See above, pp. 279–80.

27 On 16 July (T230/176).

I attended a meeting of the official steering committee on the various international organisations under the chairmanship of Gladwyn Jebb of the Foreign Office. It is all in the stage of constitution-mongering, at which I am no good, and my presence at the meeting was a pure waste of time. I have, however, in this connection made the acquaintance of North, the new Registrar-General. I lunched with him at the Athenaeum and talked to him again after Jebb's meeting about the Demographic Commission of the Economic and Social Council which it is proposed to set up.[28] He and I agree that it should be a body of independent status since demographic problems and their economic and social implications are going to be very important and do stand on their own feet. There is a prospect of happy co-operation between the Economic Section and the Registrar-General's Office on all this, particularly after the end of the year when Bryan Hopkin (whom North tried to persuade to go to the Registrar-General's Office) comes to the Economic Section from the Royal Commission on Population. Both North and I are prepared to consider him as the United Kingdom member of the Demographic Commission.

I attended a meeting of officials, with the Minister of State Noel-Baker in the chair, in the Foreign Office discussing the brief which is being prepared for the United Kingdom delegate to the Commission of the Economic and Social Council on Devastated Regions, which meets in London next week.[29] It was an amusing meeting. Noel-Baker arrived, as usual late, after the meeting had started under the chairmanship of Troutbeck of the Foreign Office. We made a third start when Lord Pakenham, who is to be the United Kingdom delegate and who knows, as he admits, nothing about the subject, arrived from Oxford. After a short time the Foreign Office officials and Sir David Waley of the Treasury, who clearly wanted to get Pakenham aside and coach him intensively without the eagle eye of Noel-Baker watching all the time, said there was nothing more to discuss and the meeting broke up! I wonder if anything will come of this. There is clearly behind it the old jealousy of the Bank and the Fund against the Economic and Social Council. No doubt briefed by Grigg and Bolton (our representatives at the Bank and the Fund), Waley did all he could to make sure that we should prevent any of the devastated countries from expressing any desires for outside aid; and yet, with UNRRA about to be dissolved, how they can many of them reconstruct their economies without outside financial aid is hard to see.[30] Noel-Baker took me out to lunch afterwards. He expressed all his old enthusiasms, which are really *so* sensible, for getting all these specialised agencies properly co-ordinated at the centre. But he has a hard row to hoe in the case of the Fund and the Bank, and I advised him just to try quietly to see that these two bodies were

[28] IOC(46) 3rd meeting, 25 July 1946, and IOC(46)27, 'Demographic Commission of the Economic and Social Council, Note by the Registrar General', CAB134/377.

[29] IOC(D)(46)1, 'Record of a meeting held at the Foreign Office on 27th July preparatory to the Sessions of the Temporary Sub-commission on Devastated Areas', CAB134/414. See also below, p. 317.

[30] In August 1945 it had been agreed that UNRRA's operations would end in Europe by December 1946 and in the Far East by March 1947.

brought along as far as possible in their relationship agreements with UNO. Nothing dramatic in my view had any chance of success.

I have spent a day with the Civil Service Commissioners doing preparatory work for the selection of Economic Assistants for the Economic Section. The Selection Board of which I am to be a member sits for two days next week seeing candidates.

# 22

## August 1946

*15 August 1946*

What a year this has been! I am just about to go on our family summer holiday for three weeks to Selsey, and this time last year we were on holiday from which I came back to a Labour Government, peace and the effective directorship of the Economic Section. It has certainly not been an idle twelve months, this first year of Social Democracy, though one is too near to events to judge how much Liberal-Socialism there has been about these innumerable policy decisions.

This has also been an active three weeks. After Ministers had gone off on holiday I reviewed with Bridges the work which we have on hand for the Economic Plan. This falls into eight parts:- (1) We have the Survey for 1950 which the Economic Survey Working Party has on hand.[1] (2) We have now to prepare a Survey for 1947. In this connection I have held a meeting of the Economic Survey Working Party at which our liaison officers from all the departments were present.[2] It was a monster gathering but went quite well. We are making an innovation this time in our treatment of the requirements which the departments should put in for consumption goods. We are no longer asking them to put in what they consider to be reasonable programmes for the supply of such goods (which is appropriate when everything is rationed or controlled); but we are starting from the centre to estimate, on the basis of our forecasts of personal spendable incomes etc., the total amount which people would like to spend on such goods and services if the supplies were available, then to break this down into demand for the main categories of goods and services. This technique, which should reveal the total inflationary or deflationary pressure in consumption markets, is clearly the appropriate normal peace-time procedure. We have also tried to get more consistency into our treatment of prices, costs and productivity. We are trying to get departments to put in their first estimates of demands, values of supplies etc. on the basis of existing prices of imports and existing wage-rates (modified for any known future changes) and existing rates of productivity. Our idea is then to make modifications in the results after central

[1] See above, p. 271.
[2] On 2 August 1946: ESWP(46)14 (Revise), Tress, 'Economic Survey for 1947–48', 6 August 1946, T230/56.

discussion of the probable departures from these assumed levels. (3) Next there is the problem of deciding whether we should plan on the basis of a calendar or financial year. I have, with some hesitation, executed a *volte-face* on this issue. On the understanding that for the internal purposes of the Budget Committee we will prepare a further set of the main estimates on a financial year basis, I have agreed that the Plan should be prepared on a calendar year basis. This would (a) permit publication in February, which would incidentally in fact have the effect in the end of forcing the hands of the Chancellor of the Exchequer to use his Budget in April to implement the published Plan, so that the use of budgetary policy for this sort of purpose would ultimately be assured by this time table, (b) not over-emphasise the relationship between the Plan and the Budget and therefore not scare the old-fashioned in financial ideas as much as my frontal attack might have done, and (c) permit – what the CSO so much desire – the existing national income estimates on the calendar year basis to be used for the measurement of the outcome of the Plan. The removal of our opposition to the calendar year basis has enabled Proctor to draft an agreed paper submitting the issue to Ministers, and this is to be discussed at an official meeting next week which Tress will attend on my behalf.[3]

(4) I mentioned to Bridges our paper on international employment policy (which was to form not only a brief for our delegation to the forthcoming trade conference, but also part of the Steering Committee's answer to the Lord President's remit how we should deal with an external depression) and how, after consulting Grigg and Bolton our representatives on the International Fund and Bank, the Treasury through Waley had wished us to modify to practically nothing our references to the use of these institutions for the avoidance of world depressions. I said that I thought that this was an issue which, in the end, might have to go to Ministers, and was encouraged by his remark that if it did he had little doubt that Ministers would decide in our favour. I also mentioned this position off the record to the Lord President and was also emboldened by his reaction. As a result I have written a letter to John Henry Woods in the Board of Trade saying that I do not think that we can go as far as Waley suggests in the direction of removing all reference to the use of these bodies as mechanisms for the control of world depressions, but that we will try to tone down our references to the Fund and the Bank as much as we possibly can consistently with our major objective to use the international institutions as far as possible to prevent world booms and depressions. I have suggested that if we cannot get an agreed draft the issue ought to go to Ministers. Meanwhile Marcus Fleming is redrafting the paper.[4] (5) Dow is now engaged on writing a paper on the possible magnitude of the next depression (e.g. how much may home investment and exports fall and how much would this through the multiplier mean in the form of reduced

[3] See Proctor to Meade, 13 August (enclosing draft to be discussed on 21 August), and Meade to Proctor, 15 August 1946, T161/1295/S53261/5. Proctor's paper was circulated as ED(46)24, 'The period to be covered by the annual White Paper on Economic Planning, Report of Working Party', 4 September 1946, CAB134/188.

[4] See above p. 302; Meade to J. H. Woods, 12 August 1946, T236/702.

consumption) in order to have a measure of the fiscal and other weapons which we must have at our disposal to fight a slump.[5] (6) Following this we intend to write up in a paper our review of the various fiscal mechanisms (variations in national insurance contributions, variations in income tax, in indirect taxes, timing of repayment of post-war credits, etc.).[6]

(7) Of all people Fergusson, Permanent Secretary of the Ministry of Fuel and Power, has sent a request to Bridges asking that the Economic Section should do a job for him. He wants there to be prepared periodically a general economic review of the present and prospective economic position for the use of members of the Coal Board, of the Boards of other Socialised Industries and of Civil Servants generally.[7] This means another job for the Economic Section. I think we should do something of this kind on the basis of the Economic Plan after it has been published in the spring and we might revise it six months later. It is certainly important to keep people of this kind in touch with the general economic background. Murrie held a meeting of myself, Campion and Nicholson to discuss this. (8) Finally I discussed with Bridges the way in which we ought to tackle the most recent remit of the Lord President's Committee, namely by what mechanisms were we to carry out the general economic plan which we now had a prospect of having on paper. I suggested that we must seek a combination of direct controls and financial inducements and should have ingredients of all the following measures in our armoury during the next 1½ to 2 years as means of getting one thing rather than another produced: production controls; allocation of raw materials; import controls to see that we gave priority of imports to those machines or raw materials which were required to produce what we wanted to see produced; investment control to give priority to investment in those industries where we wanted to see production expanded; possible limitations on production (e.g. by use of licensing the production of machinery) of those industries in which we wished to see a contraction, even if this meant some temporary unemployment in the contracted industries; measures to facilitate the mobility of labour and possibly the stiffening-up of the conditions on which unemployment benefit could be obtained in order to force men into the new jobs where they were most wanted; a development of wages policy whereby wage-rates could be put up in the industries where it was desired to attract more labour without consequential sympathetic increases elsewhere; a use of the control of prices and profit margins to make some things more, and other things less, profitable to produce; a use of particular taxes and subsidies for the same purpose; and a general fiscal policy of removing the overall inflationary pressure so that while there would be some markets in which there was an excess of demand over supply there would be others where there was some surplus of resources. Bridges asked us to draft a paper for him to circulate to the Steering Committee setting

[5] See above, pp. 284 and 299.

[6] The major paper on this subject was Dow, 'The Control of Consumption Expenditure in the Interests of Employment Policy', 17 December 1946, EC(S)(46)46 (Revise), T230/23 and Meade Papers 3/2. It was circulated to the Budget Committee in early 1947 (T171/389), and revised again in August 1947 (EC(S)(47)29, T230/25 and Meade Papers 3/2).

[7] Fergusson to Bridges, 2 August 1946, T230/107.

out these possibilities so that there could be a general discussion on it in September. After some discussion of the draft with Proctor this has been done.[8]

There has been a meeting of the Budget Committee at which various investigations by the Customs and Excise and the Inland Revenue have been put in hand.[9] Unfortunately the Chancellor cannot be attracted by the idea of an annual capital tax, so that is out. Nor by the idea of a change from the Estate Duty basis to an Inheritance Tax (with or without my frill of a graduation of the tax according to the amount which the individual had inherited from all sources up to date), though he still likes the idea of taking over in return for an annuity all estates over a certain figure and wants the possibility of a gifts tax investigated (which is very sensible with present rates of death duty, which in themselves are very sensible and would be more so if they were inheritance taxes). He is still bent on a profits tax. In this connection I pleaded strongly that if we were to have such a tax we should have one which could differentiate between distributed and undistributed profits and could be used now to differentiate in favour of undistributed profits and later against them, when we had to deal with a deflation. I argued that this should be very carefully distinguished from taxation on, or tax reliefs in respect of, investment in bricks and mortar. What one required in times of inflation was taxation which discriminated in favour of undistributed profits but against real capital investment, from whatever source financed. And vice versa in times of deflation. The Chancellor obviously wants a Budget with some more rather general tax remissions but he also wants a balanced Budget. I put in my usual plea for a budget surplus in times of inflationary pressure such as the present.

David Butt who has now joined the Section after working for Douglas Jay at No. 10 (the latter on becoming an MP being no longer the PM's economic adviser) has taken over our work on the Distribution of Industry and on the Investment Panels dealing with the problems of working out a public investment programme.[10]

Tress is preparing to visit the United States and Canada to discuss with their experts the problems of forecasting national income and expenditure.[11]

A Dutchman called Witteveen from Tinbergen's Planning Bureau came to call on us and Tress and I tried to explain to him how we were tackling some of these problems.

I have attended another lunch of the meetings of accountants and economists where we continued our discussions of accountants' and economists' use of such terms as income, profits, expenditure, etc.[12]

Philip Chantler and I have been to call on de Peyer at the Ministry of

[8] Bridges, 'Means of Implementing Planning Decisions', 12 August 1946, ED(46)22, CAB134/188. The Steering Committee discussed the paper on 8 October: ED(46) 7th meeting, CAB134/187 and T228/20.

[9] Into a profits tax, taxation of gifts and capital gains, and inheritance taxes: the resulting memoranda are on T171/391. Meade subsequently put in a memorandum on 'Stabilisation and the Taxation of Company Profits' (T171/391 and Meade Papers 3/10).

[10] Butt to Meade, 'Investment Working Party: Joint Panels', 1 August, and Butt to Meade and Tress, 'Local Authorities and Investment Policy', 9 August 1946, T230/85.

[11] See above, p. 271.

[12] On 7 August 1946: Meade Papers 3/12.

Fuel and Power to discuss with him the paper which we prepared some time ago on how the Coal Board should use the price mechanism to decide how much coal, what qualities and in what localities to produce.[13] We had once again an interesting discussion and tried hard to describe the advantages of a market mechanism and the disadvantages of being without one. But I fear that our success was negligible.

Miss Kilroy has had two meetings of her official committee on Supervisory Boards and Restrictive Practices which Philip Chantler and I attended and at which we have, I think, had considerably more success. We have accepted her general proposition that our terms of reference do not invite us to consider whether restrictive practices as such are good or bad, but merely to discover how one can apply to Supervisory Boards the principles relating to restrictive practices which the Board of Trade propose should be applied to industry generally. The President of the Board of Trade has now circulated a paper on this subject. The proposals are broadly that Restrictive Practices are not in themselves good or bad but are liable to serious misuse. Such practices should be investigated on complaint by a Commission and there should be power (a) to disallow harmful agreements between producers, (b) to prohibit certain practices by individual producers and (c) to use price control. The problem is how to apply this sort of thing to Statutory Boards. We have agreed that all existing statutory schemes should be investigated to see whether there were any restrictive powers which could be discarded, that wherever possible alternative methods which do not involve restriction should be used (I regard this as very important. Our case is that stability should be given to farmers by e.g. price insurance schemes rather than by e.g. production quotas), and that there should be drafted a set of principles governing the use of any restrictive powers which do remain. At the end of the first meeting and throughout the second meeting we discussed the special problem of Herrings. The Herring Board have put in an amended scheme which includes every conceivable restrictive power – over the number of boats, the number of processors, the amount of fishing, the minimum prices of first sale and of all sales up to the final consumer. We argued very hard on this and finally got agreement (the Fishery Ministries apart, I believe) (i) that licensing the number of boats or the number of processors on grounds of redundancy should not be allowed, (ii) that the control of the amount of fishing (either by the number of nets or the number of boats that might go out on any night) should be permitted but only up to the point of limiting the catches to the physical possibility of handling the catches, and (iii) that as a long-run programme one should aim at a price insurance system or a system whereby the Board or the state purchased the whole catch at an assured price, so that the fishermen could just go ahead and catch as much as they could without anxiety about the market. The central purchasing agency would have to dispose of the supplies as best it could, though the assured price might be lowered gradually if there were a perpetual loss on the resale. Before the system could be introduced and made acceptable to the fisherman, the rest of the

[13] Above, p. 253.

Committee wished to recommend the continuation of minimum prices for the catches. I said that I did not know whether the Section could accept this.[14]

All this is closely connected with a big row which has arisen between the Ministry of Food and the Ministry of Agriculture about the division of their responsibilities. Agriculture want to take over from Food the responsibility of marketing and processing in order to install once more the whole apparatus of restriction through the Agricultural Marketing Board. Food want to take over the products from Agriculture 'at the farm gate' or 'at the quay side'. They are much more prepared to work schemes without any element of restrictionism and to give the producer an assurance that they will take over everything which he produces at an assured price, the Ministry being responsible for resale. The issue was put up to the Lord President's Committee in the form of two papers in which the respective Ministers went for each other. It was referred to Sir Alan Barlow of the Treasury to consider at the official level as a problem in the machinery of government. I briefed the Lord President strongly on the lines that an extremely important issue of economic policy lay behind this dispute. Nicholson briefed him saying that it was a machinery-of-government question. I rebriefed him that it wasn't at all exclusively that; and Nicholson rebriefed him. I had sent to the Lord President with my first brief a copy of the long paper which we had prepared for Miss Kilroy's Committee on 'Supervisory Boards and Restrictive Practices' [above, p. 286]. The Lord President wrote me back a very patronising minute saying that I was being anti-producer! Anyhow it all obviously had some effect, as he asked us to produce a boiled-down version of our paper for him to circulate to his ministerial colleagues. Meanwhile Barlow's committee has met and the issue is clearly going rather in the direction of the Ministry of Food.[15] It is recognised that it turns largely on the question how far can we expect there to be a high and sustained demand for the produce of UK agriculture and whether the Treasury or the producers will stand the financial risk of gluts and price collapses. We have been asked to write a background economic paper on all this (which will, I hope, take the place of the paper which the Lord President suggested circulating himself). I have spent a great deal of time writing this paper. In it I say that the post-war position is likely to differ from the pre-war position in four vital ways. I. There is likely as a result of full employment, social security measures, nutritional policies and fiscal measures for the redistribution of incomes from rich to poor to be a very substantial increase in the demand

[14] Minutes of 2nd and 3rd meetings on 30 July and 9 August 1946; SBC9, 'Restrictive Practices: Memorandum by the President of the Board of Trade', 13 August 1946, and SBC5, 'Herring Industry Amending Scheme: Memorandum by the Scottish Home Department' and 'Herring Industry (Amending) Scheme, 1947', 26 July 1946, BT64/306.

[15] LP(46) 29th meeting, 2 August 1946, CAB132/1; LP(46)204, 'Marketing of Agricultural Products and Fish, Division of Responsibility between Ministry of Food and Agriculture and Fisheries Departments, Memorandum by Minister of Agriculture and Fisheries, Secretary of State for Scotland and Home Secretary', 22 July 1946, and LP(46)206, 'Marketing and Processing of Home-Produced Foodstuffs, Memorandum by Minister of Food', 28 July 1946, CAB132/4. Meade's and Nicholson's briefs have not been found. On Barlow's committee see below, p. 318.

for foodstuffs. We give quantitative illustrations of all these factors and also try to assess the possible result of a full nutritional policy on the demand for agricultural products. II. Full employment will mean on the supply side that if any particular line of production is depressed it will be much easier to turn to the production of something else. III. Externally (a) to get our balance of payments right we shall in any case have to expand exports by 50–75 per cent, which means that over the whole range of our industries and agriculture we must reckon either with heavy protection through the restriction of imports or with a relative improvement in our general level of prices and costs (if necessary by further exchange depreciation). Either of these will benefit agriculture. (b) Other countries will have nutritional policies or there will be World Food Plans which will increase the foreign demand for foodstuffs. (c) The American Trade Proposals will limit the possibilities of foreigners dumping their agricultural surpluses on our markets and the development of commodity agreements under ITO will decrease the probability of external price collapses. (d) Other countries will also have full employment policies; but if there is an external general collapse it is likely, through the decline in the demand for our exports, to put us in balance of payments difficulties, in which case we could control our imports quantitatively. All these factors are likely to improve the competitive position of UK agriculture. IV. The war experience has given us new techniques of control. We can now have a system of state purchases of all production without limit and resale to consumers, with an annual price review at which the price can be gradually (but not abruptly) reduced if there is a persistent glut of any one product. We should plan with this technique and on the assumption that there will be a high demand for UK agricultural produce. If the opposite turns out to be the case, the guaranteed prices will give the farmers security, the blow will fall on the Treasury; there will accordingly be at least a breathing space so far as the farmers are concerned during which one could consider giving over to a system of restrictions. Chantler, Shackle and Brown have all helped in preparing the paper.[16]

On the external side the most important event has been the production by Sir John Orr of the FAO's proposal for a World Food Board. His proposals are very vague. But as far as policy is concerned they would seem to come down to (a) a vast scheme of Buffer Stocks and (b) a scheme for eleemosynary grants of foodstuffs in surplus at little or no price to poor countries. We (i.e. Marcus Fleming and myself) welcome (a) and the proposals have in fact put life once more into the Buffer Stock idea, I am glad to say. Strachey, the Minister of Food, has been attracted and has had a long talk with Lionel Robbins on the subject.[17] (b), however, is much more dangerous from our point of view, because it might involve schemes whereby the poor countries got their food cheap which was financed by a high price for sales of food to countries like this, a tax which would serve

[16] Meade, Chantler, Brown and Shackle, 'The Marketing of Home-Produced Foodstuffs', 11 September 1946, EC(S)(46)34 (Revise), T230/22.

[17] The 'Proposals for a World Food Board', 5 July 1946, were initially comunicated to Whitehall in a series of cables (T236/92); Robbins, Liesching and Broadley met Strachey on 9 August 1946 (Waley to Rowe-Dutton, 12 August 1946, T236/92).

to solve those agricultural problems in the high-cost North American continent and the nutritional problems of, e.g., China at our expense. If there is to be some international socialism, which I should support though I doubt whether Ministers would do so with their eyes open, let it be by way of direct contributions from the rich countries to the poor (e.g. by way of subscriptions by the rich countries into a fund out of which the poor could buy more food). On the problem of institutions it is universally agreed in Whitehall that Orr has gone off the rails. A world food board would be a fifth wheel in the coach, where the Fund and the Bank are to deal with finance, ITO with commodity policy, the FAO with technical problems of Food and Agriculture and the Economic and Social Council with the general co-ordination of policies. I have lunched with Robert Hall of the Board of Trade and Marcus Fleming to discuss this. (Incidentally they together with John Wall of the Ministry of Food are reconsidering our whole Commodity Policy for the trade conference.)[18] I have also lunched with Lamartine Yates of FAO who is over here with Orr, and have put this general line to him. Marcus Fleming has also briefed the Lord President in this sense. He and I have attended a meeting in Liesching's room in the Ministry of Food to discuss, on the basis of a draft telegram to Washington, the line which we should take on this. The Treasury had put in a redraft of the telegram in which they very much played down the possibility of Buffer Stocks but put little emphasis on the dangers to us of perpetual eleemosynary grants. We put in a re-re-draft on these topics, which was more or less accepted.[19]

Helmore who has succeeded to Liesching's position at the Board of Trade (the latter having become Permanent Secretary at the Ministry of Food) has held a meeting of the Trade Negotiations Committee to consider certain matters which arise out of the draft commercial convention which the Americans have now produced and are intending to circulate. Marcus Fleming and I attended.[20]

I have at last managed to read a paper which the Bank of England have prepared for the Sterling Area Negotiations Committee on our relations with the non-sterling area countries. In the course of this paper they deal with the problem of our getting paid for the goods which we export to such countries, i.e. the problem of converting the foreign currencies into sterling. In many of the countries which they have in mind they say that we cannot expect the countries for a long time to accept convertibility of their currencies under Article VIII of the Fund. Moreover, they rule out (a) a system whereby we insisted on our exports being invoiced in sterling and (b) the introduction of a free exchange market for the currencies of these countries in London so that our exporters could sell these currencies for what they would fetch. They therefore conclude that we must continue and develop with these countries for a long time ahead the nexus of

[18] Trade Negotiations Committee: Sub-Committee on International Commodity Policy (CAB134/714).

[19] The meeting was on 15 August 1946. The minutes and the draft telegrams are on T236/92. The final version was dispatched as No. 8112 Foreign Office to Washington, 17 August 1946.

[20] TN(46) 4th meeting, 9 August 1946, CAB134/711.

monetary and payments agreements which we are developing with them. Waley of the Treasury has put in a plea for considering moving more quickly towards a free exchange market here. I have written a minute to Marcus Fleming on all this, suggesting that he should prepare a note for us to send to the Treasury on it.[21] First, we can develop the objections to the existence of monetary and payments agreements where the foreign currencies are overvalued, which A. J. Brown and I developed in the recent working party on trade with South East Europe [above, pp. 228, 303]. Secondly, if we could develop a free exchange market to the extent of in fact being willing to buy and sell gold freely for all international transactions, under Article IV of the Fund we should (like the USA) be free from any obligation not to allow the exchange value of foreign currencies to depreciate on the London Market. If these currencies are overvalued and if trade cannot start with these countries because this overvaluation means that we won't import their goods so that they have no sterling with which to purchase our goods, then a system which allowed our exporters to sell the currency proceeds of their exports for what they would fetch on a free London exchange market might enable trade to start up. But would such a willingness to buy and sell gold freely be compatible with the control of capital movements?

A. J. Brown has come back from leave. I have immediately set him four tasks. (i) The Lord President who has circulated as a Cabinet paper the paper which Brown prepared on the subject of how Germany maintained full employment before the war, now wants a similar paper on how the USSR maintained full employment.[22] (ii) Brown is doing something on the competitive prospects of our agricultural produce vis-à-vis that of other countries for our paper on the economic background of the dispute between the Ministry of Food and the Ministry of Agriculture.[23] (iii) This, however, is likely to be part of a much wider enquiry. After reading Brown's overseas survey the Lord President asked Marquand's Committee on Export Trade Problems (i.e. the Board of Trade) in consultation with the Economic Section to report in full on our prospects of exporting in the coming competitive conditions, on which subject he thought that our Overseas Economic Survey might be too optimistic. Austin Robinson having left the Board of Trade, they are at their wits' end how to tackle this and have applied to us. So we are to have the resources of the Board of Trade at our disposal to test the accuracy of our own statements! It is a great opportunity. Tomorrow Brown and I are to discuss with Plumb of the Board of Trade how we should go about this.[24] I have suggested that George Shackle should do some econometric work with Brown on the

[21] SAN(46)7, 'The U.S. Financial Agreement as it Affects Relations with Non-Sterling Countries', 29 June, and Waley, 'Sterling Balances Negotiations', 2 August 1946, T236/1660; Meade to Fleming, 13 August 1946, T230/138.

[22] CP(46)309, 'Full Employment in Germany before the War, Memorandum by the Lord President of the Council', 30 July 1946, CAB129/12; CP(43)355, 'Full Employment in the Soviet Union, Memorandum by the Lord President of the Council', 24 September 1946, CAB129/13.

[23] See above, pp. 313–14.

[24] See note by M. E. Hill, 30 August, T230/134, and below, p. 318.

basis of Board of Trade information about the elasticity of substitution between our goods and the goods of other countries in export markets. (iv) The sub-committee of the Economic and Social Council on devastated areas is meeting in London. I have been to one or two meetings with Noel-Baker and Lord Pakenham (who is our delegate to this sub-committee) in the Foreign Office on the subject in the absence of Marcus Fleming and A. J. Brown on leave.[25] But really life is too short to do everything! I have turned this over, lock, stock and barrel, to Brown.

Nita Watts is about to go on leave. She has just produced a background paper on our existing monetary and payments agreements which I have sent on to Marcus Fleming with the other papers in connection with our financial relations with non-sterling area countries. She has also prepared a draft paper for which the Lord President had asked on the economic effects to us of the loss of the Empire.[26] This I have sent to R. J. Shackle in the Board of Trade and R. W. B. Clarke in the Treasury for their comments before sending it to the Lord President.

I have spent much time in discussions with the Lord President, Max Nicholson, Waley and Rowe-Dutton in the Treasury, Hall-Patch, Gore-Booth and Stevens in the Foreign Office, and David Owen of UNO on the problems of finding staff for the Fund, the Bank, the secretariat of UNO and our representation on the Economic and Employment Commission of the Economic and Social Council.

I had to spend two whole full days, at the moment when Ministers were busiest before going on leave and when most of the Section seemed to be on leave, on the Civil Service Commission Selection Board for Economic Assistants. We have selected Dow, Jefferies and another very good LSE product – D. O. Henley. We have put a Miss Forsyth and a Mr Winegarten on the reserve list.

I have had lunch with Rosenstein-Rodan who has just come back from Poland. He was very interesting on the political atmosphere there.

## *16 August 1946*

This morning we were called in by Liesching at the Ministry of Food, as he described it as 'The Harley Street Specialists', to advise on a general problem which they are up against. At the moment the distribution of unrationed foodstuffs regionally is on a pre-war quantity basis. This means that areas which were depressed before the war now get less than their fair share. The Ministry of Food have made certain *ad hoc* specific adjustments for particular foodstuffs in particular regions, but it has all been a matter of giving in to particular pressures. They now want to find a 'scientific' basis for re-allocating supplies. The supplies cannot merely be allocated on a *per caput* basis because of regional differences in tastes. On the other hand, since the pre-war period there have been many changes (e.g. population

[25] Above, pp. 306–7, IOC(D)(46)3, '2nd meeting of UK Delegation to Sub-commission on Economic Reconstruction of Devastated Areas', 2 August 1946, FO371/50329. The sub-commission met 29 July–14 August 1946.

[26] 'The Economic Effects of Giving Up the Empire', 10 September 1946, T230/276.

movements, unemployment changes, changes in relative earnings) which have affected the relative demands of the various regions. We have suggested that the best criterion of present distribution might be to take the pre-war quantities of any commodity for each region and multiply it by an index of the increase in the money earnings of the working classes in that region. The pre-war datum takes account of the pre-war regional distribution of tastes for various products and the index of changes in working-class earnings weights this for changes in all the relevant other factors (population, unemployment, earnings changes). Of course, the thing is crude because (i) it assumes a unit income elasticity of demand for each foodstuff and (ii) neglects such facts as that a uniform national cheese ration (a commodity for which there were great regional differences pre-war) will have greatly modified pre-war tastes for other foods. Now the question remains of seeing whether the Central Statistical Office and the Ministry of Labour statisticians can provide the necessary regional statistics. Liesching is now going to take this up.

We have received drafts of the reports of Miss Kilroy's Committee on Supervisory Boards and Restrictive Practices (a) on Herrings and (b) on the principles which should govern the use of restrictive practices by such Boards.[27] I have discussed with Chantler various ways in which these should be tightened up.

I have had a meeting in my room of Plumb and Mrs Daniel of the Board of Trade, Miss Lidderdale of the Lord President's Office, and A. J. Brown and G. L. Shackle to discuss the way in which we should help the Board of Trade with their investigation into the prospects of the competitive position for our exports. All went well and I hope that we should now be able to organise a fairly profound enquiry into this subject. We explained how essential it was to get some idea of the order of magnitude of the elasticity of demand for our various products in various markets.[28]

I forgot to record yesterday the profound impression made on me by the meeting under Barlow of the Food and Agriculture officials to consider the demarcation line between the two ministries.[29] Here was a first-rate economic issue being discussed and it was all done in terms of administrative machinery and responsibility *without any reference to or appreciation of the market mechanism*. On both sides there was a general agreement that somehow the Ministry of Food had to decide what amounts of commodities they wanted and for what purposes and the Ministry of Agriculture had to decide what amounts should be produced and how. The idea that consumers decided or should be enabled to decide how much they wanted of various things at various prices and that producers could follow or should be encouraged to follow this lead was totally absent. The idea that the Government could intervene, not to destroy, but to improve the workings of the price mechanism was not present because no one was aware of the existence of any such animal. It reminded me of a meeting of medieval doctors discussing how to deal with an epidemic before the

27 See above, pp. 312–13; the drafts and the report are on BT64/306.
28 Above, p. 316; Note of a meeting in Mr Plumb's room on 16 August 1946, T230/134.
29 No minutes of this meeting have been located.

existence of bacteria was discovered. It made me feel (i) what dangerous seas we are sailing into when the state is taking on more and more economic functions while those responsible for them are, quite frankly, not properly trained technically and (ii) what an important long-run contribution the economist in government service has to make. But I fear one must stress the words 'long-run'. (All this also leads to planning gone wild. As they can see no force leading to a rational scale of production or distribution other than administrative decree, every output and sale must be controlled by a Department. The most amusing riddle was should the Production or the Consumption department be responsible for eggs and poultry, since eggs may be eaten or used to produce birds and birds may be eaten or used to produce eggs. It was generally agreed that some department must change a scheme to ensure that the proper amount of eggs and birds were produced for each use! Not a single mention of prices and costs at this point. May nothing be kept to a free market?)

Have discussed with Barlow the composition of the proposed Interdepartmental Economic and Social Research Committee, which is to be set up with outside experts to consider the use of information within Government Departments for academic research purposes. I realise to my sorrow that it is all focused on sociological rather than economic research. I think that this is a pity. I am suggesting that Sayers should normally represent us but that I might from time to time attend.[30]

[30] The Clapham Committee on the Provision for Social and Economic Research which reported in July 1945 (Cmd. 6868) had recommended that an interdepartmental committee be 'charged with the duty of bringing to the notice of departments the potential value for research of the materials they collect and suggestions for new methods and areas of collection'. The interdepartmental committee was set up on 1 October 1946 with Meade as a member and Sayers as his alternate (CAB124/529).

# 23

## September 1946

*21 September 1946*

I have returned from three weeks' leave to find, as always, a great accumulation of matters to attend to, in spite of the fact that this has been the holiday season. The problems of the Economic Plan have restarted in the form of activity in the Investment Working Party. In particular the Central Electricity Board, through the Ministry of Fuel and Power, have put in for the approval of the Investment Working Party all the schemes for new electrical generating plants costing £500,000 or more which they wish to start in the near future. This programme was very large in amount and was put in with very much the attitude that the need for it all must be accepted on the word of the CEB. David Butt with Philip Chantler has been working on this in the Section. We concocted a letter which I sent to Gilbert as chairman of the Investment Working Party, in which we argued that on general employment policy grounds one must be prepared now to delay and postpone capital expenditure even at considerable social cost and inconvenience and that we must go through this programme item by item to see what parts might be at least postponed for a little time. We made the point that the CEB really gave no indication at all about the assumptions which they were making in estimating the future demand for electricity. Was there nothing which could be done (e.g. by continuation of summer time or of the ban on display lighting) to hold back the peak demands? The Investment Working Party itself went quite well. The CEB demands were not merely rubber-stamped. A group was set up of the Economic Section, Central Statistical Office and Treasury to consider with the statisticians of the Central Electricity Board and of the Ministry of Fuel and Power the assumptions being made about the future demand for electricity. Fuel and Power made the point that the electricity services must supply the demands and that their programme followed inevitably upon other programmes (e.g. the electrification of the railways, the housing programme with its supplies of e.g. electric refrigerators, the mechanisation of coal mining which would require electricity as a motive power, etc.). I replied that this was the reason why an exhaustive analysis of the future demand was required, so that if necessary it could be decided to go a bit slower with those other programmes which led to increased demand for electricity. There is to be another meeting of the Investment Working Party next week to hear the report of the statistical enquiry.[1]

Another development on the Investment Working Party has been the presentation of a paper by the Board of Trade (the last will and testament of Austin Robinson before returning to Cambridge) on the problem of forecasting private investment. I feel that this paper is rather off the mark. It suggests that we should remain content for the next period ahead with dealing with private investment not by asking the firms which wish to install new plant, equipment or buildings what their plans for capital expenditure are, but by relying on estimates on the supply side of the resources which can be allocated to private investment, resting on the assumption that the demand will in any case be much in excess of this and can be held down to this through the issue of building licences. The paper suggests, however, that on the basis of a voluntary sample enquiry from all firms of over a very moderate level one should attempt to get the investment expenditure plans from the different firms for five years ahead. Our view is that both these major propositions are wrong. We believe that it is really rather meaningless to ask any but the monster concerns (e.g. ICI [Imperial Chemical Industries] or the Iron and Steel Federation) what they plan to spend on capital development five years ahead. On the other hand, we believe that one should start at once asking firms of all sizes what they intend to spend on capital development in the next twelve months, if for no other reason than because some experience of the routine provision of such information both by the firms preparing it and by us who have to interpret it will be necessary before it can be very useful. We must have had as much practice at this as possible before the next slump comes. We have accordingly put in a paper on these lines.[2]

Dow has now prepared a very interesting draft paper on the probable or possible magnitude of a future depression, showing how much decline in expenditure might occur (a) in exports, (b) in private investment and (c), through the multiplier, in private consumption, and giving some indication of the specific and structural problems that might be involved (e.g. how far resources previously producing exports could produce for home investment or consumption). I have suggested some alterations and we are going to submit a redraft as an Economic Survey Working Party paper. This is the first, I hope, of a whole series on how to deal with the next slump. Dow is already quite advanced on the first, which will be on the problem of the counteraction which one might take by fiscal and

[1] INV.WP(46)15, Tables prepared by the Electricity Commissioners, T230/86; Meade to Gilbert, 16 September 1946, T230/85; INV.WP(46) 5th meeting, 19 September 1946, T161/1297/S53555/02; INV.WP(46)17, Investment Working Party: Generating Stations Construction Programme, 23 September 1946, T230/86; INV.WP(46) 6th meeting, 25 September 1946, T161/1297/S53555/02.

[2] Robinson's paper is 'Estimate of Capital Investment in Private Industry', 1 August 1946 (see Robinson to Barnes, 1 August 1946), T161/1297/S53555/05. Subsequent dispute between the economists, not involving Meade, 'conducted more in the tones of a Reformation theological dispute than of a sober examination of practical means of getting information', (Vinter to Proctor, 12 October 1946), is recorded on the same file.

similar action to 'break the multiplier' and maintain the demand for consumption goods and services.[3]

George Shackle has prepared a paper on the Propensity to Consume in 1951. He attempts in the first part to examine the propensity to consume of various income groups in the United States (there being no such information for the United Kingdom) and on this basis and the basis of the overall United Kingdom propensity to consume in 1938 to make guesses, about the effect which the more equal distribution of income in 1951 may have on the propensity to consume in that year. It is all, admittedly, almost valueless; but there is really no information to work on. In the second part of the paper he mentions qualitatively a number of reasons for believing that the propensity to consume in 1951 is likely to be very appreciably higher than in 1938:- (i) the greater equality in the distribution of income and, in particular, the fact that the rich are likely for a time to try to maintain certain conventional expenditures (e.g. on education) although they really have no longer the income to do it with; (ii) the fact that with Death Duties, low interest rates and highly progressive and heavy sur-tax the rich cannot hope to 'found a family fortune' by saving; (iii) the change in the age distribution which means that those who are 'saving up' for old age will no longer exceed, but may be exceeded by, the old who are living on their savings; (iv) the fact that the state through national insurance etc. has taken over many of the functions of saving; and (v) the fact that there may still be some war-time backlog of consumers' demands for goods. I have sent the paper for comments by Stafford in the Central Statistical Office, and am considering circulating it to the Economic Survey Working Party as a background paper for our 1951 Economic Survey.[4]

I have asked George Shackle now to do an examination of the present budget expenditure and in particular of the expenditure 'below the line'. The point is that from the point of view of the inflationary or deflationary influence of public finance one has to take into account certain items (e.g. repayment of post-war income tax credits) which may properly for other accounting purposes be kept 'below the line' in the ordinary national Budget. I have asked him to do me an analysis of the present budgetary returns from this point of view.[5]

Stafford, Jackson and Saunders of the Central Statistical Office have been to see me about the collection of information from the various departments (and in particular the Board of Trade) for the next Economic Survey. We had agreed that as far as consumption expenditure was concerned we should on this occasion start with a regular 'propensity to consume' guess rather than with the supplies which Departments would

[3] See above, p. 299. Dow's depression paper was circulated as ESWP(46)18 on 6 November 1946 (T230/56). His 'The Control of Consumption Expenditure in the interests of Employment Policy', was circulated in the Section in December (EC(S)(46)46 (Revise), T230/23 and Meade Papers 3/2).

[4] 'The United Kingdom Propensity to Consume in 1950', September 1946, and Meade to Stafford, 20 September 1946, CAB139/168. Stafford agreed Shackle's paper should be circulated to the ESWP, but work on the 1951 survey came to a halt in October 1946 (see Cairncross to Meade, 18 December 1946, T230/163).

[5] This has not been found.

consider it reasonable to sponsor on the market. The Central Statistical Office now want to supplement that by asking for information from all the Departments concerned about what they would consider a reasonable objective to aim at for these supplies of consumption goods. I have, rather weakly, agreed to their doing this; but it is sure to cause trouble with Reddaway at the Board of Trade, to whom we had rather given an undertaking that we would ask for these departmental programmes of minimum essential supplies only in the case of essentials, such as clothing. But I can see the point of view of the Central Statistical Office. If we merely work out a 'propensity to consume' figure, it may for these various miscellaneous consumption goods give a demand which is so enormously greater than any possible available supplies, that it may be rather meaningless to show, for example, manpower requirements based on such a propensity to consume. It might be more helpful to show Ministers a manpower table in which the requirements were once more of the 'reasonable objective' type rather than of the type which shows the total amount of manpower which would be needed fully to satisfy a completely uncontrolled demand.

We have been consulted by Brigadier Cornwall-Jones about the implications in the Civilian Sector of the economy of the manpower demands which would materialise in, say, 1950 from the proposals which the military are about to put forward for an eighteen months period of military conscription. Patrick Jefferies has been looking into this with Christopher Saunders of the Central Statistical Office. It appears that with these high demands and allowing for (i) the associated demand for labour for supplies for the forces, (ii) the demand for labour for increased exports, and (iii) the increased demand for labour for building, there would still be as much and probably more labour than in 1938 for producing civilian goods for the home market, the difference being caused primarily by (a) the lower level of unemployment assumed and (b) the larger total working population. But on the other side one has to put many considerations: (i) it does not allow for any raising of the school leaving age above 15, (ii) it does not allow for a reduction in hours of work (a 10 per cent reduction from 47 to 42 or 43 a week is equivalent to 2,000,000 men), (iii) it does not allow for the increased army of 'bureaucrats' which we shall need in the brave new world, (iv) it does not allow for the increased labour required for the higher investment programme in plant and machinery for the re-equipment of industry, and (v) it does not allow for the fact that conscription will take out the youngest and most productive workers. It is most unlikely that any increase in industrial efficiency will anywhere near make up for all this, and one must remember that the civilian targets are not merely the restoration of, but the raising of, 1939 standards of living. We shall produce some cold water of this kind at the meeting of the Manpower Working Party at which this will be discussed next week.[6]

Stafford of the Central Statistical Office and I have been honoured by a very personal and confidential request from John Henry Woods, Permanent Secretary of the Board of Trade, about the information to be

[6] MP(0)(46) 8th meeting, 23 September 1946, CAB134/510.

sought in the 1946 trial Census of Production from the Building Industry. The proposal is to ask fairly detailed information about the volume as well as the value of work done under a large number of detailed heads of type of work. There is an acute row with the Building Industry who are on strike about the amount of detail asked. We advised Woods that one must have information about volume as well as value of work done; but that it was just conceivable that one might in the Census only ask for value of work done, and obtain a 'price index' for the deflation of these value figures by a separate sample enquiry. I spoke later to Woods about this. He thinks that they may be able to get away with some considerably smaller concession – e.g. that for the 1946 Census but not necessarily for the subsequent ones they should ask for the information under a smaller number of headings about the type of work done.

I have had a visit from a number of Swedish and Norwegian Government economists who are visiting this country and explained to them what we were doing in the way of forecasting National Income and Expenditure and our general technique of the Economic Surveys and turning them into an Economic Plan for a Free Society.[7] I have delivered the same old lecture on the same old subject yet once more to one of the Foreign Office summer conferences in Oxford, where I stayed the weekend in Jesus College. I think it is very useful to keep our Foreign Service people *au fait* in this way with the main things which the Social Democratic (or dare I say Liberal-Socialist) United Kingdom is doing.

I have attended two more lunches of the joint Economist-Accountant group to discuss the common problems of Social Accounting.[8]

A. J. Brown has prepared a note at the Lord President's request, which we have now sent down to him, on the methods by which Soviet Russia maintained Full Employment. We have drawn the obvious comparisons. In particular we stressed the fact that Russia with all her direct controls had to use the method of fixing relative wage-rates as an important means of getting labour into the desired occupations.[9]

During my absence on leave Philip Chantler had prepared a draft brief for the Lord President on the memorandum by the President of the Board of Trade on how to deal with 'Restrictive Practices'. I have done a covering minute and we have sent it down to the Lord President.[10] Broadly speaking we have taken the line that the onus of proving that any restrictive practice was anti-social should not be on the Government; but rather a list of practices should be generally prohibited unless the private industry could show cause why it should be allowed to indulge in them. I have stressed

[7] The visitors were I. Ohlsson from Sweden and P. J. Bjerve and O. Aukrust from Norway (Richard Stone, 'The development and use of national income and expenditure estimates', in Chester, *Lessons of the British War Economy*, p. 99.)

[8] On 10 and 18 September 1946. The group continued to meet regularly until June 1947 and produced a first report on 'Terms and Concepts in Common Use', issued jointly by the Institute of Chartered Accountants and the National Institute of Economic and Social Research, in February 1948 (Meade Papers 3/12).

[9] CP(43)355, 'Full Employment in the Soviet Union, Memorandum by the Lord President of the Council', 24 September 1946, CAB129/13.

[10] Chantler to Lord President, 'Restrictive Practices: Memorandum by the President of the Board of Trade', and Meade to Lord President, 17 September 1946, CAB124/497.

two fundamental points in my minute:- *The first* relating to Industrial Structure, namely that there is a place for public ownership and for direct public control, but where there is not public ownership or control one should make sure that there is the maximum degree of competition; what one does not want is a monopolistically organised 'private unenterprise'. *The second* relating to Industrial Efficiency, namely that most of these practices hold down output per head; (for example, quota restrictions on production or limits on new entry stop the low-cost producer from driving out the high-cost producer, or fixation of minimum retail prices or margins prevents the low-cost distributive outlet from driving out the inefficient retail shop) and that our salvation depends upon increased industrial efficiency (e.g. a 5 per cent increase in output per man – equivalent to only about 3 years normal progress – corresponds to the work of 1,000,000 men). I wonder what will happen. Not, I fear, much.

Meanwhile the Lord President has sent up to us a request for an enquiry into the industry producing electrical equipment where – he has heard – there are many restrictive practices which impede increased output per man. Chantler is taking on this commission.

David Butt, besides his work for the Investment Working Party, is considering doing a general paper on problems of industrial location.[11] He and some people in the Board of Trade are concerned about the possibility of some regions which are not now at all depressed becoming so at some date in the future (e.g. when the shipbuilding boom ends) and think that, apart from considering the very immediate *ad hoc* tactics of bringing work to the doorstep of every individual unemployed man in South Wales, one should consider now in the broad the wider strategy of preparing for these possible future issues. I very much agree with this; and have suggested that he should in all this bear in mind two points. (i) We all now tend to forget that a major plank in the distribution of industry was the diversification of industry in all regions including those which are prosperous but may later become depressed; and the policy was not in its conception confined to taking work to districts of existing unemployment. (ii) The enquiry should concentrate just as much on the possibilities of promoting the future occupational and geographical mobility of workers as on the possibilities of bringing work of the old kind to groups of workers who in the future may become unemployed.

Sayers, who has now come back after the operation on his spine, has got into touch with Frank Lee at the Ministry of Supply on the future of the Iron and Steel Industry. Apparently there is some reversal of policy in process and the attempt is being made to devise some sort of joint-public ownership-private ownership arrangement. It seems to me that this might go in either of two ways:- first, the consolidation of the private monopoly capitalist organisation (the Iron and Steel Federation) with a show of public control over prices etc.; secondly, the development of true 'Socialist competition' between private firms and state firms or firms jointly owned as far as prices and output are concerned with some considerable measure of public control over investment plans. Sayers is to represent us on two

[11] There is no indication that he did so (CAB124/647).

working parties, one on the organisation and the other on the economic policy of the industry.[12] We shall work for the second alternative.

Since Douglas Jay has left No. 10 in order to become a Member of Parliament, it seems that the Prime Minister has decided not to find another personal adviser on economic matters. We are, accordingly, beginning to brief the PM on economic matters as they come up for decision at the Cabinet. This is an interesting new development. Since the beginning of the Economic Section the PM has up to now had his own economic adviser (Lord Cherwell in the case of Churchill and Jay in the case of Attlee). We have done briefs so far for the PM on Silver (in which the Chancellor of the Exchequer is making the sensible suggestion to save silver and foreign exchange by substituting a cheap alloy for silver in our coinage); on Tin Prices (in which we backed the proposal of the Board of Trade to make an upward adjustment of tin prices in this country in order to bring them more into line with world prices); on Prisoner of War Labour (in which we suggested that there should be further development of the proposals to give prisoners of war a greater incentive to work by increasing the bonus for good work and allowing them to remit more of it to their families in Germany – a proposal which was part of the general scheme for the programme of their repatriation); and on Economic Sanctions (in which we backed the proposal of the Minister of State – itself emanating in the first place from Marcus Fleming in the Economic Section – that steps should be taken at the forthcoming meeting of the Economic and Social Council to start enquiries to set up an Economic Staff Committee parallel with the Military Staff Committee to advise the Security Council on the possibility of using Economic as well as Military Sanctions).[13]

Sayers, A. J. Brown and I all went to call on the military group – consisting of a Brigadier, an Admiral and an Air Commodore – which has been asked in the Cabinet Offices to consider the general military and strategic situation some five years ahead. We have arranged, both through our work for the internal Economic Survey and through A. J. Brown's work on the Overseas Economic Survey, to keep them briefed on our general economic potential.

During my absence on leave A. J. Brown with Marcus Fleming had drafted a note for us to send to R. W. B. Clarke on how we should keep our balance of payments statistics for purposes of the Economic Survey and for other purposes. I did not altogether like the draft which had been prepared and, with Stafford and Jackson of the Central Statistical Office, held a meeting with A. J. Brown as a result of which Stafford drafted a joint Economic Section-Central Statistical Office note which we have now sent to Clarke. The main points which we have raised are:- (i) Clarke

[12] On this issue and the working parties, see Chester, *The Nationalisation of British Industry 1945–51*, pp. 159–65.

[13] The first two of these issues were raised in, respectively, CP(46)337, 'Silver, Memorandum by the Chancellor of the Exchequer', 6 September 1946, and CP(46)338, 'Increases in Buying and Selling Prices of Tin, Memorandum by the Minister of Supply', 5 September 1946, CAB129/12. One of the Section's briefs has been found: Dow to Prime Minister, 'Silver, Memorandum by the Chancellor of the Exchequer (CP(46)337)', 10 September 1946, PREM8/340.

proposed to record imports and exports on a payments basis as opposed to a transactions basis. We argued for a transactions basis on a number of grounds:- (a) For Survey purposes it has to be a transactions basis since we are interested in the actual claims made on our real resources in any period and not in the payments made for those claims. For example, in the present period when, because of the lag between exports and payments for exports, payments for exports are lower than transactions in exports, we have to adjust the payments figures for National Expenditure purposes by adding in a special item for goods exported and not yet paid for. (b) From the point of view of our foreign exchange-foreign asset position, sums owed to us on short-term credits for our exports are a more important and a more liquid foreign asset than many for which we do take account, and we should therefore take credit for our exports not yet paid for. (c) We want to preserve the maximum of comparability with the trade returns, which are of course on a transactions basis. (ii) Clarke proposes that our imports should be recorded fob and not cif. We argued for cif on the grounds (a) of comparability with our trade returns which themselves could not be altered unless the basis of tariff valuation was changed, (b) of the greater ease of estimating shipping earnings if one has only to reckon the total earnings of our shipping and not only that part of the earnings of our shipping which derives from activities other than importing into this country, (c) of the greater convenience of cif in the case of planning that increasing range of imports which will be privately imported and not as in the war purchased by a state trading body, and (d) of the fact that it is only the USA and Canada which at present adopt the fob basis. (iii) We criticised Clarke's proposal to treat as current payments such items as the amortisation of our debts overseas and our granting of certain loans to foreign governments. (iv) We also made some miscellaneous points about the treatment of re-exports and the split up of the very important item of Government Overseas Expenditure.[14]

Preparations are now on foot for the Dominions talks (on 3 October) and then the Preparatory Committee talks (on 15 October) for the World Conference on Trade and Employment. In the absence of Marcus Fleming in New York on the United Kingdom delegation to the Economic and Social Council, I have had to try to cope with our part in this myself. (1) I have now managed to read through – I will not say study – the United States draft charter which they have put in spelling out in detailed clauses the whole of the Trade Proposals. It is a grand sign of the intention, at least of the Administration, really to take this all seriously; and I personally confess that I am rather glad to hear that they propose next week to publish the whole draft charter, though the official view here is that this is dangerous since it will frighten off a number of countries.[15] On the contrary, I believe now that anything which brings it all nearer finality is to the good.

[14] 'Economic Survey 1947, Balance of Payments', and Meade to Clarke, 16 September 1946, T230/7. See also above, pp. 264–5.

[15] 'Suggested Charter for an International Trade Organisation of the United Nations', TN(46)34, CAB134/712, and *Report of the First Session of the Preparatory Committee of the United Nations Conference on Trade and Employment*. London: 1946, pp. 52–67.

(2) I attended a meeting in the Board of Trade under Shackle with R. W. B. Clarke from the Treasury and with representatives from the Dominions Office to consider the attitude of New Zealand to quantitative import restrictions under the Trade Proposals. The New Zealanders argue (a) that their exports of primary products are so chancy and so liable to unforeseen fluctuations that they must have a permanent machinery of import restrictions to deal with sudden and unforeseen balance of payments difficulties, and (b) that they have such a stored-up liquid position of excess internal purchasing power that for the foreseeable future there will be a chronic tendency for New Zealanders to overspend on imports unless there is continuing import restriction. The meeting was to consider the line on which this should be combatted. There was some tendency to suggest the line that there were transitional period let-outs and that New Zealand's problem would probably not prove as lasting as might at the moment appear probable. I deprecated this and argued that we should say to the New Zealanders: 'If your difficulties last, you can continue the control of imports just so long as and just to the extent necessary to avoid a balance of payments difficulty. You, New Zealand, will judge how long and how severe your restrictions will be on this score. Your only obligation is to liberalise them just to the extent necessary to avoid a substantial or persistent growth in your reserves. There is no question of just having to abolish them at the end of the transitional period. The only sanction against you is that any other member of ITO can have you up to complain that you are abusing their use and ITO can in the last resort allow other countries to take counteraction if the charge is considered justified.' This line ought really to make it clear whether (as I fear) the real intention of the New Zealanders is not to use import restrictions permanently in order to give protection to particular industries. As to the argument that New Zealand's exports are peculiarly variable, this would justify New Zealand claiming that her reserves would have to be so much the higher on the average to give a proper safety margin, and could accordingly be taken into account in the criteria determining whether import restrictions were justifiable. I have written a note on all this to act as our delegation's brief in arguing the case.[16]

(3) I have been in correspondence with Shackle on the clauses of the draft charter relating to exchange control. The Americans have produced a whole set of clauses on this subject for the trade charter. We take the line that these clauses must be left to the International Monetary Fund. This would all be all right if there were a common membership of the International Monetary Fund and of the International Trade Organisation. But what if some countries which are not members of IMF join ITO? The Treasury and the Bank of England have produced articles making such a country subject to IMF obligations on exchange control. But I am asking what this means in respect of the transitional period provisions

[16] 'Summary of a discussion held in Mr Shackle's room on 16 September to consider the line to be taken with New Zealand on the Use of Quantitative Restrictions', T236/698; Meade, 'The Attitude of New Zealand to the Use of Import Restrictions on Balance of Payments Grounds', and Meade to Shackle, 18 September 1946, T230/9. T230/9 also contains earlier and subsequent correspondence on the same subject.

(Article XIV of IMF). Can the country in question determine when it can make its currency convertible? This must clearly be ruled out, or it could in effect continue import restrictions for ever. Does the Fund decide? Or does ITO decide after consultation with the Fund? I suggest the latter course.[17]

(4) I am making a last desperate effort to see if room cannot be left in the framework of ITO for the device of auctioning import licences as a technique of using non-discriminatory quantitative restrictions on Balance of Payments grounds. As at present drafted, such import licence charges would presumably come under the general limitations on import duties. And yet the device would (a) provide the one real guarantee that import restrictions were non-discriminatory and (b) would just fill the gap between the foreign supply price and the domestic selling price which would otherwise either accrue to the foreign supplier (which would militate against the objective of saving foreign exchange) or constitute an unnecessary monopoly profit in the hands of the privileged group of importers. This is a very good example of the principles of Liberal-Socialism, of attaining a quantitative result by manipulation of the pricing system which leaves everyone free to do what they want to do in view of the (rigged) market conditions with which they are faced. A Board of Trade report has come in for the Trade Negotiations Committee on this subject, which rules out this possibility in very short and unsatisfactory terms. (For example, it uses the argument that such a levy on imports would give rise to the growth of an additional vested interest behind the taxed imports; but this, of course, is not so. The domestic producers would be neither more nor less protected, since they would in either case enjoy the higher price due to the scarcity of imports on the market. The question at issue is whether the gap between external and domestic price should go to the Government, the foreign exporter or the privileged importer.) I have written to Shackle with a draft of the case for this device which I have asked to be included in the document.[18]

(5) There has been a meeting in the Board of Trade under Sir John Woods' chairmanship of Forsyth of the Ministry of Fuel and Power, Gridley of the National Coal Board, Clarke of the Treasury and Helmore, Shackle and Young of the Board of Trade and myself to consider the position of Coal under ITO.[19] Fuel and Power wanted to exclude coal from the provisions of ITO and to make a special commodity agreement about coal. This was strenuously resisted and turned down. They also hanker after the possibility of bilateral commercial deals so that we can force our coal in competition with cheaper Polish coal by using our offer to purchase other goods in exchange. This was also successfully resisted. It was also agreed that we should not go for special permission for export subsidies for coal. I argued that if our comparative costs really had become such as to make coal exports unprofitable to the country we had better abandon

[17] These memoranda have not been located. The relevant clauses of the draft chapter were articles 23 and 24 of Chapter IV.

[18] 'Restrictions to Safeguard the Balance of Payments: Note by the Board of Trade', 5 September 1946, and Meade to Shackle, 18 September, T230/9.

[19] Minutes of this meeting have not been found.

them and, in any case, the whole question was completely academic for the next five years or so. We should not plan to put so much of our scarce resources into coal as expressly to cause an intractable coal export problem if those resources could have gone into industries producing other goods which we were better qualified to export. If, as a result of successful coal mechanisation, we were faced with a coal surplus which we wanted to export in order to prevent unemployment, then – I argued – our costs would have fallen as the surplus grew. If this fall in costs was not sufficient to enable us to compete abroad, we might consider a general production subsidy to prevent unemployment. We might conceivably, within the rules of ITO, be able to confine the production subsidy to production in those districts in which there was special unemployment; and provided the subsidy was in respect of sales both in the home market and in foreign markets, we might be able to get away with it even if the district subsidised produced predominantly for the export market. A firm front was maintained on this line; and it now remains to be seen whether the Ministry of Fuel and Power will or will not insist on taking the issue up to Ministers.

(6) Finally, there have been some developments in the matter of our paper on International Employment Policy, which we had prepared to form a brief for the United Kingdom delegation on the Employment Policy side of the Trade Conference, but which has become bogged down as a result of the intervention of Bolton of the International Monetary Fund and Grigg of the International Bank [above, pp. 302 and 309]. (Incidentally, à propos of the revised version of our draft paper Grigg has telegraphed home a most offensive cable in which he talks of the Mead memorandum – I wonder whether I should reciprocate by spelling his name wrong? – as impinging at no point on reality. Luckily, however, he also expresses his profound view that 'full employment is not a snark but a boojum'. This is apparently the level at which this astonishing representative of our new Liberal-Socialist government on international finance treats what is perhaps the most firmly held conviction of the Ministers whom he professes to serve. I cannot help feeling that this telegram may in the end have played into my hands!) Woods has now written to Waley suggesting that the Economic Section should draft a lot more papers on the subject. Waley has written to agree to this. I have spoken to Woods, Helmore and Shackle. I also spoke to Rowe-Dutton and then Bridges about this in order to try to prevent the Chancellor on the visit which he is now about to pay to the Fund and the Bank [18 September-10 October] from throwing out an ill-considered commitment not to back the 'Mead memorandum'.) What I shall do is to draft a short covering note to our paper just putting the issue to Ministers – do they or do they not want us to throw our weight into using the existing international institutions for the purpose of maintaining full employment?[20] This astonishing situation almost leaves me speechless with anger.

[20] Cable REMAC 461, 6 September, Woods to Waley, 12 September, Waley to Woods, 18 September 1946, Meade to Rowe-Dutton, 16 September, and Meade to Woods (sending final version of memorandum plus draft covering note), 24 September 1946, T236/702. The final version of the paper was circulated to the Cabinet by Morrison on 30 September: CP(46)364, 'International Employment Policy, Note prepared in the Treasury, Board of

I have asked Nita Watts to prepare a draft of an Economic Section paper on the whole problem of our external financial arrangements covering (a) the need for us to arrange fixed and precise minimum balance arrangements with our sterling creditors in order to preserve our foreign exchange position (Incidentally, I see that Sir Wilfrid Eady's new agreement with Argentina contains the provision that, in addition to the small sums that are to be released to her from the sterling balances in any case, she can spend just as much more as she likes in the sterling area provided that she has an adverse balance of payments with the sterling area. Are we going to tell India that she can use her sterling balances *ad lib* to spend on British goods? Is this compatible with our undertaking to the Americans to release these balances for equal conversion into any currency? Are we prepared to let these country buy our exports without limit to get payment of their debts and if so how are we going to finance our imports?) and (b) the whole problem of our payments and monetary agreements and the effect of them on our trade if exchange rates are not properly fixed.[21]

A. J. Brown is going ahead with the enquiry which he is doing with the Board of Trade on our export prospects and is also considering a second overseas economic survey.[22]

I have lunched with Noel-Baker, Penson of the Treasury and McKenzie of the Board of Trade, the day on which he started out with our delegation to the Economic and Social Council meeting in New York. He wanted to discuss the problem of financing the balance of payments of devastated countries when UNRRA closes down at the end of this year.

I have lunched with Rosenstein-Rodan.

I have spent an afternoon with the Civil Service Commission going through the overseas entrants to our Economic Assistants. They do not seem to be very promising. Also there is a danger that D. O. Henley will go into the Foreign Service instead of coming to the Section. In spite of all this we are certainly much better staffed up than one might have feared a year or more ago.

Trade and Economic Section', CAB129/13. Waley commented: 'The main author of the document is Mr James Meade. It is perhaps a bit on the theoretical and utopian side, but on the whole it seems to me good socialism and good sense.' (Waley to Trend, 13 October 1946, T236/703.)

21 Watts, 'The Settlement of the Sterling Balances', 6 December 1946, EC(S)(46)56, T230/23 and 276. On the Argentine agreement, initiated by a mission headed by Sir Wilfrid Eady in July-September 1946, see Pressnell, *External Economic Policy since the war*, p. 365, and Meade to Eady and Bridges, 24 September 1946, T273/368.

22 On the Board of Trade enquiry see above, pp. 316 and 318; on the second Overseas Economic Survey, see Brown, 'Headings for a Survey of the Overseas Economic Position as it Affects the United Kingdom – December 1946', 15 October 1946, EC(S)(46)35, and subsequent drafts of the report on T230/22 and 23. (The final version, EC(S)(47)3, 25 January 1947, is on T230/24.)

# Appendix: *Dramatis Personae*

**Note:**This cast of characters does not include persons on which we have no information additional to that given in Meade's diary, namely: Ami (p. 16), Mr and Mrs Boyle (p. 228), Forge (p. 111), Hardraba (p. 220), the Nawab from Hyderabad (p. 300), Tait (p. 43), and Zenkl (p. 75).

Acheson, Dean Goodenham (1893–1973) US Assistant Secretary of State, 1941, Under-Secretary of State, 1945–7, Secretary of State, 1949–53.

Addison, Christopher (Lord Addison) (1869–1951) Minister of Health, 1919–21; Parliamentary Secretary, Ministry of Agriculture, 1929–30; Minister of Agriculture and Fisheries, 1930–31; Secretary of State for Commonwealth Relations, 1945–7; Paymaster-General, 1948–9; Lord Privy Seal, 1947–51.

Aldrich, Winthrop William (1885–1974) Chase National Bank, 1930–34, Chairman of the Board, 1945–53; US Ambassador to Britain, 1953–7.

Alexander, Albert Victor (Later Lord Alexander) (1885–1965) First Lord of the Admiralty, 1929–31, 1940–45, 1945–6; Minister of Defence, 1947–50; Chancellor of the Duchy of Lancaster, 1950–51.

Alsop, Joseph Wright Jr. (b. 1910) US journalist, columnist, writer; reporter for *New York Herald Tribune*, 1932–5; syndicated columnist, *Matter of Fact*, 1945–58, *Washington Post* and then LA Times Syndicate, 1958–74.

Amery, Leopold Charles Maurice Stennett (1873–1955) Conservative MP 1911–45; First Lord of the Admiralty, 1922–4; Secretary of State for the Colonies, 1924–9, for Dominion Affairs, 1925–9, for India and Burma, 1940–45.

Anderson, Sir John (later Lord Waverley) (1882–1958) Entered Colonial Office, 1905; Chairman, Board of Inland Revenue, 1919–22; Permanent Secretary, Home Office, 1922–32; Governor of Bengal, 1932–7; MP for Scottish Universities, 1938–50; Lord Privy Seal, 1938–9; Home Secretary, 1939–40; Lord President of the Council, 1940–43; Chancellor of the Exchequer, 1943–5.

Andrew, George Herbert (later Rev. Sir Herbert Andrew) (1910–85) Patent Office, 1931; Board of Trade, 1938, Assistant Secretary, 1945, Second Secretary, 1955; Permanent Secretary, Ministry of Education, 1963–4, Department of Education and Science, 1964–70.

Archer, George (1896–1960) Entered Civil Service, 1913; served in various departments, including Ministry of Supply (Under-Secretary); British Raw Materials Mission, Washington, and UK Secretary, Combined Raw Materials Board, 1942–5; later Director, Mond Nickel Co. Ltd (Managing Director 1955).

Asquith, Cyril (later Lord Asquith) (1890–1954) Judge; Lord Justice of Appeal, 1946; Chairman, Royal Commission on Equal Pay, 1944–6.

Ashton, Thomas Southcliffe (1889–1968) Reader in Currency and Public Finance, University of Manchester, 1927–44; Professor of Economic History, University of London, 1944–54.

Attlee, Clement Richard (later Lord Attlee) (1883–1967) Labour MP 1922–50; Leader of the Opposition, 1935–40, 1951–5; Lord Privy Seal, 1940–42; Secretary of State for Dominion Affairs, 1942–3; Lord President of the Council, 1943–5; Deputy Prime Minister, 1942–5; Prime Minister, 1945–51.

Aukrust, Odd (b. 1915) Norwegian economist; Ministry of Supply, Oslo, 1941–5; Economic Co-ordination Council, 1945–6; Chief, National Accounts Division, Central Bureau of Statistics, Oslo, 1946–51, 1955–68; Assistant Professor, Norwegian College of Agriculture, 1951–5.

Balogh, Thomas (later Lord Balogh) (1905–85) Economist in the City of London, 1931–9; National Institute of Economic and Social Research, 1938–47; Institute of Economics and Statistics, Oxford, 1940–55; Fellow of Balliol College, Oxford, 1945–73; Reader in Economics, Oxford University, 1960–73.

Bamford, Sir Eric St John (1891–1957) Treasury, 1919–39; Ministry of Information, 1939–46; Third Secretary, Treasury, 1946–8; Chairman, Board of Inland Revenue, 1948–55.

Barlow, Sir James Alan Noel (1881–1968) Clerk, House of Commons, 1906; Board of Education, 1907–16; Principal Assistant Secretary, Ministry of Labour, 1916–34; Under-Secretary, Treasury, 1934, Joint Second Secretary, 1938–48.

Barnes, Alfred (1887–1975), Labour MP 1922–31, 1935–55; Minister of Transport, 1945–51.

Beaverbrook, Lord (William Maxwell Aitken) (1879–1964) Newspaper proprietor; Minister for Aircraft Production, 1940–41; Minister of State, 1941; Minister of Supply, 1941–2; Lord Privy Seal, 1943–5.

Beckhart, Benjamin Haggott (b. 1897) Professor of Banking, Columbia University, 1939–63; Director of Research, Chase National Bank, 1939–49.

Belcher, John William (1905–64) Labour MP 1945–9; Parliamentary Secretary, Board of Trade, 1946–8.

Benham, Frederic Charles Courtenay (d. 1962) Professor of Commerce, University of London, 1945–7; Economic Adviser to UK Commissioner-General in S.E. Asia, 1947–55; later Price Professor, Royal Institute of International Affairs, London.

Berlin, Isaiah (later Sir Isaiah) (b. 1909) Fellow, All Souls' College, Oxford, 1932–8, 1950–56, 1975– , New College, Oxford, 1938–50; war service with Ministry of Information in New York, 1941–2, UK Embassy in Washington, 1942–6, UK Embassy in Moscow, 1945–6; Chichele Professor of Social and Political Theory, University of Oxford, 1957–67; President, Wolfson College, Oxford, 1966–75.

Bevan, Aneurin (1897–1960), Labour MP 1929–60; Minister of Health, 1945–51; Minister of Labour and National Service, 1951.

Beveridge, Sir William (Lord Beveridge) (1879–1963) Director of Labour Exchanges, 1909–16; Director, LSE, 1919–37; Master of University College, Oxford, 1937–45; Liberal MP 1944–5.

Bevin, Ernest (1881–1951) General Secretary of Transport and General Workers Union, 1921–40; Minister of Labour and National Service, 1940–45; Foreign Secretary, 1945–51; Labour MP 1940–51.

Biddle, Eric H. (b. 1898) Head, US Special Mission to UK and missions to European, Middle East and Occupied Territories, for various US Government Departments 1942–6; Adviser, US Delegation, UNRRA, 1945, UNESCO, 1946, UN, 1945–6.

Bjerve, Petter Jakob (b. 1913) Norwegian economist and statistician; instructor, University of Oslo, then Director, Central Bureau of Statistics, Oslo, from 1949; Minister of Finance, 1960–63.

Blagburn, C. H., Agricultural economist; temporary Assistant Secretary, Ministry of Food in Second World War, University of Reading after 1945.

Blaker, George (b. 1919) Private Secretary to Minister of State in Middle East, 1941–3; Cabinet Office, 1943–5; Principal Private Secretary to Minister of

Production and President of Board of Trade, 1945–7; Treasury, 1947, Under-Secretary, 1955–63; Under-Secretary, Department of Education and Science, 1963–71.

Bolton, George Lewis French (later Sir George Bolton) (1900–82) Bank of England, 1933, Adviser, 1941–8, Executive Director, 1948–57; Chairman, Bank of London and South America, 1957–70.

Boothby, Robert John Graham (later Lord Boothby) (1900–86), Conservative MP 1924–58; PPS to Chancellor of Exchequer (Churchill), 1926–9; Parliamentary Secretary, Ministry of Food, 1940–41.

Boyd-Orr, Sir John (later Lord Boyd-Orr) (1880–1971) Professor of Agriculture, University of Aberdeen, 1942–5; MP (Independent) 1945–6; Director-General FAO, 1945–48; Nobel Peace Prize, 1949.

Brand, Robert Henry (Lord Brand) (1878–1963) Director, Lazard Bros., merchant bankers; Head of British Food Mission, Washington, 1941–4; Treasury Representative in Washington, 1944–6; Chairman, British Supply Council in North America, 1942, 1945–6.

Bretherton, Russell Frederick (b. 1906) Temporary civil servant, Ministry of Supply and Board of Trade, 1939–45; Under-Secretary, Raw Materials Department, Board of Trade, 1946–8; Economic Section, 1949–51; Under-Secretary, Ministry of Materials, 1951–4, Board of Trade, 1954–61, Treasury, 1961–8.

Bridges, Sir Edward (later Lord Bridges) (1892–1969) Treasury, 1919–38; Secretary to the Cabinet, 1938–45; Permanent Secretary, Treasury, 1945–56.

Brittain, Sir Herbert (1894–1961) Entered Treasury, 1919, Third Secretary, 1942–53, Second Secretary, 1953–7.

Broadley, Herbert (later Sir Herbert) (1892–1983) Board of Trade, 1920–26; Ministry of Food, 1939, Second Secretary, 1945–8; Leader, UK Delegation to International Wheat Conferences, 1947 and 1948; Deputy Director-General FAO, 1948–58.

Brook, Norman Craven (later Lord Normanbrook) (1902–67) Principal Private Secretary to Sir John Anderson, 1938–42; Deputy Secretary, Cabinet, 1942–6; Permanent Secretary, Ministry of Reconstruction, 1943–5; Secretary to the Cabinet, 1947–62; Joint Permanent Secretary, Treasury, and Head, Home Civil Service, 1956–62.

Brooks, H. E. Assistant Principal, Treasury, 1938–9, Principal, 1940–45, Assistant Secretary, 1946.

Brown, Arthur Joseph (b. 1914) Staff of Foreign Research and Press Service, 1940–43; Foreign Office Research Department, 1943–5; Economic Section 1945–7; Professor of Economics, University of Leeds, 1947–79.

Bruce, Stanley Melbourne (later Lord Bruce of Melbourne) (1883–1967) Prime Minister of Australia and Minister for External Affairs, 1923–9; Australian Minister in London, 1932–3; High Commissioner for Australia in London, 1933–45.

Butt, David Bensusan (b. 1914) Civil servant 1938–62, Economic Section, 1946–52, then Assistant Secretary, Treasury; Australian National University, 1962–76.

Cadbury, Paul Strangman (1895–1984) Vice-Chairman, Cadbury Bros. Ltd., 1943–59, Chairman, 1959–65.

Cahan, John Flint (1912–61) Secretary, National Institute of Economic and Social Research, 1938–9; Ministry of Economic Warfare, 1939–44; Treasury, 1944–6; Director of Trade and Payments, OEEC, Paris, 1951–6.

Caine, Sydney (later Sir Sydney) (1902–67) Colonial Office, 1926, Assistant Secretary, 1940, Financial Adviser to Secretary of State for Colonies, 1942, Assistant Under-Secretary, 1944, Deputy Under-Secretary, 1947–8; Director, LSE, 1957–67.

Cairncross, Alexander Kirkland (later Sir Alec Cairncross) (b. 1911) Civil servant, 1940–45; Economic Adviser, Board of Trade, 1946–9; OEEC, 1949–50; Professor of Applied Economics, University of Glasgow, 1951–61; Economic Adviser to HM Government, 1961–4; Head, Government Economic Service, 1964–9; Master of St Peter's College, Oxford, 1969–78.

Campion, Harry (later Sir Harry) (b. 1905) Reader in Statistics, University of Manchester, 1933–9; Offices of the War Cabinet, 1939; Director, CSO, 1941–67.

Carr-Saunders, Sir Alexander (Morris) (1886–1966) Director, LSE, 1937–56; Chairman, Statistics Committee, Royal Commission on Population, 1944–9.

Carter, Sir, (Richard Henry) Archibald (1887–1958) India Office, 1924–36; Chairman, Board of Customs and Excise, 1942–7; Permanent Secretary for India, 1947; Joint Permanent Secretary for Commonwealth Relations, 1948; Chairman, Monopolies Commission, 1949–53.

Catto, Thomas Sivewright (Lord Catto) (1879–1959) Director of Yule, Catto and Co.; Financial Adviser, Treasury, 1939–44; Governor, Bank of England, 1944–9.

Chamberlain, Neville (1869–1940) Conservative MP 1918–40; Chancellor of Exchequer, 1923–4, 1931–7; Prime Minister, 1937–40.

Chambers, Stanley Paul (later Sir Paul) (1904-81) Income Tax Adviser to Government of India, 1937–40; Assistant Secretary and Director of Statistics and Intelligence, Board of Inland Revenue, 1942–5; Commissioner of Inland Revenue, 1942–7; Director, Imperial Chemical Industries, 1947–68, Chairman 1960–8; President, National Institute of Economic and Social Research, 1955–62.

Chantler, Philip (b. 1911) Economic Section, 1941–7; Economic Adviser, Ministry of Fuel and Power, 1947–60; Director of Economic Planning, Cyprus, 1969–70, Swaziland, 1970–71.

Chegwidden, Sir Thomas Sydney (1895–1984) Under-Secretary, Ministry of Production, 1942–6; Civilian Director of Studies, Imperial Defence College, 1946–7; Chairman, Public Services Board and Police Advisory Board, South Rhodesia, 1947–53; Chairman, Interim Federal Public Service Commission, Federation of Rhodesia and Nyasaland, 1953–5; President, Association of Rhodesian Industries, 1958–61.

Cherwell, Lord (Frederick Alexander Lindemann) (1886–1957) Professor of Experimental Philosophy, Oxford, 1919–56; Personal Assistant to Winston Churchill as Prime Minister, 1940–45; Paymaster-General, 1942–5, 1952–3.

Chester, Daniel Norman (later Sir Norman) (1907–86) Lecturer in Public Administration, University of Manchester, 1936–45; Economic Section, 1940–45; Fellow of Nuffield College, Oxford, 1945, Warden, 1954–78.

Churchill, Winston Leonard Spencer (later Sir Winston) (1874–1965) Chancellor of the Exchequer, 1924–9; Prime Minister, 1940–45, 1951–5; Leader of the Opposition, 1945–51.

Clark, Colin (b. 1905) University Lecturer in Statistics, University of Cambridge, 1931–7; Under-Secretary of State of Labour and Industry, Queensland, Australia, 1938–52; Director, Institute for Research in Agricultural Economics, University of Oxford, 1953–69.

Clarke, Richard William Barnes (Otto) (later Sir Richard) (1910–75) Served in Ministries of Information, Economic Warfare, Supply and Production, 1939–45; Assistant Secretary, Treasury, 1945, Under-Secretary, 1947, Third Secretary, 1955, Second Secretary, 1962; Permanent Secretary, Ministry of Aviation, 1966, Ministry of Technology, 1966–70.

Clay, Sir Henry (1883–1954) Stanley Jevons Professor of Political Economy, Manchester, 1922–7, Professor of Social Economics, 1927–30; Economic Adviser, Bank of England, 1930–44; Warden, Nuffield College, Oxford, 1944–9.

Clayton, William Lockhart (1880–1966) US Federal Loan Administration and Vice-President, Export-Import Bank, 1940–42; Assistant Secretary of State, 1944–5; Under-Secretary of State for Economic Affairs, 1945–7.

Clutterbuck, Sir (Peter) Alexander (1897–1975) Assistant Secretary, Dominions Office, 1940, Assistant Under-Secretary, 1942–6; High Commissioner for UK in Canada, 1946–52, India, 1952–5; HM Ambassador to Republic of Ireland, 1955–9.

Coase, Ronald Harry (b. 1910) Assistant Lecturer, then Reader, LSE, 1935–51; Statistician, then Chief Statistician, CSO, 1941–6; Professor, University of Buffalo, 1951–8, University of Virginia, 1958–64, University of Chicago since 1964.

Cobbold, Cameron Fromanteel (later Lord Cobbold) (1904–87) Entered Bank of England as Adviser, 1933, Executive Director, 1938, Deputy Governor, 1945–9, Governor, 1949–61.

Cockfield, Francis Arthur (later Lord Cockfield) (b. 1916) Assistant Secretary to Board of Inland Revenue, 1945; Commissioner of Inland Revenue, 1951–2, Director of Statistics and Intelligence, 1945–52; Minister of State, Treasury, 1979–82; Secretary of State for Trade, 1982–3; Member of the Commission of the European Communities, 1983–8.

Coombs, Herbert Cole (b. 1906) Assistant Economist, Commonwealth Bank of Australia, 1935; Economist, Commonwealth Treasury, 1939; Director General, Post-War Reconstruction, 1943; Governor, Commonwealth Bank of Australia, 1949–60, Chairman, 1951–60; Governor and Chairman, Reserve Bank of Australia, 1960–68.

Copland, Douglas Berry (later Sir Douglas) (1894–1971) Dean, Faculty of Commerce, University of Melbourne, 1924–44; Commonwealth Prices Commissioner, 1939–45; Economic Consultant to Prime Minister, 1941–5; Australian Minister to China, 1946–8; Australian High Commissioner to Canada, 1953–6.

Cornwall-Jones, Brigadier Arthur Thomas (1900–80) Indian Army, 1920–47; Assistant Secretary, Cabinet Office, 1939–41, Ministry of Defence, 1943–4; British Secretary, Combined Chiefs of Staff, 1944–6; Senior Assistant Secretary (Military) to the Cabinet, 1946–50.

Coulson, Sir John Eltringham (b. 1909) Entered Foreign Service, 1932; FO, Ministry of Economic Warfare, and Offices of War Cabinet, 1937–46; Counsellor, Paris, 1946–8; OEEC, 1948–50; Deputy Permanent Representative to UN, 1950–52; Minister in Washington, 1955–7; HM Ambassador to Sweden, 1960–63; Deputy Under-Secretary, FO, 1963–4; Secretary-General, EFTA, 1965–72.

Cripps, Sir (Richard) Stafford (1889–1952) Solicitor-General, 1930–31; HM Ambassador to Russia, 1940–42; Lord Privy Seal and Leader of House of Commons, 1942; Minister of Aircraft Production, 1942–5; President of Board of Trade, 1945–7; Chancellor of the Exchequer, 1947–50.

Cross, Richard Basil (1881–1952) Entered Civil Service, 1904; Ministry of Health, 1920, Principal Assistant Secretary, 1936, Adviser on Special Services, 1945–7.

Crowther, Geoffrey (later Lord Crowther) (1907–72) Assistant Editor, *The Economist*, 1935, Editor, 1938–56; war-time service in Ministries of Supply, Information, and Production.

Currie, Lauchlin (b. 1902) Assistant Director of Research and Statistics, US Federal Reserve Board, 1934–9; Administrative Assistant to the President, 1939–45; Deputy Administrator, Foreign Economic Administration, 1943–5; Director of first World Bank country mission, to Colombia, 1949–50; resident in Colombia since 1950 and influential in Colombian development planning in 1960s and 1970s.

Dalton, Hugh (later Lord Dalton) (1887–1962) Lecturer in economics, LSE, 1919–25, Cassel Reader in Commerce 1920–35; Labour MP 1924–9, 1935–59; Minister of Economic Warfare, 1940–42; President of Board of Trade, 1942–5; Chancellor of the Exchequer, 1945–7.

Dalton, Ruth (née Hamilton Fox) (1890–1966) London County Council 1925–31, Alderman 1936–42, 1946–52. Married Hugh Dalton 1914.

Daniel, Mrs J. O. Principal, Board of Trade, from 1945; previously Administrative Staff, Cabinet Office.

Dennison, Stanley Raymond (b. 1912) University Lecturer in Economics and Fellow, Gonville and Caius College, Cambridge, 1945–58; Economic Section, 1940–6; Vice-Chancellor and Professor of Economics, University of Hull, 1972–9.

dePeyer, Charles Hubert (1905–83) Mines Department, 1930, Principal, 1936; Assistant Secretary, Ministry of Fuel and Power, 1942, Under-Secretary (Coal Division), 1946–52; seconded to Foreign Office, with rank of Minister, in UK Delegation to European Coal and Steel Community, 1952–6.

Derksen, Johannes B.D. Dutch economist; developed Netherlands national accounts in 1940s in Central Bureau of Statistics, The Hague; subsequently Director, National Income Unit, Statistical Office, UN.

Devons, Ely (1913–67) Economic Assistant, Joint Committee of Cotton Trade Organisations, 1935–9; Statistician, Cotton Control, Ministry of Supply, 1939–40; CSO 1940–41; Director-General of Planning, Programmes and Statistics, Ministry of Aircraft Production, 1941–5; Professor of Commerce, LSE, 1959–65, Professor of Economics, 1965–7.

Dow, John Christopher Roderick (b. 1916) Economic Section, 1945–52; Economic Adviser, Treasury, 1952–4, 1962–3; National Institute for Economic and Social Research, 1954–62; Assistant Secretary-General, OECD, 1963–73; Executive Director, Bank of England, 1973–81, Adviser to the Governor, 1981–4.

Drew, John Alexander (b. 1907) Entered Civil Service, 1928; Customs and Excise, 1935–40; employed on special duties, 1940–5; Assistant Secretary, Cabinet Office, 1945–8; Board of Trade, 1948–50; Assistant Under-Secretary, Ministry of Defence, 1951–67.

Dupriez, Leon-Hugo Service d'Etudes Economiques, Banque Nationale de Belgique, in 1920s and 1930s; Professor of Economics, University of Louvain, in 1930s and 1940s.

Durbin, Evan Frank Mottram (1906–48) Lecturer in Economics, LSE, 1930–40; Economic Section, 1940–2; Personal Assistant to Deputy Prime Minister, 1942–5; Labour MP 1945–8; Parliamentary Secretary, Ministry of Works, 1947–8.

Eady, Sir Wilfrid (Griffin) (1880–1962) Entered Civil Service, 1913; Ministry of Labour, 1917–38; Deputy Under-Secretary, Home Office, 1938–40; Deputy Chairman, Board of Customs and Excise, 1940–1, Chairman, 1941–2; Joint Second Secretary, Treasury, 1942–52.

Eastwood, Christopher Gilbert (1905–83) Entered Civil Service, 1927; Private Secretary to Secretaries of State for the Colonies, 1940–41; Principal Assistant Secretary, Cabinet Office, 1945–7; Commissioner of Crown Lands, 1952–4.

Elizabeth, Princess (b. 1926) Queen of UK and Dominions since 1952.

Elizabeth, Queen (née Lady Elizabeth Bowes-Lyon) (b. 1900) Wife of George VI.

Emmerson, Sir Harold Corti (1896-1984) Entered Ministry of Labour, 1920; Principal Private Secretary to Ministers of Labour, 1933–5; Secretary, Department of Commissioners for Special Areas, 1938–9; Under-Secretary, Ministry of Home Security, 1940–42, Ministry of Works, 1946–56, Ministry of Labour, 1956–9.

Enfield, Ralph Roscoe (later Sir Ralph) (1885–1973) Entered Civil Service, 1913; Ministry of Agriculture and Fisheries, 1919–52, Principal Assistant Secretary, 1942, Chief Economic Adviser, 1945–52.

Evans, Archibald A. Economist on staff of ILO in 1930s; war-time service in Ministry of War Transport.

Evans, Collis William (1895–1984) Principal, Air Ministry, 1938; Financial Adviser to HQ RAF, Middle East and North Africa, 1938–43; Assistant Secretary, Ministry of Civil Aviation, 1944–8, Under-Secretary, 1948–59.

Evatt, Herbert Vere (1894–1965) Minister for External Affairs, Australia, 1941–9; Deputy Prime Minister of Australia, 1946–9; Australian representative, UK War Cabinet, and Leader, Australian war-time missions to Washington, London, 1942–3; Australian delegate to UN Conference, San Francisco, 1945, and UN Preparatory Commission, London, 1946.

Fay, Charles Ryle (1884–1961) Professor of Economic History, University of Toronto, 1921–30; Reader in Economic History, University of Cambridge from 1930.

Fennelly, Reginald Daniel (later Sir Daniel) (1890–1969) Civil servant; Under-Secretary, Raw Materials Department, Board of Trade, in 1940s.

Fergusson, Sir John Donald (1891–1963) Entered Treasury, 1919, Assistant Secretary, 1934; Permanent Secretary, Ministry of Agriculture and Fisheries, 1936–45, Ministry of Fuel and Power, 1945–52.

Firestone, O. John (Jack) (b. 1913) Advisory Committee on Reconstruction and Advisory Committee on Economic Policy, Privy Council, Canada, 1942–4; Economic Research Bureau, Department of Reconstruction, 1944–6, Director of Economic Research, 1946–8; Director of Economic Research, Department of Trade and Commerce, 1948–50, Economic Adviser, 1950–60; Professor of Economics, University of Ottawa, 1960–78.

Fisher, Allan George Barnard (1895-1976) New Zealand economist; Bank of New South Wales, Australia, 1934; Counsellor, NZ Legation, Washington, 1944; International Monetary Fund 1946–60.

Fleming (John) Marcus (1911–76) Finance Section, League of Nations, 1935–7; Ministry of Economic Warfare, 1939–42; Economic Section, 1942–1951, Deputy Director, 1947–51; Visiting Professor, Columbia University, New York, 1951–5; International Monetary Fund, 1955–76, Deputy Director of Research Department, 1964–76.

Flett, Sir Martin Teall (1911–82) Entered Civil Service, 1933; Treasury, 1934; Cabinet Office, Ministry of Reconstruction, and Lord President's Office, 1944–6; Under-Secretary, Treasury, 1949–56; Deputy Secretary, Ministry of Power, 1956-61; Deputy Under-Secretary, Air Ministry, 1961–3, Permanent Secretary, 1963–4.

Florence, Philip Sargant (1890–1982) Economist; Dean of the Faculty of Commerce and Social Science, University of Birmingham, 1947–50.

Forsyth, Ian McMillan (1892–1969) Entered Treasury, 1919; Assistant Secretary, Board of Trade, 1936; Principal Assistant Secretary, Ministry of Fuel and Power, 1943, Under-Secretary, 1946–52.

Forsyth, Jennifer Mary (b. 1924) Joined Treasury, 1945; Economic Section 1947–9; UN Economic Commission for Europe, 1949–53; Under-Secretary, Treasury, 1975–80, Department of Transport, 1980–83.

Fowler, Henry Hamill (b. 1908) Assistant General Counsel, US War Planning Board, 1942–4; Economic Adviser, US Mission on Economic Affairs, London, 1944; Special Assistant to Foreign Economic Administration, 1945; Under-Secretary, US Treasury, 1961–4, Secretary, 1965–8.

Fowler, Ronald Frederick (b. 1910) Lecturer in Commerce, LSE, 1932–40; CSO 1940–50; Director of Statistics, Ministry of Labour, 1950–68; Director of Statistical Research, Department of Employment, 1968–72.

Franks, Oliver Sherwell (later Lord Franks) (b. 1905) Professor of Moral Philosophy, University of Glasgow, 1937–45; Ministry of Supply, 1939–46,

Permanent Secretary, 1945–6; HM Ambassador at Washington, 1948–52; Provost, Worcester College, Oxford, 1962–76.

French, Sir Henry Leon (1883–1966) Entered Board of Agriculture, 1901, Assistant Secretary, 1920; Permanent Secretary, Ministry of Food, 1939–45.

Gaitskell, Hugh Todd Naylor (1906–63) Lecturer in Political Economy, University College London, 1928–40; Principal Private Secretary to Minister of Economic Warfare, 1940–42; Principal Assistant Secretary, Board of Trade, 1942–5; Labour MP 1945–63; Parliamentary Secretary, Ministry of Fuel and Power, 1946–7; Minister of Fuel and Power, 1947–50; Minister of State for Economic Affairs, 1950; Chancellor of the Exchequer, 1950–51; Leader of Labour Party 1955–63.

Gardiner, J. C. Civil servant, Board of Trade, in 1940s.

George VI (1895–52) King of UK and Dominions 1936–52.

George, H. H. Under-Secretary, Ministry of Health, in 1940s.

Gilbert, Sir Bernard (William) (1891–1957) Entered Treasury, 1914, Joint Second Secretary, 1944–56.

Gillie, (Francis) Blaise (1908–81) Entered Ministry of Health, 1930, Principal, 1937; Ministry of Works, 1942, Assistant Secretary, 1943; Ministry of Town and Country Planning, 1943; Ministry of Local Government and Planning, 1951, Under-Secretary, 1954, Welsh Secretary, 1957–63; Senior Lecturer in Town and Regional Planning, American University of Beirut, 1972–6.

Goodrich, Carter (1897–1971) Professor of Economics, Columbia University, from 1931; US Labour Commissioner, League of Nations, Geneva, 1936–40; Special Assistant to US Ambassador, London, 1941; Chairman, ILO Governing Body, 1939–45.

Gordon-Walker, Patrick Chrestien (later Lord Gordon-Walker) (1907–80) BBC European Service, 1940–44; Labour MP 1945–64, 1966–74; PPS to Lord President of the Council, 1946; Parliamentary Under-Secretary, Commonwealth Relations Office, 1947–50, Secretary of State, 1950–51; Secretary of State for Foreign Affairs, 1964–5; Secretary of State for Education and Science, 1967–8.

Gore-Booth, Paul (later Lord Gore-Booth) (1909–84) Third Secretary, FO, 1933, Washington, 1942, acting First Secretary, 1943; Head, European Recovery Department, FO, 1948; High Commissioner to India, 1960–65; Permanent Secretary, FO, 1965–9; Head, Diplomatic Service, 1968–9.

Gorell Barnes, Sir William (Lethbridge) (1909–87) Diplomatic Service, 1932–9; Offices of War Cabinet, 1939–45; Personal Assistant to Lord President of the Council, 1942–5; Assistant Secretary, Treasury, 1945–6; Personal Assistant to Prime Minister, 1946–8; Assistant Under-Secretary of State, Colonial Office, 1948–59, Deputy Under-Secretary of State, 1959–63.

Gould, Robert Macdonald (later Sir Robert) (d. 1971) Civil servant in Ministry of Labour, Chief Industrial Commissioner in late 1940s, before his retirement in 1952.

Graham, Benjamin (1894–1976) Economist; Columbia University, 1928–55; University of California at Los Angeles, 1956–76.

Grant, Alexander Thomas Kingdom (1906–88) Lecturer in Political Economy, University College London, 1938–9; Treasury, 1939, Under-Secretary, 1956; Under-Secretary, Export Credits Guarantee Department, 1958–66; Fellow, Pembroke College, Cambridge, 1966–73.

Greenwood, Arthur (1880–1954) Labour MP 1922–31, 1932–54; Deputy Leader of Labour Party, 1935–54; member of War Cabinet and Minister without Portfolio, 1940–42; Lord Privy Seal, 1945–7; Paymaster-General, 1946–7.

Gregg, Sir Cornelius (Joseph) (d. 1959) Chairman, Board of Inland Revenue, 1942–8.

Gregory, Sir Theodore (1890–1970) Cassel Professor of Economics, LSE, 1927–37; Economic Adviser to Government of India, 1938–46.

Gridley, John Crandon (1904–68) Joint Chairman, North African Joint Economic Mission, 1943–4; Economic Adviser to UK Ambassador in Paris, 1944–5; Chairman, European Coal Organisation, 1945; National Coal Board, 1946–8; Chairman, Mobil Oil Co., 1949–68.

Grigg, Sir (Percy) James (1890–1964) Entered Treasury, 1913; Chairman, Board of Customs and Excise, 1930, Board of Inland Revenue, 1930–34; Permanent Under-Secretary of State for War, 1939–42; Secretary of State for War, 1942–5.

Guillebaud, Claude William (1890–1971) Economist; Fellow, St John's College, Cambridge, 1915–71; Girdlers' Lecturer, Cambridge University, 1942–56, Reader, 1956–7.

Hackett, William Thomas Gould (b. 1906) Secretary, Ontario Executive Committee of National War Finance Committee, 1941; Economic Adviser, Bank of Montreal, 1943, Assistant General Manager, 1952.

Hale, Edward (later Sir Edward) (1895–1978) Entered Treasury, 1921, Under-Secretary in 1940s; Secretary to University Grants Committee, 1951–7; Administrative Head, Historical Branch, Cabinet Office, 1958–60.

Halifax, Lord (Edward Frederick Lindley Wood) (1881–1959) Viceroy of India, 1926–31; President of Board of Education, 1932–5; Secretary of State for War, 1935; Lord Privy Seal, 1935–7; Lord President of the Council, 1937–8, 1940; Secretary of State for Foreign Affairs, 1938–40; HM Ambassador at Washington, 1941–6.

Hall (Laura) Margaret (later Lady MacDougall) Economist; US Office of Price Administration, 1941–4; UNRRA Planning Division, Washington, Sydney, and London, 1944–5; Lecturer, Lincoln College, Oxford, 1946–7, Somerville College, 1947–9; Fellow, Somerville College, and University Lecturer in Economics, Oxford, 1949–75. Married Robert Hall 1932 (marriage dissolved 1968), Donald MacDougall 1977.

Hall, Noel Frederick (later Sir Noel) (1902–83) Professor of Political Economy, University College London, 1935–8; Director, National Institute for Economic and Social Research, 1938–43; Joint Director, Ministry of Economic Warfare 1940; Minister in Charge of War Trade Department, British Embassy, Washington, 1941–3; Principal, Brasenose College, Oxford, 1960–73.

Hall, Robert Lowe (later Lord Roberthall) (1901–88) Fellow, Trinity College, Oxford, 1927–50; Ministry of Supply, 1939–46; British Raw Materials Mission, Washington, 1942–4; Adviser, Board of Trade, 1946–7; Director, Economic Section, 1947–53; Economic Adviser to HM Government, 1953–61.

Hall, William Glenvil (1887–1962) Labour MP 1929–62; Financial Secretary, Treasury, 1945–50.

Hall-Patch, Edmund Leo (later Sir Edmund) (1896–1975) Assistant Secretary, Treasury, 1935–44; Financial Commissioner in Far East, 1940; Assistant Under-Secretary of State, FO, 1944, Deputy Under-Secretary of State, 1946–8; Head of British Delegation, OEEC, 1948–52.

Hancock, Sir Henry Drummond (1895–1965) Entered Civil Service, 1920; Secretary-General, British Purchasing Commission and British Raw Materials Mission, USA, 1941–2; Deputy Secretary, Ministry of Supply, 1942–5; Deputy Secretary, Ministry of National Insurance, 1945–8, Permanent Secretary, 1949–51; Permanent Secretary, Ministry of Food, 1951–5; Chairman, Board of Inland Revenue, 1955–8.

Harrod, Roy Forbes (later Sir Roy) (1900–78) Student of Christ Church College, Oxford, 1924–67; University Lecturer in Economics, Oxford, 1929–37, 1946–52; PM's Statistical Branch, 1940, PM's Office 1940–2; Statistical Adviser to

Admiralty, 1943–45; Fellow, Nuffield College, Oxford, 1938–47, 1954–8; Nuffield Reader in Economics, Oxford, 1952–67.

Hawkins, Harry Calvin (b. 1894) Department of State, 1931–5, Assistant Chief, Division of Trade Agreements, 1935–6, Chief, 1936–40; Chief, Division of Commercial Treaties and Agreements, 1940–41; Chief, Division of Commercial Policy and Agreements, Director, Office of Economic Affairs, 1944; Economic Counsellor, US Embassy, London, 1944–8; Professor of International Economic Relations, Tufts College, from 1948.

Hawtrey, Ralph George (later Sir Ralph) (1879–1975) Entered Treasury, 1904, Director of Financial Enquiries, 1919–45.

von Hayek, Friedrich August (b. 1899) Director, Austrian Institute for Economic Research, 1927–31; Lecturer in Economics, University of Vienna, 1929–31; Tooke Professor of Economic Science and Statistics, LSE, 1931–50.

Helmore, James Reginald Carroll (later Sir James) (1906–72) Entered Board of Trade, 1929, Under-Secretary, 1946, Second Secretary, 1946–52.

Helsby, Laurence Norman (later Lord Helsby) (1908–78) Lecturer in Economics, University of Durham, 1931–45; Assistant Secretary, Treasury, 1946; Principal Private Secretary to Prime Minister, 1947–50; Deputy Secretary, Ministry of Food, 1950–54; First Civil Service Commissioner, 1954–9; Permanent Secretary, Ministry of Labour, 1959–62; Joint Permanent Secretary to the Treasury and Head of the Home Civil Service, 1963–8.

Hemming, Francis (1893–1964) Secretary, Economic Advisory Council, 1930–39; Principal Assistant Secretary, War Cabinet Offices, 1939–41; Administrative Head, Central Economic Information Service, 1940, CSO, 1941; Principal Assistant Secretary, Ministry of Home Security, 1941–4; Ministry of Fuel and Power, 1944, Under-Secretary, 1946–53.

Henderson, Sir Hubert (Douglas) (1890–1952) Lecturer in Economics, University of Cambridge, 1919–23; Editor, *The Nation & Athenaeum*, 1923–30; Joint Secretary, Economic Advisory Council, 1930–4; Fellow, All Souls' College, Oxford, 1934–51; Economic Adviser, Treasury, 1939–44; Drummond Professor of Political Economy, University of Oxford, 1945–51.

Henderson, Leon (1895–1980) Economic Advisor and Director of Research and Planning, US National Recovery Administration, 1934–5; Commissioner, Securities and Exchange Commission, 1939–41; Administrator, Price Administration and Civilian Supply, 1941–2.

Henley, Douglas Owen (later Sir Douglas) (b. 1919) Entered Treasury, 1946; Financial Counsellor, Tokyo and Singapore, 1956–9; Assistant Under-Secretary of State, Department of Economic Affairs, 1964–9; Deputy Secretary, Treasury, 1969, Second Permanent Secretary, 1972–6; Comptroller and Auditor-General, 1976–81.

Hicklin, R. P. Civil servant, Board of Trade in 1940s.

Hicks, John Richard (later Sir John) (1904–89) Lecturer in Economics, LSE, 1926–35, Cambridge, 1935–8; Professor of Political Economy, Manchester, 1938–46; Official Fellow, Nuffield College, Oxford, 1946–52; Drummond Professor of Political Economy, Oxford, 1952–65.

Hildred, Sir William Percival (1893–1986) Entered Treasury, 1919; Deputy General Manager, Export Credits Guarantee Department, 1935–8; Director-General of Civil Aviation, Ministry of Civil Aviation, 1941–6; Director-General, International Air Transport Association, 1946–66.

Hill, M. E. (Polly) (b. 1914) Temporary civil servant, Treasury and Board of Trade, 1940–51; journalist, West Africa, 1951–3; Senior Research Fellow, University of Ghana, 1954–65; Fellow, Clare Hall, Cambridge, since 1965; Smuts Reader in Commonwealth Studies, Cambridge, 1973–9.

Hill, (William) Martin (1905–76) Economic and Financial Section and Political

Section, League of Nations, 1927–46; Chief of Administrative and Budgetary Section, UN Preparatory Commission, 1945; Special Adviser to UN Secretary-General, 1946, Assistant Secretary-General for Inter-Agency Affairs, 1967–70.

Hiss, Alger (b. 1904) Special Attorney, US Department of Justice, 1935–6; Assistant to Assistant Secretary of State, 1936; Director, Office of Special Political Affairs, 1945; Executive Secretary, Dumbarton Oaks Conference, 1944; Secretary-General, San Francisco Conference, 1945; President, Carnegie Endowment for International Peace, 1945; charged with spying before House Un-American Activities Committee, 1948; tried and convicted of perjury, 1949.

Hitchman, Sir Edwin Alan (1903–80) Assistant Principal, Ministry of Labour, 1926, Principal Assistant Secretary, 1941, Under-Secretary, 1946; transferred to Treasury, 1947, Deputy to Chief Planning Officer, 1948–9, Third Secretary, 1949–51; Permanent Secretary, Ministry of Agriculture, Fisheries and Food, 1952–9.

Hollond, Mrs Marjorie (née Tappan) (1896–1977) Economist; Fellow of Girton College, Cambridge, from 1925; war-time government service in Ministry of Agriculture and Fisheries.

Hopkin, William Aylsham Bryan (later Sir Bryan) (b. 1914) PM's Statistical Branch, 1941–5; Secretary, Royal Commission on Population, 1945–8; Economic Section, 1948–50; CSO, 1950–52; Director, National Institute of Economic and Social Research, 1952–7; Deputy Director, Economic Section, Treasury, 1958–65; Head, Government Economic Service and Chief Economic Adviser, Treasury, 1974–7.

Hopkins, Harry L. (1890–1946) US Secretary of Commerce 1938–40; Adviser to President Roosevelt, 1940–5.

Hopkins, Sir Richard (1880–1955) Chairman, Board of Inland Revenue, 1922–7; Controller of Finance and Supply Services, Treasury, 1927–8, Second Secretary, 1928–42, Permanent Secretary, 1942–5.

Howell, Kit (later Mrs Jones) (b. 1925) Economic Section, 1945–60; subsequently National Institute of Economic and Social Research, Secretary since 1968.

Hull, Cordell (1871–1955) US Secretary of State, 1933–44; Nobel Peace Prize, 1945.

Hurcomb, Sir Cyril (William) (1883–1975) Permanent Secretary, Ministry of Transport, 1927–37; Director-General, Ministry of Shipping, 1939–41; Director General, Ministry of War Transport, 1941–7; Chairman, British Transport Commission, 1947–53.

Hutchinson, Herbert John (later Sir Herbert) (1889–1971) Entered Board of Trade, 1908; Under-Secretary, Ministry of Supply, 1941–6; Second Secretary, Board of Trade, 1946–7; Secretary, National Coal Board, 1947–51.

Ince, Sir Godfrey Herbert (1891–1960) Entered Ministry of Labour, 1919, Principal Assistant Secretary, 1938, Under-Secretary, 1940; Director-General of Manpower, Ministry of Labour and National Service, 1941–4, Permanent Secretary, 1944–56.

Isaacs, George Alfred (1883–1979) Labour MP 1923–4, 1929–31, 1939–59; PPS to Secretary of State for Colonies, 1924, to Secretary of State for Dominions, 1929–31, to First Lord of the Admiralty, 1942–5; Minister of Labour and National Service, 1945–51; Minister of Pensions, 1951; President, World Trade Union Conference, London, 1945.

Ismay, George (later Sir George) (1891–1984) Entered Treasury, 1911, Assistant Secretary, 1934; Comptroller and Accountant General, General Post Office, 1937, Assistant Director-General, 1942, Deputy Director-General, 1947–52.

Jackson, Edward Francis (b. 1915) War Cabinet Offices, 1941–5; CSO, 1945; Deputy Director of Research and Planning Division, UN Economic Commission for Europe, 1951–6; University Lecturer in Economic Statistics,

Oxford, and Research Fellow of St. Antony's College, Oxford, 1956–9; Director, Oxford University Institute of Economics and Statistics, 1959–82.

Jacob, Major General Edward Ian Claud (later Sir Edward) (b. 1899) Military Assistant Secretary to Cabinet, 1939–46; Controller of European Services, BBC, 1946; Director-General, BBC, 1952–60.

Jay, Douglas Patrick Thomas (later Lord Jay) (b. 1907) Financial journalist on *The Times*, 1929–33, and *The Economist*, 1933–7; City Editor, *Daily Herald*, 1937–41; Assistant Secretary, Ministry of Supply, 1941–3; Principal Assistant Secretary, Board of Trade, 1943–5; Personal Assistant to the Prime Minister, 1945-6; Labour MP 1946–83; Economic Secretary, Treasury, 1947–50, Financial Secretary, 1950–51; President of Board of Trade, 1964–7.

Jay, Peggy (née Garnett) Councillor, London County Council. Married Douglas Jay 1933 (marriage dissolved 1972).

Jeans, Sir James Hopwood (1877–1946) Mathematician, theoretical physicist, astronomer; FRS, 1906.

Jebb, Geraldine Emma May (d. 1959) Ministry of Labour, 1913–17; Director of Studies and Lecturer in Economics, Newnham College, Cambridge, 1917–19; Lecturer in Economics, Armstrong College, Newcastle upon Tyne, 1919–29; Principal, Bedford College London, 1930–51.

Jebb, Hubert Miles Gladwyn (later Lord Gladwyn) (b. 1900) Private Secretary to Permanent Secretary, FO, 1937–40; Ministry of Economic Warfare, 1940; Acting Counsellor, FO, 1941, Head of Reconstruction Department, 1942, Counsellor, 1943, Assistant Under-Secretary of State, 1949; Permanent UK Representative to UN, 1950–54; HM Ambassador to France, 1954–60.

Jefferies, G. Patrick Economic Section, 1946–9; subsequently Principal, Ministry of Supply; later Assistant Secretary, Department of Trade and Industry.

Jenks, Clarence Wilfred (1909–73) Legal Section, ILO, 1931, Legal Adviser, 1940, Assistant Director-General 1948–64, Deputy Director-General, 1964–7, Principal Deputy Director-General, 1967–70, Director-General, 1970–73.

Jennings, Miss G. M. Principal, Treasury, in 1940s.

Jewkes, John (1902–88) Professor of Social Economics, Manchester University, 1936–46; Director, Economic Section, 1941; Director-General of Statistics and Programmes, Ministry of Aircraft Production, 1943; Principal Assistant Secretary, Office of Minister of Reconstruction, 1944; Stanley Jevons Professor of Political Economy, Manchester, 1946–8; Professor of Economic Organisation Oxford University, 1948–69.

Johnston, Sir Alexander (b. 1905) Entered Home Office, 1928; Principal Assistant Secretary, Office of Minister of Reconstruction, 1943–5; Under-Secretary, Office of the Lord President of the Council, 1946–8; Deputy Secretary of the Cabinet, 1948–51; Third Secretary, Treasury, 1951–8; Chairman, Board of Inland Revenue, 1958–68; Deputy Chairman, Monopolies Commission, 1969–76.

Jones, Edgar (b. 1911) Assistant Lecturer, University College, Swansea, 1939–41; Economic Assistant to Sir Dennis Robertson and Lord Keynes at Treasury, concerned with balance of payments statistics, 1941–6; Financial Counsellor, UK Embassy, Washington, 1946–50; Assistant Secretary, Treasury, 1950–53; International Monetary Fund, 1953–9 and 1965–76; Financial Adviser, Government of Chile, 1959–61.

Jones, John Harry (1881–1973) Professor of Economics, University of Leeds, 1919–46.

Joseph, Peggy (Mrs Francis Hemming) Economist; Economic, Financial and Transit Department, League of Nations, in early 1940s; Ministry of Fuel and Power, 1943–6: Economic Section, 1946–55; Senior Research Officer, National Institute of Economic and Social Research, 1956–70.

Jussiant, Jean (b. 1907) Chief, Belgian Economic Mission to London, 1945–6; member of Belgian delegation to Preparatory Commission for UN Conference on Trade and Employment, London and Geneva, 1946–7; Chairman, Banque de Commerce SA from 1960.

Kahn, Richard Ferdinand (later Lord Kahn) (1905–89) Fellow, King's College, Cambridge; temporary civil servant in various government departments, 1939–46; Professor of Economics, University of Cambridge, 1951–72.

Kaldor, Nicholas (later Lord Kaldor) (1908–86) Lecturer and Reader in economics, LSE, 1932–47; National Institute of Economic and Social Research, 1943–5; Chief of Economic Planning Staff, US Strategic Bombing Survey, 1945; Director, Research and Planning Division, UN Economic Commission for Europe, Geneva, 1947–9; Fellow, King's College, Cambridge, 1949–86; Reader in Economics, Cambridge, 1952–65, Professor 1965–75; Special Adviser to Chancellor of the Exchequer, 1964–8 and 1974–6.

Kershaw, Raymond Newton (1898–1981) Secretariat, League of Nations, Geneva, 1924–9; Adviser, Bank of England, 1929–35, Adviser to the Governors, 1935–53; Bank of England member of East African, West African, Palestine and Burma Currency Boards during 1932–53.

Kervyn de Lettenhove, Baron (b. 1917) Economic Attaché to Belgian Embassy, London, 1946; subsequently UN Economic Commission for Europe, Assistant Lecturer, Massachusetts Institute of Technology, Economic Adviser, Banque de Bruxelles, and Economic Adviser, Belgian Ministry of Finance.

Keynes, Florence Ada (1861–1958) Married John Neville Keynes 1882; active in local politics and community affairs in Cambridge; mother of J. M. Keynes.

Keynes, John Maynard (Lord Keynes) (1883–1946) Fellow, King's College, Cambridge, 1909–46; Treasury, 1914–19 and 1940–6.

Keynes, John Neville (1852–1949) University Lecturer in Moral Science, Cambridge, 1884–1911; University Registrary, Cambridge, 1910–25.

Keynes, Lydia (Lady Keynes) (née Lopokova) (1892–1981) Ballerina. Married J. M. Keynes 1925.

Kilroy, Alix (later Dame Alix Meynell) (b. 1903) Entered Board of Trade, 1925, Under-Secretary, 1946–55; Secretary, Monopolies Commission, 1949–52.

King, William Lyon Mackenzie (1874–1950) Prime Minister of Canada, 1921–6, 1926–30, 1935–48; Secretary of State for External Affairs, 1921–30, 1935–46.

Kunosi, Alexander (1908–62) Czech author and translator; Export Institute, Prague, 1936–9; emigrated to France, 1939, subsequently to England; Foreign Ministry, Prague, 1945–7; Czech Ambassador to Argentina, 1947–51; imprisoned 1951, rehabilitated 1954.

Laithwaite, Sir (John) Gilbert (b. 1894) Private Secretary to Viceroy of India, 1936–43; Assistant Under-Secretary of State for India, 1943; Under-Secretary (Civil), War Cabinet, 1944–5; Deputy Under-Secretary of State for Burma, 1945–7, for India, 1947, for Commonwealth Relations, 1948–9; HM Ambassador to Republic of Ireland, 1950–51; High Commissioner in Pakistan, 1951–4; Permanent Secretary, Commonwealth Relations Office, 1955–9.

Laski, Harold (1893–1950) Professor of Political Science, LSE, 1926–50; Labour Party Executive Committee, 1936–49, Chairman, 1945–6.

Law, Richard Kidston (later Lord Coleraine) (1901–80) Conservative MP 1931–54; Financial Secretary, War Office, 1940–41; Parliamentary Under-Secretary, FO, 1941–3, Minister of State, 1943–5; Minister of Education, 1945.

Layton, Sir Walter (1884–1966) Lecturer in Economics, Cambridge, 1912–19; Ministry of Munitions, 1916–18; Editor, *The Economist*, 1922–8; Director-General of Programmes, Ministry of Supply, 1940–42; Chief Adviser, Programmes and Planning, Ministry of Production, 1942–3; Head of Joint War Production Staff, 1942–3.

Leak, Hector (1887–1976) Entered Board of Trade, 1911, Assistant Secretary, 1932, Director of Statistics, 1946, Adviser on Statistics, 1948–51.

Lee, Frank Godbould (later Sir Frank) (1903–70) Colonial Office, 1926–40; transferred to Treasury, 1940; Treasury Delegation, Washington, 1944–6; Ministry of Supply, 1946, Deputy Secretary, 1947; Permanent Secretary, Ministry of Food, 1949–51, Board of Trade, 1951–9; Joint Permanent Secretary, Treasury, 1960–62; Master, Corpus Christi College, Cambridge, 1962–70.

Leeper, Sir Reginald Wildig Allen (1888–1968) Assistant Under-Secretary, FO, 1940; HM Ambassador at the Court of the King of the Hellenes, 1943–6; Director, DeBeers Consolidated Mines Ltd., 1950–65.

Leggett, Sir Frederick William (1884–1983) Entered Civil Service, 1904; Assistant Secretary, Ministry of Labour, 1919, Principal Assistant Secretary, 1930, Under-Secretary, 1939, Chief Industrial Commissioner, 1941–2; Deputy Secretary, Ministry of Labour and National Service, 1942–5; Industrial Relations Adviser, Anglo-Iranian Oil Co., 1947–60.

Lerner, Abba P. (1903–82) Assistant Lecturer, LSE, 1935–7; later positions at various American universities; Professor of Economics, University of California, Berkeley, 1965–71.

Lidderdale, Miss J. H. Principal, Office of the Lord President of the Council, in 1940s.

Liesching, Sir Percivale (1895–1974) Entered Colonial Office, 1920; Dominions Office, 1925, Assistant Under-Secretary, 1939–42; Second Secretary, Board of Trade, 1942–6; Permanent Secretary, Ministry of Food, 1946–8, Commonwealth Relations Office, 1949–55.

Lindahl, Erik Robert (1891–1960) Professor of Economics, University of Lund, Sweden, 1939–58.

Lindsell, Herbert George (1903–73) Board of Trade, 1918–32; Import Duties Advisory Office, 1932–9, Principal, 1939; Ministry of Supply, 1939, Assistant Secretary, 1941, Under-Secretary, 1950–9; Principal Officer (Establishments), UK Atomic Energy Authority, 1959–63.

Litvinov, Maxim Maximovich (1876–1951) USSR Deputy Commissar of Foreign Affairs 1921–30 and 1943–6; Commissar of Foreign Affairs, 1930–39; Ambassador to USA, 1941–3.

Lloyd, Edward Mayow Hastings (1889–1968) Inland Revenue, 1913; War Office, 1914–17; Ministry of Food, 1917–19; Economic and Financial Section, League of Nations, 1919–21; Assistant Secretary, Empire Marketing Board, 1926–33; Principal Assistant Secretary, Ministry of Food, 1939–42; Economic Adviser to Minister of State, Middle East, 1942–4; UNRRA Economic and Financial Adviser for the Balkans, 1945; FAO, 1946–7; Under-Secretary, Ministry of Food, 1947–53.

Loveday, Alexander (1888–1962) Lecturer in Economics, University of Cambridge, 1913–15; League of Nations Secretariat, 1919; Director, Financial and Economic Section, 1931–9, Economic, Financial and Transit Department, 1939–46.

Lubin, Isadore (1896–1978) Commissioner US Bureau of Labor Statistics, 1933–46; Economic Adviser in the White House, 1940–5.

Lyttleton, Oliver (later Lord Chandos) (1893–1972) Conservative MP 1940–54; President of Board of Trade, 1940–41; Minister of State in Middle East and Member of War Cabinet, 1941–2; Minister of Production and Member of War Cabinet, 1942–5; President of Board of Trade and Minister of Production, 1945; Secretary of State for the Colonies, 1951–4.

Mabane, William (later Lord Mabane) (1895–1969) Liberal National MP 1931–45; Parliamentary Secretary, Ministry of Home Security, 1939–42, Ministry of Food, 1942–5; Minister of State, FO, 1945.

McDougall, Archibald (1903–84) Lecturer in Law, Victoria University of Manchester, 1931–5; Legal adviser to Iraqi Ministry of Foreign Affairs, Baghdad, 1936–40; Counsel, UK Purchasing Commission, New York, 1940–1; British Raw Materials Mission, Washington, 1941–3; Combined Production and Resources Board, 1944–5; Head of UK Economic Group, US Department of Commerce and UK Embassy Washington, 1945–6; Legal Counsellor, UK Embassy, Cairo, 1946–9; Assistant Legal Adviser, FO, 1949–50.

McDougall, Frank Lidgett (1884–1958) Economic Adviser to Australian Prime Minister at Imperial Conferences in 1920s and 1930s; Australian Representative, Imperial Economic Committee, 1935–7; also Chairman London Agency of Australian Dried Fruits Board, member of Economic Committee, League of Nations, and Permanent Committee, International Institute of Agriculture, Rome.

MacDougall, George Donald Alistair (later Sir Donald) (b. 1912) First Lord of Admiralty's Statistical Branch, 1939–40; PM's Statistical Branch, 1940–45, 1951–3; Economic Director, OEEC, Paris, 1948–9; Official Fellow, Nuffield College, Oxford 1952–64; Head, Government Economic Service and Chief Economic Adviser to the Treasury, 1969–73.

McKenzie, A. W. Assistant Secretary, Raw Materials Department, Board of Trade, in 1940s.

McKinnon, Hector (1890–1973) Secretary of Advisory Board on Tariff and Taxation, Department of Finance, Canada, 1926–30, Commissioner of Tariff, 1930–40; Chairman of Tariff Board, 1940–59; Chairman, Wartime Prices and Trade Board, 1940–1; President, Commodity Prices Stabilization Corporation, 1941–6.

Mackintosh, William Archibald (1895–1970) National Employment Commission, Canada, 1936–8; Research Adviser, Royal Commission on Dominion-Provincial Relations, 1938–9; served in Departments of Finance and Reconstruction and Supply, Ottawa, 1939–46; Professor of Economics, Queens University, Kingston, 1927–51, Principal, 1951–61.

McNeil, Hector (1907–55) Labour MP 1941–55; Parliamentary Secretary to Ministry of War Transport, 1942–5; Parliamentary Under-Secretary of State, FO, 1945–6, Minister of State, 1946–50; Secretary of State for Scotland, 1950–51; Leader, UK Delegation to UN Economic Commission for Europe, 1948.

Magowan, Sir John Hall (1893–1951) Commercial Secretary, British Embassy, Washington, 1931–4, Berlin, 1937–9; Treasury, 1939–40; Deputy Controller-General, Exports Credits Guarantee Department, 1940–42; Commercial Adviser to HM Ambassador in Washington, 1942–8.

Margaret, Princess (b. 1930) Sister of Princess Elizabeth.

Marget, Arthur William (1899–1962) Professor of Economics, University of Minnesota, 1930–48; Chief, Finance Division, US Element Allied Commission for Austria, 1945–8, Chief, Economic Division, 1947–8; Chief, Finance Division, Office of Economic Cooperation Administration, 1948–9; Director, International Finance Division, Board of Governors of Federal Reserve System, 1950–61.

Marjolin, Robert Ernest (1911–86) Joined General de Gaulle in London, 1941; Head of French Supply Mission, USA, 1944; Directeur des Relations Economiques Extérieures, Ministère de l'Economie Nationale, 1945; Secretary-General, OEEC, 1948–55; Vice-President, EEC Commission, 1958–67.

Marquand, Hilary Adair (1901–72) Professor of Industrial Relations, University College, Cardiff, 1930–45; wartime temporary civil servant, Board of Trade, Ministry of Labour and Ministry of Production; Labour MP 1945–61; Secretary for Overseas Trade, 1945–7; Paymaster-General, 1947–8; Minister of Pensions,

1948–51; Minister of Health, 1951; Director, International Institute for Labour Studies, Geneva, 1961–5; National Board of Prices and Incomes, 1965–8.

Martin, P. W. Head of Division, Ministry of Food, 1943–5.

Maud, John Primatt Redcliffe (later Lord Redcliffe-Maud) (1906–83) Master, Birkbeck College, London, 1939–43; Deputy Secretary, later Second Secretary, Ministry of Food, 1941–4; Second Secretary, Office of Minister of Reconstruction, 1944–5; Secretary, Office of Lord President of the Council, 1945; Permanent Secretary, Ministry of Education, 1945–52, Ministry of Fuel and Power, 1952–9; Member UK Delegation, UNESCO, 1946–51.

Mayhew, Christopher Paget (later Lord Mayhew) (b. 1915) Labour MP 1945–74; PPS to Lord President of the Council, 1945–6; Parliamentary Under-Secretary of State for Foreign Affairs, 1946–50; Minister of Defence, 1964–6.

Meade, Bridget Ariane (later Mrs Dommen) (b. 1940) Daughter of James and Margaret Meade.

Meade, Charlotte Elizabeth (later Mrs Lewis) (b. 1937) Daughter of James and Margaret Meade.

Meade, Diana Hippisley (Mrs John Packham, later Mrs Hewlings) (b. 1908) Sister of James Meade.

Meade, (Elizabeth) Margaret (née Wilson) (b. 1908) Married James Meade 1933.

Meade, Thomas Wilson (b. 1936) Son of James and Margaret Meade.

Meehan, Michael Joseph (1901–63) US Bureau of Foreign and Domestic Commerce, 1932–42; Director, Progress Division, War Productions Board, 1942–4; Chief of Research and Statistics Division, Bureau of Foreign and Domestic Commerce, 1944–6; Assistant Director, Office of Business Economics, Department of Commerce, 1946–8, Director, 1949–63.

Melville, Leslie Galfreid (later Sir Leslie) (1902–86) Professor of Economics, University of Adelaide, 1929–31; Economic Adviser to Commonwealth Bank of Australia, 1931–49, Assistant Governor 1949–53.

Middleton, J. R. (b. 1904) New Zealand civil servant, with Industries and Commerce Department; seconded to Prime Minister's Department as Secretary of Executive Committee, Organisation for National Development, in 1945.

Midwinter, Miss K. M. Civil servant, FO, in 1940s; Adviser to UK Delegation to UN Preparatory Commission, 1945–6.

Morgenthau, Henry Jr. (1891–1967) Under-Secretary and Acting Secretary, US Treasury, 1933–4, Secretary, 1935–45.

Morrison, Herbert Stanley (later Lord Morrison) (1888–1965) Labour MP 1923–4, 1929–31, 1935–59; Minister of Transport, 1929–31; Minister of Supply, 1940; Home Secretary and Minister of Home Security, 1940–45; Member of War Cabinet, 1942–5; Lord President of the Council and Deputy Prime Minister, 1945–51; Secretary of State for Foreign Affairs, 1951.

Murphy, James Francis (1893–1949) Secretary, Australian Department of Commerce and Agriculture, 1934–45; Commonwealth Food Controller, 1943–5; Economic Adviser to the Minister for Commerce and Agriculture, 1945–8.

Murrie, Sir William (Stuart) (b. 1903) Entered Scottish Office, 1927; Department of Health for Scotland, 1935; Under-Secretary, Cabinet Offices, 1944, Deputy Secretary (Civil), 1947; Deputy Under-Secretary of State, Home Office, 1948–52; Permanent Under-Secretary of State for Scotland, 1959–64.

Mynors, Humphrey Charles Baskerville (later Sir Humphrey) (1903–89) Fellow, Corpus Christi College, Cambridge, 1926–33; Bank of England, 1933, Director, 1949–54, Deputy Governor, 1954–64.

Myrdal, (Karl) Gunnar (1898–1987) Swedish economist; Member, Board of Bank of Sweden, Chairman, Post-War Planning Commission, Minister of Commerce, 1945–7; Executive Secretary, UN Economic Commission for Europe, 1947–57.

Nash, Sir Walter (1882–1968) Secretary, New Zealand Labour Party, 1922–32,

President 1935–6; Minister of NZ in USA, 1942–4; Minister of Finance, Customs, 1935–49; Member, War Cabinet, 1939–45; Deputy Prime Minister of New Zealand, 1940–49, Prime Minister, 1957–60.

Neale, John Ernest (later Sir John) (1890–1975) Department of History, University College London, 1919–25; Professor of Modern History, University of Manchester, 1925–7; Astor Professor of English History, University of London, 1927–56.

Nicholson, (Edward) Max (b. 1904) Head, Allocation of Tonnage Division, Ministry of War Transport, 1942–5; Secretary, Office of Lord President of the Council, 1945–52; Director-General, Nature Conservancy, 1952–66.

Niemeyer, Sir Otto (1883–1972) Controller of Finance and Supply Services, Treasury, 1922–7; Bank of England, 1927, Director, 1938–52.

Noel-Baker, Philip John (later Lord Noel-Baker) (1889–1982) Labour MP 1929–31, 1936–70; PPS to Secretary of State for Foreign Affairs, 1929–31; Joint Parliamentary Secretary, Minstry of War Transport, 1942–5; Minister of State, FO, 1945–6; Secretary of State for Air, 1946–7, for Commonwealth Relations, 1947–50; Minister of Fuel and Power, 1950–51; Nobel Peace Price, 1959.

Norris, Harry Accountant with Deloitte, Plender, Griffiths & Co., in 1940s.

North, George Cecil (later Sir George) (1895–1971) Assistant Secretary, Ministry of Health, 1937, Director of Public Relations, 1938–40, Head of Water etc. Division, 1940–45; Registrar-General, 1945–58.

Ogilvie, Sir Frederick (Wolff) (1893–1949) President and Vice-Chancellor, Queen's University, Belfast, 1934–8; Director-General, British Broadcasting Corporation, 1938–42; British Council, 1943–5; Principal, Jesus College, Oxford, 1945–9.

Ohlsson, Ingvar Swedish Government Economist in 1940s; Konjunkturinstut, Stockholm, in 1950s; published *On National Accounting*, Uppsala, 1953.

Opie, Redvers (1900–84) Economist; Counsellor and Economic Adviser, British Embassy, Washington, 1939–46; Senior Staff Member, Brookings Institution, 1947–53; Economic Counsellor, American Chamber of Commerce, Mexico City, 1966–78.

Orr, John *see* Boyd-Orr.

Overton, Sir Arnold (1893–1975) Entered Board of Trade, 1919, Permanent Secretary, 1941–5.

Owen, Arthur David Kemp (later Sir David) (1904–70) Secretary, Civic Division, PEP, 1933–6, General Secretary, 1940–41; Personal Assistant to Sir Stafford Cripps, 1942–3; Reconstruction Department, FO, 1944–5; Deputy Executive Secretary, UN Preparatory Commission, 1945–6; Assistant Secretary-General, UN, 1946–51; Chairman, UN Technical Assistance Board, 1951–65.

Owen, George Sherard (1892–1976) Minstry of Labour, 1919–34; Unemployment Assistance Board, 1934–40; Board of Trade, 1940–42; Ministry of Production, 1942–5; Under-Secretary, Board of Trade, 1945–52.

Padmore, Thomas (later Sir Thomas) (b. 1909) Board of Inland Revenue 1931–4; transferred to Treasury, 1934; Principal Private Secretary to Chancellor of Exchequer, 1943–5, Second Secretary, 1952–62.

Pakenham, Francis Aungier (Lord Pakenham, later Lord Longford) (b. 1905) Personal Assistant to Sir William Beveridge, 1941–4; Parliamentary Under-secretary of State, War Office, 1946–7; Chancellor of the Duchy of Lancaster, 1947–8; Minister of Civil Aviation, 1948–51; Lord Privy Seal, 1964–65, 1966–8; Secretary of State for the Colonies, 1965–6; Leader of the House of Lords, 1964–8.

Palmer, Sir William (1883–1964) Second Secretary, Ministry of Supply, 1939–42, Ministry of Production, 1942–4; Principal Industrial Adviser, Board of Trade, 1944–6.

Pares, Richard (1902–58) Lecturer, New College, Oxford, 1929–40; Board of Trade, 1940–45; Professor of History, University of Edinburgh, 1945–54.

Pasvolsky, Leo (1893–1953) Economist; Special Assistant to US Secretary of State, 1936–8, 1939–46; Chief, Division of Special Research, Department of State, 1941–2, Supervisor, Division of Political and Economic Studies, 1943; Executive Director, Committee on Post-War Programmes, 1944.

Penrose, E. F. (1895–1984) Economist; ILO, 1938–41; Special Assistant to US Ambassador, London, 1941–4; US Delegation, UN, 1946–7.

Penson, John Hubert (1893–1979) Commissioner for Finance, Commission of Government of Newfoundland, 1937–41; British Supply Mission in Washington, 1944–5; Attaché, British Embassy, Washington, 1947–53.

Pepler, Sir George Lionel (1882–1959) Chief Town Planning Inspector, Ministry of Health, 1919–41; Chairman, Inter-Allied Committee for Physical Planning and Reconstruction, 1942–5; Chief Technical Adviser, Ministry of Town and Country Planning, 1943–6.

Perez-Guerrero, Manuel (b. 1911) Economic and Finance Section, League of Nations, 1937–40; Commission for Imports, Venezuelan Ministry of Finance, 1940–2; Economics and Statistics Section, ILO, Montreal, 1942–3; Head of Commission on Post-War Problems, Venezuelan Ministry of Foreign Relations, 1943–4; Liaison Director, UN, 1946–7; Venezuelan Minister of Finance, 1947–8; Technical Assistance Board, UN, 1949–58, 1963; Head, Office of Co-ordination and Planning, Venezuela, 1959–62; Minister of Mines and Hydro-carbons, Venezuela, 1963–7; Venezuelan Ambassador to UN, 1967–9; Secretary General, UNCTAD, 1969–74; Minister of State, Office of President, Venezuela, 1974.

Perroux, Francois (1903–87) Professor of Economics, University of Paris, from 1935; Director of Studies, Ecole Pratique des Hautes Etudes, from 1938; Director, Institut de Science Economique Appliqué, Paris, from 1944.

Pethick-Lawrence, Frederick Wilson (Lord Pethick-Lawrence) (1871–1961) Labour MP 1922–31, 1935–45; Financial Secretary, Treasury, 1929–31; joint editor, *Votes for Women*, 1907–14.

Phillips, Herbert Moore (b. 1908) Ministry of Labour, 1934, Assistant Secretary, Manpower Department, 1942–5, Overseas Department, 1946; Foreign Office, 1946–9; Head, Division of Applied Social Sciences, and Director, Analysis Office, UNESCO, 1952–68.

Phillips, Sir Thomas (William) (1883–1966) Entered Civil Service, 1906; Assistant Secretary, Ministry of Labour, 1919, Deputy Secretary, 1924; Permanent Secretary, Ministry of Labour, 1935–44, Ministry of National Insurance, 1944–8.

Pickard, Bertram Head of Society of Friends (Quaker) Centre, Geneva, in 1930s, and official representative of the Centre with the UN after 1945.

Pimlott, John Alfred Ralph (1909–69) Entered Home Office, 1932; Private Secretary to Home Secretary, 1943–5, to Lord President of the Council, 1945–7; Office of the Lord President of the Council, 1949–51; Under-Secretary, Ministry of Materials, 1951–4, Board of Trade, 1954–5, 1956–60; Secretary, Monopolies Commission, 1955–6.

Plant, Arnold (later Sir Arnold) (1898–1978) Professor of Commerce, LSE, 1930–65; Adviser, Production Council, 1940, Production Executive, 1941, Ministry of Production, 1942–5, Cabinet Office, 1945–6; member, Monopolies Commission, 1953–6.

Plumb, C. T. Assistant Secretary, Board of Trade, in 1940s.

Plumptre, Arthur Fitzwalter Wynne (1907–77) Canadian Economist; University of Toronto, 1931–41, 1965–72; Financial Attaché, Canadian Embassy, Washington 1942–5; Wartime Prices and Trade Board, 1942–7; Head,

Economic Division, Department of External Affairs, 1949–52; Deputy Permanent Representative of Canada to North Atlantic Council and OEEC, 1952–4; Director, International Economic Relations, Department of Finance, 1954–5, Assistant Deputy Minister, 1955–65.

Polak, Jacques Jacobus (b. 1914) Economist, League of Nations, 1937–43; Economist, Netherlands Embassy, Washington, 1943–4; Assistant Financial Adviser, Economic Adviser, UNRRA, 1944–6; International Monetary Fund from 1947, Director, Research Department, 1958–79.

Polanyi, Michael (1891–1976) Professor of Physical Chemistry, Victoria University of Manchester, 1938–48, Professor of Social Studies, 1948–58.

Ponsonby, Gilbert (d. 1981) Lecturer in Commerce, LSE, in 1940s; wartime service in Ministry of Transport; Cassel Reader in Commerce, LSE, 1950–64.

Proctor, Philip Dennis (later Sir Dennis) (1905–83) Entered Ministry of Health, 1929; Treasury, 1930, Third Secretary, 1948–50; Deputy Secretary, Ministry of Transport and Civil Aviation, 1953–8; Permanent Secretary, Ministry of Power, 1958–65.

Quirk, Roger Nathanial (1901–64) Under-Secretary, Ministry of Fuel and Power, 1948, Office of the Lord President of the Council, 1952, Office of the Minister for Science, 1959.

Radice, Edward Albert (b. 1907) League of Nations Secretariat, 1939; Ministry of Economic Warfare, 1940–44; Foreign Service, 1945–53; Ministry of Defence, 1953–70; Senior Research Fellow, St Antony's College, Oxford, 1970–73.

Raisman, Sir (Abraham) Jeremy (1892–1978) Joint Secretary, Commerce Department, Government of India, 1931–4, Secretary, Finance Department, 1938–9; Finance Member, Government of India, 1939–45; Vice-President, Governor-General's Executive Council, 1944.

Rasminsky, Louis (b. 1908) Economic Section, League of Nations, 1930–40; joined Bank of Canada 1940; Foreign Exchange Control Board, Canada, 1940–3; Deputy Governor, Bank of Canada, 1955–61, Governor 1961–73.

Reddaway, William Brian (b. 1913) Fellow, Clare College, Cambridge, since 1938; Lecturer in Economics, Cambridge, 1939–55, Director, Department of Applied Economics, 1955–69, Reader in Economics, 1957–65, Professor of Political Economy, 1969–80; Statistics Division, Board of Trade, 1940–47; Economic Adviser, OEEC, 1951–2.

Reeder, A. Assistant Secretary, Employment Department, Ministry of Labour.

Rees, P. M. Chief Accountant, Unilever Ltd. in 1940s.

Rice, Stuart Arthur (1889–1969) Instructor and Assistant Professor of Sociology, Dartmouth College, 1923–6; Professor, University of Pennsylvania, 1926–40; Chairman, Central Statistical Board, 1936–40; Assistant Director, Bureau of Budget, for Statistical Standards, Executive Office of President, 1940–55; President, Surveys and Research Corporation, Washington, 1955–65.

Robbins, Lionel Charles (later Lord Robbins) (1898–1984) Lecturer in Economics, LSE, 1925–7; Fellow and Lecturer, New College, Oxford, 1927–9; Professor of Economics, University of London, 1929–61; Economic Section, 1939–41, Director, 1941–5.

Robertson, Dennis Holme (later Sir Dennis) (1890–1963) Fellow, Trinity College, Cambridge, 1914–38, 1944–63; Reader in Economics, Cambridge University, 1930–8; Cassel Professor of Economics, LSE, 1939–44; Adviser, Treasury, 1939–44; Professor of Political Economy, Cambridge, 1944–57.

Robinson, Edward Austin Gossage (later Sir Austin) (b. 1897) Lecturer in Economics, Cambridge, 1929–49; Assistant Editor, *Economic Journal*, 1934, Joint Editor, 1944–70; Economic Section, 1939–42; Ministry of Production, 1942–5; member, British Reparations Commission, Moscow and Berlin, 1945;

Economic Adviser to Board of Trade, 1945–6; Professor of Economics, Cambridge, 1950–65.

Robinson, Joan (née Maurice) (1903–83) Assistant Lecturer in Economics, Cambridge, 1931–7, Lecturer, 1937–49, Reader, 1949–65, Professor of Economics, 1965–71.

Ronald, Nigel Bruce (1894–1973) Assistant Private Secretary to Foreign Secretary, 1929–34; First Secretary, FO, 1930, Counsellor, 1939, Assistant Under-Secretary, 1942; HM Ambassador to Portugal, 1947–54.

Roosevelt, Franklin Delano (1882–1945) President of USA, 1933–45.

Rosenstein-Rodan, Paul N. (1902–85) Professor of Political Economy, University College London, 1934–47; Economic Adviser, World Bank, 1947–52; Professor of Economics, Massachusetts Institute of Technology, 1952–68, University of Texas, 1968–72, University of Boston, 1972–85.

Rousseaux, Paul P. (b. 1910, now deceased) Professor of Economics, University of Louvain.

Rowan, Thomas Leslie (later Sir Leslie) (1908–72) Assistant and later Principal Private Secretary to Prime Minister, 1941–5, 1945–7; Second Secretary, Treasury, 1947–9, 1951–8; Economic Minister, HM Embassy, Washington, 1949–51.

Rowe-Dutton, Sir Ernest (1891–1965) Entered Inland Revenue, 1914; Treasury, 1919; Financial Adviser, HM Embassy, Berlin, 1928–32, Paris, 1934–9; Third Secretary, Treasury, 1947–9.

Rowlatt, Sir John (1898–1956) Parliamentary Counsel to Treasury, 1937; Second Parliamentary Counsel, 1947–53; First Parliamentary Counsel, 1953–6.

Salter, Sir (James) Arthur (later Lord Salter) (1881–1975) Director, Economic and Finance Section, League of Nations, 1922–31; Gladstone Professor of Political Theory and Institutions, Oxford University, 1934–44; MP (Independent) for Oxford University, 1937–50; Head, British Merchant Shipping Mission, Washington, 1941–3; Senior Deputy Director-General, UNRRA, 1944; Chancellor of Duchy of Lancaster, 1945; Minister of State for Economic Affairs, 1951–2; Minister of Materials, 1952–3.

Saunders, Christopher Thomas (b. 1907) Joint Committee of Cotton Trade Organisations, Manchester, 1935–40; Cotton Control, 1940–44; Combined Production and Resources Board, Washington, 1944–5; Ministry of Labour, 1945–7; CSO, 1947–57; Director, National Institute of Economic and Social Research, 1957–64; UN Economic Commission for Europe, 1965–72.

Saunders, Sir Harold Leonard (1885–1965) Assistant Secretary, Board of Trade, 1940; Assistant Comptroller, Patent Office, 1944; Comptroller-General, Patents, Designs and Trade Marks, and Comptroller, Industrial Property Department, Board of Trade, 1944–9.

Sayers, Richard Sidney (1908–89) Assistant Lecturer in Economics, LSE, 1931–5; Fellow, Pembroke College, Oxford, 1939–45; Ministry of Supply, 1940–45; Economic Section, 1945–7; Cassell Professor of Economics, LSE, 1947–68.

Schumacher, Ernst Friedrich (1911–77) Economic Adviser, Control Commission Germany (British Element), 1946–50; Economic Adviser, National Coal Board, 1950–70, Director of Statistics, 1963–70.

Secord, Campbell H. Assistant Secretary, Office of the Lord President of the Council, 1945–8.

Sewell, Bray, F. Partner in Tansley Witt, Chartered Accountants, London, in 1940s.

Shackle, George L. S. (b. 1903) Statistical Branch, PM's Office 1939–45; Economic Section, 1945–9; Brunner Professor of Economic Science, University of Liverpool, 1951–69.

Shackle, Robert Jones (1895–1950) Assistant Principal, Board of Trade, 1920, Principal, 1929, Assistant Secretary, 1935, Principal Assistant Secretary, 1942–7, Under-Secretary, 1947.

Sharp, Evelyn A. (later Baroness Sharp) (1903–85) Entered Board of Trade, 1926; Deputy Secretary, Ministry of Town and Country Planning, 1947–50; Joint Deputy Secretary, Ministry of Housing and Local Government 1951–5; Permanent Secretary, Ministry of Housing, 1955–66.

Shillito, Edward Alan (b. 1910) Customs and Excise, 1934–6; Treasury, 1936–57, Under-Secretary, 1951; Admiralty and Ministry of Defence, 1957–69.

Shinwell, Emanuel (later Lord Shinwell) (1884–1985) Labour MP 1922–24, 1928–31, 1935–70; Financial Secretary, War Office, 1929–30; Minister of Fuel and Power, 1945–7; Secretary of State for War, 1947–50; Minister of Defence, 1950–51.

Siepmann, Harry Arthur (1889–1963) Advisor to Governors, Bank of England, 1926, Executive Director, 1945–54.

Simon, Sir John (later Lord Simon) (1873–1954) Liberal MP 1906–18, 1922–3, 1931–40; Secretary of State for Foreign Affairs, 1931–5; Home Secretary 1935–7; Chancellor of the Exchequer, 1937–40; Lord Chancellor, 1940–5.

Sinker, Algernon Paul (later Sir Algernon) (1905–77) Fellow, Jesus College, Cambridge, 1927–49; Admiralty, 1940–45; Treasury, 1945–50; First Civil Service Commissioner, 1951–4; Director-General, British Council, 1954–68; Chairman, Council for Small Industries in Rural Areas, 1968–76.

Slim, Field-Marshal Sir William Joseph (1891–1970) Commander-in-Chief, Allied Land Forces, S.E. Asia, 1945–6; Chief of Imperial General Staff, 1948–52; Governor-General and Commander-in-Chief of Australia, 1953–60.

Smith, Sir Ben (1879–1964) Labour MP 1923–46; Parliamentary Secretary, Ministry of Aircraft Production, 1942; Minister resident for Supply in Washington, 1943–5; Minister of Food, 1945–6.

Snelling, Arthur Wendell (later Sir Arthur) (b. 1914) Dominions Office, 1936, Private Secretary to Parliamentary Under-Secretary, 1939; Joint Secretary, UK Delegation to Bretton Woods Conference, 1944; Deputy High Commissioner for UK in New Zealand, 1947–50, South Africa, 1953–5; HM Ambassador to South Africa, 1970–72.

Snowden, Philip (Lord Snowden) (1864–1937) Labour MP 1906–18, 1922–31; Chancellor of the Exchequer, 1924, 1929–31; Lord Privy Seal, 1931.

Spearman, Alexander Cadwallader Mainwaring (later Sir Alexander) (1901–82) Conservative MP 1941–66; PPS to President of Board of Trade, 1951–2. Married Diana Doyle, author of *Modern Dictatorship* in 1928.

Sraffa, Piero (1898–1983) University Lecturer in Economics, Cambridge, 1927–31, Assistant Director of Research in Economics, 1935–63, Reader in Economics, 1963–5; Fellow, Trinity College, Cambridge, 1934–83.

Stafford, Jack (1909–82) CSO, 1941, Acting Director, 1946; Director of Statistics, Department of Trade and Industry, 1948–72; Chief Statistician, Price Commission, 1973–8.

Stalin, Joseph (1879–1953) Leader, USSR and Communist Party, 1924–53.

Stevens, Sir Roger Bentham (1906–80) Entered Consular Service, 1928; Secretary, British Civil Secretariat, Washington, 1944–6; FO, 1946–8, Assistant Under-Secretary of State, 1948–58, Deputy Under-Secretary of State, 1958–63; Director, British Bank of the Middle East, 1964–77; Chancellor, Leeds University, 1963–70.

Stinebower, Leroy Dean (1904–76) Economist, US Department of State, 1934, Chief, Division of Economic Studies, 1943, Adviser, Office of Economic Affairs also Deputy Director, Office of International Trade Policy, 1945, Special Assistant to Assistant Secretary of State for Economic Affairs, 1946–9, Director, Office of Financial and Development Policy, 1949–52.

Stirling, John Ashwell (1891–1965) Department of Overseas Trade, 1917–27; Export Credits Guarantee Department, 1927–35; Commercial Relations and Exports Department, Board of Trade, 1935; Assistant Secretary, Board of Trade, 1944.

Stone, John Richard Nicholas (later Sir Richard) (b. 1913) C. E. Heath and Co., Lloyd's Brokers, 1936–9; Ministry of Economic Warfare, 1939–40; Central Economic Information Service, 1940; CSO, 1940–45; Director, Department of Applied Economics, Cambridge, 1944–55; P. D. Leake Professor of Finance and Accounting, Cambridge, 1955–80; Fellow, King's College, Cambridge, since 1945.

Strachey, Evelyn John St Loe (1901–63) Labour MP 1929–31, 1945–63; Parliamentary Under-Secretary of State, Air Ministry, 1945–6; Minister of Food, 1946–50; Secretary of State for War, 1950–51.

Svennilson, Ingvar (1908–72) Swedish economist; member of 'Stockholm School' in 1930s; Director, Industrial Institute for Economic and Social Research, 1942–52; Professor, University of Stockholm, 1947–72, Vice-President, 1958–66; Chairman, Long-Term Planning Commission, 1947–67.

Swan, Trevor Australian Economist; seconded to Economic Section 1947–8 from Prime Minister's Department, Commonwealth of Australia.

Taplin, Walter (b. 1910) Editorial Staff, *The Economist*, 1938–40; Ministry of Food, 1940–42; CSO, 1942–5; Staff, later Editor, *The Spectator*, 1946–54; Senior Economist, Iron and Steel Board, 1955–6; Research Fellow in Advertising and Promotional Activity, LSE, 1957–61.

Tawney, Richard Henry (1880–1962) Professor of Economic History, University of London, 1931–49; Adviser, British Embassy in Washington, 1941–2.

Tew, John Hedley Brian (b. 1917) Iron and Steel Control, 1940–42; Ministry of Aircraft Production, 1942–5; Industrial and Commercial Finance Corp., 1946; Professor of Economics, University of Nottingham, 1950–67; Department of Trade and Industry, 1969–71; External Professor, University of Loughborough, since 1982.

Thompson-McCausland, Lucius Perronet (1904–84) *Financial News*, 1929–34; Moody's Economic Service, 1929–39; Bank of England, 1939–65, Adviser to the Governor, 1949–65.

Thorneycroft, George Edward Peter (later Lord Thorneycroft) (b. 1909) Conservative MP 1938–66; Parliamentary Secretary, Ministry of War Transport, 1945; President of Board of Trade, 1951–7; Chancellor of the Exchequer, 1957–8; Minister of Aviation, 1960–62; Minister of Defence, 1962–4; Chairman, Conservative Party, 1975–81.

Tinbergen, Jan (b. 1903) Central Bureau of Statistics, The Hague, 1929–36, 1938–45; League of Nations, Geneva, 1936–8; Director, Central Planning Bureau, The Hague, 1945–55; Professor of Development Planning, University of Rotterdam, 1933–73, Leiden, 1973–5.

Tirana, Rifat (1908–52) Albanian by birth, educated LSE; League of Nations, Geneva, in 1930s; war-time service with US Board of Economic Warfare.

Tomlinson, John Doren (1903–81) Assistant Professor, then Professor of Political Science, Wabash College, 1928–41; US State Department, 1941, Division of International Organization Affairs, 1945–6, Assistant Chief, 1946; Adviser, Office UN Economic and Social Affairs, 1948–54; Adviser, US Delegations, Dumbarton Oaks, 1944, San Francisco 1945, UN Preparatory Commission, 1945.

Topham, A. M. R. Administrative Staff, Cabinet Offices, 1945–6; previously Principal Private Secretary to Lord Privy Seal (Attlee), 1940–2.

Towers, Graham Ford (1897–1975) Assistant General Manager, Royal Bank of Canada, Montreal, 1933–4; Governor, Bank of Canada, 1934–54.

Trend, Burke St John (later Lord Trend) (1914–87) Entered Civil Service 1936; Principal Private Secretary to Chancellor of Exchequer, 1945–9; Under-secretary, Treasury, 1949, Second Secretary, 1959–62; Deputy Secretary to Cabinet, 1956–9, Secretary, 1963–73; Rector, Lincoln College, Oxford, 1972–83.

Tress, Ronald Charles (b. 1915) Economic Section 1941–7; Reader in Public Finance, University of London, 1947–51; Professor of Economics, University of Bristol, 1951–68; Master of Birkbeck College, London, 1968–77.

Troutbeck, John Monro (later Sir John) (1894–1971) Entered FO 1920; Ministry of Economic Warfare, 1939–43; Counsellor, Foreign Office, 1943; Assistant Under-Secretary, 1946–7; Head, British Middle East Office, Cairo, 1947–50; HM Ambassador to Iraq, 1951–4.

Truman, Harry S. (1884–1972) Vice-President of USA, 1945, President, 1945–53.

Turner, Bruce R. Second Secretary, New Zealand Legation, Washington, in 1940s; NZ delegate to UN Preparatory Commission, 1945–6.

Turner, Sir George Wilfred (1896–1974) War Office, 1911–39; Ministry of Supply, 1939–48, Principal Assistant Secretary, 1939, Under-Secretary, 1941, Second Secretary, 1942; Permanent Under-Secretary of State for War, 1949–56.

Turner, Sir (Ronald) Mark (Conliffe) (1906–80) Ministry of Economic Warfare, 1939–44; FO, 1944–5; Under-Secretary, Control Office for Germany and Austria, 1945–7.

Turpin, Kenneth Charlton (b. 1915) Treasury, 1940–43; Assistant Private Secretary to Deputy Prime Minister, 1943–5; University Registry, Oxford, 1945–7; Secretary of Faculties, University of Oxford, 1947–57; Provost, Oriel College, Oxford, 1957–80.

Vandepeer, Sir Donald (Edward) (1890–1968) Entered Civil Service, 1908; Private Secretary to Permanent Secretaries and successive Ministers of Agriculture, 1922–34; Permanent Secretary, Ministry of Agriculture and Fisheries, 1945–52.

Viner, Jacob (1892–1970) Economist; University of Chicago, 1916–46, Princeton, 1946–60; Special Assistant to Secretary of US Treasury 1934–9; Consultant to Department of State, 1943–52.

Vinson, Frederic Moore (1890–1953) Director, US Office of Economic Stabilization, 1943–5; Federal Loan Administrator, 1945; Director, Office of War Mobilization and Reconversion, 1945; Secretary of Treasury, 1945; Chief Justice, 1946.

Vinter, (Frederick Robert) Peter (b. 1914) Ministry of Economic Warfare, 1939; Cabinet Office, 1943; Treasury, 1945, Third Secretary, 1965–9; Deputy Secretary, Ministry of Technology and Department of Trade and Industry, 1969–73; Overseas Adviser to Central Electricity Generating Board, 1973–9.

Waley, Sir (Sigismund) David (1887–1962) Entered Treasury, 1910, Third Secretary, 1946–7; European Recovery Department, Foreign Office, 1948.

Walker, Col. Charles William Garne (1882–1974) Assistant Secretary, Committee of Imperial Defence, 1921–5; Treasury, 1936–40; Principal Officer, Southern Civil Defence Region, 1940–42; Administrative Staff, Cabinet Offices, 1943–7.

Walker, Gilbert James (1907–82) Senior Investigator, Manpower Survey, Ministry of Labour, 1940; Deputy Director of Statistics, Ministry of Supply, 1941; Director of Statistics, British Supply Mission, Washington, 1942; Professor of Commerce, University of Birmingham, 1955–74.

Wall, John Edward (later Lord Wall) (1913–80) Ministry of Food, 1939–52, Under-Secretary, 1948–52; Deputy Head, Finance Department, Unilever Ltd., 1952–6, Head, Organisation Division, 1956–8.

Wallace, Henry Agard (1888–1965) US Secretary of Agriculture, 1933–40; Vice-President of USA, 1941–5; Secretary of Commerce, 1945–6.

Ward, John Guthrie (later Sir John) (b. 1909) Entered Diplomatic Service 1931, Second Secretary, 1936, First Secretary, 1941; member of UK delegations to Moscow and Potsdam conferences 1943–5; Counsellor and Head of UN Department, FO, 1946–9; HM Ambassador to Argentina, 1957–61, Italy, 1962–6.

Watkinson, George Laurence (later Sir George) (1896–1974) Board of Inland Revenue, 1919–31; Board of Trade, 1931–46; Deputy Secretary, Ministry of Fuel and Power, 1947–55; Member, Monopolies Commission, 1960–68.

Watts, Nita G. M. (b. 1920) Bank of England, 1940–1; Economic Section, 1941–55; Research Division, UN Economic Commission for Europe, 1956, Deputy Director, 1959–64; National Economic Development Office and Department of Economic Affairs, 1964–5; Fellow, St Hilda's College, Oxford, and Senior Research Officer, Institute of Economics and Statistics, 1965–81.

Weeks, Sir Hugh (b. 1904) Research and Statistical Manager, Cadbury's Ltd until 1939; Director of Statistics, Ministry of Supply, 1939–42; Director of Statistics and Programmes, Supply Council, 1942–3; Head of Progress and Planning Division, Ministry of Production, 1943–5; Representative, Ministries of Supply and Production of Mission to North America, 1941–5; Joint Controller, Colonial Development Corporation, 1948–51.

Welch, Anthony Edward (b. 1906) Under-Secretary, Board of Trade, 1946–66.

Wheeler, Leslie Allen (1899–1968) US Department of Agriculture, 1926–39, Director, Office of Foreign Agricultural Relations, 1939–48; Vice-Chairman, Executive Committee, FAO, Chairman, International Wheat Council, 1942–8.

White, Harry Dexter (1892–1948) Assistant Director of Research, US Treasury, 1934, Director of Monetary Research, 1942; US Executive Director, International Monetary Fund, 1946–7.

Williams, Francis (later Lord Williams) (1903–70) Editor, *Daily Herald*, 1936–40; Controller of News and Censorship, Ministry of Information, 1941–5; Adviser on Public Relations to Prime Minister, 1945–7.

Wilmot, John (later Lord Selmeston) (1895–1964) Labour MP 1933–5, 1939–50; PPS to Minister of Economic Warfare, 1940–2, to President of Board of Trade, 1942–4; Joint Parliamentary Secretary, Ministry of Supply, 1944–5; Minister of Supply 1945–7.

Wilson, Joseph Vivian (1894–1977) ILO, Geneva, 1921–3; League of Nations, Geneva, 1923, Chief of Central Section, 1933–40; Assistant Director of Research, Royal Institute of International Affairs, London, 1940–44; member, New Zealand Delegation to San Francisco Conference, 1945; Assistant Secretary of External Affairs, New Zealand, 1944–56.

Wilson, Stephen Shipley (b. 1904) Ministry of Transport, 1929–47; Ministry of Supply, 1947–50; Iron and Steel Corporation of Great Britain, 1950–53; Historical Section, Cabinet Office, 1966–77. Brother of Margaret Meade.

Wilson, Thomas (b. 1916) Ministries of Economic Warfare and Aircraft Production, 1940–2; PM's Statistical Branch, 1942–5; Fellow, University College, Oxford, 1946–58; Adam Smith Professor of Political Economy, University of Glasgow, 1958–82.

Wilson-Smith, Sir Henry (1904–78) Principal Private Secretary to Chancellor of Exchequer, 1940–42; Under-Secretary, Treasury, 1942–6; Permanent Secretary, Ministry of Defence, 1947–8; Additional Second Secretary, Treasury, 1948–51.

Winant, John Gilbert (1889–1947) Governor of New Hampshire, 1925–7, 1931–5; Assistant Director, ILO, 1935, 1937–9; US Ambassador, London, 1941–6.

Winegarten, Asher (1922–1979) Educated LSE (first class honours in economics and commerce), entered civil service in 1946; Admiralty, 1946–7; Chief Economist, National Farmers' Union, 1947–79; Director General, 1978.

Witteveen, Hendrikus Johannes (b. 1921) Professor of Business Cycles and Economics, University of Rotterdam, 1948–63; Netherlands Minister of Finance, 1963–5, 1967–71, also First Deputy Prime Minister, 1967–71; Managing Director, International Monetary Fund, 1973–8.

Wood, John B. (b. 1924) Economic Section, 1944–7; subsequently Conservative Party Research Department (1948–50), *Manchester Guardian* City Office, Lazard Bros. merchant bankers, Associated Electrical Industries (head of economic section), London Merchant Securities, and, from 1968, Institute of Economic Affairs (Deputy Director).

Woods, Sir John Henry (1895–1962) Entered Treasury, 1920, Principal Assistant Secretary, 1940–43; Permanent Secretary, Ministry of Production, 1943–5, Board of Trade, 1945–51.

Woolton, Lord (1883–1964) Businessman and politician; managing director, Lewis's, Liverpool, 1928, Chairman, 1936–51; Director General, Ministry of Supply, 1939; Minister of Food, 1940–43; Minister of Reconstruction, 1943–5; joined Conservative Party, 1945, Chairman, 1946–55.

Wrong, Humphrey Hume (1894–1954) Minister Counsellor, Canadian Legation, Washington, 1941; Assistant Undersecretary of State for External Affairs, Ottawa, 1942; Associate Undersecretary of State for External Affairs, 1944–6; Canadian Ambassador to USA, 1946–53.

Yates, Paul Lamartine Worked for FAO for many years; author of several publications on primary products and world agriculture.

Young, P. S. Civil servant, Board of Trade, in 1940s.

# Index

accountants and economists meetings 220, 277, 285–6, 300, 311, 324
Acheson, Dean 13, 332
Addison, Lord 165, 332
Addison, Paul 216n
aggregate demand, maintenance of 2, 7, 41, 43, 53, 77, 79, 81, 110, 115–16, 130, 161, 162, 199, 271–4, 278, 281, 291, 297–8, 300 *see also* budgetary policy, investment, control of *and* monetary policy
agricultural policy 71, 128, 159–60, 262, 286, 301–2, 313–14, 316n *see also* wage rates, agricultural and commercial policy proposals 3–5, 8–9, 13–14, 18, 20, 31, 90, 105, 132, 160, 191
  *see also* food
Aldrich, W. W. 22, 332
Alexander, A. V. 171, 332
Allied Control Commission (Germany) 29, 85, 97
Alsop, Joseph 300, 332
American Federation of Labor 54
Amery, Leopold 98, 332
Ami, Mr 16
Anderson, Sir John 332
  Lord President of the Council x, 115
  Chancellor of the Exchequer x, xi, 13, 21n, 28–30, 32–3, 37, 70, 74, 84, 93, 95, 106
Andrew, G. H. 301, 332
Anglo-American discussions on commercial policy ix-x, 30
  Washington, 1943 *see* Law Mission
  London 1944–5 x, 4–5, 8–9, 13–15, 18, 25–6, 31, 33, 39, 63–4, 90–1, 105–6, 119–20
  Washington 1945 *see* Anglo-American Financial Agreement, negotiation of *see also* Imperial Preference
Anglo-American discussions on monetary policy 2n, 29–30 *see also* Bretton Woods
Anglo-American Financial Agreement (1945) 217, 219, 226, 265, 290, 302–4, 331
  negotiation of ix, 120, 132, 137, 143–6, 149–55, 157, 162–7, 171–2, 176–9, 185–6, 217, 238
Anglo-American talks on civil aviation (Bermuda, 1946) 207–8, 217 *see also* civil aviation
Archer, George 175, 181, 332
Argentina 55, 331
Article VII of International Monetary Fund *see* scarce currency clause
Article VII (of Mutual Aid Agreement, 1942) 2, 12–13, 15, 50, 57, 62–3, 66, 91–3, 98, 103–4, 118–21, 126, 131–2, 147, 151–3, 160, 163, 165–6, 171, 173, 207, 217, 268
Asquith, Sir Cyril 72n, 332
Ashton, T. S. 291, 332
Athens 109
Atlantic Charter (1941) 2n, 35
Attlee, Clement 332
  Lord President of the Council x, 8, 57, 67, 74, 95, 115
  Prime Minister ix, 119, 127, 132n, 145, 149, 153, 161, 165, 176, 185, 207, 215, 220, 224, 232, 242, 311, 326
Aukrust, O. 324n, 333
Australia 12–13, 15, 19–20, 44, 92–3, 165, 171, 224, 266, 268, 279

balance of payments 9, 13, 22, 125–6, 267, 278, 289, 331
  current account 127, 154, 298, 304; estimates of 6, 17, 20–1, 30–1, 40–1, 52, 56, 58, 60, 91, 94, 105, 110, 111, 169, 175, 204, 212, 215, 226, 246, 251, 255, 264, 268, 326–7
  capital account *see* capital movements
  of US *see* USA
  *see also* exports, imports *and* UK balance of payments problem
balance of payments adjustment *see* exchange rate adjustment *and* import restrictions on balance of payments grounds
Balance of Payments Working Party 19, 137–8, 173, 179–80, 187–8, 212, 215–16, 249–50, 255–6, 263–5, 326–7
Balogh, Thomas 19n, 186, 333

Bamford, Sir Eric 293, 333
Bank of England 20, 31, 40–1, 59, 70, 73–4, 137, 143, 150, 163–4, 173, 177–9, 198, 226, 265, 279–81, 288–91, 304, 315–16, 328
Barlow, Sir Alan 19n, 26, 52, 77, 87, 148, 175, 181, 233, 313, 318–19, 333
Barnes, Alfred 123n, 157n, 333
  Minister of Transport 123n, 148n, 300
Bath 9, 33, 80
Beaverbrook, Lord 8, 98, 333
Beckhart, B. H. 133, 333
Belcher, J. W. 235, 333
Belgium 37, 54, 69, 79, 156, 228
Benham, F. C. 239, 291, 333
Berlin, Isaiah 290n, 333
Berne 54
Bevan, Aneurin 171, 333
Beveridge, Sir William 63, 333
  *Full Employment in a Free Society* 6, 8, 12, 17, 19, 29, 63n
Bevin, Ernest 333
  Minister of Labour 30, 121
  Foreign Secretary 121, 127, 132n, 147
Biddle, Eric 167, 333
Bjerve, P. J. 324n, 333
Blagburn, C. H. 3, 333
Blaker, G. 115n, 333
Board of Inland Revenue x, 21, 33, 45, 65, 69, 74, 84, 91, 97, 258, 311
Board of Trade x, 3n, 14, 25–7, 31, 34–6, 62, 88–9, 90n, 92, 103–5, 112, 115, 128, 130–2, 140, 142, 153, 155, 161, 165–6, 175, 177, 179–81, 188, 203, 207, 210, 215, 218, 231, 235, 237–8, 241, 246, 249, 256, 263, 266, 271, 275, 277, 279–81, 284–5, 291, 298–9, 301, 305, 309, 316–18, 321–3, 325, 329
Bolton, G. L. F. 267, 288–9, 302, 306, 309, 330, 334
Boothby, Robert 186, 334
Borrowing (Control and Guarantees) Act, 1946 135n, 148, 170, 176, 213
Boyd-Orr, Sir John 257, 266, 314–15, 334
Boyle, Mr & Mrs 228
Brand, R. H. 165, 334
Brazil 126
Bretherton, R. F. 198, 334
Bretton Woods *see* United Nations Monetary and Financial Conference
Bretton Woods Agreement Act (US) 1945 91
Bretton Woods institutions *see* International Bank for Reconstruction and Development *and* International Monetary Fund
Bretton Woods rules *see* International Monetary Fund, Articles of Agreement
Bridges, Sir Edward 1–3, 4, 6, 11, 15, 18, 19n, 44, 46, 48, 59–60, 63–5, 69–70, 84–5, 91, 95, 103, 105, 107, 110, 116, 121, 126, 134, 135–7, 139, 144, 147, 151, 163, 165, 167, 169, 173, 176–7, 181, 185, 189–91, 193–4, 196–7, 200–3, 205, 208, 211, 213, 217–18, 223, 226, 229, 231–3, 239, 247, 250–3, 258, 260, 262, 270–1, 283, 284–5, 290–1, 293, 295, 304, 308, 310, 330, 334
  'consistent friend of the Economic Section' 45, 49, 107
  friend of employment policy xi, 16, 17, 21, 87, 89, 127–8, 133
  meetings in room 49, 52, 53, 55, 88, 102
Brighton 199, 229, 232
Brittain, Sir Herbert xi, 17, 21n, 33, 42n, 45, 61, 64, 73, 84–5, 101–2, 108, 134, 140–1, 175, 181, 260, 293, 334
Broadley, Herbert 3, 134, 142, 173, 179, 257, 314n, 334
Brook, Norman xi, 19n, 44, 49, 52–3, 68, 75, 79, 93–4, 98, 107, 116, 119, 121, 145, 155, 176, 191, 200, 206n, 207–8, 209, 218, 224, 239, 242, 244, 246, 252, 257–8, 268, 280, 334
  'consistent friend of the Economic Section' 45, 49
Brooks, H. E. 288, 334
Brown, A. J. 3, 5, 71, 75, 107, 121, 131, 137, 143, 155, 192, 211, 216–17, 225, 226, 237, 245–6, 249–50, 255, 264, 280, 288, 303, 314, 316–18, 324, 326, 331, 334
Bruce, Stanley 12, 334
Buchenwald 75–7
Budget Committee x, xi, 20–1, 36, 41–2, 49, 205, 271–2, 282, 309, 311
  meetings of 17, 36n, 41–2, 107–8, 124–5, 196, 206, 214, 223, 258–9, 271, 292–3
budget deficits 19, 41, 51, 68, 81–2, 102, 273, 282, 292
budget surpluses 41, 46, 68, 81–2, 272–3, 282, 292–3, 311
budgetary policy 2, 21, 41, 81–2, 85, 101–2, 150, 168, 271–4, 282–4, 299, 309 *see also* Budgets *and* fiscal policy
Budgets (UK) 240–1, 247, 284, 299, 309, 322
  1941 7, 102
  1945 (April) 17, 70, 84
  1945 (October) 84, 136, 160, 195
  1946 102, 196, 223, 232, 243, 252, 258–60
  1947 260, 311
  (US) 41
Budget White Paper *see* National Income and Expenditure White Papers
buffer stocks 192, 198, 208, 275, 278, 301, 314–15 *see also* commodity policy
bulk purchases (of imports) 191, 198, 234–5 *see also* state trading
Bullock, Alan 121n
Burma 216n
Butt, David Bensusan 2n, 200, 208, 311, 320, 325, 334

Cabinet meetings 5, 8, 9-10, 19–20, 40, 118, 131–2, 146n, 148n, 159n, 160–1, 170–1, 176, 179, 182n, 185, 212–13, 216, 225, 232, 326 *see also* Ministerial meetings
Cadbury, Paul Strangman 209, 334
Cahan, J. F. 146n, 179, 334
Caine, Sydney 35, 275, 334
Cairncross, Alec xi, 133, 181n, 322n, 334
Cambridge 19, 28, 41, 62, 68, 102, 250, 321
  economists, 'collusion among' 210–11, 213
Campion, Harry 15–17, 30, 49, 52–3, 59–60, 62, 68–9, 87, 96, 102–3, 105, 107, 110, 112, 116, 140, 167, 176, 181, 188, 209, 211, 240–1, 250, 252, 299–300, 310, 335
Canada 57, 83, 90, 165, 187, 190, 194, 200, 209, 224, 228, 257, 265, 304, 311, 327
  national income accounting 271
  White Paper on Employment and Income (1945) 89–90
Canberra 12, 268
capital investment *see* investment
capital issues control 61, 73–4, 135, 170, 176, 213, 221 *see also* Borrowing (Control and Guarantees) Act, 1946
Capital Levity 91
capital levy x, 21, 26–7, 33, 36, 42–3, 45–9, 64, 65, 69–70, 74, 81, 84, 91–2, 95, 112 *see also* capital taxation *and* National Debt Enquiry
capital movements, control of 13, 15, 52, 187, 237, 267, 278–80, 305, 316
capital taxation 52
  annual 21, 36, 42–3, 45–6, 125, 258, 260, 271, 311
Carr-Saunders, Sir Alexander 99, 239, 291, 335
cartels *see* commercial policy and international cartels *and* Germany
Carter, Sir Archibald 36, 42n, 260, 335
Catto, Lord 74n, 260, 335
Census of Distribution Committee 89, 92, 104, 108, 142–3, 171, 176, 185, 206–7, 235
Central Economic Information Service ix, 156n, 239
Central Electricity Board 320–1
Central Statistical Office ix, 5, 16–17, 20–1, 40, 49, 52–3, 58–60, 64–5, 68–9, 79, 87–8, 94, 102, 107–8, 115, 124, 134, 140, 143n, 169, 210–11, 219, 230, 240–1, 250, 260, 271, 298–9, 309, 318, 320, 322–3, 326 *see also* Economic Section, relations with, national income and expenditure estimates *and* statistics for employment policy
Ceylon 216n
Chamberlain, Neville 20, 258n, 335
Chambers, Paul 33, 45, 97, 335
Chantler, Philip 3, 5, 17, 30, 34, 71, 116, 118, 122–3, 125, 130n, 141, 182, 184, 191, 197–8, 207, 215–16, 224–5, 234, 236, 244, 248, 253–4, 263, 266, 275–6, 286, 311–12, 314, 318, 320, 324–5, 335
cheap money x, 63, 65, 67–8, 70, 73, 81, 274, 281 *see also* interest rates, reduction of *and* monetary policy
Chegwidden, Sir Thomas 237, 246, 335
Cherwell, Lord 6, 18, 253, 326, 335
Chester, D. N. (Sir Norman Chester) 7n, 15, 17, 32, 65, 96, 102, 111, 122–3, 125, 129–30, 137n, 141, 142n, 148, 157, 159, 161n, 189, 197n, 234n, 242n, 251n, 324n, 335
China 20n, 42, 315
Churchill, Winston 6n, 20, 335
  Prime Minister 8, 13, 50, 80, 91n, 98, 109, 326
civil aviation 55, 146, 155, 188, 207–8, 227, 235–6 *see also* shipping (Clapham) Committee on the Provision of Social and Economic Research (1945) 319
Clark, Colin 97n, 335
Clarke, R. W. B. (Otto) xi, 127, 137, 144–5, 149, 150, 152, 153–4, 163, 171–2, 175–9, 181, 190, 198, 211n, 212, 215, 226, 246, 249–50, 255, 263–4, 284, 302, 317, 326–9, 335
Clay, Henry 99, 185, 186–7, 335
Clayton, William 106, 119, 149–51, 166, 335
Clutterbuck, Sir Alexander 3, 12, 18, 31, 166, 336
coal 82, 128, 233
  industry, nationalisation of 118, 123, 141–2, 149, 158, 175, 181–4, 191, 197–8, 224, 248–9, 253, 305, 311
  miners 243, 272, 286–7
  shortage of 117, 270, 286, 293
Coal Mines Act, 1930 79
Coalition Government (UK 1940–5) ix–x, 56, 91n, 123
Coase, Ronald 5, 6, 16–17, 58–9, 336
  'Price and Output Policy of State Enterprise: A Comment' 27n
Cobbold, C. F. 150, 163–4, 178–9, 260, 288–91, 336
Cockfield, F. A. 65, 84, 97, 336
Colonial Office xi, 3n, 30, 35, 275, 291, 303, 305
Colonies 11, 155, 275–6, 291, 303, 305
(Colwyn) Committee on National Debt and Taxation (1924–7) 259
commercial policy, post-war 2, 19, 20, 31, 50–4, 57, 61–4, 66, 90, 92–3, 152
  Anglo-American discussion on *see* Anglo-American discussions
  *see also* Imperial Preference, import restrictions *and* state trading
  international cartels 23, 25, 31–2, 34–5, 39, 66, 106
Commercial Union, Meade's proposal for

Commercial Union (*cont.*)
(1942) x, 14, 132, 166, 186
'commodity money' 68, 71
commodity policy 2, 32, 106, 192, 275–6, 314–15 *see also* buffer stocks compensation
and betterment *see* control of land use
for nationalisation *see* nationalisation compensation
competition 45, 77, 79, 115, 117, 158, 168, 198, 234–5, 243, 249, 254, 291, 300, 325 *see also laissez-faire*, Liberal-Socialism *and* monopoly
Congress of Industrial Organizations 54
Conservative Party 33, 35, 56, 78–9, 98, 121, 291
consumers' choice 7, 115, 255, 318 *see also* Liberal-Socialism
consumers' surplus 107
consumption 6, 17, 52, 56, 58, 60, 72, 94, 102, 115–16, 127, 134, 169, 183, 188–9, 193, 195–6, 201, 203, 211, 215, 219, 260, 271–3, 281, 293, 297–300, 308, 310, 321–3
taxation of 21, 34, 36, 41–2, 82, 122, 136, 140, 184, 212, 248 *see also* purchase tax *and* national insurance contributions, variation of
control of land use 50, 117, 123–4, 135–6, 159, 170–1, 287
controls 2, 21, 34, 36, 41, 48, 61, 65, 70, 73, 77–8, 83–4, 124, 129–31, 162, 221–2, 229–30, 252, 272–3, 294, 310, 314, 321 *see also* investment, control of, labour controls *and* price control Official Committee on the Future of 129–30, 183
convertibility 29–30, 33, 37, 103–4, 119, 152, 164–5, 177–9, 315, 329, 331
Coombs, H. C. 12, 268, 279, 336
Copland, D. B. 12–13, 15, 44, 336
Cornwall 114
Cornwall-Jones, Brigadier A. T. 323, 336
cost of living 214, 223, 262–3, 273
stabilisation of 128, 160–1, 191, 194–5, 198, 205–6, 214, 223, 232, 243, 249, 255, 259–60, 273, 276, 280–3, 292–3, 295–6, 304
cost-of-living index, revision of 272–2, 281–2, 292–3
cotton *see* bulk purchases *and* international cotton agreement
Cotton Working Party 239, 274–5
Coulson, Sir John 256, 266–7, 336
Crimea Conference (Yalta, 1945) 50
Cripps, Sir Stafford 115–16, 124, 127, 132, 157n, 160, 165, 180, 185, 188, 194, 202, 205, 233, 235, 252, 283, 296, 336
President of the Board of Trade 123n, 132n, 139, 172, 189, 200–1, 295, 301–2, 312, 324
Cross, R. B. 102, 336
Crowther, Geoffrey 99, 336
Currie, Laughlin 54–5, 336
Customs and Excise x, 34, 36, 41, 311
Czechoslovakia 199, 220

Dachau 228
Dalton, Hugh 112n, 127, 132, 157n, 165, 180, 196, 206n, 233, 235, 252, 336
Chancellor of the Exchequer xi, 119, 123n, 128, 135, 136–7, 139, 144, 149, 155, 160, 170, 172, 176–7, 189, 194–7, 200–1, 202, 213, 223, 225, 232, 243, 258–9, 260, 274n, 276, 281, 283, 284, 292, 293, 299, 304, 309, 311, 326, 330
President of the Board of Trade x, 35, 39, 89n, 136, 166
Dalton, Ruth 260, 337
Daniel, J. O. 318, 337
death duties 42–3, 46, 82, 123, 322
reform of 206n, 214n, 223n, 259–60, 271, 311
debt repayment *see* national debt
Defence Committee 201–2
demographic problems *see* population growth
Dennison, Stanley 3, 116, 122, 124, 158, 161, 176, 184, 205, 207, 277, 337
dePeyer, C. H. 182, 191, 253, 311–12, 337
depressions 9, 13, 19, 37, 44, 64, 74, 145, 149, 152, 185, 189, 196, 201, 205, 260, 277–9, 284–6, 297, 299–300, 302, 304, 309–10, 314, 321
1930s 12–13, 37, 44, 136, 161, 174 *see also* employment policy
Derksen, J. B. D. 133, 337
development areas *see* location of industry
Devons, Ely 11, 39, 61, 94, 337
Ding, Dr Erwin 76n
distribution of income *see* income distribution
distribution of industry *see* location of industry
Dominions 5, 11, 25, 32, 34, 93, 118, 153, 155, 165–6, 265, 268, 279, 285, 327 *see also* Australia, Canada, New Zealand, South Africa
Dominions Office 3n, 166, 291, 328
Parliamentary Undersecretary to 132n
Donoughue, Bernard 142n, 190n
Dow, J. C. R. 184, 222, 248, 252, 272, 299, 309–10, 317, 321, 337
Drew, J. A. 224, 337
Dumbarton Oaks
Conference (1944) 19n, 267
organisation *see* United Nations Organisation
Dupriez, Leon-Hugo 36–7, 83, 337
Durbin, Evan 156, 186, 260, 337

Eady, Sir Wilfrid xi, 3, 5, 4n, 6, 14, 19n, 25, 28, 31–3, 42n, 45–6, 52, 63–4, 84–5, 90n, 91, 102, 109, 127, 136–7, 140, 144–5, 148–50, 153–5, 163–4, 172–3, 177–9, 187, 190, 215, 251, 260, 268, 288–9, 331, 337
'the the real menace' 138, 288–9
Eastbourne 199
Eastwood, C. G. 187, 337
Economic Development Working Party 128, 133–5, 138
Economic and Industrial Planning Staff (EIPS) 67, 78, 85–6, 92
economic forecasting 2, 7, 49, 56, 58, 60, 64–5, 69, 90, 95 *see also* national income and expenditure forecasts *and* Economic Surveys
Economic Plan 116, 122, 127–8, 137, 139–41, 148, 162, 169, 174–6, 190, 193–4, 198, 201–2, 213, 221, 229, 231–2, 240–1, 247, 252, 261, 272, 283, 293, 299, 308, 309, 310, 320, 324 *see also* Economic Surveys
economic planning *see* planning
economic sanctions 326
Economic Section
post-war staffing xi, 3, 4–6, 11, 15, 18, 28, 34, 38–9, 49, 59–62, 71, 75, 79–80, 83, 93–4, 104–5, 107–9, 113, 115–16, 121, 127, 133, 188, 200, 208–9, 239, 258, 291, 317, 331
relations with Central Statistical Office 15–16, 21, 49, 52–3, 58–9, 62, 68–9, 92, 102, 108, 110, 115, 134
relations with Treasury 2, 17, 21, 28, 33, 36, 44–5, 49, 64, 92, 96, 102–3, 111, 115, 137, 153, 176, 196–7n, 203, 212, 217, 252–3, 258, 268
staff meetings 74–5, 77–8, 82, 84, 94–5, 97, 121–3, 133, 137, 139, 155, 157–8, 167–8, 174–5, 184, 192, 198, 211, 214, 221, 228, 248–9
Economic Survey Working Party 203, 210–13, 218–19, 230–2, 240, 270, 284, 298–9, 208, 321
Economic Surveys xi, 49, 74–5, 79, 191, 241, 283–4, 237
1944 7, 17, 20–1, 33, 74–5
1945 74, 77–8, 82, 94–5, 97, 116–17, 128–9
1946 169, 181, 190, 194–5, 196, 201–4, 210–12, 225
1946/47 203, 210, 230–1, 239–41, 247, 250–1, 255, 258, 261, 270, 282–4, 286, 293–4, 303
1947/48 272, 284, 298–9, 310, 322–3
for 1950/51 201, 203, 210–12, 218–19, 231–2, 271, 308, 322
*Economist, The* 52, 56, 111–12, 251
efficiency 2, 56–7, 66, 99, 124–5, 142, 146, 158, 195, 254, 323, 325 *see also* productivity
Egypt 16, 226
elasticity of demand for UK imports 212, 216, 245–6, 249, 264, 304, 317–18
electricity 18, 26, 320–1
nationalisation 144, 158, 233, 235, 248
Elizabeth, Princess 80, 337
Elizabeth, Queen 80, 337
Emmerson, Sir Harold 195, 222–3, 337
employment policy, international *see* international economic policy
employment policy, post-war, UK ix-xi, 2, 8–9, 12–14, 16, 23, 41–3, 49, 54, 56–7, 66, 75, 83, 85, 101–2, 108, 116–17, 125, 159, 172, 202, 234, 252, 300, 320, 324 *see also* Economic Plan *and* Economic Surveys
Employment Stabilisation Fund 273–4, 282, 292–3
Employment Policy White Paper ix–xi, 5, 7, 9, 12, 15, 43, 53, 58, 69, 71, 77, 79, 88, 168, 184n
Enfield, Ralph Roscoe 3, 5, 131, 137, 266, 337
Essential Works Order 205 *see also* labour controls
Establishment matters *see* Economic Section, post-war staffing
Evans, A. A. 21–2, 29, 337
Evans, C. W. 181, 337
Evatt, Herbert Vere 93, 338
Excess Profits Tax 21, 34, 84, 125, 258, 276, 301
Exchange Control Act, 1947 135n
exchange controls 29–30, 33, 135, 177, 179, 328–9 *see also* capital movements, control of
exchange rate adjustments 15, 19, 22, 31, 256, 278, 281, 289–90
appreciation/revaluation 304
depreciation/devaluation 13, 15, 63–4, 99, 119, 172, 187, 226–8, 245, 249, 256–7, 264, 267, 276–9, 283, 289, 314, 316
exchange rates 12, 13, 65, 66, 118, 130, 212, 216, 226, 249, 256, 288
fixed 13, 22, 106, 289, 303, 331
flexible *see* exchange adjustments
Exchange Requirements Committee 30
exports 115, 154, 172, 226, 263, 328
UK *see* UK

Fay, C. R. 99, 338
Federation of British Industries 15, 88–9, 97
Fennelly, R. D. 23, 338
Fergusson, Sir Donald 3, 5, 14, 20, 39–40, 128, 160, 175, 181, 203, 213, 233, 253, 293, 310, 338
financial crisis 1931 12, 172, 225, 290
Finland 54
Firestone, O. J. 271, 338
fiscal policy 19, 21, 84, 222, 240–1, 247, 281, 294–5, 310, 313, 321–2 *see also* budgetary policy, subsidies *and* taxation

Fisher, A. G. B. 99, 188, 338
Fleming, Marcus 3, 5, 15, 22, 39, 44–5, 60–1, 67, 94, 104–7, 109, 112, 116, 119–20, 122, 126, 131–2, 145–6, 151, 154–5, 158, 168, 173–4, 177, 179–80, 191–2, 194, 198, 208, 215–18, 225, 227, 234–5, 237–8, 243, 245, 249–50, 255–7, 263–4, 266–7, 275, 278–9, 290, 302, 309, 314–17, 326–7, 338
  'Price and Output Policy of State Enterprise: A Symposium' 18, 26, 28, 239, 243
Flett, Sir Martin 176, 194, 201–2, 338
Florence, Philip Sargent 99, 338
food 215, 314–15, 317–19 *see also* agricultural policy
  controls 142, 148
  world shortage of 117, 216, 224–5, 236, 244, 248, 261, 276, 287u
Food and Agriculture Organisation 39–40, 257, 266, 314–15
foreign balance *see* balance of payments, current account
Foreign Office xi, 11, 27, 39–40, 109, 120–1, 126, 137, 146, 155, 166, 180, 218, 256, 266–7, 288, 303, 306, 317
  conferences in Oxford 109, 131, 200, 324
Forge, Mr 111–12
Forsyth, I. M. 329, 338
Forsyth, J. M. 317, 338
Fowler, Henry H. 120, 338
Fowler, R. F. 16, 68, 338
France 54, 241
Franks, Oliver 23, 25, 32, 65, 92, 169, 173, 179, 231, 247, 286, 338
French, Sir Henry 39, 338
full employment 9, 13, 15, 23–4, 41, 43–4, 51–2, 63–4, 68, 92, 106–7, 146, 172, 222, 232, 243–5, 275, 278, 295–6, 313–14, 316, 324, 330 *see also* employment policy *and* wages policy
'fundamental disequilibrium' 267

Gaitskell, Hugh 156, 186, 339
Gardiner, J. C. 179, 339
Gardner, R. N. 91n
gas industry, nationalisation of 148, 183, 233, 235
General Agreement on Tariffs and Trade (GATT) x
general election (1945) 83, 91, 114–15, 121
Geneva ix, x, 44, 54, 133, 188 *see also* League of Nations
George VI, King 80, 339
George, H. H. 102, 339
Germany 3, 29, 54–5, 67, 71, 78, 80, 85–6, 92, 131, 166, 181, 184, 216n, 225, 236–7, 244, 246, 264, 316, 326
  cartels 32, 34
  concentration camps *see* Buchenwald *and* Dachau
Gilbert, Sir Bernard xi, 7, 85, 88–9, 95–6, 102, 117, 125, 139–48, 169, 175, 181–2, 185, 189–90, 194, 197, 200–1, 204, 206, 213–14, 221, 223–4, 233, 248, 252–3, 255, 260–1, 283, 293, 297, 320, 339
Gillie, Blaise 50, 339
gold standard 22, 31 *see also* financial crisis 1931
Goodrich, Carter 36–7, 339
Gordon-Walker, Patrick 186, 255, 339
Gore-Booth, P. 317, 339
Gorell Barnes, William Lethbridge 3, 174, 207, 217, 339
Gosplan socialism 15, 118, 133, 137 *see also* planning
Gould, R. M. 272, 282–3, 295, 339
government expenditure 19, 79, 84, 140–1, 175, 212, 219, 271, 284, 327
  current 6, 17, 56, 58, 60, 94, 265, 298
  capital *see* investment, public
Graham, Benjamin 68, 339
Grant, A. T. K. 132n, 145, 150, 177–8, 290, 339
Greenwood, Arthur 239, 339
Gregg, Sir Cornelius 33, 42n, 45, 64–5, 84, 91, 97, 107–8, 260, 339
Gregory, Sir Theodore 133, 339
Gridley, J. C. 329, 339
Grigg, Sir James 285, 302, 306, 309, 330, 340
Guillebaud, Claude 99, 340

Hackett, W. T. G. 257, 340
The Hague 133
Hale, Edward 85, 340
Halifax, Lord 137, 146n, 151n, 166n, 178n, 179n
Hall, Margaret 62, 340
Hall, Noel 99, 340
Hall, Robert x, 23, 60–2, 92, 94, 315, 340
Hall, W. G. 156, 340
Hall-Patch, Ronald 120, 146n, 166–7, 227, 288, 290–1, 317, 340
Hancock, Sir Henry 189, 340
'Hansel and Gretel' 80
Hardraba, Mr 220, 231
Harrod, R. F. 27–8, 68, 98–9, 133, 173, 291, 340
Hawkins, Harry 4, 5, 8, 9–10, 13–15, 18, 20, 22–3, 25–6, 31, 34, 39, 50, 90, 105, 185, 340
Hawtrey, Ralph 99, 341
Hayek, Frederick 38, 99, 239, 341
Helmore, James 103, 105, 109, 154–5, 163, 166, 172, 180, 188, 198, 215, 217–18, 237, 265, 280–1, 284–5, 315, 329–30, 341
Helsby, L. N. 75n, 94n, 113, 200, 239, 341
Hemming, Francis 182, 191, 239, 341
Henderson, Sir Hubert 3–4, 99, 341
Henderson, Leon 44, 54, 341

Henley, D. O. 317, 331, 341
Hicklin, R. P. 92, 341
Hicks, J. R. 99, 107, 220, 277, 341
Hildred, Sir William 175, 341
Hill, M. E. 316n, 341
Hill, Martin 133, 341
Hiroshima 114
Hiss, Alger 209, 341
Hitchman, Sir Edwin 88, 297, 342
Holland 54, 112, 209, 311
Hollond, M. 218, 280, 342
Home Office 224
Hopkin, Bryan 208, 306, 342
Hopkins, Harry 50, 342
Hopkins, Sir Richard x, xi, 1, 17, 19n, 21, 26, 28, 36, 41, 42n, 44–6, 63–5, 69–70, 73–4, 81–2, 84, 92, 101, 104, 110, 206, 258–60, 292–3, 342
Hot Springs *see* United Nations Conference on Food and Agriculture
housing policy 111, 207, 230, 249
Howell, Kit 113, 342
Hull, Cordell 22, 342
Hurcomb, Sir Cyril 26, 28–9, 175, 181, 213, 243, 342
Hutchinson, H. J. 198, 342
Hydrabad, Nawab from 300

Imperial Chemical Industries 321
Imperial Preference 14, 93, 120, 132, 144, 151, 164–6, 285
import controls *see* import programming *and* import restrictions
import duties *see* tariffs
Import-Export Bank 163
import licences, auctioning of 3, 171, 173, 183, 238, 245, 257, 280, 329
import programming 122, 128–9, 132, 134, 136–8, 173, 180, 208, 215, 221, 225, 255, 302–3
import quotas *see* quantitative restrictions
import restrictions 63–4, 117, 132, 143, 177, 179, 188, 226–7, 264, 280, 286, 314, 328
  on balance of payments grounds 9, 15, 29–30, 33, 57, 66, 71, 104, 119, 136, 145, 149, 155, 171–2, 187, 215, 228, 245, 256, 278–80, 289–90, 329
  objective test for 153–4, 237, 279–80, 305
  application to state trading 198–9, 218, 227, 238, 245, 257, 280, 305
imports 154, 172, 226, 264, 290, 328–9
  restrictions on *see* import restrictions
  UK *see* UK
Ince, Sir Godfrey 88, 89, 116, 139, 169, 190, 233, 294, 342
income distribution 23, 27, 41, 48–9, 78–9, 110, 125, 142, 255, 288, 291, 313, 322
income tax 41, 81, 97, 108–10, 116, 125, 127, 193, 252, 277, 299, 310
  PAYE 108, 136, 184, 189, 196, 201, 222, 248, 252
income tax deferred credits 107–10, 196, 201, 222, 248, 260, 271, 273, 281, 285, 293, 299, 310, 322
increasing returns industries 27, 141, 156, 168, 175
India 11, 42, 104, 133, 182, 216n, 224, 226, 236, 244, 252, 283, 290, 300, 331
  Secretary of State for 132n
industrial efficiency *see* efficiency
inflation 24, 40, 45, 51, 77, 122, 161, 184, 283
  control of 46, 48–9, 58, 61, 79, 81, 190, 214, 243, 272–4, 281–2, 292–3, 296 *see also* wages policy
  in transitional period 34, 48, 56, 65, 70–1, 73–4, 83–4, 95, 108, 110, 117, 124–5
inflationary/deflationary gaps 127–8, 134, 136, 139–40, 169, 175, 183, 190, 193, 202–4, 211, 221, 240, 247, 270, 284, 299
inflationary pressure 21, 53, 134, 140, 190, 196, 212, 247, 270, 281, 295, 308, 310–11
Institute of Chartered Accountants 220n
interest rates 52, 70, 73, 81, 102, 115, 130, 168, 205, 327
  and burden of national debt 36, 41, 42, 45–6, 48–9, 56, 59, 65, 80, 83, 274
  and investment 48, 51, 54–6, 61, 67, 95, 162, 184, 205, 222, 230, 249, 274
  determination of 46, 48, 51, 55–6, 61, 70, 74
  reduction of 41, 45–6, 48–9, 51, 56, 59, 67–8, 81, 274n *see also* cheap money, monetary policy *and* national debt
International Bank for Reconstruction and Development ix, 2n, 19, 22, 26–7, 29, 37, 119–20, 192, 217, 219, 227–8, 238–9, 250, 257, 266, 278, 285, 288–90, 302, 306, 309, 315, 317, 330
International Chamber of Commerce 171
International Civil Aviation Conference (Chicago, 1944) 55
international commercial policy organisation *see* International Trade Organisation
International Conference on Employment Policy, proposed 8, 12, 19 *see also* United Nations Conference on Trade and Employment
international cotton agreement 125–6
international employment policy 19, 27, 30, 36, 106–7, 119, 217–18, 244, 266, 277–9, 285, 289, 299, 302, 309, 330 *see also* United Nations Economic and Social Council
International Labour Organisation 19, 27, 30, 36–7, 42, 54, 83, 131, 146, 158, 166–7, 192
International Monetary Fund ix, 2n, 12, 22, 27, 37, 40, 68, 78, 127, 152–3, 155, 163,

International Monetary Fund (*cont.*) 186–7, 192, 219, 227–8, 238–9, 250, 257, 266, 285, 288–90, 302–3, 306, 309, 315, 317, 328–30
Articles of Agreement 12–13, 15, 29–30, 32–3, 37, 63, 104, 106, 118–20, 172, 180, 185–7, 256–7, 304, 316, 328 *see also* scarce currency clause
Parliamentary debate on 33, 37, 121, 172, 185–6
international trade conference *see* United Nations Conference on Trade and Employment
International Trade Organisation x, 14, 19, 25, 27, 37, 64, 106, 119n, 151, 154, 180, 192, 239, 257, 263, 266, 268, 285, 289–90, 314–15, 327–30
*see also* Commercial Union *and* United Nations Conference on Trade and Employment
International Trade Union Conference (1945) 54
International Wheat Agreement 132
investment 41, 51–2, 67, 204, 222, 273, 298–300
and interest rates *see* interest rates
control of 53, 122, 170, 176, 184, 198, 204–5, 221–2, 229, 252, 274, 281, 284–5, 294, 310, 320, 325
in stocks 111–12, 220, 277
planning of 37, 42–4, 49, 66, 71, 135, 162, 167, 202, 211–14, 221, 250, 296–7
private 58, 60, 66, 71, 73, 90, 92, 94, 111–12, 115, 127, 140, 149, 170, 184, 212, 221, 252, 297, 321
public 43, 53–4, 58, 60, 82, 85, 88, 92, 94, 102, 127, 130, 184, 193, 212, 221, 284–5, 311
working party on *see* Investment Working Party
Investment (Control and Guarantees) Bill *see* Borrowing (Controls and Guarantees) Act, 1946
Investment Working Party 148, 204, 213, 221, 229–30, 252, 274, 284, 296–8, 311, 320, 325
Iron and Steel Federation 32, 208, 234, 321, 325
iron and steel industry 32, 65–7, 71, 198, 208, 214, 234, 325–6
nationalisation of 123, 134, 253
Isaacs, George 252, 342
Minister of Labour 139, 160–1, 200–1, 283, 294
Ismay, George 181, 342

Jackson, E. F. 181, 219, 322, 326, 342
Jacob, Major General Edward 209, 342
Jamaica 35
Japan 93–4, 111, 114
Jay, Douglas 112, 145, 153, 156, 161, 176–7, 187, 190–1, 200, 202, 208, 209, 211–12, 220, 222, 224, 242, 244, 247, 249, 255, 276, 283, 287, 311, 325, 342
Jay, Peggy 209, 249, 343
Jeans, Sir James 7–8, 343
Jebb, G. E. M. 239, 343
Jebb, Gladwyn 120, 306, 343
Jefferies, G. P. 39, 208, 244, 248, 317, 323, 343
Jenks, C. W. 30, 41–2, 186, 343
Jennings, G. M. 85, 343
Jewkes, John 25, 99, 112, 116, 239, 343
Johnston, Sir Alexander 169, 175, 194, 197, 207, 242, 300, 343
Joint Intelligence Board 97
Jones, Edgar 20, 39, 268, 343
Jones, J. H. 99, 343
Joseph, Peggy 182, 191, 214, 253, 343
Juissant, Jean 69, 156, 228, 343
Juissant, Mrs 228

Kahn, R. F. 32, 35, 99, 177, 188, 210–11, 213, 291, 295, 343
Kaldor, Nicholas 56, 167, 186, 344
Kaliski, S. F. 90n
Kershaw, R. N. 226, 344
Kervyn de Lettenhove, Baron 228, 344
Keynes, Florence Ada 269, 344
Keynes, John Maynard x, xi, 19n, 22, 25, 28–30, 32–3, 40, 42, 45–6, 48, 55, 58–9, 61, 63–5, 72–3, 81, 84, 91, 101–3, 105, 110, 111n, 119–20, 136, 192, 194, 196, 198, 204, 213, 216–17, 219, 223, 225–8, 247, 250–2, 255, 258–9, 260, 268, 272, 291, 344
mission to Washington (September-December 1945) 124, 132, 137, 144–5, 149–53, 162–6, 176–9
retirement party for, as editor of *Economic Journal* 98–100
*The Collected Writings of John Maynard Keynes* 26n, 29n, 33n, 37n, 48n, 65n, 97n, 101n, 103n, 119n, 132n, 162n, 192n, 238n
*The General Theory of Employment, Interest and Money* 48, 70
Keynes, John Neville 99, 269, 344
Keynes, Lydia 269, 344
Kilroy, Alix 35, 263, 275, 286, 301, 312–13, 318, 344
King, W. L. Mackenzie 51n, 344
Kunosi, A. 199, 344

labour controls 2, 21, 34, 36, 41, 83, 87–8, 129–31, 141, 160–1, 183, 202, 206, 270, 296
labour demand 77, 88, 222, 240, 248, 323
labour, foreign, use of 224, 270, 287, 293
Labour Government (1945–50) ix–xi, 114–15, 118, 308
labour mobility 7, 77–8, 112–13, 161, 184, 190, 193, 214, 262, 277, 294, 310 *see also* wages policy

Labour Party 115, 117, 156, 176, 233
Labour Party Conference (1944) 15
labour supply 77, 82, 88, 118, 125, 134, 214, 218, 222, 224, 232–3, 240, 244, 270, 293, 323
*laissez-faire* 38, 79, 112–13, 116, 119, 195
Laithwaite, Gilbert 11, 15, 344
land *see* control of land use
Land Commission 170–1, 287 *see also* control of land use
Laski, Harold 156, 344
Law Mission to Washington (1943) x, 2n, 3n, 4–5, 8–9, 13, 22
  Meade diary of x
Law, Mrs Richard 56, 291
Law, Richard 9, 33, 35n, 54, 56, 218, 291, 344
Layton, Sir Walter 99, 344
League of Nations ix, 44n, 54, 109, 111, 131, 133, 156n, 186, 188, 220n, 300
Leak, Hector 20, 92, 104, 140, 344
Lee, F. G. 91, 289, 297, 325, 344
Leeds 125, 132
Leeper, Sir Reginald 109, 345
Leggett, Sir Frederick 19–20, 30, 345
Lend-Lease 2, 30, 57, 78, 91, 103, 111, 114, 118, 127, 137, 143, 163, 216n, 219
  'consideration' for *see* Article VII
LePan, Douglas 90n
Lerner, A. P. 133, 345
  *The Economics of Control* 37–8, 44, 72, 79, 107
  'Functional Finance and the Federal Debt' 82n
Liberal-Socialism 1, 37–8, 44, 65, 79, 115–16, 118–19, 133, 136–7, 158, 160–2, 220, 228, 240, 272, 283, 286, 289, 291, 296, 310, 324, 329–30
Lidderdale, J. H. 318, 345
Liesching, Sir Percivale 3, 14, 18, 23n, 31, 34, 103, 105, 131–2, 151n, 186, 191, 199, 217–18, 227, 244, 265, 278, 314n, 315, 317–18, 345
Lindahl, Eric 167, 345
Lindsell, H. G. 297, 345
liquidity preference, theory of 43, 48, 55–6, 67–8 *see also* interest rates, determination of
Litvinov, Maxim 131, 345
Liverpool University 5, 113
Lloyd, E. M. H. 16, 345
loan negotiations *see* Anglo-American Financial Agreement, negotiation of
local authorities' investment 48, 53–4, 85, 95, 102, 135, 148, 221, 284, 297 *see also* investment, public
location of industry 7, 112–13, 161–2, 184, 190, 207, 218, 276–7, 311, 325
London ix, x, 61, 80, 114, 120, 126, 152, 199n, 207, 215, 239, 277
London School of Economics x, 33, 39, 62, 94, 104–5, 107, 109, 268
Lord Chancellor 200
Lord President's Committee x, 115, 117, 124, 137, 141, 147, 148n, 161, 215, 280, 313
  meetings of 117–18, 123–4, 128–9, 137, 141–2, 148, 166n, 182n, 194–5, 206, 235, 243, 263, 274n, 293, 295, 302–3
  Industrial Sub-Committee 129, 159–60, 215
Lord President's Office 128, 139, 175, 193–4, 211, 241, 299, 318
Lord Privy Seal 200, 224
Louvain, University of 36, 79, 83
Loveday, Alexander 219, 345
Lubin, Isadore 36–7, 41, 44, 54, 345
Lyttleton, Oliver 8, 35, 39, 104, 106, 345

Mabane, William 98, 345
McDougall, A. 250, 345
McDougall, F. L. 120, 346
MacDougall, G. D. A. (Sir Donald) 3, 18–28, 75, 94, 107, 121, 127, 181, 346
McKenzie, A. W. 331, 346
McKinnon, Hector 90, 346
Mackintosh, W. A. 89, 90, 346
McNeil, Hector 180, 346
manpower budget 2, 77, 87–9, 139, 147, 169, 175, 231, 240, 251, 323
Manpower Committee 89, 147, 201, 205
Manpower Working Party 323
Margaret, Princess 80, 346
Marget, Arthur 44, 346
marginal cost pricing 18, 26, 45, 115, 141, 158–9, 168–9, 174–5, 197, 234, 248–9, 254–5, 292, 300–1
  Meade-Fleming symposium on 18, 26, 27–8, 239, 243
  *see also* nationalised industries, price policy
Marjolin, Robert 241, 346
marketing boards *see* agricultural policy *and* restrictive practices
Marquand, H. 316, 346
Martin, P. W. 198, 218, 346
Maud, John 23, 62, 109, 111, 116–17, 128, 137, 139, 142, 159–60, 346
*Mauritania* 190m
(May) Committee on National Expenditure (1931) 225
Mayhew, C. 170, 176, 347
'Mead memorandum' 330 *see also* international economic policy
Meade, Bridget ix, 80, 109, 347
Meade, Charlotte ix, 80, 347
Meade, Diana 9, 347
Meade, James
  *An Introduction to Economic Analysis and Policy* 1, 79, 122
  *The Collected Papers of James Meade* ix, x, 6, 7n, 14n, 18n, 36n, 37n, 42n, 43n, 51n, 72n, 107n, 122n, 147n, 158n, 166n, 184n, 251n, 272n

Meade, James (*cont.*)
'Is the National Debt a Burden?' 43n
'Mr Lerner on "The Economics of Control"' 37–8, 44, 72, 78–9, 107, 133
(with Richard Stone) *National Income and Expenditure* 6, 16
'The Optimum Balance between Economies of Scale and Variety of Products: an Illustrative Model' 107n
'Population Explosion, the Standard of Living and Social Conflict' 42n
'Price and Output Policy of State Enterprise: A Symposium' 18, 26, 28, 239, 243
*World Economic Survey* 109
Meade, Margaret ix, x, 9, 80, 109, 186, 188, 200, 209, 228–9, 268, 291, 347
Meade, Thomas ix, 80, 209, 347
Meehan, M. J. 257, 347
Melville, L. G. 93, 347
Middleton, J. R. 43, 347
Midwinter, K. M. 199, 347
Ministerial meetings 5, 34–5, 39, 116–17, 124, 132, 145, 149, 165, 175n, 177–8, 200, 202, 207, 224–5, 283–4, 302
of 'socialising Ministers' 123, 130, 167 *see also* socialisation, Ministerial Committee on
*see also* Cabinet meetings, Lord President's Committee, Reconstruction Committee
Minister of Agriculture and Fisheries 132n
Minister of National Insurance 200–1
Minister of Town and Country Planning 287
Ministry of Agriculture and Fisheries xi, 3n, 5, 14, 20, 39–40, 142, 159–60, 218, 248, 262, 266, 276, 313, 316, 318–19
Ministry of Aircraft Production 10, 27, 49, 62
Ministry of Civil Aviation 175, 181, 217
Ministry of Economic Warfare 11, 27
Ministry of Food xi, 3n, 134, 142, 173, 179, 207, 215–16, 218, 257, 266, 282, 305, 313, 315–16, 317–18
Ministry of Fuel and Power 123, 128, 142, 175, 181–3, 191, 203–4, 214, 224, 253, 287, 293, 305, 310, 312, 320, 329–30
Ministry of Health 39, 80, 102, 284
Ministry of Information 237, 246
Ministry of Labour 30, 77-8, 83, 87–9, 111, 128, 139, 146, 166–7, 181, 195, 205, 210–11, 214, 218, 222–3, 231–3, 248, 262, 271, 282, 294–5, 297–8
Ministry of National Insurance 185, 189
Ministry of Production 32, 78
Ministry of Reconstruction xi, 6
Ministry of Supply 10, 32, 34, 63, 65–6, 173, 175, 179, 181, 198, 234, 297, 325
Ministry of Town and Country Planning 50
Ministry of (War) Transport 138, 175, 188, 197, 199, 233, 254, 298, 300
Ministry of Works 89, 99
monetary and payments agreements 288, 303, 316–17, 331
monetary policy x, 19, 30, 59, 61, 65, 70, 81, 106, 222 *see also* cheap money, interest rates, national debt *and* National Debt Enquiry
money, demand for 43, 61, 67–8, 74
money, supply of 61, 67–8, 74
monopoly 23, 35, 45, 66, 115, 117, 158, 161, 167–9, 174–5, 198–9, 234–5, 253, 275, 286, 296, 305, 325, 329 *see also* competition, nationalisation *and* restrictive practices
Morgenthau, Henry Jr. 30, 32, 37, 347
Morrison, Herbert 116, 119, 122, 131, 137, 147, 160, 170, 176, 194, 196, 252, 347
Lord President of the Council x, 115, 117, 123, 124–5, 127–8, 130, 132–3, 139, 141–2, 145, 147, 151, 153, 155, 157, 159, 160–3, 165–8, 170, 175–9, 182–3, 185, 188–9, 190, 200–2, 206–7, 212, 214, 216, 217, 220, 224–5, 227, 232–7, 241–4, 246, 252, 254, 262, 265, 283–4, 286–8, 293–5, 298–302, 309, 313, 315–17, 324–5
most favoured nation 13, 120 *see also* non-discrimination
Murphy, James Francis 92–3, 347
Murrie, Sir William 128, 139, 188, 200, 207, 310, 347
Mutual Aid Agreement (1942) 2n *see also* Article VII *and* Lend-Lease
Mynors, Humphrey 40, 347
Myrdal, Gunnar 146, 155, 156, 347

Nagasaki 114
Nash, Walter 285, 347
National Coal Board 141, 233, 310, 329
national debt x, 26, 33, 64, 82
burden of 36, 45–6, 48–9, 55, 65, 81–2
repayment of 36, 41, 45–7, 51, 69, 81–2
*see also* capital levy
National Debt Enquiry x, 21, 33, 70, 92
Meade papers for 21, 26–7, 36, 41–3, 45–9, 51–2, 55, 64, 69–70, 74, 81–4, 91–2
meetings of 45–6, 48–9n, 55–6, 59, 61, 63–5, 73–4, 80–4, 91, 95, 101–2
sub-committee on capital levy 64, 65, 84
National Defence Contribution 258
national income and expenditure 2, 5–7, 12, 23, 37, 71, 74, 77, 85, 111–12, 133, 208, 213, 219, 231, 284
forecasting and planning 1, 7, 16–17, 21, 37, 41, 52–3, 56, 58, 60, 69, 84–5, 94–5, 108, 110–11, 122, 124, 127, 134–5, 141, 147–8, 175, 181, 184, 193, 196, 199, 204, 219, 220, 251, 311, 324 *see also* aggregate demand
official UK estimates ix, 7, 16, 37, 44, 49, 52, 62, 68–9, 75, 102–3, 143, 265, 299, 309, 327

national income and expenditure (*cont.*)
targets for 58, 60, 69, 92, 108, 110, 135, 139, 141, 169, 181, 184, 193, 199, 204, 211, 218, 219
National Income White Papers
1941 ix, 101, 251
1945 52
1946 219, 240
National Institute of Economic and Social Research 17, 220, 277 *see also* Accountants and Economists meetings
National Insurance Bill (1946) 185, 189–90, 194, 200–1, 215
national insurance contributions, variation of 184–5, 189–90, 194, 198, 200–1, 222, 248, 252, 274, 285, 299, 310
National Investment Board 135
National Investment 135, 148, 170
National Union of Mineworkers 293 *see also* coal miners
nationalisation xi, 18, 45, 79, 122–3, 130, 141–2, 148–9, 239, 243, 325
of coal, electricity, etc. *see* coal, electricity, etc.
*see also* socialisation
nationalisation compensation 18, 123, 130, 141, 149, 157, 167–8, 174–5, 182, 197, 206
nationalised industries
investment in 157–8, 168, 221, 230, 234, 243, 297
price policy 123, 130, 141–2, 157–9, 174–5, 181–4, 191, 197, 206, 214, 233–4, 248, 253–4, 261, 300–1, 311 *see also* marginal cost pricing
wages policy 157–8, 168, 218, 223–4
Neale, J. E. 239, 347
new issues control *see* capital issues control
New York 238, 266, 278, 289, 327, 331
New Zealand 12–13, 43, 188, 285, 328
Nicholson, Max 169, 170, 183, 189, 192–5, 199–202, 204–5, 213–14, 220, 222, 224–5, 232, 241, 243–4, 247, 254, 261–2, 283, 287, 297, 300, 310, 313, 317, 348
Niemeyer, Sir Otto 291, 348
Noel-Baker, Philip 15, 21–2, 26, 29, 83, 121, 126, 131, 146, 180, 227, 290, 306, 317, 331, 348
non-discrimination 3–4, 57, 104, 137, 145, 171–2, 177, 187–8, 191, 238, 280, 329 *see also* Article VII
Norris, Harry 277, 285, 348
North, G. C. 306, 348
Norway 54, 324

Ogilvie, Sir Frederick 109, 348
Ogilvie, Lady 109
Ohlsson, I. 324n, 348
Opie, Redvers 105, 348
Orr, John *see* Boyd-Orr
Ottawa 13, 89, 271
Ottawa Agreements (1932) 151
Overseas Economic Intelligence, Committee on 11, 15–16, 155, 188, 217, 237, 246, 281
Overseas Economic Survey 15, 107, 121, 131, 192, 217, 226, 237, 246, 280–1, 304, 316, 326, 331
Overton, Sir Arnold 35, 103–4, 116, 348
Owen (Arthur) David 27, 120, 317, 348
Owen, George 130, 180, 348
Oxford 11, 28, 62, 75, 94, 109, 127, 131, 156n, 200, 255

Padmore, Thomas 42n, 348
Pakenham, Lord 253, 261, 306, 317, 348
Palestine 226
Palmer, Sir William 142, 200, 348
Pan-American Conference (Mexico City, 1945) 22–3
Pares, Richard 130, 155, 348
Paris 146, 158
Pasvolsky, Leo 26, 348
Patinkin, Don 97n
PAYE *see* income tax
Penrose, E. F. 8–9, 14, 54, 156, 349
Penson, J. H. 331, 349
Pepler, Sir George 109, 349
Perez-Guerrero, M. 186, 349
Perroux, F. 189, 239, 243, 349
Pethick-Lawrence, Lord 165, 349
Philadelphia 289
Phillips, H. M. 200, 349
Phillips, Sir Thomas 78, 349
Pickard, B. 199, 349
Pigou, A. C. 1
Pimlott, John 170, 349
planning xi, 37, 60, 79, 114, 116, 122, 124, 127–8, 132, 133–5, 139, 142, 146–7, 169–70, 199, 201–3, 213, 220, 241, 271, 286, 293–5, 297, 310, 319 *see also* Economic Plan *and* Economic Surveys
Plant, Arnold 27, 99, 112, 239, 291, 349
Plant, Mrs. A. 112
Plumb, C. T. 316, 318, 349
Plumptre, A. F. W. 186, 349
Polak, J. J. 133, 349
Poland 317, 329
Polanyi, Michael 281, 350
Political and Economic Planning 130–1
Ponsonby, Gilbert 43, 45, 53, 83, 197, 350
population, optimum 28
population problem 42, 81, 109, 208–9, 224, 249, 255, 260, 306 *see also* labour supply
post-war credits *see* income tax deferred credits
Potsdam Conference (1945) 114
Prague 75
Pressnell, L. S. xi, 30n, 93n, 331n
price controls 36, 112, 125, 129–30, 220, 238, 272, 281–2, 310, 312

prices 35, 41, 47, 51, 81, 83, 110–11, 118, 137, 142, 168–9, 211, 216, 219, 223, 226, 231, 246, 249–50, 256, 262, 264, 270, 272–3, 276, 283, 286, 294, 298, 304, 308, 314, 319, 325, 329
  agricultural 160, 236, 248, 261, 276, 296
primary products *see* buffer stocks, commodity policy *and* cotton
Prime Minister's Office xi, 242
Prime Minister's Statistical Branch 6n
Princeton 219
Proctor, Dennis xi, 52–3, 58, 60, 69, 85, 87, 91–2, 96, 102, 140, 176, 181, 195–6, 198, 203, 204, 211, 221, 240–1, 252, 272, 284, 296–7, 299, 309, 311, 321n, 350
productivity 23, 25, 68, 77, 81, 110, 149, 158–9, 211, 218, 223, 231–2, 233, 243, 249, 273, 283, 293, 296, 298, 308, 325 *see also* efficiency
profits taxation 41, 43–4, 52, 258, 260, 285, 301, 311 *see also* Excess Profits Tax
propensity to consume 48, 61, 219–20, 322–3
Proposals for Consideration by an International Conference on Trade and Employment *see* White Papers
protection *see* quantitative restrictions *and* tariffs
public expenditure *see* government expenditure *and* investment, public
Public Utility Corporations, Official Committee on 17–18, 26 *see also* electricity *and* gas
public works *see* investment, public
purchase tax 42, 99, 180, 183, 222
  Committee on Future Use of 33–4, 36, 41, 130, 248

quantitative restrictions (on imports) 3–5, 14, 90, 120, 153, 187–8, 238, 245, 267
  and balance of payments difficulties *see* import restrictions on balance of payments grounds
  *see also* agricultural policy
Quarterly Economic Survey 71
*Queen Mary* 219n
Quirk, R. N. 182, 191, 253, 350

Radice, E. A. 27, 92–3, 350
Raisman, Sir Jeremy 291, 350
Rasminsky, Louis 209, 228, 350
Raspin, Dr Angela xi
rationing 2, 61, 129–30, 236, 238, 245, 272, 282, 287, 298
Reciprocal Trade Agreements Act (US) 23, 91, 97, 151, 165, 265
Reconstruction Committees
  Cabinet 6, 18n, 19, 35, 39
  Official 34, 36
    Sub-Committee on Industrial Problems 27, 62–3, 82–3
reconstruction, European 3, 22, 26, 28–9, 97–8, 306, 331 *see also* Germany
Reddaway, W. B. 92, 143, 175, 181, 185, 210, 323, 350
Reeder, A. 88, 176, 181, 350
Rees, P. M. 277, 285, 350
Reform Club 12, 74n, 77, 97, 146, 167, 176, 219, 268
reparations 3, 67, 78, 92, 103, 181
Reparations Commission 107, 181
restrictive practices 2, 23–4, 35, 115, 124, 130, 184, 242, 275–6, 324–5
  Committee on Supervisory Boards and 235–6, 249, 263, 286, 301, 311, 313, 318
  *see also* monopoly
Rice, Stuart 167, 350
Rignano scheme *see* death duties reform of
Robbins, Lionel x, 3, 7, 8, 9n, 11, 17, 20–1, 25, 28, 32–4, 41, 44–5, 49, 52–3, 55, 57, 60–1, 64–5, 69–70, 73, 75, 78, 84, 87, 89, 94–7, 99, 102–3, 105–6, 109, 116, 131, 132n, 137, 146, 153, 166, 171, 228, 239, 288–9, 291, 314, 350
  as Director of the Economic Section ix, 14, 15, 31–2, 58–9, 67, 93–4, 160, 163
  family 112
  as 'fixer' 3, 4, 8, 11, 16, 39, 62
  *Autobiography of an Economist* 239n
Robertson, D. H. 44, 71, 98–9, 350
  *Essays in Monetary Theory* 70
Robinson, E. A. G. 20, 35, 44, 175–6, 181, 194, 202–3, 205, 210–11, 218, 231–2, 241, 249–50, 253, 263–4, 295, 302, 316, 320, 350
Robinson, Joan 99, 350
Ronald, Nigel 11, 54, 126, 155, 350
Roosevelt, Franklin Delano 36, 41, 50, 63, 91n, 351
Rosenstein-Rodan, Paul 186, 246, 258, 268, 317, 331, 351
Rousseaux, Paul 79, 351
Rowan, Leslie 176, 351
Rowe-Dutton, Sir Ernest 128, 150, 178, 226, 267, 317, 330, 351
Rowlatt, Sir John 260, 351
Royal Commission on Equal Pay 71–2
Royal Commission on Population 109, 208–9, 249, 306
Royal Economic Society 42n, 72, 98–100
Royal Institute of International Affairs 189, 199
Royal Statistical Society 72
Ruhr 225, 237, 246
Russia, *see* USSR

Sabine, B. E. V. 258n
Salter, Sir Arthur 97–8, 99, 351
San Francisco Conference (1945) 67, 114, 120, 209

Saunders, Christopher 176, 203, 211, 231, 271, 322, 323, 351
Saunders, Sir Harold 85, 351
Savannah 219n, 250
savings 41, 43–4, 48–9, 66, 73, 81–2, 84, 201, 220, 260, 298, 322
Sayers, R. S. 94, 107, 109, 121, 127, 194–5, 197, 200, 206–7, 213–14, 221–3, 229, 232, 234, 243–4, 247–8, 254, 262–3, 274–5, 286, 292, 319, 325, 351
scarce currency clause 13, 15, 119, 143–5, 149, 152–3, 155, 177, 179, 185, 187
Schumacher, E. F. 115, 351
Secord, Campbell 49, 193–4, 211, 230, 241, 299, 351
Selsey 308
Sewell Bray, F. 277, 285, 351
Shackle, G. L. S. 6, 18, 162, 184, 205, 213, 221–2, 229, 231, 249, 252, 271, 314, 316, 318, 322, 351
Shackle, R. J. 3, 132n, 207, 217, 227, 238, 245, 256–7, 265, 278, 279–80, 305, 317, 328–30, 351
Sharp, Evelyn 113, 351
Sherman Act (US) 34
Shillito, E. A., 45, 352
Shinwell, Emmanuel 15, 123n, 157n, 171, 175, 233, 235, 296, 352
  Minister of Fuel and Power 123n, 132n, 141–2, 148n, 287
shipping 131–2, 146, 148, 155, 158, 188, 207, 216–17, 327
Shipping Committee 173, 180
Siepmann, H. A. 226, 352
Simon, Sir John 258n, 352
Singapore 216n
Sinker, A. P. 109, 352
Slim, Field Marshal Sir William 275, 352
slumps *see* depressions
Smith, Ben 7, 352
  Minister of Food 216n, 236, 244
Snelling, A. W. 266, 352
Snowden, Philip 20, 352
socialisation 29, 88, 115–17, 167–9, 174–5, 181–3, 198, 220, 234, 291
Ministerial Committee on 233–4, 241–2, 254
  Official Committee on 175, 181–3, 197, 206, 213–14, 223–4, 233, 248, 253, 255, 261
  *see also* nationalisation *and* nationalised industries
social security contributions *see* national insurance contributions
South Africa 165, 285
South East Europe, trade with 256, 267, 288–9, 303, 316
Southern Ireland 55
Spearman, A. C. 33, 78, 121, 291, 352
Spearman, Mrs. Doris 33, 291, 352
Sraffa, Piero 99, 352
stabilisation policy *see* cost of living stabilisation
Stafford, Jack 3, 5, 59–60, 69, 87, 89, 94, 102, 134, 140, 147, 176, 181, 193, 196, 203–4, 211–12, 219, 229, 240, 247, 251, 261, 297, 322, 323–4, 326, 352
Stage II ix, 74
Stage III xi, 90, 103–4, 105, 111 *see also* transitional period finance *see* Anglo-American Financial Agreement, negotiation of
Stalin, Joseph 50n, 352
state trading 4n, 118, 198–9, 218, 227, 238, 245, 255, 257, 280, 305 *see also* bulk purchases
statistics 68, 111–12, 169, 179, 220n, 324
  of balance of payments *see* balance of payments estimates
  for employment policy 4–7, 17, 53, 60, 65, 69, 87–9, 96, 97, 140, 147, 191, 231, 252
  'Joy through Statistics' 97
  *see also* census of distribution *and* national income and expenditure
Steering Committee on Economic Development 89, 116, 122, 128–9, 134–5, 147, 183, 203, 229, 253, 272, 283–6, 295, 299, 309, 310
  meetings of 139–40, 169–70, 173, 181, 190–1, 231, 251, 282, 293, 311n
Steering Committee on International Negotiations 218n, 290–1, 306
sterling area 50, 57, 143–4, 152, 162–5, 177–9, 187, 226–7, 291, 331
  negotiations (1946) 217, 226–7, 290–1, 315–16
    *see also* sterling balances
sterling balances 30, 50–1, 59, 103–4, 119, 144, 152, 163, 177–9, 226–7, 290–1, 303–4, 331
Stevens, Sir Roger 317, 352
Stinebower, L. S. 120, 218, 352
Stirling, J. A. 132n, 145, 166, 352
Stone, Richard ix, 7, 16, 17, 20, 52, 60, 62, 68, 92, 99, 102, 133, 143, 196, 204, 219–20, 240, 250–1, 277, 285, 300, 324n, 352
  'The Analysis of Market Demand' 72
  *The Measurement of Consumers' Expenditure and Behaviour in the United Kingdom 1920–1938*, vol. I, 219n
  'The Development and Use of National Income and Expenditure Estimates' 7n, 251n, 324n
  (with Meade) *National Income and Expenditure* 6, 16
Strachey, John 353
  Minister of Food 314
subsidies 110–11, 115, 130, 142, 146, 158, 161, 205, 207, 222, 249, 255, 276, 286, 295, 310, 330
  agricultural *see* agricultural policy

subsidies (*cont.*)
cost-of-living *see* cost of living, stabilisation of
sur-tax 42–3, 81, 252, 322
Svennilson, Ingvar 146, 155–6, 353
Swan, Trevor 268n, 353
Swansea 39
Sweden 146–7, 155–6, 167, 304, 324
Switzerland 37, 54

Tait, Mr 43–4
Taplin, Walter 69, 353
tariffs 31, 63, 66, 71, 218, 235, 279
US *see* USA
Tawney, R. H. 291, 353
taxation 19, 41, 45–7, 51, 56, 61, 68, 73, 79, 81, 83–4, 88, 102, 110–11, 129–30, 134, 162, 183, 190, 195–6, 205, 222–3, 231, 238, 245, 255, 272, 284–5, 291–2, 295, 299, 310, 314
and incentives 41, 43, 45, 50, 84, 125, 136, 171, 258
on capital *see* capital taxation
on consumption *see* consumption
on income *see* income tax
on profits *see* profits
post-war remission of 70, 73, 84, 107–8, 110, 124–5, 134, 136, 140, 258, 311
Tew, Brian 49, 121, 353
Thompson-McCausland, L. P. 20, 67–8, 74, 154, 171, 177–8, 198, 226, 280–1, 353
Thorneycroft, Peter 78, 353
Tinbergen, Jan 112, 209, 311, 353
Tomlinson, J. D. 120, 353
Topham, A. M. R. 209, 353
Tory Reform Committee 78–9, *see also* Conservative Party
Towers, Graham 90, 353
trade barriers, reduction of 13, 22, 106, 119, 151, 165, 172, 226, 244–5, 263, 266 *see also* Imperial Preference *and* US tariff, reduction of
Trade Negotiations Committee 265, 305, 315, 329
trade unions 54, 58, 68, 112–13, 161, 195, 214, 220, 223, 254–5, 272, 296
Trades Union Congress 223
transitional period 2–3, 33–4, 36, 77–8, 114, 142, 155, 185, 187–8, 204, 262
inflation in *see* inflation
let-outs *see* import restrictions on balance of payments grounds
*see also* Stage III
transport 29, 43, 53, 197, 203, 249, 263, 298
European, reconstruction of 21–2, 26, 29
nationalisation of 45, 233–4, 241–3, 253–4, 300–1
*see also* civil aviation *and* shipping
Treasury x, 2n, 14, 21–2, 26–8, 33, 44–5, 52–3, 56, 60, 69, 71, 84–5, 87–92, 95–6, 102, 105, 122, 127–9, 132, 135–7, 139–40, 148–9, 153, 162–6, 170, 173, 175–81, 185, 195, 198, 205, 207, 215, 217, 222, 226–7, 239, 241, 249, 251–2, 279–80, 284–5, 288, 291, 298–9, 302–3, 305, 309, 314–16, 320, 328 *see also* Budgets *and* National Debt Enquiry
Trend, B. 145n, 223n, 293n, 330n, 353
Tress, Ronald 3, 21, 38, 45. 52, 68, 71, 75, 77, 79, 82, 84, 89, 97, 103, 108, 110, 112, 122, 127, 134, 140, 141, 147–8, 158, 170, 176, 181, 193, 195–6, 202–3, 205, 207–8, 211–13, 215, 224, 226, 229, 232–3, 240, 247, 249, 251, 253, 255, 261–2, 264, 272, 297, 309, 311, 353
Tress, Mrs R. 112
Troutbeck, J. M. 306, 354
Truman, Harry F. 63, 91n, 114n, 354
Turner, B. R. 188, 354
Turner, Sir George 59, 63, 354
Turner, Sir Mark 67, 354
Turpin, K. C. 124, 354

UK 20, 23, 27, 37, 236, 297, 322
balance of payments problem 3–4, 9, 13, 22, 54, 59, 63, 90, 103–4, 125–7, 143–5, 150, 152–3, 155, 165, 177, 187, 198, 216, 238, 249, 264, 281, 284–5, 304, 314
exports 7, 21, 25, 31–2, 34, 41–2, 63–4, 66, 94, 98–9, 103, 110, 117, 119, 128, 130–1, 136, 144, 150, 152–5, 163–4, 169, 187–8, 210, 212, 214–15, 226, 245–6, 249–50, 255–7, 297, 299, 302, 304–5, 309, 314–16, 318, 321, 323, 327, 329–31
elasticity of demand for 212, 216, 245–6, 249, 264, 304, 317, 318
imports 31, 62–4, 66, 90, 110, 149, 159, 162–4, 187, 212, 215, 226, 255–6, 262–3, 302–4, 310, 327, 331
USA 20–1, 23, 26–7, 32, 34–5, 37, 41, 44, 78, 103–4, 119, 125–6, 131, 143–4, 149, 152, 164, 172, 187–8, 190n, 209, 216n, 218–19, 224, 227–8, 236, 244–5, 249, 257, 265, 268, 304, 311, 316, 322, 327
balance of payments 9, 13, 22, 125–6
Congress 13, 22–3, 29, 33, 35, 37, 90–1, 98, 106, 119, 150–1, 209, 217, 236, 238, 265, 302
Embassy in London 4, 8–9, 156, 167
employment policy 9, 54, 106–7
tariff, reduction of 9, 14, 23, 91, 98, 120, 157, 165 *see also* Reciprocal Trade Agreements Act
USSR 20n, 29, 54–5, 63, 119, 131, 146–7, 199, 228, 316, 324
unemployment 7, 51, 56, 58, 64, 77, 87, 92, 106, 117, 129, 134, 161, 172, 194, 200–1, 207, 218, 231, 235, 243, 267, 271, 286, 295, 310, 318, 323, 325, 330

unemployment (*cont.*)
target rate of 7, 12, 63
*see also* employment policy
University College London 62, 239, 246, 258, 268
United Nations Conference on Food and Agriculture (Hot Springs, Virginia, 1943) 8
United Nations Conference on Trade and Employment (Havana 1948) ix–x
preparations for 22, 63, 90–1, 93, 165, 171, 191–2, 199, 215, 217–18, 227, 237, 244–6, 256, 265–6, 277–8, 285, 299, 302, 309, 327, 330
*see also* Proposals for an International Conference on Trade and Employment
United Nations Economic and Social Council 67, 192, 199, 208, 257, 265–7, 278, 289–90, 306, 315, 317
and employment policy 19, 27, 30, 36–7, 106–7, 120–1, 126–7, 146, 167, 180, 208, 217–18, 227–8, 266, 278
United Nations Monetary and Financial Conference (Bretton Woods, 1944) 2n, 15 *see also* International Bank for Reconstruction and Development *and* International Monetary Fund
United Nations Organisation 20n, 27, 37, 67n, 114, 120–1, 126, 131, 133, 180, 186, 188–9, 208–9, 218, 238, 307, 317, 338 *see also* United Nations Economic and Social Council
United Nations Relief and Rehabilitation Administration 114, 133, 306, 331

Vandepeer, Sir Donald 132n, 142, 160, 276, 354
Vienna 44
Viner, Jacob 268, 291, 354
Vinson, Frederic Moore 166, 354
Vinter, Peter 91–2, 204, 222, 297, 321n, 354

wages policy 2, 23–4, 51–2, 58, 68, 77, 183–4, 193–5, 202, 204–6, 214, 222, 310
in nationalised industries 157–9, 168, 214, 223–4
Working Parties on 161, 205, 214, 222–3, 232, 243, 247–8, 254–5, 261–2, 283, 295–6
wage-rates 41, 77, 110–13, 134, 148, 159, 161, 184, 195, 205–6, 211, 214, 218, 222–3, 231–2, 243–4, 248–9, 254, 262–3, 267, 272–3, 275, 283, 294–5, 298, 304, 308, 310, 324
agricultural 205–6, 247–8, 261–2, 271, 276, 296
Waley, Sir David 19, 20, 226, 256, 279–80, 285, 288, 290–1, 302–4, 306, 309, 316–17, 330, 354
Walker, Col. Charles 94, 121, 354
Walker, Gilbert 11, 15, 59, 61–2, 94, 354
Wall, John 218, 315, 354
Wallace, Henry 40, 354
Ward, J. G. 120, 354
War Damage Contribution 50, 124, 136, 159
War Damage Payments 101
war, end of
European ix, 17, 20–1, 33, 70–1, 74–5, 80, 82–3, 116
Far Eastern ix, 114, 117
Washington 9, 11, 13, 20n, 26, 50, 54, 61, 91, 105, 125, 132, 146, 149, 151, 153, 162–3, 166, 167, 171–2, 176, 178–9, 185, 191, 198, 238–9, 244, 250, 257, 266, 285, 289–90
Anglo-American discussions in, 1943 *see* Law Mission
Anglo-American discussions in, 1945 *see* loan negotiations
Watkinson, G. L. 35, 354
Watts, Nita xii, 5, 21, 26–8, 30–1, 36, 45, 91, 94, 105, 110–11, 155, 166, 207–8, 215, 217, 224, 226–7, 242–3, 249, 272, 281, 304, 317, 331, 355
Weeks, Sir Hugh 8, 59, 185, 355
'good friend of the Economic Section' 78
Welch, A. W. 256, 355
Wheeler, Leslie 126, 355
White, Harry Dexter 29, 355
White Papers 135, 148, 166, 220, 223, 244, 250–1, 281, 283
*An Analysis of the Sources of War Finance and an Estimate of the National Income and Expenditure* (Cmd 6261, 1941) ix, 79
*British Air Services* (Cmd 6712, 1945) 188n
*Capital Issues Control, Memorandum of Guidance to the Capital Issues Committee* (Cmd 6645, 1945) 74
*The Control of Land Use* (Cmd 6537, 1944) 50, 123n
*Employment Policy* (Cmd 6527, 1944) ix, x, xi, 2, 7, 12, 15, 43, 53, 77, 79, 88, 168, 184n
*Financial Agreement between the Governments of the United States and the United Kingdom* (Cmd 6708, 1945) 185n
*National Income and Expenditure of the United Kingdom 1938 to 1945* (Cmd 6784, 1946) 240
*Proposals for Consideration by an International Conference on Trade and Employment* (Cmd 6709, 1945) x, 185n, 186, 285, 305, 314 *see also* United Nations Conference on Trade and Employment
*Statement Relating to Defence* (Cmd 6743, 1946) 220n

White Papers (*cont.*)
*Statistical Material Presented during the Washington Negotiations* (Cmd 6707, 1945) 185n, 186
*Statistics relating to the War Effort of the United Kingdom* (Cmd 6564, 1944) 281
Whitehall xi, 1, 12, 68–9, 75, 80, 99, 105, 107, 114, 131–2, 135, 147, 170, 176, 181, 184, 189, 192, 194, 196, 208, 219, 222, 224, 244, 252–3, 289 *see also* Board of Trade, Treasury, etc.
Williams, Francis 244, 283, 355
Wilmot, John 123n, 157n, 355
Minister of Supply 123n, 234
Wilson, J. V. 188, 355
Wilson, Stephen 53–4, 115n, 197, 300, 355
Wilson, Thomas 6, 94, 122, 130, 148, 155, 157–8, 165, 174, 200, 355
Wilson-Smith, Henry 11, 200, 239, 355
Winant, J. G. 35, 54–5, 355
Winegarten, A. 317, 355
Witteveen, H. J. 311, 355
Wood, John 184, 207, 249, 263, 275, 277, 286, 355
Woods, Sir John Henry 116, 155, 169, 177, 179–80, 191, 194, 234, 263, 277, 283–4, 294, 302, 309, 323–4, 329–30, 356
Woolton, Lord x, 8, 17, 19, 28, 35, 40, 109, 356
world food crisis *see* food, world shortage of
Wrong, Hume 228, 356

Yates, Lamartine 315, 356
Young, P. S. 266, 329, 356

Zenkl, Mr 75–7

For Product Safety Concerns and Information please contact our EU representative GPSR@taylorandfrancis.com
Taylor & Francis Verlag GmbH, Kaufingerstraße 24, 80331 München, Germany

www.ingramcontent.com/pod-product-compliance
Lightning Source LLC
LaVergne TN
LVHW011108300926
849160LV00008B/311

* 9 7 8 1 1 3 8 9 9 1 5 0 7 *